Street by Street

PORTSMOUTH SOUTHAMPTON

EASTLEIGH, FAREHAM, GOSPORT, HAVANT, WINCHESTER

Chandler's Ford, Hayling Island, Hedge End, Horndean, Hythe, Lyndhurst, Portchester, Romsey, Southsea, Waterlooville

Ist edition May 2001

© Automobile Association Developments Limited 2001

Published by AA Publishing (a trading name of Automobile Association Developments Limited, whose registered office is Norfolk House, Priestley Road, Basingstoke, Hampshire, RG24 9NY. Registered number 1878835).

Mapping produced by the Cartographic Department of The Automobile Association.

ISBN 0 7495 2360 3

A CIP Catalogue record for this book is available from the British Library.

Printed by G. Canale & C. S.P.A., Torino, Italy

Ref: MX005

Key to map pages — ii-iii

Key to map symbols — iv-1

Enlarged scale pages — 2-19

Street by Street — 20-139

Index – towns & villages — 140-141

Index – streets — 141-159

Index – featured places — 159-162

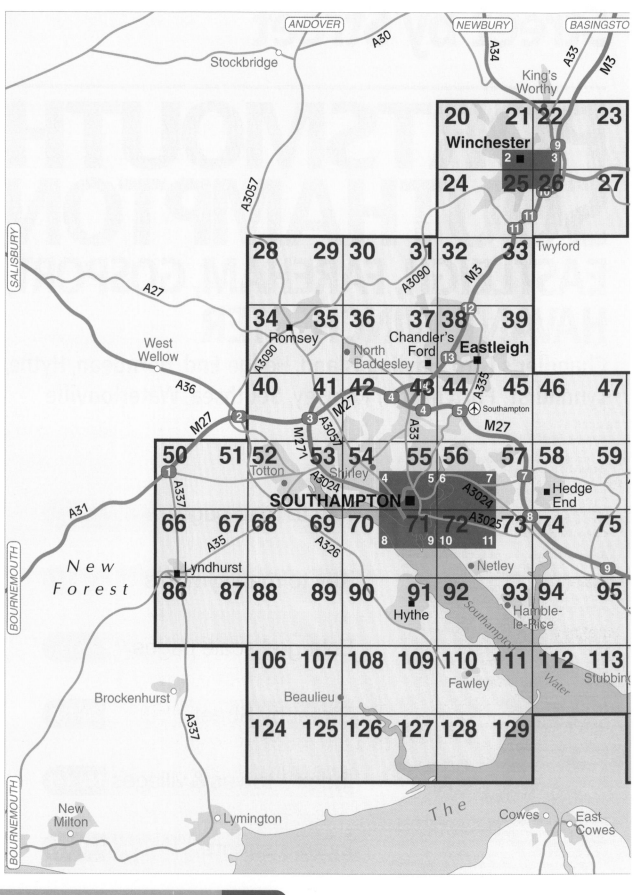

ii

ANDOVER · A30 · NEWBURY · BASINGSTO

A34 · A33 · M3

Stockbridge

King's Worthy

A3057

| 20 | 21 | 22 | 23 |

Winchester

9

2 ■

3

| 24 | 25 | 26 | 27 |

10

11

11

SALISBURY

A27

Twyford

| 28 | 29 | 30 | 31 | 32 | 33 |

A3090

M3

West Wellow

A36

A3090

| 34 | 35 | 36 | 37 | 38 | 39 |

Romsey

Chandler's Ford

Eastleigh

12

North Baddesley

13

M27

| 40 | 41 | 42 | 43 | 44 | 45 | 46 | 47 |

2

3

M27

A3057

4

43

A33

44

A335

5

Southampton

M27

| 50 | 51 | 52 | 53 | 54 | 55 | 56 | 57 | 58 | 59 |

1

A337

Totton

A3024

Shirley

4

5 6

7

A3024

7

Hedge End

SOUTHAMPTON ■

| 66 | 67 | 68 | 69 | 70 | 71 | 72 | 73 | 74 | 75 |

A31

A35

A326

8

9 10

11

A3025

8

9

New Forest

Lyndhurst ■

Netley

| 86 | 87 | 88 | 89 | 90 | 91 | 92 | 93 | 94 | 95 |

Hythe

Hamble-le-Rice

Southampton

BOURNEMOUTH

| 106 | 107 | 108 | 109 | 110 | 111 | 112 | 113 |

Fawley

Water

Stubbing

Beaulieu

| 124 | 125 | 126 | 127 | 128 | 129 |

Brockenhurst

A337

The

New Milton

Lymington

Cowes

East Cowes

BOURNEMOUTH

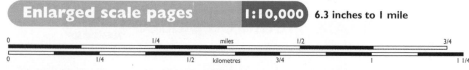

Enlarged scale pages   1:10,000   6.3 inches to 1 mile

0   1/4   miles   1/2   3/4

0   1/4   1/2   kilometres   3/4   1   1 1/4

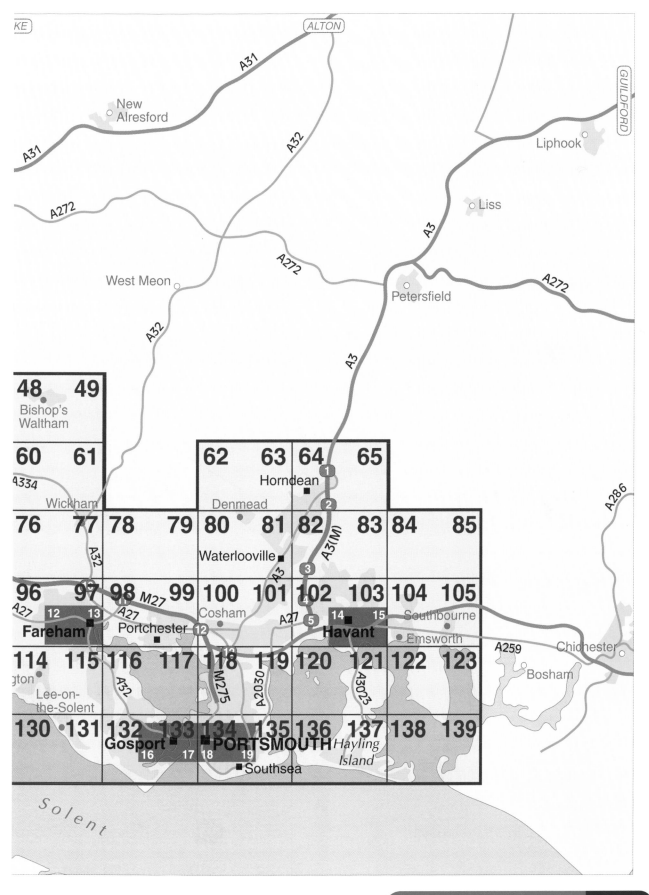

KE

ALTON

GUILDFORD

A31

New
Alresford

A31

Liphook

A272

A32

Liss

A272

West Meon

A272

A3

Petersfield

A286

A32

A3

48   49
Bishop's
Waltham

60   61

A334

Wickham

62   63   64   65

Horndean

Denmead

76   77   78   79   80   81   82   83   84   85

Waterlooville

A3(M)

A32

A3

96   97   98   99   100   101   102   103   104   105

M27

Cosham

A27

Southbourne

12   13

A27

A27

12

5

14   15

Fareham   Portchester   12   Havant   Emsworth

A259

Chichester

114   115   116   117   118   119   120   121   122   123

A32

M275

A2030

A3023

Bosham

Lee-on-
the-Solent

130   131   132   133   134   135   136   137   138   139

Gosport   PORTSMOUTH   Hayling
Island

16   17   18   19

Southsea

Solent

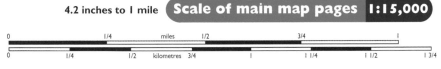

4.2 inches to 1 mile   Scale of main map pages 1:15,000

0   1/4   miles   1/2   3/4   1

0   1/4   1/2   kilometres 3/4   1   1 1/4   1 1/2   1 3/4

Junction 9	Motorway & junction
Services	Motorway service area
	Primary road single/dual carriageway
Services	Primary road service area
	A road single/dual carriageway
	B road single/dual carriageway
	Other road single/dual carriageway
	Restricted road
	Private road
← ←	One way street
	Pedestrian street
	Track/ footpath
	Road under construction
	Road tunnel
P	Parking

P+	Park & Ride
	Bus/coach station
	Railway & main railway station
	Railway & minor railway station
⊖	Underground station
⊖	Light railway & station
++++++++	Preserved private railway
LC	Level crossing
•—•—•—•—•	Tramway
--------------	Ferry route
....	Airport runway
—·—·—·—·	Boundaries- borough/ district
▼▼▼▼▼▼▼	Mounds
93	Page continuation 1:15,000
7	Page continuation to enlarged scale 1:10,000

	River/canal lake, pier	&#9855;	Toilet with disabled facilities
	Aqueduct lock, weir		Petrol station
465 ▲ Winter Hill	Peak (with height in metres)	PH	Public house
	Beach	PO	Post Office
	Coniferous woodland		Public library
	Broadleaved woodland	*i*	Tourist Information Centre
	Mixed woodland		Castle
	Park		Historic house/ building
	Cemetery	Wakehurst Place NT	National Trust property
	Built-up area	M	Museum/ art gallery
	Featured building	†	Church/chapel
⊓⊔⊓⊔⊓⊔	City wall		Country park
A&E	Accident & Emergency hospital		Theatre/ performing arts
	Toilet		Cinema

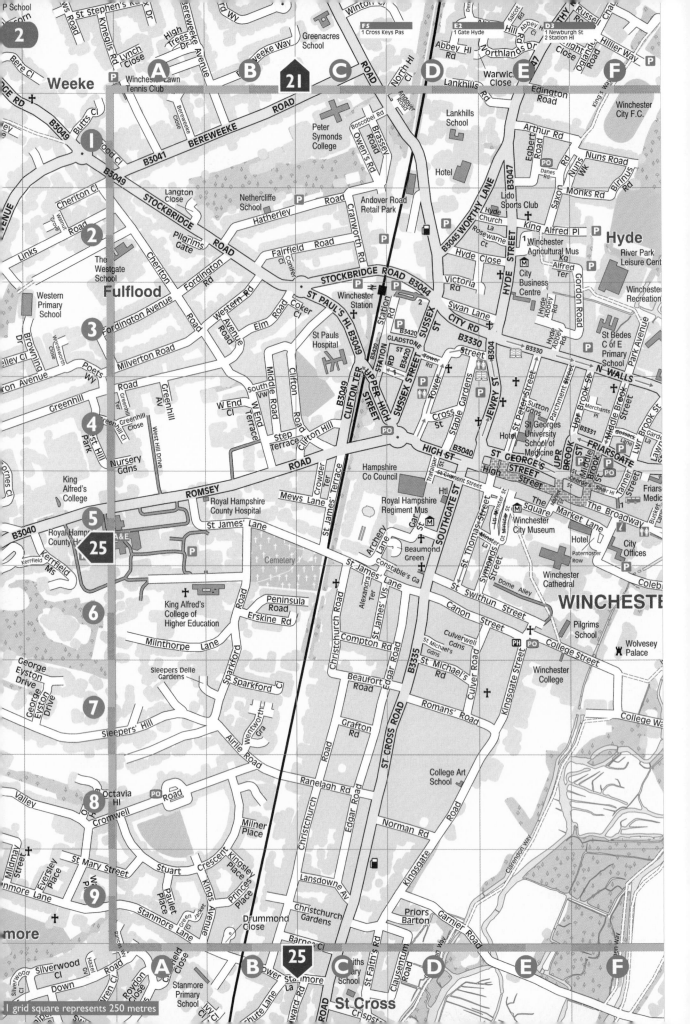

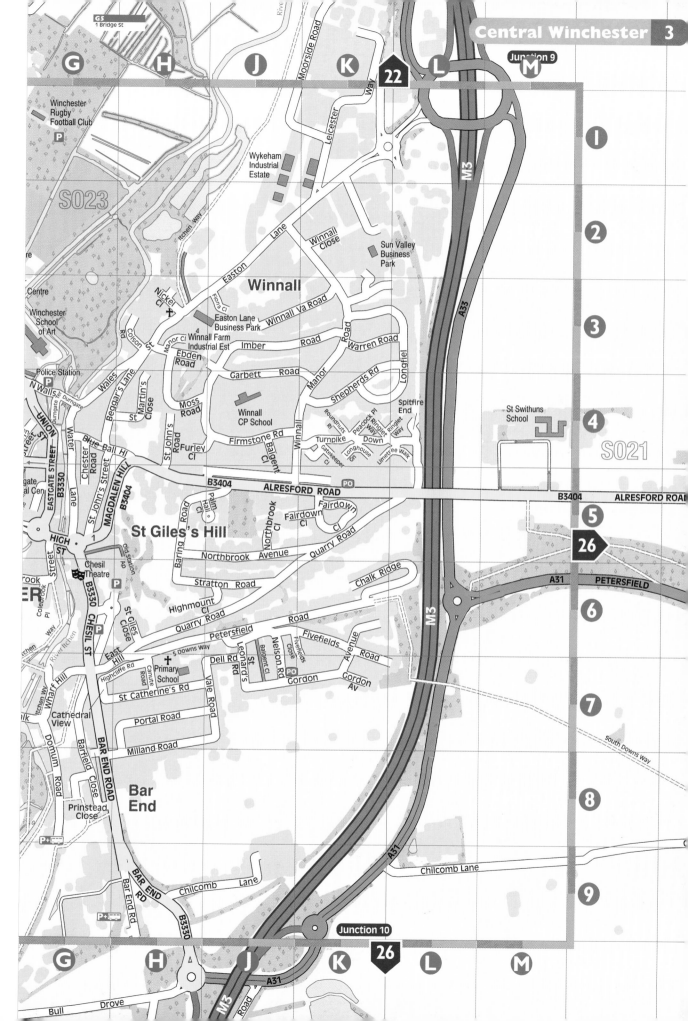

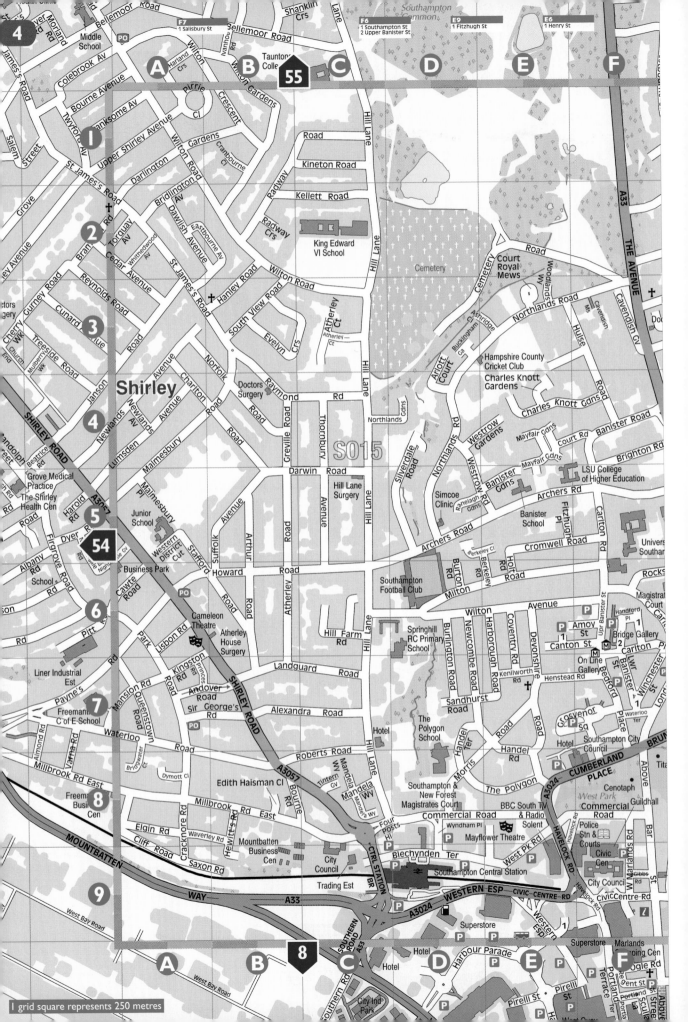

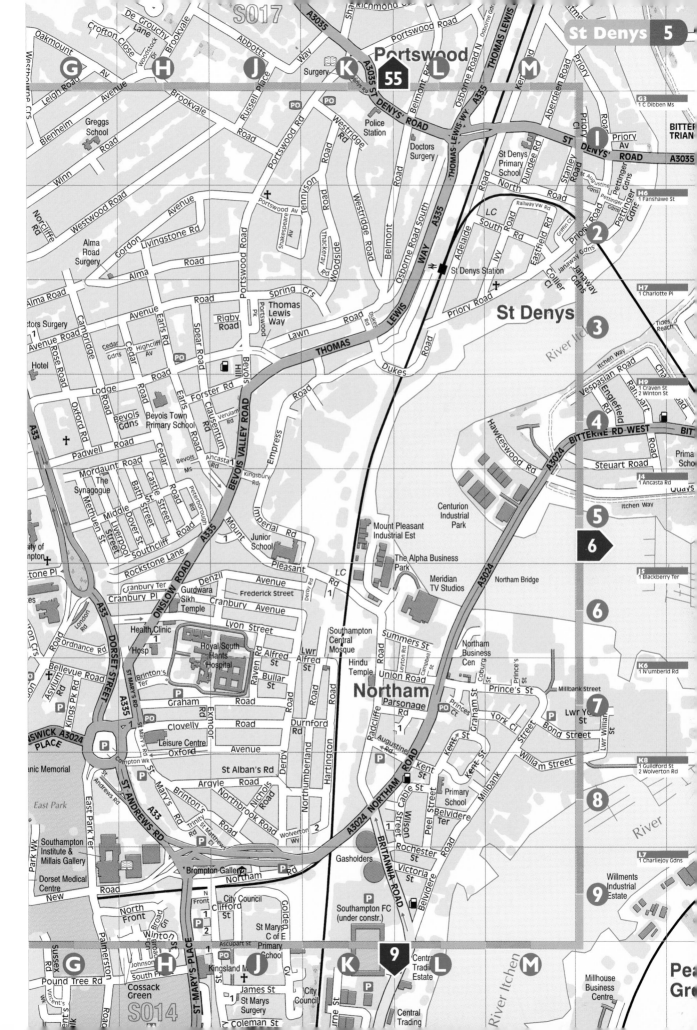

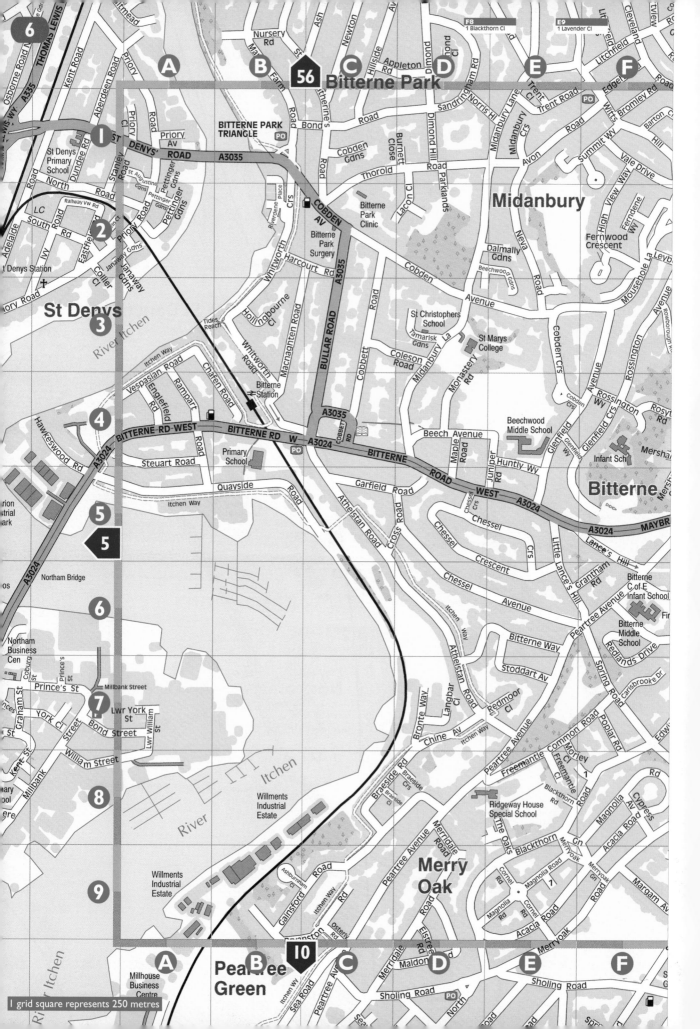

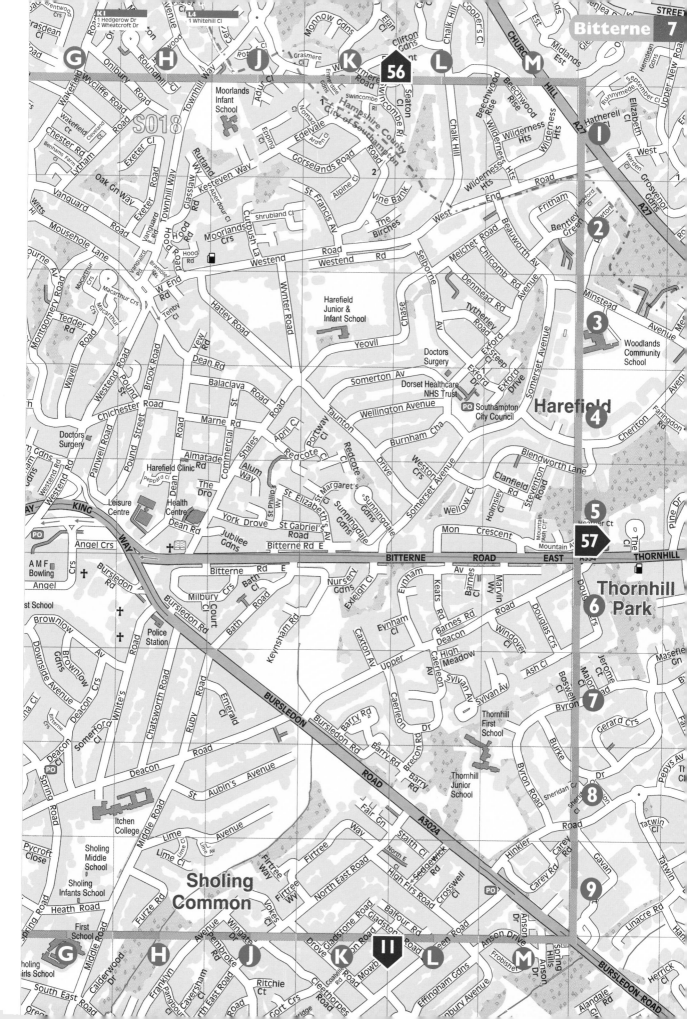

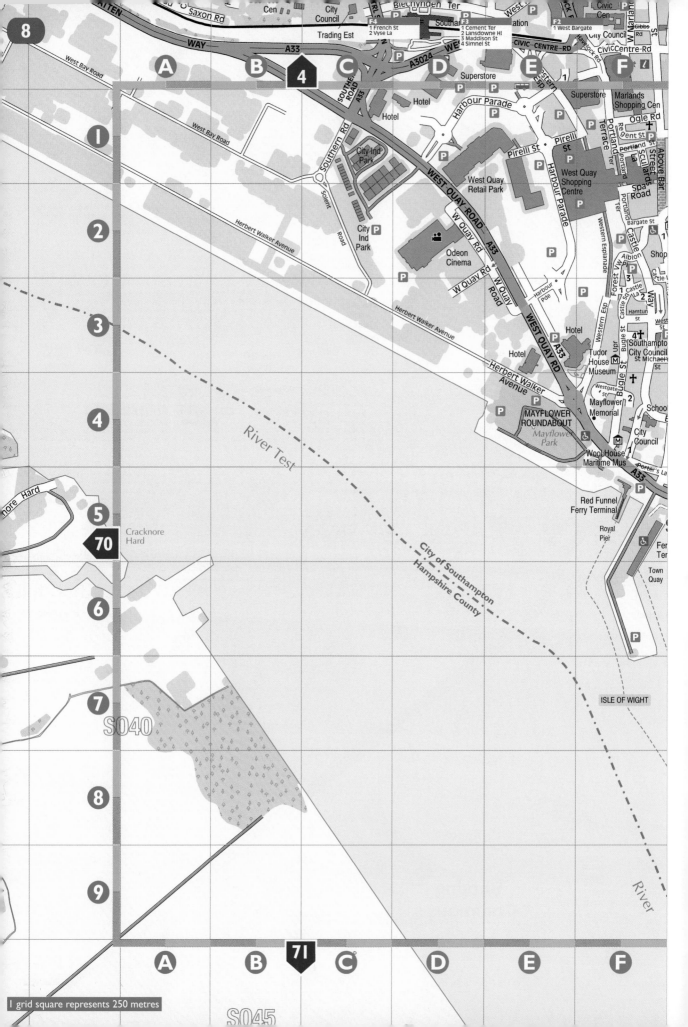

8

West Bay Road

A **B** **4** **C** **D** **E** **F**

West Bay Road

1

West Bay Road

Herbert Walker Avenue

2

Herbert Walker Avenue

3

River Test

Herbert Walker Avenue

4

Hard

5

70 Cracknore Hard

City of Southampton
Hampshire County

6

7

SO40

ISLE OF WIGHT

8

9

River

A **B** **71** **C** **D** **E** **F**

1 grid square represents 250 metres

SO45

Saxon Rd
Cen
City Council
Trading Est
1 French St
2 Vyse La
Blechynden Ter
Southa
1 Cement Ter
2 Lansdowne Hl
3 Maddison St
4 Simnel St
WAY
A33
A3024
WES
F2
1 West Bargate
City Council
CivicCentre-Rd
Civic Cen
W
Gibbs
Rd
W Marland
St
CIVIC-CENTRE-RD
Superstore
Superstore
Marlands Shopping Cen
Ogle Rd
Harbour Parade
Hotel
Southern Rd
City Ind Park
Solent
Road
City Ind Park
Regent St
Portland Terrace
Portland
Street
Scullards
Spa
Road
Above Bar
Pirelli St
Pirelli St
West Quay Shopping Centre
West Quay Retail Park
Harbour Parade
Bargate St
Castle
Albion
Shop
WEST QUAY ROAD A33
W Quay Rd
Odeon Cinema
W Quay Rd
W Quay Road
Harbour Pde
Western Esplanade
Forest Vw
Castle Sq
Castle
Way
Hamtun st
West
Hotel
Hotel
WEST QUAY RD
Herbert Walker Avenue
Western Esp
Bugle St
Upr Bugle St
Westgate St
Tudor House Museum
Southampton City Council
St Michael St
MAYFLOWER ROUNDABOUT
Mayflower Park
Mayflower Memorial
Wool House Maritime Mus
City Council
School
Red Funnel Ferry Terminal
Royal Pier
Porter's La
A33
Fer Ter
Town Quay

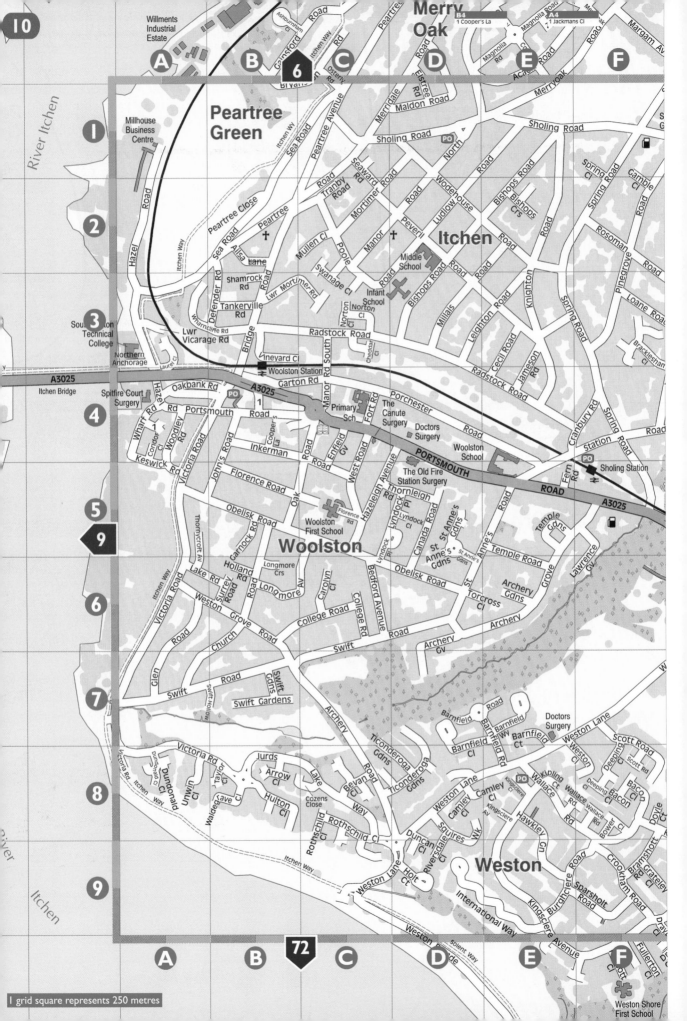

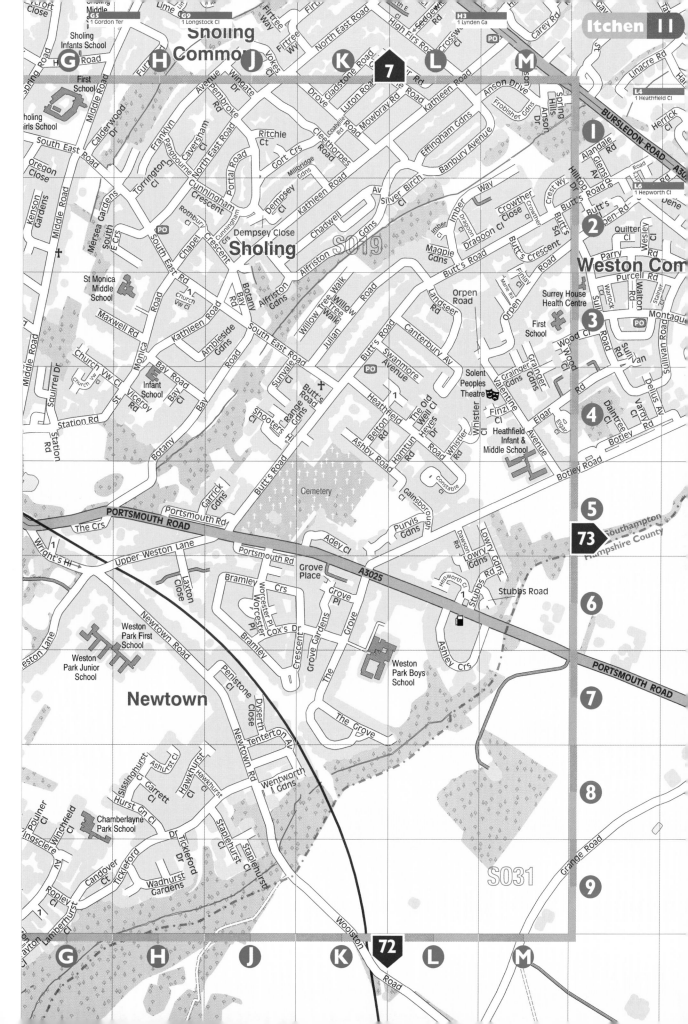

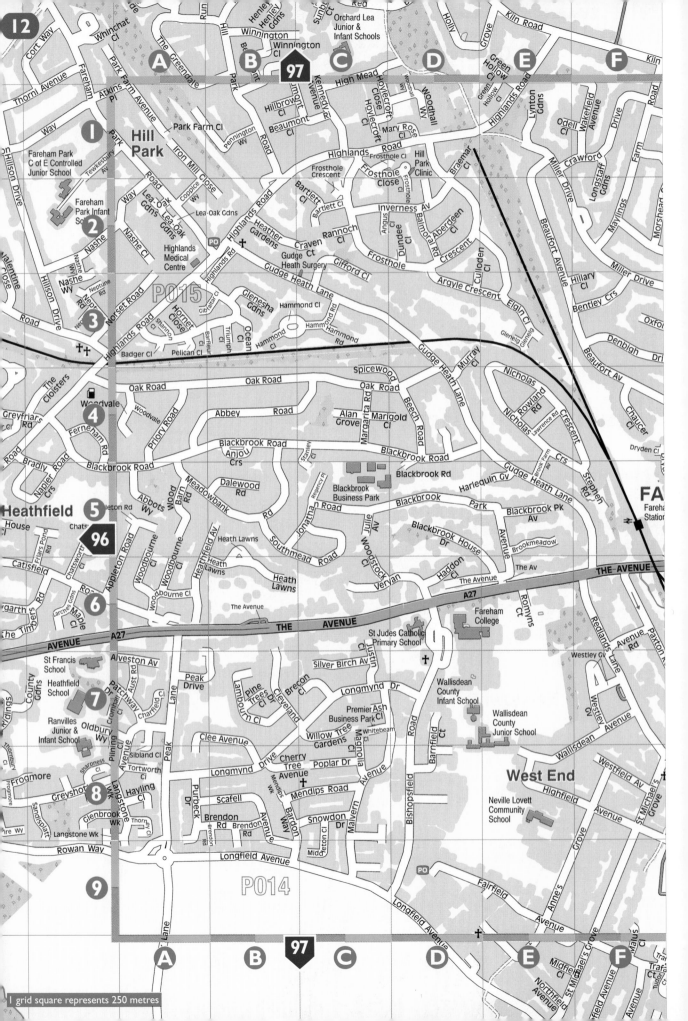

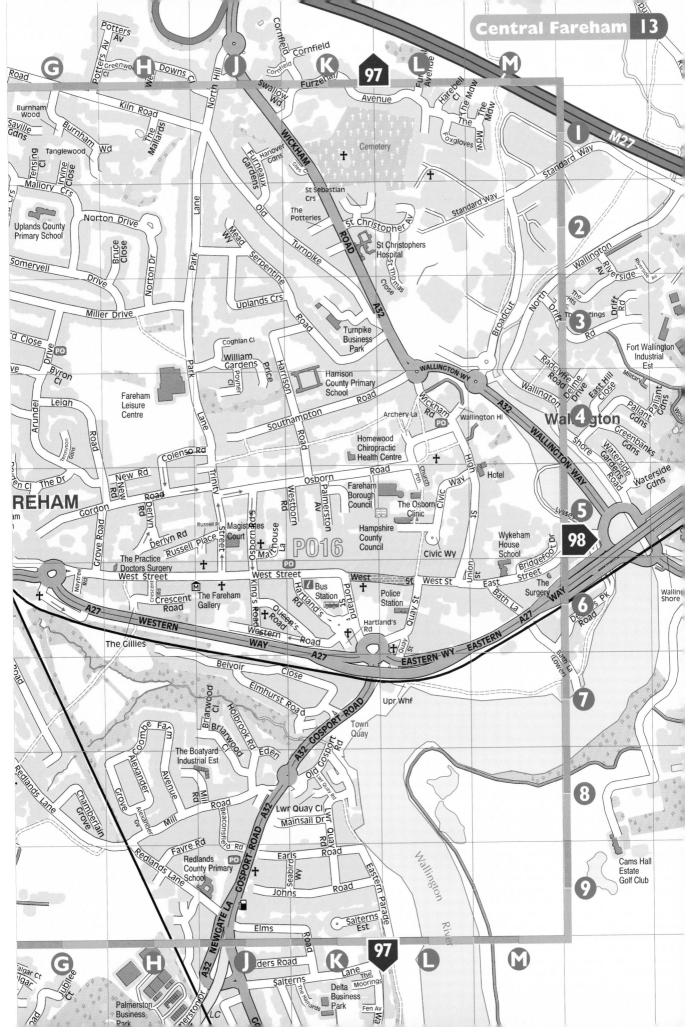

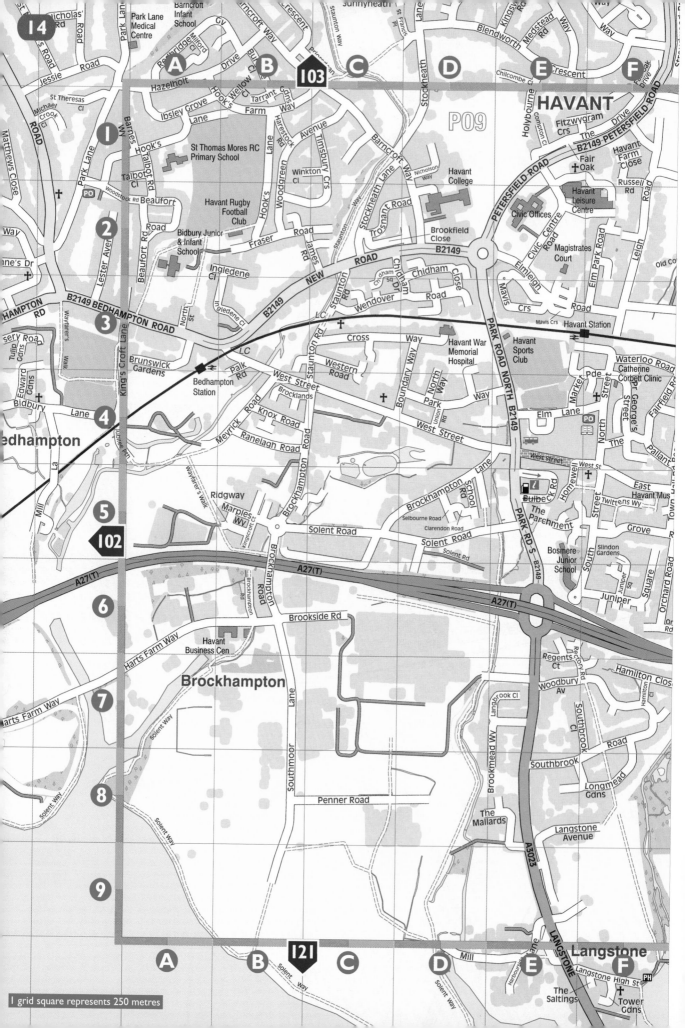

G · H · J · K · 133 · L · M

K2 1 Admiral's Wk
K7 1 Seager's Ct

L2 1 Anchor La

Shipbuilding Road
Shipbuilding Road
Boiler Rd
Navy Rd
Aldrich Road

HM Naval Base

Burrow Island

City of Portsmouth / Hampshire County

Queen's Road
Murray's La
Victoria Rd
Gloucester Rd
Anchor Ga
The Parade
Marlborough Rw
Cir

L3 1 Benbow Pl
2 South Ter

HMS Nelson

Mary Rose Ship Hall
King's Rd
Main Road
Sampson Rd
Jago Rd
Stony Lane
Short Rw
Cumberland St
Kg William St

North Street Treadgold Museum

Portse

HMS Victory
Scott Rd
Sunny Walk
Bonfire Cnr
Prince George St
Queen Street

L4 1 Beneficial St
2 College La
3 Havant St
4 Rosemary La
5 Ship Leopard St
6 Victory Rd

Royal Naval Museum
College Rd
Admiralty Rd
Hanover St
Bishop
Aylward St
Que
Lion St

Dockyard Apprentice Exhibition
Queen Street
PO
Portland St

Main Road
Mary Rose Exhibition
Old Star
Hawke St
Union St
Curzon Road
University of Portsmouth

L7 1 French St
2 Lombard St
3 Oyster Ms

University of Portsmouth

Portsmouth Harbour

Yacht Marina

HMS Warrior
Station
The Hard
B2154
ORDNANCE RW
Clock
College St
Kent Street
St George's Wy
Britain St
Richmond Road
Burnaby Road

The Hard Interchange Bus & Coach Station
Portsmouth Harbour Station

St Georges Business Centre

United Services Rugby Club

M3 1 Aylward St

University of Portsmouth

BROAD ROAD
Minnitt Rd
SOUTH STREET
Bus Station

PARK RD

United Services Cricket Ground

ST GEORGE'S RD
Old Portsmouth

18

M4 1 Dean St
2 Margery's Ct
3 St Georges Sq
4 Solent Wy
5 Sun St

Trinity Cl
Haslar Road
Trinity Gn
The Esplanade
Solent Way

Isle of Wight Car Ferry Terminal

Way Road
ST GEORGE'S RD
B2154
A3
CAMBRIDGE RD

Gunwharf
Armory La
Armory Ct
Crays
King Charles St
Warblington St
Street
University of Portsmouth

The Pascoe Practice

Portsmouth Grammar School
MUSEUM ROAD

PO

City of Portsmouth / Hampshire County

Royal Navy Submarine Museum Offices

Bath Sq
PH
Bathing La
West St
East Street
Captains Rw
Camber Place
Round Tower
Town Walls
Square Tower
Battery Row

BROAD STREET
Tower St
HIGH ST
White Hart Road
Oyster St
Thomas's St
Highbury St
St Nicholas St
Street
Peacock La

Goldfield Gallery
Cathedral Church of St Thomas of Canterbury
Grand Pde
Penny St
Pembroke Road

Portsmouth City Council

City Museum & Art Gallery
Chadderton Guns Museum

M6 1 Beehive Wk
2 Nobbs La

Judes of E Primary School
Woodville Dr
Blount Rd
King's Ter

Chatham Dr
Hotel
Gordon Road

M7 1 Halfpenny La
2 Wyndham Ms

P

The Long Curtain (Old Town Defences)

BELLEVUE
PIER ROAD
A288
SOUTH TERR

PO

Long Curtain Road

Clarence Pier & Amusement Centre

Clarence Esplanade

M8 1 Pembroke Cl

Hovercraft Terminal
Clarence Esplanade
Solent Way

G · H · J · K · 133 · L · M

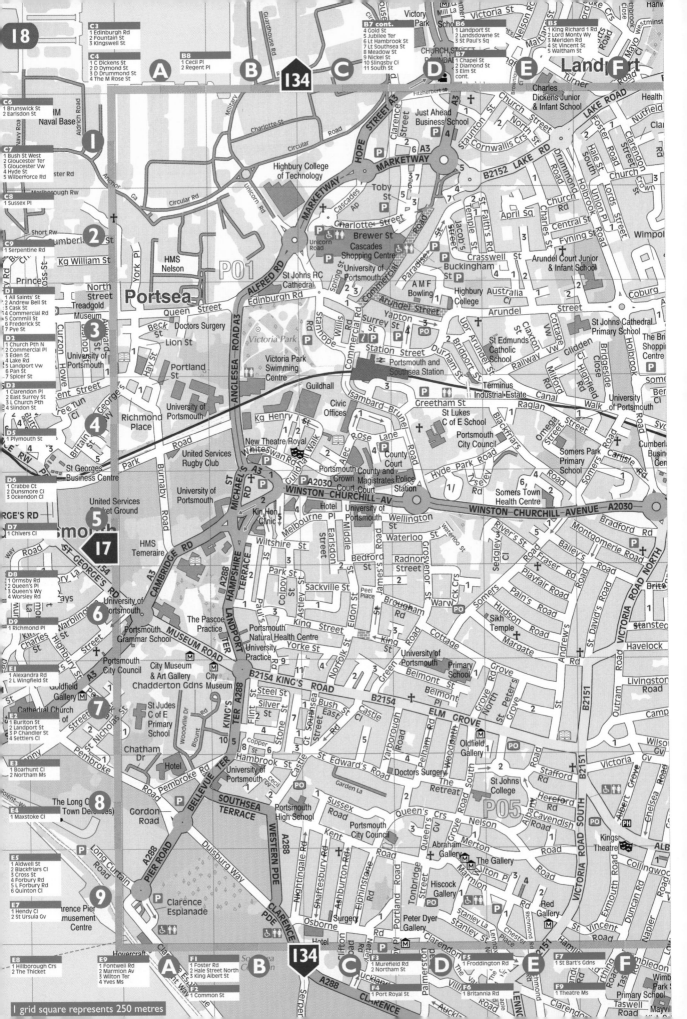

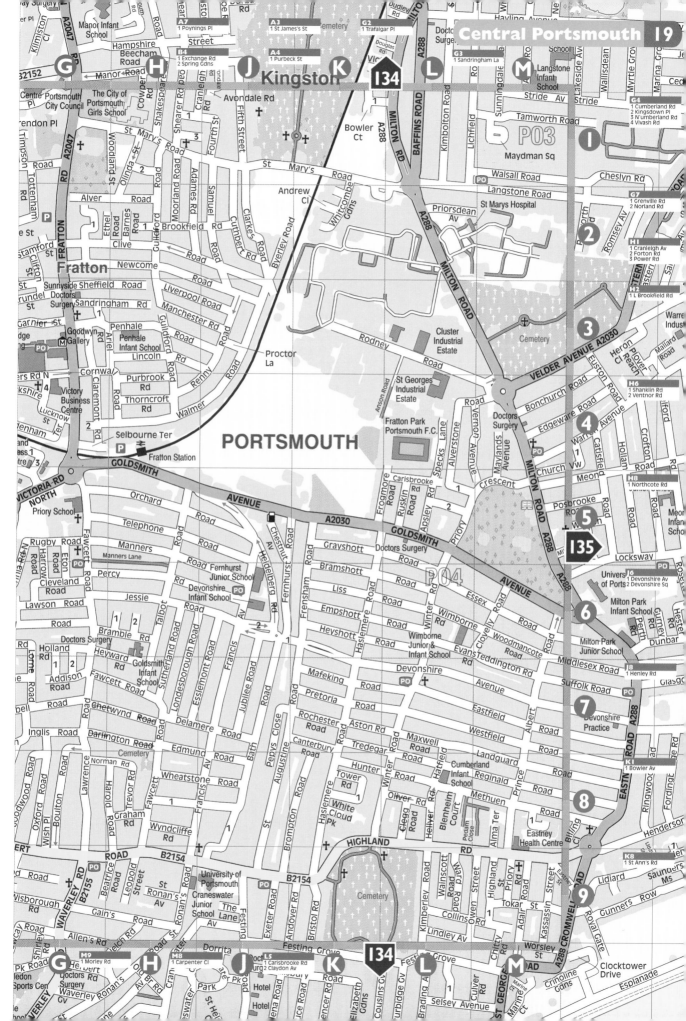

A B C D E

1

B3049

Northwood Park

Church Lane

✝

Main Road

New Road

Littleton

Rozelle Close
Holm Oak Cl
Fairclose
Drive
The Hall Way
Pitter Cl
Westfield
Hilden
Way
Eyfield Way
North Drive
Dale Close
Valley Road
Bercote Close
Chestn
Ave
2

e

STOCKBRIDGE ROAD B3049

South Drive
PO
Kenn

3

Watley Lane

Lainston House
Hotel

Deane Down Drove

Lock's
Lane

Lock's Lane

PH

Woodman Lane

Dean

4

Church

Home
Lane

Lambourne
Close

✝

PO

Sparsholt Primary School

Bostock
Close

Dean Lane

Close
Rapoow

Littleton Lane

5

Westview Road

Downside Road

Burrow Road

Grovelands Road
Sawyer Cl
Sern

Lanham
Lane

Teg
Beech
Copse

Wabste

Cro

Do

6

SO22

Crab
Wood

7

Crabwood Farm House

Lanham Lane

Teg
Down

Clarendon Way

Royal
Winchester
Golf Club

A B 24 C D E

1 grid square represents 500 metres

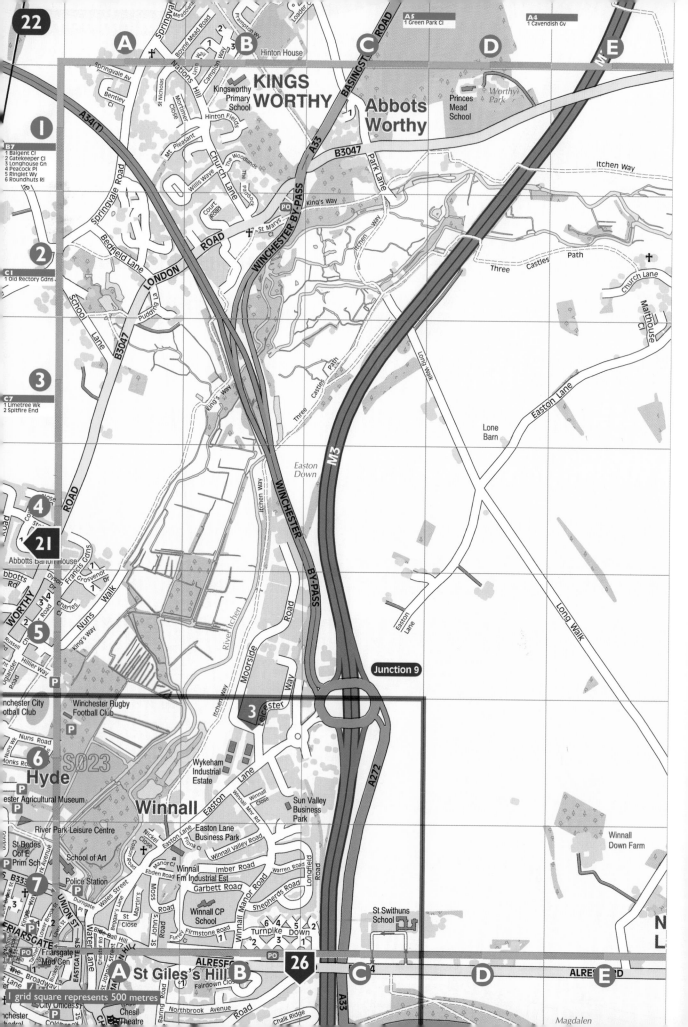

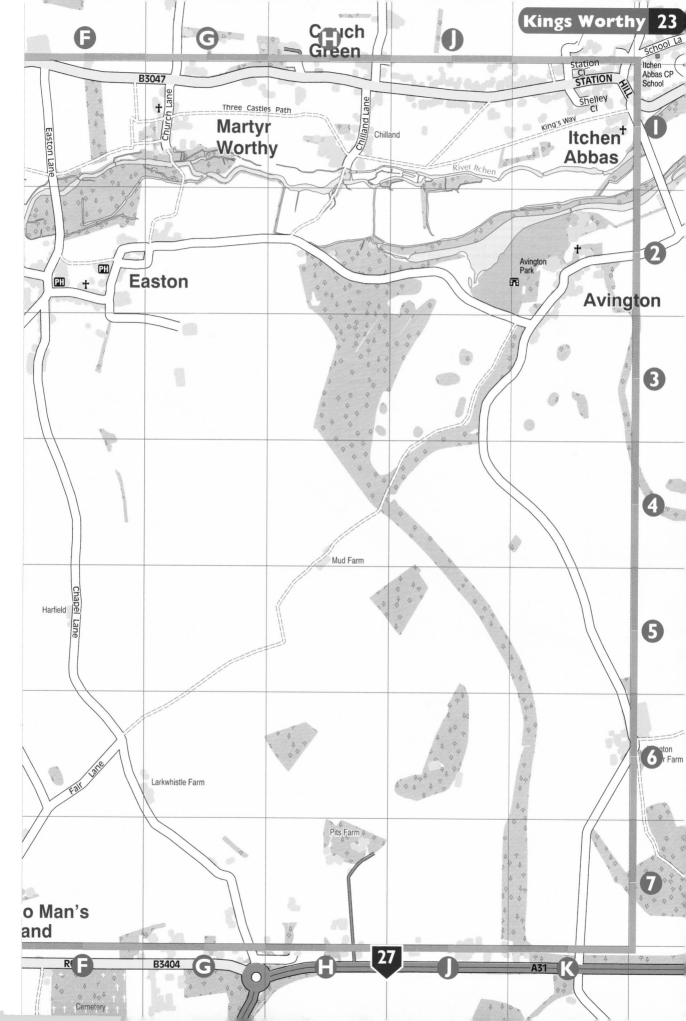

F G H J

Church
Green

I

B3047

Easton Lane

Church Lane

✝

Three Castles Path

**Martyr
Worthy**

Chilland Lane

Chilland

River Itchen

Station
CI

STATION

Itchen
Abbas CP
School

School La

Shelley
CI

HILL

King's Way

Itchen ✝
Abbas

PH ✝ PH **Easton**

Avington
Park

✝

Avington

2

3

Chapel Lane

Harfield

Mud Farm

4

5

Fair Lane

Larkwhistle Farm

...gton
...r Farm

6

Pits Farm

7

o Man's
...and

R...

Cemetery

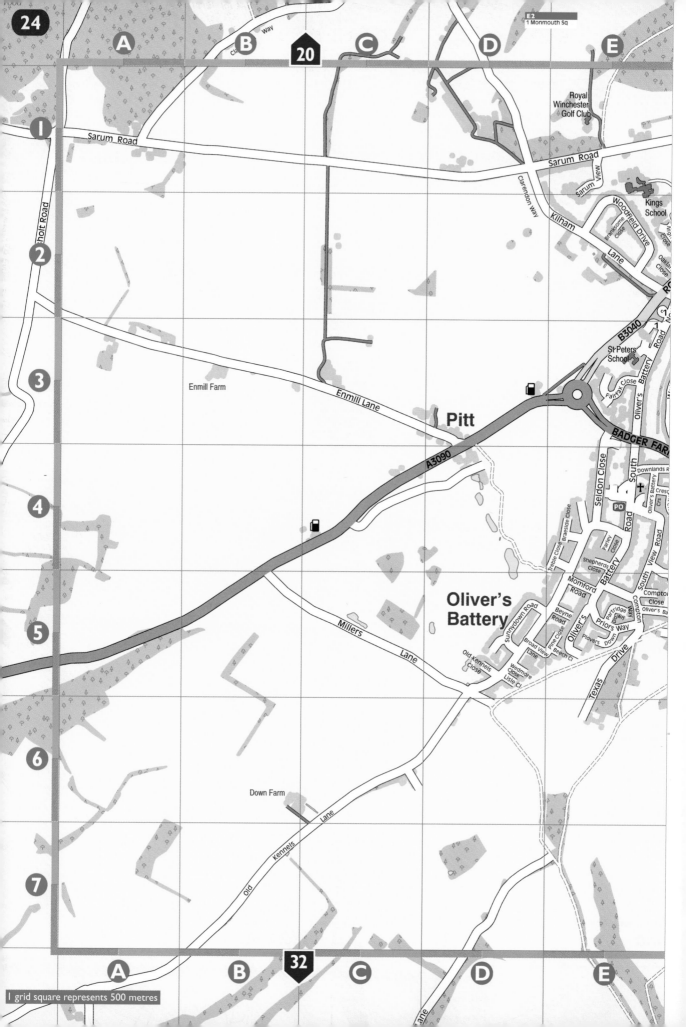

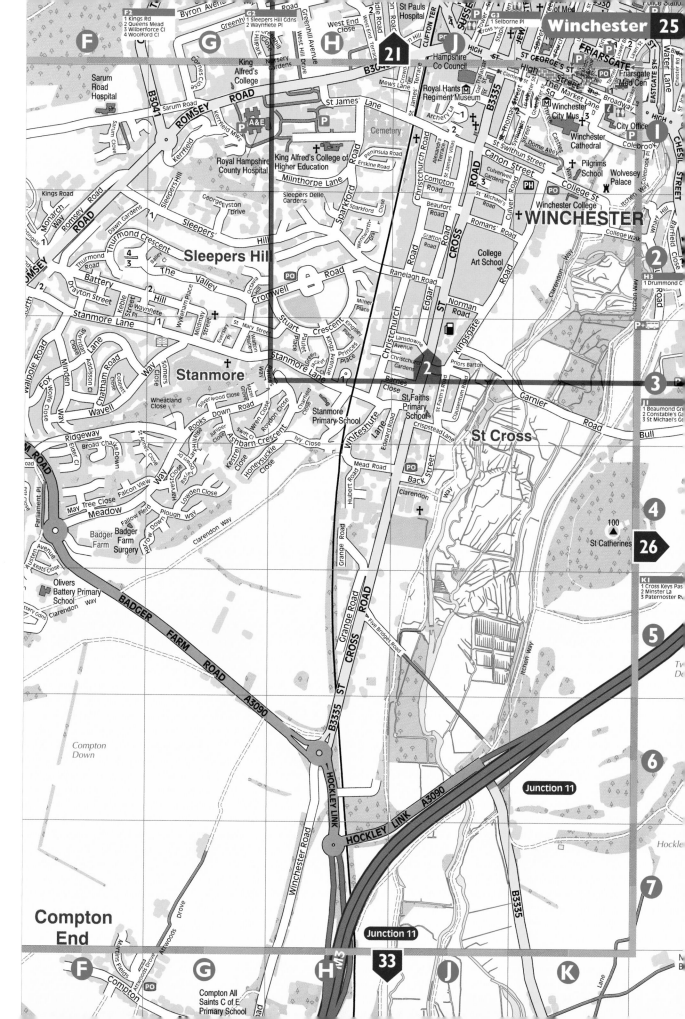

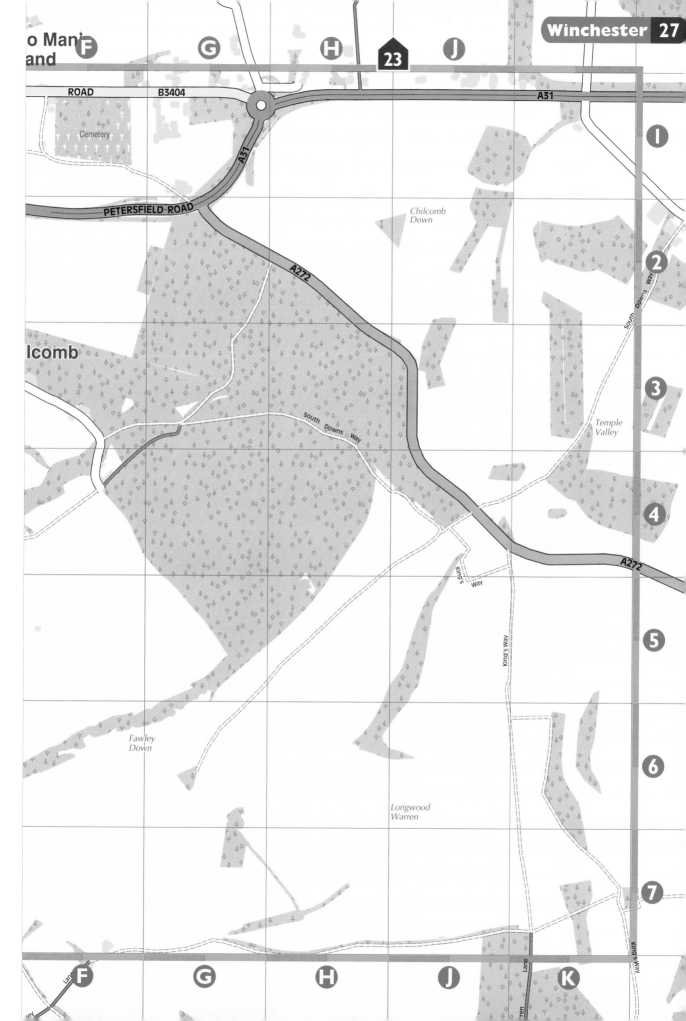

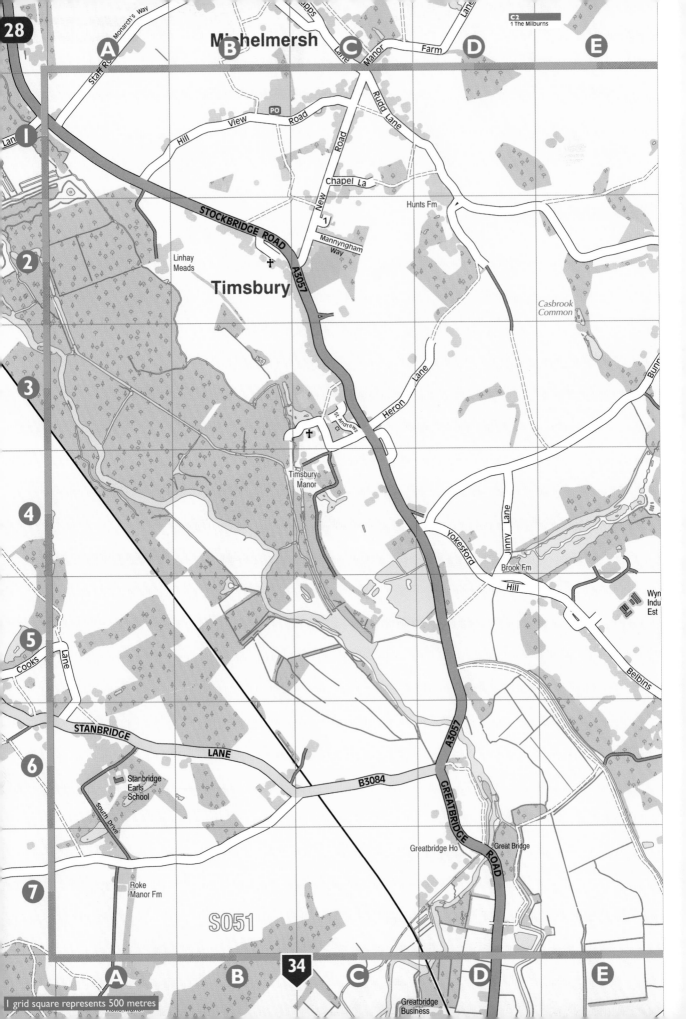

G7
1 Cavendish Cl

H7
1 Anderson Cl
2 Ganger Rd
3 The Green
4 Norris Cl
5 Woodley Wy

Farley Lane

F
G
H
J

I

Paynes Hay

Braishfield Road

Monarch's Way

Hill

Lane

Fern

2

Paynes Hay
Farm

Church Lane

Lower St

Sharpes Fm

Braishfield

Dummers

Rd

Monarch's Way

Pud

Rudd Lane

Newport
Lane

Common Hill Road

Hill Vw
Rd PO

Braishfield
CP School

3

Kiln

Lane

30

4

Megana
Wy

Fairbornes Fm

ford Farm
strial

Abbotswood Fm

Jermyns Ho

5

Braishfield Road

Sandy
Lane

Belbins
Business Park

Jermyns Lane

6

Abbotswood

Cemetery

Cupernham
Lane

Ganger Fm

THE
STRAIGHT
MILE

7

Woodley
Cl

Woodley
Close

Ganger Farm Lane

Fotner
Cl

2
5

1

4

Woodley Lane

Cavendish Cl

Stapleford

Horseshoe Dr

Short Hi

Hunters

Braishfield Road

North

6

35
dley

Cupernham
F

Brook Way

Brook Wy

Kinver Cl

Kinver Cl

Richmond Lane

Anstey
Road

Bransley Cl

G

Ashley

Halden Cl

Pinewood Cl

Oakwood Cl

Bourne

5

8

Cedar
Lawn

School Road

H

Peel
Cl

J

K

Grovely Wy

Lane

Oxlease

7

PO

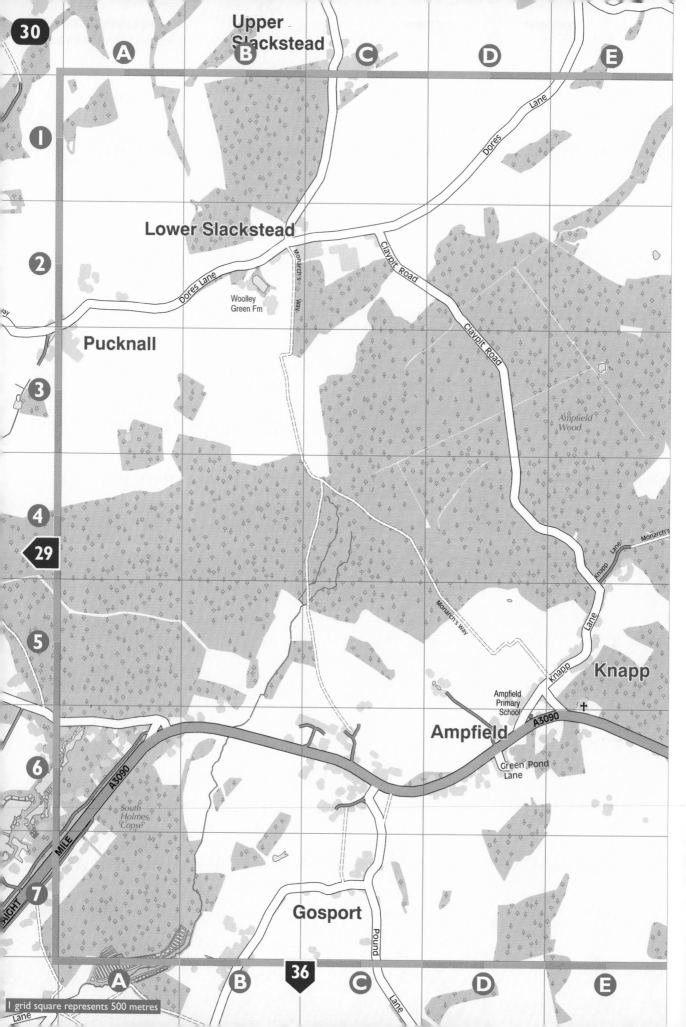

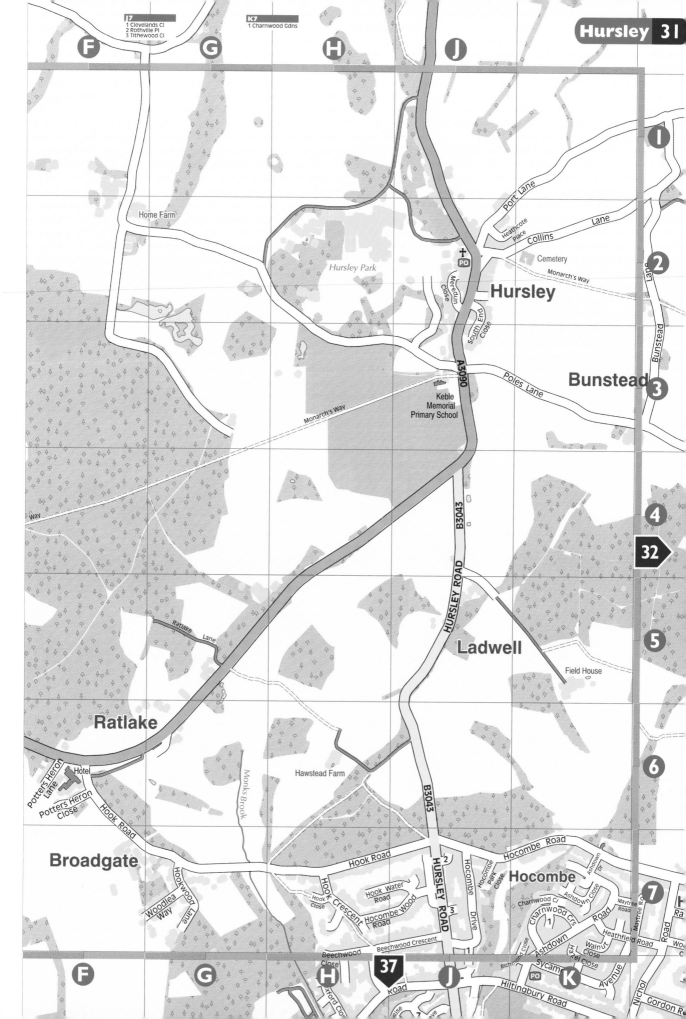

F G H J

17
1 Clevelands Cl
2 Rothville Pl
3 Tithewood Cl

K7
1 Charnwood Gdns

I

2

Port Lane

Heathcote Place

Collins Lane

Cemetery

Monarch's Way

Home Farm

Hursley Park

Meredun Close

Hursley

South End Close

A3090

Poles Lane

Bunstead

3

Bunstead Lane

Monarch's Way

Keble Memorial Primary School

B3043

4

32

Hursley Road

Ladwell

Field House

5

Ratlake Lane

Ratlake

Monks Brook

Hawstead Farm

B3043

6

Potters Heron Lane

Hotel

Potters Heron Close

Hook Road

Broadgate

Hookwood Lane

Woodlea Way

Hook Road

Hook Crescent

Hook Water Road

Hocombe Wood Road

Hursley Road

Hocombe Drive

Hocombe Road

Hocombe Park Close

Hocombe

Charnwood Cl

Charnwood Crs

Ashdown Dr

Ashdown Close

Maytree Rd

7

Heathfield Road

Ashdown Road

Wainut Close

Hazel Close

Maytree Rd

Beechwood Close

Beechwood Crescent

Oxford Close

Richmond Close

Ashdown

Sycamore

PO

Hiltingbury Road

Nichol Gordon R

K

F G H **37** J K

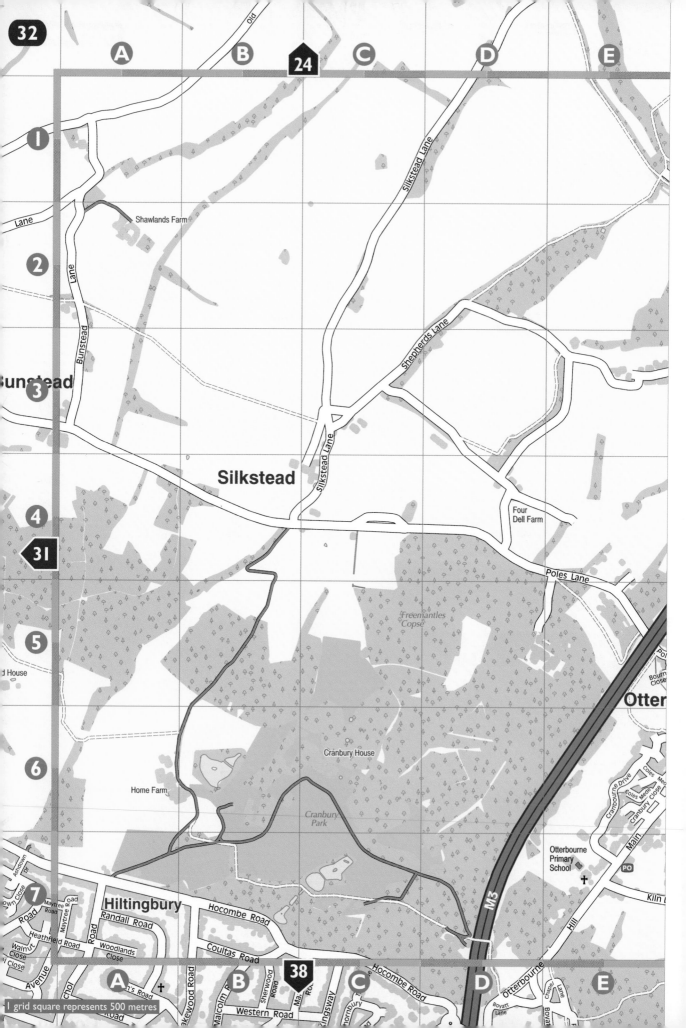

A   B   24   C   D   E

1

Old

Silkstead Lane

Lane

2

Bunstead Lane

Shawlands Farm

Bunstead

3

Bunstead

Shepherds Lane

Silkstead

Silkstead Lane

Four
Dell Farm

4

31

Poles Lane

House

Freemantles
Copse

5

d House

Bourn
Close

Otter

6

Cranbury House

Cranbury
Park

Home Farm

Cranborne Drive
Coles Mede
Coles Mede
Cranbury Close

Main

Otterbourne
Primary
School

PO

7

Ashdown Dr

Maytree Road

Road

Hiltingbury

Randall Road

Hocombe Road

M3

Kiln

own Close

Maytree Road

Heathfield Road

Woodlands
Close

Coultas Road

Hill

Otterbourne

Walnut
Close

l Close

Avenue

chol

n's Road

akewood Road

Malcolm R

Sherwood
Road

Ma

Kingsway

Thornbury

Hocombe Road

Boyatt
Lane

Chapel
Lane

Boyatt

A   B   38   C   D   E

Western Road

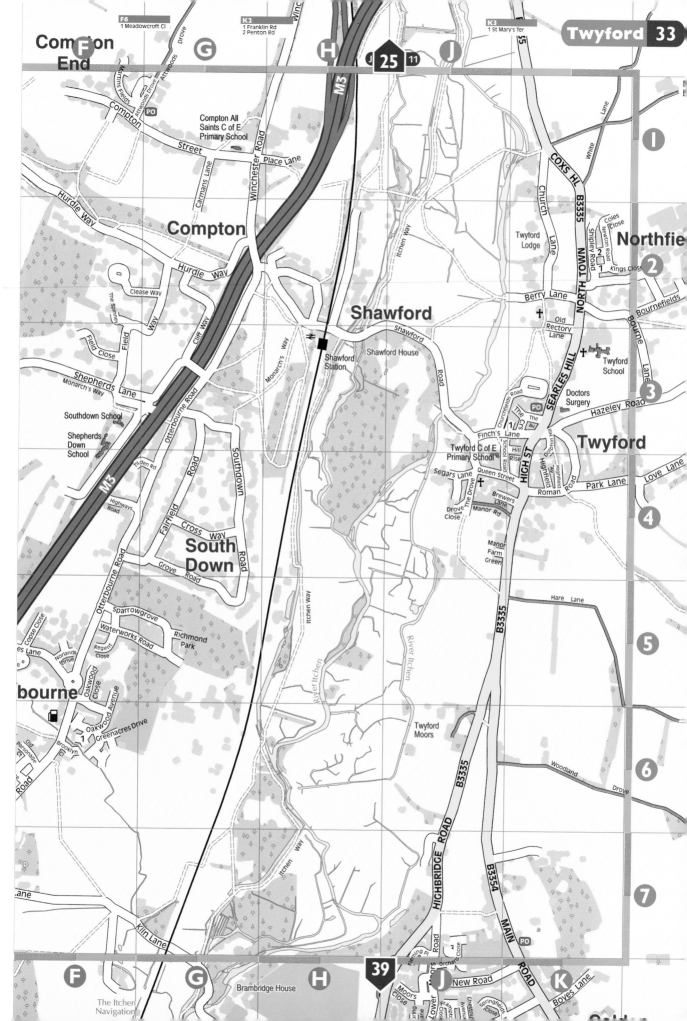

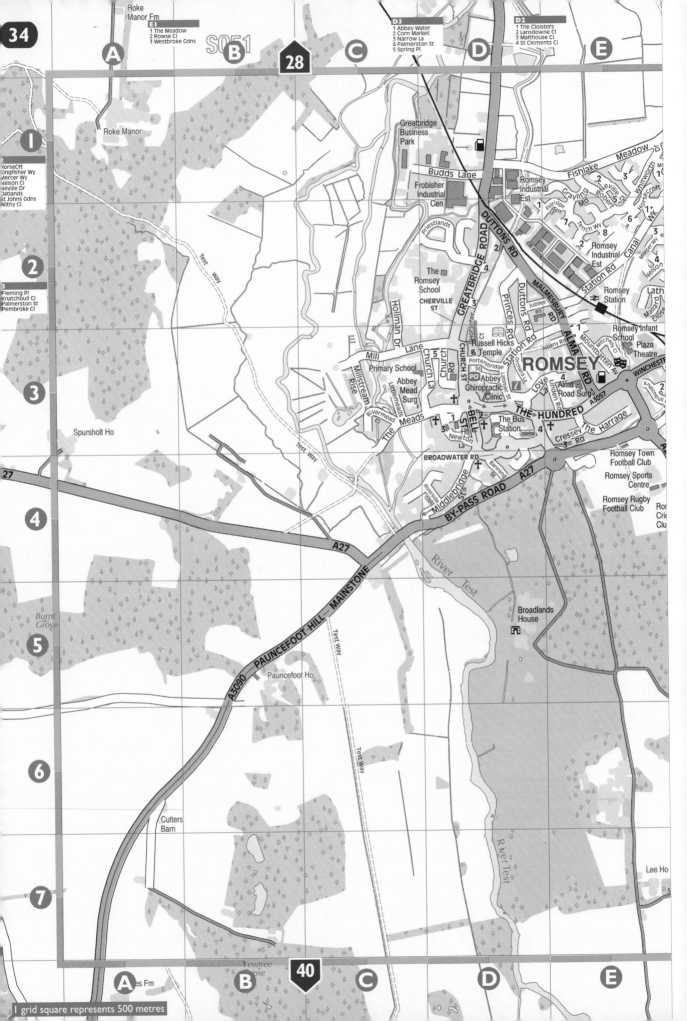

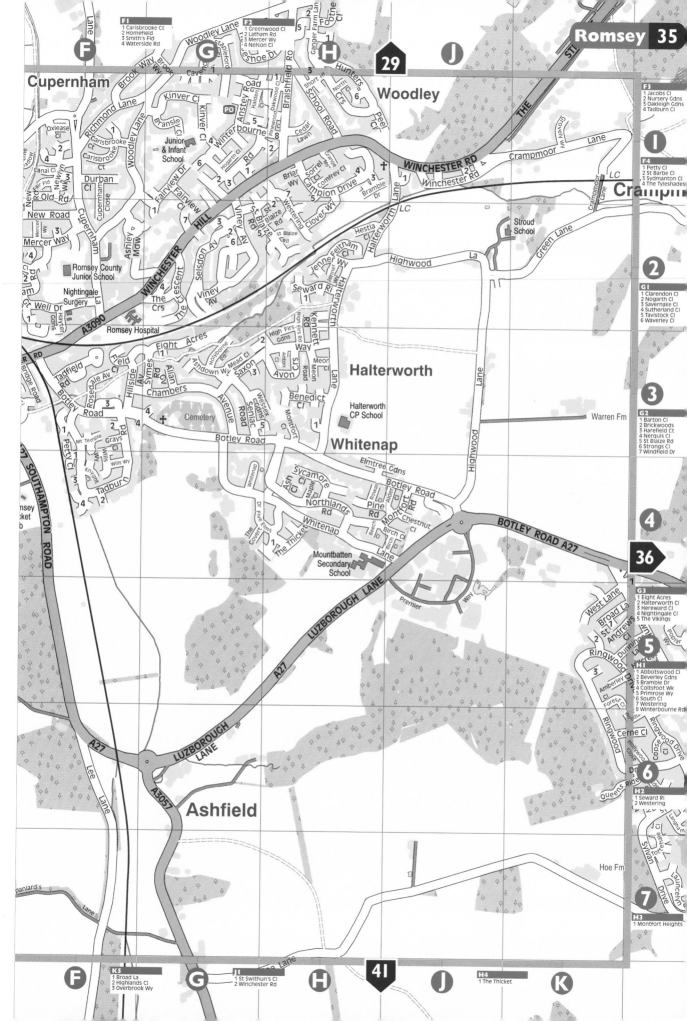

F
G
H
J

29

Woodley

I

Crampm

2

3

Cupernham

Woodley Lane

Halterworth

Whitenap

Warren Fm

4

36

5

6

Ashfield

Hoe Fm

7

F
G
H
41
J

K

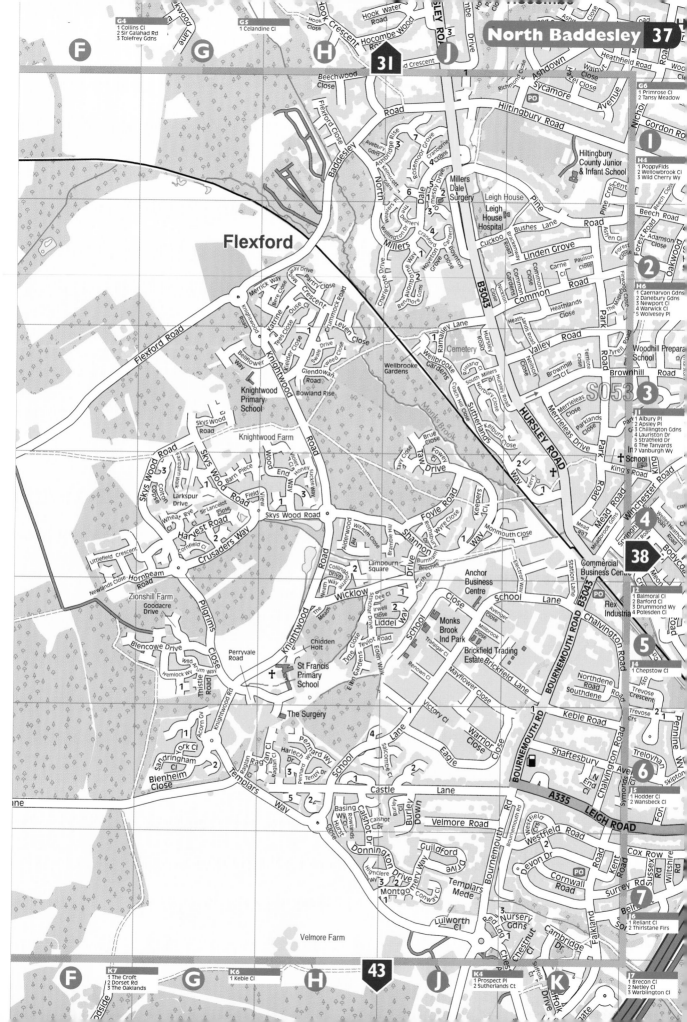

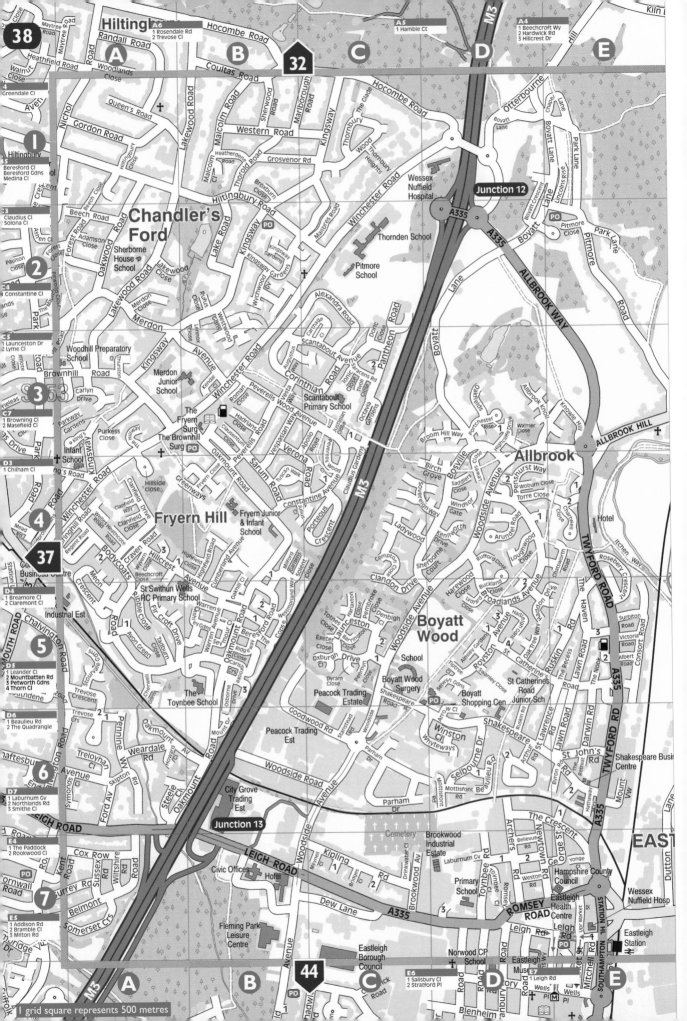

40

A   B   **34**   C   D   E

1

Ranvilles Fm

Yewtree Copse

A3090

Ridge Lane

Ridge

2

Lee Park Fm

Moorcourt Copse

3

Lee Church L

Test Way

Moorcourt

4

Test Way

River Test

River Blackwater

Test Way

Wade Hill Fm

5

Hill Street

Nursling Ho

Chu

Hillstreet   Colbury Ho

6

Broadlands Lake

Brooke's Hill

7

Nursling Mill

Mill Lane

Brookes Hill Industrial Estate

Green La

Manor Ho Fm

SALISBURY

A   B   **52**   C   D   E

ROA

Testwood Lakes

Little Testwood Fm

I grid square represents 500 metres

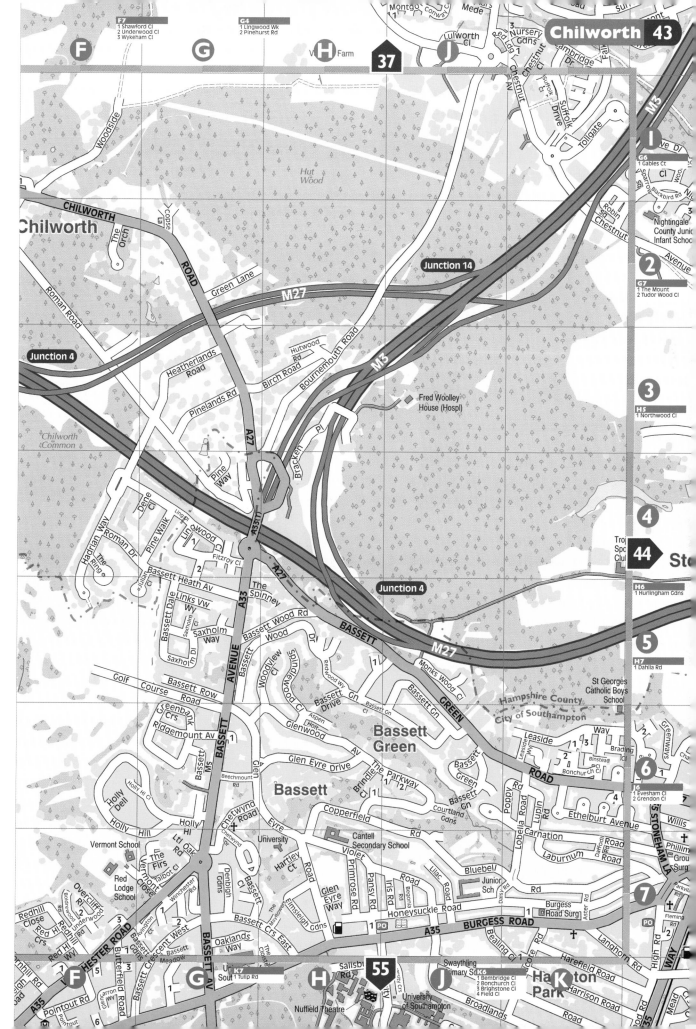

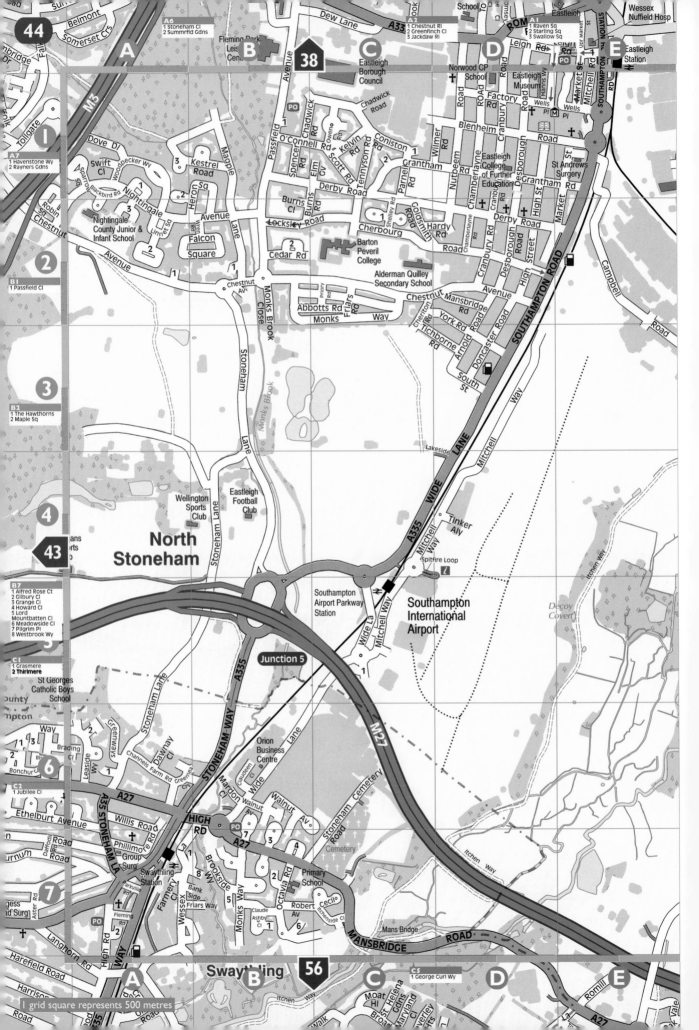

F

G

H

J WINCHESTER ROAD

Woolstreet Farm

Stakes La

I

LANE

Dairy Farm

Alma Lane

Scivier's Lane

Crescent

The

Durley Hall Lane

Wintershill Hall

Wintershill

Durley Hall Farm

Winters Hill

King's Way

2

Greenwood Lane

Scivier's Lane

Durley Street

3

Durley Street

The Drove

PO

Manor Road

Durley Manor Farm

4

48

5

Brook Road

Durley Primary School

Durley

Parsonage Lane

Lower Farm

Kytes Lane

Brown Heath

Mincingfield Farm

Mincingfield Lane

6

White Street

Heathen Street

Gregory Lane

Stapleford Farm

7

River Ham

Calcot H

Calcot

Hill Farm

Durley Mill

Mill Lan

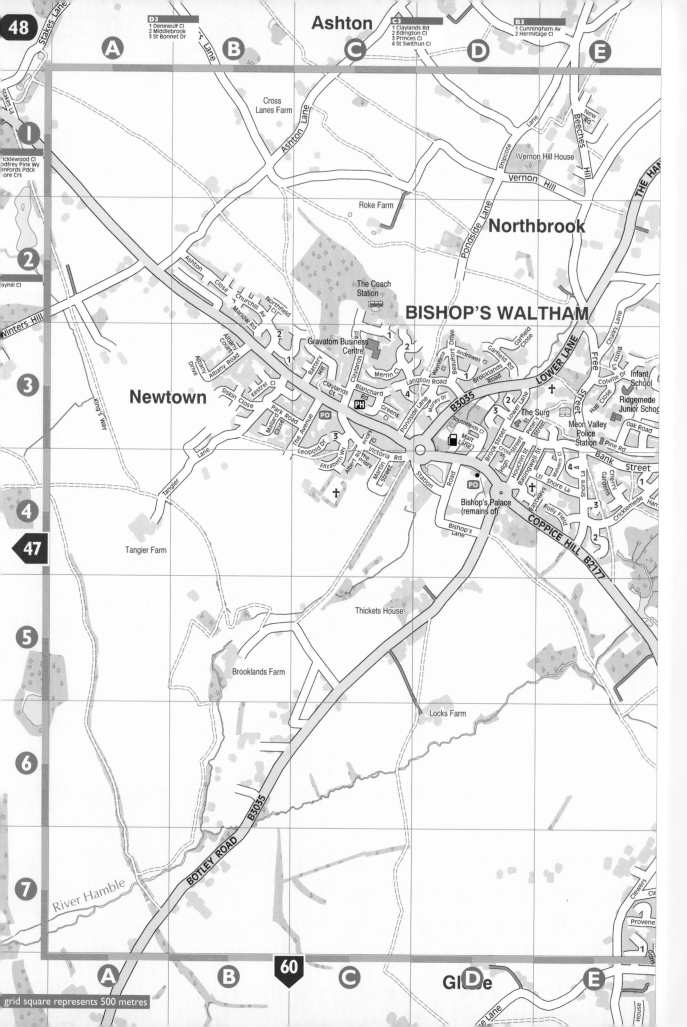

F Lane
F7
1 Meadow Cl

The Hang

J6
1 Beverley Gdns
2 Coronation Rd

Galley Down

B3032

I
I7
1 Rowan Cl
2 Russett Cl

Bishopsdown Stud Farm

Duncombe

Dundridge

Dundridge Lane

2

Swanmore Park House

Park La

Hill

Damson

Hill Top

3

Park

Park La

Upper Swanmore

Tennyson Cl

Wordsworth Cl

Byron Close

Rareridge

Elm Rd

Willow Rd

Sycamore Rd

Gunners Pk

Lane

West Hoe Lane

Cemetery

Jervis

Court

Lane

Green Lane

4

Mayhill

Hoe Road

Hoe

Suetts Lane

Swanmore Road

Moorlands Road

Well Lane

Hill

Vicarage Lane

Cut Throat Lane

5

Donigers Dell

Hampton

Paradise Lane

Swanmore Business Park

Lower Chase Road

Broad Lane

Foxcombe Close

Church Road

PO

Swanmore Church of England School

Buckets Farm

Vicarage Lane

Church Lane

Swanmore

6

The Drove

Chapel Road

Greenways

Larkspur Cl

New Road

Spring Vale

Myers Cl

Spring Lane

Leacock

Spring Vale

Dodds Lane

Crofton Way

Swanmore County Secondary School

King's Way

Hill

Lower Chase Road

Ludwell's La

wers Lane

Evelyn

Meadow Gdns

Proyene

Cardens

The Ridings

B2177

New Road

Waltham Business Park

The Lakes

Martin Cl

Medlicott Wy

Glendale

Droxford Road

Hillpound

7

Hill Crest

Chase Grove

Linden Close

F 1

G

Brickyard Road

H

61

J

Orchardlea

K

Mislingfor

Forest Road

Dirty Copse

Forest Farm

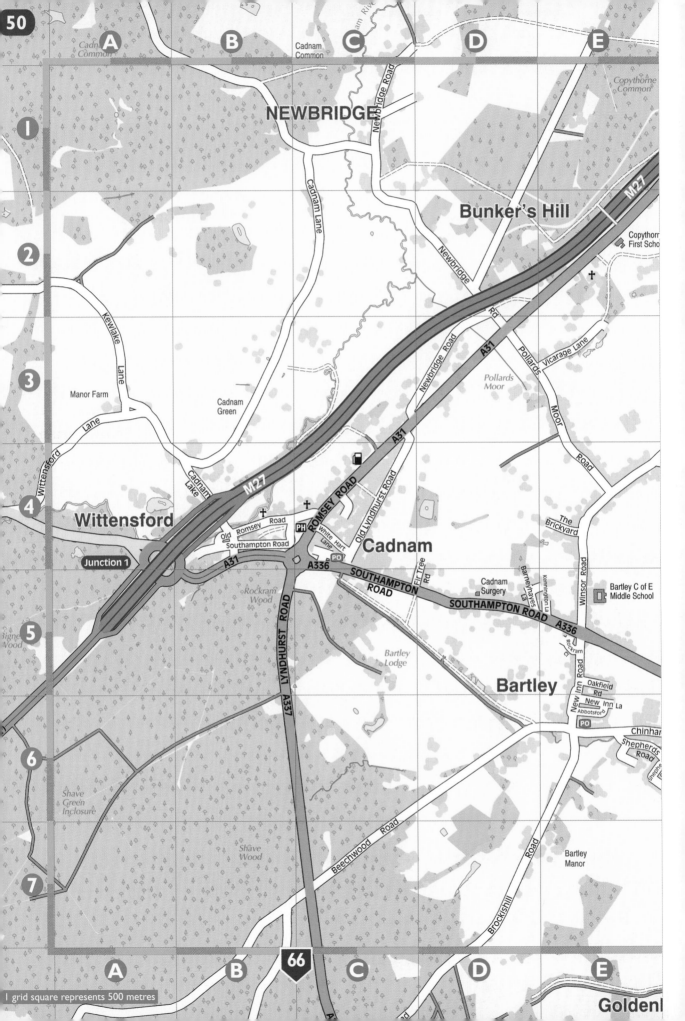

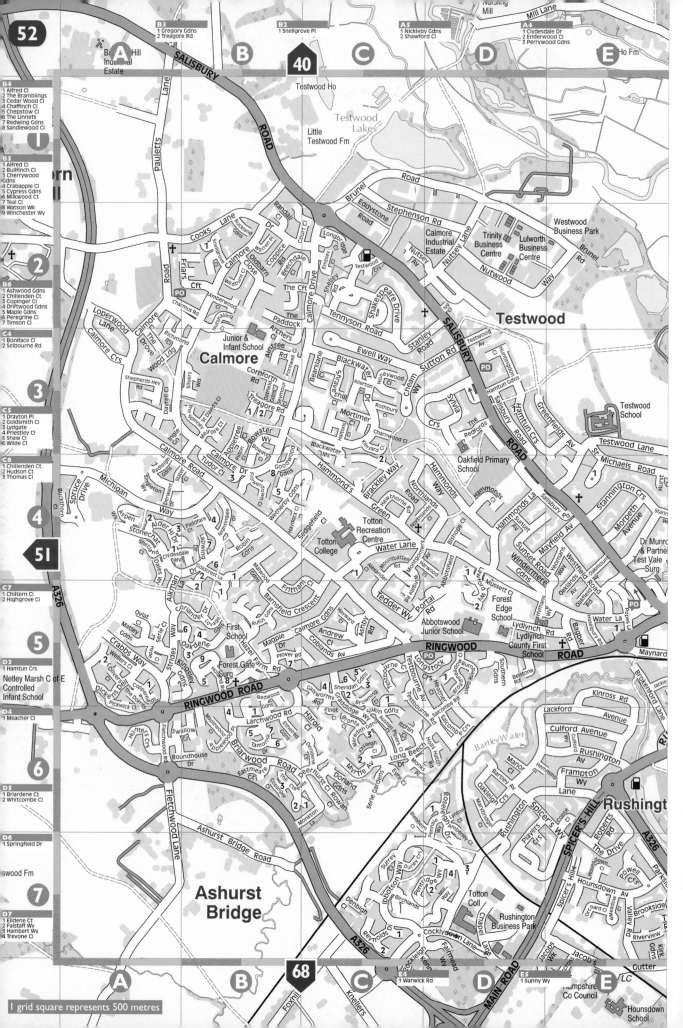

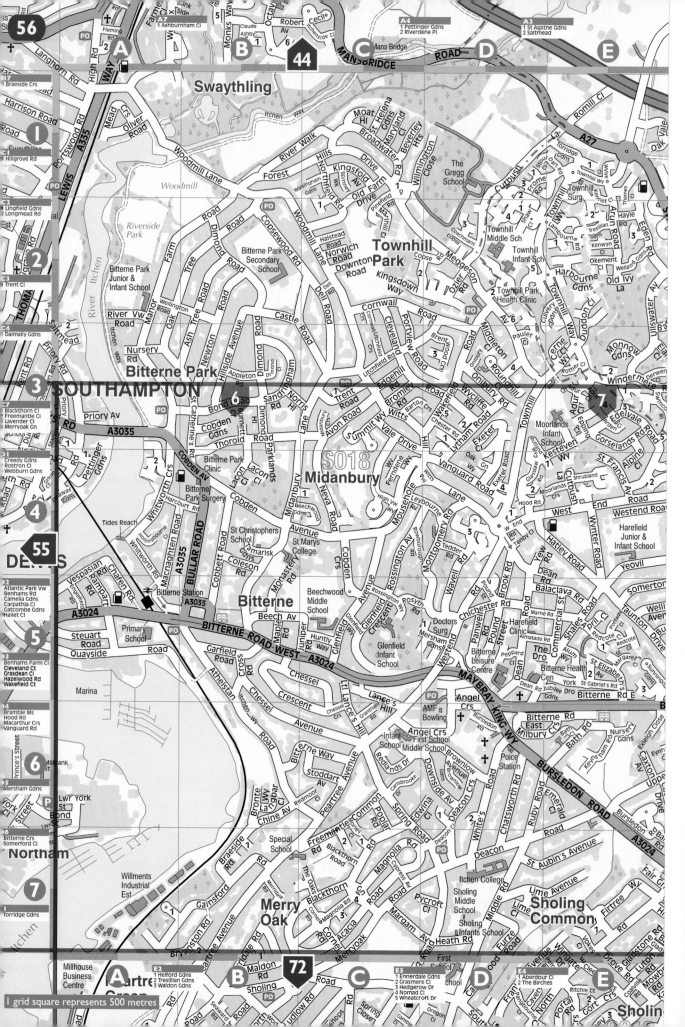

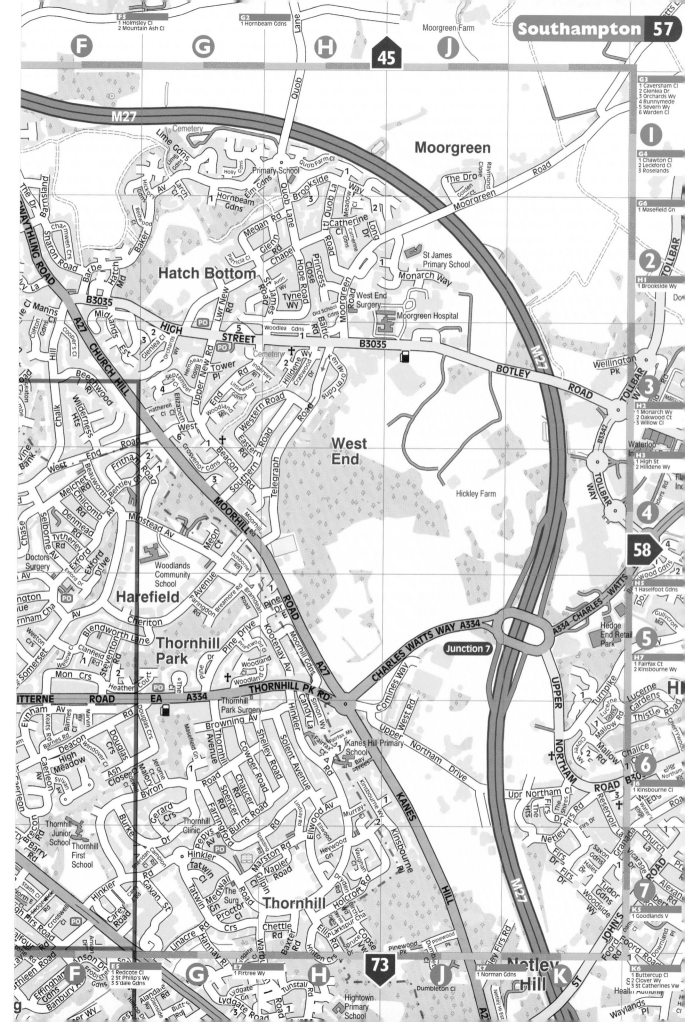

A **B** **C** **D** **E**

46

74

Croft House

Chancellors Lane

WINCHESTER ROAD

Botley Park
Hotel &
Country Club

**Boorley
Green**

Hedge End
Station

Dowd's Farm

Nelson
Ind Park

Solent
Industrial Est

St Lukes.
Surg.

Hedge End
Busi Cen

Waterloo
Industrial Est

Berrywood
Primary
School

Giles
Close

Flanders
Ind Park

Taplin
Drive

Shamblehurst
CP School

Wildern

Wildern Clinic

Hotel

Grange Dr

Broadoak

BROAD OAK A334 A334

Holmesland

Woodhills School

Hedge
Retail

**HEDGE
END**

Lucerne
Gardens

Freeground Junior &
Infant School

Police
Station
Freegrounds

Kings Copse
Primary School

South West
Health Authority

1 grid square represents 500 metres

F4
1 Glebe Ct

F **G** **H** **47** **J**

I

Calcot House

Durley
Mill

Mill Lane

Calcot Hill

Hill Farm

Blind Lane

2

Breach
Hill

Nether Hill Lane

The
Plantation

Calcot Lane

Capers End Lane

3

Maddoxford Farm

Kestrel Close
Ravenscroft Wy
Falcon Wy
ws Nest Lane

Hill Farm

Curdridge
Primary
School

†

Long Common

River Hamble

Wangfield Farm

Wangfield Lane

Church La

Curdridge

B3035

Chapel Lane

Lockhams

4

The Vine
School

Botley Road

Reading Room Lane

60

CKS H

Uplands Farm

WINCHESTER STREET

Park View

Pern Drive
Alexandra Wy

Botley Junior &
Infant School

Vicarage Lane

Botley
Station

Hillsons Road

STATION HILL

A334

Kitnocks

Outlands Lane

5

E4
1 Rowley Cl

Jenkins Cl

Mayfair
Cypress Gdns

HIGH STREET
†

PO

Kilford Court
Mortimer Road

Cheping
Gardens

Four
Acre

MILL HILL A334

Harelbwood

Botley

6

A3051

Steeple Court

Church Lane

Fairthorne Manor

7

†

F D2
1 Watkin Rd **G** D6
1 Montrose Cl **H** **75** **J** E2
1 Pear Tree Cl **K**

Barn Farm

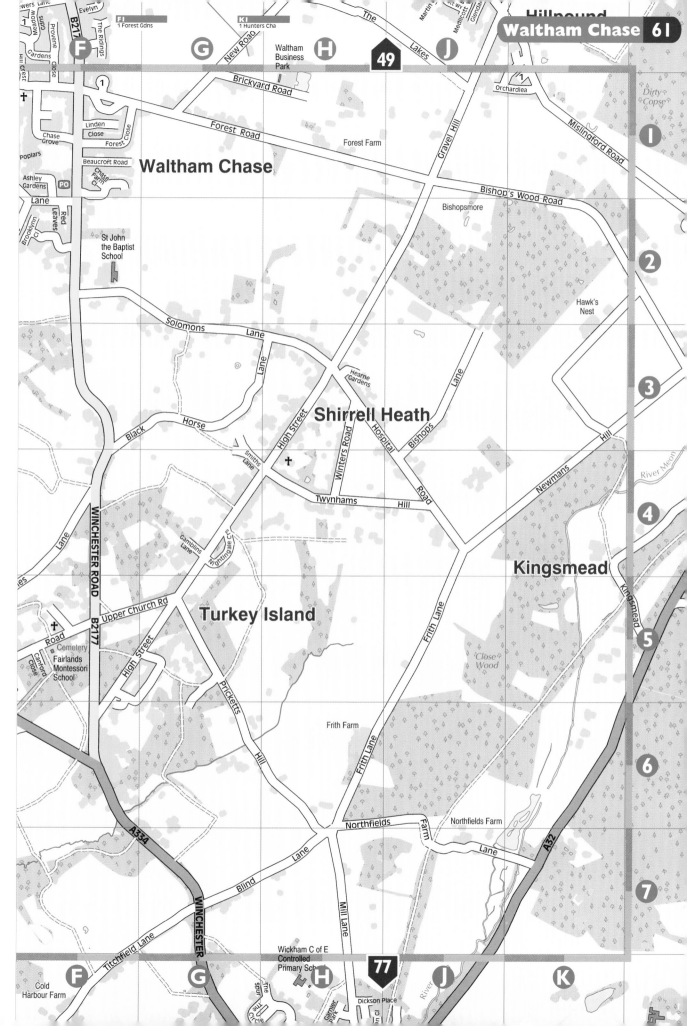

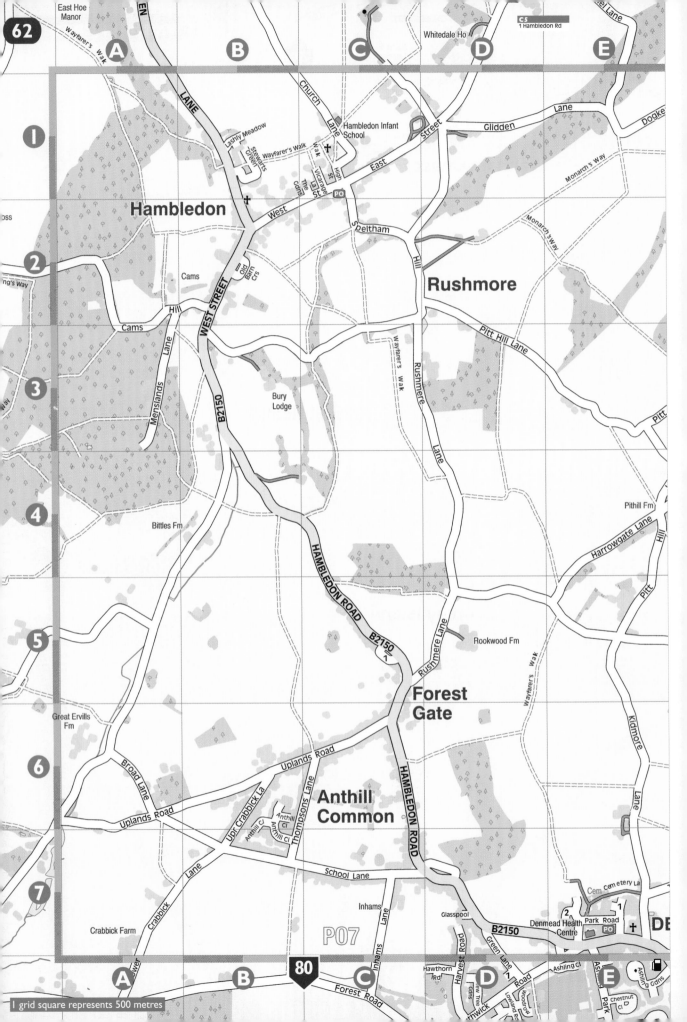

A B C D E

1

East Hoe Manor
Wayfarer's Walk

EN LANE

Church Lane

Hambledon Infant School

Whitedale Ho

C5
1 Hambledon Rd

el Lane

Glidden Lane

Dogke

Monarch's Way

Lashly Meadow

Stewarts Green

Wayfarer's Walk

Vicarage La

High St

St

The Gdns

PO

East Street

Hill Street

Hambledon

West Street

Spaltham

Monarch's way

2

ng's Way

Cams

Old Barn Crs

Cams Hill

Rushmore

Pitt Hill Lane

3

Way

Menslands Lane

WEST STREET

Bury Lodge

Wayfarer's Walk

Rushmere Lane

Pitt

4

Bittles Fm

B2150

Pithill Fm

Harrowgate Lane

Pitt Hill

5

Great Ervills Fm

HAMBLEDON ROAD B2150

Rushmere Lane

Rookwood Fm

Forest Gate

Wayfarer's Walk

6

Broad Lane

Uplands Road

Thompsons Lane

Anthill Common

HAMBLEDON ROAD

Kidmore Lane

Uplands Road

Upr Crabbick La

Anthill Cl

Anthill Cl

7

Great Ervills Fm

Crabbick Lane

School Lane

Inhams Lane

Glasspool

Cem Cemetery La

Crabbick Farm

P07

Inhams Lane

Harvest Road

B2150

Green Lane

Denmead Health Centre

Park Road

PO

DE

80

Forest Road

Hawthorn Rd

Lowland Rd

Ashling Cl

Park

Ashling Gdns

Chestnut Cl

A B C D E

F G H J

Dookenne Lane

I

Glidden Fm

Monarch's Way

2

Hinton Manor Lane

Old Mill Lane

Horsepost Lane

Pitt Hill Lane

Harrowgate Lane

3

Monarch's Way

Denmead Mill

Monarch's Way

Harrowgate Lane

Hinton Daubnay

Broadway Lane

Monarch's Way

Old Mill Lane

Lovedean Lane

4

Taggell

64

5

Day Lane

Coldhill Lane

The Crossways

Broadway Fm

New Road

The Curve

Portland View

Loxwood

Whitley Rd

6

Lovedean

White

Broadway Lane

Lovedean Lane

Horse

Ashley Cl

Edneys

Eastland Gate

7

Tanner's Lane

Lane

Meadowlands Junior School

Woodcroft La

ENMEAD

Shrover

Woodcroft Lane

Meadowlands Infant School

F

Anmore

G

Road

H

81

J

K

Denmead

Martin Avenue

the Heath

Fulmer Walk

Kite Cl

Partridge Gardens

Eagle Av

Crebe Cl

Dove Cl

Sparrow

Eagle Av

Chaffinch Cl

Curlew Gdns

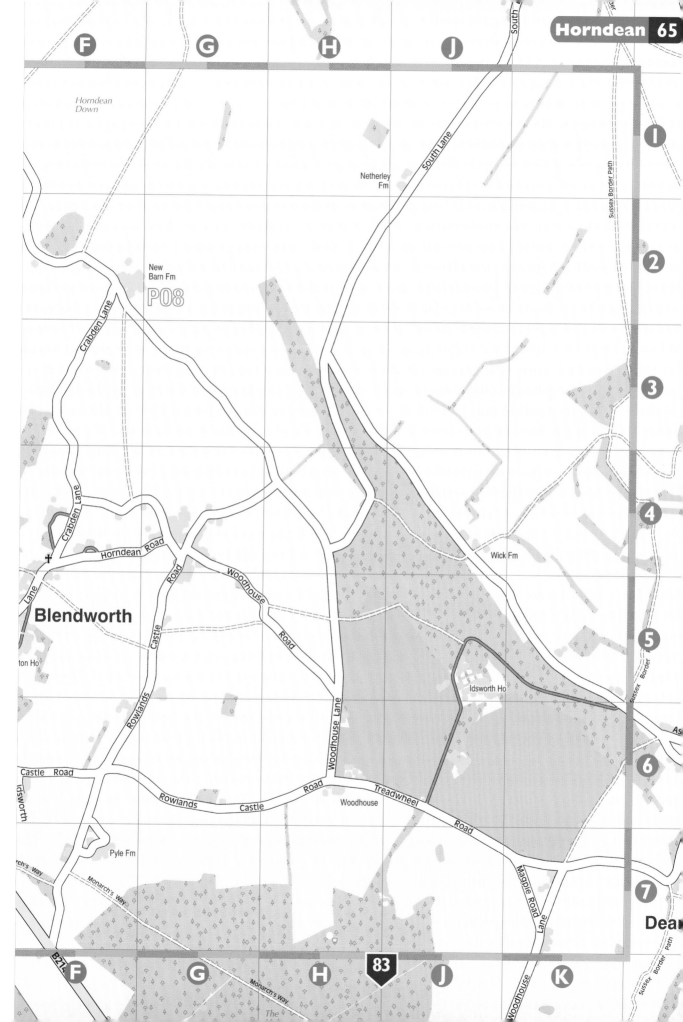

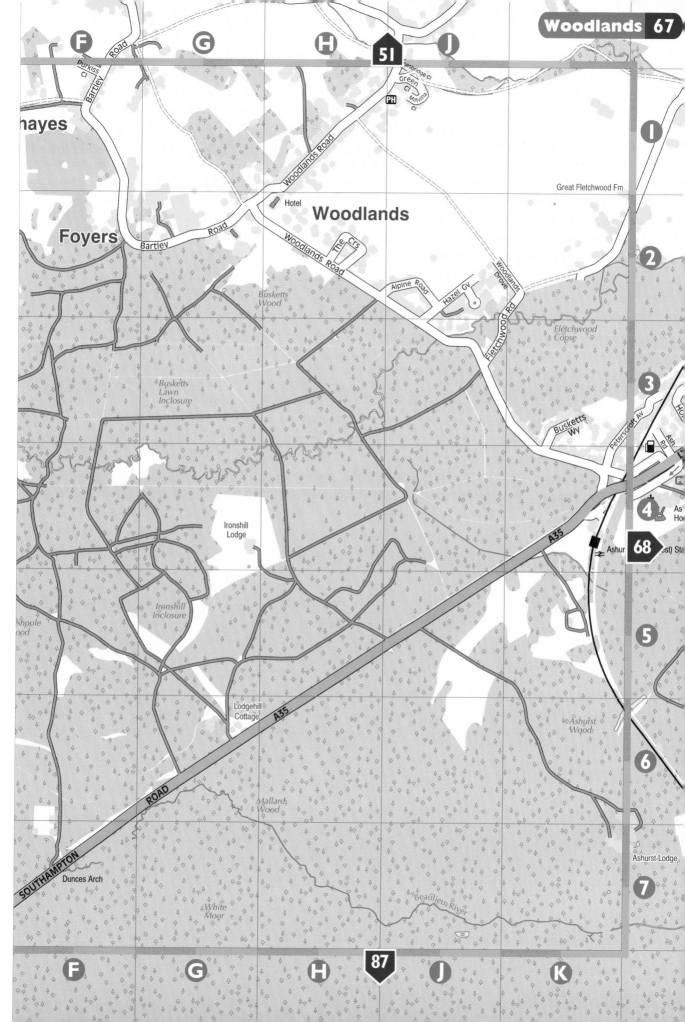

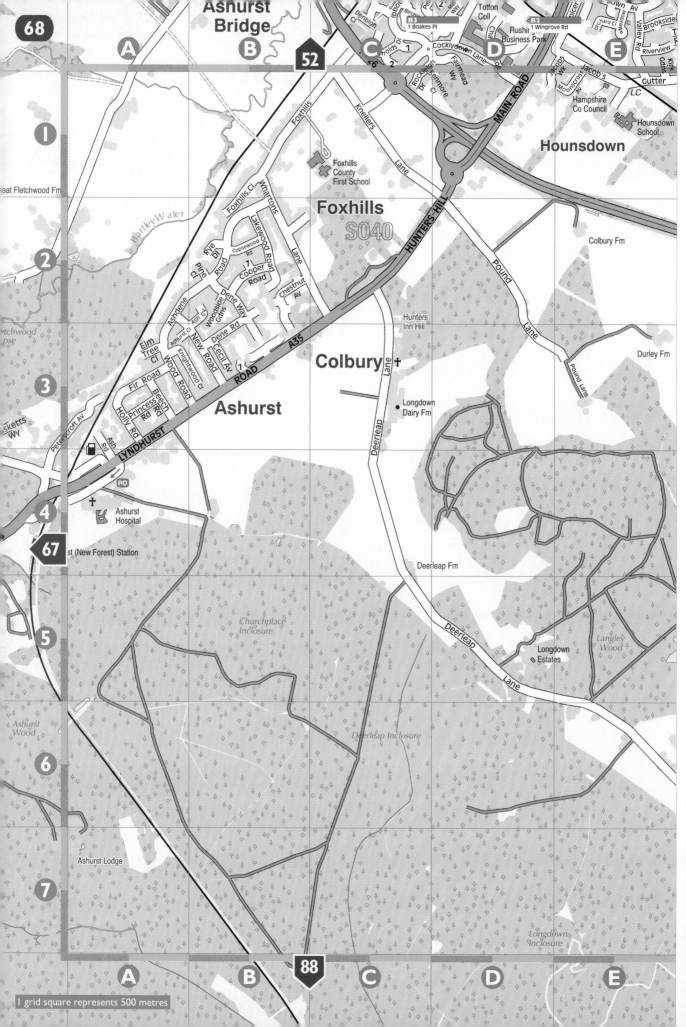

F G Bury Lane H 53 J

K4
1 Lakeland Gdns
2 Lloyd Av

Hill

The Retreat
Lane

BY-PASS

A326

A326

Marchwood
Road

Trotts Lane

City of South ampton
Hampshire County

I

2

Bury Fm

Bury Road

Normandy

Bury Rd

Cork La

The

LC
Trotts Lane

Trotts

LC

LC

Reed Dr

3

Marchwood

The Rushes

Bilberry

Alder Cl

The Rowans

Mar Juni Sch

Pooksgreen

Pooksgreen

Kingfisher W

Woodpecker Drive

Osprey

Sandpiper

4

PO

Marshfield Cl

LC

Tavell's

Tavells

Park Lane

Bohunton Av

Park Cl

Langley
Lodge

Staplewood
Lane

BY-PASS

MARCHWOOD

Long

Poplar

Dr

Kestrel
Cl

Woodside Cl

St Johns

Plantation Dr

Mulberry Rd

Main

70

Lane The Crs

2

LC

Lansdpur Dr

Willow

Spind

Bythe R

Staplewood La

5

Marchwo
C of E
Infant School

MARCH

Staplewood
Lane

6

Arters
Lawn

Twiggs Lane

7

End

Lane

Twiggs

Beaulieu Road

Birchlands Farm

Foxhill Farm

A
B
C
D
E

B4
1 Acorn Cl
2 The Limes
3 Malcroft Ms
4 Ripplewood
5 Tanglewood
6 Woodmoor Cl

A4
1 Crooked Hays Cl
2 St Johns Ct

A3
1 Pebble Ct

Saxon Rd
Bus Cen
MOUNTB
W

54

City of Southampton
Hampshire County

Cracknore H La

Imperial Way

Herbert Walker Avenue

West Bay Road

River Test

City of Southampton
Hampshire County

I

2

Quayside Wk
Maritime Av
Ordnance Way
Admiralty Wy
Magazine La

Cork La

Normandy Way

Cardiner

Cl

Cracknore Hard

3

Bury Rd
Cork La
The Gulls
Shorefield
Tide's Way
Old Magazine Cl
Main Road
Gage Cl

Hard

Lane

7

Cracknore
Hard

The Rushes
Reed Dr
The Tussocks
Moss
Uchen
Drake Cl
Old Cracknore Cl

Bilberry
Alder La
Melick Cl
Pond
Frome Cl

Cracknore

4

Lane
Kingfisher Wy
The Rowans
Cranp
Aumble
Elder
Rosewood Gdns
6

Sandpipet
Woodpecker Drive
Aspen
St
Evergreen Cl
The Hawthorns
Kingswood
Normandy Way

Marchwood
Junior
School
The Surg
Wood Cl
Ferndale
1

4

Maryvale
Malthouse Gdns
Dapple Pl

Africa Dr
Burma Wy
Philpott Dr
Adams Wd Dr

69

Main
Mulberry Rd
Oakland Dr
2

Larkspur Dr
Willow Dr
Spindlewood Wy
Hythe Road
LC
Pumpfield Farm

5

Marchwood
C of E
Infant School

MARCHWOOD

Veal's Lane

6

BY-PASS
Main Road
A326

Marchwood
Priory
Hospital

Church Farm Close

Lock's Farm

7

Gdn City
Church Farm

Dibde

A
B
C
D
E

90

The Old
Manor

I grid square represents 500 metres

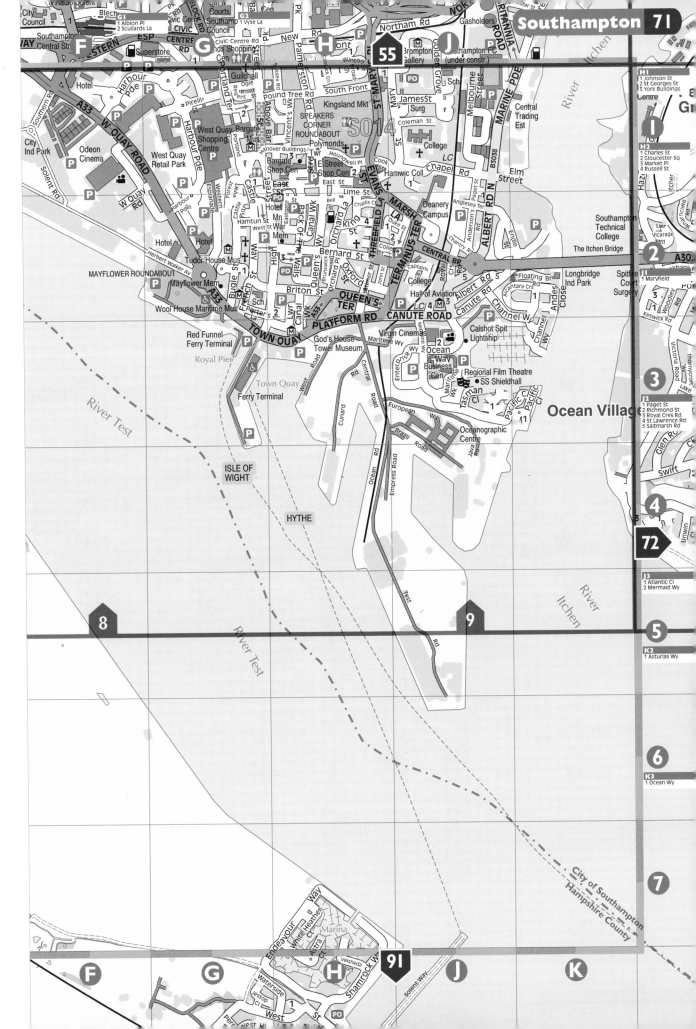

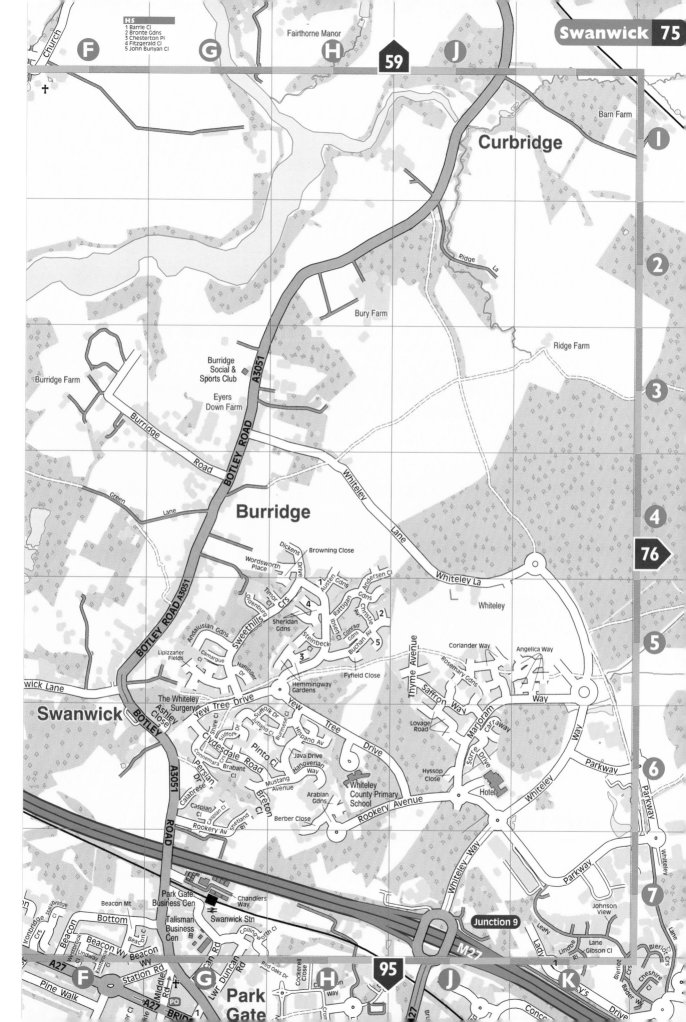

HS
1 Barrie Cl
2 Bronte Gdns
3 Chesterton Pl
4 Fitzgerald Cl
5 John Bunyan Cl

F
G
H
59
J

Curbridge

Church

Fairthorne Manor

Barn Farm

I

Ridge La

2

Bury Farm

Ridge Farm

3

Burridge Farm

Burridge
Social &
Sports Club

A3051

Eyers
Down Farm

BOTLEY ROAD

Whiteley Lane

4

76

Green

Lane

Burridge

Dickens Drive
Browning Close

Whiteley La

Wordsworth Place

Whiteley

Austen Gdns
Andersen Cl
Christie Gdns

5

BOTLEY ROAD A3051

Timor Crs

Oldenburg

Sheridan Gdns

Rattigan

Ibsen Av

Conrad Gdns

Buchan Av

Andalusian Gdns

Sweethills

Steinbeck Cl

Coriander Way

Rosemary Gdns

Angelica Way

Lipizzaner Fields

Camargue Cl

Haflinger Dr

Hemmingway Gardens

Fyfield Close

Thyme Avenue

Saffron Way

Way

wick Lane

Swanwick

The Whiteley
Surgery

Ashey Close

BOTLEY

Yew Tree Drive

Suffolk Dr

Yew Tree Drive

Hispano Av

Lovage Road

Marjoram

Caraway

Way

Clydesdale Road

Shire Cl

Suffolk Cl

Burmese Cl

Suntana Cl

Java Drive

Hanoverian Way

Hyssop Close

Sorrel Drive

Parkway

A3051 ROAD

Pinto Cl

Connemara
Brabant
Cl

Persian Dr

Mustang Avenue

Whiteley County Primary School

Hotel

6

Calabrese

Caspian Cl

Caspian Cl

Shetland Rd

Breton Cl

Arabian Gdns

Rookery Avenue

Whiteley Way

Parkway

Caspian Cl

Rookery Av

Berber Close

Parkway

7

Park Gate
Business Cen

Chandlers Way

Swanwick Stn

Whiteley Way

Johnson View

Ironbridge

Beacon Mt

Talisman
Business
Cen

Collingworth Way

Junction 9

Lindfe

Lane
Gibson Cl

Bierlot

Beacon
Bottom

Beacon Wy

Beacon Wy

Beacon

Lwr Duncan Rd

Lower Duncan Rd

Red Oaks Dr

95

M27

Leafy

Lady's

Cheshire

Bader

A27

Station Rd

PO

Pine Walk

A27

F

G

H

J

K

**Park
Gate**

Cockerell Close

Concor

Drive

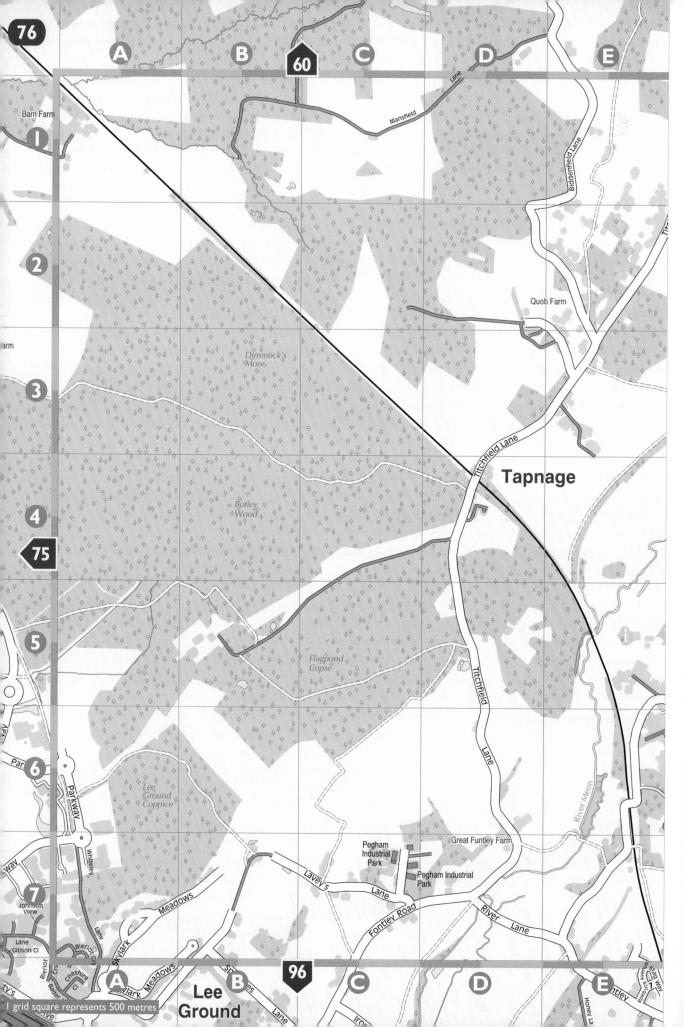

76

A B 60 C D E

Barn Farm

1

Mansfield Lane

Biddenfield Lane

2

Quob Farm

arm

3

Dimmock's Moor

Titchfield Lane

Tapnage

4

Botley Wood

75

5

Flagpond Copse

Titchfield Lane

Par

6

Lee Ground Coppice

River Meon

Great Funtley Farm

Parkway

Whiteley

Pegham Industrial Park

Pegham Industrial Park

7

Johnson View

Skylark Meadows

Lavey's Lane

Fontley Road

River Lane

Lane

Gibson Cl

Bleriot Crs

Cheshire Cl

A Skylark Meadows B 96 C D E

Lee Ground

1 grid square represents 500 metres

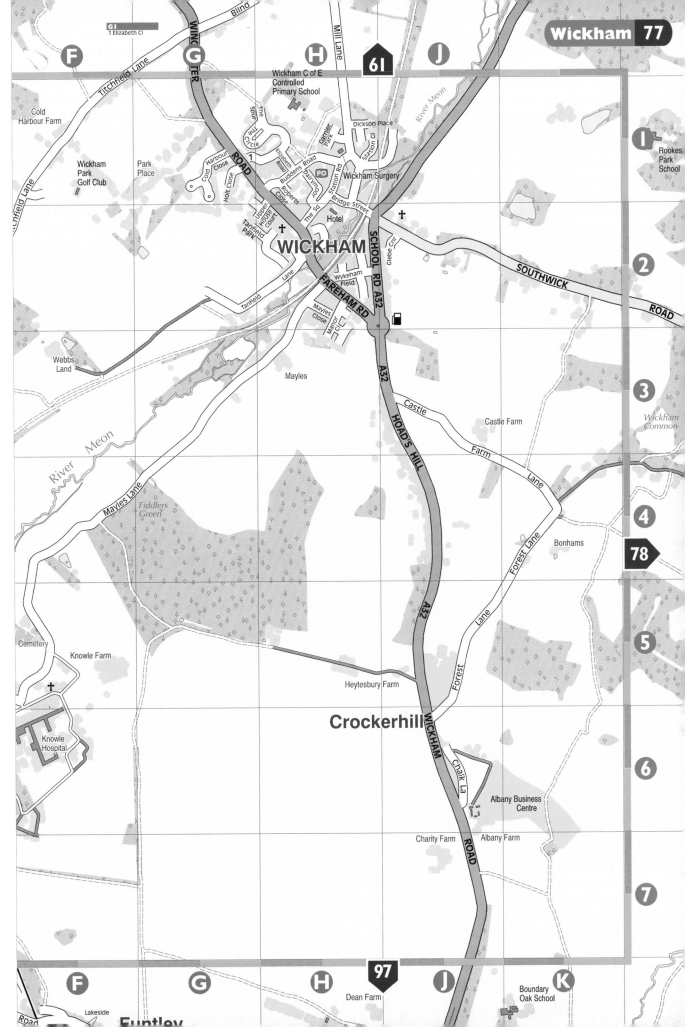

A **B** 62 P07 **C** **D** 2150 **E** DE

E2
1 The Tithe

Inhams
Lane

D2
1 The Pastures

Glasspool

D1
1 Frenchies Vw
2 Furdies
3 Peakfield

Crabbie... **A**

Crab...

Crabbie... **B**

Inhams

Denmead Health Centre

Cem Cemetery La

Park Road

1

Forest Road

Hawthorn Rd

Harvest Road

Green Lane

Southwick Road

Ashling Cl

Ashling Park Road

Chestnut Cl

Bere Road

Denm...
Ju...
Sch...

I

Forest of Bere

Bunkers Hill

Bunkers Hill

Southwick Rd

Yew Tree Gdns

Woodrow

Lowland Rd

The Smithy

The Meadow

Home Mead

The Orchard

Field Wy

2

Creech Woods

The Willows

The Liberty

Forest Road

Pond Piece

Cottage Cl

The Spring

Old River

Forest Rd

Kilnside

3

The Spinney

Paddock End

Parklands Business Park

Furzeley Road

79

Creech Farm

Sheepwash Lane

Furzeley Road

Newlands

Furzeley Corner

4

Closewood

Belney Farm

Belney Lane

Sheepwash Lane

Wayfarer's Wk

5

Place Wood

Sheepwash Farm

Wanstead Farm

6

... Wood Lane

North Road E

South Rd

Priory Rd

East Road

Drive

Pitymoor Lane

Wayfarer's Walk

7

Southwick Park
Naval Recreation Centre

Purb...

A **B** 100 **C** **D** **E**

Comphouse Farm

65

F G H J

Monarch's Way

B2149

The Holt

Monarch's Way

Links Lane

Holt Gdns

Wellsworth La

Bowes

Wellsworth Gdns

Meadowlands

Wellsworth

Broad Crt

2

Greatfield Way

The Peak

Hill

Sussex Border Path

Uplands Road

Rowlands Castle Station

Havant Thicket

Links Lane

The Fairway

Doctors Surgery

PH PO PH

Finchdean Rd

3

B2149

Kings Cl

Castle Road

Royal Gdns

Nightingale Cl

Kingfisher Close

Nuthatch Cl

Blackcap

Brambling Rd

Jaunock Rd

Mallard Road

Red Hill

Redhill

College Road

Stansted Ct

English Gallery

Yardlea Cl

Hill Brow Cl

The Drift

4

Hazeldean Dr

84

Durrants

St Johns C of E Primary School

Durrants Gdns

Whichers Cl

Durrants Road

B2149

WHICHERS GATE ROAD B2148

COMLEY

5

LC

Staunton Way

P09

Prospect Lane

6

Staunton Park Community School

Well Meadow

Winterslow Drive

Marchwood Rd

Crondall Av

Silkstead Av

Bitterne Cl

Bondfields Crs

Park Way

Gt Copse Drive

Middle Park Way

Front Lawn GM Junior School

PETERSFIELD ROAD

Crawley Avenue

Millbrook Drive

Kimbridge Crs

Malwood

Stansted Crs

Wakefords

Longstock Rd

Leckford Rd

Burghclere Rd

Wyndham Rd

Bradley Rd

Ken Berry Court

Penton Court

HILL

B2149

7

103

Exbury Rd

Sherfield Av

Oakshott

PO Baybridge

Sharps Copse Junior & Infant School

Prospect Lane

Forest

Whitsbury Rd

Froxfield

F G H J K

Dean Lane End

Warren Down

Firtree Piece

Drews Fm

Wellsworth

Stansted Forest

Hare Warren

Rowlands Castle Station

Doctor Surgery

PO

Finchdean Rd

Rowland's Castle

Sussex Border Path

Monarch's Way

Monarch's Wy

Horsepasture Fm

Woodberry La

Sussex Border Path

Sussex Border Path

Holme Farm

Glen Dr

83

LC

Stubbermere

Park Lane

West Sussex County
Hampshire County

Woodberry Lane

COMLEY

Southleigh Forest

Sussex Border Path

Emsworth Common Road

Monk's

HILL

Hill

104

Monk's Fm

West Sus

B2148

Finchdean Rd

Uplands Road

Broad Cft

Wellswood Gdns

Midlands

F G H J

Watergate

Watergate
Hanger

I

Broadreed Fm

B2146

2

Lumley Seat

Monarch's Way
Lane

Monarch's Way

3

Monarch's Wy

Woodlands

Woodlands
Cotts

B2146

4

Stanstead House

Newbarn Lane

B2146

5

Park Lane

Sindle's Fm

Monument La

6

Racton
Park Fm

B2146

B2147

†

Aldsworth

7

Ractonpark
Wood

B2147 Common Road

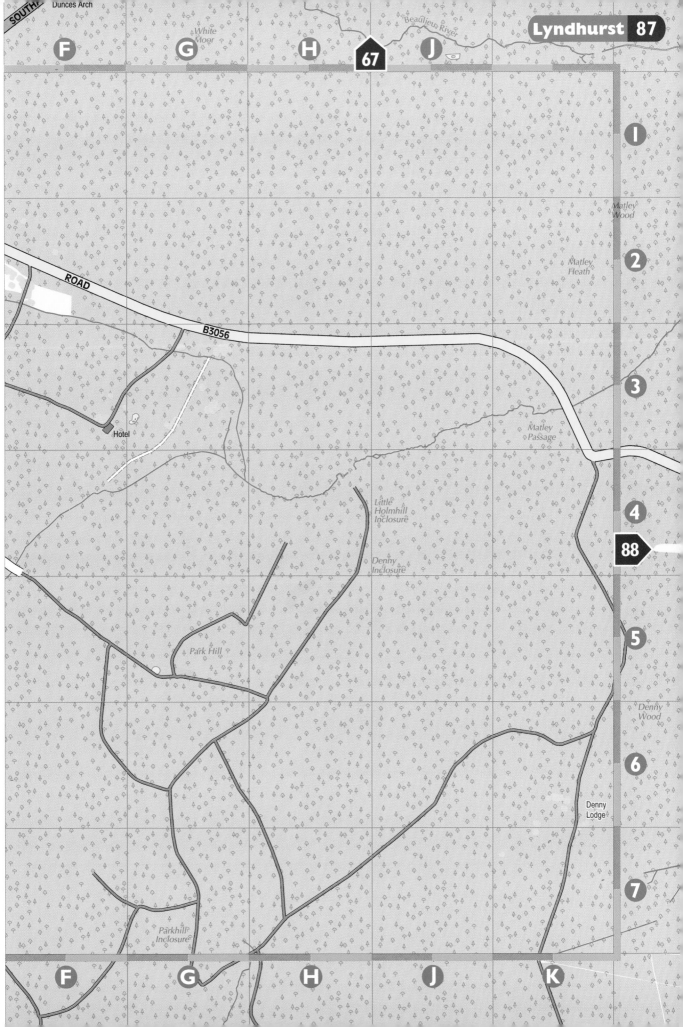

SOUTH

Dunces Arch

White Moor

Beaulieu River

F

G

H

67

J

I

Matley Wood

2

ROAD

Matley Heath

B3056

3

Matley Passage

Hotel

Little Holmhill Inclosure

4

88

Denny Inclosure

5

Park Hill

Denny Wood

6

Denny Lodge

7

Parkhill Inclosure

F

G

H

J

K

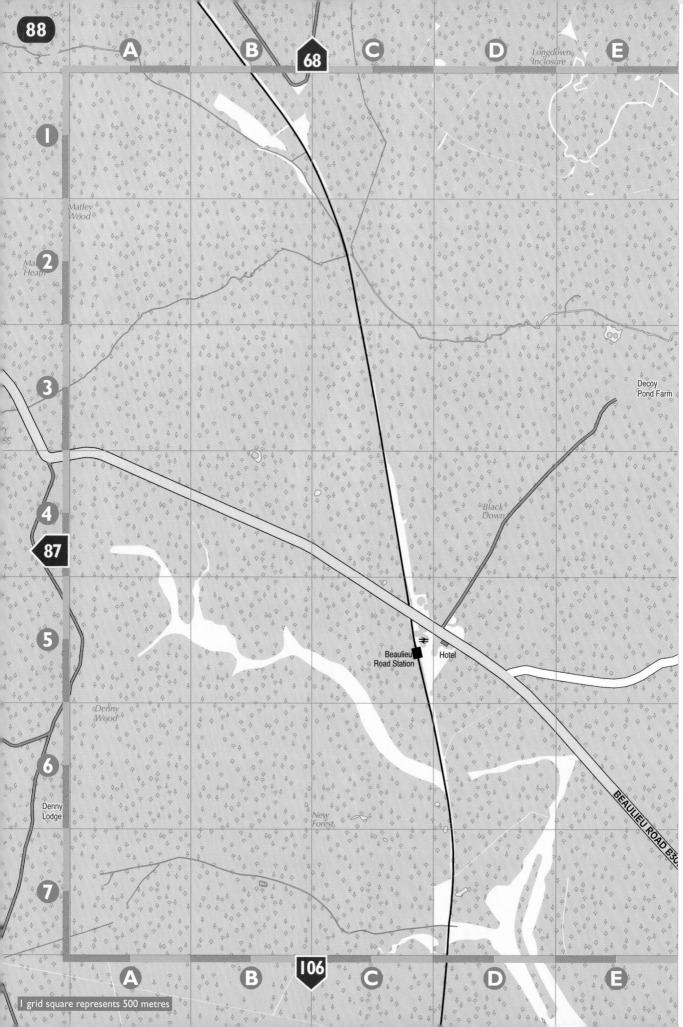

A B **68** C D E

Longdown
Inclosure

I

Matley
Wood

2

Ma
Heath

3

Decoy
Pond Farm

ge

4

87

Black
Down

5

Beaulieu
Road Station   Hotel

Denny
Wood

6

Denny
Lodge

New
Forest

BEAULIEU ROAD B30

7

A B **106** C D E

I grid square represents 500 metres

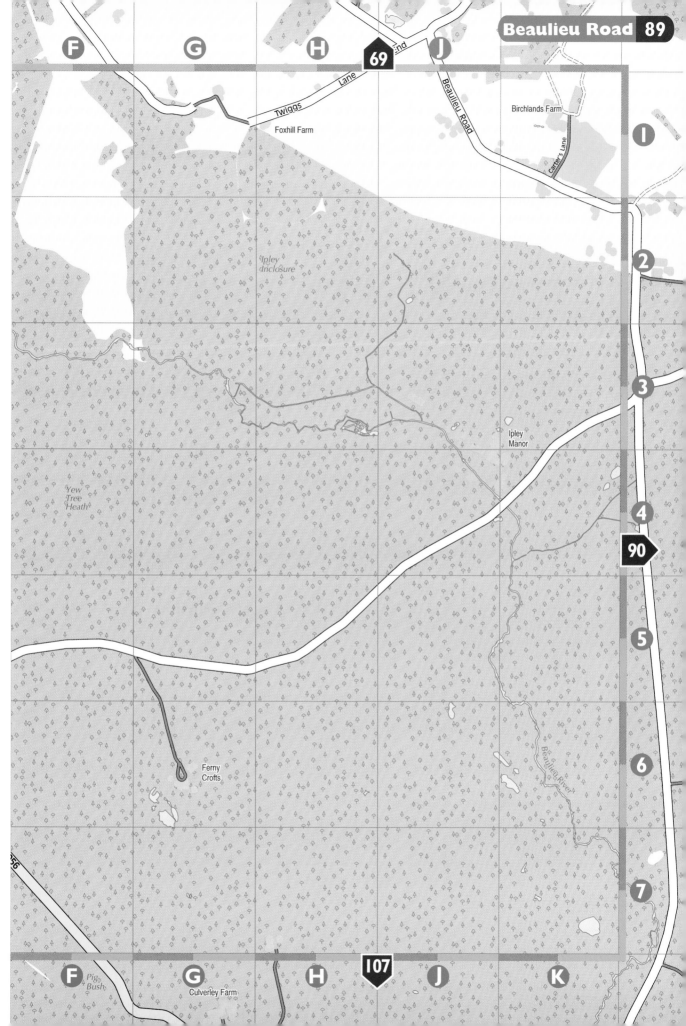

F

G

H

69

J

Twiggs Lane

Lane End

Foxhill Farm

Beaulieu Road

Birchlands Farm

Carter's Lane

I

Ipley
Inclosure

2

3

Ipley
Manor

Yew
Tree
Heath

4

90

5

Beaulieu River

Ferny
Crofts

6

7

356

F

Pig
Bush

G

Culverley Farm

H

107

J

K

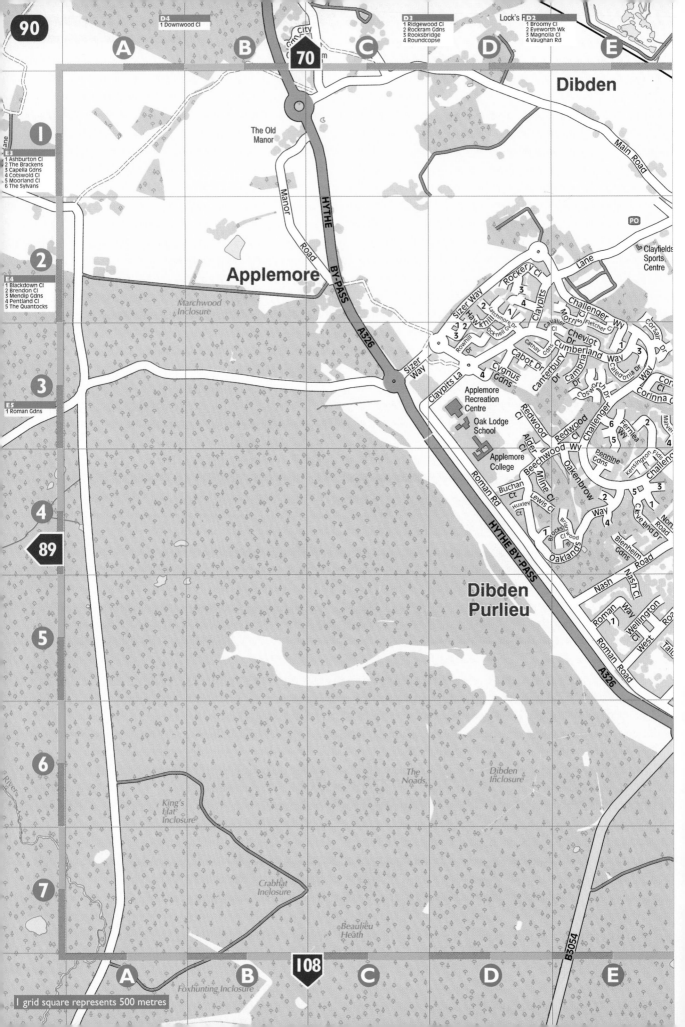

A   B   C   D   E

70

Dibden

D4
1 Downwood Cl

D3
1 Ridgewood Cl
2 Rockram Gdns
3 Rooksbridge
4 Roundcopse

Lock's Rd D2
1 Broomy Cl
2 Eyeworth Wk
3 Magnolia Cl
4 Vaughan Rd

1

E3
1 Ashburton Cl
2 The Brackens
3 Capella Gdns
4 Cotswold Cl
5 Moorland Cl
6 The Sylvans

The Old Manor

Main Road

PO

Clayfields Sports Centre

2

E4
1 Blackdown Cl
2 Brendon Cl
3 Mendip Gdns
4 Pentland Cl
5 The Quantocks

Applemore

Marchwood Inclosure

Lane

Rockery Cl

Sizer Way

Hawkhill

Larchmore Dr

Claypits

Challenger Wy

Morris

Fletcher

Cheviot Dr

Cavalier

Corsair Dr

3

E5
1 Roman Gdns

Sizer Way

Claypits La

Cabot Dr

Canterbury Dr

Cumberland Way

Cambria

Cosworth Dr

Caledonia Dr

Corinna Cl

Cygnus Gdns

Applemore Recreation Centre

Oak Lodge School

Redwood

Redwood Cl

Challenger Cl

Fernlea Wk

Pennine Gdns

Alder

Beechwood Dr

Milne Cl

Oakenbrow

Applemore College

Buchan Ct

Lewis Cl

Huxley Ct

Roman Rd

4

89

Oaklands

Brocks Cl

Blenheim Gdns

Road

Cleveland Dr

Nash Cl

Nash

Dibden Purlieu

HYTHE BY-PASS

A326

5

Roman Way

Wellington Cl

West

6

The Noads

Dibden Inclosure

River

King's Hat Inclosure

7

Crabhat Inclosure

Beaulieu Heath

B3054

Foxhunting Inclosure

A   B   **108**   C   D   E

1 grid square represents 500 metres

A

B

72

C

D

E

NETLE

Rd

E1

1 Sedgemead

Garffi

Victoria

aham Road

Vw

Chamberlayne

Mortimer Cl

New Monk

Road

Station

Road

Denham
Gdns

Netley
Court
School

PO

1

I

2

3

Southampton W

4

91

rostlane

5

West

Road

Road

East

Charleston

Road

First street

Second St

6

Av C

AV D

Avenue E

Av
C

Cadland
Creek

oad

Cadland Road

7

I grid square represents 500 metres

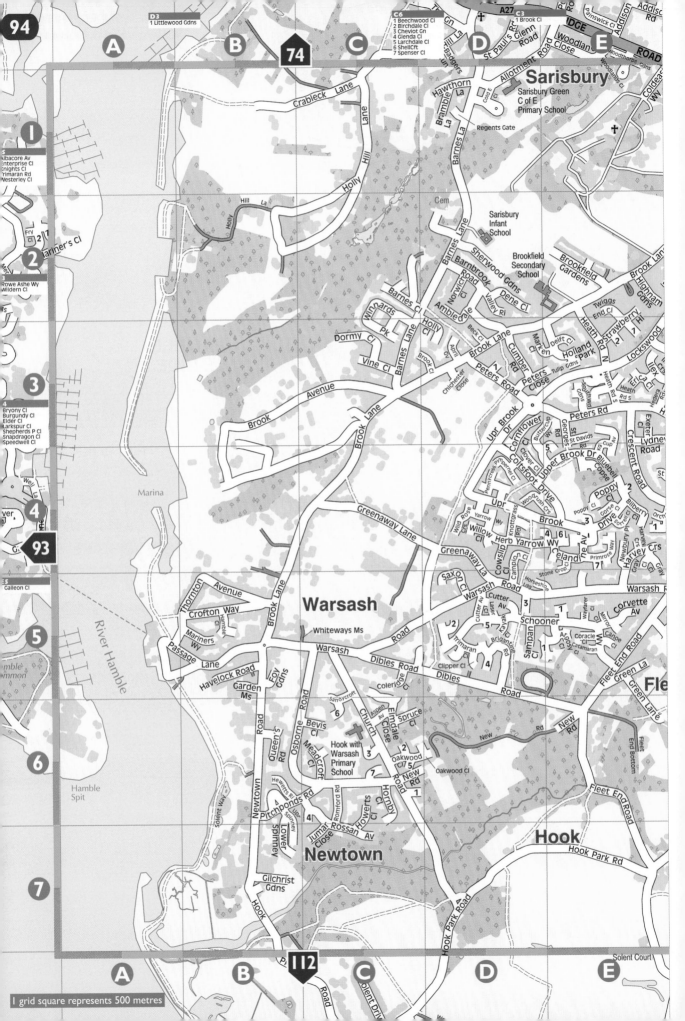

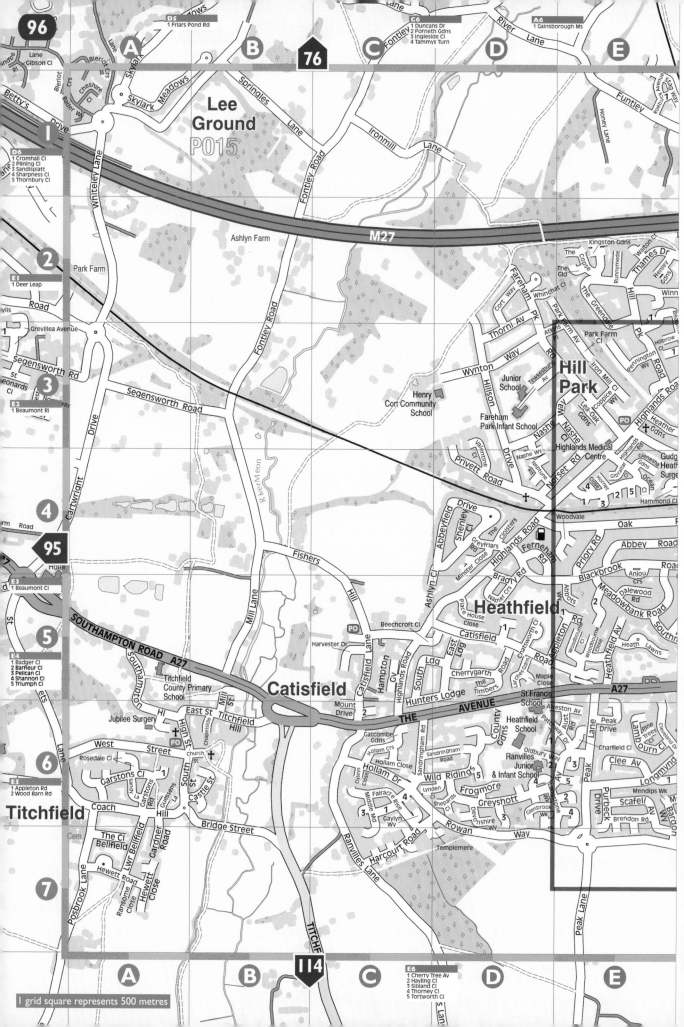

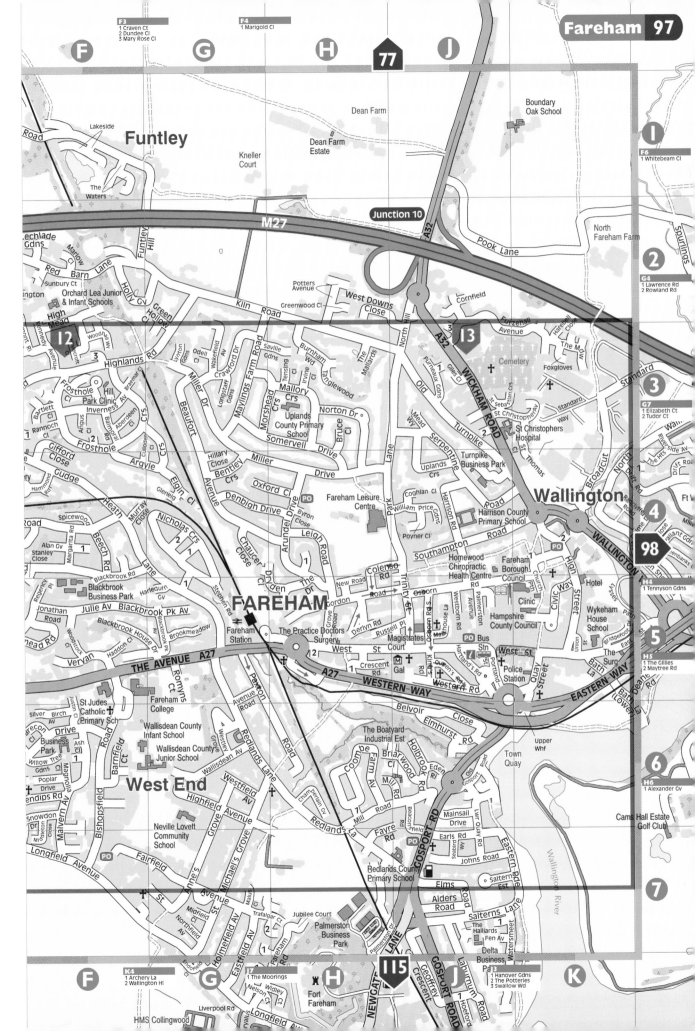

Southwick

F5
1 Canon's Barn Cl
2 Steep Cl

F7
1 Gladstone Gdns

West Street

Back Lane

North

Doctors
Surger

79

Southwick Park
Naval Recreation Centre

Southwick Park Lake

G5
1 Conifer Ms

Offwell Farm

Drove Road

New
Barns

Crooked Walk Lane

H5
1 Rowland Rd

Portchester Lane

Portsdown Hill Road

Portsdown Hill Road

Fort Southwick

Workshop Rd

North Rd

The Circus
Road

Hilltop Rd

South Rd

James Callaghan

H6
1 Elgar Cl
2 Hopkins Cl

Nelson Lane

Skew Road

M27

Ports Down

Link Road

East

100

Butterfly
Drive

Rockrose Wy

J5
1 Ridgeway Cl
2 Winterbourne Cl

Waltham

Kilmiston Dr

Exton Cl

Weyhill Cl

Dore Avenue

High Vw

Harting Gdns

Rogate Gdns

Froxfield Gdns

Junior &
Infant School

Laverock Lea

Richmond Rise

Hill View Rd

Dore Avenue

Burton close

Hill Rd

Anson Grove

Carlton Road

Pentland Rise

Pentland Rd

Montrose Av

Portobello Rd

Southwick Rd

Edward Gv

Seaview Av

Browning Avenue

Keats Av

Chaucer Av

Shelley Av

Dryden Av

Wordsworth Av

Masefield Av

Macaulay Av

Coleridge Rd

Coleridge Rd

Hillsley

Kingscote Rd

Almondsbury Road

Tintern Cl

Longdean Cl

Chetworth Crs

Woofferton Road

Deernhurst Crescent

Beverston Road

Elkstone Rd

Birdlip Rd

K5
1 Dellfield Cl
2 Desborough Cl
3 Rothwell Cl

Leith Avenue

Linden Lea

Simpson Cl

Red Barn

Portsview Gdns

Colinton Av

Morningside Av

Mountview Av

Raymond Rd

Newbolt

Truro Rd

Mousehole Rd

Bude Cl

Falmouth Road

Pendennis Rd

Helston Rd

Allaway Avenue

Allaway Av

Bourne

Doctors
Surgery

St Pauls RC
Primary Sch

arn County
y School

The Hillway

Portsview Avenue

Kelvin Grove

Jubilee Avenue

Junior School

Saxon Shore Infant Sch

Sedgefield Close

Pamela Rd

King Richard School

Paulsgrove

Portchester Station

PO

Portsdown Rd

The Crossway

New Town

Portsdown Rd

Neelands Gv

Sullivan Cl

Parry Cl

Coitsmead

Beach Dr

Shorehaven

Farmlea Rd

Port Wy

K6
1 Bodmin Rd
2 Watersedge Rd

CHESTER

The Close

The Kingsway

The Fairway

The Downsway

St Helena Wy

St James Wy

The Leaws

A27

Portchester Health Centre

PO

Westlands Medical Centre

Allenby Gv

Clive Grove

Vincent Gv

Frobisher Gv

Marlborough Gv

Portchester Community School

Wellington Gv

Kg George Road

Priory Rd

Qu Mary Rd

Sunningdale Rd

Castle Grove

Myrtle Avenue

Castle Street

The Keep

Station Rd

Cow Lane

Hamilton Road

Hampshire County City of Portsmouth

Port W

117

A27 SOUTHAMPTON ROAD

Lock View

Port Wy

Sennen Pl

Carbis Cl

Lock Approach

Newlyn Wy

Bryher Island

Mullion

Marina

Westlands Gv

Hart Lane

Seaway Gv

rberry Dr

Coral Cl

Kent Gv

Marina Gv

Harbour Vw

White Hart La

Westbrook Rd

Merton Crs

Roman Gv

Olive Crs

PO

Edgar Gv

Denville Gv

Benham Gv

Norman Gv

Castle View Rd

Bayly Avenue

Windsor Rd

Castle St

York Rd

Castle County Primary School

Westlands Medical Centre

F

G

H

J

K

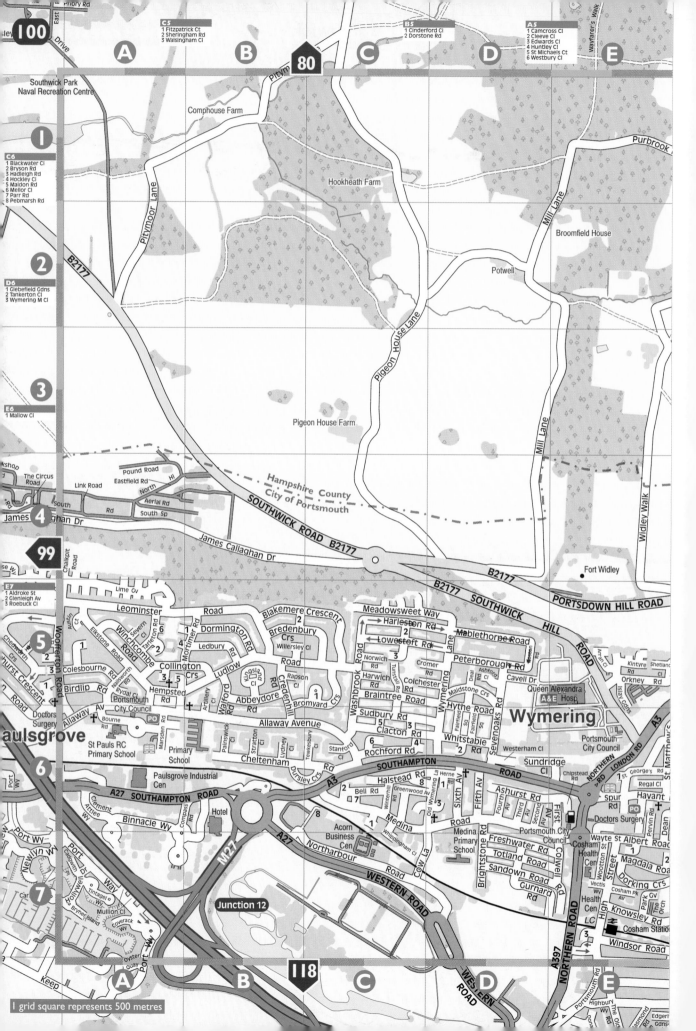

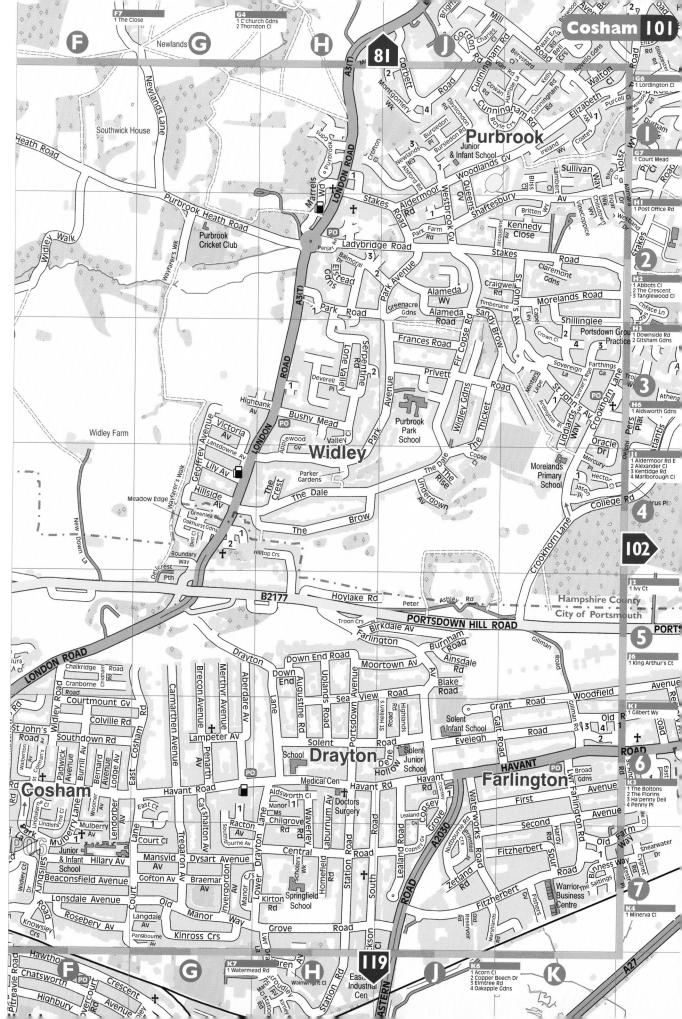

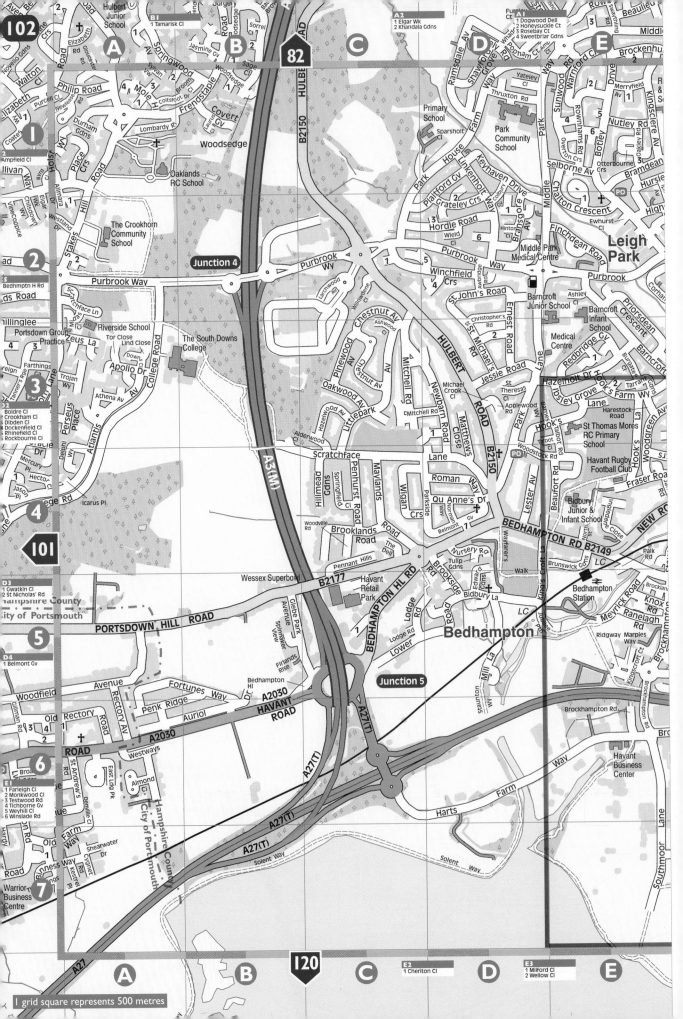

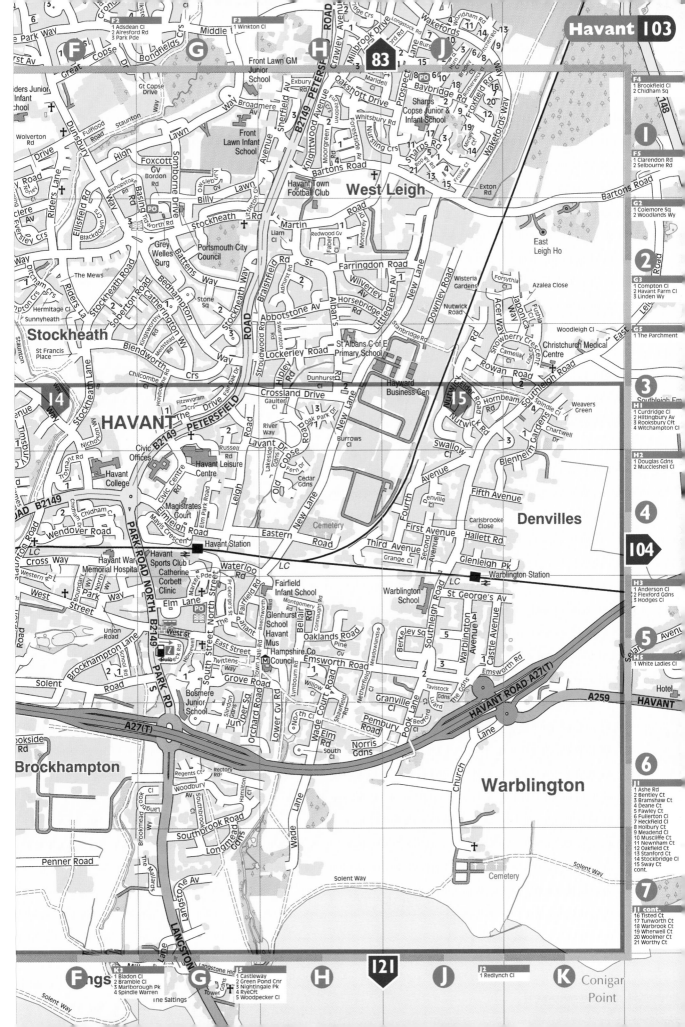

88

124

A B C D E

I
2
3
4
5
6
7

Denny
Lodge
Inclosure

LC

Frame
Heath
Inclosure

SO42

Ladycross
Lodge

B3055

Stockley
Inclosure

Frame
Wood

Moon
Hill

Hawkhill
Inclosure

Rowl

A B C D E

1 grid square represents 500 metres

F G H **89** J I

Pig Bush

Culverley Farm

North Gate

North Lane

Shepton Bridge

2

arrow

Tanfany Wood

Penerley Lodge

3 Hi Cl

Leygreen Farm

Stubbs Wood

4

108

National Motor Museum

5

Palace House

Furzey Lodge

6

Furzey Lane

Beaulieu

Hatchet Gate

HIGH ST B305

B3055

HATCHET

LANE **B3054**

7

F G **125** J K

Masseys La

Swinesleys Farm

F   G   H   **91**   J

J1
1 Forest La
2 Henry Cl
3 Hunter Cl

J2
1 Hadley Fld
2 Tennyson Cl

A326

New Rd

Roman Rd

Hardley

Chevron
Business Park

Old School Cl

Falconer Ct

Main Rd

Cadlands Pk Est

A326

LONG

14th Street

Harrier Wy

The Mill Pond

Lane

Larch Av

Sycamore Dr

Hardley
School

Lime Kiln Lane

The Warren

Little Holbury

Long Lane

LANE

I
J3
1 Shapton Cl
2 Teachers Wy

2

J4
1 Cherryton Gdns
2 Stagbrake Cl
3 Westcot Rd

Stonyford
Pond

Holbury
Purlieu

Larkspur
Gdns

Manor
Infant
School

Wedgewood
Cl

Southbourne Avenue

Ivor Close

Westbourne Av

Albany Rd

Manor
Road

Drove

Renda Road

Ruxley Cl

Oakley Cl

Watton Rd

Nelson Rd

3

K3
1 Broadley Cl
2 Hayward Ct
3 Ridley Cl

Park Lane

Lime Kiln La

Depedene

Holbury
Drove

Bower
Cl

Studley
Av

BroadOak

Redrise

School

Burbush Rd

Park Hl

Beechwood Rd

Bramble

Holbury

William Cl

Hunters

Raymond Rd

4

Whyte Cl

Moat Cl

Foxcroft Dr

Eastcot
Cl

Ct Elms

Henery Cl

Whitefield

Stonymoor Cl

Perrywood

Fair>cross

Roew Cl

Myvern Way

110

K4
1 Pondhead Cl
2 Roewood Cl
3 Stockley Cl

Rollestone Road

Rollstone Farm

Roughdown Lane

5

6

Otterwood
Gate

Stock Water

Summer Lane

Cowleys Lane

Row Down

King's Copse

Kings
Copse
Inclosure

Blackwell
Common

7

ood

Summer Lane

Steerleys
Copse

92

A · B · C · D · E

A5
1 Wentworth Gdns

A5
1 Ashleycross Cl
2 Hobson Wy

A3
1 Sloane Av
2 Sloane Ct

1

B5
1 The Greenwich
2 Harvey Ct

LONG Long LANE

2

B6
1 Edward Cl
2 Fields Cl
3 Pendleton Gdns

3

C5
1 Foursheils Cl
2 Thornhill Cl

Holbury

4

109

C6
1 Valley Cl

5

E4
1 Admirals Cl
2 ChurchFlds
3 Denny Cl
4 The Lane
5 Linda Rd
6 Meadow Wy
7 The Paddocks
8 Rhyme Hall Ms
9 The Square
10 Whites La

6

7

13th Street
12th Avenue
11th Street
10th Street
9th Street
8th Street
7th Street
6th Street
5th Street
4th Street
3rd Street
2nd St
1st Street

H Avenue
Avenue
Avenue
E Avenue
E Avenue

Oil Refinery

S045

Foreshore North
Foreshore
South
Foreshore Rd
P.L.P.H.
Burman Road South
Cadland Road
Marsh Lane
Salterns La

Fawley County First School
Fawley Business Centre

Church Forest
Orchard Edge
Woodcoleville Rd
Willow Rd
Sherringham

School Rd

B3053

Fawley

FAWLEY ROAD
Ashdown
South Avenue

Long Lane Close
The Close
Springfield
Stanley Rd
Waltons Avenue
Nelson
William
Winters Cl
Raymond
Hobson Cl
May Close
May Crs
Alum Cl
Crawte Avenue
Wentworth Gv
Long Copse

Myvern Cl
Rollestone Rd
Newlands Road

Ashdown Road
Slades Hill
Fry Cl
Heather Rd
Thornhill Rd
Smith Rd
Milliken Cl
Glyn Jones
Heather Rd
Furzey Cl
Hedley
Dark Lane

Blackfield Rd
The Pentagon
Chapel La

Fields Heath
Fields Farm

Blackfield Health Centre
Priest Cft Dr
The Fowey
Hampton Lane
Wilverley Pl
The Drove
Hugh's Cl
Blackfield Junior & Infant School

New Rd
St Michaels Cl
Newlands Copse
Walkers Walk
Newlands Cl
Hartsgrove Close
Exbury Rd
Janes Cl
Wheelers Walk
Saxon Rd
Wessex Cl
Viking
Norman Rd
Cedric

Blackfield
Tom's Down
Mopley Pond
Badminston Common

King's Copse Road
Blackwell Common

Hampton Lane
Hampton Gdns
Hampton Cl
Northampton La
Cem
Holly Rd
Thornbury Avenue
Green Lane
Walker's Lane South

Langley
Lea Road
Chalewood Rd
Clare Gdns

128

A · B · C · D · E

F G H **93** J

I

2

3 ISL

4

112

5

6

7

North Trestle Road

Burmah Road N

South Trestle Road

Old Agwi Road

Flume Rd

Copthorne Lane

Stonehills Lane

Ashlett Cl

Ashlett

Ashlett Road

ast Clinic

Ashlett

Ashlett Creek

LEY BY-PASS

B3053

Stonehills

Northern Access Road

Northern Access Rd

Badminston Farm

Badminston Lane

Badminston Drove

Ower

B3053

Calshot

PO

Calshot Cl

Sprat's Down

Stanswood Road

F G H **129** J K

Castle Lane

B3053

Solent Court

1

Hook
Park

Solent Way

Hook Pk Road

Cowes Lane

Solent Drive

Workman's
Lane

Chilling Lane

Chilling

Workman's La

Solent Way

2

3

ISLE OF WIGHT

III

4

5

Calshot
Castle

6

7

A B C D E

F G H ⬖ 95 J

I

Singledge

2

Little Posbrook

Brownwich Lane

Posbrook Lane

Triangle Lane

3

Brownwich Lane

Brownwich Farm

Meon

4

114

Solent Way

Solent Way

5

Titchfield Haven

Cliff

6

7

F G H J K

F · G · H · **97** · J

Fleetlar

I

2
J4
1 Honeysuckle Cl
2 The Mead
3 Myrtle Cl
4 Nesbitt Cl
5 Puffin Gdns

3
J5
1 Dandelion Cl
2 Mallard Gdns

4

116

5
K2
1 Bridgemary Wy

6
K3
1 Harwood Cl
2 Mountbatten Cl

7
K5
1 Beaulieu Pl
2 Birchmore Cl
3 Clover Cl
4 Nicholl Pl
5 Niton Cl
6 Ramsay Pl
7 Warsash Gv

K4
1 Cameron Cl

H5
1 Keyhaven Cl

I1
1 Farrier Wy

J6
1 Ankerwyke
2 Calshot Wy

F · G · H · **131** · J · K

K7
1 Davis Cl
2 Snape Cl

K6
1 Hoylake Cl
2 The Fairway
3 Sunningdale Cl

Woodcot

Peel Common

Bridgemary

Rowner

Gosport Airfield

Crofton School

Newlands Farm

HMS Collingwood

Collingwood Business Park

Fareham Megabowl

Fort Fareham

Chark Common

P013

Holbrook County Junior & Infant School

Bridgemary Community School

Bedenham County Junior & Infant Sch

Rowner Health Centre

Grange County Junior & Infant School

Junior & Infant School

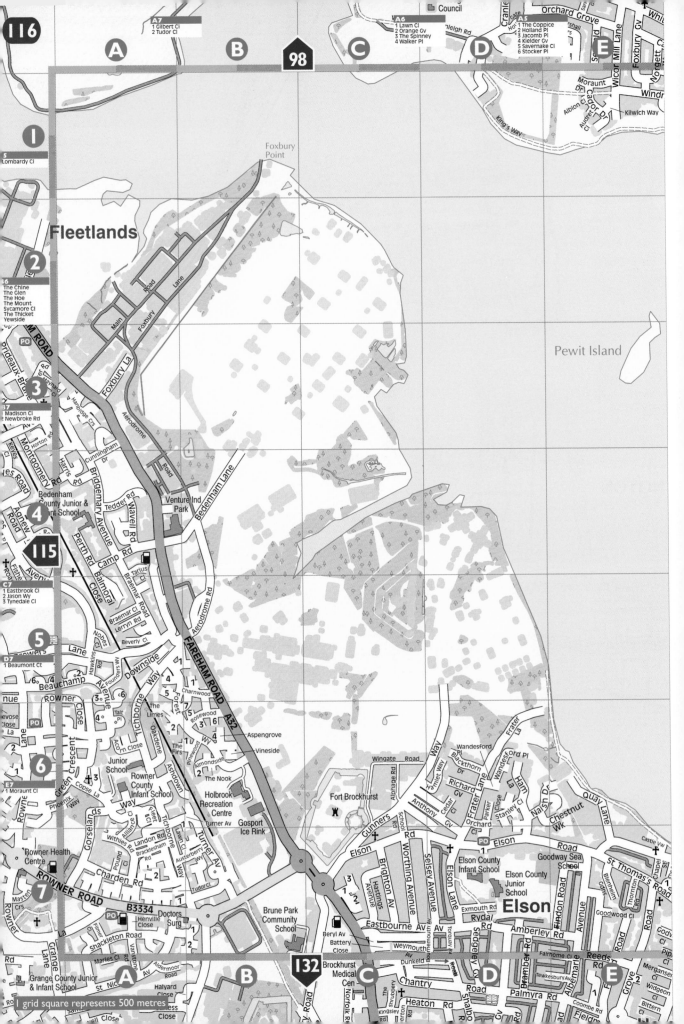

F

G

99

H

J

Community

Marlborou **F7**

1 Alencon Cl
2 Kynon Cl

Castle Grove

Cow Lane

Castle County
Primary School

White Hart La

Marina

Keep

Coral Cl

mill

Grove

e Hart Lane

rberry Dr

Clif

Gv

White Hart La

PO

Edgar
Crs

Cooper
Gv

Denville
Av

Windsor
Gns

York Gdns

Castle St

Waterside La

Coppins

Seaway

Kent Gv

Grove Avenue

Merton Avenue

Westbrook Rd

Olive
Crs

Neville

Benham
Gv

Norman
Cl

Wicor Pth

Waterside

Harbour Vw

Lansdown
Av

Lonsdale Av

Merton
Crs

Roman Gv

Kenwood Rd

Bavy Avenue

Castle View Rd

Hospital Lane

Church Rd

Portchester
Castle

Alton Gv

Beachway

Webb
Rd

Cemetery

King's Way

1

2

Lock Approa

Carbis Cl

3

4

118

Portsmouth Harbour

5

Whale
Island

N Battery

1

Wha

Wardr

Roa

Quarterdec

Y Rd

Guardroom

AV

Chatfield

Pier

6

7

1

2

e Lane

Bucklers
Road

Green

wit

F

G

H

133

J

K

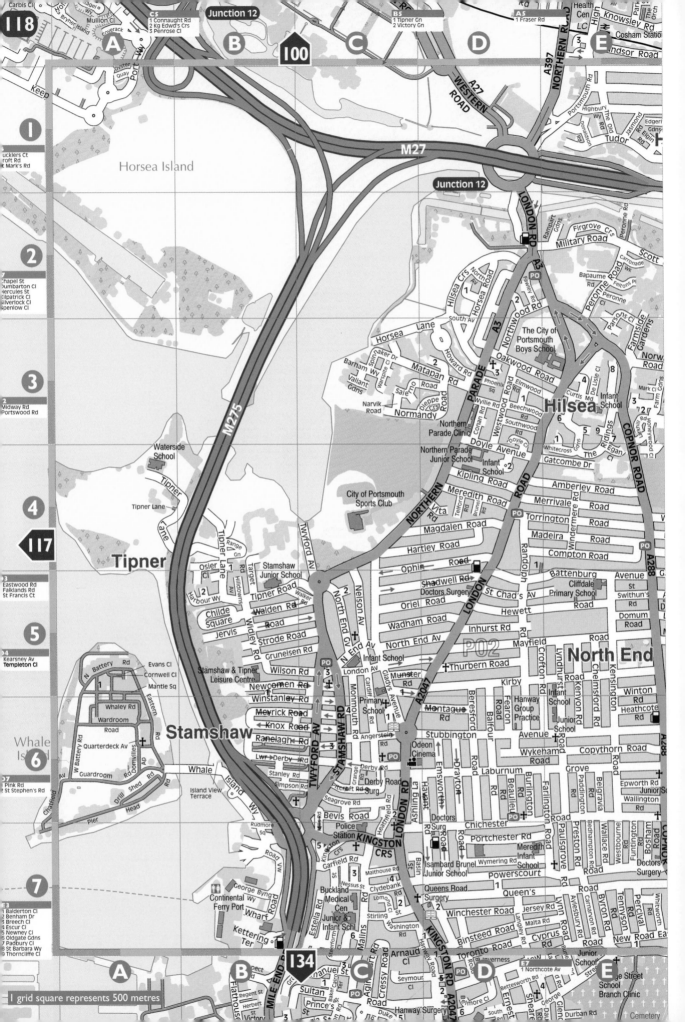

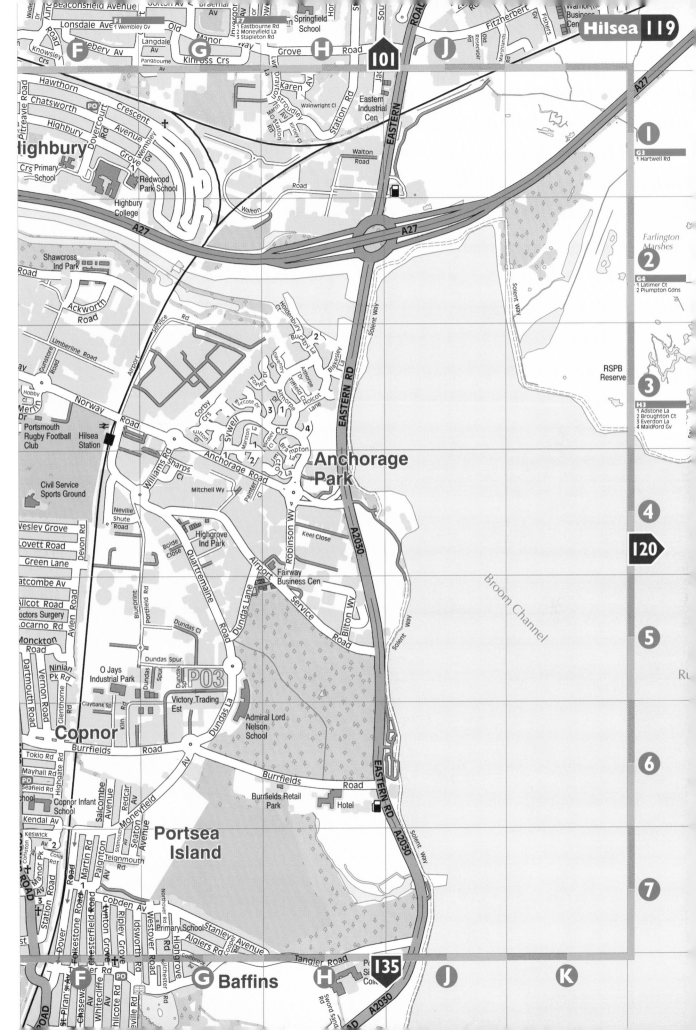

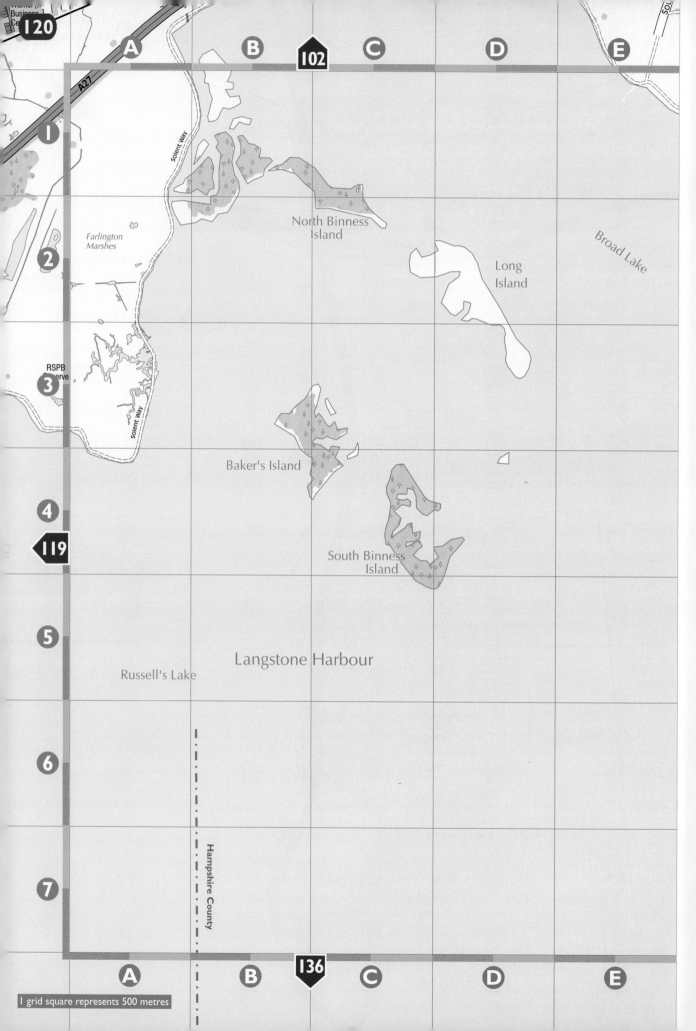

A B 102 C D E

A27

I

Farlington
Marshes

2

RSPB
Reserve

3

Solent Way

North Binness
Island

Long
Island

Broad Lake

Baker's Island

South Binness
Island

4

119

5

Langstone Harbour

Russell's Lake

6

Hampshire County

7

A B 136 C D E

1 grid square represents 500 metres

Langstone

Conigar Point

Langstone Road

Langstone Bridge

Northney Road

Hotel

Spinnaker Grange

Northney Road

Northney La

Northney

St Peter's Rd

Clovelly Rd

New Cut

Island Cl

Kingsway

Queensway

Pycroft Close

Avenue Road

Church Lane

North 122

Meadow Cl

Rogers Md

St Peter's Av

Victoria Road

Mill Close

St Peter's Road

HAYLING ISLAND

Stoke

Croft Lane

Chichester Road

Northwood Lane

Tye

Castlemans Lane

Gutner Lane

Woodgason Lane

West Lane

Copse Lane

PO

Fleet

Daw Lane

Yew Tree Rd

HAVANT ROAD

137

EMSWORTH

A **B** **104** **C** **D** **E** Sussex Border

Conigar
Point

Fowley
Island

Sweare

Deep

Wickor
Point

Great Deep

naker
nge

No3ney

Hunter Rd

Swift Road

Spartan Cl Sabre Rd

N Bay

S Bay

Meteor Road

Culver Road

Canberra Rd

Emsworth Rd

urch
ane

No121 Hayling

ter's Av

Hornet Road

Thorney County
Primary School

Sussex Border Path

Hampshire County
West Sussex County

Chichester Road

Cutner Lane

ve

Emsworth Rd

son Lane

Marker Point

Emsworth Channel

A **B** **138** **C** **D** **E**

Path

F   **G**   **H**   **105**   **J**

Lane

I

Chidham Point

2

Prinsted
Point

Sussex Border Path

PH
Marsh
La

Marsh   Lane

3

4

Thorney Island

Stanbury
Point

New
Barn

5

West Thorney

Thorney Island
Airfield

Smith
Lane

Church

Pleasant Lane

Victor Rd

Road

Vulcan
Road

Valiant
Road

Valetta Road

Varsity Road

Thorney Old Pk

✝

Thorney
Channel

6

Sussex Border

7

F   **G**   **H**   **139**   **J**   **K**

A   B   C   D   E

1

2

3

4

5

6

7

Hatchet
Moor

Beaulieu Heath

Greenmoor

B3054

Crockford Bridge

Crockford Stream

Pilley

Wooden House La.

Pilley St.

Pilley
Bailey

PO

ucky

Jordans Lane

Holly Lane

Bull Hill

Bull
Hill

B3054

Norley
Inclosure

Norleywood Road

Norley Farm

Norleyw

Thatch

A   B   C   D   E

1 grid square represents 500 metres

F G H **107** J

I

Swinesleys Farm

Beufre Farm

Hatchet Pond

Masseys La

East

Heath La

Whithers La

Pages Lane

Gaza Av

Matthews Lane

Sweyns Lease

Warton Cl

Lane

2

Lodge

Boldre Road

PO

Chapel

Wallace La

Knights Copse

Cripple

Gate

Lane

3

New Inn La

East Boldre

Church La

4

126

Newhouse Copse

B3054

HATCHET LANE

B3054

5

Newlands

6

Horsemoor Copse

Newlands Plantation

7

Ⓐ   Ⓑ   108   Ⓒ   Dock Lane   Ⓓ   *Spearbed Copse*   Ⓔ

Ⓘ

Beufre Farm

Solent Way

Keeping
Copse

Beaulieu River

Lane

Lode

❷

Keeping

❸

Ashen
Wood

**Bucklers
Hard**

PH

Hotel

Little Purnel

Ⓜ Ma
Mu

❹

125

Lodge Farm

Clobb

Tylers
Copse

❺

Salte

❻

Drokes

Coopers
Wood

St Leonards
Grange

❼

Gins

Ⓐ   Ⓑ   Ⓒ   Ⓓ   Ⓔ

B3054

Warren Lane

1 grid square represents 500 metres

Bergerie

F G H J

109

I

2

3

Exbury

4

128

5

6

7

Steerleys
Copse

Summer Lane

Yard
Wood

Main

Drive

Gilbury
Hard

Exbury House

aritime
useum

Salternshill
Copse

Haxland
Pits

ernshill

Lower
Exbury

Gins

Lane

Beaulieu River

Gins House

F G H J K

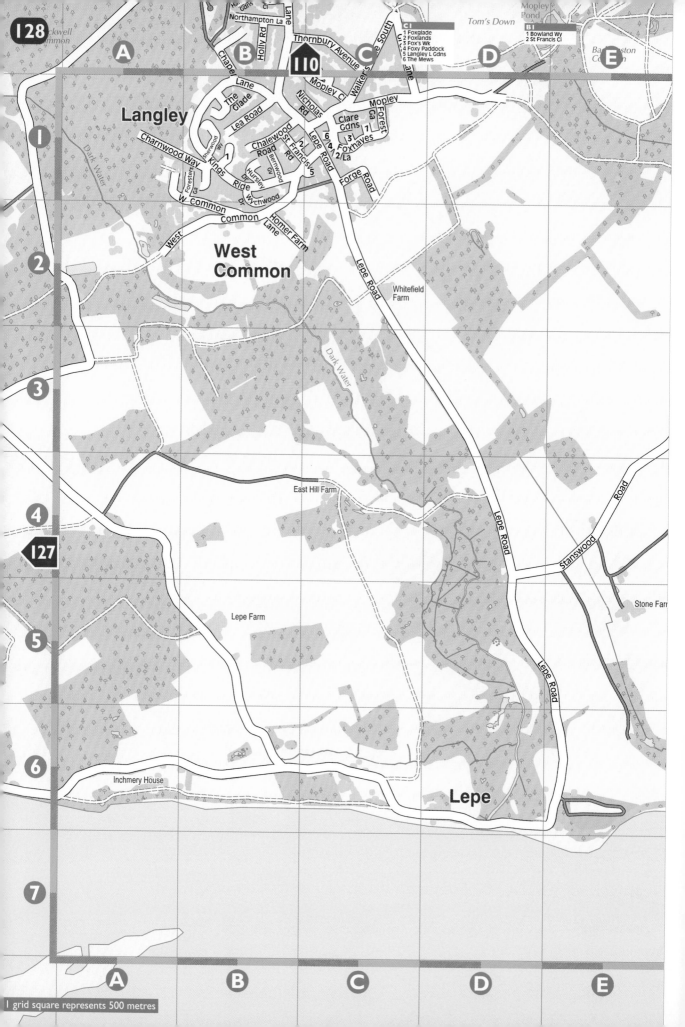

Calshot

Sprat's Down

Stanswood Road

F
G
H
J
I

PO

Cals...
Cl...

Triste...
Close

Castle
Lane

B3053

Hillhead

Eaglehurst

Stanswood
Bay

Stanswood Farm

Stanswood Road

Nelson's
Place

Stanswood Road

Cadland House

Stansore
Point

1

2

3

4

5

6

7

F
G
H
J
K

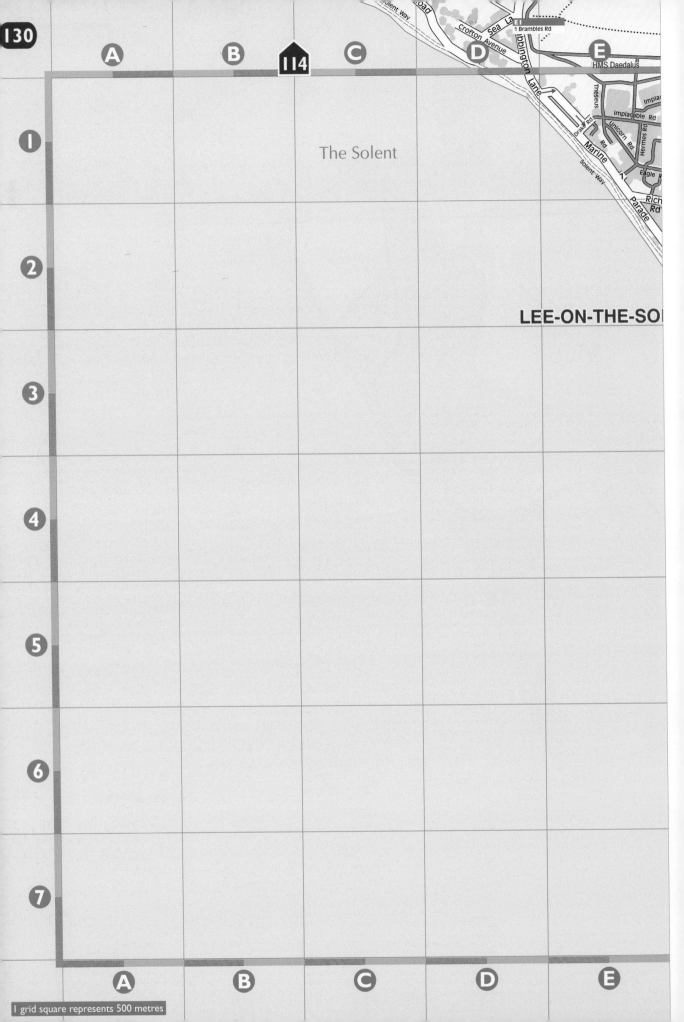

The Solent

LEE-ON-THE-SO

114

HMS Daedalus

Crofton Avenue

1 Brambles Rd

Sea La

Ibbington Lane

Theseus

Implac

Implacable Rd

Drake Rd

Unicorn Rd

Hermes Rd

Rd

Marine

Eagle R

Solent Way

Parade

Rich

Rd

Solent Way

A B C D E

1 grid square represents 500 metres

Rowner

F1
1 Inverkip Cl
2 Nottingham Pl
3 Southcliff

F2
1 Olave Cl
2 Osborne Rd
3 Queens Cl

G1
1 Chaffinch Wy
2 Common Barn La
3 Empson Wk
4 Kenilworth Cl
5 Magpie La
6 Martin Cl
7 Sparrow Ct
8 Swallow Ct
9 Swift Cl

G2
1 Chilcomb Cl
2 Esmonde Cl
3 Gibson Cl
4 Harrier Cl
5 Headley Cl
6 Kimpton Cl
7 Osprey Gdns
8 Trent Wy
9 Waveney Cl

G3
1 Cheyne Wy
2 Maple Cl

H3
1 Larch Cl

H4
1 The Seagulls

K1
1 Connigar Cl

K2
1 Davenport Cl
2 Hudson Cl

Browndown

Browndown Point

The Solent

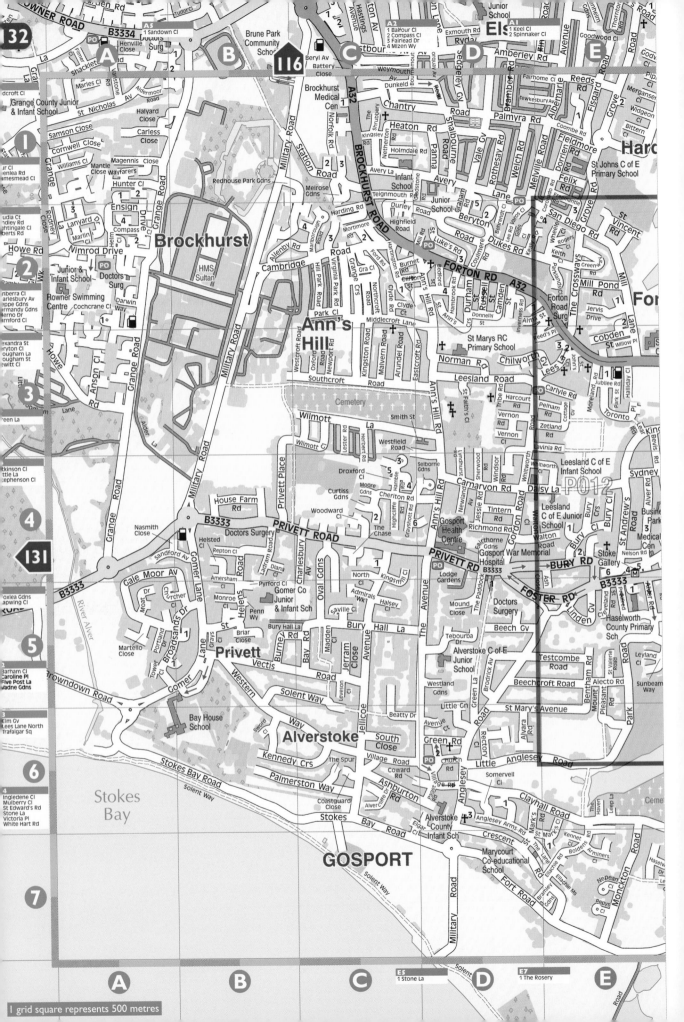

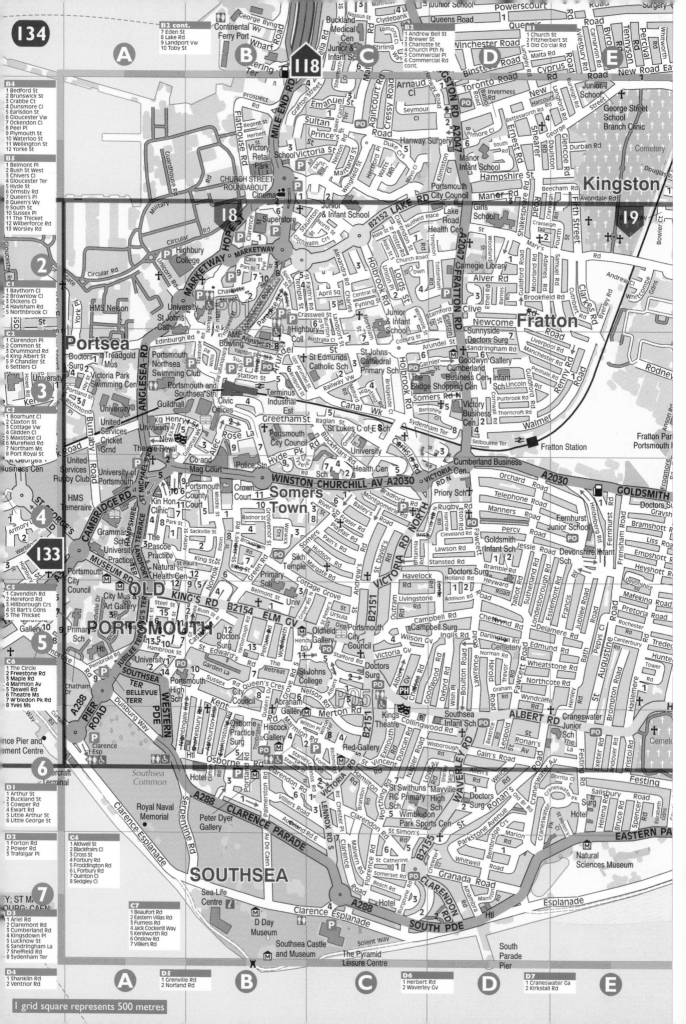

119

136

Baffins

Milton

Eastney

West Winner

Portsmouth Sixth Form College

F G H J

F G H J K

120

A B C D E

1

Langstone Channel

2

Sinah
Lake

3

Hampshire County
City of Portsmouth

University
of Portsmouth

4

135

Ferry Road

North Shore Road

Hayling Billy
Business
Cen
Station Theatre

Furniss W

PO

Harbour Road

Warren Cl

Warren Close

Park Road

St Thomas
Av

St Thomas Road

Richm

Fort
Cumberland

Lime Gv

Ferry Road

Sinah La

St Catherine's

St Aubin's Park

St Aubin's

Staunton Avenue

Fernhurst Clo

5

Ferry Road

Links Lane

St Helen's Road

St George's Road

Sea Front

Bacon

Westme

Sinah Common

6

East Winner

7

A B C D E

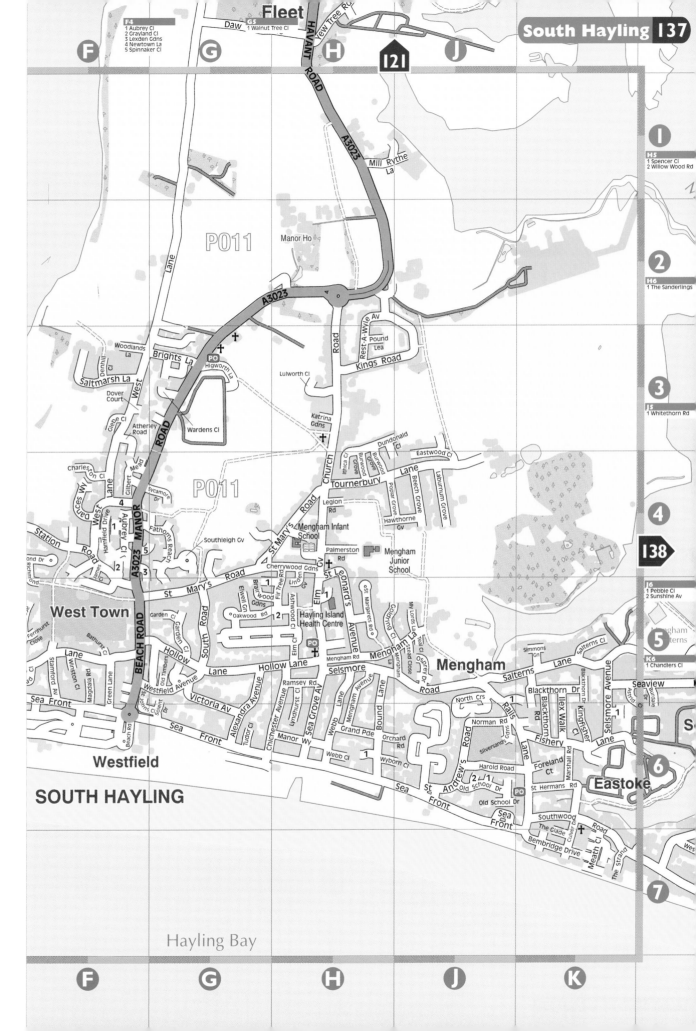

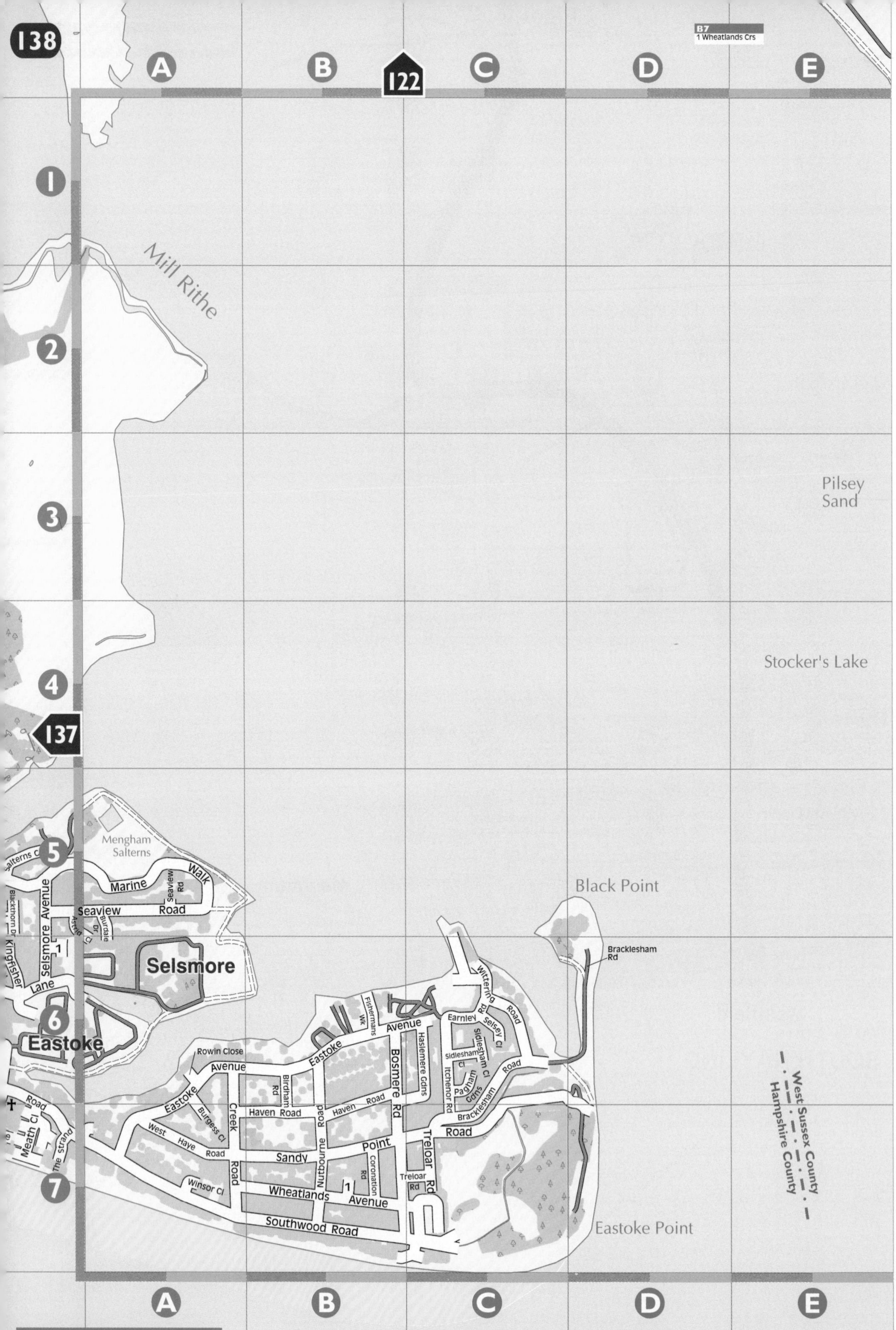

B7
1 Wheatlands Crs
122
137
A
B
C
D
E
1
2
3
4
5
6
7
Mill Rithe
Pilsey Sand
Stocker's Lake
Mengham Salterns
Black Point
Bracklesham Rd
Eastoke Point
West Sussex County
Hampshire County
Selsmore
Eastoke
Salterns Cl
Marine Walk
Seaview Rd
Seaview Road
Selsmore Avenue
Blackthorn Dr
Kingfisher
Burdale Dr
Selsmore Lane
Rowin Close
Eastoke Avenue
Fishermans Wk
Haslemere Gdns
Bosmere Rd
Wittering Road
Earnley Rd
Selsey Cl
Sidlesham Cl
Itchenor Rd
Pagham Gdns
Bracklesham Road
Birdham Rd
Haven Road
Burgess Cl
Creek Road
West Haye Road
Meath Cl
The Strand
Nutbourne Road
Coronation Rd
Sandy Point Road
Treloar Rd
Winsor Cl
Wheatlands Avenue
Southwood Road

1 grid square represents 500 metres

F G H J

123

I

2

3

4

Rookwood
Lane

5

6

East Head

Chichester Harbour

Longmere
Point

Pilsey
Island

Sussex

Border

Path

Rookwood Lane

Rookwood Road

ROOKWOOD RD

Ellanore Lane

Summerfield
Rd

Summerfield Road

PO

Cunliffe
Close

Elmstead
Park Road

Elms
Wy

Elmstead Pk Rd

Elms Lane

Meadow Wy

Locksash

Elmstead
Gdns

B2179

Roman Landing

Roman Landing

Roman Landing

Coastguard Lane

West Wittering
Parochial School

Pound Rd

The Wad

Royce
Close

Royce Way

Elms
Ride

Elms
Ride

Middlefield

The Byeway

Seaward
Dr

Wellsfield

West Witter 7

F G H J K

CAKEHAM

West

Strand

Berrybarn Lane

Abbotswood 29 F6
Abbots Worthy 22 C1
Abshot 95 F6
Aldermoor 54 B1
Allbrook 38 D4
Alverstoke 132 B6
Ampfield 30 D6
Anchorage Park 119 H4
Anmore 81 G1
Ann's Hill 132 C3
Anthill Common 62 C6
Applemore 90 B2
Ashfield 35 G6
Ashlett 111 F4
Ashurst 68 B3
Ashurst Bridge 52 B7
Avington 23 K2
Baffins 135 G1
Bank 86 A3
Bar End 3 H8
Barrow Hill 51 G2
Bartley 50 D5
Bassett 43 H6
Bassett Green 43 H6
Beaulieu 107 K6
Bedhampton 102 D5
Bishopstoke 45 F1
Bishop's Waltham 48 C2
Bitterne 6 F5
Bitterne Park 56 A3
Blackfield 110 D7
Blendworth 64 E5
Boarhunt 98 E1
Boorley Green 58 D2
Botley 59 G6
Boyatt Wood 38 C5
Braishfield 29 H2
Brambridge 39 G2
Breach 105 G5
Bridgemary 115 J4
Broadgate 31 F7
Broadoak 58 D5
Brockhampton 14 A7
Brockhurst 132 A2
Brooke's Hill 40 A7
Brown Heath 47 H6
Bucket Corner 36 D3
Bucklers Hard 126 D3
Bull Hill 124 A7
Bunker's Hill 50 D2
Bunstead 31 K3
Burridge 75 G4
Bursledon 73 K5
Butlocks Heath 73 G6
Buttsash 91 J6
Cadnam 50 C4
Calmore 52 B3
Calshot 111 J7
Catherington 64 B3
Catisfield 96 B5
Causeway 64 C7
Chandler's Ford 38 A2
Chilcomb 26 E3
Chilworth 42 E2
Chilworth Old Village 42 D1
Clayhall 133 F6
Clayhill 86 D3
Colbury 68 C3
Colden Common 39 K1
Compton 33 G2
Compton End 25 F7
Copnor 119 F6
Copythorne 51 F2
Cosham 101 F6
Cowplain 82 A2
Coxford 54 B2
Crampmoor 35 K1
Crockerhill 77 H6
Cupernham 35 F1
Curbridge 75 J1
Curdridge 59 K4
Custards 86 D1
Dean 20 B4
Denmead 62 E7
Denvilles 15 L2
Dibden 90 E1
Dibden Purlieu 90 D5
Drayton 101 H6
Dundridge 49 J2
Durley 47 G5
Durley Street 47 H3
Durrants 83 J5
East Boldre 125 J3
Eastland Gate 63 J7
Eastleigh 38 E7
Eastney 135 H5
Easton 23 F2
Eling 53 G7
Elson 116 D7
Emery Down 66 A7
Emsworth 104 B7
Exbury 127 J3
Fair Oak 46 B1
Fareham 12 F5
Farlington 101 J6
Fawley 110 E5
Fleet 121 G7
Fleetend 94 E5
Fleetlands 115 K2
Flexford 37 G2
Forest Gate 62 C5
Forton 16 A2
Foxhills 68 C2
Foyers 67 F2
Fratton 19 G2
Freemantle 54 D6
Frostlane 91 K4
Fryern Hill 38 A4
Fulflood 21 G7
Funtley 97 F1
Furzeley Corner 80 E4
Furzey Lodge 107 G6
Glebe 60 D1
Goldenhayes 66 E1
Goose Green 86 D2
Gosport 30 B7
Gosport 16 D4
Halterworth 35 H3
Hambledon 62 B2
Hamble-le-Rice 93 J3
Hambrook 105 K4
Hampton Park 55 K1
Hardley 109 K1
Hardway 132 E1
Harefield 7 M4
Harestock 21 F4
Hatch Bottom 57 G2
Hatchet Gate 107 G7
Havant 14 E1
Hayling Island 121 H5
Headbourne Worthy 21 J2
Heathfield 96 D5
Hedge End 58 A5
Hermitage 104 D5
Hides Close 108 A3
Highbridge 39 G3
Highbury 118 E1
Highfield 55 H2
Hightown 73 H1
Hill Head 114 A6
Hill Park 12 A1
Hillpound 49 K7
Hillstreet 40 A6
Hill Top 108 D3
Hillyfields 41 H7
Hilsea 118 E3
Hiltingbury 32 A7
Hocombe 31 K6
Hoe 49 G4
Holbury 109 K4
Hook 94 D7
Hook Park 112 C1
Horndean 64 D6
Horton Heath 46 C4
Hound 73 H7
Hounsdown 68 D1
Hursley 31 J2
Hyde 2 F2
Hythe 91 J2
Itchen 10 D2
Itchen Abbas 23 K1
Kingsmead 61 K4
Kingston 134 E1
Kings Worthy 22 B1
Knapp 30 E5
Ladwell 31 J5
Langdown 91 J3
Langley 128 A1
Langstone 121 F1
Lee 41 F3
Lee Ground 96 B1
Lee-on-the-Solent 130 D2
Leigh Park 102 E2
Lepe 128 D6
Little Holbury 109 J2
Little Posbrook 113 K2
Littleton 20 E2
Locks Heath 95 G2
Long Common 58 E3
Lord's Hill 42 B7
Lordswood 42 E7
Lovedean 63 K6
Lower Slackstead 30 A2
Lower Swanwick 74 B5
Lowford 73 K4
Lumley 104 D5
Lyndhurst 86 B1
Marchwood 69 K3
Martyr Worthy 23 G1
Maybush 53 K2
Mead End 81 F2
Meon 113 K4
Merry Oak 6 D9
Midanbury 6 E2
Millbrook 53 K5
Milton 135 H4
Moorcourt 40 B4
Moorgreen 57 J1
Netley 72 E7
Netley Hill 73 K1
Netley Marsh 51 K6
New Brighton 104 D3
New Town 11 H7
Newbridge 50 B1
Newtown 48 A3
Newtown 94 C7
No Man's Land 22 E7
Nob's Crook 39 K3
North Baddesley 36 B6
North Boarhunt 78 D3
North End 118 E5
North Hayling 121 J4
North Stoneham 44 A4
Northam 5 K7
Northbrook 48 D2
Northfields 33 K2
Northney 121 K3
Nursling 41 H6
Nutbourne 105 J7
Nutburn 36 C5
Ocean Village 9 K5
Old Netley 73 H4
Old Portsmouth 17 L5
Old Shirley 54 B3
Oliver's Battery 24 D5
Otterbourne 32 E5
Otterwood 108 E7
Park Gate 95 G1
Paulsgrove 99 K6
Peartree Green 10 B1
Peel Common 115 G5
Pikeshill 66 B7
Pilley 124 A6
Pitt 24 D3
Pooksgreen 69 J3
Portchester 98 E6
Portsea 18 A3
Portsea Island 119 G7
Portsmouth 19 J4
Portswood 55 J3
Prinsted 105 F7
Privett 132 B5
Pucknall 30 A3
Purbrook 101 J1
Ratlake 31 F6
Red Hill 83 J4
Redbridge 53 H4
Ridge 40 B2
Romsey 34 D3
Row Ash 60 B4
Rowland's Castle 83 K3
Rowner 115 K7
Rownhams 42 A4
Rushington 52 E6
Rushmore 62 D2
St Cross 25 J3
St Denys 5 M3
St Giles's Hill 3 H5
Sarisbury 94 D1
Shawford 33 H2
Shedfield 60 E5
Shirley 4 A4
Shirley Warren 54 C2
Shirrell Heath 61 H3
Sholing 11 J2
Sholing Common 7 H9
Shorn Hill 51 K1
Silkstead 32 B4
Sleepers Hill 25 G2
Soake 81 G2
Southampton 8 F5
Southbourne 105 H6
South Down 33 G4
South Hayling 137 F6
Southwick 79 H7
Stamshaw 118 A6
Stanmore 25 G3
Stockheath 103 F3
Stoke 121 H6
Stoke Common 39 F5
Stonehills 111 F5
Stubbermere 84 D5
Stubbington 114 E4
Swanmore 49 J6
Swanwick 75 F6
Swaythling 56 B1
Tapnage 76 D4
Testwood 52 D2
Thorney Island 123 F4
Thornhill 57 H7
Thornhill Park 57 G5
Timsbury 28 B2
Tipner 118 A4
Titchfield 95 K6
Titchfield Common 95 F5
Titchfield Park 95 J3
Toothill 41 K2
Totton 53 F4
Townhill Park 56 C2
Trotts 69 H2
Turkey Island 61 G5
Twyford 33 K3
Tye 121 K6
Upper Shirley 54 E2
Upper Swanmore 49 K3
Upton 41 J4
Wallington 13 M4
Waltham Chase 61 F1
Walton Heath 79 F6
Warblington 15 L6
Warsash 94 C5
Waterlooville 82 A5
Wecock 81 K1
Weeke 21 G5
West Common 128 B2
West End 57 H4
West End 12 E8
West Leigh 103 H1
West Thorney 123 G5
Westbourne 104 E2
Weston 10 E9
Whitenap 35 H3
Wickham 77 H2
Widley 101 H4
Wildern 58 B5
Wimpson 53 K3
Winchester 2 E6
Winnall 3 J3
Winsor 51 G3
Wintershill 47 J2
Wittensford 50 A4
Woodcot 115 H4
Woodlands 67 H2
Woodley 35 H1
Woodmancote 105 J2
Woolston 10 B6
Wymering 100 D6

USING THE STREET INDEX

Street names are listed alphabetically. Each street name is followed by its postal town or area locality, the Postcode District, the page number, and the reference to the square in which the name is found.

Example: **Abbey Cl** *FAWY* SO45 **91** H3 1

Some entries are followed by a number in a blue box. This number indicates the location of the street within the referenced grid square. The full street name is listed at the side of the map page.

GENERAL ABBREVIATIONS

ACC ACCESS
ALY ALLEY
AP APPROACH
AR ARCADE
ASS ASSOCIATION
AV AVENUE
BCH BEACH
BLDS BUILDINGS
BND BEND
BNK BANK
BR BRIDGE
BRK BROOK
BTM BOTTOM
BUS BUSINESS
BVD BOULEVARD
BY BYPASS
CATH CATHEDRAL
CEM CEMETERY
CEN CENTRE
CFT CROFT
CH CHURCH
CHA CHASE
CHYD CHURCHYARD
CIR CIRCLE
CIRC CIRCUS
CL CLOSE
CLFS CLIFFS
CMP CAMP
CNR CORNER
CO COUNTY
COLL COLLEGE
COM COMMON
COMM COMMISSION
CON CONVENT
COT COTTAGE
COTS COTTAGES
CP CAPE
CPS COPSE
CR CREEK
CREM CREMATORIUM
CRS CRESCENT
CSWY CAUSEWAY
CT COURT
CTRL CENTRAL
CTS COURTS
CTYD COURTYARD
CUTT CUTTINGS
CV COVE
CYN CANYON
DEPT DEPARTMENT
DL DALE
DM DAM
DR DRIVE
DRO DROVE
DRY DRIVEWAY
DWGS DWELLINGS
E EAST
EMB EMBANKMENT
EMBY EMBASSY
ESP ESPLANADE
EST ESTATE
EX EXCHANGE
EXPY EXPRESSWAY
EXT EXTENSION
F/O FLYOVER
FC FOOTBALL CLUB
FK FORK
FLD FIELD
FLDS FIELDS
FLS FALLS
FLS FLATS
FM FARM
FT FORT
FWY FREEWAY
FY FERRY
GA GATE
GAL GALLERY
GDN GARDEN
GDNS GARDENS
GLD GLADE
GLN GLEN
GN GREEN
GND GROUND
GRA GRANGE
GRG GARAGE
GT GREAT
GTWY GATEWAY
GV GROVE
HGR HIGHER
HL HILL
HLS HILLS
HO HOUSE
HOL HOLLOW
HOSP HOSPITAL
HRB HARBOUR
HTH HEATH
HTS HEIGHTS
HVN HAVEN
HWY HIGHWAY
IMP IMPERIAL
IN INLET
IND EST INDUSTRIAL ESTATE
INF INFIRMARY
INFO INFORMATION
INT INTERCHANGE
IS ISLAND
JCT JUNCTION
JTY JETTY
KG KING
KNL KNOLL
L LAKE
LA LANE
LDG LODGE
LGT LIGHT
LK LOCK
LKS LAKES
LNDG LANDING
LTL LITTLE
LWR LOWER
MAG MAGISTRATE
MAN MANSIONS
MD MEAD
MDW MEADOWS
MEM MEMORIAL
MKT MARKET
MKTS MARKETS
ML MALL
ML MILL
MNR MANOR
MS MEWS
MSN MISSION
MT MOUNT
MTN MOUNTAIN
MTS MOUNTAINS
MUS MUSEUM
MWY MOTORWAY
N NORTH
NE NORTH EAST
NW NORTH WEST
O/P OVERPASS
OFF OFFICE
ORCH ORCHARD
OV OVAL
PAL PALACE
PAS PASSAGE
PAV PAVILION
PDE PARADE
PH PUBLIC HOUSE
PK PARK
PKWY PARKWAY
PL PLACE
PLN PLAIN
PLNS PLAINS
PLZ PLAZA
POL POLICE STATION
PR PRINCE
PREC PRECINCT
PREP PREPARATORY
PRIM PRIMARY
PROM PROMENADE
PRS PRINCESS
PRT PORT
PT POINT
PTH PATH
PZ PIAZZA
QD QUADRANT
QU QUEEN
QY QUAY
R RIVER
RBT ROUNDABOUT
RD ROAD
RDG RIDGE
REP REPUBLIC
RES RESERVOIR
RFC RUGBY FOOTBALL CLUB
RI RISE
RP RAMP
RW ROW
S SOUTH
SCH SCHOOL
SE SOUTH EAST
SER SERVICE AREA
SH SHORE
SHOP SHOPPING
SKWY SKYWAY
SMT SUMMIT
SOC SOCIETY
SP SPUR
SPR SPRING
SQ SQUARE
ST STREET
STN STATION
STR STREAM
STRD STRAND
SW SOUTH WEST
TDG TRADING
TER TERRACE
THWY THROUGHWAY
TNL TUNNEL
TOLL TOLLWAY
TPK TURNPIKE
TR TRACK
TRL TRAIL
TWR TOWER
U/P UNDERPASS
UNI UNIVERSITY
UPR UPPER
V VALE
VA VALLEY
VIAD VIADUCT
VIL VILLA
VIS VISTA
VLG VILLAGE
VLS VILLAS
VW VIEW
W WEST
WD WOOD
WHF WHARF
WK WALK
WKS WALKS
WLS WELLS
WY WAY
YD YARD
YHA YOUTH HOSTEL

POSTCODE TOWNS AND AREA ABBREVIATIONS

BPWT ....Bishop's Waltham
BROC ....Brockenhurst
CHAM ....Cosham
CHFD ....Chandler's Ford
ELGH ....Eastleigh
EMRTH ....Emsworth/Southbourne
ENEY ....Eastney
FAWY ....Fawley/Hythe
FHAM ....Fareham

FHAM/PORC ....Fareham/Portchester
FHAM/STUB ....Fareham/Stubbington
GPORT ....Gosport
HAV ....Havant
HEND ....Hedge End
HISD ....Hayling Island
HLER ....Hamble-le-Rice
HORN ....Horndean
HSEA ....Hilsea

ITCH ....Itchen
LSOL/BMARY ....Lee-on-the-Solent/Bridgemary
LYMN ....Lymington
LYND ....Lyndhurst
NBAD ....North Baddesley
NEND ....North End
PSEA ....Portsea
PTSW ....Portswood

RCCH ....Rural Chichester
ROMY ....Romsey
ROWN ....Rownhams
RWIN ....Rural Winchester
SELS ....Selsey
SHAM ....Southampton
SSEA ....Southsea
TOTT ....Totton
WEND ....West End

WHAM ....Wickham
WINC ....Winchester
WINW ....Winchester west
WSHM ....Southampton west
WVILLE ....Waterlooville/Denmead

Index - streets

10th - Ays

10th St *FAWY* SO45 .... 110 A3
11th St *FAWY* SO45 .... 110 A2
12th St *FAWY* SO45 .... 110 A2
13th St *FAWY* SO45 .... 110 A1
14th St *FAWY* SO45 .... 109 K2
1st St *FAWY* SO45 .... 110 D4
2nd St *FAWY* SO45 .... 110 D2
3rd St *FAWY* SO45 .... 110 C3
4th St *FAWY* SO45 .... 110 C3
5th St *FAWY* SO45 .... 110 C2
6th St *FAWY* SO45 .... 110 B2
7th St *FAWY* SO45 .... 110 B3
8th St *FAWY* SO45 .... 110 B3
9th St *FAWY* SO45 .... 110 A3

A

Aaron Ct *TOTT* SO40 .... 70 A3
A Av *FAWY* SO45 .... 110 A2
Abbey Cl *FAWY* SO45 .... 91 H3 🖸
Abbeydore Rd *CHAM* PO6 .... 100 B5
Abbeyfield Dr *FHAM* PO15 .... 96 D4
Abbey Hl *ITCH* SO19 .... 72 B5
Abbey Hill Cl *WINC* SO23 .... 21 K5 🖸
Abbey Hill Rd *WINC* SO23 .... 21 J5
Abbey Rd *FHAM* PO15 .... 12 B4
Abbey Water *ROMY* SO51 .... 34 D3 🖸
Abbotsbury Rd *ELGH* SO50 .... 45 J1
Abbots Cl *WVILLE* PO7 .... 101 H2 🖸
Abbotsfield *TOTT* SO40 .... 52 D5
Abbotsfield Cl *ROWN* SO16 .... 42 D6
Abbotsford *TOTT* SO40 .... 50 E6
Abbotstone Av *HAV* PO9 .... 103 H2
Abbots Wy *FHAM* PO15 .... 12 A5
  HLER SO31 .... 73 G7
Abbotswood Cl *ROMY* SO51 .... 35 H1 🖸
Abbotts Rd *ELGH* SO50 .... 44 B2
  WINC SO23 .... 21 K5
Abbotts Wy *PTSW* SO17 .... 55 J3
Abercrombie Gdns *ROWN* SO16 .... 42 B7
Aberdare Av *CHAM* PO6 .... 101 G5
Aberdeen Cl *FHAM* PO15 .... 12 D2
Aberdour Cl *WEND* SO18 .... 7 H2
Abingdon Gdns *ROWN* SO16 .... 55 F1 🖸
Above Bar St *SHAM* SO14 .... 4 F8
Abraham Cl *HEND* SO30 .... 58 C7
Abshot Cl *FHAM/STUB* PO14 .... 95 G5
Abshot Rd *FHAM/STUB* PO14 .... 95 G5
Acacia Gdns *HORN* PO8 .... 64 C7
Acacia Rd *ITCH* SO19 .... 6 E9
Acer Wy *HAV* PO9 .... 103 J2
Ackworth Rd *HSEA* PO3 .... 119 F2
Acorn Cl *CHAM* PO6 .... 101 K6 🖸
  WINW SO22 .... 21 G5
  LSOL/BMARY PO13 .... 116 A6
  TOTT SO40 .... 70 B4 🖸
Acorn Ct *HLER* SO31 .... 93 J5 🖸
Acorn Dr *ROWN* SO16 .... 41 K4
Acorn Gv *NBAD* SO52 .... 37 G6
The Acorns *HLER* SO31 .... 73 J5
Acre La *HORN* PO8 .... 82 D4
Adair Rd *ENEY* PO4 .... 19 M9
Adames Rd *PSEA* PO1 .... 19 H1
Adams Cl *HEND* SO30 .... 58 A1
Adamson Cl *CHFD* SO53 .... 38 A2
Adams Rd *HAV* PO9 .... 91 H4
Adams Wood Dr *TOTT* SO40 .... 70 A4
Adderbury Av *EMRTH* PO10 .... 104 C2
Addison Cl *ELGH* SO50 .... 38 E5 🖸
  ENEY PO4 .... 19 G7
  HLER SO31 .... 74 E7
Addisson Cl *WINW* SO22 .... 25 F3
Adelaide Rd *PTSW* SO17 .... 5 L2
Adela Verne Cl *ITCH* SO19 .... 73 H2 🖸
Adey Cl *ITCH* SO19 .... 11 K5
Adhurst Rd *HAV* PO9 .... 103 H2
Admirals Cl *FAWY* SO45 .... 110 E4 🖸
Admirals Rd *HLER* SO31 .... 95 G2
Admirals Wk *GPORT* PO12 .... 132 C5
  PSEA PO1 .... 17 K2 🖸
Admiralty Rd *PSEA* PO1 .... 17 L3
Admiralty Wy *TOTT* SO40 .... 70 A2
Adsdean Cl *HAV* PO9 .... 103 F2 🖸
Adstone La *HSEA* PO3 .... 119 H3 🖸
Adur Cl *GPORT* PO12 .... 132 C1 🖸
  WEND SO18 .... 7 J1
Aerial Rd *CHAM* PO6 .... 100 A4
Aerodrome Rd
  LSOL/BMARY PO13 .... 116 B5
Africa Dr *TOTT* SO40 .... 70 A4
Agincourt Rd *NEND* PO2 .... 134 C1
Agitor Rd *FAWY* SO45 .... 111 F2
Agnew Rd *LSOL/BMARY* PO13 .... 115 K4
Aikman La *TOTT* SO40 .... 52 A5
Ailsa La *ITCH* SO19 .... 10 B2
Ainsdale Rd *CHAM* PO6 .... 101 J5
Ainsley Gdns *ELGH* SO50 .... 38 D5
Aintree Cl *ELGH* SO50 .... 46 C4 🖸
Aintree Dr *WVILLE* PO7 .... 82 C4
Aintree Rd *TOTT* SO40 .... 52 A6
Airlie Rd *WINW* SO22 .... 2 B7
Airport Service Rd *HSEA* PO3 .... 119 G4
Ajax Cl *FHAM/STUB* PO14 .... 114 E6
Alameda Rd *WVILLE* PO7 .... 101 J2
Alameda Wy *WVILLE* PO7 .... 101 J2
Alandale Rd *ITCH* SO19 .... 73 H2
Alan Drayton Wy *ELGH* SO50 .... 45 H1
Alan Gv *FHAM* PO15 .... 12 C4

Albacore Av *HLER* SO31 .... 94 D5 🖸
Albany Ct *BPWT* SO32 .... 48 B3
Albany Dr *BPWT* SO32 .... 48 B3
Albany Rd *BPWT* SO32 .... 48 B3
  FAWY SO45 .... 109 K3
  ROMY SO51 .... 34 D3
  SSEA PO5 .... 18 E8
  WSHM SO15 .... 54 D6
Albatross Wk
  LSOL/BMARY PO13 .... 115 J5
Albemarle Av *HLER* SO31 .... 93 F1
Albert Cl *HLER* SO31 .... 18 F8
Albert Gv *SSEA* PO5 .... 18 F8
Albert Rd *BPWT* SO32 .... 48 C4
  CHAM PO6 .... 100 E7
  ELGH SO50 .... 38 E5
  FHAM/STUB PO14 .... 115 G5
  HEND SO30 .... 58 A7
  SSEA PO5 .... 18 F9
Albert Rd North *SHAM* SO14 .... 9 K3
Albert Rd South *SHAM* SO14 .... 9 K4
Albert St *GPORT* PO12 .... 16 C4
Albion Cl *FHAM/PORC* PO16 .... 116 E1
Albion Pl *SHAM* SO14 .... 8 F2
Albretia Av *HORN* PO8 .... 81 J2
Albury PI *CHFD* SO53 .... 37 J1 🖸
Alcantara Crs *SHAM* SO14 .... 9 K4
Alder Cl *FAWY* SO45 .... 90 D3
  ROMY SO51 .... 35 J4
  RWIN SO21 .... 39 K2
  TOTT SO40 .... 70 A3
Alder Hill Dr *TOTT* SO40 .... 52 A4
Alder La *LSOL/BMARY* PO13 .... 132 A3
Aldermoor Av *ROWN* SO16 .... 42 B7
Aldermoor Cl *ROWN* SO16 .... 42 D7
Aldermoor Rd
  LSOL/BMARY PO13 .... 132 A1
  ROWN SO16 .... 42 C7
  WVILLE PO7 .... 101 J2
Aldermoor Rd East
  WVILLE PO7 .... 101 J1 🖸
Alderney Cl *ROWN* SO16 .... 41 K7
Alder Rd *ROWN* SO16 .... 54 A1
Alders Rd *FHAM/PORC* PO16 .... 97 J7
Alderwood Cl *CHFD* SO53 .... 37 H4
Alderwood Cl *HAV* PO9 .... 102 B3
Aldrich Rd *PSEA* PO1 .... 17 M1
Aldroke St *CHAM* PO6 .... 100 E7 🖸
Aldsworth Cl *CHAM* PO6 .... 101 H6
Aldsworth Gdns *CHAM* PO6 .... 101 H6 🖸
Aldwell St *SSEA* PO5 .... 18 E5 🖸
Alec Rose La *PSEA* PO1 .... 18 C4
Alecto Rd *GPORT* PO12 .... 16 A3
Alencon Cl *GPORT* PO12 .... 117 F7 🖸
Alexander Cl *TOTT* SO40 .... 52 C4
  WVILLE PO7 .... 101 J1 🖸
Alexander Gv
  FHAM/PORC PO16 .... 13 H8
Alexandra Av *HISD* PO11 .... 137 G6
Alexandra Cl *FAWY* SO45 .... 91 H2 🖸
Alexandra Rd *CHFD* SO53 .... 38 C2
  FAWY SO45 .... 91 H2
  HEND SO30 .... 58 A7
  PSEA PO1 .... 18 E1 🖸
  WSHM SO15 .... 4 B7
Alexandra St *GPORT* PO12 .... 132 D2 🖸
Alexandra Ter *WINC* SO23 .... 2 C6
Alexandra Wy *HEND* SO30 .... 59 F5
Alfred Cl *TOTT* SO40 .... 52 B4 🖸
  TOTT SO40 .... 52 B5 🖸
Alfred Rd *FHAM/STUB* PO14 .... 114 E4
  PSEA PO1 .... 18 B3
Alfred Rose Ct *WEND* SO18 .... 44 B7 🖸
Alfred St *SHAM* SO14 .... 5 J6
Alfrey Cl *EMRTH* PO10 .... 105 F6
Alfriston Gdns *ITCH* SO19 .... 11 K3
Algiers Rd *HSEA* PO3 .... 119 G7
Alhambra Rd *ENEY* PO4 .... 134 D7
Allan Gv *ROMY* SO51 .... 35 G3
Allaway Av *CHAM* PO6 .... 99 J4
Allbrook Cl *HAV* PO9 .... 82 E7
Allbrook Hl *ELGH* SO50 .... 38 E3
Allbrook Knoll *ELGH* SO50 .... 38 D3
Allbrook Wy *ELGH* SO50 .... 38 D2
Allcot Rd *HSEA* PO3 .... 118 E5
Allenby Gv *FHAM/PORC* PO16 .... 99 F7
Allenby Rd *GPORT* PO12 .... 132 B2
Allendale Av *EMRTH* PO10 .... 104 B3
Allen Rd *HEND* SO30 .... 58 B5
Allen's Rd *SSEA* PO5 .... 19 G3
Allerton Cl *TOTT* SO40 .... 52 C3
Alliance Cl *LSOL/BMARY* PO13 .... 116 A7
Allington La *HEND* SO30 .... 45 H6
Allington Rd *WSHM* SO15 .... 53 J5
Allmara Dr *WVILLE* PO7 .... 101 K1
Allotment Rd *HLER* SO31 .... 94 D1
All Saint's Rd *PSEA* PO1 .... 134 C1
All Saint's St *PSEA* PO1 .... 18 D1 🖸
Alma La *BPWT* SO32 .... 47 G1
Alma Rd *ROMY* SO51 .... 34 E3
  SHAM SO14 .... 4 F3
Alma St *GPORT* PO12 .... 132 D2
Almatade Rd *WEND* SO18 .... 7 H4
Alma Ter *ENEY* PO4 .... 19 M8
Almond Cl *CHAM* PO6 .... 102 A6
  HORN PO8 .... 82 D1
Almond Rd *WSHM* SO15 .... 54 D1
Almondsbury Rd *CHAM* PO6 .... 99 J4
Almondside
  LSOL/BMARY PO13 .... 116 B6
Alpine Cl *WEND* SO18 .... 7 K2
Alpine Rd *TOTT* SO40 .... 67 J2

Alresford Rd *HAV* PO9 .... 103 F2 🖸
  RWIN SO21 .... 26 E1
  WINC SO23 .... 3 J5
Alsford Rd *WVILLE* PO7 .... 101 J1
Alten Rd *WVILLE* PO7 .... 81 H3
Althorpe Dr *HSEA* PO3 .... 119 H3
Alton Cl *ELGH* SO50 .... 46 A1
Alton Gv *FHAM/PORC* PO16 .... 117 F1
Alum Cl *FAWY* SO45 .... 110 A4
Alum Wy *FHAM/PORC* PO16 .... 98 B5
  WEND SO18 .... 7 J5
Alvara Rd *GPORT* PO12 .... 132 D6
Alvercliffe Dr *GPORT* PO12 .... 132 C6
Alver Rd *GPORT* PO12 .... 16 B7
  PSEA PO1 .... 19 G2
Alverstone Rd *ENEY* PO4 .... 19 L4
Alveston Av *FHAM/STUB* PO14 .... 96 D6
Amarylis Cl *FHAM* PO15 .... 95 K2
Amberley Cl *HEND* SO30 .... 58 E4
  NBAD SO52 .... 35 K5
Amberley Rd *TOTT* SO40 .... 52 D6
Amberley Rd *GPORT* PO12 .... 116 D7
  NEND PO2 .... 118 E4
Amberslade Wk *FAWY* SO45 .... 91 G5
Amberwood Cl *TOTT* SO40 .... 52 B2
Ambledale *HLER* SO31 .... 94 D2
Ambledale Rd *CHFD* SO53 .... 37 H4
Ambleside *HEND* SO30 .... 58 C7
Ambleside Gdns *ITCH* SO19 .... 11 H3
Amersham Cl *GPORT* PO12 .... 132 B4
Amethyst Gv *WVILLE* PO7 .... 82 C5
Amoy St *WSHM* SO15 .... 4 E6
Ampfield Cl *HAV* PO9 .... 102 C2 🖸
Amport Cl *WINW* SO22 .... 21 F4
Amport Ct *HAV* PO9 .... 82 E7
Ampthill Rd *WSHM* SO15 .... 54 C5
Amyas Ct *ENEY* PO4 .... 135 H4
Ancasta Rd *SHAM* SO14 .... 5 J4 🖸
Anchorage Rd *HSEA* PO3 .... 119 G4
The Anchorage *GPORT* PO12 .... 16 D6
Anchor Ga *PSEA* PO1 .... 17 M1
Anchor La *PSEA* PO1 .... 17 L2 🖸
Andalusian Gdns *HLER* SO31 .... 75 G5
Anderby Rd *ROWN* SO16 .... 53 J2
Andersen Cl *HLER* SO31 .... 75 H5
Anderson Cl *HAV* PO9 .... 15 G1
  ROMY SO51 .... 29 H7 🖸
Anderson's Rd *SHAM* SO14 .... 9 K3
Andes Cl *SHAM* SO14 .... 9 L4
  SHAM SO14 .... 9 L4
Andes Rd *ROWN* SO16 .... 53 G1
Andover Rd *ENEY* PO4 .... 19 K9
  WINW SO22 .... 21 H5
  WSHM SO15 .... 4 B5
Andrew Bell St *PSEA* PO1 .... 18 D1 🖸
Andrew Cl *FAWY* SO45 .... 91 H5 🖸
  PSEA PO1 .... 19 J2
  TOTT SO40 .... 52 C5
Andrew Crs *WVILLE* PO7 .... 81 J4
Andrewes Cl *BPWT* SO32 .... 48 D3
Andrew Pl *FHAM/STUB* PO14 .... 114 C5
Andromeda Rd *ROWN* SO16 .... 41 K7
Anfield Cl *ELGH* SO50 .... 46 B2
Angel Crs *ITCH* SO19 .... 7 G6
Angelica Gdns *ELGH* SO50 .... 46 B4
Angelica Wy *FHAM* PO15 .... 75 K5
Angelo Cl *WVILLE* PO7 .... 82 B5
Angelus *FHAM/STUB* PO14 .... 114 D5
Angerstein Rd *NEND* PO2 .... 118 C6
Anglers Wy *HLER* SO31 .... 74 C5
Anglesea Rd
  LSOL/BMARY PO13 .... 131 H4
  PSEA PO1 .... 18 B4
  WSHM SO15 .... 54 C3
Anglesea Ter *SHAM* SO14 .... 9 K3

Ann's Hill Rd *GPORT* PO12 .... 132 D3
Anson Cl *LSOL/BMARY* PO13 .... 132 A3
Anson Dr *ITCH* SO19 .... 7 M9
Anson Gv *FHAM/PORC* PO16 .... 99 G5
Anson Rd *ELGH* SO50 .... 46 B4
  ENEY PO4 .... 19 K4
Anstey Rd *ROMY* SO51 .... 35 G1
Anthill Cl *WVILLE* PO7 .... 62 B6
Anthony Gv *GPORT* PO12 .... 116 C6
  LSOL/BMARY PO13 .... 116 C6
Anton Cl *ROMY* SO51 .... 35 H3
Anvil Cl *HORN* PO8 .... 82 B2
Anzac Cl *FHAM/STUB* PO14 .... 114 D3
Apex Dr *FHAM* PO15 .... 96 D5
Apley Pl *CHFD* SO53 .... 37 J1 🖸
Apley Rd *ENEY* PO4 .... 19 L5
Apollo Dr *WVILLE* PO7 .... 102 A3
Apollo Pl *ITCH* SO19 .... 10 E6
Apollo Rd *CHFD* SO53 .... 38 C3
Appleshaw Cl *WINW* SO22 .... 21 G3
Appleton Rd *FHAM* PO15 .... 96 D5
  WEND SO18 .... 56 B3
Appletree Cl *TOTT* SO40 .... 52 B4
Appletree Ct *HEND* SO30 .... 59 F5
Applewood Gv *WVILLE* PO7 .... 101 H4
Applewood Pl *TOTT* SO40 .... 52 B6
Applewood Rd *HAV* PO9 .... 102 B3
April Cl *WEND* SO18 .... 7 J4

April Gv *HLER* SO31 .... 94 D3
April Sq *PSEA* PO1 .... 18 E2
Apsley Pl *CHFD* SO53 .... 37 J1 🖸
Apsley Rd *ENEY* PO4 .... 19 L5
Aquila Wy *HLER* SO31 .... 93 J4
Arabian Gdns *FHAM* PO15 .... 75 H6
Arcadia Cl *ROWN* SO16 .... 54 C1
Archers Cl *TOTT* SO40 .... 52 B2
Archers Rd *ELGH* SO50 .... 38 D6
  WSHM SO15 .... 4 D5
Archery Gdns *ITCH* SO19 .... 10 E6
Archery Gv *ITCH* SO19 .... 10 D6
Archery La *FHAM/PORC* PO16 .... 13 L4
  WINC SO23 .... 2 C5
Archery Rd *ITCH* SO19 .... 10 C7
Arden Cl *WEND* SO18 .... 7 K1
Ardingly Crs *HEND* SO30 .... 58 C2
Ardington Ri *WVILLE* PO7 .... 101 K3
Argosy Cl *HLER* SO31 .... 94 E5
Argus Rd *LSOL/BMARY* PO13 .... 131 G1
Argyle Crs *FHAM* PO15 .... 12 D3
Argyle Rd *SHAM* SO14 .... 5 H3
Ariel Rd *PSEA* PO1 .... 19 G3
Ark Royal Crs
  LSOL/BMARY PO13 .... 131 F1
Arliss Rd *ROWN* SO16 .... 54 B3
Arlott Cl *WSHM* SO15 .... 4 D4
Armada Cl *ROWN* SO16 .... 41 K4
Armada Dr *FAWY* SO45 .... 91 G4
Arminers Cl *GPORT* PO12 .... 132 E7
Armitage Av *FAWY* SO45 .... 91 G5
Armory La *PSEA* PO1 .... 17 M6
Armstrong Cl *WVILLE* PO7 .... 81 J4 🖸
Armstrong Ct *ROWN* SO16 .... 42 A6 🖸
Arnaud Cl *NEND* PO2 .... 134 C1
Arnheim Cl *ROWN* SO16 .... 42 D7
Arnheim Rd *ROWN* SO16 .... 42 E7
Arnold Rd *ELGH* SO50 .... 44 D3
  PTSW SO17 .... 55 K2
Arnside Rd *WVILLE* PO7 .... 81 K5
Arnwood Av *FAWY* SO45 .... 91 G6
Arragon Ct *WVILLE* PO7 .... 82 B5
Arran Cl *CHAM* PO6 .... 100 E5
Arreton *HLER* SO31 .... 73 F7 🖸
Arrow Cl *ELGH* SO50 .... 38 D6
  ITCH SO19 .... 10 B8
Arters Lawn *TOTT* SO40 .... 69 G7
Arthur Rd *ELGH* SO50 .... 38 D6
  WINC SO23 .... 2 E1
  WSHM SO15 .... 4 B5
Arthurs Gdns *HEND* SO30 .... 58 A1 🖸
Arthur St *NEND* PO2 .... 134 D1 🖸
Artillery Cl *NEND* PO2 .... 100 B6
Arundel Dr *FHAM/PORC* PO16 .... 13 G4
Arundel Rd *ELGH* SO50 .... 38 D4
  GPORT PO12 .... 132 C3
  TOTT SO40 .... 53 F4
Arundel St *PSEA* PO1 .... 18 F3
Arun Rd *WEND* SO18 .... 56 E2
Ascot Cl *FHAM/STUB* PO14 .... 95 H4
Ascot Rd *ELGH* SO50 .... 46 C4
  HSEA PO3 .... 135 F1
Ascupart St *SHAM* SO14 .... 9 J1
Asford Gv *ELGH* SO50 .... 39 G6
Ashbarn Crs *WINW* SO22 .... 25 G3
Ashbridge Ri *CHFD* SO53 .... 37 H1
Ashburnham Cl *ITCH* SO19 .... 6 B9
Ashburton Cl *FAWY* SO45 .... 90 E3 🖸
Ashburton Rd *GPORT* PO12 .... 132 C6
  SSEA PO5 .... 18 C9
Ashby Rd *ITCH* SO19 .... 11 K4
  TOTT SO40 .... 52 C5
Ash Cl *FAWY* SO45 .... 91 H6
  FHAM/STUB PO14 .... 12 C7
  GPORT PO12 .... 16 A6
  HLER SO31 .... 73 J5 🖸
  HORN PO8 .... 81 K2
  ITCH SO19 .... 7 M7
  NBAD SO52 .... 36 A5
  ROMY SO51 .... 35 H4
  RWIN SO21 .... 39 J2
Ash Copse *HORN* PO8 .... 64 A7
Ashdene *WSHM* SO15 .... 54 C4 🖸
Ashdene Rd *TOTT* SO40 .... 68 A3 🖸
Ashdown *FAWY* SO45 .... 110 C4
  LSOL/BMARY PO13 .... 116 A6
Ashdown Cl *CHFD* SO53 .... 31 K7
Ashdown Dr *CHFD* SO53 .... 31 K7
Ashdown Rd *CHFD* SO53 .... 37 K1
  FAWY SO45 .... 110 C4
Ashdown Wy *ROMY* SO51 .... 35 G3
Ashen Cl *CHFD* SO53 .... 37 K2
Ashe Rd *HAV* PO9 .... 103 J1 🖸
Ashford Cl *CHAM* PO6 .... 100 D5
Ashford Crs *FAWY* SO45 .... 91 J3
Ash Gv *TOTT* SO40 .... 68 B3
Ashington Cl *HORN* PO8 .... 82 B2
Ashlea Cl *ELGH* SO50 .... 46 C1
Ashleigh Cl *FAWY* SO45 .... 91 H6
Ashlett Cl *FAWY* SO45 .... 111 F4
Ashlett Rd *FAWY* SO45 .... 111 F4
Ashley Cl *WINW* SO22 .... 21 F4
  HAV PO9 .... 102 E2
  HLER SO31 .... 75 G6
  HORN PO8 .... 64 A7
Ashley Ct *HLER* SO31 .... 73 K3 🖸
Ashley Crs *ITCH* SO19 .... 11 L6
Ashleycross *FAWY* SO45 .... 110 A4 🖸
Ashley Gdns *BPWT* SO32 .... 61 F1
  CHFD SO53 .... 38 B5
Ashley Mdw *ROMY* SO51 .... 35 F2
Ashling Cl *WVILLE* PO7 .... 80 E1

Ashling Gdns *WVILLE* PO7 .... 80 E1
Ashling La *NEND* PO2 .... 118 C7
Ashling Park Rd *WVILLE* PO7 .... 80 E1
Ashlyn Cl *FHAM* PO15 .... 96 C5
Ashmead Rd *ROWN* SO16 .... 54 A1
Ashmore Rd *WINW* SO22 .... 21 F6 🖸
Ashridge Cl *WSHM* SO15 .... 4 D3
Ash Rd *TOTT* SO40 .... 68 A3
Ashtead Cl *FHAM/PORC* PO16 .... 98 D6
Ashton Cl *BPWT* SO32 .... 48 B2
Ashton La *BPWT* SO32 .... 48 B2
Ashton Wy *FHAM/STUB* PO14 .... 114 E7
Ash Tree Rd *WEND* SO18 .... 56 B3
Ashurst Bridge Rd *TOTT* SO40 .... 52 B6
Ashurst Cl *WINW* SO22 .... 21 G4
  ITCH SO19 .... 11 H8
  TOTT SO40 .... 68 A3
Ashurst Rd *CHAM* PO6 .... 100 D6
Ashwood *FHAM* PO15 .... 95 K1 🖸
  HLER SO31 .... 95 H4
Ashwood Cl *HAV* PO9 .... 102 C3
  HISD PO11 .... 137 H5
Ashwood Gdns *ROWN* SO16 .... 55 F1 🖸
  TOTT SO40 .... 52 B6 🖸
Aspen Av *HLER* SO31 .... 94 C6
Aspen Cl *HEND* SO30 .... 58 C5
  RWIN SO21 .... 39 K2
Aspengrove
  LSOL/BMARY PO13 .... 116 B6
Aspen Holt *ROWN* SO16 .... 43 H6
Aspen Wk *TOTT* SO40 .... 52 A4
Aspen Wy *HORN* PO8 .... 64 B7
Aster Rd *ROWN* SO16 .... 43 K7
Astley St *SSEA* PO5 .... 18 C6
Aston Rd *ENEY* PO4 .... 19 K7
  WEND SO18 .... 7 L3
Astra Ct *FAWY* SO45 .... 91 H1
Astral Gdns *HLER* SO31 .... 93 J3
Astrid Cl *HISD* PO11 .... 137 K5
Asturias Wy *SHAM* SO14 .... 9 L4
Asylum Rd *WSHM* SO15 .... 5 F2
Atalanta Cl *ENEY* PO4 .... 135 H3
Atheling Rd *FAWY* SO45 .... 110 D4
Athelstan Rd *ITCH* SO19 .... 6 C5
Athena Av *WVILLE* PO7 .... 102 A3
Athena Cl *ELGH* SO50 .... 39 K7
Atherfield Rd *ROWN* SO16 .... 53 K1
Atherley Ct *WSHM* SO15 .... 4 C3
Atherley Rd *HISD* PO11 .... 137 F3
  WSHM SO15 .... 4 B6
Atkinson Cl *GPORT* PO12 .... 132 D6 🖸
Atkins Pl *FHAM* PO15 .... 96 C5
Atlantic Cl *SHAM* SO14 .... 9 H5
Atlantic Park Vw *WEND* SO18 .... 56 D2 🖸
Atlantis Av *WVILLE* PO7 .... 102 A4
Attwoods Dro *RWIN* SO21 .... 33 F1
Aubrey Cl *HISD* PO11 .... 137 F4 🖸
Auckland Rd *WSHM* SO15 .... 54 A5
Auckland Rd East *SSEA* PO5 .... 134 B6
Auckland Rd West *SSEA* PO5 .... 134 B6 🖸
Audret Cl *FHAM/PORC* PO16 .... 116 E1
Augustine Rd *CHAM* PO6 .... 101 H5
  SHAM SO14 .... 5 K7
Augustus Wy *CHFD* SO53 .... 38 B3
Auriol Dr *CHAM* PO6 .... 102 B6
Austen Av *WINW* SO22 .... 25 F5
Austen Cl *TOTT* SO40 .... 52 C6
  WINC SO23 .... 21 K5 🖸
Austen Gdns *HLER* SO31 .... 75 H5
Austerberry Wy
  LSOL/BMARY PO13 .... 116 A7
Austin Ct *CHAM* PO6 .... 100 A5
Australia Cl *PSEA* PO1 .... 18 E3
Aust Rd *FHAM/STUB* PO14 .... 12 A7
Autumn Rd *TOTT* SO40 .... 70 B4
Avebury Gdns *CHFD* SO53 .... 37 H1
Avenger Cl *CHFD* SO53 .... 37 J3
Avens Cl *ELGH* SO50 .... 46 B5
Avenue C *FAWY* SO45 .... 92 B6
Avenue Ct *GPORT* PO12 .... 132 D6
Avenue D *FAWY* SO45 .... 92 B6
Avenue De Caen *SSEA* PO5 .... 134 B7
Avenue E *FAWY* SO45 .... 92 B6
Avenue Rd *FHAM/STUB* PO14 .... 12 F6
  WINW SO22 .... 2 B3
  GPORT PO12 .... 16 C4
  HISD PO11 .... 121 G4
  SHAM SO14 .... 5 H3
The Avenue *BPWT* SO32 .... 48 C3
  FHAM PO15 .... 12 E6
  GPORT PO12 .... 132 D6
  PTSW SO17 .... 5 G4
  RWIN SO21 .... 33 K3
Avery La *GPORT* PO12 .... 132 C1
Avington Cl *ELGH* SO50 .... 39 G5 🖸
Avington Ct *ROWN* SO16 .... 43 G7
Avocet Quay *EMRTH* PO10 .... 104 D7
Avocet Wk *LSOL/BMARY* PO13 .... 115 J5
Avonborne Wy *CHFD* SO53 .... 37 J2
Avon Cl *LSOL/BMARY* PO13 .... 131 G3
Avon Crs *ROMY* SO51 .... 35 H3
Avondale Rd *PSEA* PO1 .... 19 H1
  WVILLE PO7 .... 82 A5
Avon Gn *CHFD* SO53 .... 38 A5
Avon Rd *WEND* SO18 .... 6 E1
Avon Wy *HEND* SO30 .... 57 H2
Awbridge Rd *HAV* PO9 .... 102 D2
Aylen Rd *HSEA* PO3 .... 119 F5
Aylesbury Rd *NEND* PO2 .... 118 E2
Ayling Cl *LSOL/BMARY* PO13 .... 131 K1 🖸
Aylward St *PSEA* PO1 .... 17 M3 🖸
Aysgarth Rd *WVILLE* PO7 .... 81 K5

Azalea Cl *HAV* PO9........... 103 K2

B

Back La *WHAM* PO17.......... 79 H7
Back of the Walls *SHAM* SO14.... 9 G3
Back St *WINC* SO23 .... 25 J4
Bacon Cl *ITCH* SO19 .... 10 F8
Bacon La *HISD* PO11 .... 136 E5
Baddesley Cl *NBAD* SO52 ...... 36 A5
Baddesley Rd *CHFD* SO53 ...... 37 H1
Bader Cl *HEND* SO30 .... 58 B4 ⬛
Bader Wy *FHAM* PO15 .... 95 K1
Badger Brow *WVILLE* PO7 ...... 82 B7
Badger Cl *ELGH* SO50 .... 45 J1
  FHAM PO15.......... 12 A3
Badger Farm Rd *WINW* SO22 .... 24 E3
Badgers Run *HLER* SO31 ...... 74 D7
The Badgers *HLER* SO31 ...... 73 F7 ⬛
Badgers Wk *FAWY* SO45 ...... 91 G4 ⬛
Badminston Dro *FAWY* SO45.... 111 F7
Badminston La *FAWY* SO45.... 111 F6
Baffins Rd *HSEA* PO3 .... 19 L1
Bagber Rd *TOTT* SO40 .... 52 E5
Baigent Cl *WINC* SO23 .... 3 J4
Bailey Cl *WINW* SO22 .... 25 G2
  HEND SO30 .... 58 E6
Bailey's Rd *SSEA* PO5 .... 18 E5
Bakers Dro *ROWN* SO16 ...... 41 K6
Baker St *NEND* PO2 .... 134 C1
Balaclava Rd *WEND* SO18 ...... 7 H4
Balderton Cl *NEND* PO2 ...... 118 E3 ⬛
Balfour Cl
  LSOL/BMARY PO13 .... 132 A2 ⬛
Balfour Rd *ITCH* SO19 .... 7 K9
  NEND PO2 .... 118 D6
Ballard Cl *ROWN* SO16 .... 53 H3
Balliol Cl *FHAM/STUB* PO14 .... 95 H5
Balliol Rd *NEND* PO2 .... 134 D1
Balmoral Cl *CHFD* SO53 ...... 37 J2 ⬛
  LSOL/BMARY PO13 .... 116 A4
  ROWN SO16 .... 42 D6
Balmoral Dr *WVILLE* PO7 ...... 101 K4
Balmoral Rd *FHAM* PO15 ...... 12 D2
Balmoral Wy *ROWN* SO16 ...... 41 J5
Baltic Rd *HEND* SO30 .... 57 H2
Banbury Av *ITCH* SO19 ...... 11 L1
Bangor Rd *WSHM* SO15 ...... 54 C6
Banister Gdns *WSHM* SO15 ...... 4 F5
Banister Rd *WSHM* SO15 ...... 4 F4
Bank Side *WEND* SO18 .... 44 A7
Bank St *BPWT* SO32 .... 48 E4
Banning St *ROMY* SO51 ...... 34 D4
Bapaume Rd *HSEA* PO3 ...... 118 E2
Barbe Baker Av *HEND* SO30 .... 57 F2
Bardon Wy *FHAM/STUB* PO14 .. 12 B8
Bar End Rd *WINC* SO23 .... 3 G7
Barfield Cl *WINC* SO23 .... 3 G7
Barfleur Cl *FHAM* PO15 ...... 12 A3
Barfleur Rd *FHAM/STUB* PO14 .. 115 H2
Barford Cl *CHFD* SO53 ...... 37 J2 ⬛
Bargate St *SHAM* SO14 ...... 8 F7
Barham Cl *GPORT* PO12 ...... 16 A2
Barham Rd *WINC* SO23 .... 3 H6
Baring Rd *WINC* SO23 .... 3 H6
Barker Mill Cl *ROWN* SO16 .... 41 K5
Barle Cl *WEND* SO18 .... 56 E3
Barley Down Dr *WINW* SO22 .... 25 G4
Barlow Cl *FHAM/STUB* PO14 .... 114 C5
Barnbrook Rd *HLER* SO31 ...... 94 D2
Barn Cl *EMRTH* PO10 .... 104 A6
Barncroft Wy *HAV* PO9 ...... 102 E5
Barnes Cl *HLER* SO31 .... 94 C2
  ITCH SO19 .... 7 L6
  WINC SO23 .... 2 B9
Barnes La *HLER* SO31 .... 94 D2
Barnes Rd *ITCH* SO19 .... 7 L6
  PSEA PO1 .... 19 H2
Barnes Wallis Rd *FHAM* PO15 .. 95 J2 ⬛
Barnes Wy *HAV* PO9 .... 102 D3
Barney Evans Crs *HORN* PO8 .... 81 J2
Barneyhayes La *TOTT* SO40 .... 50 D4
Barnfield Cl *EMRTH* PO10 ...... 105 H4
  ITCH SO19 .... 10 D8
Barnfield Ct *FHAM/STUB* PO14 .. 12 D8
  ITCH SO19 .... 10 E7
Barnfield Rd *ITCH* SO19 ...... 10 D7
Barnfield Wy *ITCH* SO19 ...... 10 E7
Barn Fold *HORN* PO8 .... 82 C4
Barn Green *WVILLE* PO7 ...... 80 E1
Barn Piece *NBAD* SO52 ...... 37 G4
Barnsfield Crs *TOTT* SO40 .... 52 B5
Barnsland *HEND* SO30 .... 57 F2
Baron Rd *HLER* SO31 .... 93 J3
Barons Md *ROWN* SO16 ...... 53 K1
Barrie Cl *HLER* SO31 .... 75 H5 ⬛
Barrington Cl *ELGH* SO50 ...... 38 C5
Barrow Down Gdns *ITCH* SO19 .. 73 H2
Barrow Hill Rd *TOTT* SO40 .... 51 G1
Barry Rd *ITCH* SO19 .... 7 H4
Barters Cl *ROWN* SO16 ...... 54 A3
Bartlett Cl *FHAM* PO15 ...... 12 C2
The Bartletts *HLER* SO31 ...... 93 K4
Bartley Av *TOTT* SO40 ...... 52 D6
Bartley Rd *TOTT* SO40 ...... 50 B8
Barton Cl *ROMY* SO51 ...... 35 G2 ⬛
Barton Crs *WEND* SO18 ...... 6 F1
Barton Cross *HORN* PO8 ...... 64 C5
Barton Dr *HEND* SO30 ...... 58 C5
  HLER SO31 .... 93 J3
Barton Rd *ELGH* SO50 ...... 39 F7
Bartons Rd *HAV* PO9 .... 103 H1
Bartram Rd *TOTT* SO40 ...... 53 F6
Barwell Gv *EMRTH* PO10 ...... 104 B3 ⬛
Basing Rd *HAV* PO9 .... 103 F1
Basingstoke Rd *WINC* SO23 .... 22 C1
Basing Wy *CHFD* SO53 ...... 37 H5
Basingwell St *BPWT* SO32 .... 48 D4
Basin St *NEND* PO2 .... 118 C4
Bassett Av *ROWN* SO16 ...... 43 G2
Bassett Cl *ROWN* SO16 ...... 43 G3
Bassett Crs East *ROWN* SO16 .. 43 G4
Bassett Crs West *ROWN* SO16 .. 55 G1
Bassett Dl *ROWN* SO16 ...... 43 G4
Bassett Gdns *ROWN* SO16 .... 43 G4
Bassett Gn *ROWN* SO16 ...... 43 G5
Bassett Green Cl *ROWN* SO16 .. 43 H5
Bassett Green Dr *ROWN* SO16.. 43 H6

Bassett Green Rd *ROWN* SO16 .. 43 H5
Bassett Heath Av *ROWN* SO16 .. 43 G1
Bassett Meadow *ROWN* SO16 .. 55 G1
Bassett Ms *ROWN* SO16 ...... 43 G6
Bassett Rw *ROWN* SO16 ...... 43 G5
Bassett Wood Dr *ROWN* SO16 .. 43 G5
Bassett Wood Rd *ROWN* SO16 .. 43 G5
Batchelor Gn *HLER* SO31 ...... 73 K5 ⬛
Bathing La *PSEA* PO1 .... 17 K6
Bath La *FHAM/PORC* PO16 .... 13 M6
Bath La (Lower)
  FHAM/PORC PO16 .... 13 M7
Bath Rd *EMRTH* PO10 .... 104 C6
  ENEY PO4 .... 19 J8
  ITCH SO19 .... 7 J6
Bath Sq *PSEA* PO1 .... 17 K6
Bath St *SHAM* SO14 .... 5 H5
Bathurst Cl *HISD* PO11 ...... 137 F5
Bay Trees *ITCH* SO19 .... 57 H6
Beach Dr *CHAM* PO6 .... 99 J6
Beach Rd *EMRTH* PO10 ...... 104 B6
  HISD PO11 .... 137 F5
  LSOL/BMARY PO13 ...... 131 F3
  SSEA PO5 .... 134 C7
Beachway *FHAM/PORC* PO16 .... 117 J1
Beacon Bottom *HLER* SO31 .... 75 F7
Beacon Cl *HLER* SO31 ...... 75 F7
Beacon Mt *HLER* SO31 ...... 75 F7
Beacon Rd *HEND* SO30 ...... 57 G4
Beaconsfield Av *CHAM* PO6 .... 101 F7
Beaconsfield Rd
  FHAM/PORC PO16 .... 13 J8
  WVILLE PO7 .... 81 K5 ⬛
Beacon Sq *EMRTH* PO10 ...... 104 B7
Beacon Wy *HLER* SO31 ...... 95 F1
Bealing Cl *ROWN* SO16 ...... 43 J7
Bearslane Cl *TOTT* SO40 ...... 52 C3
Beatrice Rd *ENEY* PO4 ...... 19 H9
  WSHM SO15 .... 54 D5 ⬛
Beattie Ri *HEND* SO30 ...... 58 B2 ⬛
Beatty Cl *HLER* SO31 ...... 95 G4
Beatty Dr *GPORT* PO12 ...... 132 C6
Beauchamp Av
  LSOL/BMARY PO13 .... 115 K5
Beaucroft Rd *BPWT* SO32 .... 61 F1
Beaufort Av *FHAM/PORC* PO16 .. 12 E2
Beaufort Dr *BPWT* SO32 ...... 48 D3
Beaufort Rd *HAV* PO9 ...... 14 A3
  SSEA PO5 .... 134 C7 ⬛
  WINC SO23 .... 2 C7
Beaulieu Av *FHAM/PORC* PO16.. 98 D6
  HAV PO9 .... 82 E7
Beaulieu Cl *WINW* SO22 ...... 21 G3 ⬛
  ROWN SO16 .... 42 D6
Beaulieu Pl
  LSOL/BMARY PO13 .... 115 K5 ⬛
Beaulieu Rd *BROC* SO42 ...... 88 E6
  BROC SO42 .... 108 D3
  ELGH SO50 .... 38 D6 ⬛
  FAWY SO45 .... 91 H3
  LYND SO43 .... 86 E2
  NEND PO2 .... 118 D6
  TOTT SO40 .... 89 J1
Beaumaris Gdns *FAWY* SO45 .. 91 G2
Beaumond Gn *WINC* SO23 .... 2 D5
Beaumont Cl *FHAM* PO15 .... 12 B1
  ROWN SO16 .... 55 F1 ⬛
Beaumont Ct *GPORT* PO12 .... 116 D7 ⬛
Beaumont Ri *FHAM* PO15 .... 96 E2 ⬛
Beaumont Rd *TOTT* SO40 .... 53 F5
Beauworth Av *WEND* SO18 .... 7 M2
Beaver Dr *ELGH* SO50 ...... 45 K1
Beck Cl *HLER* SO31 ...... 94 D3
Beckford La *WHAM* PO17 ...... 79 H4
Beck St *PSEA* PO1 .... 18 A3
Bedenham La
  LSOL/BMARY PO13 .... 116 B4
Bedfield La *WINC* SO23 ...... 22 A2
Bedford Av *ITCH* SO19 ...... 10 C6
Bedford Cl *HAV* PO9 ...... 15 J6
  HEND SO30 .... 58 C6 ⬛
Bedford Pl *WSHM* SO15 ...... 4 F7
Bedford St *GPORT* PO12 ...... 132 D2
  SSEA PO5 .... 18 C5
Bedhampton Hl *CHAM* PO6 .... 102 B5
Bedhampton Hill Rd
  HAV PO9 .... 102 C5 ⬛
  NEND PO2 .... 118 E6
Bedhampton Wy *HAV* PO9 .... 103 G2
Bedwell Cl *ROWN* SO16 ...... 42 A6
Beecham Rd *PSEA* PO1 ...... 134 D1
Beech Av *WEND* SO18.......... 6 D4
Beech Cl *CHFD* SO53 .... 38 A2
  FAWY SO45 .... 91 H6
  FHAM PO15 .... 96 C5
  WINW SO22 .... 24 E5
  HLER SO31 .... 93 H4
  HORN PO8 .... 82 A3
  ROMY SO51 .... 35 H4
Beech Copse *WINW* SO22 .... 20 E6
Beech Crs *FAWY* SO45 ...... 91 H6
Beechcroft Cl *CHFD* SO53 .... 38 A5
  FHAM PO15 .... 96 C5
Beechcroft Rd *GPORT* PO12 .. 132 D5
Beechcroft Wy *CHFD* SO53 .... 38 A4 ⬛
Beechdale Cl *TOTT* SO40 ...... 52 B2
Beechen La *LYND* SO43 ...... 86 E4
Beeches Hl *BPWT* SO32 ...... 48 E1
The Beeches *ELGH* SO50 ...... 46 C2 ⬛
Beechfield Ct *WSHM* SO15 .... 54 B4
Beech Gdns *HLER* SO31 ...... 93 H4
Beech Gv *GPORT* PO12 ...... 132 D5
  HISD PO11 .... 137 J4
Beechmount Rd *ROWN* SO16 .. 43 G6

Beech Rd *CHFD* SO53 .... 38 A2
  FHAM PO15 .... 12 D4
  HEND SO30 .... 58 C5
  TOTT SO40 .... 68 A3
  WSHM SO15 .... 54 C6
Beech Wy *HORN* PO8 .... 64 C7
Beechwood Av *HAV* PO9 ...... 81 K7
Beechwood Cl *CHFD* SO53 .... 37 H1
  HLER SO31 .... 94 C6 ⬛
Beechwood Crs *CHFD* SO53.... 31 H7
Beechwood Gdns *WEND* SO18 .. 6 D2
Beechwood Ri *WEND* SO18 .... 7 L1
  NEND PO2 .... 118 D3
  TOTT SO40 .... 50 C7
Beechwood Rd *FAWY* SO45 .. 109 K4
Beechwood Wy *FAWY* SO45 .. 90 D4
Beechworth Rd *HAV* PO9 ...... 15 G4
Beehive Wk *PSEA* PO1 ...... 17 M6 ⬛
Beggar's La *WINC* SO23 ...... 3 G4
Begonia La *ROWN* SO16 ...... 43 J7
Behrendt Cl *GPORT* PO12 .... 132 D2
Belbins *ROMY* SO51 .... 28 E5
Belfry Wk *FHAM/STUB* PO14 .. 95 H4
Belgrave Rd *PTSW* SO17 ...... 55 K2
Belgravia Rd *NEND* PO2 ...... 118 E6
Bellair Rd *HAV* PO9 ...... 15 G5
Bell Crs *WVILLE* PO7 ...... 81 K7
Bell Davies Rd
  FHAM/STUB PO14.......... 114 C6
Bellemoor Rd *WSHM* SO15 .... 54 E3
Bellevue La *EMRTH* PO10 .... 104 C4
Bellevue Rd *ELGH* SO50 ...... 38 D7
  WSHM SO15 .... 5 G7
Bellevue Ter *SSEA* PO5 ...... 18 A8
Bellflower Wy *NBAD* SO52 .... 37 G3
Bell Hl *CHAM* PO6 .... 100 C6
Bells La *FHAM/STUB* PO14 .... 114 D5
Bell St *ROMY* SO51 .... 34 D3
  SHAM SO14 .... 9 H5
Belmont Cl *FHAM* PO15 ...... 91 H4
  FHAM/STUB PO14 .... 114 E4 ⬛
  HORN PO8 .... 64 D2
Belmont Gv *HAV* PO9 .... 102 D4 ⬛
Belmont Pl *SSEA* PO5 ...... 18 D7
Belmont Rd *CHFD* SO53 ...... 38 A7
  PTSW SO17 .... 5 K2
Belmont St *SSEA* PO5 ...... 18 D7
Belmore Cl *PSEA* PO1 ...... 134 D1
Belney La *WHAM* PO17 ...... 80 D5
Belstone Rd *TOTT* SO40 ...... 52 D5
Belton Rd *ITCH* SO19 ...... 11 K4
Belvedere Rd *FAWY* SO45 .... 91 H4
Belvidere Rd *SHAM* SO14 ...... 5 L5
Belvidere Ter *SHAM* SO14 .... 5 L8
Belvoir Cl *FHAM/PORC* PO16 .. 13 J7
Bembridge *HLER* SO31 ...... 73 F7
Bembridge Cl *ROWN* SO16 .... 43 K6 ⬛
Bembridge Crs *ENEY* PO4 .... 134 D7
Bembridge Dr *HISD* PO11 .... 137 K7
Benbow Cl *HORN* PO8 ...... 64 D5
Benbow Pl *PSEA* PO1 ...... 17 L3 ⬛
Benedict Cl *ROMY* SO51 ...... 35 H3
Benedict Wy *FHAM/PORC* PO16 .. 99 H4
Beneficial St *PSEA* PO1 ...... 17 L4 ⬛
Benham Dr *HSEA* PO3 .... 118 E2
Benham Gv *FHAM/PORC* PO16 .. 117 G1
Benhams Farm *WEND* SO18 .... 7 G1
Benhams Rd *WEND* SO18 ...... 56 D2 ⬛
Benmore Gdns *CHFD* SO53 .... 37 J3
Benson Rd *WSHM* SO15 ...... 54 C4
Bentham Rd *GPORT* PO12 ...... 16 A8
Bentham Wy *HLER* SO31 ...... 74 C5
Bentley Cl *HORN* PO8 ...... 64 D4
Bentley Ct *HAV* PO9 ...... 103 J1 ⬛
Bentley Crs *FHAM/PORC* PO16 .. 12 F3
Bentley Gn *WEND* SO18 ...... 7 M2
Berber Cl *FHAM* PO15 ...... 75 H6
Bercote Cl *WINW* SO22 ...... 20 E2
Bere Cl *CHFD* SO53 .... 37 H2
  WINW SO22 .... 21 G5
Bere Farm La *WHAM* PO17 .... 78 C5
Bere Rd *WVILLE* PO7 ...... 80 E1
Beresford Cl *CHFD* SO53 ...... 38 B5 ⬛
  WVILLE PO7 .... 81 K7
Beresford Gdns *WVILLE* PO7 .. 81 K7
Beresford Rd *CHFD* SO53 ...... 38 B5
  FHAM/STUB PO14 .... 114 E4
  NEND PO2 .... 118 D5
Bereweeke Av *WINW* SO22 .... 21 H4
Bereweeke Cl *WINW* SO22 .... 2 A1
Bereweeke Rd *WINW* SO22 .... 2 A1
Bereweeke Wy *WINW* SO22.... 21 H5
Bergen Crs *HEND* SO30 ...... 58 A4 ⬛
Berkeley Cl *FHAM/STUB* PO14 .. 115 J5
  WSHM SO15 .... 4 D5
Berkeley Gdns *HEND* SO30 .... 58 B4
Berkeley Rd *WSHM* SO15 ...... 4 D5
Berkeley Sq *HAV* PO9 ...... 14 D2
Berkshire Cl *PSEA* PO1 ...... 18 F4
Bernard Av *CHAM* PO6 ...... 101 F6
Bernard St *SHAM* SO14 ...... 9 G3
Berney Rd *ENEY* PO4 ...... 135 H4
Bernina Av *WVILLE* PO7 ...... 81 H3
Bernina Cl *WVILLE* PO7 ...... 81 H3
Bernwood Gv *FAWY* SO45 .... 128 B1
Berry Cl *HEND* SO30 ...... 58 C5
Berrydown Rd *HAV* PO9 ...... 82 D6
Berry La *FHAM/STUB* PO14 .... 114 B5
  RWIN SO21 .... 33 K2
Berrywood Gdns *HEND* SO30 .. 58 A4 ⬛
Beryl Av *GPORT* PO12 ...... 116 C7
Beryton Cl *GPORT* PO12 ...... 132 D2 ⬛
Beryton Rd *GPORT* PO12 ...... 132 D2
Betteridge Dr *ROWN* SO16 .... 41 J5
Bettesworth Rd *PSEA* PO1 .... 134 D1
Betula Cl *WVILLE* PO7 ...... 82 B7
Beulah Rd *ROWN* SO16 ...... 54 B3
Bevan Cl *ITCH* SO19 .... 11 L1
Bevan Rd *HORN* PO8 .... 64 A7
Beverley Cl *HLER* SO31 ...... 95 H2
Beverley Gdns *BPWT* SO32 .... 49 J6 ⬛
  HLER SO31 .... 73 H4
  ROMY SO51 .... 35 H1 ⬛
Beverley Hts *WEND* SO18 .... 6 F1
Beverley Rd *FAWY* SO45 ...... 91 G6
  FHAM/STUB PO14 .... 114 E4
Beverly Cl *LSOL/BMARY* PO13.. 116 A5
Beverston Rd *CHAM* PO6 ...... 99 K5

Bevis Cl *FAWY* SO45 .... 110 C5
  HLER SO31 .... 94 C6
  NEND PO2 .... 118 C3
Bevis Rd *GPORT* PO12 ...... 16 B4
Bevois Gdns *SHAM* SO14 ...... 5 G4
Bevois Hl *PTSW* SO17 ...... 5 J3
Bevois Valley Rd *SHAM* SO14 .. 5 J3
Bidbury La *HAV* PO9 .... 102 D5
Biddenfield La *WHAM* PO17 .... 76 B1
Bideford Cl *ROWN* SO16 ...... 53 K3
Bilberry Cl *HLER* SO31 ...... 94 E4
Bilberry Dr *TOTT* SO40 ...... 69 K3
Billett Av *WVILLE* PO7 ...... 82 A4
Billing Cl *PSEA* PO4 ...... 135 G5 ⬛
Billington Gdns *HEND* SO30 .... 58 C3
Billy Lawn Av *HAV* PO9 ...... 103 G2
Bilton Wy *HSEA* PO3 .... 119 H5
Bindon Cl *ROWN* SO16 ...... 54 B2
Bindon Rd *ROWN* SO16 ...... 54 B2
Binnacle Wy *CHAM* PO6 ...... 100 A6
Binness Wy *CHAM* PO6 ...... 101 K7
Binsey Cl *ROWN* SO16 ...... 53 K4
Binstead Cl *ROWN* SO16 ...... 43 K6
Binsteed Rd *NEND* PO2 ...... 118 D7
Birch Cl *HORN* PO8 .... 81 K2
  ROMY SO51 .... 35 H4
  ROWN SO16 .... 54 B2
Birchdale Cl *HLER* SO31 ...... 94 C6 ⬛
Birch Dr *LSOL/BMARY* PO13 .... 115 K3
Birchen Cl *HLER* SO31 ...... 95 H2 ⬛
The Birches Cl *NBAD* SO52 .... 36 A5
The Birches *WEND* SO18........ 7 K2
Birch Gv *ELGH* SO50 .... 38 C4
Birchlands *TOTT* SO40 ...... 52 C7
Birchmore Cl
  LSOL/BMARY PO13 .... 115 K5 ⬛
Birch Rd *HEND* SO30 ...... 58 C5
  HLER SO31 .... 43 H3
  ROWN SO16 .... 54 B2
Birch Tree Cl *EMRTH* PO10 .... 104 C2
Birch Tree Dr *EMRTH* PO10 .... 104 C2
Birch Wd *ITCH* SO19 ...... 57 H7
Birchwood Gdns *HEND* SO30 .. 58 B4 ⬛
Birdham Rd *HISD* PO11 ...... 138 B6
Birdlip Cl *HORN* PO8 .... 64 B6
Birdlip Rd *CHAM* PO6 ...... 100 A5
Birdwood Gv *FHAM/PORC* PO16.. 99 G1
Birinus Rd *WINC* SO23 ...... 2 F2
Birkdale Av *WEND* SO18 ...... 6 E6
Biscay Cl *FHAM/STUB* PO14 .... 114 C4 ⬛
Bishops Cl *TOTT* SO40 ...... 52 D4
Bishops Ct *ELGH* SO50 ...... 39 G5
Bishops Crs *ITCH* SO19 ...... 10 E2
Bishopsfield Rd
  FHAM/STUB PO14.......... 12 D8
Bishops Ga *FHAM/STUB* PO14 .. 95 H3
Bishop's La *BPWT* SO32 ...... 48 D4
  BPWT SO32 .... 61 J3
Bishops Rd *ITCH* SO19 ...... 10 D3
Bishop St *PSEA* PO1 ...... 17 M3
Bishop's Wood Rd *BPWT* SO32.. 61 J1
Bittern Cl *GPORT* PO12 ...... 132 C1
Bitterne Cl *HAV* PO9 .... 83 G7
Bitterne Crs *ITCH* SO19 ...... 7 G7
Bitterne Pk Triangle *WEND* SO18.. 6 B1
Bitterne Rd East *WEND* SO18.... 7 J6
Bitterne Rd West *WEND* SO18.... 6 C4
Bitterne Wy *ITCH* SO19 ...... 6 E6
Blackberry Ter *SHAM* SO14 .... 5 J5
Blackbird Cl *HORN* PO8 ...... 82 A1
Blackbird Rd *ELGH* SO50 ...... 44 A1
Blackbird Wy
  LSOL/BMARY PO13 .... 131 G1
Blackbrook House Dr
  FHAM PO15 .... 12 D5
Blackbrook Park Av
  FHAM PO15 .... 12 C5
Blackbrook Rd *FHAM* PO15 .... 12 D5
Blackbushe Cl *ROWN* SO16 .... 42 A6 ⬛
Blackcap Cl *HAV* PO9 ...... 83 H4
Blackdown Cl *FAWY* SO45 .... 90 E4 ⬛
Blackdown Crs *HAV* PO9 ...... 103 F2
Blackfield Rd *FAWY* SO45 .... 110 B6
Blackfriars Cl *SSEA* PO5 ...... 18 E5
Blackfriars Rd *SSEA* PO5 ...... 18 E4
Black Horse La *BPWT* SO32 .... 61 F3
Blackhouse La *WHAM* PO17 .... 78 D5
Blackthorn Cl *ITCH* SO19 ...... 6 F8 ⬛
  HISD PO11 .... 137 K5
Blackthorn Dr *GPORT* PO12 .... 116 D6
Blackthorn Gn *RWIN* SO21 .... 39 K2
Blackthorn Rd *HISD* PO11 .... 137 K5
  ITCH SO19 .... 6 G1
Blackwater Dr *TOTT* SO40 .... 52 B3
Blackwater Ms *TOTT* SO40 .... 52 C3
Bladon Cl *HAV* PO9 .... 15 L1
Bladon Rd *ROWN* SO16 ...... 54 A4
Blake Cl *ROWN* SO16 ...... 41 H6 ⬛
Blakemere Crs *CHAM* PO6 .... 100 B5
Blakeney Rd *ROWN* SO16 ...... 53 J2
Blake Rd *CHAM* PO6 .... 101 F4
  GPORT PO12 .... 16 C4
Blakesley La *HSEA* PO3 ...... 119 H4
Blanchard Rd *BPWT* SO32 ...... 61 F3
Blankney Cl
  FHAM/STUB PO14 .... 114 C5 ⬛
Blann Cl *ROWN* SO16 ...... 41 H6 ⬛
Bleaklow Cl *ROWN* SO16 ...... 54 A4
Blechynden Ter *WSHM* SO15.... 4 D9
Blencowe Dr *NBAD* SO52 ...... 37 F5
Blendon Dr *HAV* PO9 ...... 103 F5
Blendworth Crs *HAV* PO9 .... 103 H3
Blendworth La *HORN* PO8 .... 64 E5
  WEND SO18 .... 7 M4
Blendworth Rd *ENEY* PO4 .... 135 G3 ⬛
Blenheim Av *PTSW* SO17 ...... 5 H4
Blenheim Cl *NBAD* SO52 ...... 37 G6
  TOTT SO40 .... 52 C6
Blenheim Ct *FAWY* SO45 ...... 19 L8
Blenheim Gdns *FAWY* SO45 .... 90 E4
  GPORT PO12 .... 116 E7
  HAV PO9 .... 15 L2
  PTSW SO17 .... 55 J2

Blenheim Rd *ELGH* SO50 ...... 44 D1
  HORN PO8 .... 64 B7
Bleriot Crs *FHAM* PO15 ...... 95 K1
Blighmont Crs *WSHM* SO15 .... 54 C6
Blind La *BPWT* SO32 .... 46 B6
  BPWT SO32 .... 59 K2
  WHAM PO17 .... 61 G7
Bliss Cl *WVILLE* PO7 ...... 101 K1
Blissford Cl *HAV* PO9 .... 83 J7 ⬛
Blossom Cl *HEND* SO30 ...... 58 B5
Blount Rd *PSEA* PO1 ...... 17 K8
Blue Ball Hl *WINC* SO23 ...... 3 G4
Bluebell Cl *WVILLE* PO7 ...... 82 A7
Bluebell Copse *HLER* SO31 .... 94 E4
Bluebell Rd *ROWN* SO16 ...... 43 J7
Bluestar Gdns *HEND* SO30 .... 58 B2
Blundell La *HLER* SO31 ...... 74 B3
Blyth Cl *ROWN* SO16 .... 53 J2
Boakes Pl *TOTT* SO40 ...... 68 B3 ⬛
Boarhunt Cl *PSEA* PO1 ...... 18 E3 ⬛
Boarhunt Rd *WHAM* PO17 .... 98 B3
Bodmin Rd *CHAM* PO6 ...... 99 K6 ⬛
  ELGH SO50 .... 39 H7
Bodycoats Rd *CHFD* SO53 .... 38 A4
Bolde Cl *HSEA* PO3 .... 119 G4
Boldens Rd *GPORT* PO12 ...... 132 E7
Bolderwood Cl *ELGH* SO50 .... 39 J7
Boldre Cl *HAV* PO9 .... 102 D2 ⬛
Boldrewood Rd *ROWN* SO16 .. 43 F3
Bolhinton Av *TOTT* SO40 ...... 69 J4
The Boltons *WVILLE* PO7 ...... 101 K3 ⬛
Bonchurch Cl *ROWN* SO16 .... 43 K6 ⬛
Bonchurch Rd *ENEY* PO4 ...... 19 M4
Bondfields Crs *HAV* PO9 ...... 83 G7
Bond Rd *WEND* SO18 ...... 6 B1
Bond St *SHAM* SO14 .... 5 M7
Bonfire Cnr *PSEA* PO1 ...... 17 L2
Boniface Cl *TOTT* SO40 ...... 52 C4 ⬛
Boniface Crs *ROWN* SO16 ...... 53 K1
Boothby Cl *TOTT* SO40 ...... 53 F6 ⬛
Bordon Rd *HAV* PO9 .... 103 G1
Borrowdale Rd *ROWN* SO16 .. 53 K3
Boscobel Rd *WINW* SO22 ...... 2 C1
Bosham Rd *NEND* PO2 ...... 118 E7
Bosham Wk
  LSOL/BMARY PO13 .... 115 J5
Bosmere Gdns *EMRTH* PO10 .. 104 B5
Bosmere Rd *HISD* PO11 ...... 138 B6
Bossington Cl *ROWN* SO16 .... 41 K6 ⬛
Bostock Cl *RWIN* SO21 ...... 20 A4
Boston Rd *CHAM* PO6 ...... 100 D5
Bosuns Cl *FHAM/PORC* PO16 .. 115 J1
Bosville *ELGH* SO50 .... 38 D4
Boswell Cl *HEND* SO30 ...... 58 E5
  ITCH SO19 .... 11 H5
Botany Bay Rd *ITCH* SO19 .... 11 H5
Botley Dr *HAV* PO9 .... 102 E1
Botley Gdns *ITCH* SO19 ...... 73 H2 ⬛
Botley Rd *BPWT* SO32 ...... 48 B7
  ELGH SO50 .... 46 C3
  HEND SO30 .... 57 J3
  HLER SO31 .... 75 F5
  ITCH SO19 .... 11 M5
  ITCH SO19 .... 73 G2 ⬛
  NBAD SO52 .... 36 D7
  ROMY SO51 .... 35 F3
Boulter La *WHAM* PO17 ...... 79 K6
Boulton Rd *SSEA* PO5 ...... 19 G8
Boundary Cl *WSHM* SO15 .... 54 C6
Boundary Rd *HLER* SO31 ...... 73 J5
Boundary Wy *CHAM* PO6 ...... 101 G4
  HAV PO9 .... 14 D4
Bound La *HISD* PO11 ...... 137 H6
Boundstone *FAWY* SO45 ...... 91 G3 ⬛
Bourne Av *WSHM* SO15 ...... 54 C6
Bourne Cl *HORN* PO8 ...... 64 C6
  RWIN SO21 .... 32 E5
Bourne La *RWIN* SO21 ...... 33 K2
  TOTT SO40 .... 51 G7
Bournemouth Av *GPORT* PO12.. 132 C1
Bournemouth Rd *CHFD* SO53 .. 37 K5
  LYND SO43 .... 86 B3
  ROWN SO16 .... 43 H3
Bourne Rd *CHAM* PO6 ...... 100 A6
  TOTT SO40 .... 51 F7
  WSHM SO15.......... 4 B8
Bourne View *EMRTH* PO10 .... 105 G4
Bowater Cl *TOTT* SO40 ...... 52 B3
Bowater Wy *TOTT* SO40 ...... 52 B3
Bowcombe *HLER* SO31 ...... 73 F6
Bowden La *PTSW* SO17 ...... 55 K2
Bower Cl *FAWY* SO45 ...... 109 K4
  ITCH SO19 .... 10 F8
Bowers Cl *HORN* PO8 ...... 82 B1
Bowes Hl *HAV* PO9 .... 83 K2
Bowland Ri *CHFD* SO53 ...... 37 H3
Bowland Wy *FAWY* SO45 .... 128 B1 ⬛
Bowler Av *HSEA* PO3 ...... 19 K1 ⬛
Bowler Ct *HSEA* PO3 ...... 19 K1
Boxwood Cl
  FHAM/PORC PO16 .... 98 E5 ⬛
  WVILLE PO7 .... 81 K7
Boyatt Crs *ELGH* SO50 ...... 38 D2
Boyatt La *CHFD* SO53 ...... 38 D1
  ELGH SO50 .... 38 D3
Boyd Cl *FHAM/STUB* PO14 .... 114 C6 ⬛
Boyd Rd *LSOL/BMARY* PO13 .. 115 J4
Boyes La *RWIN* SO21 ...... 39 K1
Boyle Crs *WVILLE* PO7 ...... 101 K1
Boynton Cl *CHFD* SO53 ...... 37 J2
Brabant Cl *HLER* SO31 ...... 75 G6
Brabazon Rd *FHAM* PO15 ...... 95 J1
Bracken Cl *NBAD* SO52 ...... 36 B7
Bracken Crs *ELGH* SO50 ...... 45 J1
Bracken Heath *HORN* PO8...... 82 C4
Bracken La *ROWN* SO16 ...... 54 A4
Bracken Pl *ELGH* SO50 ...... 43 H4
Bracken Rd *NBAD* SO52 ...... 36 B7
The Brackens *FAWY* SO45 .... 90 E3 ⬛
  WINC SO23 .... 3 G4
Brackenway Rd *CHFD* SO53 .... 37 K2
Bracklesham Cl *ITCH* SO19 .... 10 F3
Bracklesham Rd *HISD* PO11 .. 138 C7
  LSOL/BMARY PO13.......... 116 A2
Brackley Av *ELGH* SO50 ...... 46 A1
Brackley Wy *TOTT* SO40 ...... 52 C4
Bradford Rd *SSEA* PO5 ...... 18 F5
Brading Av *ENEY* PO4 ...... 135 H4
  LSOL/BMARY PO13 .... 115 K5
Brading Cl *ROWN* SO16.......... 43 K6

Bradley Ct *HAV* PO9 .... 103 J1
Bradley Gn *ROWN* SO16 .... 42 C7
Bradley Peak *WINW* SO22 .... 21 F6
Bradley Rd *WINW* SO22 .... 21 F4
Bradly Rd *FHAM* PO15 .... 96 D5
Braehead *FAWY* SO45 .... 91 C4
Braemar Av *CHAM* PO6 .... 101 G7
Braemar Cl *FHAM* PO15 .... 12 D1
   LSOL/BMARY PO13 .... 116 A5
Braemar Rd
   LSOL/BMARY PO13 .... 116 A4
Braeside Cl *WINW* SO22 .... 24 E4
   ITCH SO19 .... 6 C8
Braeside Crs *ITCH* SO19 .... 6 D8
Braeside Rd *ITCH* SO19 .... 6 C8
Braintree Rd *CHAM* PO6 .... 100 C5
Brairwood Gdns *HISD* PO11 .... 137 G5
Braishfield Cl *ROWN* SO16 .... 54 A3
Braishfield Rd *HAV* PO9 .... 103 H2
   ROMY SO51 .... 35 H1
Bramber Rd *GPORT* PO12 .... 132 C5
Bramble Cl *ELGH* SO50 .... 38 E5
   FAWY SO45 .... 109 K4
   FHAM/STUB PO14 .... 114 B6
Bramble Dr *ROMY* SO51 .... 35 H1
Bramble La *HLER* SO31 .... 94 D1
Bramble Ms *WEND* SO18 .... 7 H2
Bramble Rd *ENEY* PO4 .... 19 C6
Brambles Rd
   LSOL/BMARY PO13 .... 130 E1
Bramble Wy
   LSOL/BMARY PO13 .... 115 H5
Brambling Cl *ROWN* SO16 .... 42 C5
Brambling Rd *HAV* PO9 .... 83 J4
The Bramblings *TOTT* SO40 .... 52 B4
Bramdean Dr *HAV* PO9 .... 102 E1
Bramdean Rd *WEND* SO18 .... 57 C5
Bramham Moor
   FHAM/STUB PO14 .... 114 C3
Bramley Cl *WVILLE* PO7 .... 82 A5
Bramley Crs *ITCH* SO19 .... 11 J5
Bramley Gdns *EMRTH* PO10 .... 104 E6
   GPORT PO12 .... 132 D7
Brampton La *PSEA* PO3 .... 119 H3
Bramshaw Cl *WINW* SO22 .... 21 F4
Bramshaw Ct *HAV* PO9 .... 103 J1
Bramshott Rd *ENEY* PO4 .... 19 K6
   ITCH SO19 .... 10 F9
Bramston Rd *WSHM* SO15 .... 54 D4
Brandon Rd *SSEA* PO5 .... 134 C6
Branksome Av *WSHM* SO15 .... 54 D3
Branksome Cl *WINW* SO22 .... 24 E2
Bransbury Cl *ROWN* SO16 .... 42 D7
Bransbury Rd *ENEY* PO4 .... 135 C5
Bransgore Av *HAV* PO9 .... 102 D2
Bransley Cl *ROMY* SO51 .... 35 G1
Brasenose Cl *FHAM/STUB* PO14 .... 95 H5
Brasher Cl *ELGH* SO50 .... 45 K1
Brassey Rd *WINW* SO22 .... 2 C1
Brasted Ct *ENEY* PO4 .... 135 H3
Brazil Rd *SHAM* SO14 .... 9 J6
Breach Av *EMRTH* PO10 .... 105 C4
Breamore Cl *ELGH* SO50 .... 38 D4
Breamore Rd *WEND* SO18 .... 57 C5
Brean Cl *ROWN* SO16 .... 53 K1
Brecon Av *CHAM* PO6 .... 101 G5
Brecon Cl *CHFD* SO53 .... 37 J7
   FAWY SO45 .... 91 F3
   FHAM/STUB PO14 .... 12 B7
Brecon Rd *ITCH* SO19 .... 7 L8
Bredenbury Crs *CHAM* PO6 .... 100 B5
Breech Cl *HSEA* PO3 .... 118 E3
Brenchley Cl *FHAM/PORC* PO16 .... 98 D7
Brendon Cl *FAWY* SO45 .... 90 E4
Brendon Gn *ROWN* SO16 .... 54 A4
Brendon Rd *FHAM/STUB* PO14 .... 12 A8
Brent Ct *EMRTH* PO10 .... 104 B6
Brentwood Crs *WEND* SO18 .... 56 D3
Breton Cl *FHAM* PO15 .... 75 G6
Brewer Cl *HLER* SO31 .... 95 G2
Brewers La *LSOL/BMARY* PO13 .... 115 K5
   RWIN SO21 .... 33 J4
Brewer St *PSEA* PO1 .... 18 C2
Brewhouse Sq *GPORT* PO12 .... 16 E3
Brewster Cl *HORN* PO8 .... 82 B2
Briar Ct *GPORT* PO12 .... 132 B5
   HORN PO8 .... 64 C7
Briardene Ct *TOTT* SO40 .... 52 D5
Briarfield Gdns *HORN* PO8 .... 64 C6
Briarswood *ROWN* SO16 .... 54 C3
Briarswood Ri *FAWY* SO45 .... 90 E4
Briar Wy *ROMY* SO51 .... 35 H1
Briarwood Cl *FHAM/PORC* PO16 .... 13 J7
Briarwood Rd *TOTT* SO40 .... 52 B6
Brickfield La *CHFD* SO53 .... 37 J5
Brickfield Rd *PTSW* SO17 .... 55 K2
Brickmakers La *RWIN* SO21 .... 39 J2
Brickwoods *ROMY* SO51 .... 35 G2
Brickyard Rd *BPWT* SO32 .... 61 G1
The Brickyard *TOTT* SO40 .... 50 E4
Bridefield Cl *HORN* PO8 .... 81 J2
Bridefield Crs *HORN* PO8 .... 81 J2
Bridge Cl *HLER* SO31 .... 74 A4
Bridgefoot Dr
   FHAM/PORC PO16 .... 13 M5
Bridgefoot Pth *EMRTH* PO10 .... 104 C6
Bridgemary Av
   LSOL/BMARY PO13 .... 116 A4
Bridgemary Gv
   LSOL/BMARY PO13 .... 115 K3
Bridgemary Rd
   LSOL/BMARY PO13 .... 115 K2
Bridgemary Wy
   LSOL/BMARY PO13 .... 115 K2
Bridge Rd *EMRTH* PO10 .... 104 C3
   HLER SO31 .... 74 D7
   ITCH SO19 .... 10 B3
   ROMY SO51 .... 34 E3
Bridgers Cl *ROWN* SO16 .... 41 K6
Bridges Cl *ELGH* SO50 .... 38 C7
Bridgeside Cl *PSEA* PO1 .... 18 F3
Bridge St *FHAM/STUB* PO14 .... 96 B6
   WHAM PO17 .... 77 H1
   WHAM PO17 .... 79 G7
   WINC SO23 .... 2 E5
Bridget Ct *HORN* PO8 .... 64 D5
Bridgwater Ct *WSHM* SO15 .... 4 A8

Bridlington Av *WSHM* SO15 .... 4 A2
Bridport St *PSEA* PO1 .... 18 D3
Brigantine Av *HLER* SO31 .... 94 D5
Brighstone Cl *ROWN* SO16 .... 43 K6
Brighton Av *GPORT* PO12 .... 116 C7
Brighton Rd *WSHM* SO15 .... 4 F4
Brightside *WVILLE* PO7 .... 81 J7
Brightside Rd *ROWN* SO16 .... 54 A2
Brights La *HISD* PO11 .... 137 G3
Brightstone Rd *CHAM* PO6 .... 100 D7
Brindle Cl *ROWN* SO16 .... 43 H6
Brinton La *FAWY* SO45 .... 91 H1
Brinton's Rd *SHAM* SO14 .... 5 H8
Brinton's Ter *SHAM* SO14 .... 5 H7
Bristol Rd *ENEY* PO4 .... 19 K9
Britain St *PSEA* PO1 .... 17 M4
Britannia Gdns *HEND* SO30 .... 58 A1
Britannia Rd *SHAM* SO14 .... 5 K8
   SSEA PO5 .... 18 F6
Britannia Rd North *SSEA* PO5 .... 18 F6
Briton St *SHAM* SO14 .... 8 F4
Britten Rd *LSOL/BMARY* PO13 .... 131 F2
Britten Wy *WVILLE* PO7 .... 101 K2
Broadbent Cl *ROWN* SO16 .... 41 J5
Broad Chalke Down *WINW* SO22 .... 25 F4
Broad Cft *HAV* PO9 .... 83 K3
Broadcut *FHAM/PORC* PO16 .... 13 M3
Broad Gdns *CHAM* PO6 .... 101 K6
Broad Gn *SHAM* SO14 .... 5 H9
Broadlands Av *ELGH* SO50 .... 38 D5
   WVILLE PO7 .... 81 K7
Broadlands Rd *PTSW* SO17 .... 55 J1
   NBAD SO52 .... 35 K5
   WVILLE PO7 .... 62 A6
Broadley Cl *FAWY* SO45 .... 109 K3
Broadmeadow Cl *TOTT* SO40 .... 52 D5
Broadmeadows La
   WVILLE PO7 .... 82 B6
Broadmead Rd *ROWN* SO16 .... 41 J5
Broadmere Av *HAV* PO9 .... 103 G1
Broad Oak *HEND* SO30 .... 58 D5
Broadoak Cl *FAWY* SO45 .... 109 K4
Broadsands Dr *GPORT* PO12 .... 132 A5
Broad St *PSEA* PO1 .... 17 K7
Broad View La *WINW* SO22 .... 24 D5
Broadwater Rd *ROMY* SO51 .... 34 D4
   WEND SO18 .... 56 C1
Broad Wy *HLER* SO31 .... 93 H1
Broadway La *HORN* PO8 .... 63 J6
The Broadway *WINC* SO23 .... 3 F5
Brockenhurst Av *HAV* PO9 .... 82 E7
Brockhampton La *HAV* PO9 .... 14 B5
Brockhampton Rd *HAV* PO9 .... 14 B5
Brockhurst Rd *GPORT* PO12 .... 132 C1
Brockishill Rd *LYND* SO43 .... 66 C1
   TOTT SO40 .... 50 D7
Brocklands *HAV* PO9 .... 14 B4
Brocks Cl *FAWY* SO45 .... 90 E3
Brodrick Av *GPORT* PO12 .... 132 D5
Brokenford Av *ENEY* PO4 .... 19 K9
Brokenford La *TOTT* SO40 .... 52 E5
Bromley Rd *WEND* SO18 .... 6 F1
Brompton Rd *ENEY* PO4 .... 19 K9
Bromyard Crs *CHAM* PO6 .... 100 B6
Bronte Cl *TOTT* SO40 .... 52 C6
Bronte Gdns *FHAM* PO15 .... 75 H5
Bronte Wy *ITCH* SO19 .... 6 D7
Brook Av *HLER* SO31 .... 94 B3
Brook Cl *HLER* SO31 .... 94 C3
   NBAD SO52 .... 36 B7
Brookdale Cl *WVILLE* PO7 .... 81 K5
Brookers La
   LSOL/BMARY PO13 .... 115 H4
Brook Farm Av *FHAM* PO15 .... 12 C5
Brookfield Gdns *HLER* SO31 .... 94 D2
Brookfield Rd *ELGH* SO50 .... 46 A1
   PSEA PO1 .... 19 H7
Brook Gdns *EMRTH* PO10 .... 104 D7
Brooklands Rd *BPWT* SO32 .... 48 D3
   HAV PO9 .... 102 C4
Brook La *HEND* SO30 .... 58 E6
   HLER SO31 .... 94 D3
Brooklyn Cl *RWIN* SO21 .... 33 F6
Brooklyn Dr *WVILLE* PO7 .... 82 A5
Brooklynn Cl *BPWT* SO32 .... 61 F2
Brookmeadow *FHAM* PO15 .... 12 E5
Brookmead Wy *HAV* PO9 .... 14 E8
Brook Rd *ELGH* SO50 .... 46 B1
   WEND SO18 .... 7 H4
Brook St *BPWT* SO32 .... 48 D4
Brookvale Rd *PTSW* SO17 .... 55 H3
Brook Va *ROWN* SO16 .... 54 B3
Brook Wy *ROMY* SO51 .... 29 G7
Brookwood Av *ELGH* SO50 .... 38 C7
Brookwood Rd *ROWN* SO16 .... 53 J4
Broom Cl *ENEY* PO4 .... 135 J1
   WVILLE PO7 .... 102 B1
Broomfield Crs
   LSOL/BMARY PO13 .... 131 J1
Broom Hill Wy *ELGH* SO50 .... 38 C3
Brooms Gv *ITCH* SO19 .... 73 G2
Broom Sq *ENEY* PO4 .... 135 J4
Broom Wy *LSOL/BMARY* PO13 .... 131 C1
Broomy Cl *LSOL/BMARY* PO13 .... 90 D2
Brougham La *GPORT* PO12 .... 132 D2
Brougham Rd *SSEA* PO5 .... 18 C6
Brougham St *GPORT* PO12 .... 132 D2
Broughton Cl *ROWN* SO16 .... 54 B3
Broughton Rd *HSEA* PO3 .... 119 H3
Broughton St *LYND* SO43 .... 66 B7
Browndown Rd
   LSOL/BMARY PO13 .... 131 K5
Brownhill Cl *CHFD* SO53 .... 37 K3
Brownhill Ct *ROWN* SO16 .... 53 K1
Brownhill Rd *CHFD* SO53 .... 37 K3
   NBAD SO52 .... 36 B5
Brownhill Wy *ROWN* SO16 .... 53 H1
Browning Av *CHAM* PO6 .... 99 H5
   ITCH SO19 .... 6 D7
Browning Cl *ELGH* SO50 .... 38 C1
   HLER SO31 .... 75 H5

   TOTT SO40 .... 52 C5
Browning Dr *WINW* SO22 .... 21 G7
Brownlow Av *ITCH* SO19 .... 7 G6
Brownlow Cl *PSEA* PO1 .... 134 C1
Brownlow Gdns *ITCH* SO19 .... 7 G7
Brownwich La
   FHAM/STUB PO14 .... 113 J2
The Brow *WVILLE* PO7 .... 101 H4
Broxburn Cl *CHFD* SO53 .... 38 B1
Broxhead Rd *HAV* PO9 .... 83 H7
Bruce Cl *FHAM/PORC* PO16 .... 13 H2
Bruce Rd *ENEY* PO4 .... 134 C6
Brue Cl *CHFD* SO53 .... 37 J3
Brune La *LSOL/BMARY* PO13 .... 115 H4
Brunel Cl *HEND* SO30 .... 58 C3
Brunel Rd *NEND* PO2 .... 118 D4
   TOTT SO40 .... 52 C1
   WSHM SO15 .... 53 H5
Brunei Wy *FHAM* PO15 .... 95 J1
Brunswick Gdns *HAV* PO9 .... 14 A3
Brunswick Ms *WSHM* SO15 .... 4 F7
Brunswick Sq *SHAM* SO14 .... 9 G4
Brunswick St *SSEA* PO5 .... 18 C6
Bryanston Rd *ITCH* SO19 .... 10 B1
Bryher Island *CHAM* PO6 .... 100 A8
Bryony Cl *HLER* SO31 .... 94 E4
Bryony Gdns *ELGH* SO50 .... 46 B5
Bryony Wy *WVILLE* PO7 .... 82 B7
Bryson Rd *CHAM* PO6 .... 100 C6
Bubb La *BPWT* SO32 .... 46 B7
   HEND SO30 .... 58 A1
Buchanan Rd *ROWN* SO16 .... 42 A6
Buchan Av *FHAM* PO15 .... 75 H5
Buchan Ct *FAWY* SO45 .... 90 D4
Buckby La *HSEA* PO3 .... 119 H3
Bucketts Farm Cl *BPWT* SO32 .... 49 J6
Buckingham Ga *WSHM* SO15 .... 4 D3
Buckingham St *PSEA* PO1 .... 18 D2
Buckland Cl *ELGH* SO50 .... 38 D5
   WVILLE PO7 .... 81 J3
Buckland Gdns *TOTT* SO40 .... 52 B2
Buckland St *NEND* PO2 .... 134 D1
Bucklers Ct *HAV* PO9 .... 82 E6
   NEND PO2 .... 118 C6
Bucklers Rd *GPORT* PO12 .... 117 F7
Bucksey Rd
   LSOL/BMARY PO13 .... 115 K7
Buckthorn Cl *TOTT* SO40 .... 51 K4
Buddens Rd *WHAM* PO17 .... 77 H1
Budds La *ROMY* SO51 .... 34 D1
Bude Cl *ROWN* SO16 .... 99 J5
Bugle St *SHAM* SO14 .... 8 F4
Bulbeck Rd *HAV* PO9 .... 14 E5
Bullar Rd *WEND* SO18 .... 6 C3
Bullar St *SHAM* SO14 .... 5 J7
Bull Dro *WINC* SO23 .... 26 A3
Bullfinch Cl *TOTT* SO40 .... 52 B5
Bull HI *LYMN* SO41 .... 124 A1
Bull La *BPWT* SO32 .... 60 E1
Bullrush Cl *FAWY* SO45 .... 91 G5
Bulls Copse La *HORN* PO8 .... 64 B6
Bunkers HI *WVILLE* PO7 .... 80 C2
Bunny La *ROMY* SO51 .... 28 E3
Bunstead La *RWIN* SO21 .... 32 A3
Bunting Gdns *HORN* PO8 .... 82 A1
Burbidge Gv *ENEY* PO4 .... 135 F6
Burbush Cl *FAWY* SO45 .... 109 K4
Burcote Dr *HSEA* PO3 .... 119 G3
Burdale Dr *HISD* PO11 .... 138 A5
Burgate Cl *HAV* PO9 .... 102 E3
Burgess Cl *HISD* PO11 .... 138 A7
Burgess Gdns *ROWN* SO16 .... 55 F1
Burgess Rd *PTSW* SO17 .... 43 J7
   WSHM SO15 .... 54 E2
Burghclere Rd *HAV* PO9 .... 83 J7
   ITCH SO19 .... 10 E9
Burgogne Rd *ITCH* SO19 .... 73 H1
   SSEA PO5 .... 18 C7
Burgundy Cl *HLER* SO31 .... 94 E4
Buriton Cl *FHAM/PORC* PO16 .... 99 G5
Buriton Rd *WINW* SO22 .... 21 G3
Buriton St *PSEA* PO1 .... 18 E2
Burke Dr *ITCH* SO19 .... 7 M7
Burleigh Rd *NEND* PO2 .... 118 E7
Burley Cl *CHFD* SO53 .... 37 J6
   HAV PO9 .... 83 J7
Burley Down *CHFD* SO53 .... 37 J6
Burley Rd *WINW* SO22 .... 21 G3
Burlington Rd *NEND* PO2 .... 118 D6
   WSHM SO15 .... 4 D6
Burmah Rd North *FAWY* SO45 .... 111 F1
Burmah Rd South *FAWY* SO45 .... 110 E2
Burma Wy *TOTT* SO40 .... 70 A5
Burmese Cl *FHAM* PO15 .... 75 H5
Burnaby Rd *PSEA* PO1 .... 18 A4
Burnbank Gdns *TOTT* SO40 .... 52 D5
Burnett Cl *FAWY* SO45 .... 91 J4
   WINW SO22 .... 21 F5
   WEND SO18 .... 6 C1
Burnett Rd *GPORT* PO12 .... 132 C2
Burnetts Flds *ELGH* SO50 .... 46 B4
Burnetts Gdns *ELGH* SO50 .... 46 C4
Burnetts La *HEND* SO30 .... 46 A7
Burney Rd *GPORT* PO12 .... 132 B5
Burnham Beeches *CHFD* SO53 .... 37 J4
Burnham Cha *WEND* SO18 .... 7 K4
Burnham Rd *CHAM* PO6 .... 101 J5
Burnham Wd
   FHAM/PORC PO16 .... 13 G1
Burns Cl *ELGH* SO50 .... 44 B1
Burnside *LSOL/BMARY* PO13 .... 115 J2
   WVILLE PO7 .... 82 B4
Burns Pl *ROWN* SO16 .... 54 B2
Burns Rd *ELGH* SO50 .... 44 C2
   ITCH SO19 .... 57 G7
Burnt House La
   FHAM/STUB PO14 .... 114 E4
Burr Cl *RWIN* SO21 .... 39 J2
Burrfields Rd *HSEA* PO3 .... 119 G5
Burridge Rd *HLER* SO31 .... 75 F5
Burrill Av *CHAM* PO6 .... 101 G5
Burrows Cl *HAV* PO9 .... 15 H1
Bursledon Hts *HLER* SO31 .... 74 A4
Bursledon Pl *WVILLE* PO7 .... 101 J1
Bursledon Rd *HEND* SO30 .... 58 A7
   ITCH SO19 .... 57 G7
   WVILLE PO7 .... 101 J1
Burton Rd *WSHM* SO15 .... 4 D5
Burwood Gv *HISD* PO11 .... 137 H4
Bury Cl *GPORT* PO12 .... 16 B6

   TOTT SO40 .... 52 C5
Bury Crs *GPORT* PO12 .... 16 A6
Bury Hall La *GPORT* PO12 .... 132 C5
Bury La *TOTT* SO40 .... 53 C7
Bury Rd *GPORT* PO12 .... 16 A6
   TOTT SO40 .... 69 J2
Bush Saint West *SSEA* PO5 .... 18 C7
Bush St East *SSEA* PO5 .... 18 C7
Bushy Md *WVILLE* PO7 .... 101 H3
Busket La *WINC* SO23 .... 2 F5
Busketts Wy *TOTT* SO40 .... 67 K3
Butcher St *PSEA* PO1 .... 17 K6
Buttercup Cl *FAWY* SO45 .... 91 H5
   HEND SO30 .... 57 K6
Buttercup Wy *HLER* SO31 .... 94 D3
Butterfield Rd *ROWN* SO16 .... 43 F7
Butterfly Dr *CHAM* PO6 .... 99 K4
Buttermere Cl *ROWN* SO16 .... 53 K2
Buttsash Av *FAWY* SO45 .... 91 H5
Butts Ash Gdns *FAWY* SO45 .... 91 H5
Butts Ash La *FAWY* SO45 .... 91 H5
Butts Bridge HI *FAWY* SO45 .... 91 H4
Buttsbridge Rd *FAWY* SO45 .... 91 H5
Butts Cl *WINW* SO22 .... 21 G6
   ITCH SO19 .... 73 G1
Butt's Crs *ITCH* SO19 .... 11 M2
Butts La *BPWT* SO32 .... 48 E3
Butt's Rd *ITCH* SO19 .... 73 G1
Butt's Sq *ITCH* SO19 .... 11 M2
Byerley Cl *EMRTH* PO10 .... 104 E1
Byerley Rd *PSEA* PO1 .... 19 J2
Byeways *FAWY* SO45 .... 91 G4
The Byeway *SELS* SO20 .... 139 K7
By-pass Rd *ROMY* SO51 .... 34 D4
Byrd Cl *WVILLE* PO7 .... 101 K1
Byron Av *WINW* SO22 .... 21 G7
Byron Cl *BPWT* SO32 .... 49 F3
   FHAM/PORC PO16 .... 13 G3
Byron Rd *ELGH* SO50 .... 38 E6
   ITCH SO19 .... 7 M8
   NEND PO2 .... 118 E7

C

Cable St *SHAM* SO14 .... 5 L8
Cabot Dr *FAWY* SO45 .... 90 E3
Cadgwith Pl *CHAM* PO6 .... 100 A7
Cadland Rd *FAWY* SO45 .... 92 A7
Cadlands Park Est *FAWY* SO45 .... 109 K1
Cadnam La *TOTT* SO40 .... 50 C1
Cadnam Rd *ENEY* PO4 .... 135 C5
Cador Dr *FHAM/PORC* PO16 .... 116 E1
Caerleon Av *ITCH* SO19 .... 7 L7
Caerleon Dr *ITCH* SO19 .... 7 L7
Caernarvon Gdns *CHFD* SO53 .... 37 H6
Cains Cl *FHAM/STUB* PO14 .... 114 D4
Cairo Ter *NEND* PO2 .... 134 C1
Caistor Cl *ROWN* SO16 .... 42 B7
Calabrese *HLER* SO31 .... 75 G6
Calbourne *HLER* SO31 .... 73 F6
Calcot HI *BPWT* SO32 .... 59 K1
Calcot La *BPWT* SO32 .... 59 K2
Calder Cl *ROWN* SO16 .... 53 K4
Calderwood Dr *ITCH* SO19 .... 11 C1
Caledonia Dr *FAWY* SO45 .... 90 E3
Calmore Crs *TOTT* SO40 .... 52 A3
Calmore Gdns *TOTT* SO40 .... 52 B5
Calmore Rd *TOTT* SO40 .... 52 A3
Calpe Av *LYND* SO43 .... 66 C7
Calshot Cl *FAWY* SO45 .... 111 J7
Calshot Dr *CHFD* SO53 .... 37 H6
Calshot Rd *FAWY* SO45 .... 110 E4
   HAV PO9 .... 82 D6
Calshot Wy
   LSOL/BMARY PO13 .... 115 J6
Camargue Cl *HLER* SO31 .... 75 C5
Camber Pl *PSEA* PO1 .... 17 K7
Cambria Dr *FAWY* SO45 .... 90 E3
Cambrian Cl *HLER* SO31 .... 73 K3
Cambridge Dr *CHFD* SO53 .... 37 K7
Cambridge Gn
   FHAM/STUB PO14 .... 95 H4
Cambridge Rd *GPORT* PO12 .... 132 B2
   LSOL/BMARY PO13 .... 131 C3
   PSEA PO1 .... 18 A6
Camcross Cl *CHAM* PO6 .... 100 A5
Camden St *GPORT* PO12 .... 132 D2
Camelia Cl *HAV* PO9 .... 103 J3
   NBAD SO52 .... 36 B5
Camelia Gdns *WEND* SO18 .... 56 D2
Camelia Gv *ELGH* SO50 .... 46 D1
Camelot Crs *FHAM/PORC* PO16 .... 98 E5
Cameron Cl
   LSOL/BMARY PO13 .... 115 K4
Camley Cl *ITCH* SO19 .... 10 D8
Campbell Rd *ELGH* SO50 .... 44 E2
   SSEA PO5 .... 18 F7
Campbell St *SHAM* SO14 .... 5 L7
Campbell Wy *ELGH* SO50 .... 46 B1
Campion Cl *ELGH* SO50 .... 46 B5
   HLER SO31 .... 94 D5
   WVILLE PO7 .... 82 B7
Campion Dr *ROMY* SO51 .... 35 H1
Campion Rd *ITCH* SO19 .... 57 G7
Campion Wy *WINC* SO23 .... 22 B1
Camp Rd *LSOL/BMARY* PO13 .... 116 A4
Cams Bay Cl
   FHAM/PORC PO16 .... 98 C5
Cams HI *FHAM/PORC* PO16 .... 98 B5
   WVILLE PO7 .... 62 A3
Canada Rd *ITCH* SO19 .... 10 D6
Canal Cl *ROMY* SO51 .... 35 F1
Canal La *ROMY* SO51 .... 34 E2
   SHAM SO14 .... 9 G3
   SSEA PO5 .... 18 E8
Canberra Cl *GPORT* PO12 .... 132 C4
Canberra Rd *EMRTH* PO10 .... 122 D4
   ROWN SO16 .... 41 G7
Candover Ct *ITCH* SO19 .... 11 C9
Candy La *WEND* SO18 .... 57 H1
Canford Cl *BPWT* SO32 .... 61 F5
   ROWN SO16 .... 53 J2
Cannon St *WSHM* SO15 .... 54 D4
Canoe Cl *HLER* SO31 .... 94 E5
Canon's Barn Cl
   FHAM/PORC PO16 .... 99 F5
Canon St *WINC* SO23 .... 2 D6

Canterbury Av *ITCH* SO19 .... 11 L3
Canterbury Cl
   LSOL/BMARY PO13 .... 131 J4
Canterbury Dr *ENEY* PO4 .... 90 D3
Canterbury Rd *ENEY* PO4 .... 19 K7
   FHAM/STUB PO14 .... 114 D4
Canton St *WSHM* SO15 .... 4 E6
Canute Rd *SHAM* SO14 .... 9 K4
   WINC SO23 .... 3 H7
Capella Gdns *FAWY* SO45 .... 90 E3
Capel Ley *WVILLE* PO7 .... 101 K2
Capers End La *BPWT* SO32 .... 59 K3
Captains Pl *SHAM* SO14 .... 9 J4
Captains Rw *PSEA* PO1 .... 17 K7
Carberry Dr *FHAM/PORC* PO16 .... 98 E7
Carbery Ct *HAV* PO9 .... 82 E6
Carbis Cl *CHAM* PO6 .... 99 K7
Cardiff Rd *NEND* PO2 .... 118 C5
Cardinal Dr *WVILLE* PO7 .... 82 C4
Cardinal Wy *HLER* SO31 .... 95 G3
Carey Rd *ITCH* SO19 .... 7 M9
Carisbrooke *HLER* SO31 .... 73 F6
Carisbrooke Av
   FHAM/STUB PO14 .... 114 B5
Carisbrooke Cl *HAV* PO9 .... 15 J3
Carisbrooke Ct *ROMY* SO51 .... 35 F1
Carisbrooke Crs *CHFD* SO53 .... 38 C5
Carisbrooke Dr *ITCH* SO19 .... 6 F7
Carisbrooke Rd *ENEY* PO4 .... 19 L5
   LSOL/BMARY PO13 .... 115 J4
Carless Cl *LSOL/BMARY* PO13 .... 132 A1
Carlisle Rd *ROWN* SO16 .... 54 C4
   SSEA PO5 .... 18 F4
Carlton Crs *WSHM* SO15 .... 4 F6
Carlton Pl *WSHM* SO15 .... 4 F7
Carlton Rd *FHAM/PORC* PO16 .... 99 F7
   GPORT PO12 .... 16 D5
   WSHM SO15 .... 4 E5
Carlton Wy *GPORT* PO12 .... 16 D4
Carlyle Rd *GPORT* PO12 .... 16 A3
Carlyn Dr *CHFD* SO53 .... 38 A3
Carmans La *RWIN* SO21 .... 33 G2
Carmarthen Av *CHAM* PO6 .... 101 G5
Carnarvon Rd *GPORT* PO12 .... 132 D4
   NEND PO2 .... 118 E7
Carnation Rd *ROWN* SO16 .... 43 K7
Carne Cl *CHFD* SO53 .... 37 K2
Caroline Pl *GPORT* PO12 .... 16 B2
Carolyn Cl *ITCH* SO19 .... 10 C6
Carpathia Cl *WEND* SO18 .... 56 D2
Carpenter Cl *ENEY* PO4 .... 19 M8
   FAWY SO45 .... 91 H2
Carraway *FHAM* PO15 .... 75 J6
Carroll Cl *ELGH* SO50 .... 46 C2
Carronade Wk *HSEA* PO3 .... 118 C2
Carshalton Av *CHAM* PO6 .... 101 G6
Carter's La *TOTT* SO40 .... 89 K1
Carthage Cl *CHFD* SO53 .... 38 C3
Cartwright Dr *FHAM* PO15 .... 96 A4
Cascades Ap *PSEA* PO1 .... 18 C2
Cask St *PSEA* PO1 .... 18 D1
Caspar John Cl
   FHAM/STUB PO14 .... 114 C6
Caspian Cl *HLER* SO31 .... 75 C6
Castle Av *HAV* PO9 .... 15 K5
Castle Cl *SSEA* PO5 .... 18 C7
Castle Ct *WSHM* SO15 .... 54 B6
Castle Farm La *WHAM* PO17 .... 77 J3
Castle Gv *FHAM/PORC* PO16 .... 99 C7
Castle La *CHFD* SO53 .... 37 H6
   FAWY SO45 .... 129 J1
   NBAD SO52 .... 36 E6
   SHAM SO14 .... 8 F4
Castlemans La *HISD* PO11 .... 121 H6
Castle Rd *HAV* PO9 .... 83 H3
   HLER SO31 .... 72 E7
   SSEA PO5 .... 18 B8
   WEND SO18 .... 56 B2
   WHAM PO17 .... 79 J7
Castleshaw Cl *ROWN* SO16 .... 54 A5
Castle Sq *SHAM* SO14 .... 8 F4
Castle St *FHAM/PORC* PO16 .... 99 G7
   FHAM/STUB PO14 .... 96 A6
   SHAM SO14 .... 5 H5
Castle Vw *GPORT* PO12 .... 116 E7
Castle View Rd
   FHAM/PORC PO16 .... 117 G1
Castleway *HAV* PO9 .... 15 K5
Castle Wy *SHAM* SO14 .... 8 F4
Catamaran Cl *HLER* SO31 .... 94 E5
Cateran Cl *ROWN* SO16 .... 54 A4
Cathay Gdns *FAWY* SO45 .... 90 D3
Cathedral Vw *WINC* SO23 .... 3 G7
Catherine Cl *HEND* SO30 .... 57 H2
Catherine Gdns *HEND* SO30 .... 57 H2
Catherington La *HORN* PO8 .... 64 B3
Catherington Wy *HAV* PO9 .... 103 G2
Catisfield La *FHAM* PO15 .... 96 C5
Catisfield Rd *ENEY* PO4 .... 135 G3
   FHAM PO15 .... 96 D5
Causeway Crs *TOTT* SO40 .... 53 F4
Causeway Farm *HORN* PO8 .... 64 C7
The Causeway
   FHAM/PORC PO16 .... 98 B5
Cavalier Cl *FAWY* SO45 .... 90 D3
Cavanna Cl *LSOL/BMARY* PO13 .... 115 J3
Cavell Dr *CHAM* PO6 .... 100 D5
Cavendish Cl *ROMY* SO51 .... 29 G7
   WVILLE PO7 .... 82 A5
Cavendish Dr *WVILLE* PO7 .... 82 A6
Cavendish Gv *WINC* SO23 .... 22 A4
   WSHM SO15 .... 4 F3
Cavendish Ms *WSHM* SO15 .... 4 F3
Cavendish Rd *SSEA* PO5 .... 18 E8
C Av *FAWY* SO45 .... 110 A2
Caversham Cl *HEND* SO30 .... 57 G3
   ITCH SO19 .... 11 H1
Cawte Rd *WSHM* SO15 .... 4 A6
Caxton Av *ITCH* SO19 .... 7 K6
Cecil Av *ROWN* SO16 .... 54 C3
   TOTT SO40 .... 68 B3
Cecil Gv *SSEA* PO5 .... 18 B8
Cecil Pl *SSEA* PO5 .... 18 B8
Cecil Rd *ITCH* SO19 .... 10 C4
Cedar Cl *GPORT* PO12 .... 116 D5
   HEND SO30 .... 58 B5
   HLER SO31 .... 73 J5
   WVILLE PO7 .... 81 K7
Cedar Crs *HORN* PO8 .... 64 D7
   NBAD SO52 .... 36 A5

Cedar Gdns *HAV* PO09 .... 15 G2
Cedar Gv *HSEA* PO3.......... 135 G1
Cedar Lawn *ROMY* SO51 .... 35 H1
Cedarmount *LYND* SO43 .... 86 C2
Cedar Rd *ELGH* SO50 .... 44 B2
  FAWY SO45 .... 91 H7
  SHAM SO14 .... 5 H4
Cedar Wood Cl *ELGH* SO50 .... 46 D1
  TOTT SO40 .... 52 B4
Cedric Cl *FAWY* SO45 .... 110 C7
Celandine Av *HLER* SO31 .... 94 E4
  HORN PO08 .... 82 D2
Celandine Cl *NBAD* SO52 .... 37 G5
Celia Cl *WVILLE* PO07 .... 82 C5
Cement Ter *SHAM* SO14 .... 8 F3
Cemetery La *EMRTH* PO10.......... 105 F3
  WVILLE PO07 .... 62 E7
Cemetery Rd *WSHM* SO15 .... 4 D3
Centaur St *NEND* PO02 .... 118 C7
Centaury Gdns *ELGH* SO50 .... 46 B4
Central Br *SHAM* SO14 .... 9 J3
Central Rd *CHAM* PO6 .... 101 H7
  FHAM/PORC PO16 .... 98 E7
  SHAM SO14 .... 9 H5
Central Station Br *WSHM* SO15 .... 4 C9
Central St *PSEA* PO01 .... 18 E2
Centre Wy *HLER* SO31 .... 95 F3
Cerdic Ms *HLER* SO31 .... 93 K2
  WEND SO18 .... 56 E3
Cerne Cl *NBAD* SO52 .... 35 K6
Chadderton Gdns *PSEA* PO01 .... 18 A7
Chadwell Av *ITCH* SO19 .... 11 K2
Chadwick Rd *ELGH* SO50 .... 44 B1
Chafen Rd *WEND* SO18 .... 6 A3
Chaffinch Cl *TOTT* SO40 .... 52 B4
Chaffinch Gn *HORN* PO08 .... 81 K1
Chaffinch Wy
  FHAM/PORC PO16 .... 98 C6
  LSOL/BMARY PO13 .... 131 G1
Chale Cl *LSOL/BMARY* PO13 .... 115 K5
Chalewood Rd *FAWY* SO45 .... 128 B1
Chalice Ct *HEND* SO30 .... 58 A6
Chalk HI *WEND* SO18 .... 7 L1
Chalk La *WHAM* PO17 .... 77 J6
Chalkpit Rd *CHAM* PO6 .... 100 A4
Chalk Rdg *HORN* PO08 .... 64 E1
  WINC SO23 .... 3 K6
Chalkridge Rd *CHAM* PO6 .... 101 F5
Chalky La *BPWT* SO32 .... 48 E3
Challis Ct *SHAM* SO14 .... 9 H3
Challenger Wy *FAWY* SO45 .... 90 E2
Chaloner Crs *FAWY* SO45 .... 91 H5
Chalton Crs *HAV* PO09 .... 102 E1
Chalvington Rd *CHFD* SO53 .... 37 K5
Chalybeate Cl *ROWN* SO16.......... 54 C2
Chamberlain Gv
  FHAM/STUB PO14.......... 13 G8
Chamberlain Rd *PTSW* SO17 .... 55 H1
Chamberlayne Rd *ELGH* SO50.......... 44 D2
  HLER SO31 .... 73 J5
Chambers Av *ROMY* SO51 .... 35 G3
Chambers Cl *ROWN* SO16.......... 41 H6
Chancellors La *BPWT* SO32 .... 58 D1
Chancel Rd *HLER* SO31 .... 95 G3
Chandlers Cl *HISD* PO11 .... 137 K6
Chandlers Wy *HLER* SO31 .... 75 G7
Chandos St *SHAM* SO14 .... 9 H3
Channels Farm Rd *ROWN* SO16 .. 44 A6
Channel Wy *SHAM* SO14.......... 9 K4
Chantry Rd *GPORT* PO12 .... 132 C1
  HORN PO08 .... 64 C5
  SHAM SO14 .... 9 K3
The Chantry *FHAM/STUB* PO14.......... 95 H3
Chapel Crs *ITCH* SO19 .... 11 H2
Chapel Dro *ELGH* SO50 .... 46 B4
  HEND SO30 .... 58 A6
Chapel La *BPWT* SO32 .... 59 K4
  BROC SO42 .... 125 J4
  ELGH SO50 .... 38 E1
  FAWY SO45 .... 110 B7
  FAWY SO45 .... 110 D4
  LYND SO43 .... 86 C2
  ROMY SO51 .... 28 C1
  RWIN SO21 .... 23 F5
  TOTT SO40 .... 52 D7
Chapel Rd *BPWT* SO32 .... 49 J6
  HEND SO30 .... 57 H7
  HLER SO31 .... 74 D7
  SHAM SO14 .... 9 J2
Chapelside *FHAM/STUB* PO14.......... 96 B6
Chapel St *GPORT* PO12 .... 116 E7
  NEND PO02 .... 118 C7
  SSEA PO5 .... 18 B7
Chaplains Av *HORN* PO08 .... 81 J2
Chaplains Cl *HORN* PO08 .... 81 J1
Charden Rd *ELGH* SO50 .... 45 K2
  LSOL/BMARY PO13 .... 116 A7
Charfield Cl *FHAM/STUB* PO14 .. 12 A7
  WINW SO22 .... 25 H3
Chark La *LSOL/BMARY* PO13 .... 115 G7
Charlecote Dr *CHFD* SO53 .... 37 H2
Charlesbury Av *GPORT* PO12 .. 132 C4
Charles Cl *WINC* SO23 .... 21 K5
  WVILLE PO07 .... 81 J7
Charles Dickens St *PSEA* PO01 .. 18 C4
Charles Knott Gdns
  WSHM SO15.......... 4 E4
Charles St *PSEA* PO01 .... 18 E2
  SHAM SO14 .... 9 H3
Charleston Cl *HISD* PO11 .... 137 F4
Charleston Rd *FAWY* SO45 .... 92 A6
Charles Watts Wy *HEND* SO30 .. 57 H5
Charlesworth Dr *WVILLE* PO07.. 81 J4
Charlesworth Gdns *WVILLE* PO7.. 81 J4
Charliejoy Gdns *SHAM* SO14 .. 5 L7
Charlotte Pl *SHAM* SO14 .... 5 H7
Charlotte St *PSEA* PO01 .... 18 B1
Charlton Rd *WSHM* SO15.......... 4 A4
Charminster Cl *WVILLE* PO07.......... 82 C5
Charmus Rd *TOTT* SO40 .... 52 A2
Charmwen Crs *HEND* SO30 .... 57 F2
Charnwood
  LSOL/BMARY PO13 .... 116 A5
Charnwood Cl *CHFD* SO53 .... 31 K7
  TOTT SO40 .... 52 C2
Charnwood Crs *CHFD* SO53 .... 31 K7
Charnwood Gdns *CHFD* SO53 .. 31 K7
Charterhouse Wy *HEND* SO30.......... 58 A3

Chartwell Cl *ELGH* SO50 .... 38 E4
  FHAM/STUB PO14.......... 95 H5
Chartwell Dr *HAV* PO09 .... 15 L1
Chase Farm Cl *BPWT* SO32 .... 61 F1
Chase Gv *BPWT* SO32 .... 61 F1
The Chase *FHAM/STUB* PO14.......... 95 J4
  GPORT PO12 .... 132 C4
Chasewater Av *HSEA* PO3 .... 135 F1
Chatburn Av *HORN* PO08 .... 81 K2
Chatfield Av *NEND* PO02 .... 117 K6
Chatfield Rd
  LSOL/BMARY PO13 .... 115 K3
Chatham Dr *PSEA* PO01 .... 18 A7
Chatham Rd *WINW* SO22 .... 25 F3
Chatsworth Av *CHAM* PO6 .... 119 F1
Chatsworth Rd *ELGH* SO50 .... 38 E4
  ITCH SO19 .... 7 H7
Chaucer Av *CHAM* PO6 .... 99 H5
Chaucer Cl *FHAM/PORC* PO16 .... 12 F4
  WVILLE PO07 .... 81 K3
Chaucer Rd *ITCH* SO19 .... 57 G6
Chaundler Rd *WINC* SO23 .... 21 K5
Chaveney Cl *FAWY* SO45 .... 91 F5
  FAWY SO45 .... 91 G5
Chawton Cl *WINW* SO22 .... 21 G3
  WEND SO18 .... 57 G4
Cheam Wy *TOTT* SO40 .... 52 C3
Cheddar Cl *ITCH* SO19 .... 10 C3
Chedworth Crs *CHAM* PO6 .... 99 K5
Chelmsford Rd *NEND* PO02 .... 118 C5
Chelsea Rd *SSEA* PO5 .... 18 F8
Cheltenham Crs
  LSOL/BMARY PO13 .... 131 G2
Cheltenham Gdns *HEND* SO30 .. 58 B1
Cheltenham Rd *CHAM* PO6 .... 100 B5
Chelveston Crs *ROWN* SO16 .... 42 A7
Cheping Gdns *HEND* SO30 .... 59 F6
Chepstow Cl *CHFD* SO53 .... 37 J4
  TOTT SO40 .... 52 B4
Chepstow Ct *WVILLE* PO07 .... 82 C4
Cherbourg Rd *ELGH* SO50 .... 44 C2
Cheriton Cl *WINW* SO22 .... 21 G6
  HORN PO08 .... 64 B5
Cheriton Rd *ELGH* SO50 .... 44 C3
  WINW SO22 .... 2 A2
  GPORT PO12 .... 132 C4
Cherque La *LSOL/BMARY* PO13.. 115 H7
Cherry Cl *LSOL/BMARY* PO13 .... 131 G3
Cherry Dro *ELGH* SO50 .... 46 B5
Cherry Gdns *BPWT* SO32 .... 48 E4
Cherrygarth Rd *FHAM* PO15 .... 96 D5
Cherryton Gdns *FAWY* SO45 .... 109 J4
Cherry Tree Av
  FHAM/STUB PO14.......... 12 B8
  HORN PO08 .... 82 C3
Cherry Wk *WSHM* SO15 .... 54 D4
Cherrywood *HEND* SO30 .... 58 A6
Cherrywood Gdns *TOTT* SO40 .. 52 B5
  HISD PO11 .... 137 G4
Chervil Cl *HORN* PO08.......... 64 D3
Cherville St *ROMY* SO51 .... 34 D2
Cherwell Crs *ROWN* SO16.......... 53 K4
Cherwell Gdns *CHFD* SO53 .... 38 A5
Cheshire Cl *FHAM* PO15 .... 96 A1
Cheshire Wy *EMRTH* PO10.......... 105 H4
Chesil St *WINC* SO23 .... 3 G6
Cheslyn Rd *HSEA* PO3 .... 135 G2
Chessel Av *ITCH* SO19 .... 6 D6
Chessel Crs *ITCH* SO19 .... 6 D5
Chester Crs *LSOL/BMARY* PO13.. 131 J4
Chesterfield Rd *HSEA* PO3 .... 135 F1
Chester Pl *SSEA* PO5 .... 18 E9
  SSEA PO5 .... 134 C6
Chester Rd *WEND* SO18 .... 7 G1
  WINC SO23 .... 3 G5
Chesterton Gdns *HORN* PO08 .. 81 K2
Chesterton Pl *FHAM* PO15 .... 75 H5
Chestnut Av *CHFD* SO53 .... 37 K7
  ELGH SO50 .... 43 K2
  ENEY PO4 .... 19 K7
  WINW SO22 .... 20 E3
  HAV PO09 .... 102 C3
  HORN PO08 .... 64 D7
  RWIN SO21 .... 39 J1
  TOTT SO40 .... 68 B2
  ROMY SO51 .... 35 J4
  WVILLE PO07 .... 80 E1
Chestnut Ri *ELGH* SO50 .... 44 A2
Chestnut Rd *ROWN* SO16.......... 54 B2
The Chestnuts *HLER* SO31 .... 95 F4
Chestnut Wk *GPORT* PO12.......... 116 E6
Chestnut Wy *FHAM/STUB* PO14 .. 95 H5
Chettle Rd *ITCH* SO19 .... 57 H7
Chetwynd Dr *ROWN* SO16.......... 43 G7
Chetwynd Rd *ENEY* PO4 .... 19 G7
  ROWN SO16.......... 43 G7
Chevening Ct *ENEY* PO4 .... 135 G3
Cheviot Dr *FAWY* SO45 .... 90 E3
Cheviot Gn *HLER* SO31 .... 94 C6
Cheviot Rd *ROWN* SO16.......... 53 K4
Chewter Cl *SSEA* PO5 .... 134 D7
Cheyne Wy
  LSOL/BMARY PO13 .... 131 G3
Chichester Av *HISD* PO11 .... 137 G6
Chichester Cl *HEND* SO30.......... 58 B3
  HLER SO31 .... 94 D3
  LSOL/BMARY PO13 .... 115 J5
Chichester Rd *HISD* PO11 .... 121 K6
  NEND PO02 .... 118 D7
  WEND SO18 .... 7 G1
Chickenhall La *ELGH* SO50 .... 45 F1
Chidden Holt *CHFD* SO53 .... 37 H5
Chidham Cl *HAV* PO09 .... 14 C2
Chidham Dr *HAV* PO09 .... 14 C2
Chidham Rd *CHAM* PO6 .... 101 F5
Chidham Sq *HAV* PO09 .... 14 C3
Chilbolton Av *WINW* SO22 .... 2 C4
Chilbolton Ct *HAV* PO09 .... 83 J7
Chilcomb Cl
  LSOL/BMARY PO13 .... 131 G2
Chilcombe Cl *HAV* PO09 .... 103 J3
Chilcomb La *RWIN* SO21 .... 3 L9
  WINC SO23.......... 3 H9
Chilcomb Rd *WEND* SO18.......... 7 L2
Chilcote Rd *HSEA* PO3 .... 135 F1
Childe Sq *NEND* PO02 .... 118 B5
Chilgrove Rd *CHAM* PO6 .... 101 H6

Chilham Cl *ELGH* SO50 .... 38 D3
Chilland La *RWIN* SO21 .... 23 H1
Chillenden Ct *TOTT* SO40 .... 52 B6
  TOTT SO40 .... 52 C6
Chillerton *HLER* SO31 .... 73 F7
Chilling La *HLER* SO31 .... 112 D2
Chillingham Gdns *CHFD* SO53 .. 37 J1
Chilsdown Wy *WVILLE* PO07 .... 101 K1
Chiltern Cl *TOTT* SO40 .... 52 C7
Chiltern Gn *ROWN* SO16.......... 53 K4
Chilworth Cl *ROWN* SO16.......... 42 E2
Chilworth Dro *ROWN* SO16.......... 42 D3
Chilworth Gv *GPORT* PO12.......... 132 D3
Chilworth Rd *ROWN* SO16.......... 43 F3
Chine Av *ITCH* SO19 .... 6 D7
Chine Cl *HLER* SO31 .... 95 F2
The Chine
  LSOL/BMARY PO13 .... 116 B6
Chinham Rd *TOTT* SO40 .... 50 E6
Chipstead Rd *CHAM* PO6 .... 100 E6
Chisholm Cl *ROWN* SO16.......... 42 A4
Chitty Rd *ENEY* PO4 .... 19 M9
Chivers Cl *SSEA* PO5 .... 18 D7
Christchurch Gdns
  CHAM PO6 .... 101 G4
  WINC SO23 .... 2 B9
Christchurch Rd *WINC* SO23 .... 2 C9
Christie Av *HLER* SO31 .... 75 H5
Christopher Wy *EMRTH* PO10 .. 104 C4
Church Cl *ELGH* SO50 .... 39 F6
  HLER SO31 .... 95 G3
  NBAD SO52 .... 36 B6
Churcher Cl *GPORT* PO12 .... 132 A5
Churcher Rd *EMRTH* PO10 .... 104 E2
Church Farm Cl *FAWY* SO45 .... 70 C7
Churchfields *FAWY* SO45 .... 110 E4
Churchfields Rd *RWIN* SO21 .... 33 J3
Church HI *HEND* SO30 .... 57 F3
Churchill Av *BPWT* SO32 .... 48 B2
Churchill Cl *FHAM/STUB* PO14 .. 95 H5
Churchill Ct *HORN* PO08 .... 64 B6
Churchill Dr *EMRTH* PO10 .... 104 C2
Church La *BPWT* SO32 .... 46 E5
  BPWT SO32 .... 49 K5
  BPWT SO32 .... 59 J4
  BROC SO42 .... 125 J3
  ELGH SO50 .... 39 H2
  FAWY SO45 .... 110 D4
  WINW SO22 .... 20 D1
  HAV PO09 .... 15 K7
  HEND SO30 .... 58 A7
  HEND SO30 .... 59 F7
  HISD PO11 .... 121 K4
  HLER SO31 .... 74 A5
  LYND SO43 .... 86 C1
  PTSW SO17 .... 55 J2
  ROMY SO51 .... 29 H2
  ROMY SO51 .... 34 D3
  ROWN SO16.......... 40 E6
  RWIN SO21 .... 22 E2
  RWIN SO21 .... 23 C1
  RWIN SO21 .... 33 K1
  RWIN SO21 .... 39 J2
  WINC SO23 .... 22 B1
  WVILLE PO07 .... 62 C1
Church Pth *EMRTH* PO10 .... 104 C6
  FHAM/PORC PO16 .... 13 L5
  GPORT PO12 .... 16 F6
  HORN PO08 .... 64 B6
Church Pth North *PSEA* PO01 .. 18 D2
  BPWT SO32 .... 49 J5
  ELGH SO50 .... 60 E5
  EMRTH PO10 .... 104 E3
  EMRTH PO10 .... 105 G7
  EMRTH PO10 .... 123 G6
  FHAM/PORC PO16 .... 117 H1
  GPORT PO12 .... 132 D6
  HISD PO11 .... 137 H3
  HLER SO31 .... 94 C6
  HLER SO31 .... 95 G3
  ITCH SO19 .... 10 B7
  ROMY SO51 .... 34 D3
Church St *FHAM/STUB* PO14 .... 96 A1
  PSEA PO01 .... 18 E1
  PSEA PO01 .... 134 B1
  ROMY SO51 .... 34 D3
  WSHM SO15 .... 54 C4
  WSHM SO15 .... 54 D4
Church Street Rbt *PSEA* PO01 .. 134 B1
Church Vw *EMRTH* PO10 .... 104 E3
  ENEY PO4 .... 19 M5
Church View Cl *ITCH* SO19 .... 11 G4
Churchward Gdns
  HEND SO30 .... 58 B2
Cinderford Cl *CHAM* PO6 .... 100 B5
The Circle *SSEA* PO5 .... 134 C6
  WHAM PO17 .... 77 G1
Circular Rd *PSEA* PO01 .... 18 A2
The Circus *WVILLE* PO07 .... 99 K4
Cirrus Gdns *HLER* SO31 .... 93 J4
City Rd *WINC* SO23 .... 2 D5
Clacton Rd *CHAM* PO6 .... 100 C6
Claire Gdns *HORN* PO08 .... 64 D2
Clandon Dr *ELGH* SO50 .... 38 C4
Clanfield Cl *CHFD* SO53 .... 38 A4
Clanfield Dr *CHFD* SO53 .... 38 A4
Clanfield Rd *WEND* SO18 .... 7 M1
Clanfield Wy *CHFD* SO53 .... 38 A4
Clanwilliam Rd
  LSOL/BMARY PO13 .... 131 F2
Clare Cl *FHAM/STUB* PO14 .... 95 H5
Clare Gdns *FAWY* SO45 .... 128 C1
Claremont Cl *ELGH* SO50 .... 38 D4
Claremont Crs *WSHM* SO15 .... 54 B5
Claremont Gdns *WVILLE* PO07 .. 101 K2
  WSHM SO15 .... 54 B5
Clarence Esp *SSEA* PO5 .... 18 A9
Clarence Pde *SSEA* PO5 .... 18 B9
Clarence Rd *GPORT* PO12.......... 16 F4
  LYND SO43 .... 86 C1
  SSEA PO5 .... 134 C7
Clarence St *PSEA* PO01 .... 18 D1
Clarendon Rd *ROMY* SO51 .... 35 G1
Clarendon Crs
  FHAM/STUB PO14.......... 95 G5

Clarendon Pl *PSEA* PO01 .... 18 D3
Clarendon Rd *HAV* PO09 .... 14 D5
  ROWN SO16.......... 54 B4
  SSEA PO5 .... 18 D9
Clarendon St *PSEA* PO01 .... 18 F1
Clarendon Wy *WINC* SO23 .... 2 E9
Clarkes Rd *PSEA* PO01 .... 19 J2
Claude Ashby Cl *WEND* SO18.......... 44 B7
Claudeen Cl *WEND* SO18 .... 44 B7
Claudia Ct *GPORT* PO12 .... 132 C2
Claudius Cl *CHFD* SO53 .... 38 C5
Claudius Gdns *CHFD* SO53 .... 38 C4
Clausentum Cl *CHFD* SO53 .... 38 B3
Clausentum Rd *SHAM* SO14.......... 5 H4
  WINC SO23 .... 25 J3
Claxton St *PSEA* PO01 .... 18 E3
Claybank Sp *HSEA* PO3 .... 119 F6
Claydon Av *ENEY* PO4 .... 19 L5
Clayhall Rd *GPORT* PO12 .... 132 C5
Clay HI *BROC* SO42 .... 86 D5
Clayhill Cl *BPWT* SO32 .... 48 E7
Claylands Cl *BPWT* SO32 .... 48 C3
Claylands Rd *BPWT* SO32 .... 48 C3
Clay La *LYND* SO43 .... 86 C2
Claypit Rd *ROMY* SO51 .... 30 D2
Claypits La *FAWY* SO45 .... 90 D2
Cleasby Cl *ROWN* SO16.......... 53 K5
Clease Wy *RWIN* SO21 .... 33 F2
Clee Av *FHAM/STUB* PO14 .... 12 A7
Cleethorpes Rd *ITCH* SO19 .... 11 K5
Cleeve Cl *CHAM* PO6 .... 100 A5
The Cleeves *TOTT* SO40 .... 52 B6
Clegg Rd *ENEY* PO4 .... 19 L8
Clement Attlee Wy *CHAM* PO6 .. 100 A6
Cleric Ct *FHAM/STUB* PO14 .... 95 J3
Cleveland Cl *WEND* SO18 .... 7 G1
Cleveland Dr *FAWY* SO45 .... 90 E2
  WEND SO18 .... 12 B7
Cleveland Rd *GPORT* PO12 .... 16 B7
  SSEA PO5 .... 19 G6
  WEND SO18 .... 56 C2
Clevelands Cl *CHFD* SO53 .... 31 J7
Clewers HI *BPWT* SO32 .... 48 E7
Clewers La *BPWT* SO32 .... 48 E7
Cliffe Av *HLER* SO31 .... 93 H3
Clifford Dibben Ms *SHAM* SO14 .. 5 G3
Clifford Pl *ELGH* SO50 .... 46 B1
Clifford St *SHAM* SO14 .... 5 J9
Cliff Rd *FHAM/STUB* PO14 .... 114 A6
  WSHM SO15.......... 4 A8
Cliff Wy *RWIN* SO21 .... 33 G3
Clifton Crs *WVILLE* PO07 .... 81 G1
Clifton Gdns *WEND* SO18 .... 57 F3
Clifton HI *WINW* SO22 .... 2 C4
Clifton Rd *WINW* SO22 .... 2 B3
  LSOL/BMARY PO13 .... 131 H4
  SSEA PO5 .... 134 B6
  WSHM SO15.......... 54 B4
Clifton St *GPORT* PO12 .... 132 C2
  PSEA PO01 .... 19 G2
Clifton Ter *WINW* SO22 .... 2 C4
Clinton Rd *WVILLE* PO07 .... 81 K2
Clipper Cl *HLER* SO31 .... 94 D5
Clive Gv *FHAM/PORC* PO16 .... 99 F7
Clive Rd *PSEA* PO01 .... 19 H2
Clock St *PSEA* PO01 .... 17 L4
Clocktower Dr *ENEY* PO4 .... 135 G4
The Cloisters *FHAM* PO15.......... 96 D4
  ROMY SO51 .... 34 D2
  ROMY SO51 .... 43 H7
The Close Bellfield
  FHAM/STUB PO14.......... 96 A7
The Close *CHAM* PO6 .... 101 F7
  FAWY SO45 .... 110 A4
  FHAM/PORC PO16 .... 99 F6
  WEND SO18 .... 58 A6
  WEND SO18 .... 57 G5
Closewood Rd *WVILLE* PO07 .... 81 F4
Clovelly Rd *EMRTH* PO10 .... 104 B6
  ENEY PO4 .... 19 M6
  HISD PO11 .... 121 K3
  SHAM SO14 .... 5 H7
Clover Cl *HLER* SO31 .... 94 C5
  LSOL/BMARY PO13 .... 115 K5
Clover Wy *HEND* SO30 .... 57 K6
  ROMY SO51 .... 35 H2
Club House La *BPWT* SO32 .... 60 E1
Clydebank Rd *NEND* PO02 .... 118 C7
Clyde Ct *GPORT* PO12 .... 132 C2
Clyde Rd *GPORT* PO12 .... 132 C2
Clydesdale Dr *TOTT* SO40 .... 52 A4
Clydesdale Rd *HLER* SO31 .... 75 G7
Clydesdale Wy *TOTT* SO40 .... 52 A4
Coach HI *FHAM/STUB* PO14 .... 96 A6
Coach Hill Cl *CHFD* SO53 .... 38 A4
Coachmans Copse *WEND* SO18 .. 56 D2
Coach Rd *HLER* SO31 .... 93 H4
Coal Park La *HLER* SO31 .... 74 D4
Coalville Rd *ITCH* SO19 .... 11 K1
Coastguard Cl *GPORT* PO12 .... 132 C5
Coastguard La *SELS* SO20 .... 139 H7
Coates Rd *ITCH* SO19 .... 73 C1
Coates Wy *WVILLE* PO07 .... 101 K1
Coat Gdns *FAWY* SO45 .... 91 H3
Cobbett Cl *WINW* SO22 .... 25 F3
Cobbett Rd *WEND* SO18.......... 6 C4
Cobbett Wy *HEND* SO30 .... 58 D5
Cobblewood *EMRTH* PO10 .... 104 C3
Cobden Av *HSEA* PO3 .... 119 F7
  WEND SO18 .... 6 C5
Cobden Crs *WEND* SO18 .... 6 C5
Cobden Gdns *WEND* SO18 .... 6 C1
Cobden St *GPORT* PO12 .... 16 B7
Coblands Av *TOTT* SO40 .... 52 C5
Coburg St *PSEA* PO01 .... 18 F3
  SHAM SO14 .... 5 L7
Cochrane Cl
  LSOL/BMARY PO13 .... 132 A2
Cockleshell Gdns *ENEY* PO4 .... 135 H5
Cocklydown La *TOTT* SO40 .... 52 A5
Coghlan Cl *FHAM/PORC* PO16 .. 13 J3
Coker Cl *WINW* SO22 .... 2 B3
Colburn Cl *ROWN* SO16.......... 53 J2
Colbury Gv *HAV* PO09 .... 102 D2
Colchester Av *CHFD* SO53 .... 38 B4
Colchester Rd *CHAM* PO6 .... 100 C5
Cold East Cl *HLER* SO31 .... 94 D1
Coldeast Wy *HLER* SO31 .... 94 D1
Cold Harbour Cl *WHAM* PO17.......... 77 G1

Coldharbour Farm Rd
  EMRTH PO10.......... 104 C5
Coldharbour La *ROWN* SO16.......... 41 K5
Coldhill La *HORN* PO08 .... 63 K5
Colebrook Av *HSEA* PO3.......... 135 C1
  WSHM SO15 .... 54 D3
Colebrook Pl *WINC* SO23 .... 3 G6
Colebrook St *WINC* SO23 .... 3 F6
Coleman St *SHAM* SO14 .... 9 J1
Colemore Sq *HAV* PO09 .... 103 G2
Colenso Rd *FHAM/PORC* PO16 .. 13 H4
Coleridge Cl *HLER* SO31 .... 94 C5
Coleridge Gdns *HORN* PO08 .... 82 A1
Coleridge Rd *CHAM* PO6 .... 99 J5
Colesbourne Rd *CHAM* PO6 .... 100 A5
Coles Cl *RWIN* SO21 .... 33 K2
Coles Mede *RWIN* SO21 .... 32 E6
Coleson Rd *WEND* SO18 .... 6 C3
Coleville Av *FAWY* SO45 .... 110 E4
Colinton Av *FHAM/PORC* PO16 .. 99 G5
College La *HAV* PO09 .... 83 K4
  HLER SO31 .... 93 J4
College La *PSEA* PO01 .... 17 L4
  PSEA PO01 .... 17 L3
  WVILLE PO07 .... 81 L4
College Rd *ITCH* SO19 .... 10 C6
  PSEA PO01 .... 17 L3
College St *PSEA* PO01 .... 17 L4
  SHAM SO14 .... 9 H3
  WINC SO23 .... 2 E6
College Wk *WINC* SO23 .... 2 F7
Collett Cl *HEND* SO30 .... 58 A2
Colley Cl *WINC* SO23 .... 21 K4
Collier Cl *PTSW* SO17 .... 5 M2
Collingbourne Dr *CHFD* SO53 .. 37 H4
Collington Crs *CHAM* PO6 .... 100 A5
Collingwood Rd *FAWY* SO45.......... 18 F9
Collingworth Cl *HLER* SO31 .... 75 G7
Collins Cl *NBAD* SO52 .... 37 G4
Collins La *RWIN* SO21 .... 33 K2
Collins Rd *ENEY* PO4 .... 19 L9
Collis Rd *HSEA* PO3 .... 119 F7
Colne Av *ROWN* SO16.......... 53 J1
Colpoy St *SSEA* PO5 .... 18 B6
Colson Rd *WINC* SO23 .... 3 H3
Colt Cl *ROWN* SO16.......... 42 A6
Coltsfoot Cl *HEND* SO30 .... 58 A5
Coltsfoot Dr *HLER* SO31 .... 94 D4
  WVILLE PO07 .... 102 A1
Coltsfoot Wk *ROMY* SO51 .... 35 H1
Coltsmead *CHAM* PO6 .... 99 J5
Colville Rd *CHAM* PO6 .... 101 F6
Colville Rd *CHAM* PO6 .... 101 F6
Colwell Cl *ROWN* SO16.......... 53 J4
Colwell Rd *FHAM/STUB* PO14.......... 100 E7
Comfrey Cl *HORN* PO08 .... 64 D3
  ROMY SO51 .... 35 H1
Comines Wy *HEND* SO30 .... 57 H6
Comley HI *HAV* PO09.......... 83 K6
Commercial Pl *PSEA* PO01 .... 18 D2
Commercial Rd *PSEA* PO01 .... 18 C3
  PSEA PO01 .... 18 D1
  TOTT SO40 .... 53 F5
  WSHM SO15.......... 4 F8
Commercial St *WEND* SO18 .... 7 J5
Common Barn La
  LSOL/BMARY PO13 .... 131 G1
Common Cl *CHFD* SO53 .... 37 K2
Common Gdns *CHFD* SO53 .... 37 K2
Common Hill Rd *ROMY* SO51.......... 29 J3
Common La *FHAM/STUB* PO14 .. 95 J6
  WHAM PO17 .... 79 H7
Common Rd *CHFD* SO53 .... 37 K2
  EMRTH PO10.......... 105 J5
Commonside *EMRTH* PO10 .... 104 E1
Common St *PSEA* PO01 .... 18 F2
Compass Cl
  LSOL/BMARY PO13 .... 132 A2
Compass Rd *CHAM* PO6 .... 100 A6
Compton Cl *ELGH* SO50 .... 38 C4
  WINW SO22 .... 24 E5
  HAV PO09.......... 14 E1
Compton Rd *LSOL/BMARY* PO13 .... 131 H2
Compton Rd *NEND* PO02 .... 118 E4
  TOTT SO40 .... 52 D5
  WINC SO23 .... 2 C6
Compton St *SHAM* SO21 .... 33 F1
Compton Wk *SHAM* SO14 .... 5 G8
Conan Rd *NEND* PO02 .... 118 D3
Concorde Wy *FHAM* PO15 .... 95 K1
Condor Av *FHAM/PORC* PO16 .. 98 C6
Condor Cl *ITCH* SO19 .... 10 A4
Conference Dr *HLER* SO31 .... 95 G3
Conford Ct *HAV* PO09 .... 82 E7
Conifer Av *FAWY* SO45 .... 91 G3
  WINW SO22 .... 2 B2
  HORN PO08 .... 82 B3
Conifer Gv *LSOL/BMARY* PO13 .. 115 K3
Conifer Ms *FHAM/PORC* PO16 .. 99 G5
Conifer Rd *ROWN* SO16.......... 42 B7
Conigar Rd *EMRTH* PO10 .... 104 C3
Coniston Av *HSEA* PO3 .... 119 F7
Coniston Gdns *HEND* SO30 .... 58 A7
Coniston Rd *ELGH* SO50 .... 44 C1
  ROWN SO16.......... 53 H4
Connaught Rd *HAV* PO09 .... 15 G4
  NEND PO02 .... 118 C5
Connemara Crs *HLER* SO31.......... 75 G6
Connigar Cl
  LSOL/BMARY PO13 .... 131 K1
Conqueror Wy
  FHAM/STUB PO14.......... 114 E5
Conrad Gdns *FHAM* PO15.......... 75 H5
Consort Rd *ELGH* SO50 .... 38 C5
Constable Cl *GPORT* PO12 .... 133 F7
  ITCH SO19 .... 11 L5
Constable's Ga *WINC* SO23 .... 2 B5
Constantine Av *CHFD* SO53 .... 38 C4
Constantine Cl *CHFD* SO53 .... 38 C4
Convent La *EMRTH* PO10 .... 104 C6
Conway Cl *CHFD* SO53 .... 37 J7
Cooks La *EMRTH* PO10 .... 105 H5
  TOTT SO40 .... 52 B2
Cook St *SHAM* SO14 .... 9 H2
Coombedale *HLER* SO31 .... 95 G4
Coombe Farm Av
  FHAM/PORC PO16 .... 13 H8
Coombe Rd *GPORT* PO12.......... 132 E1
Coombs Cl *HORN* PO08 .... 64 D3

Cooper Gv *FHAM/PORC* PO16 .... 117 G1
Cooper Rd *HSEA* PO3 .... 135 G1
   TOTT SO40 .... 68 B2
Cooper's Cl *WEND* SO18 .... 57 F3
Cooper's La *ITCH* SO19 .... 10 B4
Copeland Rd *ROWN* SO16 .... 53 J3
Copinger Cl *TOTT* SO40 .... 52 B6 🔟
Copnor Rd *NEND* PO2 .... 118 E3
Copper Beech Dr *CHAM* PO6 .. 101 K6 🔟
Copperfield Rd *ROWN* SO16 ...... 43 H6
Copperfields *TOTT* SO40 .... 52 A5
Copper St *SSEA* PO5 .... 18 B7
Coppice Cl *WINW* SO22 .... 21 F6
Coppice Hl *BPWT* SO32 .... 48 D4
Coppice Rd *TOTT* SO40 .... 52 B2
The Coppice *HORN* PO8 .... 64 B6
   LSOL/BMARY PO13 .... 116 A5 🔟
Coppice Vw *FHAM* PO15 .... 12 A2
Coppins Gv *FHAM/PORC* 117 F1
Copse Cl *NBAD* SO52 .... 36 A6
   RWIN SO21 .... 33 F5
   TOTT SO40 .... 52 E6
   WVILLE PO7 .... 101 J4
Copse La *HISD* PO11 .... 121 H7
   HLER SO31 .... 93 J4
   LSOL/BMARY PO13 .... 116 A6
   ROWN SO16 .... 43 G2
Copse Rd *WEND* SO18 .... 56 C2
The Copse *CHFD* SO53 .... 38 B5
   FHAM PO15 .... 96 E2
Copse Vw *ITCH* SO19 .... 57 H7
Copsewood Rd *FAWY* SO45 .... 91 G3
   TOTT SO40 .... 68 B2
   WEND SO18 .... 56 B2
Copsey Cl *CHAM* PO6 .... 101 J6
Copsey Gv *CHAM* PO6 .... 101 J7
Copthorne La *FAWY* SO45 .... 110 E4
Copythorne Crs *TOTT* SO40 .... 51 F2
Copythorn Rd *NEND* PO2 .... 118 E6
Coracle Cl *HLER* SO31 .... 94 E5
Coral Cl *FHAM/PORC* PO16 .... 117 F1
Coralin Gv *WVILLE* PO7 .... 82 C4
Coram Cl *WINC* SO23 .... 21 K5 🔟
Corbett Rd *WVILLE* PO7 .... 81 J7
Corbiere Cl *ROWN* SO16 .... 53 K1
Corbould Rd *FAWY* SO45 .... 91 G6 🔟
Corby Crs *HSEA* PO3 .... 119 G3
Cordelia Cl *FAWY* SO45 .... 90 E3
Corfe Cl *FHAM/STUB* PO14 ..... 114 B5
Corhampton Crs *HAV* PO9 .... 102 C2
Coriander Dr *TOTT* SO40 .... 52 A5
Coriander Wy *FHAM* PO15 .... 75 J5
Corinna Gdns *FAWY* SO45 .... 90 D3
Corinthian Rd *CHFD* SO53 .... 38 B3
Cork La *TOTT* SO40 .... 70 A2
Cormorant Cl
   FHAM/PORC PO16 .... 98 C6 🔟
Cormorant Dr *FAWY* SO45 .... 91 J4
Cornaway La *FHAM/PORC* PO16.. 98 E7
Cornbrook Gv *HORN* PO8 .... 82 D4
Cornelius Dr *WVILLE* PO7 .... 82 C4
Cornel Rd *ITCH* SO19 .... 6 E9
Corner Md *WVILLE* PO7 .... 80 E1
Cornes Cl *WINW* SO22 .... 21 G7
Cornfield *FHAM/PORC* PO16 ...... 97 J2
Cornfield Cl *NBAD* SO52 .... 37 G4
Cornfield Rd
   LSOL/BMARY PO13 .... 131 G2
Cornflower Cl *HLER* SO31 .... 94 D4
Cornforth Rd *TOTT* SO40 .... 52 B5
Corn Market *ROMY* SO51 .... 34 D3 🔟
Cornmill St *PSEA* PO1 .... 18 D1 🔟
Cornwall Crs *WEND* SO18 .... 56 C2
Cornwall Cl *CHFD* SO53 .... 37 K7
   PSEA PO1 .... 19 C4
   WEND SO18 .... 56 C2
Cornwell Cl *LSOL/BMARY* PO13 .. 132 A1
   NEND PO2 .... 118 A5
Coronado Rd *GPORT* PO12 .... 16 A1
Coronation Pde *HLER* SO31 .... 93 H3 🔟
Coronation Rd *BPWT* SO32 .... 49 J6 🔟
   HISD PO11 .... 138 B7
Corsair Dr *FAWY* SO45 .... 90 E4
Cortina Wy *HEND* SO30 .... 58 B7
Cort Wy *FHAM* PO15 .... 96 D2
Corvette Av *HLER* SO31 .... 94 E5
Cosford Cl *ELGH* SO50 .... 45 K1 🔟
Cosham Park Av *CHAM* PO6 ..... 100 E7
Cossack Gn *SHAM* SO14 .... 9 H1
Cossack La *WINC* SO23 .... 2 F1
Cosworth Dr *FAWY* SO45 .... 90 E3
Cotsalls *ELGH* SO50 .... 46 B2
Cotswold Cl *FAWY* SO45 .... 90 E3 🔟
   HAV PO9 .... 83 F7 🔟
Cotswold Rd *ROWN* SO16 .... 54 A4
Cottage Cl *WVILLE* PO7 .... 80 E4
Cottage Gv *GPORT* PO12 .... 16 A4
   SSEA PO5 .... 18 D6
Cottage Vw *PSEA* PO1 .... 18 E3
Cottes Wy *FHAM/STUB* PO14 .. 114 B6
Cottesway East
   FHAM/STUB PO14. .... 114 B6
Cotton Cl *ELGH* SO50 .... 39 H7
Cotton Dr *EMRTH* PO10 .... 104 B3
Cotwell Av *HORN* PO8 .... 82 C1
Coulmere Rd *GPORT* PO12 .... 132 D2
Coulsdon Rd *HEND* SO30 .... 58 B6
Coultas Rd *CHFD* SO53 .... 32 B7
Country Vw *FHAM/STUB* PO14 .. 114 C4
County Gdns *FHAM/STUB* PO14 .. 96 D6
Course Park Crs
   FHAM/STUB PO14. .... 95 H4
Court Barn La
   LSOL/BMARY PO13 .... 131 G1
Court Cl *CHAM* PO6 .... 101 E7
   ITCH SO19 .... 7 J6
   TOTT SO40 .... 52 B2
Courtenay Rd *WINC* SO23 ...... 21 K5 🔟
Court House Rd *FAWY* SO45 ... 91 H2 🔟
Courtland Gdns *ROWN* SO16 ..... 43 J6
Court La *CHAM* PO6 .... 101 E7
Court Md *CHAM* PO6 .... 101 G2 🔟
Courtmount Gv *CHAM* PO6 ...... 101 F6
Court Rd *LSOL/BMARY* PO13 ... 131 F1
   WINC SO23 .... 22 B1
   WSHM SO15 .... 4 E4
Court Royal Ms *WSHM* SO15 .... 4 E4
Cousins Gv *ENEY* PO4 .... 135 F6
Coventry Rd *WSHM* SO15 .... 4 E6

Coverack Wy *CHAM* PO6 .... 100 A7
Covert Gv *WVILLE* PO7 .... 102 B1
The Covert *ROMY* SO51 .... 35 G4
Covington Rd *EMRTH* PO10...... 104 E1
Cowan Rd *WVILLE* PO7 .... 101 J1
Coward Rd *GPORT* PO12 .... 132 C6
Cowdray Cl *ELGH* SO50 .... 45 J1 🔟
   ROWN SO16 .... 42 C7
Cowdray Pk *FHAM/STUB* PO14.. 114 B5
Cowes La *HLER* SO31 .... 112 C1
Cow La *CHAM* PO6 .... 100 C1
   FHAM/PORC PO16 .... 99 H7
Cowley Rd *ROWN* SO16 .... 53 K2
Cowleys La *BROC* SO42 .... 109 F7
Cowper Rd *ITCH* SO19 .... 57 G6
   PSEA PO1 .... 134 D7 🔟
Cowslip Cl *HLER* SO31 .... 94 D5
   LSOL/BMARY PO13 .... 115 K5
Cox Dl *FHAM/STUB* PO14 .... 95 H5
Coxford Cl *ROWN* SO16 .... 54 B2
Coxford Dro *ROWN* SO16 .... 54 A2
Coxford Rd *ROWN* SO16 .... 54 A2
Cox Rw *CHFD* SO53 .... 38 A7
Cox's Dr *ITCH* SO19 .... 11 J6
Coxs Hl *RWIN* SO21 .... 33 K1
Cozens Cl *ITCH* SO19 .... 10 B8
Crabapple Cl *TOTT* SO40 .... 52 B5 🔟
Crabbe Ct *SSEA* PO5 .... 18 D6 🔟
Crabbs Wy *TOTT* SO40 .... 52 A5
Crabden La *HORN* PO8 .... 65 H4
Crableck La *HLER* SO31 .... 94 B1
Crabthorne Farm La
   FHAM/STUB PO14 .... 114 C4 🔟
Crabtree *ROWN* SO16 .... 54 A3 🔟
Crabwood Cl *ROWN* SO16 .... 54 A3
Crabwood Ct *HAV* PO9 .... 82 E6 🔟
Crabwood Dr *HEND* SO30 .... 57 H3
Crabwood Rd *ROWN* SO16 .... 53 K2
Cracknore Hard *TOTT* SO40 ...... 70 D3
Cracknore Hard La
   TOTT SO40 .... 70 D3 🔟
Cracknore Rd *WSHM* SO15 .... 4 A9
Craigwell Rd *WVILLE* PO7 .... 101 J1
Crampmoor La *ROMY* SO51........ 35 J1
Cranberry Cl *TOTT* SO40 .... 70 A4
Cranborne Gdns *CHFD* SO53 ...... 37 J1
Cranborne Rd *CHAM* PO6 .... 101 F5
Cranbourne Cl *WSHM* SO15 .... 4 H3
Cranbourne Dr *RWIN* SO21 .... 32 E6
Cranbourne La *GPORT* PO12 ...... 16 C7
Cranbury Av *SHAM* SO14 .... 5 H6
Cranbury Cl *RWIN* SO21 .... 32 E6
Cranbury Gdns *HLER* SO31 .... 73 J4
Cranbury Pl *SHAM* SO14.............. 5 H6
Cranbury Rd *ELGH* SO50 .... 44 D1
   ITCH SO19 .... 10 F4
Cranbury Ter *SHAM* SO14............. 5 H6
Craneswater Av *ENEY* PO4 ...... 134 D6
Craneswater Ga *ENEY* PO4 .... 134 D7 🔟
Cranesater Pk *ENEY* PO4 .... 134 D6
Cranford Gdns *CHFD* SO53 .... 37 J2
Cranford Wy *PTSW* SO17 .... 55 H2
Cranleigh Av *PSEA* PO1 .... 19 H1 🔟
Cranleigh Rd *FHAM/PORC* PO16.. 98 D7
   HEND SO30 .... 58 B6
   PSEA PO1 .... 19 H1
Cranmer Dr *ROWN* SO16 .... 41 H6
Cranmore *HLER* SO31 .... 73 F6
Cranworth Rd *WINW* SO22 .... 2 F2
Crasswell St *PSEA* PO1 .... 18 D2
Craven Ct *FHAM* PO15 .... 12 B2
Craven Cl *CHFD* SO53 .... 38 A4
Craven St *SHAM* SO14 .... 5 H9 🔟
Crawford Cl *ROWN* SO16 .... 41 J6
Crawford Dr *FHAM/PORC* PO16 .. 12 E1
Crawley Av *HAV* PO9 .... 83 H7
Crawte Av *FAWY* SO45 .... 110 A5
Credenhill Rd *CHAM* PO6 .... 100 B5
Creedy Gdns *WEND* SO18 ...... 56 D1 🔟
Creek End *EMRTH* PO10 .... 104 C7
Creek Rd *GPORT* PO12 .... 16 C5
   HISD PO11 .... 138 A6
Creighton Rd *WSHM* SO15 .... 54 A6
Cremyll Cl *FHAM/STUB* PO14 ... 114 D5
Crescent Cl *WINW* SO22 .... 24 E4
Crescent Rd *FHAM/PORC* PO16.. 13 H6
   GPORT PO12 .... 132 D7
   HLER SO31 .... 94 E3
   NBAD SO52 .... 36 A5
The Crescent *BPWT* SO32 .... 47 H1
   ELGH SO50 .... 38 D6
   EMRTH PO10 .... 105 G6
   HLER SO31 .... 72 E7
   ITCH SO19 .... 11 G5
   ROMY SO51 .... 35 G2
   RWIN SO21 .... 33 K3
   TOTT SO40 .... 67 H2
   WVILLE PO7 .... 101 H2 🔟
Cressey Rd *ROMY* SO51 .... 34 E3
Cressy Rd *NEND* PO2 .... 134 C1
Crest Cl *FHAM/PORC* PO16 .... 98 A5
Crestland Cl *HORN* PO8 .... 82 B2
The Crest *WVILLE* PO7 .... 101 H4
Crest Wy *ITCH* SO19 .... 11 M2
Crete La *FAWY* SO45 .... 91 G5
Crete Rd *FAWY* SO45 .... 91 G6
Cricket Dr *HORN* PO8 .... 64 D6
Cricklemede *BPWT* SO32 .... 48 E4
Cricklewood Cl *BPWT* SO32 .... 48 E4 🔟
Crigdon Cl *ROWN* SO16 .... 53 K4
Crinoline Gdns *ENEY* PO4 .... 135 G4
Cripple Gate La *BROC* SO42 ..... 125 J3
Crispin Cl *ELGH* SO50 .... 46 B5
   HLER SO31 .... 95 G2
Crispstead La *WINC* SO23 .... 25 J3
Crisspyn Cl *HORN* PO8 .... 64 C6
Crockford Br *LYMN* SO41 .... 124 C6
Crockford Rd *EMRTH* PO10 ...... 104 C4
Croftlands Av
   FHAM/STUB PO14 .... 114 C4
Croft La *HISD* PO11 .... 121 H6
Crofton Av *LSOL/BMARY* PO13 .. 114 D7
Crofton Cl *PTSW* SO17 .... 55 H3 🔟
   WVILLE PO7 .... 101 H1
Crofton La *FHAM/STUB* PO14 ... 114 C6
Crofton Rd *ENEY* PO4 .... 135 G3
   NEND PO2 .... 118 D5
Crofton Wy *BPWT* SO32 .... 49 H6 🔟

Croft Rd *NEND* PO2 .... 118 C6 🔟
The Croft *CHFD* SO53 .... 37 K7 🔟
   FHAM/STUB PO14. .... 114 D3
   TOTT SO40 .... 52 B2
Cromarty Av *ENEY* PO4 .... 135 G4
Cromarty Cl *FHAM/STUB* PO14 .. 114 C4
Cromarty Rd *ROWN* SO16 .... 41 K6
Crombie Cl *HORN* PO8 .... 82 A1
Cromer Rd *CHAM* PO6 .... 100 C5
   ROWN SO16 .... 41 K6
Cromhall Cl *FHAM/STUB* PO14 .. 96 D6 🔟
Crompton Wy *FHAM* PO15 .... 95 H1
Cromwell Rd *ENEY* PO4 .... 135 G4
   WINW SO22 .... 25 G2
   WSHM SO15 .... 4 E5
Crondall Av *HAV* PO9 .... 83 F7
Crooked Hays Cl *TOTT* SO40 .. 70 A4 🔟
Crooked Walk La *WHAM* PO17 .. 99 H3
Crookham Cl *HAV* PO9 .... 102 D2 🔟
Crookham Rd *ITCH* SO19 .... 10 F9
Crookhorn La *WVILLE* PO7 .... 101 K5
Crossbill Cl *HORN* PO8 .... 64 B5
Crosshouse Rd *SHAM* SO14 .... 9 L4
Cross Keys Pas *WINC* SO23 .... 2 F5 🔟
Crossland Cl *GPORT* PO12 .... 16 C8
Crossland Dr *HAV* PO9 .... 15 J1
Cross La *HORN* PO8 .... 64 B7
Cross Rd *ITCH* SO19 .... 6 C5
   LSOL/BMARY PO13 .... 131 H4
Cross St *BPWT* SO32 .... 48 D3
   PSEA PO1 .... 17 M3
   SSEA PO5 .... 18 E5 🔟
   WINC SO23 .... 2 D4
Cross Wy *HAV* PO9 .... 14 C3
   RWIN SO21 .... 33 G4
The Crossways *GPORT* PO12 ..... 16 A2
The Crossway
   FHAM/PORC PO16 .... 99 F6
Crosswell Cl *ITCH* SO19 .... 7 L9
Croucher's Cft *WINW* SO22 .... 20 E6
Crouch La *HORN* PO8 .... 64 B5
Crowder Ter *WINW* SO22 .... 2 C5
Crown Cl *WVILLE* PO7 .... 101 K5
Crown St *PSEA* PO1 .... 18 F1
   WSHM SO15 .... 54 C4
Crowsbury Cl *EMRTH* PO10 ...... 104 B3
Crows Nest La *BPWT* SO32 .... 58 E5
Crowsport *HLER* SO31 .... 93 K3
Crowther Cl *ITCH* SO19 .... 11 M1
Croydon Cl *ROWN* SO16 .... 42 B7
Crummock Rd *CHFD* SO53 .... 37 H5
Crusader Rd *HEND* SO30 .... 58 C7
Crusaders Wy *NBAD* SO52 .... 37 G4
Crystal Wy *WVILLE* PO7 .... 82 C5
Cuckmere La *ROWN* SO16 .... 53 J4
Cuckoo Bushes La *CHFD* SO53 .. 37 J2
Cuckoo La *FHAM/STUB* PO14 ... 114 C3
Cudworth Md *HEND* SO30 .... 58 C3
Culford Av *TOTT* SO40 .... 52 E6
Culford Wy *TOTT* SO40 .... 52 E6
Culloden Cl *FHAM* PO15 .... 12 D3
Culloden Rd *FHAM/STUB* PO14 .. 115 G1
Culver Cl *HLER* SO31 .... 73 F6 🔟
Culver Cl *ROWN* SO16 .... 53 J2
Culver Dr *HISD* PO11 .... 137 K7
Culver Rd *ENEY* PO4 .... 135 F6
   WINC SO23 .... 2 D7
Culverwell Gdns *WINC* SO23 ...... 2 D6
Culvery Gdns *WEND* SO18 .... 56 D2
Cumberland Av *CHFD* SO53 .... 38 B5
   EMRTH PO10 .... 104 B2
Cumberland Pl *WSHM* SO15 .... 4 E8
Cumberland St *SSEA* PO5 .... 19 G4 🔟
Cumberland St *PSEA* PO1 .... 17 M2
   SHAM SO14 .... 9 J1
Cumberland Wy *FAWY* SO45 ...... 90 E3
Cumber Rd *HLER* SO31 .... 94 D3
Cumbrian Wy *ROWN* SO16 .... 53 K4
Cunard Av *WSHM* SO15 .... 54 D4
Cunard Rd *SHAM* SO14 .... 9 H6
Cunliffe Cl *SELS* SP20 .... 139 K6
Cunningham Av *BPWT* SO32 .... 48 E3 🔟
Cunningham Crs *ITCH* SO19 .... 11 H2
Cunningham Dr *HLER* SO31 .... 95 F2
   LSOL/BMARY PO13 .... 116 A4
   WVILLE PO7 .... 101 J1
Cupernham Cl *ROMY* SO51 .... 35 F2
Cupernham La *ROMY* SO51 .... 29 F6
Curdridge Cl *HAV* PO9 .... 103 H1 🔟
Curdridge La *BPWT* SO32 .... 60 B2
Curlew Cl *EMRTH* PO10 .... 104 B6
   ROWN SO16 .... 42 C6
Curlew Dr *FAWY* SO45 .... 91 J4
   FHAM/PORC PO16 .... 98 C6
Curlew Gdns *HORN* PO8 .... 82 A1
Curtis Md *NEND* PO2 .... 118 E3
Curtiss Gdns *GPORT* PO12 ...... 132 C4
The Curve *HORN* PO8 .... 64 A6
   LSOL/BMARY PO13 .... 115 J5
Curzon Howe Rd *PSEA* PO1 ...... 17 M3
Curzon Rd *WVILLE* PO7 .... 81 K6
Custards Rd *LYND* SO43 .... 66 C7
Cutbush La *WEND* SO18 .... 7 J2
Cuthbert Rd *PSEA* PO1 .... 19 J2
Cutlers La *FHAM/STUB* PO14 ... 114 D4
Cutter Av *HLER* SO31 .... 94 D5
Cut Throat La *BPWT* SO32 .... 49 K5
Cygnet Ct *FHAM/PORC* PO16 .. 98 C6 🔟
Cygnet Cl *CHAM* PO6 .... 102 A7
Cygnus Gdns *FAWY* SO45 .... 90 D3
Dene Cl *HLER* SO31 .... 94 D2
   ROWN SO16 .... 43 G4
Dene Hollow *CHAM* PO6 .... 101 J6
Dene Rd *TOTT* SO40 .... 68 B3
Dene Wy *TOTT* SO40 .... 68 B3
Denewulf Cl *BPWT* SO32 .... 48 D3 🔟
Cygnus Av *ITCH* SO19 .... 6 F8
Cypress Crs *HORN* PO8 .... 64 B5
Cypress Gdns *HEND* SO30 .... 59 F5
   TOTT SO40 .... 52 B5 🔟
Cyprus Rd *FHAM/STUB* PO14 .... 95 H5
   NEND PO2 .... 118 D7

Daisy Rd *ROWN* SO16 .... 43 K7
Dale Dr *LSOL/BMARY* PO13 ...... 115 J2
Dale Rd *FAWY* SO45 .... 91 G3
   FHAM/STUB PO14. .... 114 E4
   NEND PO2 .... 54 D2
Dales Wy *TOTT* SO40 .... 52 A4
The Dale *WVILLE* PO7 .... 101 H4
Dale Valley Cl *ROWN* SO16 .... 54 D1
Dale Valley Gdns *ROWN* SO16 ... 54 D1
Dale Valley Rd *ROWN* SO16 .... 54 D1
Dalewood Rd *FHAM* PO15 .... 12 B5
Dallington Cl
   FHAM/STUB PO14 .... 114 D6 🔟
Dalmally Gdns *WEND* SO18 .... 6 D2
Damask Gdns *WVILLE* PO7 .... 82 C4
Damen Cl *HEND* SO30 .... 58 A7
Dampier Cl *LSOL/BMARY* PO13 .. 131 K1
Damson Dr *CHFD* SO53 .... 37 K7
Danbury Ct *EMRTH* PO10.......... 104 D4
Dances Wy *HISD* PO11 .... 137 F4
Dandelion Cl
   LSOL/BMARY PO13 .... 115 J5 🔟
Dando Rd *WVILLE* PO7 .... 83 F7 🔟
Danebury Cl *HAV* PO9 .... 83 F7 🔟
Danebury Gdns *CHFD* SO53 .... 37 H6 🔟
Danebury Wy *ROWN* SO16 .... 53 J1
Dane Cl *FAWY* SO45 .... 110 C6
Danesbrook La *WVILLE* PO7 ... 82 B6 🔟
Danes Rd *FHAM/PORC* PO16 ..... 98 E5
   WINC SO23 .... 2 E1
Dapple Pl *TOTT* SO40 .... 70 B4
Dark La *FAWY* SO45 .... 110 C6
Darlington Gdns *WSHM* SO15 ...... 4 A1
Darlington Rd *ENEY* PO4 .... 19 G7
Darren Cl *FHAM/STUB* PO14 .... 114 E3
Dartington Rd *ELGH* SO50 .... 39 G5
Dartmouth Rd *HSEA* PO3 .... 119 F5
Dart Rd *WEND* SO18 .... 56 E1
Darwin Rd *ELGH* SO50 .... 38 E6
   WSHM SO15. .... 4 E5
Darwin Wy *LSOL/BMARY* PO13 .. 132 A2
Daulston Rd *PSEA* PO1 .... 134 D1
Davenport
   LSOL/BMARY PO13 .... 131 K2 🔟
Daventry La *HSEA* PO3 .... 119 H3
D Av *FAWY* SO45. .... 110 A1
Davis Cl *LSOL/BMARY* PO13 ... 115 K7 🔟
Daw La *HISD* PO11 .... 121 G7
Dawlish Av *WSHM* SO15 .... 4 A2
Dawnay Cl *ROWN* SO16 .... 44 A4
Dawn Gdns *WINW* SO22 .... 25 F2
Dawson Rd *ITCH* SO19 .... 11 L5
Dayrell Cl *TOTT* SO40 .... 52 A3
Dayshes Cl *LSOL/BMARY* PO13 .. 115 J4
Dayslondon Rd *WVILLE* PO7 ..... 101 J1
Deacon Cl *ITCH* SO19 .... 7 G8
Deacon Crs *ITCH* SO19 .... 7 G7
Deacon Rd *HLER* SO31 .... 95 G3
   ITCH SO19 .... 7 H8
Deal Cl *FHAM/STUB* PO14 .... 114 D3
Deal Rd *CHAM* PO6 .... 100 D5
Dean Cl *WINW* SO22 .... 21 F1
Dean Rd *HEND* SO30 .... 103 J1 🔟
Deane Ct *HAV* PO9 .... 103 J1 🔟
Deane Down Dro *WINW* SO22 .... 20 E3
The Deanery *CHFD* SO53 .... 37 J2
Deane's Park Rd
   FHAM/PORC PO16 .... 98 A5
Deanfield Cl *HLER* SO31 .... 93 J4
Dean La *RWIN* SO21 .... 20 B1
Dean Rd *CHAM* PO6 .... 100 E7
   ELGH SO50 .... 46 A2
   HLER SO31 .... 7 H5
Deans Ga *FHAM/STUB* PO14 .... 114 D6
Dean St *PSEA* PO1 .... 17 M4 🔟
Deanswood Dr *WVILLE* PO7 ...... 81 K4
Dearing Cl *LYND* SO43 .... 86 C1
Dee Cl *CHFD* SO53 .... 37 H5
Deeping Cl *ITCH* SO19 .... 10 F8
Deeping Ga *WVILLE* PO7 .... 82 B6
Deerhurst Cl *TOTT* SO40 .... 52 C6
Deerhurst Crs *CHAM* PO6 .... 99 K5
Deer Leap *FHAM* PO15 .... 96 E1 🔟
Deerleap La *TOTT* SO40 .... 68 C4
Deerleap Wy *FAWY* SO45 .... 91 H3
Defender Rd *ITCH* SO19 .... 10 B3
De Grouchy La *PTSW* SO17 .... 55 H3
Delamere Rd *ENEY* PO4 .... 19 H7
Delft Cl *HLER* SO31 .... 94 E3
Delft Gdns *WVILLE* PO7 .... 81 J3
De Lisle Cl *NEND* PO2 .... 118 B4
Delius Av *ITCH* SO19 .... 73 G2
Dell Cl *CHAM* PO6 .... 101 G4
   ELGH SO50 .... 46 B2
Dellcrest Pth *CHAM* PO6 .... 101 G5
Dellfield Cl *CHAM* PO6 .... 99 K5 🔟
Dell Piece East *HORN* PO8 .... 64 E7
Dell Piece West *HORN* PO8 .... 64 D7
Dell Quay Cl *FHAM/STUB* PO14 .. 115 H5
Dell Rd *WEND* SO18 .... 56 C2
   WINC SO23 .... 3 J1
The Dell *FHAM/PORC* PO16 .... 98 A5
   HAV PO9 .... 102 C4
Delme Dr *FHAM/PORC* PO16 ..... 98 A4
Delphi Wy *WVILLE* PO7 .... 102 A4
Dempsey Cl *ITCH* SO19 .... 11 J2
Denbigh Cl *WSHM* SO15 .... 55 C5
   TOTT SO40 .... 52 C7
Denbigh Dr *FHAM/PORC* PO16 .. 12 F3
Denbigh Gdns *ROWN* SO16 .... 43 G7
Dene Cl *HLER* SO31 .... 94 D2
   ROWN SO16 .... 43 G4
Dene Hollow *CHAM* PO6 .... 101 J6
Dene Rd *TOTT* SO40 .... 68 B3
Dene Wy *TOTT* SO40 .... 68 B3
Denewulf Cl *BPWT* SO32 .... 48 D3 🔟
Denham Cl *FHAM/STUB* PO14 .. 114 C5
   WINC SO23 .... 21 J5
Denham Gdns *HLER* SO31 .... 92 E1
Denhill Cl *HISD* PO11 .... 137 F3
Denmead Rd *WEND* SO18 .... 7 J3
Denny Cl *FAWY* SO45 .... 110 E4
Denville Av *FHAM/PORC* PO16 .. 117 F5
Denville Cl *CHAM* PO6 .... 100 A6
Denvilles Cl *HAV* PO9 .... 15 J2
Denzil Av *HLER* SO31 .... 73 F7
   SHAM SO14 .... 5 H6
Depedene Cl *FAWY* SO45 .... 109 J3

Derby Rd *ELGH* SO50 .... 44 C1
   NEND PO2 .... 118 C6
   SHAM SO14 .... 5 J8
Deridene Ct *TOTT* SO40 .... 52 C2
Derlyn Rd *FHAM/PORC* PO16 .... 13 H5
Derwent Cl
   FHAM/STUB PO14 .... 114 E3
   HORN PO8 .... 64 D2
   WEND SO18 .... 56 E3
Derwent Dr *TOTT* SO40 .... 52 A4
Derwent Rd
   LSOL/BMARY PO13 .... 131 G3
   ROWN SO16 .... 53 K1
Desborough Cl *CHAM* PO6 ...... 99 K5 🔟
Desborough Rd *ELGH* SO50 .... 44 D1
Devenish Rd *WINW* SO22 .... 21 G4
Deverell Pl *WVILLE* PO7 .... 101 H3
Devine Gdns *ELGH* SO50 .... 45 H1 🔟
Devon Dr *CHFD* SO53 .... 37 K7
Devon Rd *HSEA* PO3 .... 119 F4
Devonshire Av *ENEY* PO4 .... 19 J6 🔟
   HLER SO31 .... 73 J5 🔟
   HLER SO31 .... 73 K3 🔟
Devonshire Rd *WSHM* SO15 .... 4 E5
Devonshire Sq *ENEY* PO4 .... 19 J6 🔟
Devonshire Wy
   FHAM/STUB PO14. .... 96 D6
Dew La *ELGH* SO50 .... 38 C7
Diamond St *SSEA* PO5 .... 18 B7 🔟
Diana Cl *EMRTH* PO10 .... 104 B2
   GPORT PO12 .... 132 B4
Dibble Dr *NBAD* SO52 .... 36 A7
Dibden Cl *HAV* PO9 .... 102 D2 🔟
Dibden Lodge Cl *FAWY* SO45 ..... 91 G1
Dibles Rd *HLER* SO31 .... 94 C5
Dickens Cl *NEND* PO2 .... 134 C1 🔟
Dickens Dell *TOTT* SO40 .... 52 A5
Dickens Dr *HLER* SO31 .... 75 H5
Dickson Pl *WHAM* PO17 .... 77 H1
Didcot Rd *WSHM* SO15 .... 54 D3 🔟
Dieppe Crs *NEND* PO2 .... 118 D3
Dieppe Gdns *GPORT* PO12 ...... 132 C4 🔟
Diligence Cl *HLER* SO31 .... 73 K4
Dimond Cl *WEND* SO18 .... 56 B3
Dimond Hl *WEND* SO18 .... 56 B1
Dimond Rd *WEND* SO18 .... 56 B2
Dingle Wy *HLER* SO31 .... 95 F2
Discovery Cl
   FHAM/STUB PO14 .... 114 D2 🔟
Ditcham Crs *HAV* PO9 .... 103 F3
Ditton Cl *FHAM/STUB* PO14 ..... 114 D4
Dockenfield Cl *HAV* PO9 .... 102 D2 🔟
Dock La *BROC* SO42 .... 108 D7
Dodds La *BPWT* SO32 .... 49 J6
Dodwell La *HLER* SO31 .... 74 A2
Dogkennel La *WVILLE* PO7 .... 63 G1
Dogwood Dell *WVILLE* PO7 .... 102 A1 🔟
Dolman Rd *GPORT* PO12 .... 16 D7
Dolphin Cl *ELGH* SO50 .... 45 J1
Dolphin Ct
   FHAM/STUB PO14 .... 114 C3 🔟
Dolphin Crs *GPORT* PO12 ...... 16 B5 🔟
Dolphin Hl *RWIN* SO21 .... 33 K4
Dolphin Wy *GPORT* PO12 .... 133 G7
Dolton Rd *ROWN* SO16 .... 54 A1
Dome Aly *WINC* SO23 .... 2 E6
Domum Rd *NEND* PO2 .... 118 E5
   WINC SO23 .... 3 G7
Domvilles Ap *NEND* PO2 .... 118 A6
Donaldson Rd *CHAM* PO6 .... 118 E1
Doncaster Rd *ELGH* SO50 .... 44 D3
Donigers Dell *BPWT* SO32 .... 48 E5
Donnelly St *GPORT* PO12 .... 132 D2
Donnington Dr *CHFD* SO53 .... 37 H7
Donnington Gv *PTSW* SO17 .... 55 J2
Dorcas Cl *WVILLE* PO7 .... 82 B4
Dore Av *FHAM/PORC* PO16 .... 98 E6
Dores La *ROMY* SO51 .... 30 D1
Doric Cl *CHFD* SO53 .... 38 C3
Dorking Crs *CHAM* PO6 .... 100 E7
Dorland Gdns *TOTT* SO40 .... 52 C6
Dormington Rd *CHAM* PO6 ...... 100 B5
Dormy Cl *HLER* SO31 .... 94 C3
Dormy Wy *LSOL/BMARY* PO13 .. 115 J2
Dormere La *WVILLE* PO7 .... 82 B6 🔟
Dorothy Dymond St
   PSEA PO1 .... 18 C4 🔟
Dorrien Rd *GPORT* PO12.......... 132 E1
Dorrita Av *HORN* PO8 .... 82 B1
Dorrita Cl *ENEY* PO4 .... 134 E6
The Dorrits *TOTT* SO40 .... 52 A5
Dorset Cl *HORN* PO8 .... 64 C6
Dorset Ct *CHFD* SO53 .... 37 K7 🔟
Dorset St *SHAM* SO14 .... 5 G6
Dorstone Rd *CHAM* PO6 .... 100 B5 🔟
Douglas Crs *ITCH* SO19 .... 7 M6
Douglas Gdns *HAV* PO9 .... 103 H2 🔟
Douglas Rd *PSEA* PO1 .... 134 E1
Douglas Wy *FAWY* SO45 .... 91 F2
Dove Cl *HORN* PO8 .... 82 A1
Dove Dl *ELGH* SO50 .... 45 J1
Dove Gdns *HLER* SO31 .... 95 G1 🔟
Dover Cl *FHAM/STUB* PO14 ...... 114 C4
Dover Ct *HISD* PO11 .... 137 F3
Dovercourt Rd *CHAM* PO6 .... 119 F1
Dover Rd *HSEA* PO3 .... 119 F7
Dover St *SHAM* SO14 .... 5 H5
Dowds Cl *HEND* SO30 .... 58 A4
Down End *CHAM* PO6 .... 101 H5
Down End Rd *CHAM* PO6 .... 101 H5
Downend Rd *FHAM/PORC* PO6 .. 98 C5
Down Farm Pl *HORN* PO8 .... 64 D3 🔟
Downham Cl *HORN* PO8 .... 82 A2
Downland Cl *HEND* SO30 .... 58 E5
   HLER SO31 .... 95 F2
Downland Pl *HEND* SO30 .... 74 A1
Downlands Rd *WINW* SO22 .... 24 E4
Downley Rd *HAV* PO9 .... 103 J2
Down Rd *HORN* PO8 .... 64 C3
Downs Cl *WVILLE* PO7 .... 102 A3
Downscroft Gdns *HEND* SO30 .. 58 A4 🔟
   HEND SO30 .... 58 A5 🔟
Downside *LSOL/BMARY* PO13 .. 116 A5
Downside Av *ITCH* SO19 .... 7 G6
Downside Rd *WINW* SO22 .... 20 E5
   WVILLE PO7 .... 101 H3 🔟
Down's Park Av *TOTT* SO40 .... 53 F6
Down's Park Crs *TOTT* SO40 ...... 53 F6

D

Daffodil Rd *ROWN* SO16.............. 43 K7
Dahlia Rd *ROWN* SO16............ 43 H7 🔟
Daintree Cl *ITCH* SO19 .... 73 G2
Dairy La *ROWN* SO16................. 41 F7
Dairymoor *WHAM* SO17 .... 77 H1
Daisy La *GPORT* PO12 .... 132 D4
   HLER SO31 .... 95 G3
Daisy Md *WVILLE* PO7 .... 82 B7

Down's Park Rd *TOTT* SO40........ 53 F6
The Downsway
  FHAM/PORC PO16 .... 99 J5
Downton Rd *WEND* SO18............ 56 C2
Downwood Cl *FAWY* SO45 .. 90 D4 ⓵
Downwood Wy *HORN* PO8 ...... 64 D3
Doyle Av *NEND* PO2 .... 118 D3
Doyle Cl *NEND* PO2 .... 118 D3
Doyle Ct *ITCH* SO19 .... 10 F8
Dragoon Cl *ITCH* SO19 .... 11 L2
Drake Cl *HLER* SO31 .... 95 G1
  TOTT SO40 .... 70 A3
Drake Rd *ELGH* SO50 .... 39 H6
  LSOL/BMARY PO13 .... 130 E1
Drakes Cl *FAWY* SO45 .... 91 G4 ⓵
Draycote Rd *HORN* PO8 .... 64 D1
Drayton Cl *ITCH* SO19 .... 10 F9
Drayton La *CHAM* PO6 .... 101 G5
Drayton Pl *TOTT* SO40 .... 52 C5 ⓵
Drayton Rd *NEND* PO2 .... 118 D6
Drayton St *WINC* SO22 .... 25 F2
Dreadnought Rd
  FHAM/STUB PO14.............. 115 F2
Dresden Dr *HORN* PO8 .... 81 J3
Drift Rd *FHAM/PORC* PO16 ... 13 M3
The Drift *HAV* PO9 .... 83 J4
Driftwood Gdns *ENEY* PO4 .. 135 H6
  TOTT SO40 .... 52 B6 ⓵
Drill Shed Rd *NEND* PO2 .... 118 A6
Drinkwater Cl *ELGH* SO50 ..... 38 C7
The Drive *EMRTH* PO10 .... 105 G6
  FHAM/PORC PO16 .... 13 C5
  HAV PO9 .... 14 E1
  HEND SO30 .... 56 B1
  LSOL/BMARY PO13 .... 115 H5
  TOTT SO40 .... 52 E7
Drove Cl *RWIN* SO21 .... 33 J4
Drove Rd *ITCH* SO19 .... 11 K1
  WHAM PO17 .... 99 K2
The Drove *BPWT* SO32 .... 47 J3
  ELGH SO50 .... 46 C5
  FAWY SO45 .... 110 B6
  HEND SO30 .... 57 J1
  RWIN SO21 .... 33 J4
  TOTT SO40 .... 52 A3
  WEND SO18 .... 7 H5
Droxford Cl *GPORT* PO12 ..... 132 C2
Droxford Rd *BPWT* SO32 ...... 49 K7
Drummond Cl *WINN* SO22 .... 25 H3 ⓵
Drummond Rd *FAWY* SO45 .. 91 H2 ⓵
  HEND SO30 .... 58 B3
  PSEA PO1 .... 18 E1
Drummond Wy *CHFD* SO53 .. 37 J2 ⓶
Dryden Av *CHAM* PO6 .... 99 H5
Dryden Cl *FHAM/PORC* PO16.. 12 F4
  WVILLE PO7 .... 81 J3
Dryden Rd *ITCH* SO19 .... 57 H7
Drysdale Ms *ENEY* PO4 ...... 135 G6 ⓶
Duddon Cl *WEND* SO18.......... 56 E3
Dudleston Heath Dr *HORN* PO8 .. 82 C3
Dudley Rd *HSEA* PO3 .... 135 F1 ⓵
Duffield La *EMRTH* PO10 ...... 105 G3
Dugald Drummond St
  PSEA PO1 .... 18 C4 ⓵
Duisburg Wy *SSEA* PO5 .... 18 A8
Duke Crs *PSEA* PO1 .... 134 C1
Duke Rd *HEND* SO30 .... 58 B1
Dukes Rd *GPORT* PO12 .... 132 D2
  PTSW SO17 .... 5 K3
  SHAM SO14 .... 5 K3
Duke St *SHAM* SO14 .... 9 J3
Dukeswood Dr *FAWY* SO45 .... 91 G3
Dumbarton Cl *NEND* PO2 .... 118 C7 ⓵
Dumbleton Cl *ITCH* SO19 ...... 57 J7
Dummer Ct *HAV* PO9 .... 82 E7
Dummers Rd *ROMY* SO51 ..... 29 J2
Dumpers Dro *ELGH* SO50 ..... 46 C5
Dunbar Cl *ROWN* SO16 .... 42 A6
Dunbar Rd *ENEY* PO4 .... 135 G4
Duncan Cl *ITCH* SO19 .... 10 D8
Duncan Rd *HLER* SO31 .... 95 G1
  SSEA PO5 .... 18 F9
Duncans Dr
  FHAM/STUB PO14.............. 96 C6 ⓵
Dundas Cl *HSEA* PO3 .... 119 G5
Dundas La *HSEA* PO3 .... 119 G4
Dundas Sp *HSEA* PO3 .... 119 C5
Dundee Cl *FHAM* PO15 .... 12 C2
Dundee Rd *PTSW* SO17 .... 5 M1
Dundonald Cl *HISD* PO11 ..... 137 H5
  ITCH SO19 .... 10 A8
Dundridge La *BPWT* SO32 .... 49 F2
Dundry Wy *HEND* SO30 .... 58 B5
Dunhurst Cl *HAV* PO9 .... 103 H3
Dunkeld Rd *GPORT* PO12 .... 132 C1
Dunkirk Cl *ROWN* SO16 .... 42 E7
Dunkirk Rd *ROWN* SO16 .... 42 E7
Dunlin Cl *ENEY* PO4.............. 135 J3
Dunn Cl *ENEY* PO4 .... 135 G5
Dunnings La *NBAD* SO52 .... 35 K5
Dunnock Cl *HAV* PO9 .... 83 J4
Dunsbury Wy *HAV* PO9 .... 103 F1
Dunsmore Cl *SSEA* PO5 .... 18 D6 ⓶
Dunster Cl *ROWN* SO16 .... 42 D6
Dunvegan Dr *ROWN* SO16 .... 42 D6
Durban Cl *ROMY* SO51 .... 35 F1
Durban Rd *PSEA* PO1 .... 134 C1
Durford Ct *HAV* PO9 .... 82 E7 ⓵
Durham Gdns *WVILLE* PO7 .. 102 A1
Durham St *GPORT* PO12 ...... 132 D2
  PSEA PO1 .... 18 D3
Durlands Rd *HORN* PO8 ..... 64 D4 ⓵
Durley Av *HORN* PO8 .... 82 A2
Durley Brook Rd *BPWT* SO32 .. 46 E5
Durley Crs *TOTT* SO40 .... 52 C7
Durley Hall La *BPWT* SO32 .... 47 G2
Durley Rd *ELGH* SO50 .... 46 D4
  GPORT PO12 .... 132 C2
Durley St *BPWT* SO32 .... 47 J4
Durnford Rd *SHAM* SO14 .... 5 J7
Durngate Pl *WINC* SO23 .... 3 G4
Durngate Ter *WINC* SO23 .... 3 G4
Durrants Gdns *HAV* PO9 .... 83 J3
Durrants Rd *HAV* PO9 .... 83 J4
Dursley Crs *CHAM* PO6 .... 100 B6
Dutton La *ELGH* SO50 .... 38 C7
Duttons Rd *ROMY* SO51 .... 34 D2
Dyer Rd *WSHM* SO15 .... 54 D5

Dymoke St *EMRTH* PO10 ..... 104 B2
Dymott Cl *WSHM* SO15.......... 4 A8
Dyram Cl *ELGH* SO50 .... 38 C5
Dysart Av *CHAM* PO6 .... 101 G7
Dyserth Cl *ITCH* SO19 .... 11 J7
Dyson Dr *WINC* SO23 .... 21 K5

E

Eadens La *TOTT* SO40 .... 51 G3
Eagle Av *HORN* PO8 .... 81 J1
Eagle Cl *CHFD* SO53 .... 37 J6
  FHAM/PORC PO16 .... 98 C6 ⓶
Eagle Rd *LSOL/BMARY* PO13 .. 130 E1
Earls Cl *ELGH* SO50 .... 45 K1
Earlsdon St *SSEA* PO5 .... 18 C6 ⓵
Earls Rd *FHAM/PORC* PO16 ... 13 J9
  SHAM SO14 .... 5 H3
Earnley Rd *HISD* PO11 .... 138 C6
East Boldre Rd *BROC* SO42 .. 125 H1
Eastbourne Av *GPORT* PO12 .. 116 C7
  WSHM SO15 .... 4 A2
Eastbourne Rd *HSEA* PO3 .... 119 F7 ⓶
Eastbrook Cl *GPORT* PO12 .. 116 C7 ⓵
  HLER SO31 .... 95 F1
East Cams Cl
  FHAM/PORC PO16 .... 98 C5 ⓶
Eastchurch Cl *ROWN* SO16 ... 42 A7
Eastcliff Cl *LSOL/BMARY* PO13 .. 131 F1
East Cosham Rd *CHAM* PO6 .. 101 G6
Eastcot Cl *FAWY* SO45 .... 109 J4
East Ct *CHAM* PO6 .... 101 G6
Eastcroft Rd *GPORT* PO12 ... 132 D3
East Dr *ELGH* SO50 .... 39 G6
Eastern Av *CHAM* PO6 .... 135 G2
Eastern Pde *ENEY* PO4 .... 134 E7 ⓵
  FHAM/PORC PO16 .... 13 K9
Eastern Rd *CHAM* PO6 .... 119 J1
  ENEY PO4 .... 135 G3
  HAV PO9 .... 15 G3
  HEND SO30 .... 57 G3
  HSEA PO3 .... 135 G2
  NEND PO2 .... 118 A5
Eastern Villas Rd *ENEY* PO4 .. 134 C7 ⓶
Eastern Wy *FHAM/PORC* PO16 .. 13 L6
Eastfield Av *FHAM/STUB* PO14 .. 115 G1
Eastfield Rd *CHAM* PO6 .... 100 A4
  ENEY PO4 .... 19 L7
  PTSW SO17 .... 5 M2
Eastgate St *SHAM* SO14 .... 9 G3
  WINC SO23 .... 3 J3
East HI *WINC* SO23 .... 3 G7
East Hill Cl *FHAM/PORC* PO16 .. 98 A4
East House Av
  FHAM/STUB PO14.............. 114 E5
Eastleigh Rd *ELGH* SO50 .... 46 B2
East Leigh Rd *HAV* PO9 .... 103 K3
East Ldg *FHAM* PO15 .... 96 D5
East Lodge Pk *CHAM* PO6 ... 102 A4
Eastmeare Ct *TOTT* SO40 ..... 52 B6
Eastney Farm Rd *ENEY* PO4 .. 135 H5 ⓵
Eastney Rd *ENEY* PO4 .... 135 G6 ⓶
Eastoke Av *HISD* PO11 .... 138 A7
Easton La *RWIN* SO21 .... 22 C5
  WINC SO23 .... 3 J3
Eastover Rd *HAV* PO9 .... 82 E7
East Park Ter *SHAM* SO14 .... 5 C8
East Rd *FAWY* SO45 .... 92 A6
  WHAM PO17 .... 79 K7
East St *EMRTH* PO10 .... 104 E3
  FHAM/PORC PO16 .... 13 M6
  FHAM/STUB PO14.............. 96 A6
  HAV PO9 .... 14 F5
  PSEA PO1 .... 17 K6
  SHAM SO14 .... 9 G2
  WHAM PO17 .... 62 C1
East Surrey St *PSEA* PO1 ..... 18 D3 ⓶
Eastville Rd *ELGH* SO50 .... 46 B2 ⓶
Eastways *BPWT* SO32 .... 48 D4
Eastwood Cl *HISD* PO11 ...... 137 J4 ⓶
East Woodhay Rd *WINW* SO22 .. 21 G3 ⓶
Eastwood Rd *NEND* PO2 .... 118 D3 ⓶
E Av *FAWY* SO45 .... 110 B2
Ebden Rd *WINC* SO23 .... 3 H3
Ebery Gv *HSEA* PO3 .... 135 G2
Ecton La *HSEA* PO3 .... 119 H4
Edelvale Rd *WEND* SO18 .... 7 J1
Edenbridge Rd *ENEY* PO4 ... 135 G3
Eden Ri *FHAM/PORC* PO16 ... 13 J8
Eden St *PSEA* PO1 .... 18 D2 ⓶
Eden Wk *CHFD* SO53 .... 37 H5
Edgar Crs *FHAM/PORC* PO16 .. 117 G1
Edgar Rd *WINC* SO23 .... 2 C8
Edgecombe Crs
  LSOL/BMARY PO13 .... 115 H5
Edgefield Gv *HORN* PO8 .... 82 C4
Edgehill Rd *WEND* SO18 .... 6 F1
Edgell Rd *EMRTH* PO10 .... 104 C2
Edgerly Gdns *CHAM* PO6 .... 118 C1
Edgeware Rd *ENEY* PO4 .... 19 M4
Edinburgh Rd *PSEA* PO1 ..... 18 C3 ⓵
Edington Cl *BPWT* SO32 ...... 48 C3 ⓶
Edington Rd *WINC* SO23 ...... 21 K5
Edith Haisman Cl *WSHM* SO15 .. 4 A8
Edmund Rd *ENEY* PO4 .... 19 H7
Edmunds Cl *HEND* SO30 .... 58 C7
Edneys La *WVILLE* PO7 .... 63 F7
Edward Av *ELGH* SO50 .... 38 D2
Edward Cl *FAWY* SO45 .... 110 B6 ⓵
Edward Gdns *HAV* PO9 .... 102 D5
Edward Gv *FHAM/PORC* PO16.. 99 H5
Edward Rd *FAWY* SO45.......... 91 H2
  WINC SO23 .... 25 H4
  WSHM SO15 .... 54 C5
Edwards Cl *CHAM* PO6 ...... 100 A3 ⓶
  WVILLE PO7 .... 82 A3
Edwina Cl *ITCH* SO19 .... 6 F7
Edwin Rd
  NBAD SO52 .... 36 B6
Effingham Gdns *ITCH* SO19 ... 11 L1
Egan Cl *NEND* PO2 .... 118 E4
Egbert Rd *WINC* SO23 .... 2 E1
Eglantine Cl *HORN* PO8 .... 82 C1
Eglantine Wk *HORN* PO8 ...... 82 C1
Eight Acres *ROMY* SO51 ...... 35 G3 ⓵
Elaine Gdns *HORN* PO8.......... 64 A7

Elan Cl *WEND* SO18 .... 56 E3
Elcombes Cl *LYND* SO43 .... 86 C1
Elderberry Wy *HORN* PO8 ..... 82 C1
Elder Cl *WINW* SO22 .... 25 F4
  HLER SO31 .... 94 E4 ⓶
  TOTT SO40 .... 70 B4
Elderfield Cl *EMRTH* PO10 ... 104 D3
Elderfield Rd *HAV* PO9 .... 82 E6
Elder Gn *RWIN* SO21 .... 39 K2
Elder Rd *HAV* PO9 .... 15 K1
Eldon Cl *SSEA* PO5 .... 18 C6
Eldridge Gdns *ROMY* SO51 ... 34 E2
Electron Wy *CHFD* SO53 .... 37 K4
Elgar Cl *CHAM* PO6 .... 99 H6 ⓵
  GPORT PO12 .... 132 C6
  ITCH SO19 .... 11 M4
Elgar Rd *ITCH* SO19 .... 11 M4
Elgar Wk *WVILLE* PO7 .... 102 A2 ⓵
  FHAM PO15 .... 12 E3
Elgin Cl *FAWY* SO45 .... 91 H3
Elgin Rd *CHAM* PO6 .... 118 E1
Eling Cl *WINW* SO22 .... 21 G4
Eling Ct *HAV* PO9 .... 82 E7
Eling HI *TOTT* SO40 .... 53 G7
Elizabeth Cl *HEND* SO30 .... 57 G3
  WHAM PO17 .... 77 G1 ⓶
Elizabeth Ct
  FHAM/STUB PO14.............. 97 G7 ⓶
Elizabeth Gdns *ENEY* PO4 ... 134 E6
  FAWY SO45 .... 91 H5
Elizabeth Rd
  FHAM/STUB PO14.............. 114 E5
  WHAM PO17 .... 77 H1
  WVILLE PO7 .... 101 K1
Elizabeth Wy *FHAM/STUB* PO14 .. 48 C4
Elkstone Cl *CHAM* PO6 .... 100 A5
Ellachie Ms *GPORT* PO12 ..... 132 E7 ⓶
Ellachie Rd *GPORT* PO12 ..... 132 E7
Elland Cl *ELGH* SO50 .... 46 B2
Ellanore La *SELS* PO20 .... 139 J5
Elldene Ct *TOTT* SO40 .... 52 D7 ⓵
Ellen Gdns *CHFD* SO53 .... 37 H5
Ellerslie Cl *FHAM/STUB* PO14 .. 114 B6
Ellesmere Orch *EMRTH* PO10 .. 104 E2
Elliot Cl *TOTT* SO40 .... 52 C6
Elliot Ri *HEND* SO30 .... 58 B2
Ellisfield Rd *HAV* PO9 .... 103 F2
Ellis Rd *ITCH* SO19 .... 57 H7
Ellwood Av *ITCH* SO19 .... 57 H7
Ellwood Cl *ITCH* SO19 .... 57 H7
Elm Cl *HISD* PO11 .... 137 H5
Elm Crs *FAWY* SO45 .... 91 H7
Elmdale Cl *HLER* SO31 .... 94 C6
Elmes Dr *WSHM* SO15 .... 54 A5
Elmeswelle Rd *HORN* PO8 .... 64 B6
Elmfield La *HEND* SO30 .... 57 G2
Elm Gv *ELGH* SO50 .... 44 C1
  GPORT PO12 .... 16 B3
  HISD PO11 .... 137 H5
  SSEA PO5 .... 18 D6 ⓵
Elmhurst Rd *FHAM/PORC* PO16 .. 13 J7
  GPORT PO12 .... 16 C5
Elm La *HAV* PO9 .... 14 E4
Elmleigh Rd *HAV* PO9 .... 14 E4
Elmore Av *LSOL/BMARY* PO13 .. 131 G3
Elmore Cl *LSOL/BMARY* PO13 .. 131 G3
Elmore Rd *LSOL/BMARY* PO13 .. 131 G3
Elm Rd *BPWT* SO32 .... 49 F3
  WINW SO22 .... 2 B5
  HAV PO9 .... 15 H6
Elms La *SELS* PO20 .... 139 K6
Elmsleigh Gdns *ROWN* SO16 .. 43 H7
Elmslie Gdns *HLER* SO31 .... 73 J4
Elms Ride *SELS* PO20 .... 139 K7
Elms Rd *FHAM/PORC* PO16 ... 13 J9
Elmstead Gdns *SELS* PO20 ... 139 K6
Elmstead Park Rd *SELS* PO20 .. 139 K6
Elm St *SHAM* SO14 .... 9 K2
Elm Ter *SHAM* SO14 .... 9 K3
Elm Tree Cl *TOTT* SO40 .... 68 A3
Elmtree Gdns *ROMY* SO51 ... 35 H4
Elmtree Rd *CHAM* PO6 .... 101 K6 ⓶
Elmwood Av *WVILLE* PO7 ..... 81 K7
Elmwood Rd *NEND* PO2 ...... 118 D3
Elphinstone Rd *SSEA* PO5 ..... 18 C9
Elsfred Rd *FHAM/STUB* PO14 .. 114 B6
Elson Cl *GPORT* PO12 .... 116 D7
Elson Rd *GPORT* PO12 .... 116 C7
Elstead Gdns *WVILLE* PO7 .. 101 H2
Elstree Rd *ITCH* SO19 .... 6 D9
Elwell Gn *HISD* PO11 .... 137 G5
Emanuel St *NEND* PO2 .... 134 C1
Embley Cl *TOTT* SO40 .... 52 C2
Embsay Rd *HLER* SO31 .... 74 C5
Emerald Cl *ITCH* SO19 .... 11 J7
  WVILLE PO7 .... 82 B6
Emer Cl *NBAD* SO52 .... 36 B5 ⓵
Emmanuel Cl
  FHAM/STUB PO14.............. 95 H4 ⓵
Emmett Rd *ROWN* SO16 .... 42 A6
Emmons Cl *HLER* SO31 .... 93 J5
Empress Rd *LYND* SO43 .... 86 C1 ⓶
  SHAM SO14 .... 5 J5
  SHAM SO14 .... 9 J7
Empshott Rd *ENEY* PO4 .... 19 K6
Empson Wk
  LSOL/BMARY PO13 .... 131 G1 ⓵
Emsbrook Dr *EMRTH* PO10 .. 104 C4 ⓵
Emsworth Common Rd
  EMRTH PO10 .... 104 A1
Emsworth House Cl
  EMRTH PO10 .... 104 B5
Emsworth Rd *HAV* PO9 .... 15 K5
  EMRTH PO10 .... 122 E3
  HAV PO9 .... 15 G5
  NEND PO2 .... 118 D6
  WSHM SO15 .... 54 C4
Endeavour Cl *GPORT* PO12 ... 16 E6
  WVILLE PO7 .... 54 C5 ⓶
Enderwood Cl *TOTT* SO40 .... 52 A4 ⓶
Endle St *SHAM* SO14 .... 9 K3
Endofield Cl *FHAM/STUB* PO14.. 115 G1
Enfield Gv *ITCH* SO19 .... 10 C1

Englefield Rd *WEND* SO18 .... 6 A4
English Rd *WSHM* SO15 .... 54 C5
Enmill La *WINW* SO22 .... 24 C3
Ennel Copse *NBAD* SO52 .... 36 B6
Ennerdale Cl *HORN* PO8 ..... 64 D2 ⓵
Ennerdale Gdns *WEND* SO18 .. 56 E3 ⓵
Ennerdale Rd
  FHAM/STUB PO14.............. 114 E3
  ROWN SO16 .... 53 G3
Ensign Dr *LSOL/BMARY* PO13 .. 132 A2
Ensign Wy *HLER* SO31 .... 94 D5
Enterprise Cl *HLER* SO31 ...... 94 D5 ⓶
Enterprise Rd *ROWN* SO16 ... 42 D2
Enterprise Wy *SHAM* SO14 ..... 9 J5
Epping Cl *WEND* SO18.............. 7 J1
Epsom Cl *ELGH* SO50 .... 46 C4 ⓶
Epworth Rd *NEND* PO2 .... 118 E6
Erica Cl *HLER* SO31 .... 94 E3
  HORN PO8 .... 82 C2
Erica Wy *HORN* PO8 .... 82 C1
Eric Rd *FHAM/STUB* PO14 .... 114 D5
Ernest Cl *EMRTH* PO10 .... 104 C5
Ernest Rd *HAV* PO9 .... 102 D2
  PSEA PO1 .... 134 D1
Erskine Rd *WINN* SO22 .... 2 B6
Escombe Rd *ELGH* SO50 .... 39 G7
Escur Cl *HORN* PO8 .... 118 E3 ⓶
Esher Gv *WVILLE* PO7 .... 81 H3
Eskdale Cl *HORN* PO8 .... 64 D2
Esmond Cl *EMRTH* PO10 ...... 104 C6
Esmonde Cl
  LSOL/BMARY PO13 .... 131 G2 ⓶
Esplanade *ENEY* PO4 .... 134 D7
Esplanade Gdns *ENEY* PO4 .. 135 H6
The Esplanade *GPORT* PO12 .. 17 H6
Essex Rd *ENEY* PO4 .... 19 L6
Esslemont Rd *ENEY* PO4 .... 19 L6
Estella Rd *NEND* PO2 .... 118 C7
Estridge Cl *HLER* SO31 .... 73 K4 ⓶
Ethelburt Av *ROWN* SO16 ..... 43 K6
Ethelred Gdns *TOTT* SO40 ..... 52 B6
Ethel Rd *PSEA* PO1 .... 19 G2
Eton Rd *SSEA* PO5 .... 19 G5
European Wy *SHAM* SO14 .... 9 J6
Euryalus Rd *FHAM/STUB* PO14 .. 115 G3
Euston Rd *ENEY* PO4 .... 135 G3
Evans Rd *ENEY* PO4 .... 19 L6
Evans St *SHAM* SO14 .... 9 H2
Evelegh Rd *CHAM* PO6 .... 101 J6
Evelyn Crs *WSHM* SO15 .... 4 B3
Evelyn Crs *WSHM* SO15 .... 4 B3
Evenlode Rd *ROWN* SO16 ..... 53 K3
Everdon La *HSEA* PO3 .... 119 H3 ⓵
Everglades Av *HORN* PO8 ..... 82 A2
Evergreen Cl *TOTT* SO40 .... 70 A4
  WVILLE PO7 .... 81 J6 ⓵
Eversley Crs *HAV* PO9 .... 102 E2
Eversley Pl *WINW* SO22 .... 25 G3
Evesham Cl *ROWN* SO16 .... 43 J6 ⓵
Ewart Cl *FAWY* SO45 .... 110 C6
Ewart Rd *PSEA* PO1 .... 134 D1 ⓵
Ewell Wy *TOTT* SO40 .... 52 C3
Ewhurst Cl *HAV* PO9 .... 102 E2
Exbury Cl *ELGH* SO50 .... 46 A3
Exbury Rd *FAWY* SO45 .... 110 B7
  HAV PO9 .... 103 H1
Excellent Rd
  FHAM/STUB PO14.............. 115 G2
Exchange Rd *PSEA* PO1 ...... 18 B4 ⓵
Exeter Cl *ELGH* SO50 .... 38 C5
  EMRTH PO10 .... 104 C3
  HLER SO31 .... 94 E3
  WEND SO18 .... 7 H1
Exeter Rd *ENEY* PO4 .... 19 J9
  WEND SO18 .... 7 H2
Exford Av *WEND* SO18 .... 7 L3
Exford Dr *WEND* SO18 .... 7 M4
Exleigh Cl *ITCH* SO19 .... 7 K6
Exmoor Rd *NEND* PO2 .... 118 D6
Exmouth Gdns *ELGH* SO50 .. 46 B4 ⓶
Exmouth Rd *GPORT* PO12 ... 116 D7
  SSEA PO5 .... 18 F9
Exton Gdns *FHAM/PORC* PO16 .. 99 F5
Exton Rd *HAV* PO9 .... 103 J1
Eyebright Cl *ELGH* SO50 ...... 46 B5 ⓶
Eyeworth Wk *FAWY* SO45 .... 90 D2 ⓶
Eynham Av *ITCH* SO19 .... 7 L6
Eynham Cl *ITCH* SO19 .... 7 L6
Eyre Cl *TOTT* SO40 .... 52 C6

F

Faber Cl *HAV* PO9 .... 103 H2
Fabian Cl *WVILLE* PO7 .... 82 B5 ⓵
Factory Rd *ELGH* SO50 .... 44 D1
Fairacre Rd *FHAM/STUB* PO14 .. 96 C6
Fairbairn Wk *NBAD* SO52 ...... 37 G4
Fairbourne Cl *HORN* PO8 ...... 81 K3
Faircross Cl *FAWY* SO45 ...... 109 K4
Fairdown Cl *WINC* SO23 .... 3 J5
Fairfax Cl *WINW* SO22 .... 24 E3
Fairfax Ct *ITCH* SO19 .... 57 H7 ⓵
Fairfax Ms *ITCH* SO19 .... 57 H6
Fair Fld *ROMY* SO51 .... 35 F1
Fairfield Av *FHAM/STUB* PO14 .. 12 D9
Fairfield Cl *EMRTH* PO10 ..... 104 C4
  FAWY SO45 .... 91 H2 ⓶
Fairfield Rd *WINW* SO22 .... 2 B4
  HAV PO9 .... 14 F4
  RWIN SO21 .... 33 G4
Fairfield Sq *CHAM* PO6 .... 100 D6
Fair Gn *ITCH* SO19 .... 7 K8
Fairhome Cl *GPORT* PO12 ... 132 D1
Fair Isle Cl *FHAM/STUB* PO14.. 96 C6
Fairisle Rd *ROWN* SO16 .... 41 K7
Fair La *RWIN* SO21 .... 23 G5
Fairlawn Cl *ROWN* SO16 .... 42 A5
Fairlead Dr
  LSOL/BMARY PO13 .... 132 A2 ⓶
Fairlea Rd *EMRTH* PO10 ...... 104 C3
Fairlie Cl *HEND* SO30 .... 58 B1 ⓶
Fairmead Wk *HORN* PO8 .... 82 C2
Fairmead Wy *TOTT* SO40 ...... 52 D7
Fair Oak Rd *HAV* PO9 .... 14 E1
Fairoak Rd *ELGH* SO50 .... 45 G1
Fairthorne Gdns *GPORT* PO12.. 132 D4

Fairview Cl *FAWY* SO45 .... 91 H3
  ROMY SO51 .... 35 G1
Fairview Dr *FAWY* SO45 .... 91 G4
  ROMY SO51 .... 35 G2
Fairview Pde *FAWY* SO45 ...... 91 H4
Fairwater Ct
  LSOL/BMARY PO13 .... 115 J6
Fairway Gdns *ROWN* SO16 .... 41 K6
The Fairway *FHAM/PORC* PO16 .. 99 F6
  HAV PO9 .... 83 K3
  LSOL/BMARY PO13 .... 115 K6 ⓶
Fairy Crossway *HORN* PO8 .... 82 C3
Falaise Cl *ROWN* SO16 .... 42 D7
Falcon Cl *FHAM/PORC* PO16 .. 98 C6 ⓶
Falconer Ct *FAWY* SO45 ...... 109 J1
Falcon Flds *FAWY* SO45 ...... 110 C4
Falcon Rd *HORN* PO8 .... 64 B5
Falcon Sq *ELGH* SO50 .... 44 A2
Falcon Vw *WINW* SO22 .... 25 F4
Falcon Wy *BPWT* SO32 .... 59 F3
Falkland Cl *CHFD* SO53 .... 37 K7
Falkland Cl
  LSOL/BMARY PO13 .... 131 G1
Falklands Cl
  LSOL/BMARY PO13 .... 131 G1
Falklands Rd *NEND* PO2 ..... 118 D3 ⓶
Fallow Fld *WINW* SO22 .... 25 F4
Falmouth Rd *CHAM* PO6 .... 99 J5
Falstaff Wy *TOTT* SO40 .... 52 D7 ⓶
Fanshawe St *SHAM* SO14 .... 5 H6 ⓵
Fareham Park Rd *FHAM* PO15 .. 96 D3
Fareham Rd
  LSOL/BMARY PO13 .... 115 K2
  WHAM PO17 .... 77 H2
  WHAM PO17 .... 99 H1
Faringdon Rd *WEND* SO18 .... 57 G5
Farleigh Cl *HAV* PO9 .... 102 E1 ⓶
Farley Cl *ELGH* SO50 .... 46 C2
  WINC SO22 .... 24 E4
Farlington Av *CHAM* PO6 ..... 101 H5
Farlington Rd *NEND* PO2 ..... 118 D6
Far Meadow Wy *EMRTH* PO10 .. 104 C6
Farm Edge Rd
  FHAM/STUB PO14.............. 114 D6
Farmery Cl *ELGH* SO50 .... 44 A7
Farm Gdns *HSEA* PO3 .... 118 E3
Farmhouse Wy *HORN* PO8 .... 64 B7
Farm La *RCCH* PO18 .... 105 J7
Farmlea Rd *CHAM* PO6 .... 99 J6
Farm Rd *FHAM/STUB* PO14 .... 95 K4
Farmside Gdns *HSEA* PO3 .... 118 E3
Farm Vw *EMRTH* PO10 .... 104 C3
Faroes Cl *FHAM/STUB* PO14 .. 114 C4 ⓶
Farriers Wy *HORN* PO8 .... 82 D4
Farrier Wy
  FHAM/PORC PO16 .... 115 J1 ⓵
Farringdon Rd *HAV* PO9 ...... 103 H2
Farringford Rd *ITCH* SO19 ..... 57 G6
Farthings Ga *WVILLE* PO7 .... 101 K3
Fastnet Cl *ROWN* SO16 .... 41 K6 ⓵
Fastnet Wy
  FHAM/STUB PO14.............. 114 C4 ⓵
Fathoms Reach *HISD* PO11 .. 137 F4
F Av *FAWY* SO45 .... 110 C1
Fawcett Rd *ENEY* PO4 .... 19 G5
Fawley By-pass *FAWY* SO45 .. 110 G4
Fawley Ct *HAV* PO9 .... 103 J1 ⓶
Fawley Rd *FAWY* SO45 .... 91 J6
  NEND PO2 .... 118 D2
  WSHM SO15 .... 54 B6
Fay Cl *FHAM/STUB* PO14 ...... 114 D5
Fayre Rd *FHAM/PORC* PO16 .. 13 H9
Fearon Rd *NEND* PO2 .... 118 D5
Felix Rd *GPORT* PO12 .... 132 E1
Fell Cl *HLER* SO31 .... 95 F2
Fell Dr *LSOL/BMARY* PO13 ... 131 G1
Feltham Cl *ROMY* SO51 .... 35 H2
Feltons Pl *HSEA* PO3 .... 118 E2
Fen Av *FHAM/PORC* PO16 ..... 97 J7
Fennell Cl *WVILLE* PO7 .... 81 J4
Ferncroft Cl
  FHAM/STUB PO14.............. 114 D6 ⓶
  WVILLE PO7 .... 82 A4
Ferndale *HEND* SO30 .... 58 D7
Ferndale Ms
  LSOL/BMARY PO13 .... 115 J3
Ferndale Rd *TOTT* SO40 .... 70 A4
Ferndene Wy *WEND* SO18 ...... 6 F2
Fern Dr *HAV* PO9 .... 15 G2
Ferneham Rd *FHAM* PO15 ..... 96 D4
Fern Hill La *ROMY* SO51 .... 29 J1
Fernhills Rd *FAWY* SO45 .... 91 J5
Fernhurst Cl *HISD* PO11 .... 136 E5
Fernhurst Rd *ENEY* PO4 .... 19 J6
Fernie Cl *FHAM/STUB* PO14 .. 114 C5
Fernlea Gdns *ROWN* SO16 ... 55 F1 ⓶
Fernlea Wy *FAWY* SO45 .... 90 E3
Fern Rd *FAWY* SO45 .... 91 G3
  ITCH SO19 .... 10 E5
Fern Wy *FHAM* PO15 .... 95 J3
Fernwood Crs *WEND* SO18 ..... 6 F2
Fernyhurst Av *ROWN* SO16 ... 42 A5
Ferrol Rd *GPORT* PO12 .... 16 C2
Ferry Rd *ENEY* PO4 .... 135 G1
  FAWY SO45 .... 91 G3
  HISD PO11 .... 136 B4
Festing Gv *ENEY* PO4 .... 134 E6
Festing Rd *ENEY* PO4 .... 19 J9
Fey Rd *GPORT* PO12 .... 16 C4
Field Cl *HLER* SO31 .... 95 G4
  LSOL/BMARY PO13 .... 115 J2
  ROMY SO51 .... 35 F3
  ROWN SO16 .... 43 K6 ⓶
  RWIN SO21 .... 33 F3
Fielden Cl *NBAD* SO52 .... 36 A6
Fieldfare Ct *TOTT* SO40 .... 52 B4
Fieldhouse Dr
  LSOL/BMARY PO13 .... 115 G7
Fieldmore Rd *GPORT* PO12 .. 132 C1
Fields Cl *FAWY* SO45 .... 110 B6 ⓶
Field Vw *NBAD* SO52 .... 37 G4
Field Wy *RWIN* SO21 .... 33 K3
  WVILLE PO7 .... 80 E1
Fifth Av *CHAM* PO6 .... 100 D6
  HAV PO9 .... 15 K2
Fifth St *PSEA* PO1 .... 134 E1
Filmer Cl *LSOL/BMARY* PO13 .. 116 A7
Filton Cl *TOTT* SO40 .... 52 B4
Finchdean Rd *HORN* PO8 ...... 83 K3
  HAV PO9 .... 102 E2

Finch Rd *ENEY* PO4..... 135 J5
Finch's La *RWIN* SO21..... 33 J3
Findon Rd *GPORT* PO12..... 116 E7
Finisterre St *FHAM/STUB* PO14.. 114 C3
Finlay Cl *ITCH* SO19..... 11 M2
Finzi Cl *ITCH* SO19..... 11 M4
Fiona Cl *WINC* SO23..... 3 J3
Fir Cl *LYND* SO43..... 86 C2
Fir Copse Rd *WVILLE* PO7..... 101 J3
Fir Croft Dr *CHFD* SO53..... 38 A5
Firecrest Cl *ROWN* SO16..... 42 C6
Firgrove Cl *NBAD* SO52..... 36 A6
Firgrove Crs *HSEA* PO3..... 118 C2
Firgrove La *WHAM* PO17..... 78 C3
Firgrove Rd *NBAD* SO52..... 36 B5
  WSHM SO15..... 54 D5
Firlands Ri *CHAM* PO6..... 102 B5
Firmstone Rd *WINC* SO23..... 3 J4
Fir Rd *TOTT* SO40..... 68 A3
Firs Av *WVILLE* PO7..... 82 A3
Firs Dr *HEND* SO30..... 57 K6
First Av *CHAM* PO6..... 100 E6
  CHAM PO6..... 101 K6
  EMRTH PO10..... 105 G6
  HAV PO9..... 15 J3
  HORN PO8..... 64 D1
  WSHM SO15..... 53 J6
The Firs *LSOL/BMARY* PO13..... 116 A6
  ROWN SO16..... 43 G7
First St *FAWY* SO45..... 92 B6
Fir Tree Cl *ELGH* SO50..... 46 B4
Firtree Gdns *HORN* PO8..... 64 D7
Fir Tree La *ELGH* SO50..... 46 A4
Fir Tree Rd *HISD* PO11..... 137 H5
  TOTT SO40..... 50 D5
Firtree Wy *ITCH* SO19..... 7 K9
Firwood Cl *CHFD* SO53..... 37 K2
Fisgard Rd *GPORT* PO12..... 132 E1
Fisher Cl *FHAM/STUB* PO14.. 114 C4
The Fishermans
  EMRTH PO10..... 104 D6
Fishermans Wk *HISD* PO11..... 138 B6
Fisher Rd *LSOL/BMARY* PO13.. 115 K4
Fishers Gv *CHAM* PO6..... 101 K7
Fishers Hl *FHAM* PO15..... 96 B4
Fisher's Rd *TOTT* SO40..... 53 F6
Fishery La *HISD* PO11..... 137 K6
Fishlake Mdw *ROMY* SO51..... 34 E1
Fitzgerald Cl *HLER* SO31..... 75 H5
Fitzherbert Rd *CHAM* PO6..... 101 J7
Fitzherbert Spur *CHAM* PO6..... 101 K7
Fitzherbert St *PSEA* PO1..... 134 B1
Fitzhugh Pl *SHAM* SO14..... 4 E5
Fitzhugh St *SHAM* SO14..... 4 E9
Fitzpatrick Ct *CHAM* PO6..... 100 C5
Fitzroy Cl *ROWN* SO16..... 43 G4
Fitzwilliam Av
  FHAM/STUB PO14..... 114 B5
Fitzwygram Crs *HAV* PO9..... 14 E1
Five Bridges Rd *WINC* SO23..... 25 H5
Five Elms Dr *ROMY* SO51..... 35 C4
Fivefields Cl *WINC* SO23..... 3 J6
Fivefields Rd *WINC* SO23..... 3 K6
Five Heads Rd *HORN* PO8..... 64 B4
Five Post La *GPORT* PO12..... 16 A1
Flag Staff Gn *GPORT* PO12..... 16 E2
Flag Wk *HORN* PO8..... 64 A7
Flamborough Cl *ROWN* SO16..... 53 J2
Flamingo Ct *FHAM/PORC* PO16.. 98 C6
Flanders Rd *HEND* SO30..... 58 A4
Flathouse Rd *PSEA* PO1..... 134 B1
Fleet Cl *LSOL/BMARY* PO13.. 116 A6
Fleetend Cl *HAV* PO9..... 83 F7
Fleet End Bottom *HLER* SO31.. 94 E6
Fleet End Rd *HLER* SO31..... 94 E6
Fleming Av *NBAD* SO52..... 36 B6
Fleming Pl *ROMY* SO51..... 34 E3
  RWIN SO21..... 39 J1
Fleming Rd *WINW* SO22..... 21 F4
  ROWN SO16..... 44 A7
Fletcher Cl *FAWY* SO45..... 90 E3
Fletchwood La *TOTT* SO40..... 52 A6
Fletchwood Rd *TOTT* SO40..... 52 A6
Fleuret Cl *FAWY* SO45..... 91 H6
Flexford Cl *CHFD* SO53..... 37 H1
Flexford Rd *NBAD* SO52..... 36 D4
Flint Cl *ITCH* SO19..... 73 H1
Flint St *SSEA* PO5..... 18 B7
Floating Bridge Rd *SHAM* SO14.. 9 L4
Florence Rd *ITCH* SO19..... 10 B5
  SSEA PO5..... 134 C7
Florentine Wy *WVILLE* PO7..... 82 B5
The Florins *HLER* SO31..... 95 F5
  WVILLE PO7..... 101 K3
Flowerdown Cl *TOTT* SO40..... 52 B4
Flowers Cl *HLER* SO31..... 93 H3
Flume Rd *FAWY* SO45..... 111 F3
Foldsgate Cl *LYND* SO43..... 66 C7
Folkestone Rd *HSEA* PO3..... 135 F1
Folly Fld *BPWT* SO32..... 48 E4
Font Cl *FHAM/STUB* PO14..... 95 H3
Fontley Rd *FHAM* PO15..... 96 B3
Fontwell Cl *TOTT* SO40..... 52 B4
Fontwell Gdns *ELGH* SO50..... 46 C4
Fontwell Ms *HORN* PO8..... 64 C2
Fontwell Rd *SSEA* PO5..... 18 E9
Foord Rd *HEND* SO30..... 74 A1
Footner Cl *ROMY* SO51..... 29 H7
Forbes Rd *ROWN* SO16..... 42 C6
Forbury Rd *PSEA* PO5..... 18 E5
Ford Av *CHFD* SO53..... 38 A6
Fordingbridge Rd *ENEY* PO4.. 135 G5
Fordington Rd *WINW* SO22..... 2 A3
Ford Rd *GPORT* PO12..... 132 C2
Foreland Ct *HISD* PO11..... 137 K6
Foreshore North *FAWY* SO45.. 110 E1
Foreshore South *FAWY* SO45.. 110 E1
Forest Av *HORN* PO8..... 82 A2
Forest Cl *BPWT* SO32..... 61 F1
  CHFD SO53..... 37 K2
  HORN PO8..... 82 A2
  NBAD SO52..... 35 K5
Forest Edge *FAWY* SO45..... 110 D4
Forest End *WVILLE* PO7..... 81 J6
Foresters Ga *FAWY* SO45..... 128 B1
Foresters Rd *FAWY* SO45..... 110 C5
Forest Front *FAWY* SO45..... 91 G6
Forest Gdns *BPWT* SO32..... 61 F1
  LYND SO43..... 86 C1
Forest Ga *FAWY* SO45..... 128 C1

Forest Hills Dr *WEND* SO18..... 56 B1
Forest Hill Wy *FAWY* SO45..... 91 G4
Forest La *FAWY* SO45..... 109 J1
  WHAM PO17..... 77 J3
Forest Meadow *FAWY* SO45..... 91 H6
Forest Rd *BPWT* SO32..... 61 G1
  CHFD SO53..... 38 A2
  WVILLE PO7..... 79 K1
Forestside Av *HAV* PO9..... 103 H1
Forest Vw *SHAM* SO14..... 8 F3
Forest Vw *LSOL/BMARY* PO13.. 116 A3
  TOTT SO40..... 51 K2
Forge Cl *HLER* SO31..... 73 K4
Forge Rd *FAWY* SO45..... 128 C1
Forneth Gdns *FHAM* PO15..... 96 C6
Forster Rd *SHAM* SO14..... 5 H4
Forsythia Cl *HAV* PO9..... 103 J2
  HEND SO30..... 58 A4
Fort Cumberland Rd
  ENEY PO4..... 135 J5
Fort Fareham Rd
  FHAM/STUB PO14..... 115 G1
Forth Cl *CHFD* SO53..... 37 J5
  FHAM/STUB PO14..... 114 C4
Forties Cl *FHAM/STUB* PO14 .. 114 C3
Forton Rd *GPORT* PO12..... 16 A3
  PSEA PO1..... 19 H1
Fort Rd *GPORT* PO12..... 132 E7
  ITCH SO19..... 10 C4
Fortunes Wy *CHAM* PO6..... 102 A5
Foster Cl *FHAM/STUB* PO14..... 114 D3
Foster Rd *GPORT* PO12..... 16 A7
  PSEA PO1..... 18 F1
Founders Wy
  LSOL/BMARY PO13..... 116 A5
Foundry La *WSHM* SO15..... 54 C4
Fountain St *PSEA* PO1..... 18 D3
Four Acre *HEND* SO30..... 59 F6
Four Posts Hl *WSHM* SO15..... 4 C8
Fourshells Cl *FAWY* SO45..... 110 C5
Fourth Av *CHAM* PO6..... 100 D6
  HAV PO9..... 15 J3
Fourth St *PSEA* PO1..... 19 J1
Fowey Cl *CHFD* SO53..... 37 J3
The Fowey *FAWY* SO45..... 110 B5
Fowlers Rd *HEND* SO30..... 58 A4
Fowler's Wk *NBAD* SO52..... 42 E1
Foxbury Cl *FAWY* SO45..... 91 H4
Foxbury Gv *FHAM/PORC* PO16.. 98 E7
Foxbury La *EMRTH* PO10..... 105 F2
  LSOL/BMARY PO13..... 116 A3
Fox Cl *ELGH* SO50..... 45 J1
Foxcombe Cl *BPWT* SO32..... 49 H5
Foxcott Cl *ITCH* SO19..... 72 C5
Foxcott Gv *HAV* PO9..... 103 J1
Foxcroft Dr *FAWY* SO45..... 109 J4
Foxes Cl *WVILLE* PO7..... 81 K7
Foxglade *FAWY* SO45..... 128 C1
Foxgloves *FHAM/PORC* PO16 .. 13 L1
The Foxgloves *HEND* SO30..... 58 C7
Foxhayes La *FAWY* SO45..... 128 C1
Foxhills *TOTT* SO40..... 68 B1
Foxhills Cl *TOTT* SO40..... 68 B2
Foxlands *FAWY* SO45..... 128 C1
Fox La *WINW* SO22..... 25 F3
Foxlea Gdns *GPORT* PO12..... 132 E1
Foxley Dr *HSEA* PO3..... 119 G3
Fox's Wk *FAWY* SO45..... 128 C1
Foxtail Dr *FAWY* SO45..... 91 G5
Foxy Paddock *FAWY* SO45..... 128 C1
Foy Gdns *HLER* SO31..... 94 B5
Foyle Rd *CHFD* SO53..... 37 J4
Frampton Cl *RWIN* SO21..... 39 J1
Frampton Wy *TOTT* SO40..... 52 E6
Frances Rd *WVILLE* PO7..... 101 J3
Francis Av *ENEY* PO4..... 19 J8
Francis Cl *LSOL/BMARY* PO13 .. 116 A1
Francis Gdns *WINC* SO23..... 22 A5
Francis Pl *FHAM/STUB* PO14.. 114 F5
Francis Rd *HORN* PO8..... 64 D1
Frankland Ter *EMRTH* PO10.. 104 D6
Franklin Rd *LSOL/BMARY* PO13.. 131 K1
  RWIN SO21..... 33 K2
Franklyn Av *ITCH* SO19..... 11 H1
Frarydene *EMRTH* PO10..... 105 G6
Fraser Cl *ROWN* SO16..... 42 A5
Fraser Gdns *EMRTH* PO10..... 105 H4
Fraser Rd *HAV* PO9..... 14 B2
  LSOL/BMARY PO13..... 115 K3
  NEND PO2..... 118 A5
  SSEA PO5..... 18 E5
Frater La *GPORT* PO12..... 116 D6
Fratton Pk *PSEA* PO1..... 19 G2
Fratton Wy *ELGH* SO50..... 46 B2
Frayslea *FAWY* SO45..... 91 H4
Freda Routh Gdns *ELGH* SO50 .. 46 C1
Frederick St *PSEA* PO1..... 18 D1
  SHAM SO14..... 5 J6
Freedom Ct *FAWY* SO45..... 91 H3
Freegrounds Av *HEND* SO30.. 58 B6
Freegrounds Cl *HEND* SO30.. 58 B6
Freegrounds Rd *HEND* SO30.. 58 B6
Freemantle Cl *ITCH* SO19..... 6 E8
Freemantle Common Rd
  ITCH SO19..... 6 E8
Freemantle Rd *GPORT* PO12.. 132 E1
Freestone Rd *SSEA* PO5..... 134 C6
Free St *BPWT* SO32..... 48 E3
Frenchies Vw *WVILLE* PO7..... 80 D1
French St *PSEA* PO1..... 17 L7
  SHAM SO14..... 8 F4
Frendstaple Rd *WVILLE* PO7.. 102 B1
Frensham Cl *HEND* SO30..... 58 B6
Frensham Rd *ENEY* PO4..... 19 K6
Freshfield Gdns *WVILLE* PO7.. 81 K5
Freshfield Rd *WSHM* SO15..... 54 A5
Freshfield Sq *WSHM* SO15..... 54 C5
Freshwater Rd *CHAM* PO6..... 100 D7
Friarscroft *HLER* SO31..... 72 E6
Friars Cft *TOTT* SO40..... 52 A2
Friars Pond Rd *FHAM* PO15.. 96 D5
Friars Rd *ELGH* SO50..... 44 C2
Friars Wy *WEND* SO18..... 44 A1
Friary Cl *SSEA* PO5..... 134 B6
Fritham Cl *TOTT* SO40..... 52 B5
Fritham Rd *WEND* SO18..... 7 M2
Frith La *WHAM* PO17..... 61 H6

Frobisher Cl
  LSOL/BMARY PO13..... 131 K2
Frobisher Gdns
  EMRTH PO10..... 104 C6
  ITCH SO19..... 11 M1
Frobisher Gv *FHAM/PORC* PO16.. 99 F7
Froddington Rd *SSEA* PO5..... 18 F5
Froghall *FAWY* SO45..... 91 G5
Frogmore *FHAM/STUB* PO14..... 96 D6
  ROWN SO16..... 53 J1
Frogmore La *HORN* PO8..... 64 B6
Frogmore Rd *ENEY* PO4..... 19 K5
Frome Cl *TOTT* SO40..... 70 B3
Frome Rd *WEND* SO18..... 56 D1
Fromond Rd *WINW* SO22..... 21 F4
Frosthole Cl *FHAM* PO15..... 12 D1
Frosthole Crs *FHAM* PO15..... 12 C1
Frost La *FAWY* SO45..... 91 K4
Froxfield Cl *WINW* SO22..... 21 G3
Froxfield Gdns
  FHAM/PORC PO16..... 99 F5
Froxfield Rd *HAV* PO9..... 103 J1
Froyle Ct *HAV* PO9..... 103 J1
Fry Cl *FAWY* SO45..... 110 C5
  HLER SO31..... 93 K2
Fryern Cl *CHFD* SO53..... 38 B4
Fulflood Rd *HAV* PO9..... 103 F1
Fullerton Cl *HAV* PO9..... 103 J1
  ITCH SO19..... 72 C5
Fulmar Cl *ROWN* SO16..... 42 C6
Fulmar Dr *FAWY* SO45..... 91 J4
Fulmer Wk *HORN* PO8..... 81 K1
  HORN PO8..... 81 K1
Funtington Rd *NEND* PO2..... 118 E7
Funtley Hl *FHAM/PORC* PO16.. 97 F2
Funtley Rd *FHAM* PO15..... 96 E1
Furdies *WVILLE* PO7..... 80 D1
Furley Cl *WINC* SO23..... 3 H4
Furneaux Gdns
  FHAM/PORC PO16..... 13 J1
Furness Rd *SSEA* PO5..... 134 C7
Furniss Wy *HISD* PO11..... 136 E4
Furnston Gv *EMRTH* PO10..... 105 H5
Fury Wy *FHAM/STUB* PO14..... 114 C4
Furzedale Gdns *FAWY* SO45..... 91 J5
Furzedale Pk *FAWY* SO45..... 91 J5
Furzedown Crs *HAV* PO9..... 103 H1
Furzedown Ms *FAWY* SO45..... 91 J5
Furzedown Rd *PTSW* SO17..... 55 H2
Furzehall Av *FHAM/PORC* PO16.. 13 L1
Furze La *ENEY* PO4..... 135 J3
Furzeley Rd *WVILLE* PO7..... 80 C3
Furze Rd *ITCH* SO19..... 7 H9
Furze Wy *HORN* PO8..... 82 C1
Furzey Cl *FAWY* SO45..... 110 C6
Furzey La *BROC* SO42..... 107 G6
Furzley Ct *HAV* PO9..... 82 D7
Fushia Cl *HAV* PO9..... 103 K2
Fushia Gdns *ROWN* SO16..... 54 E2
Fyeford Cl *ROWN* SO16..... 42 A5
Fyfield Cl *FHAM* PO15..... 75 H1
Fyfield Wy *WINW* SO22..... 20 E2
Fyning St *PSEA* PO1..... 18 F2

G

Gables Ct *ROWN* SO16..... 43 G6
Gage Cl *TOTT* SO40..... 70 B3
Gainsborough Cl *ITCH* SO19..... 11 L5
Gainsborough Ms
  FHAM/STUB PO14..... 96 A6
Gainsford Rd *ITCH* SO19..... 6 B9
Gain's Rd *ENEY* PO4..... 19 G9
Galaxie Rd *HORN* PO8..... 82 C1
Gale Moor Av *GPORT* PO12.. 132 A5
Galleon Cl *HLER* SO31..... 94 E5
The Gallops *FHAM/STUB* PO14 .. 95 J4
Galsworthy Rd *TOTT* SO40..... 52 C5
Galt Rd *CHAM* PO6..... 101 J6
Gamble Cl *ITCH* SO19..... 10 F1
Gamblins La *BPWT* SO32..... 61 G4
Ganger Farm La *ROMY* SO51.. 29 H7
Ganger Rd *ROMY* SO51..... 29 H7
Gannet Cl *FAWY* SO45..... 91 J4
  ROWN SO16..... 42 C6
The Gannets
  FHAM/STUB PO14..... 114 C5
Garbett Rd *WINC* SO23..... 3 J4
Garden City *FAWY* SO45..... 70 B7
Garden Cl *HISD* PO11..... 137 G5
  LYND SO43..... 86 B1
Garden La *SSEA* PO5..... 18 C8
  WINC SO23..... 2 F4
Garden Ms *HLER* SO31..... 94 B5
The Gardens *HAV* PO9..... 15 K6
  WVILLE PO7..... 62 C1
Gardiner Cl *TOTT* SO40..... 70 B3
Gardner Rd *FHAM/STUB* PO14.. 96 A7
Garfield Cl *BPWT* SO32..... 48 D3
Garfield Rd *BPWT* SO32..... 48 D3
  HLER SO31..... 72 D7
  ITCH SO19..... 11 H5
  NEND PO2..... 118 C7
Garland Av *EMRTH* PO10..... 104 C3
Garnett Cl *FHAM/STUB* PO14.. 114 D3
Garnier Pk *WHAM* PO17..... 77 H1
Garnier Rd *WINC* SO23..... 2 D9
Garnier St *PSEA* PO1..... 18 D3
Garnock Rd *ITCH* SO19..... 10 B6
Garratt Cl *HEND* SO30..... 58 C7
Garrett Cl *ITCH* SO19..... 11 H8
Garrick Gdns *ITCH* SO19..... 11 H5
Garsons Rd *EMRTH* PO10..... 105 G6
Garstons Cl *FHAM/STUB* PO14.. 96 A6
Garstons Rd *FHAM/STUB* PO14.. 96 A6
Gar St *WINC* SO23..... 2 D5
Garton Rd *ITCH* SO19..... 10 B4
Gatcombe Av *HAV* PO9..... 15 H5
Gatcombe Cl *HLER* SO31..... 73 F6
Gatcombe Dr *NEND* PO2..... 118 E4
Gatcombe Gdns
  FHAM/STUB PO14..... 96 C6
  WEND SO18..... 56 D2
Gate House Rd
  FHAM/PORC PO16..... 98 D7
Gate Hyde *WINC* SO23..... 2 E1
Gatekeeper Cl *WINC* SO23..... 3 K4
Gatwick Cl *ROWN* SO16..... 42 B7

Gaulter Cl *HAV* PO9..... 15 G1
Gavan St *ITCH* SO19..... 57 G7
G Av *FAWY* SO45..... 110 C1
Gaylyn Wy *FHAM/STUB* PO14.. 96 C6
Gaza Av *BROC* SO42..... 125 H2
Gento Cl *HEND* SO30..... 58 D6
Geoffrey Av *WVILLE* PO7..... 101 C4
Geoffrey Crs
  FHAM/PORC PO16..... 115 J1
George Byng Wy *NEND* PO2 .. 118 D7
George Curl Wy *ELGH* SO50..... 44 C5
George Eyston Dr *WINW* SO22 .. 25 G2
George St *ELGH* SO50..... 38 D7
  GPORT PO12..... 16 D4
  PSEA PO1..... 134 D1
Gerard Crs *ITCH* SO19..... 57 G6
Gibbs Rd *SHAM* SO14..... 4 F9
Gibraltar Cl *FHAM* PO15..... 12 C1
Gibraltar Rd *ENEY* PO4..... 135 J5
  FHAM/STUB PO14..... 115 G1
Gibson Cl *FHAM* PO15..... 75 K7
  LSOL/BMARY PO13..... 131 G2
Gifford Cl *FHAM* PO15..... 12 C2
Gilbert Cl *LSOL/BMARY* PO13 .. 116 A7
Gilbert Md *HISD* PO11..... 137 F4
Gilbert Wy *WVILLE* PO7..... 101 K1
Gilbury Cl *WEND* SO18..... 44 B7
Giles Cl *FHAM/PORC* PO16..... 13 K1
  GPORT PO12..... 132 D2
  HEND SO30..... 58 C3
Gilkicker Rd *GPORT* PO12..... 133 F7
Gillcrest *FHAM* PO15..... 95 H2
The Gillies *FHAM/PORC* PO16.. 13 H6
Gillman Rd *CHAM* PO6..... 101 K6
Gilpin Cl *ITCH* SO19..... 57 C7
Gins La *BROC* SO42..... 126 C3
Girton Cl *FHAM/STUB* PO14..... 95 H5
Gitsham Gdns *WVILLE* PO7..... 101 H3
Gladstone Gdns
  FHAM/PORC PO16..... 99 F7
Gladstone Rd *GPORT* PO12.. 132 D1
  ITCH SO19..... 7 K9
Gladstone St *WINC* SO23..... 2 D3
Gladys Av *HORN* PO8..... 82 B1
  NEND PO2..... 118 C5
Glamis Cl *WVILLE* PO7..... 82 B5
Glamorgan Rd *HORN* PO8..... 64 C2
Glasgow Rd *ENEY* PO4..... 135 G5
Glasslaw Rd *WEND* SO18..... 7 H2
Glasspool *WVILLE* PO7..... 62 D7
Glebe Cl *HISD* PO11..... 137 F3
Glebe Cnr *WHAM* PO17..... 77 J2
Glebe Ct *ELGH* SO50..... 46 C1
  HEND SO30..... 59 F4
  PTSW SO17..... 55 J1
Glebe Dr *LSOL/BMARY* PO13.. 115 J6
Glebefield Gdns *CHAM* PO6..... 100 D6
Glebe Park Av *CHAM* PO6..... 102 B5
The Glebe *FHAM/STUB* PO14.. 114 D6
Glenbrook Wk
  FHAM/STUB PO14..... 96 D6
Glencarron Wy *ROWN* SO16..... 55 F1
Glencoe Rd *PSEA* PO1..... 134 E1
Glencoyne Gdns *ROWN* SO16 .. 54 A2
Glenda Cl *HLER* SO31..... 94 C6
Glendale *BPWT* SO32..... 49 J7
Glen Dl *HAV* PO9..... 84 A4
Glendale *HLER* SO31..... 95 G4
Glendowan Rd *CHFD* SO53..... 37 H3
Gleneagles Dr *HORN* PO8..... 82 C3
Glenelg *FHAM* PO15..... 12 E5
Glen Eyre Dr *ROWN* SO16..... 43 H6
Glen Eyre Rd *ROWN* SO16..... 43 H6
Glen Eyre Wy *ROWN* SO16..... 43 H7
Glenfield Av *WEND* SO18..... 6 E4
Glenfield Crs *WEND* SO18..... 6 F4
Glenfield Wy *WEND* SO18..... 6 E4
Glenlea Cl *HEND* SO30..... 57 G3
Glenlea Dr *HEND* SO30..... 57 G3
Glenleigh Av *HEND* SO30..... 57 G3
Glenleigh Pk *HAV* PO9..... 15 K3
Glenn Rd *HEND* SO30..... 57 G2
  HLER SO31..... 74 D7
Glen Rd *HLER* SO31..... 74 D6
  ITCH SO19..... 10 A7
Glenside *FAWY* SO45..... 91 G3
Glenside Av *ITCH* SO19..... 73 C1
The Glen *LSOL/BMARY* PO13.. 116 B6
Glenthorne Cl
  FHAM/STUB PO14..... 114 E6
Glenthorne Rd *HSEA* PO3..... 119 F6
Glenwood Av *ROWN* SO16..... 43 H6
Glenwood Cl *ELGH* SO50..... 46 D1
Glenwood Gdns *HORN* PO8..... 82 A2
Glenwood Rd *EMRTH* PO10..... 105 C5
Glidden Cl *PSEA* PO1..... 18 E3
Glidden La *BPWT* SO32..... 62 D1
Gloucester Rd *PSEA* PO1..... 17 M1
  WVILLE PO7..... 82 A7
Gloucester Sq *SHAM* SO14..... 9 G4
Gloucester Ter *SSEA* PO5..... 18 C7
Gloucester Vw *SSEA* PO5..... 18 C7
Glyn Dr *FHAM/STUB* PO14..... 114 D5
Glyn Jones Cl *FAWY* SO45..... 110 C5
Glyn Wy *FHAM/STUB* PO14..... 114 D5
Godfrey Pink Wy *BPWT* SO32.. 48 E4
Godwin Cl *EMRTH* PO10..... 104 B3
  WINW SO22..... 21 F4
Godwit Cl *GPORT* PO12..... 116 E7
Godwit Rd *ENEY* PO4..... 135 H2
Gofton Av *CHAM* PO6..... 101 C7
Goldcrest Cl
  FHAM/PORC PO16..... 98 B6
  HORN PO8..... 64 B5
Goldcrest Gdns *ROWN* SO16.. 42 B6
Goldcrest La *TOTT* SO40..... 52 B6
Golden Ct *HEND* SO30..... 57 J2
Golden Gv *SHAM* SO14..... 5 J3
Golden Hind Pk *FAWY* SO45..... 91 G4
Goldfinch La
  LSOL/BMARY PO13..... 131 G1

Goldring Cl *HISD* PO11..... 137 H1
Goldsmith Av *ENEY* PO4..... 19 H4
Goldsmith Cl *TOTT* SO40..... 52 C5
Goldsmith Rd *ELGH* SO50..... 44 C2
Gold St *SSEA* PO5..... 18 B7
Golf Course Rd *ROWN* SO16..... 43 F5
Gomer La *GPORT* PO12..... 132 B4
Goodacre Dr *NBAD* SO52..... 37 G5
Goodison Cl *ELGH* SO50..... 46 A2
Goodlands V *HEND* SO30..... 57 K5
Goodsell Cl
  FHAM/STUB PO14..... 114 C5
Goodwin Cl *ROWN* SO16..... 53 J2
Goodwood Cl
  FHAM/STUB PO14..... 95 H4
  GPORT PO12..... 116 E7
  WVILLE PO7..... 82 C4
Goodwood Rd *EMRTH* PO10..... 105 H6
Goodwood Gdns *TOTT* SO40.. 52 B4
Goodwood Rd *ELGH* SO50..... 38 B5
  SSEA PO5..... 19 G8
Gordon Av *SHAM* SO14..... 5 C2
  WINC SO23..... 3 J7
Gordon Rd *BPWT* SO32..... 60 A3
  CHFD SO53..... 38 A4
  EMRTH PO10..... 104 E7
  FHAM/PORC PO16..... 13 G5
  GPORT PO12..... 132 D4
  PSEA PO1..... 18 A8
  WINC SO23..... 2 F2
  WVILLE PO7..... 81 J7
Gordon Ter *ITCH* SO19..... 11 G5
Goring Fld *WINW* SO22..... 21 F6
Gorley Ct *HAV* PO9..... 82 D7
Gorran Av *LSOL/BMARY* PO13 .. 115 K6
Gorse Cl *HLER* SO31..... 94 E4
Gorselands Rd *WEND* SO18..... 7 J1
Gorselands Wy
  LSOL/BMARY PO13..... 116 A7
Gort Crs *ITCH* SO19..... 11 J1
Gosport La *LYND* SO43..... 86 D2
Gosport Rd *FHAM/PORC* PO16.. 13 K7
  FHAM/STUB PO14..... 114 C5
  LSOL/BMARY PO13..... 131 G3
Gover Rd *ROWN* SO16..... 53 H3
Grace Dieu Gdns *HLER* SO31.. 73 J4
Graddidge Wy *TOTT* SO40..... 52 C5
Grafton Gdns *ROWN* SO16..... 42 D6
Grafton Rd *WINC* SO23..... 2 F3
Grafton St *NEND* PO2..... 134 B1
Graham Rd *ENEY* PO4..... 19 H8
  GPORT PO12..... 132 D2
  SHAM SO14..... 5 H7
Graham St *SHAM* SO14..... 5 L7
Grainger Gdns *ITCH* SO19..... 11 M4
Granada Cl *HORN* PO8..... 82 B2
Granada Rd *ENEY* PO4..... 134 D7
  HEND SO30..... 57 K7
Granby Gv *PTSW* SO17..... 55 J1
Grand Pde *WINW* SO22..... 21 F2
  HISD PO11..... 137 H6
  PSEA PO1..... 17 L8
Grange Cl *GPORT* PO12..... 132 C2
  HAV PO9..... 15 J3
  WEND SO18..... 44 B7
Grange Crs *GPORT* PO12..... 132 C2
Grange Dr *HEND* SO30..... 58 C4
Grange La *LSOL/BMARY* PO13 .. 115 K7
Grange Ms *ROMY* SO51..... 35 H1
Grange Rd *HEND* SO30..... 58 B4
  HLER SO31..... 72 E7
  LSOL/BMARY PO13..... 132 A3
  NEND PO2..... 118 C6
  ROWN SO16..... 54 C3
  WINC SO23..... 25 H5
Grangewood Gdns
  ELGH SO50..... 46 A1
Grantham Av *HLER* SO31..... 93 H3
Grantham Rd *ELGH* SO50..... 44 C1
  ITCH SO19..... 6 E6
Grant Rd *CHAM* PO6..... 101 J6
Granville Cl *HAV* PO9..... 15 H5
Granville St *SHAM* SO14..... 9 K2
Grasdean Cl *WEND* SO18..... 56 D3
Grasmere *ELGH* SO50..... 44 C1
Grasmere Cl *WEND* SO18..... 56 E3
Grasmere Wy
  FHAM/STUB PO14..... 114 E3
Grassmere Wy *HORN* PO8..... 82 C3
Grassymead *FHAM* PO15..... 95 H2
Grateley Cl *ITCH* SO19..... 10 F9
Grateley Crs *HAV* PO9..... 102 D7
Gravel Hl *BPWT* SO32..... 61 J1
Gray Cl *HLER* SO31..... 94 E4
Grayland Cl *HISD* PO11..... 137 F4
Grayling Md *ROMY* SO51..... 34 E1
Grays Av *FAWY* SO45..... 91 J3
Grays Cl *ELGH* SO50..... 39 J2
  GPORT PO12..... 132 B5
  ROMY SO51..... 35 F3
Grays Ct *PSEA* PO1..... 17 M4
Grayshott Cl *WINW* SO22..... 21 C3
Grayshott Rd *ENEY* PO4..... 19 K5
  GPORT PO12..... 132 C4
Great Br *ROMY* SO51..... 28 D7
Greatbridge Rd *ROMY* SO51..... 28 D6
Great Copse Dr *HAV* PO9..... 103 J1
Great Elms Cl *FAWY* SO45..... 109 J4
Great Field Rd *WINW* SO22..... 21 G4
Greatfield Wy *HAV* PO9..... 83 J3
Great Gays *FHAM/STUB* PO14.. 114 B6
Great Md *LYND* SO43..... 86 C2
  WVILLE PO7..... 81 J7
Great Minster St *WINC* SO23.. 2 E5
Great Southsea St *SSEA* PO5.. 18 C7
Great Well Dr *ROMY* SO51..... 34 E2
Greatwood Cl *FAWY* SO45..... 91 H4
Grebe Cl *FHAM/PORC* PO16..... 98 C6
  HORN PO8..... 81 K1
Greenacre Gdns *WVILLE* PO7.. 101 J4
Greenacres Dr *ROMY* SO51..... 33 F6
Greenaway La *HLER* SO31..... 94 C4
Greencrss La *ROWN* SO16..... 43 G6
Greenbanks Gdns
  FHAM/PORC PO16..... 98 A4
Green Cl *FAWY* SO45..... 91 H2
  TOTT SO40..... 67 J1
Green Crs *LSOL/BMARY* PO13.. 115 H4
Grendale Cl *CHFD* SO53..... 38 B4
The Greendale *FHAM* PO15..... 96 E2

reenfield Crs HORN PO8 82 C2
reenfield Ri HORN PO8 82 C2
reenfields Av TOTT SO40 52 D3
reenfinch Cl ELGH SO50 44 A2 2
reenhill Av WINW SO22 2 A4
reenhill Cl WINW SO22 2 A4
reenhill La ROWN SO16 41 K3
reenhill Rd WINW SO22 21 G7
reenhill Ter WINW SO22 2 A4
reen Hollow Cl
FHAM/PORC PO16 12 D1
reen Jacket Cl WINW SO22 2 A9
reen La BPWT SO32 49 K4
FAWY SO45 110 C7
GPORT PO12 132 D5 1
GPORT PO12 133 F1
HISD PO11 137 F6
HLER SO31 73 H4
HLER SO31 74 C5
HLER SO31 75 F4
HLER SO31 93 K4
HLER SO31 94 E5
HSEA PO3 119 F4
ROMY SO51 35 K2
ROWN SO16 43 G2
ROWN SO16 53 K2
TOTT SO40 40 A7
WVILLE PO7 62 D7
Greenlea Cl CHAM PO6 101 G4
Greenlea Crs ROWN SO16 44 A6
Greenlea Rd GPORT PO12 132 C1 2
Green Park Cl WINC SO23 22 A5 1
Green Park Rd ROWN SO16 53 K5
Green Pond Cnr HAV PO9 15 J5
Green Pond La ROMY SO51 30 D6
Green Rd FHAM/STUB PO14 114 D3
GPORT PO12 132 D6
SSEA PO5 18 C7
Greens Cl BPWT SO32 48 C3
ELGH SO50 45 K2
The Green HLER SO31 74 C7
ROMY SO51 29 H7 3
Greenway Rd GPORT PO12 16 A2
Greenways BPWT SO32 49 J6
CHFD SO53 38 A4
ROWN SO16 44 A6
The Greenwich FAWY SO45 110 B5 1
Greenwood Av CHAM PO6 100 C6
ROWN SO16 41 J5
Greenwood Cl
FHAM/PORC PO16 97 H2
ROMY SO51 35 F2 1
Greenwood La BPWT SO32 47 F3
Greetham St SSEA PO5 18 D4
Gregory Gdns TOTT SO40 52 B3 1
Gregory La BPWT SO32 47 G6
Gregson Cl LSOL/BMARY PO13 115 K4
Grenadier Cl HLER SO31 95 G4
Grendon Cl ROWN SO16 43 J6 2
Grenville Gdns FAWY SO45 91 H5
Grenville Rd ENEY PO4 19 G7 1
Gresley Gdns HEND SO30 58 B2 3
Grevillea Av FHAM PO15 95 K3
Greville Gn EMRTH PO10 104 B3
Greville Rd WSHM SO15 4 B4
Greyfriars Rd FHAM PO15 96 D4
Greyhound Cl HEND SO30 58 A1 3
Greyshott Av FHAM/STUB PO14 96 D6
Greywell Av ROWN SO16 42 C7
Griffen Cl ELGH SO50 45 H1 2
Griffin Ct PTSW SO17 5 M2
Griffin Wk LSOL/BMARY PO13 131 K2
Griffon Cl HLER SO31 73 K4
Gritanwood Rd ENEY PO4 135 G5
Grosvenor Cl PTSW SO17 55 K2
Grosvenor Dr WINC SO23 22 A5
Grosvenor Gdns HEND SO30 57 G3
PTSW SO17 55 K2 1
Grosvenor Rd CHFD SO53 38 B1
PTSW SO17 55 K2
Grosvenor Sq WSHM SO15 4 F7
Grosvenor St SSEA PO5 18 D5
Grove Av FHAM/PORC PO16 117 F1
GPORT PO12 16 C4
Grove Gdns ITCH SO19 11 K7
Grovelands Rd WINW SO22 20 E6
Grovely Wy ROMY SO51 35 K1
Grove Pl ITCH SO19 11 K6
Grove Rd CHAM PO6 101 H7
FHAM/PORC PO16 13 G6
GPORT PO12 16 A1
HAV PO9 14 F5
LSOL/BMARY PO13 131 F2
RWIN SO21 33 G4
WSHM SO15 54 D5
Grove Rd North SSEA PO5 18 D7
Grove Rd South SSEA PO5 18 D8
The Grove EMRTH PO10 104 E3
FHAM/STUB PO14 114 C5
HLER SO31 73 G6
ITCH SO19 11 K7
Gruneisen Rd NEND PO2 118 B5
Guardhouse Rd PSEA PO1 134 A1
Guardroom Rd NEND PO2 118 A6
Gudge Heath La FHAM PO15 12 B2
Guernsey Cl ROWN SO16 53 K1
Guessens La FHAM/STUB PO14 96 A6
Guest Rd ELGH SO50 39 G7
Guildford Cl EMRTH PO10 105 G5
Guildford Dr CHFD SO53 37 J7
Guildford Rd PSEA PO1 19 H2
Guildford St SHAM SO14 5 K8 1
Guildhall Wk PSEA PO1 18 B5
Guillemot Cl FAWY SO45 91 J3
Guillemot Gdns
LSOL/BMARY PO13 115 J4
Gull Cl LSOL/BMARY PO13 115 J5
The Gulls TOTT SO40 70 A3
Gullycroft Md HEND SO30 58 A5
Gunners Pk BPWT SO32 49 F3
Gunners Rw ENEY PO4 135 G6
Gunners Wy GPORT PO12 116 C7
LSOL/BMARY PO13 116 D6
Gunwharf Rd PSEA PO1 17 L6
Gurnard Rd CHAM PO6 100 D7
Gurney Rd ENEY PO4 135 G4
WSHM SO15 54 D4
Gutner La HISD PO11 121 K6
Gwatkin Cl HAV PO9 102 D3 1
Gypsy La HORN PO8 64 A7

H

Hack Dr RWIN SO21 39 J2
Hackworth Gdns HEND SO30 58 B2
Haddon Cl FHAM PO15 12 D6
Haddon Dr ELGH SO50 38 D5
Hadleigh Gdns ELGH SO50 38 D5
Hadleigh Rd CHAM PO6 100 C6 3
Hadley Fld FAWY SO45 109 J2 1
Hadrians Cl CHFD SO53 38 B3
Hadrian Wy ROWN SO16 43 F4
Haflinger Dr HLER SO31 75 G5
Haig Rd ELGH SO50 45 K2
Haileybury Gdns HEND SO30 58 B3 1
Halden Cl ROMY SO51 35 G1
Hales Dr HEND SO30 57 K7
Hale St North PSEA PO1 18 F1 2
Hale St South PSEA PO1 18 F1
Halfpenny La PSEA PO1 17 M7 1
Halifax Ri WVILLE PO7 82 A6
Hall Cl BPWT SO32 48 E3
Hallet Cl WEND SO18 56 D2 6
Hallett Rd HAV PO9 15 K3
Halletts Cl FHAM/STUB PO14 114 D4
The Halliards FHAM/PORC PO16 97 J7
Halliday Cl GPORT PO12 16 B4
Halliday Crs ENEY PO4 135 H5
Hall Lands La ELGH SO50 46 C1
Halls Farm Cl WINW SO22 21 H4
The Hall Wy WINW SO22 20 E2
Halsey Cl GPORT PO12 132 C5
Halstead Rd CHAM PO6 100 C6
WEND SO18 56 C2
Halterworth Cl ROMY SO51 35 G3 2
Halterworth La ROMY SO51 35 H2
Haltons Cl TOTT SO40 52 C3
Halyard Cl LSOL/BMARY PO13 132 A1
Hambert Wy TOTT SO40 52 D7 3
Hamble Cl HLER SO31 94 B5
Hamble Ct CHFD SO53 38 A5 1
Hambledon Cl WINW SO22 21 G3
Hambledon Rd WVILLE PO7 62 C5 1
Hamble House Gdns
HLER SO31 93 K4 1
Hamble La HLER SO31 73 J3
WVILLE PO7 101 K1
Hamble Rd GPORT PO12 132 C4
Hamble Springs BPWT SO32 48 E4
Hamblewood HEND SO30 59 F6
Hambrook Rd GPORT PO12 132 D2
Hambrook St SSEA PO5 18 B8
Hameldon Cl ROWN SO16 54 A5 2
Hamfield Dr HISD PO11 137 F4
Hamilton Cl HAV PO9 14 F7
Hamilton Gv
LSOL/BMARY PO13 115 J6
Hamilton Ms FAWY SO45 91 J5 2
Hamilton Rd CHAM PO6 99 H6
ELGH SO50 39 G7
FAWY SO45 91 J6
SSEA PO5 18 E9
Ham La EMRTH PO10 105 G7
GPORT PO12 116 D6
HORN PO8 64 A4
Hamlet Wy GPORT PO12 116 D6
LSOL/BMARY PO13 116 C6
Hammond Cl FHAM PO15 12 B3
Hammond Rd FHAM PO15 12 C3
Hammonds Cl TOTT SO40 52 D4
Hammond's Gn TOTT SO40 52 C4
Hammonds La TOTT SO40 52 D4
Hammonds Wy TOTT SO40 52 D4
Hampshire St PSEA PO1 134 D1
Hampshire Ter PSEA PO1 18 B6
Hampton Cl FAWY SO45 110 B7
WVILLE PO7 82 B6 4
Hampton Gdns FAWY SO45 110 B7
Hampton Gv FHAM PO15 96 C5
Hampton Hl BPWT SO32 49 J5
Hampton La FAWY SO45 110 B5
WINW SO22 21 F6
Hamtun Crs TOTT SO40 52 D3 1
Hamtun Gdns TOTT SO40 52 D3
Hamtun Rd ITCH SO19 11 L5
Hamtun St SHAM SO14 8 F3
Hanbidge Crs
LSOL/BMARY PO13 116 A3
Handel Rd WSHM SO15 4 E8
Handel Ter WSHM SO15 4 D8
Handford Pl WSHM SO15 4 F6
Handley Rd GPORT PO12 132 C2 2
The Hangers BPWT SO32 48 E1
Hanley Rd WSHM SO15 4 B3
Hannah Gdns WVILLE PO7 82 A5 3
Hannay Ri ITCH SO19 57 G7
Hannington Rd HAV PO9 82 E6 2
Hann Rd ROWN SO16 41 K5
Hanns Wy ELGH SO50 44 D1
Hanover Buildings SHAM SO14 9 G2
Hanover Gdns
FHAM/PORC PO16 13 J1
Hanoverian Wy FHAM PO15 75 H6
Hanover St PSEA PO1 17 L3
Hanway Rd NEND PO2 118 C7
Ha'penny Dell WVILLE PO7 101 K3 3
Harborough Rd WSHM SO15 4 E6
Harbourne Gdns WEND SO18 56 E2
Harbour Pde SHAM SO14 8 E1
WSHM SO15 8 D1
Harbour Rd GPORT PO12 16 F4
HISD PO11 136 D4
Harbourside HAV PO9 121 G1
Harbour Vw
FHAM/PORC PO16 117 F1
Harbour Wy EMRTH PO10 104 D6 3
NEND PO2 118 B5
Harbridge Ct HAV PO9 82 E6
Harcourt Cl HORN PO8 82 B1
Harcourt Rd FHAM/STUB PO14 96 C7
GPORT PO12 132 D3
PSEA PO1 134 D1
WEND SO18 6 B2
Harding Rd GPORT PO12 132 C2
Hardley La FAWY SO45 91 J7
The Hard PSEA PO1 17 L3
Hardwicke Cl ROWN SO16 54 A2
Hardwicke Wy HLER SO31 93 H3 2
Hardwick Rd CHFD SO53 38 A4 2
Hardy Cl HLER SO31 95 G2
WSHM SO15 54 C6
Hardy Dr FAWY SO45 91 J5
Hardy Rd CHAM PO6 101 K7
ELGH SO50 44 C2
Harebell Cl FHAM/PORC PO16 13 L1
Harefield Ct ROMY SO51 35 G2 3
Harefield Rd PTSW SO17 55 K1
Hare La RWIN SO21 33 K5
Harestock Cl WINW SO22 21 G2
Harestock Rd WINW SO22 21 G3
HAV PO9 14 B1
Harewood Cl ELGH SO50 38 D5
Harkness Dr WVILLE PO7 82 C5
Harland Crs WSHM SO15 54 E3
Harlaxton Cl ELGH SO50 38 C5
Harlech Dr CHFD SO53 37 H6
Harlequin Gv FHAM PO15 12 D5
Harleston Rd CHAM PO6 100 C5
Harlyn Rd ROWN SO16 54 A3
Harold Cl TOTT SO40 52 C6
Harold Rd EMRTH PO10 104 E2
ENEY PO4 19 H8
FHAM/STUB PO14 114 E4
HISD PO11 137 J6
WSHM SO15 54 D5
The Harrage ROMY SO51 34 E3
Harrier Cl HORN PO8 64 B5
LSOL/BMARY PO13 131 G2 4
ROWN SO16 42 C5
Harrier Wy FAWY SO45 109 J1
Harriet Cl FHAM/STUB PO14 114 C5
Harris Av HEND SO30 58 B4 3
Harrison Rd FHAM/PORC PO16 13 J3
PTSW SO17 55 K1
Harris Rd LSOL/BMARY PO13 115 K4
Harrow Down WINW SO22 25 G4
Harrowgate La WVILLE PO7 62 E4
Harrow Rd SSEA PO5 19 G5
Hart Hl FAWY SO45 91 K5
Harting Gdns FHAM/PORC PO16 99 F5
Hartington Rd GPORT PO12 132 C2
SHAM SO14 5 K8
Hartland Ct EMRTH PO10 105 G5
Hartland's Rd
FHAM/PORC PO16 13 K6
Hartley Av PTSW SO17 55 J2
Hartley Cl ELGH SO50 45 K2
FAWY SO45 91 H5 5
Hartley Ct ROWN SO16 43 H7
Hartley Rd ELGH SO50 45 K1
NEND PO2 118 C4
Hartley Wk FAWY SO45 91 G5 2
Hart Plain Av HORN PO8 81 K3
Harts Farm Wy HAV PO9 102 D6
Hartsgrove Cl FAWY SO45 110 B7
Hartwell Rd HSEA PO3 119 G4 2
Hartwood Gdns HORN PO8 81 K3
Harvest Cl WINW SO22 25 G4
Harvester Dr FHAM PO15 96 C5
Harvest Rd NBAD SO52 37 G4
WVILLE PO7 80 D1
Harvey Ct FAWY SO45 110 B5 2
Harvey Crs HLER SO31 94 E4
Harvey Gdns FAWY SO45 91 J3
Harvey Rd ELGH SO50 39 H7
Harwich Rd CHAM PO6 100 C5
Harwood Cl
LSOL/BMARY PO13 115 K3 1
TOTT SO40 52 C4
Harwood Rd
LSOL/BMARY PO13 115 K4
Haselbury Rd TOTT SO40 52 E5
Haselfoot Gdns WEND SO18 57 H5 1
Haselworth Dr GPORT PO12 132 E7
Haskells Cl LYND SO43 86 B1 1
Haslar Crs WVILLE PO7 81 H3
Haslar Rd GPORT PO12 16 E9
Haslemere Gdns HISD PO11 138 C6
Haslemere Rd EMRTH PO10 105 G4
ENEY PO4 19 K8
The Hassocks WVILLE PO7 82 B6
Hastings Av GPORT PO12 116 C7
Hatch Ct HAV PO9 82 D6
Hatchet La BROC SO42 107 J7
Hatch Md HEND SO30 57 F2
Hatfield Rd ENEY PO4 19 L8
Hathaway Cl ELGH SO50 38 E6
Hathaway Gdns WVILLE PO7 82 C4
Hatherell Cl HEND SO30 57 G3
Hatherley Crs
FHAM/PORC PO16 98 E7
Hatherley Dr
FHAM/PORC PO16 98 E6 1
Hatherley Rd CHAM PO6 99 K5
WINW SO22 2 B2
Hatley Rd WEND SO18 7 H3
Havant Farm Cl HAV PO9 14 F1
Havant Rd CHAM PO6 101 K6
EMRTH PO10 15 M5
HAV PO9 15 J6
HISD PO11 121 G4
HORN PO8 64 E6
NEND PO2 118 C6
Havant St PSEA PO1 17 L4 3
Havelock Rd HLER SO31 94 B5
SHAM SO14 4 E8
SSEA PO5 18 F6
WSHM SO15 4 E8
Haven Crs FHAM/STUB PO14 114 A6
Havendale HEND SO30 58 C7 3
Haven Rd HISD PO11 138 B7
Havenstone Wy WEND SO18 44 A7 1
The Haven ELGH SO50 38 E5
ENEY PO4 135 G3
GPORT PO12 132 E6
H Av FAWY SO45 110 C1
Havisham Rd NEND PO2 134 C1 4
Hawfinch Cl ROWN SO16 42 C5
Hawk Cl FHAM/STUB PO14 114 C5
Hawke St PSEA PO1 17 L3
Hawkeswood Rd WEND SO18 5 M4
Hawkewood Av WVILLE PO7 81 J3
Hawkhill FAWY SO45 90 D2
Hawkhurst Cl ITCH SO19 11 H8
Hawkins Rd
LSOL/BMARY PO13 116 A5
Hawkley Cl HAV PO9 83 F7 4
Hawkley Gn ITCH SO19 10 E8
Hawkwell FHAM/PORC PO16 98 C6
Hawswater Cl ROWN SO16 54 A3 2
Hawthorn Cl ELGH SO50 46 B1 1
FHAM/PORC PO16 98 E5
HEND SO30 58 C6 2
RWIN SO21 39 K2
Hawthorn Crs CHAM PO6 119 F1
Hawthorne Gv HISD PO11 137 H4
Hawthorne Rd TOTT SO40 52 C4
Hawthorn La HLER SO31 94 D1
Hawthorn Rd FAWY SO45 91 G3 3
HORN PO8 64 D2
PTSW SO17 55 H2
WVILLE PO7 80 C1
The Hawthorns ELGH SO50 44 B2 1
TOTT SO40 70 B4
Hayburn Rd ROWN SO16 53 J2
Haydock Cl TOTT SO40 52 B4
Haydock Ms WVILLE PO7 82 C4
Hayes Md FAWY SO45 109 J2
Hayle Rd WEND SO18 56 E2
Hayley Cl FAWY SO45 91 G6
Hayling Av HSEA PO3 135 G1
Hayling Cl FHAM/STUB PO14 12 A8
Hay St PSEA PO1 18 A4
Hayter Gdns ROMY SO51 35 F2
Hayward Cl TOTT SO40 52 C5
Hayward Ct FAWY SO45 109 K3 2
Hazel Cl CHFD SO53 31 K7
RWIN SO21 39 K1
Hazeldean Dr HAV PO9 83 J4
Hazeldown Cl ROWN SO16 41 K6
Hazeleigh Av ITCH SO19 10 C5
Hazeley Rd RWIN SO21 33 K3
Hazel Farm Rd TOTT SO40 52 B5
Hazel Gv WINW SO22 25 G3
HLER SO31 95 G4
TOTT SO40 67 J2
Hazelholt Dr HAV PO9 14 A1
Hazel Rd ITCH SO19 10 A2
Hazelwood
FHAM/STUB PO14 114 C2 1
Hazelwood Av HAV PO9 102 C3
Hazelwood Rd WEND SO18 56 D3 4
Hazleton Wy HORN PO8 64 C7
Headland Dr HLER SO31 95 F2
Headley Cl
LSOL/BMARY PO13 131 G2 5
Hearne Gdns BPWT SO32 61 H3
Heath Cl ELGH SO50 46 C2
HORN PO8 64 C5
Heathcote Pl RWIN SO21 31 J2
Heathcote Rd CHFD SO53 38 A4
NEND PO2 118 E6
Heathen St BPWT SO32 47 G7
Heatherbrae Gdns
NBAD SO52 36 A6 1
Heather Cha ELGH SO50 45 K1 2
Heather Cl LSOL/BMARY PO13 115 J5
TOTT SO40 52 D5
WVILLE PO7 82 A7
Heatherdeane Rd PTSW SO17 55 H2
Heatherdene Rd CHFD SO53 38 B1
Heather Gdns FHAM PO15 12 B2
Heatherlands Rd ROWN SO16 43 G3
Heather Rd FAWY SO45 110 C5
Heatherstone Av FAWY SO45 91 G6
Heatherton Ms EMRTH PO10 104 C3
Heatherview Cl NBAD SO52 36 A5 1
Heathfield FAWY SO45 91 G4 5
Heathfield Av FHAM PO15 12 A6
Heathfield Cl ITCH SO19 11 L4 1
Heathfield Rd CHFD SO53 31 K7
ITCH SO19 11 K4
NEND PO2 118 C7
Heath Gdns HLER SO31 73 G6
Heath House Cl HEND SO30 74 A1
Heath House Gdns HEND SO30 74 A1
Heathhouse La HEND SO30 74 A1
Heathlands Cl CHFD SO53 37 K2
Heathlands Rd CHFD SO53 37 K2
Heath La BROC SO42 125 H1
Heath Lawns FHAM PO15 12 B6
Heath Rd HLER SO31 94 E3
ITCH SO19 7 G9
NBAD SO52 36 B7
Heath Rd North HLER SO31 94 E3
Heath Rd South HLER SO31 94 E3
The Heath WVILLE PO7 81 F1
Heaton Rd GPORT PO12 132 C1
Hebrides Cl
FHAM/STUB PO14 114 C4 7
Heckfield Cl HAV PO9 103 J1 7
Hector Cl WVILLE PO7 101 K4
Hector Rd FHAM/STUB PO14 115 H2
Hedera Rd HLER SO31 94 E3
Hedgerow Cl ROWN SO16 41 K5
Hedgerow Dr WEND SO18 7 K1 1
Hedgerow Gdns EMRTH PO10 104 C3
Hedley Cl FAWY SO45 110 C6
Hedley Gdns HEND SO30 58 A1 4
Heidelberg Rd ENEY PO4 19 J5
The Heights FHAM/PORC PO16 98 A4
HEND SO30 57 K6
Helena Rd ENEY PO4 134 E6
Helford Gdns WEND SO18 56 E2 1
Hellyer Rd ENEY PO4 19 L8
Helm Cl LSOL/BMARY PO13 132 A2
Helsted Cl GPORT PO12 132 B4
Helston Dr EMRTH PO10 104 B3
Helston Rd CHAM PO6 99 J5
Helvellyn Rd ROWN SO16 54 A4
Hemdean Gdns HEND SO30 57 G3
Hemlock Rd HORN PO8 81 K1
Hemlock Wy NBAD SO52 37 G5
Hemming Cl TOTT SO40 52 D6
Hemmingway Gdns
FHAM PO15 75 H5
Hempsted Rd CHAM PO6 100 A5
Hemsley Wk HORN PO8 82 B1
Henderson Rd ENEY PO4 135 G5
Hendy Cl SSEA PO5 18 E7 1
Henery St GPORT PO12 16 D5 1
Henley Gdns FHAM PO15 96 E2
Henley Rd ENEY PO4 19 J8 1
Henry Cl FAWY SO45 109 J1 2
Henry Rd ELGH SO50 39 G6 1
WSHM SO15 54 D5
Henry St WSHM SO15 4 E6 1
Henstead Rd WSHM SO15 4 E7
Henty Rd ROWN SO16 54 B4
Henville Cl LSOL/BMARY PO13 116 A7
Hepworth Cl ITCH SO19 11 L6 1
Herbert Rd ENEY PO4 134 D6 1
GPORT PO12 132 C3
Herbert St PSEA PO1 134 B1
Herbert Walker Av WSHM SO15 8 E3
Hercules St NEND PO2 118 C7 3
Hereford Rd SSEA PO5 18 E8
Hereward Cl ROMY SO51 35 G3 3
Hermes Rd LSOL/BMARY PO13 130 E1
Hermitage Cl BPWT SO32 48 B3 2
HAV PO9 103 F2
Herne Rd CHAM PO6 100 D6
Heron Cl ENEY PO4 135 G3
Heron La ROMY SO51 28 C3
Heron Quay EMRTH PO10 104 D7
Herons Cl FHAM/STUB PO14 114 D3
Heron Sq ELGH SO50 44 B2
Heron Wy LSOL/BMARY PO13 115 H4
Herrick Cl ITCH SO19 73 G1
Herriott Cl HORN PO8 64 B7
Hertford Pl PSEA PO1 134 C1
Hertsfield FHAM/STUB PO14 95 H2
Hester Rd ENEY PO4 135 G4 1
Hestia Cl ROMY SO51 35 H2
Hewett Cl FHAM/STUB PO14 96 A7
Hewett Rd FHAM/STUB PO14 96 A7
NEND PO2 118 D5
Hewetts Ri HLER SO31 94 B6
Hewitt Cl GPORT PO12 132 D2 5
Hewitt's Rd WSHM SO15 4 B9
Heyes Dr ITCH SO19 11 L4
Heysham Rd WSHM SO15 54 C4
Heyshott Rd ENEY PO4 19 K6
Heyward Rd ENEY PO4 19 G6
Heywood Gn ITCH SO19 57 H7
Hickory Dr WINW SO22 21 F3
Hickory Gdns HEND SO30 57 G1
Highbank Av WVILLE PO7 101 G3
Highbridge Rd ELGH SO50 39 G3
Highbury Cl ELGH SO50 46 B2
Highbury Gv CHAM PO6 119 F1
Highbury St PSEA PO1 17 M6
Highbury Wy CHAM PO6 118 E1
Highclere Av HAV PO9 102 E2
Highclere Rd ROWN SO16 54 E1
Highclere Wy CHFD SO53 37 H7
Highcliff Av SHAM SO14 5 H3
Highcliffe Dr ELGH SO50 38 D3
Highcliffe Rd GPORT PO12 132 C4
WINC SO23 3 G7
Highcroft La HORN PO8 64 D4
Highcrown St PTSW SO17 55 H2
High Dr LSOL/BMARY PO13 115 K6
Highfield RWIN SO21 33 K4
Highfield Av FHAM/STUB PO14 12 E8
PTSW SO17 55 G1
RWIN SO21 33 K4
WVILLE PO7 82 B5
Highfield Cl CHFD SO53 38 A4
PTSW SO17 55 H2 1
WVILLE PO7 82 A4
Highfield Crs PTSW SO17 55 J2
Highfield La PTSW SO17 55 H2
Highfield Rd CHFD SO53 38 B4
GPORT PO12 132 C2
PSEA PO1 18 F3
PTSW SO17 55 G3
High Firs Gdns ROMY SO51 35 H3
High Firs Rd ITCH SO19 7 K9
ROMY SO51 35 H2
Highgate Rd HSEA PO3 119 F6
Highgrove Cl TOTT SO40 52 C7 2
Highgrove Rd HSEA PO3 119 G7
Highland Cl EMRTH PO10 104 B6
Highland Rd EMRTH PO10 104 B5
ENEY PO4 19 K8
Highlands Cl FAWY SO45 91 H4
NBAD SO52 35 K5 2
Highlands Rd CHAM PO6 101 J6
FHAM PO15 12 A2
Highland St ENEY PO4 19 M9
Highlands Wy FAWY SO45 91 G4
High Lawn Wy HAV PO9 103 F1
High Md FHAM PO15 12 C1
High Meadow ITCH SO19 7 L7
Highmount Cl WINC SO23 3 H6
Highnam Gdns HLER SO31 94 E2
High Oaks Cl HLER SO31 95 F3
High Rd ELGH SO50 44 A6
ROWN SO16 56 A1
High St BPWT SO32 48 D4
BPWT SO32 61 F5
BROC SO42 108 A7
CHAM PO6 100 E7
ELGH SO50 44 D2
EMRTH PO10 104 C6
FAWY SO45 91 H1
FHAM/PORC PO16 13 L4
FHAM/STUB PO14 96 A6
GPORT PO12 16 F5
HEND SO30 57 H3 1
HEND SO30 59 F5
HLER SO31 74 A6
LSOL/BMARY PO13 131 F2
LYND SO43 86 C1
PSEA PO1 17 L7
RWIN SO21 33 K4
SHAM SO14 9 G4
TOTT SO40 53 F5
WHAM PO17 79 J7
WINC SO23 2 D4
WVILLE PO7 62 C1
High Trees ELGH SO50 46 D1
WVILLE PO7 82 A5
High Trees Dr WINW SO22 21 H5
High Vw FHAM/PORC PO16 99 F5
High View Wy WEND SO18 6 F2
Highways Rd RWIN SO21 33 F4
Highwood La ROMY SO51 35 J2
Highwood Rd
LSOL/BMARY PO13 131 K1
Higworth La HISD PO11 137 G3
Hilary Av CHAM PO6 101 F7
Hilda Gdns WVILLE PO7 81 F1
Hilden Wy WINW SO22 20 D2
Hillary Cl FHAM/PORC PO16 12 E3
LYND SO43 86 D3
Hillborough Crs SSEA PO5 18 E8 2
Hillbrow Cl FHAM PO15 12 B1

Hill Brow Cl *HAV* PO9 .... 83 J4
Hillcrest Av *CHFD* SO53 .... 38 A4
Hillcrest Cl *NBAD* SO52 .... 36 A5
Hillcrest Dr *CHFD* SO53 .... 38 A4 ⑤
Hill Crest Rd *BPWT* SO32 .... 48 E7
Hill Cft *FHAM* PO15 .... 95 J3
Hilldene Wy *HEND* SO30 .... 57 H3 ②
Hilldowns Rd *NEND* PO2 .... 118 B5
Hill Farm Rd *WSHM* SO15 .... 4 C6
Hillgrove Rd *WEND* SO18 .... 56 C1 ①
Hill Head Rd *FHAM/STUB* PO14 .. 114 B6
Hillier Wy *WINC* SO23 .... 21 K5
Hill La *ROWN* SO16 .... 54 E1
  RWIN SO21 .... 39 J1
  WSHM SO15 .... 55 F3
Hillmead Gdns *HAV* PO9 .... 102 C4
Hill Park Rd *FHAM* PO15 .... 96 E2
  GPORT PO12 .... 132 C2
Hill Pl *HLER* SO31 .... 74 A5
Hill Ri *RWIN* SO21 .... 33 K3
Hill Rd *FHAM/PORC* PO16 .... 99 G5
Hillside *WINW* SO22 .... 21 F2
Hillside Av *ROMY* SO51 .... 35 F3
  WEND SO18 .... 56 B3
  WVILLE PO7 .... 101 G4
Hillside Cl *CHFD* SO53 .... 38 A4
  WINW SO22 .... 21 F2
Hillside Crs *CHAM* PO6 .... 99 J5
Hillside Rd *WINW* SO22 .... 21 F6
Hillsley Rd *CHAM* PO6 .... 99 J4
Hillson Dr *FHAM* PO15 .... 96 D3
Hill St *ROMY* SO51 .... 40 B5
Hilltop *WINW* SO22 .... 21 F2
Hilltop Crs *CHAM* PO6 .... 101 G4
Hilltop Dr *ITCH* SO19 .... 11 M1
Hilltop Gdns *HORN* PO8 .... 64 C7
Hilltop Rd *WVILLE* PO7 .... 99 K4
Hillview *HORN* PO8 .... 64 D7
Hillview Rd *FAWY* SO45 .... 91 G3
Hill View Rd *FHAM/PORC* PO16 ... 99 F5
  ROMY SO51 .... 28 B1
  ROMY SO51 .... 29 H3
The Hillway *CHFD* SO53 .... 38 A3
  FHAM/PORC PO16 .... 99 F6
Hillyfields *ROWN* SO16 .... 41 H7
Hilsea Crs *NEND* PO2 .... 118 D2
Hiltingbury Av *HAV* PO9 .... 103 H1 ②
Hiltingbury Cl *CHFD* SO53 .... 38 A1
Hiltingbury Rd *CHFD* SO53 .... 37 J1
Hilton Rd *GPORT* PO12 .... 16 D8
Hinkler Rd *ITCH* SO19 .... 7 M9
Hinton Cl *HAV* PO9 .... 102 D2
Hinton Crs *ITCH* SO19 .... 57 H7
Hinton Flds *WINC* SO23 .... 22 B1
Hinton Manor La *HORN* PO8 ...... 63 K3
Hipley Rd *HAV* PO9 .... 103 H3
Hirst Rd *FAWY* SO45 .... 91 J3
Hispano Av *FHAM* PO15 .... 75 H6
Hither Gn *EMRTH* PO10 .... 105 H4
Hitherwood Cl *HORN* PO8 .... 82 C4
Hoad's Hl *WHAM* PO17 .... 77 J3
Hobart Dr *FAWY* SO45 .... 91 J4
Hobb La *HEND* SO30 .... 58 C6
Hobby Cl *HSEA* PO3 .... 119 F3
Hobson Wy *FAWY* SO45 .... 110 A4 ②
Hockham Ct *HAV* PO9 .... 82 D6
Hockley Cl *CHAM* PO6 .... 100 C6 ④
Hockley Link *RWIN* SO21 .... 25 H6
Hocombe Dr *CHFD* SO53 .... 31 J7
Hocombe Park Cl *CHFD* SO53 ..... 31 J7
Hocombe Rd *CHFD* SO53 .... 31 J7
Hocombe Wood Rd *CHFD* SO53 ... 31 H7
Hodder Cl *CHFD* SO53 .... 37 J5 ⑥
Hodges Cl *HAV* PO9 .... 15 G1
Hoeford Cl *FHAM/PORC* PO16 .... 115 J1
Hoe La *ROMY* SO51 .... 41 H1
Hoe Rd *BPWT* SO32 .... 49 F4
The Hoe *LSOL/BMARY* PO13 ..... 116 B6 ③
Hogarth Cl *ROMY* SO51 .... 35 G1
Hogwood La *HEND* SO30 .... 45 H5
Holbrook Rd *FHAM/PORC* PO16 ... 13 J7
  PSEA PO1 .... 18 F1
Holbury Ct *HAV* PO9 .... 103 J1 ⑧
Holbury Dro *FAWY* SO45 .... 109 J3
Holcot La *HSEA* PO3 .... 119 H3
Holcroft Rd *ITCH* SO19 .... 57 H7
Holdenbury Ct *HSEA* PO3 .... 119 H2
Holdenhurst Cl *HORN* PO8 ...... 64 D3 ④
Hole La *BPWT* SO32 .... 60 B3
Holkham Cl *ROWN* SO16 .... 53 K1 ②
Hollam Cl *FHAM/STUB* PO14 ...... 96 C6
Hollam Crs *FHAM/STUB* PO14 .... 96 C6
Hollam Dr *FHAM/STUB* PO14 ..... 96 C6
Hollam Rd *ENEY* PO4 .... 135 G4
Holland Pk *HLER* SO31 .... 94 E3
Holland Pl
  LSOL/BMARY PO13 .... 116 A5 ④
  ROWN SO16 .... 54 C3
Holland Rd *ENEY* PO4 .... 19 G6
  ITCH SO19 .... 10 B6
  TOTT SO40 .... 52 B5
Hollingbourne Cl *WEND* SO18 ...... 6 B3
Holliman Dr *ROMY* SO51 .... 34 C2
Hollow La *HISD* PO11 .... 137 G5
Hollybank Cl *HORN* PO8 .... 64 D7
Hollybank Crs *FAWY* SO45 .... 91 G3
Hollybank La *EMRTH* PO10 ...... 104 C2
Hollybank Rd *FAWY* SO45 .... 91 G3
Hollybrook Av *ROWN* SO16 .... 54 D1
Hollybrook Cl *ROWN* SO16 .... 54 C1
Hollybrook Gdns *HLER* SO31 ..... 95 F1
Hollybrook Rd *ROWN* SO16 ...... 54 C1
Holly Cl *FAWY* SO45 .... 91 H7
  HLER SO31 .... 94 D3
Holly Dell *ROWN* SO16 .... 43 F6
Holly Dr *WVILLE* PO7 .... 82 B7
Holly Gdns *HEND* SO30 .... 57 G1
Holly Gv *FHAM/PORC* PO16 ...... 97 F2
Holly Hatch Rd *TOTT* SO40 ...... 52 C6
Holly Hl *ROWN* SO16 .... 43 F6
Holly Hill La *HLER* SO31 .... 74 D7
Holly La *LYMN* SO41 .... 124 A7
Holly Oak Rd *ROWN* SO16 .... 54 B1
Holly Rd *FAWY* SO45 .... 110 B7
  TOTT SO40 .... 68 A3
Holly St *GPORT* PO12 .... 16 D5
Hollywell Dr *CHAM* PO6 .... 100 A7

Hill Brow Cl *HAV* PO9 .... 83 J4
Hollywood Cl *NBAD* SO52 .... 36 A6
Holman Cl *HORN* PO8 .... 82 B3
Holmdale Rd *GPORT* PO12 .... 132 C1
Holmefield Av
  FHAM/STUB PO14 .... 115 G1
Holmesland Dr *HEND* SO30 .... 58 E5
Holmesland La *HEND* SO30 .... 58 E5
Holmgrove *FHAM/STUB* PO14 .... 95 H3 ②
Holm Oak Cl *WINW* SO22 .... 20 D2
Holmsley Cl *WEND* SO18 .... 7 M5
Holne Ct *FHAM* PO15 .... 135 H5
Holst Wy *WVILLE* PO7 .... 102 A1
Holt Cl *WHAM* PO17 .... 77 C1
Holt Ct *ITCH* SO19 .... 10 D9
Holt Gdns *HAV* PO9 .... 83 J2
Holt Rd *WSHM* SO15 .... 4 E5
Holyborne Rd *ROMY* SO51 .... 35 G3
Holybourne Rd *HAV* PO9 .... 14 E1
Holyrood Av *PTSW* SO17 .... 55 J2
Holyrood Cl *WVILLE* PO7 .... 82 B6 ⑤
Home Farm Cl *FAWY* SO45 .... 91 J4
Homefield *ROMY* SO51 .... 35 F1 ②
  EMRTH PO10 .... 104 E2
Home Md *WVILLE* PO7 .... 80 E2
Homer Cl *HORN* PO8 .... 81 K3
  LSOL/BMARY PO13 .... 115 J7
Homer Farm La *FAWY* SO45 ...... 128 B2
Home Rule Rd *HLER* SO31 .... 95 F2
Homewell *HAV* PO9 .... 14 E5
Honey La *FHAM* PO15 .... 96 E1
Honeysuckle Cl *WINW* SO22 ...... 25 C4
  HLER SO31 .... 95 F1
  LSOL/BMARY PO13 .... 115 J4 ④
Honeysuckle Ct *WVILLE* PO7 .... 102 A1 ④
Honeysuckle Rd *ROWN* SO16 ..... 43 J2
Honeysuckle Wy *NBAD* SO52 ..... 37 H4
Honeywood Cl *HSEA* PO3 .... 118 C3
  TOTT SO40 .... 52 C3
Hood Cl *HLER* SO31 .... 95 G2
Hood Rd *WEND* SO18 .... 7 H2
Hook Cl *CHFD* SO53 .... 31 H7
Hook Crs *CHFD* SO53 .... 31 H7
Hook La *HLER* SO31 .... 95 F7
Hook Park Rd *HLER* SO31 .... 112 D1
Hook Rd *ROMY* SO51 .... 31 F6
Hook Water Rd *CHFD* SO53 ...... 31 H7
Hookwood La *ROMY* SO51 .... 31 G7
Hook's Farm Wy *HAV* PO9 .... 14 A1
Hook's La *HAV* PO9 .... 14 A1
Hope Cl *HEND* SO30 .... 57 H2
Hope St *PSEA* PO1 .... 18 C1
Hopfield Cl *WVILLE* PO7 .... 81 K7
Hopfield Ms *WVILLE* PO7 .... 81 K7 ①
Hopkins Cl *CHAM* PO6 .... 99 H6 ②
Hordle Rd *HAV* PO9 .... 102 D2
Hornbeam Cl *HEND* SO30 .... 58 C6 ③
Hornbeam Gdns *HEND* SO30 ..... 57 G2 ①
Hornbeam Rd *HAV* PO9 .... 15 K1
  NBAD SO52 .... 37 F5
Hornby Cl *HLER* SO31 .... 94 C6
Hornchurch Rd *ROWN* SO16 ...... 42 A6
Horndean Rd *EMRTH* PO10 ..... 104 A2
  HORN PO8 .... 65 F4
Hornet Cl *FHAM* PO15 .... 12 A3
  GPORT PO12 .... 16 B8
  FHAM PO14 .... 115 G2
Hornet Rd *EMRTH* PO10 .... 122 D4
  FHAM PO14 .... 115 G2
Horns Dro *ROWN* SO16 .... 41 K5
Horsea Cl *NEND* PO2 .... 118 C3
Horsea Rd *NEND* PO2 .... 118 D2
Horsebridge Rd *HAV* PO9 .... 103 H2
Horsebridge Wy *ROWN* SO16 .... 41 K6
Horsecroft *ROMY* SO51 .... 34 E2 ⑥
Horsefair Ct *ROMY* SO51 .... 34 D3
Horsepost La *WVILLE* PO7 ...... 63 G2
Horse Sands Cl *ENEY* PO4 ...... 135 J5
Horseshoe Cl
  FHAM/STUB PO14 .... 95 J4 ①
Horseshoe Ldg *HLER* SO31 ...... 94 E3
Horton Rd *LSOL/BMARY* PO13 .. 115 K3
Horton Wy *ELGH* SO50 .... 45 J2
Hospital La *FHAM/PORC* PO16 .. 117 H1
Hospital Rd *BPWT* SO32 .... 61 H5
Hotspur Cl *FAWY* SO45 .... 91 G1
Houchin St *BPWT* SO32 .... 48 D4
Houghton Cl *HAV* PO9 .... 83 J7 ⑥
Hound Cl *HLER* SO31 .... 93 G1
Hound Rd *HLER* SO31 .... 73 G7
Hound Road Gdns *HLER* SO31 ... 93 G1
Hound Wy *HLER* SO31 .... 73 G7
Houndwell Pl *SHAM* SO14 .... 9 H2
Hounsdown Av *TOTT* SO40 ...... 52 E7
Hounsdown Cl *TOTT* SO40 ...... 52 E7
House Cl *RWIN* SO21 .... 39 K1
House Farm Rd *GPORT* PO12 ... 132 B4
Hoveton Gv *CHFD* SO53 .... 37 J2
Howard Cl *CHFD* SO53 .... 38 A6
  ELGH SO50 .... 46 B1
  WEND SO18 .... 44 B7 ①
Howard Rd *NEND* PO2 .... 118 D3
  WSHM SO15 .... 4 B6
Howard's Gv *WSHM* SO15 .... 54 D4
Howe Cl *LSOL/BMARY* PO13 .... 131 K2
Howerts Cl *HLER* SO31 .... 94 C7
Hoylake Cl
  LSOL/BMARY PO13 .... 115 K6 ①
Hoylake Rd *CHAM* PO6 .... 101 H5
Hoylecroft Cl *FHAM* PO15 .... 12 C1
Hubert Rd *WINC* SO23 .... 25 H4
Hudson Cl
  LSOL/BMARY PO13 .... 131 K2 ②
Hudson Ct *TOTT* SO40 .... 52 C6 ②
Hudson Rd *SSEA* PO5 .... 18 E5
Hugh's Cl *FAWY* SO45 .... 110 B6
Hulbert Rd *HAV* PO9 .... 102 C1
  WVILLE PO7 .... 82 B6
Hulles Wy *NBAD* SO52 .... 36 A6
Hulse Rd *WSHM* SO15 .... 4 F3
Hulton Cl *ITCH* SO19 .... 10 B8
Humber Cl
  FHAM/STUB PO14 .... 114 C4 ①
Humber Gdns *HLER* SO31 .... 73 K4 ③
The Hummicks *BROC* SO42 ...... 108 C7 ①
Hundred Acres Rd *WHAM* PO17 .. 78 B2
The Hundred *ROMY* SO51 .... 34 D3
  WVILLE PO7 .... 81 J4
Hungerford *HLER* SO31 .... 73 J6
Hunt Av *HLER* SO31 .... 73 F7

Hunter Cl *FAWY* SO45 .... 109 J1 ⑤
  LSOL/BMARY PO13 .... 132 A1
Hunter Rd *EMRTH* PO10 .... 122 D3
  ENEY PO4 .... 19 K8
Hunters Cha *FHAM/STUB* PO14 .. 61 K1 ①
Hunters Crs *ROMY* SO51 .... 29 H7
  TOTT SO40 .... 52 A6
Hunters Hl *TOTT* SO40 .... 68 C2
Hunters Ldg *FHAM* PO15 .... 96 C6
Hunters Ride *WVILLE* PO7 .... 81 K6
Hunters Wy *ELGH* SO50 .... 45 K1
Huntingdon Cl
  FHAM/STUB PO14 .... 95 H5 ②
  TOTT SO40 .... 52 D3
Huntley Cl *CHAM* PO6 .... 100 A5 ⑤
Huntly Wy *WEND* SO18 .... 6 A1
Hunton Cl *ROWN* SO16 .... 54 E1
Hunts Pond Rd *HLER* SO31 ...... 95 G3
The Hurdles *FHAM/STUB* PO14 ... 95 J4
Hurdle Wy *RWIN* SO21 .... 33 J1
Hurlingham Gdns
  ROWN SO16 .... 43 H6 ⑤
Hurn Cl *HAV* PO9 .... 83 J7
Hurricane Dr *ROWN* SO16 .... 41 K5
Hursley Dr *FAWY* SO45 .... 128 B1
Hursley Rd *CHFD* SO53 .... 31 J7
  HAV PO9 .... 102 A3
  RWIN SO21 .... 33 J1
Hurstbourne Cl *HAV* PO9 .... 82 E7 ②
Hurst Cl *CHFD* SO53 .... 37 H6
  FHAM/STUB PO14 .... 114 B6
  TOTT SO40 .... 52 E4
Hurst Gn *LSOL/BMARY* PO13 ... 115 J5
Hurst Green Cl *HORN* PO8 .... 82 C3
  ITCH SO19 .... 11 H1
Hurstville Dr *WVILLE* PO7 .... 82 A6
Hurstwood Av *EMRTH* PO10 .... 105 H6
Hussey Cl *WINC* SO23 .... 21 K5 ③
Hutwood Rd *ROWN* SO16 .... 43 H3
Huxley Cl *HLER* SO31 .... 95 G4
Huxley Ct *FAWY* SO45 .... 90 D4
Hyde Abbey Rd *WINC* SO23 .... 2 E3
Hyde Church La *WINC* SO23 ...... 2 E3
Hyde Cl *TOTT* SO40 .... 52 A5
  WINC SO23 .... 2 D2
  WSHM SO15 .... 54 D3
Hyde Park Rd *SSEA* PO5 .... 18 D5
Hyde St *SSEA* PO5 .... 18 C7 ①
  WINC SO23 .... 2 C2
Hymans Wy *TOTT* SO40 .... 52 D5
Hyssop Cl *FHAM* PO15 .... 75 J6
Hythe By-pass *FAWY* SO45 ...... 90 C2
Hythe Rd *CHAM* PO6 .... 100 D6
  TOTT SO40 .... 70 A5

I

Ibbotson Wy *TOTT* SO40 .... 52 C7
Ibsen Cl *HLER* SO31 .... 75 H5
Ibsley Gv *HAV* PO9 .... 14 A1
Icarus Pl *WVILLE* PO7 .... 102 A4
Idsworth Cl *HORN* PO8 .... 64 E6
Idsworth Rd *HORN* PO8 .... 82 C3
  HSEA PO3 .... 119 F7
Iford Ct *HAV* PO9 .... 83 J7 ⑤
Ilex Crs *HLER* SO31 .... 94 E3
Ilex Wk *HISD* PO11 .... 137 K5
Imber Cl *ITCH* SO19 .... 11 L2
Imber Rd *WINC* SO23 .... 3 J3
Imber Wy *ITCH* SO19 .... 11 L2
Imperial Av *WSHM* SO15 .... 54 C5
Imperial Rd *SHAM* SO14 .... 5 J3
Implacable Rd
  LSOL/BMARY PO13 .... 130 E1
Ingersley Ri *HEND* SO30 .... 57 J3
Ingledene Cl *GPORT* PO12 .... 16 A6
  HAV PO9 .... 14 A3
Ingle Gln *FAWY* SO45 .... 91 H5 ⑤
Ingle Gn *TOTT* SO40 .... 52 A3
Ingleside *HLER* SO31 .... 73 F6
Ingleside Cl *FHAM/STUB* PO14 .. 96 C6 ③
Ingleton Rd *ROWN* SO16 .... 53 J3
Inglis Rd *SSEA* PO5 .... 19 G7
Inhams La *WVILLE* PO7 .... 80 C1
Inhurst Av *WVILLE* PO7 .... 82 B5
Inhurst Rd *NEND* PO2 .... 118 D3
Inkerman Rd *ITCH* SO19 .... 10 B4
Inlands Rd *RCCH* PO18 .... 105 J3
International Wy *ITCH* SO19 .... 10 D9
Invergordon Av *CHAM* PO6 ..... 101 G7
Inverkip Cl
  LSOL/BMARY PO13 .... 131 F1 ①
Inverness Av *FHAM* PO15 .... 12 C3
Inverness Rd *GPORT* PO12 ..... 132 D3
  NEND PO2 .... 134 D1
Ionic Cl *CHFD* SO53 .... 38 C3
Iping Av *HAV* PO9 .... 102 E1
Ipley Wy *FAWY* SO45 .... 91 H4
Ireland Wy *WVILLE* PO7 .... 101 K1
Iris Rd *ROWN* SO16 .... 43 J7
Ironbridge Crs *HLER* SO31 ...... 75 F7
Ironbridge La *ENEY* PO4 .... 135 H4
Iron Mill Cl *FHAM* PO15 .... 12 A1
Ironmill La *FHAM* PO15 .... 96 C1
Irvine Cl *FHAM/PORC* PO16 ...... 13 G2
Irving Rd *ROWN* SO16 .... 54 A3
Irwell Cl *CHFD* SO53 .... 37 H5
Isambard Brunel Rd *PSEA* PO1 .. 18 D5 ⑧
Isis Cl *ROWN* SO16 .... 53 K4
Island Cl *HISD* PO11 .... 121 H4
Island View Ter *NEND* PO2 ..... 118 B6
Islay Gdns *CHAM* PO6 .... 100 E5
Itchen Av *ELGH* SO50 .... 45 J1
Itchenor Rd *HISD* PO11 .... 138 C6
Itchen Rd *HAV* PO9 .... 83 J7
Itchenside Cl *WEND* SO18 .... 44 C7
Itchen Vw *ELGH* SO50 .... 38 E4
Itchin Cl *TOTT* SO40 .... 52 C6
Ithica Cl *HISD* PO11 .... 137 H4
Ivanhoe Rd *WSHM* SO15 .... 54 E3
Ivor Cl *FAWY* SO45 .... 109 K3
Ivy Cl *WINW* SO22 .... 25 H5
  TOTT SO40 .... 52 D2
Ivy Ct *WVILLE* PO7 .... 101 J2 ⑥
Ivy Dene *ITCH* SO19 .... 73 G1
Ivydene Gdns *HORN* PO8 .... 82 B1

Ivy La *HEND* SO30 .... 56 E2
Ivy Rd *PTSW* SO17 .... 5 M2

J

Jacaranda Cl *FHAM* PO15 .... 95 K3 ⑧
Jack Cockerill Wy *SSEA* PO5 ... 134 C7 ④
Jackdaw Cl *HORN* PO8 .... 81 K1
Jackdaw Ri *ELGH* SO50 .... 44 A2 ③
Jackie Wigg Gdns *TOTT* SO40 ... 52 E5
Jackmans Cl *ITCH* SO19 .... 10 A4 ②
Jackson Cl *CHAM* PO6 .... 119 H1
Jacob Cl *ROMY* SO51 .... 35 F3 ③
Jacob's Gutter La *TOTT* SO40 ... 52 E7
Jacob's St *PSEA* PO1 .... 18 D2
Jacobs Wk *TOTT* SO40 .... 68 D1
Jacomb Pl
  LSOL/BMARY PO13 .... 116 A5 ③
Jacqueline Av *WVILLE* PO7 ..... 101 J2
Jago Rd *PSEA* PO1 .... 17 K2
Jamaica Pl *GPORT* PO12 .... 16 C6
Jamaica Pl *GPORT* PO12 .... 16 C6
Jamaica Rd *GPORT* PO12 .... 16 C6 ①
James Callaghan Dr *CHAM* PO6 .. 99 K4
James Cl *HISD* PO11 .... 137 F5
James Copse Rd *HORN* PO8 ..... 64 A7
James Grieve Av *HLER* SO31 .... 95 F4
James Rd *HAV* PO9 .... 14 B2
  LSOL/BMARY PO13 .... 115 K3
James St *SHAM* SO14 .... 9 J1
Janaway Gdns *PTSW* SO17 .... 5 M2
Janes Cl *FAWY* SO45 .... 110 B7
Janson Rd *WSHM* SO15 .... 54 D5
Japonica Wy *HAV* PO9 .... 103 K2
Jarvis Flds *HLER* SO31 .... 74 A5
Jasmine Gv *WVILLE* PO7 .... 82 B7
Jasmine Rd *HEND* SO30 .... 58 A4
Jasmond Rd *CHAM* PO6 .... 118 E1
Jason Pl *WVILLE* PO7 .... 101 K4
Jason Wy *GPORT* PO12 .... 116 C7 ②
Java Dr *FHAM* PO15 .... 75 H6
Java Rd *SHAM* SO14 .... 9 K7
Javelin Rd *EMRTH* PO10 .... 122 D4
J Av *FAWY* SO45 .... 110 C1
Jay Cl *FHAM/STUB* PO14 .... 114 C3
  HORN PO8 .... 64 B5
Jeffries Cl *ROWN* SO16 .... 41 K6
Jellicoe Av *GPORT* PO12 .... 132 C6
Jenkins Cl *HEND* SO30 .... 59 F5
Jenkins Gv *HSEA* PO3 .... 135 G1
Jenner Wy *ROMY* SO51 .... 35 H2
Jennings Rd *TOTT* SO40 .... 53 F4
Jermyns La *ROMY* SO51 .... 29 H6
Jerome Ct *ITCH* SO19 .... 57 G6
Jerram Ct *GPORT* PO12 .... 132 C5
Jerrett's La *ROWN* SO16 .... 53 J1
Jersey Cl *FHAM/STUB* PO14 .... 114 E6
  ROWN SO16 .... 53 K1
Jervis Court La *BPWT* SO32 ..... 49 H3
Jervis Dr *GPORT* PO12 .... 16 A2
Jervis Rd *NEND* PO2 .... 118 B5
Jesmond Gv *HLER* SO31 .... 95 F5
Jessamine Rd *ROWN* SO16 ...... 54 C2
Jessica Cl *WVILLE* PO7 .... 82 C4
Jessie Rd *ENEY* PO4 .... 19 H6
  GPORT PO12 .... 132 D4
  HAV PO9 .... 102 D3
Jessop Cl *FAWY* SO45 .... 91 G1
Jetty Rd *FAWY* SO45 .... 110 E2
Jewry St *WINC* SO23 .... 2 E4
Jex Blake Cl *ROWN* SO16 .... 42 C7
Jinny La *ROMY* SO51 .... 28 D3
Jockey La *ELGH* SO50 .... 39 H5
Jodrell Cl *HORN* PO8 .... 64 D5
John Bunyan Cl *FHAM* PO15 .... 75 H5 ⑤
Johnson St *SHAM* SO14 .... 9 H1 ④
Johnson Vw *FHAM* PO15 .... 75 K7
Johns Rd *FHAM/PORC* PO16 ..... 13 J9
  ITCH SO19 .... 10 B5
John St *SHAM* SO14 .... 9 H4
Jonathan Rd *FHAM* PO15 .... 12 C5
Jones La *FAWY* SO45 .... 91 G2
Jordans La *LYMN* SO41 .... 124 A7
Joseph St *GPORT* PO12 .... 16 D5 ⑧
Jubilee Av *CHAM* PO6 .... 99 H6
Jubilee Cl *ELGH* SO50 .... 44 C2 ①
Jubilee Cl *FHAM/STUB* PO14 .... 97 F3
Jubilee Gdns *WEND* SO18 .... 7 J5
Jubilee Pth *HAV* PO9 .... 102 D5
Jubilee Rd *ENEY* PO4 .... 19 J7
  FHAM/PORC PO16 .... 99 G6
  GPORT PO12 .... 16 A4
  ROMY SO51 .... 34 D2
  WVILLE PO7 .... 81 K5
Jubilee Ter *SSEA* PO5 .... 18 B7 ③
Julian Cl *ROWN* SO16 .... 43 G5
Julian Rd *ITCH* SO19 .... 11 K3
Julie Av *FHAM* PO15 .... 12 C5
Juliet Ct *WVILLE* PO7 .... 82 B5 ⑤
Julius Cl *CHFD* SO53 .... 38 B4
Jumar Cl *HLER* SO31 .... 94 C7
Junction Rd *TOTT* SO40 .... 52 E5
Juniper Cl *WINC* SO23 .... 25 G3
  NBAD SO52 .... 36 A5
Juniper Rd *HORN* PO8 .... 64 D3 ⑧
  WEND SO18 .... 6 E5
Juniper Sq *HAV* PO9 .... 14 F5
Jupiter Cl *ROWN* SO16 .... 41 K7
Jura Cl *CHAM* PO6 .... 100 E5
Jurds Lake Wy *ITCH* SO19 ...... 10 B8
Jurd Wy *HLER* SO31 .... 73 J4
Justin Cl *FHAM/STUB* PO14 ..... 12 C3
Justinian Cl *CHFD* SO53 .... 38 C3
Jute Cl *FHAM/PORC* PO16 .... 98 E5
Jutland Cl *FHAM* PO15 .... 75 G6

K

Kanes Hl *ITCH* SO19 .... 57 J6
Karen Av *CHAM* PO6 .... 119 H1
Kassassin St *ENEY* PO4 .... 19 M9
Kassel Cl *WVILLE* PO7 .... 82 C4
Kathleen Rd *ITCH* SO19 .... 11 H3

Katrina Gdns *HISD* PO11 .... 137 H3
Katrine Crs *CHFD* SO53 .... 37 H3
Kayak Cl *HLER* SO31 .... 94 D5
Kayleigh Cl *TOTT* SO40 .... 52 C6
Kealy Rd *GPORT* PO12 .... 132 D2
Kearsney Av *NEND* PO2 .... 118 D4 ③
Keats Cl *CHAM* PO6 .... 99 H5
Keats Cl *WINW* SO22 .... 82 A1
  HORN PO8 .... 64 B5
Keats Rd *ITCH* SO19 .... 7 L6
Keble Cl *CHFD* SO53 .... 37 K6 ④
Keble Rd *CHFD* SO53 .... 37 K6
Keble St *WINW* SO22 .... 25 F2
Keel Cl *HSEA* PO3 .... 119 H4
  LSOL/BMARY PO13 .... 132 A1 ④
Keepers Cl *CHFD* SO53 .... 37 J4
The Keep *FHAM/PORC* PO16 ..... 99 H6
Kefford Cl *HORN* PO8 .... 64 C6
Keith Cl *GPORT* PO12 .... 132 C2
Kelburn Cl *CHFD* SO53 .... 37 J3
Kellett Rd *WSHM* SO15 .... 4 C2
Kelly Rd *WVILLE* PO7 .... 101 K1
Kelmscott Gdns *CHFD* SO53 ..... 37 H1
Kelsey Av *EMRTH* PO10 .... 105 H5
Kelsey Cl *FHAM/STUB* PO14 ..... 96 G5
Kelvin Cl *FAWY* SO45 .... 91 H3
Kelvin Gv *FHAM/PORC* PO16 .... 99 G6
  HLER SO31 .... 73 F7
Kelvin Rd *ELGH* SO50 .... 44 C1
Kempton Pk *WVILLE* PO7 .... 82 E7
Kemshott Ct *HAV* PO9 .... 82 E7
Ken Berry Ct *HAV* PO9 .... 83 J7
Kendal Av *HSEA* PO3 .... 119 F6
  ROWN SO16 .... 53 K4
Kendal Cl *CHFD* SO53 .... 38 B3
  HORN PO8 .... 82 B1
Kenilworth Cl
  LSOL/BMARY PO13 .... 131 G1 ④
Kenilworth Dr *ELGH* SO50 ...... 38 D4
Kenilworth Gdns *HEND* SO30 ... 57 F3
Kenilworth Rd *SSEA* PO5 ...... 134 C7 ③
  WSHM SO15 .... 4 E7
Kenmore Cl *TOTT* SO40 .... 52 C7
Kennedy Av *FHAM* PO15 .... 97 F2
Kennedy Cl *WVILLE* PO7 .... 101 K2
Kennedy Crs *GPORT* PO12 ..... 132 B6
Kennedy Rd *ROWN* SO16 .... 54 A1
Kennel Rd *WINW* SO22 .... 20 E3
Kennet Cl *GPORT* PO12 .... 132 E7
  WEND SO18 .... 56 E1
Kennett Rd *WINC* SO23 .... 35 H2
Kennington La *TOTT* SO40 ...... 50 E5
Kensington Cl *ELGH* SO50 ...... 39 G5 ③
Kensington Flds *FAWY* SO45 .... 90 E4
Kensington Gdns
  FHAM/STUB PO14 .... 95 H4 ②
Kensington Rd *GPORT* PO12 .... 16 C7
  NEND PO2 .... 118 E5
Kenson Gdns *ITCH* SO19 .... 11 G2
Kent Gv *FHAM/PORC* PO16 ..... 117 F1
Kentidge Rd *WVILLE* PO7 ...... 101 J1 ⑧
Kentish Rd *WSHM* SO15 .... 54 D5
Kent Rd *CHFD* SO53 .... 37 K7
  LSOL/BMARY PO13 .... 115 J3
  SSEA PO5 .... 18 B7
Kent St *PSEA* PO1 .... 17 M4
  SHAM SO14 .... 5 L8
Kenwood Rd
  FHAM/PORC PO16 .... 117 G2
Kenwyn Cl *WEND* SO18 .... 56 E2
Kenya Rd *FHAM/PORC* PO16 ..... 98 E7
Kenyon Rd *NEND* PO2 .... 118 C5
Kern Cl *ROWN* SO16 .... 54 A1
Kerrfield *WINW* SO22 .... 25 C1
Kerrfield Ms *WINW* SO22 .... 25 C1
Kerry Cl *CHFD* SO53 .... 37 K4
Kesteven Wy *WEND* SO18 .... 7 H2
Kestrel Cl *BPWT* SO32 .... 59 F3
  BPWT SO32 .... 59 F3
  FHAM/STUB PO14 .... 114 C3
  WINW SO22 .... 25 G4
  ROWN SO16 .... 54 C6
  TOTT SO40 .... 69 G4
Kestrel Pl *CHAM* PO6 .... 102 A7
Kestrel Rd *ELGH* SO50 .... 44 B1
Keswick Av *HSEA* PO3 .... 119 F6
Keswick Rd *ITCH* SO19 .... 10 A4
Kettering Ter *NEND* PO2 .... 118 B7
Kevlyn Crs *HLER* SO31 .... 73 J4 ③
Kewlake La *ROMY* SO51 .... 50 A2
Kew La *HLER* SO31 .... 73 K6
Keydell Cl *HORN* PO8 .... 64 B7
Keyes Cl *LSOL/BMARY* PO13 ... 115 K3
Keyes Rd *LSOL/BMARY* PO13 ... 115 K4
Keyhaven Cl
  LSOL/BMARY PO13 .... 115 H5 ④
Keyhaven Dr *HAV* PO9 .... 102 D1
Keynsham Rd *ITCH* SO19 .... 7 J7
Khandala Gdns *WVILLE* PO7 .... 102 A2 ②
Khartoum Rd *PTSW* SO17 .... 55 H2
Kidmore La *WVILLE* PO7 .... 62 E6
Kielder Cl *CHFD* SO53 .... 37 H3
Kielder Gv
  LSOL/BMARY PO13 .... 116 A5 ④
Kilford Ct *HEND* SO30 .... 59 F6
Kilham La *WINW* SO22 .... 24 E2
Killarney Cl *ITCH* SO19 .... 73 H2 ③
Kilmiston Cl *PSEA* PO1 .... 134 D1
Kilmiston Dr *FHAM/PORC* PO16 .. 99 F5
Kiln Cl *FAWY* SO45 .... 91 F3
Kiln La *ROMY* SO51 .... 29 G3
  RWIN SO21 .... 32 E7
  WVILLE PO7 .... 79 G1
Kiln Rd *FHAM/PORC* PO16 ...... 97 G2
Kilnside *WVILLE* PO7 .... 80 E2
Kilnyard Cl *TOTT* SO40 .... 52 C3
Kilpatrick Cl *NEND* PO2 ...... 118 C7 ④
Kilwich Wy *FHAM/PORC* PO16 .. 116 E1
Kimberley Cl *ELGH* SO50 .... 46 C1
Kimberley Rd *ENEY* PO4 .... 19 L5
Kimbolton Rd *HSEA* PO3 .... 19 L1
Kimbridge Crs *HAV* PO9 .... 83 H7
Kimpton Cl
  LSOL/BMARY PO13 .... 131 G2 ⑧
Kimpton Ct *HAV* PO9 .... 83 J7 ⑨
Kineton Rd *WSHM* SO15 .... 4 C1
King Albert St *PSEA* PO1 .... 18 F1 ⑤
King Alfred Pl *WINC* SO23 .... 2 E2
King Alfred Ter *WINC* SO23 ...... 2 E2 ①
King Arthur's Ct *CHAM* PO6 ... 101 J4 ④

Kings Rd *WINW* SO22 ...... 25 F2
King Charles St *PSEA* PO1 ...... 17 L6
King Cup Av *HLER* SO31 ...... 94 E4
King Edward Av *ROWN* SO16 ...... 54 B4
King Edward's Crs
　NEND PO2 ...... 118 C5
Kingfisher Cl *HAV* PO9 ...... 83 J4
　HISD PO11 ...... 137 K6
　HLER SO31 ...... 93 K2
　HORN PO8 ...... 81 K1
Kingfisher Copse *HLER* SO31 ...... 95 G3
Kingfishers *FHAM/PORC* PO16 ...... 98 C6
Kingfisher Wy *ROMY* SO51 ...... 34 K2
　TOTT SO40 ...... 69 K4
King George Rd
　FHAM/PORC PO16 ...... 99 F7
King George's Av *WSHM* SO15 ...... 54 A6
King Henry I St *PSEA* PO1 ...... 18 B4
King John Av *FHAM/PORC* PO16 ...... 98 E7
King Richard 1 Rd *PSEA* PO1 ...... 18 B5
Kings Av *WINW* SO22 ...... 2 A9
　HLER SO31 ...... 93 H3
Kingsbury Rd *SHAM* SO14 ...... 5 J5
Kingsclere Av *HAV* PO9 ...... 102 E1
　ITCH SO19 ...... 10 E8
Kingsclere Cl *ITCH* SO19 ...... 10 E8
King's Cl *CHFD* SO53 ...... 38 A3
　HAV PO9 ...... 83 H3
　LYND SO45 ...... 86 C1
　RWIN SO21 ...... 33 K2
Kings Copse Av *HEND* SO30 ...... 58 C5
King's Copse Rd *FAWY* SO45 ...... 109 K7
　HEND SO30 ...... 58 B7
Kingscote Rd *CHAM* PO6 ...... 99 J4
　HORN PO8 ...... 81 J2
Kingscroft Ct *HAV* PO9 ...... 14 B5
King's Croft La *HAV* PO9 ...... 102 D3
Kingsdown Pl *PSEA* PO1 ...... 19 G4
Kingsdown Rd *WVILLE* PO7 ...... 81 K3
Kingsdown Wy *WEND* SO18 ...... 56 C2
Kingsey Av *EMRTH* PO10 ...... 104 B6
Kings Fld *HLER* SO31 ...... 73 K4
Kings Field Gdns *HLER* SO31 ...... 73 K4
Kingsfold Av *WEND* SO18 ...... 56 C1
Kingsgate Rd *WINC* SO23 ...... 2 D9
Kingsgate St *WINC* SO23 ...... 2 E7
Kingsland Cl *CHAM* PO6 ...... 100 B5
Kings La *RWIN* SO21 ...... 26 E5
Kingsley Gdns *TOTT* SO40 ...... 52 A5
Kingsley Pl *WINW* SO22 ...... 2 B9
Kingsley Rd *ENEY* PO4 ...... 135 G5
　GPORT PO12 ...... 132 C1
　WSHM SO15 ...... 54 C5
Kingsmead *WHAM* PO17 ...... 61 K3
Kingsmead Av
　FHAM/STUB SO14 ...... 114 E6
Kings Mede *HORN* PO8 ...... 64 C6
Kingsmill Cl *GPORT* PO12 ...... 132 C4
Kings Park Rd *WSHM* SO15 ...... 5 G7
Kings Ride *FAWY* SO45 ...... 128 B1
King's Rd *CHFD* SO53 ...... 37 K4
　EMRTH PO10 ...... 104 B6
　FHAM/PORC PO16 ...... 13 G6
　GPORT PO12 ...... 16 B5
　HISD PO11 ...... 137 H3
　LSOL/BMARY PO13 ...... 131 F1
　PSEA PO1 ...... 17 K2
　SSEA PO5 ...... 18 C6
King's Ter *EMRTH* PO10 ...... 104 C6
　PSEA PO1 ...... 18 A6
Kingston *HLER* SO31 ...... 73 F6
Kingston Crs *NEND* PO2 ...... 118 C7
Kingston Gdns *FHAM* PO15 ...... 96 E2
Kingston Rd *GPORT* PO12 ...... 132 C5
　NEND PO2 ...... 118 D7
　WSHM SO15 ...... 4 A7
King St *EMRTH* PO10 ...... 104 E3
　GPORT PO12 ...... 16 F4
　SHAM SO14 ...... 9 H3
　SSEA PO5 ...... 18 B6
King's Wy *FHAM/PORC* PO16 ...... 98 C6
　RWIN SO21 ...... 23 K1
　RWIN SO21 ...... 27 J4
　WHAM PO17 ...... 79 J4
　WINC SO23 ...... 2 F1
Kingsway *CHFD* SO53 ...... 38 A4
　HISD PO11 ...... 121 H4
Kingsway Gdns *CHFD* SO53 ...... 38 B2
The Kingsway
　FHAM/PORC PO16 ...... 99 F6
Kingswell St *PSEA* PO1 ...... 18 C3
Kingswood *TOTT* SO40 ...... 70 B4
Kingsworthy Rd *HAV* PO9 ...... 103 G3
King William St *PSEA* PO1 ...... 17 M2
Kinnell Cl *EMRTH* PO10 ...... 104 C6
Kinross Crs *CHAM* PO6 ...... 101 G7
Kinross Rd *TOTT* SO40 ...... 52 E5
Kinsbourne Cl *ITCH* SO19 ...... 57 J6
Kinsbourne Ri *ITCH* SO19 ...... 57 J7
Kinsbourne Wy *ITCH* SO19 ...... 57 H7
Kintyre Rd *CHAM* PO6 ...... 100 E5
Kinver Cl *ROMY* SO51 ...... 35 G1
Kipling Ct *ITCH* SO19 ...... 10 E8
Kipling Rd *ELGH* SO50 ...... 38 C7
　NEND PO2 ...... 118 D4
Kirby Rd *NEND* PO2 ...... 118 D5
Kirk Gdns *TOTT* SO40 ...... 52 E7
Kirkstall Rd *ENEY* PO4 ...... 134 D7
Kirtley Cl *CHAM* PO6 ...... 119 H1
Kirton Rd *CHAM* PO6 ...... 101 H7
Kitchener Rd *PTSW* SO17 ...... 55 K1
Kite Cl *HORN* PO8 ...... 81 K1
Kites Croft Cl *FHAM/STUB* SO14 ...... 95 H5
Kitnocks Hl *BPWT* SO32 ...... 59 K4
Kittiwake Cl
　LSOL/BMARY PO13 ...... 115 J3
Knapp La *ROMY* SO51 ...... 30 E5
Knatchbull Cl *ROWN* SO51 ...... 34 E3
Knellers La *TOTT* SO40 ...... 68 C1
Knight Cl *WINC* SO23 ...... 21 K5
Knighton Rd *ITCH* SO19 ...... 10 E7
Knights Bank Rd
　FHAM/STUB SO14 ...... 114 A6
Knights Cl *HLER* SO31 ...... 94 D5
Knightstone Gra *FAWY* SO45 ...... 91 H4
Knightwood Av *HAV* PO9 ...... 103 H1
　LYND SO43 ...... 86 C1
Knightwood Cl *LYND* SO43 ...... 86 C1
　TOTT SO40 ...... 68 A3
Knightwood Rd *FAWY* SO45 ...... 91 J4

NBAD SO52 ...... 37 G2
Knottgrass Rd *HLER* SO31 ...... 94 D4
Knowle Hl *ELGH* SO50 ...... 38 E3
Knowle La *ELGH* SO50 ...... 46 C4
Knowsley Crs *CHAM* PO6 ...... 101 F7
Knowsley Rd *CHAM* PO6 ...... 100 E7
Knox Rd *HAV* PO9 ...... 14 B4
　NEND PO2 ...... 118 B6
Knyght Cl *ROMY* SO51 ...... 35 F4
Kootenay Av *WEND* SO18 ...... 57 H5
Kynegils Rd *WINW* SO22 ...... 21 G5
Kynon Ct *GPORT* PO12 ...... 117 F7
Kytes La *BPWT* SO32 ...... 47 G6

L

Laburnum Av *CHAM* PO6 ...... 101 H7
Laburnum Cl *NBAD* SO52 ...... 36 B5
Laburnum Crs *FAWY* SO45 ...... 91 J6
Laburnum Gv *ELGH* SO50 ...... 38 D7
　HISD PO11 ...... 137 J4
　NEND PO2 ...... 118 D6
Laburnum Rd
　FHAM/PORC PO16 ...... 115 J1
　HEND SO30 ...... 58 C6
　ROWN SO16 ...... 43 K7
　WVILLE PO7 ...... 81 K7
Lackford Av *TOTT* SO40 ...... 52 D6
Lacon Cl *WEND* SO18 ...... 6 D2
Ladram Rd *GPORT* PO12 ...... 132 B4
Lady Betty's Dr *FHAM* PO15 ...... 75 K7
Ladybridge Rd *WVILLE* PO7 ...... 101 H2
Ladycross Rd *FAWY* SO45 ...... 91 H4
Ladywood *ELGH* SO50 ...... 38 C4
Lainston Cl *WINW* SO22 ...... 21 F5
Lake Farm Cl *HEND* SO30 ...... 58 B4
Lakeland Gdns *TOTT* SO40 ...... 69 K4
Lakelands Dr *WSHM* SO15 ...... 54 D6
Lake Rd *BPWT* SO32 ...... 60 A4
　CHFD SO53 ...... 38 B2
　ITCH SO19 ...... 10 A6
　PSEA PO1 ...... 18 D2
Lakeside *ELGH* SO50 ...... 44 C3
　LSOL/BMARY PO13 ...... 131 G4
　WHAM PO17 ...... 97 F1
Lakeside Av *HSEA* PO3 ...... 135 G2
　ROWN SO16 ...... 41 K6
Lakeside Gdns *HAV* PO9 ...... 15 G2
Lakesmere Rd *HORN* PO8 ...... 64 D6
The Lakes *BPWT* SO32 ...... 49 H7
Lakewood Cl *CHFD* SO53 ...... 38 A3
Lakewood Rd *CHFD* SO53 ...... 38 A3
　TOTT SO40 ...... 68 B2
Lamberhurst Cl *ITCH* SO19 ...... 72 D5
Lambert Cl *WVILLE* PO7 ...... 101 K1
Lambourn Cl *FHAM/STUB* SO14 ...... 12 B7
Lambourne Cl *FAWY* SO45 ...... 91 G5
Lambourne Dr *HLER* SO31 ...... 95 F3
Lambourne Rd *WEND* SO18 ...... 56 E2
Lambourn Sq *CHFD* SO53 ...... 37 H4
Lammas Rd *FAWY* SO45 ...... 91 H4
Lampeter Av *CHAM* PO6 ...... 101 G6
Lancaster Cl *FHAM/PORC* PO16 ...... 98 C1
　HLER SO31 ...... 73 K4
　LSOL/BMARY PO13 ...... 131 J4
Lancaster Rd *ROWN* SO16 ...... 54 A1
Lancaster Wy *WVILLE* PO7 ...... 82 A7
Lance's Hl *ITCH* SO19 ...... 6 F5
Landguard Rd *ENEY* PO4 ...... 19 J9
　WSHM SO15 ...... 4 B7
Landon Rd *LSOL/BMARY* PO13 ...... 114 K7
Landport St *PSEA* PO1 ...... 18 E2
　SSEA PO5 ...... 18 B6
Landport Ter *PSEA* PO1 ...... 18 A6
Landport Vw *PSEA* PO1 ...... 18 D2
Landsdowne St *SSEA* PO5 ...... 18 B6
Landseer Rd *ITCH* SO19 ...... 11 L3
Lands End Dr *EMRTH* PO10 ...... 104 C6
Lanehays Rd *FAWY* SO45 ...... 91 G3
Lanesbridge Cl *TOTT* SO40 ...... 51 J7
Lanes End *FHAM/STUB* SO14 ...... 114 D5
The Lane *ENEY* PO4 ...... 19 J9
　FAWY SO45 ...... 110 E4
　GPORT PO12 ...... 132 D7
Langbar Cl *ITCH* SO19 ...... 6 D7
Langbrook Cl *HAV* PO9 ...... 14 E7
Langdale Av *CHAM* PO6 ...... 101 G7
Langdale Cl *ROWN* SO16 ...... 54 A4
Langdown Lawn *FAWY* SO45 ...... 91 H4
Langdown Lawn Cl
　FAWY SO45 ...... 91 H4
Langdown Rd *FAWY* SO45 ...... 91 H3
Langford Rd *NEND* PO2 ...... 134 E1
Langham Cl *NBAD* SO52 ...... 36 A6
Langhorn Rd *ROWN* SO16 ...... 43 K7
Langley Lodge Gdns
　FAWY SO45 ...... 128 C1
Langley Rd *NEND* PO2 ...... 118 D7
　WSHM SO15 ...... 54 B6
Langrish Rd *HAV* PO9 ...... 83 H7
Langrish Rd *ROWN* SO16 ...... 42 C7
Langstone Av *HAV* PO9 ...... 14 E8
Langstone High St *HAV* PO9 ...... 121 G1
Langstone Rd *HAV* PO9 ...... 14 E8
　HSEA PO3 ...... 19 L2
Langstone Wk
　FHAM/STUB SO14 ...... 96 D6
　LSOL/BMARY PO13 ...... 115 J5
Langton Cl *WINW* SO22 ...... 2 A2
Langton Rd *BPWT* SO32 ...... 48 C3
Lanham La *WINW* SO22 ...... 20 C7
Lankhills Rd *WINC* SO23 ...... 21 J5
Lansdown Av
　FHAM/PORC PO16 ...... 117 G1
Lansdowne Av *WINC* SO23 ...... 2 C9
　WVILLE PO7 ...... 101 G3
Lansdowne Cl *ROMY* SO51 ...... 34 D2
Lansdowne Hl *SHAM* SO14 ...... 8 F3
Lansdowne Rd *WSHM* SO15 ...... 54 B5
Lantana Cl *WVILLE* PO7 ...... 82 A7
Lanyard Dr *LSOL/BMARY* PO13 ...... 132 A2
Lapthorn Cl
　LSOL/BMARY PO13 ...... 115 J3
Lapwing Cl *GPORT* PO12 ...... 132 E1
　HORN PO8 ...... 64 D7
Lapwing Dr *TOTT* SO40 ...... 52 B4

Lapwing Gv
　FHAM/PORC PO16 ...... 98 C6
Larch Av *FAWY* SO45 ...... 109 K2
Larch Cl *HEND* SO30 ...... 57 G1
　LSOL/BMARY PO13 ...... 131 H3
Larchdale Cl *HLER* SO31 ...... 94 C6
Larches Gdns *FHAM/PORC* PO15 ...... 96 D5
Larchfield Wy *HORN* PO8 ...... 64 D7
Larch Rd *ROWN* SO16 ...... 54 B1
Larch Wy *HLER* SO31 ...... 73 J5
Larchwood Av *HAV* PO9 ...... 102 C2
Larchwood Rd *TOTT* SO40 ...... 52 B6
Larg Dr *WINW* SO22 ...... 21 F3
Lark Hill Ri *WINW* SO22 ...... 25 C4
Larkhill Rd *HSEA* PO3 ...... 118 E3
Larkspur Cha *ITCH* SO19 ...... 57 H7
Larkspur Cl *BPWT* SO32 ...... 49 H6
　HLER SO31 ...... 94 E4
Larkspur Dr *NBAD* SO52 ...... 37 G4
　TOTT SO40 ...... 69 K5
Larkspur Gdns *FAWY* SO45 ...... 109 J3
　HEND SO30 ...... 58 B6
Laser Cl *HLER* SO31 ...... 94 D5
Lashly Meadow *WVILLE* PO7 ...... 62 B1
Latchmore Dr *FAWY* SO45 ...... 90 D2
Latchmore Forest Gv
　HORN PO8 ...... 82 A2
Latchmore Gdns *HORN* PO8 ...... 81 K2
Latelie Cl *HLER* SO31 ...... 93 F1
Latham Cl *ELGH* SO50 ...... 46 A1
Latham Ct *WSHM* SO15 ...... 54 C5
Latham Rd *ELGH* SO50 ...... 46 A1
　ROMY SO51 ...... 35 F2
Latimer Ct *HSEA* PO3 ...... 119 G3
Latimer Rd *ROMY* SO51 ...... 34 D3
　SHAM SO14 ...... 9 H4
Lauder Cl *EMRTH* PO10 ...... 105 G4
Launcelyn Cl *NBAD* SO52 ...... 36 B5
Launceston Dr *ELGH* SO50 ...... 38 C5
Laundry Rd *ROWN* SO16 ...... 54 C2
Laurel Cl *FAWY* SO45 ...... 91 F3
　HLER SO31 ...... 95 G2
　ITCH SO19 ...... 10 A4
Laurel Gdns *HLER* SO31 ...... 95 G2
Laurel Rd *HLER* SO31 ...... 95 G2
　HORN PO8 ...... 82 D1
Lauriston Dr *CHFD* SO53 ...... 37 J1
Laurus Cl *WVILLE* PO7 ...... 102 B1
Lavant Cl *HORN* PO8 ...... 82 C4
Lavant Dr *HAV* PO9 ...... 15 G1
Lavender Cl *ITCH* SO19 ...... 6 E9
Lavender Rd *WVILLE* PO7 ...... 82 B7
Laverock Lea
　FHAM/PORC PO16 ...... 99 F5
Laverstoke Cl *ROWN* SO16 ...... 41 K5
Lavey's La *FHAM* PO15 ...... 76 C7
Lavington Gdns *NBAD* SO52 ...... 36 A7
Lavinia Rd *GPORT* PO12 ...... 132 D3
Lawford Wy *TOTT* SO40 ...... 52 D4
Lawn Cl *LSOL/BMARY* PO13 ...... 116 A6
Lawn Dr *HLER* SO31 ...... 95 F4
Lawn Rd *ELGH* SO50 ...... 38 E5
　WINW SO22 ...... 21 F2
　PTSW SO17 ...... 5 J3
Lawn St *WINC* SO23 ...... 2 F4
Lawnside Rd *WSHM* SO15 ...... 54 B4
Lawnswood Cl *HORN* PO8 ...... 82 A3
Lawrence Av *HORN* PO8 ...... 81 K3
Lawrence Gv *ITCH* SO19 ...... 10 E6
Lawrence Rd *FHAM* PO15 ...... 12 A6
　SSEA PO5 ...... 19 G8
Lawson Cl *HLER* SO31 ...... 74 C5
Lawson Rd *SSEA* PO5 ...... 19 G6
Laxton Cl *HLER* SO31 ...... 95 G3
　ITCH SO19 ...... 11 H6
Layton Rd *LSOL/BMARY* PO13 ...... 115 K4
Lazy Acre *EMRTH* PO10 ...... 105 G4
Leacock Cl *BPWT* SO32 ...... 49 J7
Leafy La *FHAM* PO15 ...... 75 K7
Lealand Gv *CHAM* PO6 ...... 100 C1
Lealand Rd *CHAM* PO6 ...... 101 J7
Leamington Crs
　LSOL/BMARY PO13 ...... 131 G2
Leander Cl *ELGH* SO50 ...... 38 D5
Lea-oak Gdns *FHAM* PO15 ...... 12 A2
Lea Rd *FAWY* SO45 ...... 128 B1
Lear Rd *GPORT* PO12 ...... 16 B4
Leaside Wy *ROWN* SO16 ...... 43 K6
Leatherhead Gdns
　HEND SO30 ...... 58 C2
The Leaway *FHAM/PORC* PO16 ...... 99 G6
Lebanon Rd *WSHM* SO15 ...... 53 J5
Lechlade Gdns *FHAM* PO15 ...... 96 E2
Leckford Cl *FHAM/PORC* PO16 ...... 99 F5
　WEND SO18 ...... 57 G4
Leckford Rd *HAV* PO9 ...... 83 J7
Ledbury Rd *CHAM* PO6 ...... 100 B5
Lederle La *LSOL/BMARY* PO13 ...... 115 K2
Lee Church La *ROMY* SO51 ...... 40 E3
Lee Dro *ROMY* SO51 ...... 41 F2
Lee La *ROMY* SO51 ...... 35 F6
Leep La *GPORT* PO12 ...... 132 E6
Lee Rd *GPORT* PO12 ...... 132 D2
Leesland Rd *GPORT* PO12 ...... 132 D5
Lees La *GPORT* PO12 ...... 16 A3
Legion Rd *HISD* PO11 ...... 137 H4
Leicester Rd *WSHM* SO15 ...... 54 E2
Leicester Wy *WINC* SO23 ...... 3 K1
Leigh Cl *CHFD* SO53 ...... 37 K6
　ELGH SO50 ...... 38 E7
　FHAM/PORC PO16 ...... 13 G4
　HAV PO9 ...... 82 D1
　PTSW SO17 ...... 5 G1
Leighton Av *WSHM* SO15 ...... 54 C5
Leighton Rd *ITCH* SO19 ...... 10 D3
Leith Av *FHAM/PORC* PO16 ...... 99 G5
Lemon Rd *WSHM* SO15 ...... 54 C5
Lendorber Av *CHAM* PO6 ...... 101 F7
Lennox Cl *CHFD* SO53 ...... 38 B7
　GPORT PO12 ...... 132 D6
　ROWN SO16 ...... 42 A6
Lennox Rd North *SSEA* PO5 ...... 18 E9
Lennox Rd South *SSEA* PO5 ...... 134 C4
Lensyd Gdns *HORN* PO8 ...... 64 A6
Leofric Ct *ENEY* PO4 ...... 135 H5
Leominster Rd *CHAM* PO6 ...... 100 A5
Leonard Rd *GPORT* PO12 ...... 16 D4
Leopold Dr *BPWT* SO32 ...... 48 C4
Leopold St *ENEY* PO4 ...... 19 H9
Lepe Rd *FAWY* SO45 ...... 128 E4

Lerryn Rd *LSOL/BMARY* PO13 ...... 116 A5
Lester Av *HAV* PO9 ...... 102 D4
Lester Rd *GPORT* PO12 ...... 132 C3
Leven Cl *CHFD* SO53 ...... 37 H2
Leventhorpe Ct *GPORT* PO12 ...... 16 C3
Leveson Cl *GPORT* PO12 ...... 132 C5
Leviathan Cl *FHAM/STUB* SO14 ...... 114 A1
Lewes Cl *ELGH* SO50 ...... 38 D4
Lewin Cl *RWIN* SO21 ...... 39 K2
Lewis Cl *FAWY* SO45 ...... 90 D4
Lewis Rd *EMRTH* PO10 ...... 104 D3
Lewis Silkin Wy *ROWN* SO16 ...... 42 B7
Lewry Cl *HEND* SO30 ...... 58 B5
Lexby Rd *TOTT* SO40 ...... 53 F6
Lexden Gdns *HISD* PO11 ...... 137 F4
Leybourne Av *WEND* SO18 ...... 6 C1
Leyland Cl *GPORT* PO12 ...... 16 B8
Leyton Rd *SHAM* SO14 ...... 5 L7
Liam Cl *HAV* PO9 ...... 103 H2
The Liberty *WVILLE* PO7 ...... 80 D2
Library Rd *TOTT* SO40 ...... 53 F5
Lichen Wy *TOTT* SO40 ...... 70 A3
Lichfield Rd *FHAM/STUB* SO14 ...... 95 H3
　HSEA PO3 ...... 19 L1
Liddel Wy *CHFD* SO53 ...... 37 H2
Liddiards Wy *WVILLE* PO7 ...... 101 K3
Lidiard Gdns *ENEY* PO4 ...... 135 K3
Lilac Cl *HAV* PO9 ...... 103 K3
Lilac Rd *ROWN* SO16 ...... 43 K7
Lily Av *WVILLE* PO7 ...... 101 G4
Lime Av *ITCH* SO19 ...... 7 H9
Lime Cl *FAWY* SO45 ...... 91 F4
　ITCH SO19 ...... 7 H9
　RWIN SO21 ...... 39 K2
Lime Gdns *HEND* SO30 ...... 57 G1
Lime Gv *CHAM* PO6 ...... 100 A5
　HISD PO11 ...... 136 D5
Lime Kiln La *FAWY* SO45 ...... 109 J3
The Limes *LSOL/BMARY* PO13 ...... 116 A6
　TOTT SO40 ...... 70 B4
Lime St *SHAM* SO14 ...... 9 H5
Limetree Wk *WINC* SO23 ...... 3 K4
Lime Wy *FAWY* SO45 ...... 91 F4
Linacre Rd *ITCH* SO19 ...... 73 G3
Lincoln Cl *FHAM/STUB* SO14 ...... 95 H3
Lincoln Ct *WSHM* SO15 ...... 54 E2
Lincoln Ri *HORN* PO8 ...... 82 B1
Lincoln Rd *PSEA* PO1 ...... 19 H5
Lincolns Ri *ELGH* SO50 ...... 38 E2
Linda Gv *HORN* PO8 ...... 82 A2
Linda Rd *FAWY* SO45 ...... 110 E4
Lindberg Ri *FHAM* PO15 ...... 75 K7
Lind Cl *WVILLE* PO7 ...... 102 A3
Linden Gdns *HEND* SO30 ...... 58 C7
Linden Gv *CHFD* SO53 ...... 37 K2
　GPORT PO12 ...... 16 A7
　HISD PO11 ...... 137 H5
Linden Lea *FHAM/PORC* PO16 ...... 99 F5
Linden Rd *ROMY* SO51 ...... 34 E3
　ROWN SO16 ...... 42 B7
Lindens Cl *EMRTH* PO10 ...... 104 C3
Linden Wk *NBAD* SO52 ...... 36 A5
Linden Wy *HAV* PO9 ...... 103 G3
　HORN PO8 ...... 64 C7
Lindisfarne Cl *CHAM* PO6 ...... 101 F7
Lindley Av *ENEY* PO4 ...... 19 L9
Lind Rd *GPORT* PO12 ...... 133 F7
Lindsay Rd *ITCH* SO19 ...... 57 H6
Lindway *HLER* SO31 ...... 75 F7
Linford Ct *HAV* PO9 ...... 82 D1
Linford Crs *ROWN* SO16 ...... 54 E1
Ling Dl *ROWN* SO16 ...... 43 G4
Lingfield Gdns *WEND* SO18 ...... 56 C2
Lingwood Cl *ROWN* SO16 ...... 43 G4
Lingwood Wk *ROWN* SO16 ...... 43 G4
Linkenholt Wy *HAV* PO9 ...... 102 D1
Link Rd *CHAM* PO6 ...... 100 A4
　ROWN SO16 ...... 54 A1
Links La *HAV* PO9 ...... 83 J2
　HISD PO11 ...... 136 D5
The Links *WINW* SO22 ...... 21 G6
Links View Wy *ROWN* SO16 ...... 43 G5
The Link *WVILLE* PO7 ...... 82 B4
Linkway *FHAM/STUB* SO14 ...... 114 C6
Linnet Cl *HORN* PO8 ...... 81 K1
Linnet Sq *ELGH* SO50 ...... 44 A7
The Linnets
　FHAM/PORC PO16 ...... 98 C6
　TOTT SO40 ...... 52 B4
Linwood Cl *FAWY* SO45 ...... 91 H4
Lionheart Wy *HLER* SO31 ...... 73 J4
Lion St *PSEA* PO1 ...... 18 A3
Lipizzaner Flds *HLER* SO31 ...... 75 G5
Lisbon Rd *WSHM* SO15 ...... 4 A1
Lisle Cl *WINW* SO22 ...... 24 D5
Lisle Wy *EMRTH* PO10 ...... 104 B3
Liss Rd *ENEY* PO4 ...... 19 K6
Litchfield Crs *WEND* SO18 ...... 56 C3
Litchfield Rd *WINW* SO22 ...... 21 G3
　WEND SO18 ...... 56 C3
Lith Av *HORN* PO8 ...... 64 D4
Lith La *HORN* PO8 ...... 64 D3
Little Abshot Rd
　FHAM/STUB SO14 ...... 95 G6
Little Anglesey Rd
　GPORT PO12 ...... 132 D6
Little Arthur St *NEND* PO2 ...... 134 D1
Little Bull La *BPWT* SO32 ...... 60 E2
Little Cnr *WVILLE* PO7 ...... 80 E2
Littlefield Crs *NBAD* SO52 ...... 37 H4
Little Gays *FHAM/STUB* SO14 ...... 114 A4
Little George St *PSEA* PO1 ...... 134 D1
Little Gn *GPORT* PO12 ...... 132 D6
Littlegreen Av *HAV* PO9 ...... 83 G4
Little Hambrook St *SSEA* PO5 ...... 18 B7
Little Lance's Hl *ITCH* SO19 ...... 6 E5
Little La *GPORT* PO12 ...... 132 D6
Little Md *WVILLE* PO7 ...... 81 F2
Littlemeads *ROMY* SO51 ...... 34 C3
Little Minster St *WINC* SO23 ...... 2 E5
Little Oak Rd *ROWN* SO16 ...... 43 G7
Littlepark Av *HAV* PO9 ...... 102 C3
Little Park Cl *HEND* SO30 ...... 58 A6
Little Quob La *HEND* SO30 ...... 57 H2
Little Shore La *BPWT* SO32 ...... 48 D4
Little Southsea St *SSEA* PO5 ...... 18 B7
Littleton Gv *HAV* PO9 ...... 103 G2

Littleton La *RWIN* SO21 ...... 20 A5
Littlewood Gdns *HEND* SO30 ...... 57 G3
　WSHM SO15 ...... 94 D3
Little Woodham La
　LSOL/BMARY PO13 ...... 131 K3
Liverpool Rd
　FHAM/STUB PO14 ...... 115 G1
　PSEA PO1 ...... 19 H3
Liverpool St *ROWN* SO16 ...... 5 H2
Livingstone Rd *SHAM* SO14 ...... 5 G1
　SSEA PO5 ...... 18 F7
Lloyd Av *TOTT* SO40 ...... 69 K4
Loane Rd *ITCH* SO19 ...... 10 F3
Lobelia Rd *ROWN* SO16 ...... 43 K7
Locarno Rd *HSEA* PO3 ...... 118 G5
Lock Approach *CHAM* PO6 ...... 99 K7
Lockerley Crs *ROWN* SO16 ...... 54 A2
Lockerley Rd *HAV* PO9 ...... 103 H5
Locke Rd *HEND* SO30 ...... 58 B4
Lockhams Rd *BPWT* SO32 ...... 60 A4
Locksash Cl *SELS* PO20 ...... 139 J6
Locksheath Cl *HAV* PO9 ...... 82 E7
Locksheath Park Rd *HLER* SO31 ...... 95 G5
Lock's La *RWIN* SO21 ...... 20 A4
Locksley Rd *ELGH* SO50 ...... 44 B2
Locks Rd *HLER* SO31 ...... 95 F2
Locksway Rd *ENEY* PO4 ...... 135 G4
Lockswood Rd *HLER* SO31 ...... 94 E3
Lock Vw *CHAM* PO6 ...... 99 K7
Lodge Av *FAWY* SO45 ...... 101 F6
Lodgebury Cl *EMRTH* PO10 ...... 105 H6
Lodge Dr *FAWY* SO45 ...... 91 G5
Lodge Gdns *GPORT* PO12 ...... 132 C4
Lodge La *BROC* SO42 ...... 125 K2
Lodge Rd *HAV* PO9 ...... 102 C5
　HLER SO31 ...... 95 G3
　SHAM SO14 ...... 5 G4
Lofting Cl *ELGH* SO50 ...... 45 H1
Logan Cl *ROWN* SO16 ...... 42 A6
Lomax Cl *HEND* SO30 ...... 58 B5
Lombard St *PSEA* PO1 ...... 17 L7
Lombardy Cl
　LSOL/BMARY PO13 ...... 116 B5
Lombardy Ri *WVILLE* PO7 ...... 102 A1
Lomond Cl *NEND* PO2 ...... 118 C5
Londesborough Rd *ENEY* PO4 ...... 19 H7
London Av *NEND* PO2 ...... 118 C5
London Rd *CHAM* PO6 ...... 100 E6
　HORN PO8 ...... 64 C1
　NEND PO2 ...... 118 D5
　WINC SO23 ...... 22 A2
　WSHM SO15 ...... 4 F7
　WVILLE PO7 ...... 81 K5
　WVILLE PO7 ...... 101 H2
Lone Va *WVILLE* PO7 ...... 101 H3
Longacres *FHAM/STUB* SO14 ...... 95 H4
Long Beech Dr *TOTT* SO40 ...... 52 C2
Longbridge Rd *EMRTH* PO10 ...... 104 B3
Longclose Rd *HEND* SO30 ...... 58 C5
Long Copse *FAWY* SO45 ...... 110 B4
Long Copse La *EMRTH* PO10 ...... 104 C2
Long Curtain Rd *PSEA* PO1 ...... 17 M8
Longdean Cl *CHAM* PO6 ...... 99 K5
Long Dr *HEND* SO30 ...... 57 H2
　LSOL/BMARY PO13 ...... 115 K6
Longfield Av *FHAM/STUB* PO14 ...... 12 B9
Longfield Cl *ENEY* PO4 ...... 135 H3
Longfield Rd *EMRTH* PO10 ...... 104 B3
　WINC SO23 ...... 3 L4
Longhouse Gn *WINC* SO23 ...... 3 L4
Longlands Rd *EMRTH* PO10 ...... 105 G6
　FAWY SO45 ...... 109 K2
　HLER SO31 ...... 73 K4
　TOTT SO40 ...... 69 J4
Long Lane *FAWY* SO45 ...... 110 A4
Longleat Gdns *ROWN* SO16 ...... 42 C6
Longmead Av *ELGH* SO50 ...... 39 G6
Longmead Gdns *HAV* PO9 ...... 14 F8
Longmeadow Gdns *FAWY* SO45 ...... 91 J4
Longmead Rd *WEND* SO18 ...... 56 D3
Longmore Av *ITCH* SO19 ...... 10 B6
Longmore Crs *ITCH* SO19 ...... 10 B6
Longmynd Dr
　FHAM/STUB PO14 ...... 12 B8
Longridge Rd *HEND* SO30 ...... 58 B6
Longshore Wy *ENEY* PO4 ...... 135 J4
　HSEA PO3 ...... 135 J3
Longs La *FHAM/STUB* PO14 ...... 114 D4
Longstaff Gdns
　FHAM/PORC PO16 ...... 12 F2
Longstock Crs *TOTT* SO40 ...... 52 C5
Longstock Rd *HAV* PO9 ...... 83 J7
Long Wk *RWIN* SO21 ...... 22 C5
Long Water Dr *GPORT* PO12 ...... 133 F7
Longwood Av *HORN* PO8 ...... 82 A2
Lonsdale Av *CHAM* PO6 ...... 101 F7
Loperwood *TOTT* SO40 ...... 51 J2
Loperwood La *TOTT* SO40 ...... 52 A2
Lordington Cl *CHAM* PO6 ...... 101 G6
Lord Montgomery Wy
　SSEA PO5 ...... 18 B5
Lord Mountbatten Cl
　WEND SO18 ...... 44 B7
Lord's HI Centre East
　ROWN SO16 ...... 42 A6
Lord's HI Centre West
　ROWN SO16 ...... 42 A7
Lord's Hill Wy *ROWN* SO16 ...... 42 A6
Lords St *PSEA* PO1 ...... 18 F1
Lordswood *ELGH* SO50 ...... 39 H3
Lordswood Cl *ROWN* SO16 ...... 54 E1
Lordswood Gdns *ROWN* SO16 ...... 42 D7
Lordswood Rd *ROWN* SO16 ...... 42 D7
Loreille Cl *ROWN* SO16 ...... 41 K4
Lorne Rd *SSEA* PO5 ...... 19 G6
Loughwood Cl *HEND* SO30 ...... 38 D4
Lovage Gdns *TOTT* SO40 ...... 52 B5
Lovage Rd *FHAM* PO15 ...... 75 J6
Lovage Wy *HORN* PO8 ...... 64 D3
Lovedean La *HORN* PO8 ...... 63 K4
Love La *ROMY* SO51 ...... 34 C3
Lovett Rd *HSEA* PO3 ...... 118 G4
Lowcay Rd *SSEA* PO5 ...... 19 G9
Lowden Cl *WINW* SO22 ...... 25 G4
Lower Alfred St *SHAM* SO14 ...... 5 J7
Lower Banister St *WSHM* SO15 ...... 4 F7
Lower Bellfield
　FHAM/STUB PO14 ...... 96 A7

Lower Bere Wd *WVILLE* PO7 ...... 82 A6
Lower Brookfield Rd
  PSEA PO1 .... 19 H2
Lower Brook St *WINC* SO23 ...... 2 F4
Lower Brownhill Rd
  ROWN 53 H2
Lower Canal Wk *SHAM* SO14 ...... 9 C5
Lower Chase Rd *BPWT* SO32 ...... 49 H1
Lower Church Pth *PSEA* PO1 .. 18 D3
Lower Church Rd
  FHAM/STUB PO14 .... 95 H3
Lower Crabbick La *WVILLE* PO7 .. 80 A1
Lower Derby Rd *NEND* PO2 ...... 118 B6
Lower Drayton La *CHAM* PO6 .. 101 H7
Lower Duncan Rd *HLER* SO31 .. 95 C1
Lower Farlington Rd
  CHAM PO6 .... 101 K6
Lower Forbury Rd *SSEA* PO5 .. 18 E5
Lower Grove Rd *HAV* PO9 ...... 15 C6
Lower La *BPWT* SO32 .... 48 E3
Lower Moors Rd *RWIN* SO21 .. 32 A2
Lower Mortimer Rd *ITCH* SO19 .. 10 B3
Lower Mullin's La *FAWY* SO45 .. 91 F2
Lower New Rd *HEND* SO30 .. 57 C3
Lower Northam Rd *HEND* SO30 .. 58 B5
Lower Quay Cl
  FHAM/PORC PO16 .... 13 J8
Lower Quay Rd
  FHAM/PORC PO16 .... 13 K8
Lower Rd *HAV* PO9 .... 102 C5
Lower St Helens Rd *HEND* SO30.. 58 B7
Lower Spinney *HLER* SO31 .... 94 B7
Lower St *ROMY* SO51 .... 29 G2
Lower Swanwick Rd
  HLER SO31 .... 74 C5
Lower Vicarage Rd *ITCH* SO19 .. 10 A7
Lower William St *SHAM* SO14 .. 6 A4
Lower Wingfield St *PSEA* PO1 .. 18 E1
Lower York St *SHAM* SO14 .... 5 M7
Lowestoft Rd *CHAM* PO6 ...... 100 C5
Lowford HI *HLER* SO31 .... 73 J4
Lowland Rd *WVILLE* PO7 ...... 80 D1
Lowry Gdns *ITCH* SO19 ...... 11 L6
Loxwood Rd *HORN* PO8 ...... 64 A6
Luard Ct *HAV* PO9 .... 15 J5
Lucas Cl *ROWN* SO16 .... 42 A6
Luccombe Pl *WSHM* SO15 .... 54 E2
Luccombe Rd *WSHM* SO15 .... 54 E2
Lucerne Av *WVILLE* PO7 ...... 81 J3
Lucerne Gdns *HEND* SO30 .... 57 K6
Lucknow St *PSEA* PO1 .... 19 C4
Ludcombe *WVILLE* PO7 .... 62 E7
Ludlow Rd *CHAM* PO6 .... 100 B5
  ITCH SO19 .... 10 D2
Ludwell's La *BPWT* SO32 .... 49 C7
Lugano Cl *WVILLE* PO7 .... 81 J4
Lukin Dr *ROWN* SO16 .... 41 H6
Lulworth Cl *CHFD* SO53 ...... 37 J7
  HISD PO11 .... 137 H5
  ROWN SO16 .... 53 K2
Lulworth Gn *ROWN* SO16 .... 53 K2
Lulworth Rd
  LSOL/BMARY PO13 .... 131 F2
Lumley Rd *EMRTH* PO10 ...... 104 D5
Lumsden Av *WSHM* SO15 .... 54 D5
Lumsden Rd *ENEY* PO4 ...... 135 J5
Lundy Cl *ROWN* SO16 .... 41 K6
Lunedale Rd *FAWY* SO45 .... 91 F6
Lupin Rd *ROWN* SO16 .... 43 K6
Lutman St *EMRTH* PO10 ...... 104 B2
Luton Rd *ITCH* SO19 .... 11 K1
Luxton Cl *HEND* SO30 .... 58 E4
Luzborough La *ROMY* SO51.... 35 G6
Lyburn Cl *ROWN* SO16 .... 42 D7
Lychgate Rd *HORN* PO8 ...... 64 C5
Lychgate Gn *FHAM/STUB* PO14.. 114 D2
Lydgate *TOTT* SO40 .... 52 C5
Lydgate Cl *ITCH* SO19 ...... 73 C1
Lydgate Gn *ITCH* SO19 ...... 73 C1
Lydgate Rd *ITCH* SO19 ...... 73 C1
Lydiard Cl *ELGH* SO50 ...... 38 D5
Lydlynch Rd *TOTT* SO40 ..... 52 D5
Lydney Cl *CHAM* PO6 .... 100 B6
Lydney Rd *HLER* SO31 .... 94 E4
Lymbourn Rd *HAV* PO9 ...... 15 C5
Lyme Cl *ELGH* SO50 .... 38 C5
Lymer La *ROWN* SO16 .... 41 H5
Lynch Cl *WINW* SO22 .... 21 H5
Lyndale Rd *HLER* SO31 ...... 95 C2
Lynden Cl *FHAM/STUB* PO14 .. 96 C6
Lynden Ga *ITCH* SO19 ...... 11 H3
Lyndhurst Rd *WINW* SO22 .... 21 C3
  HISD PO11 .... 137 H5
Lyndhurst Rd *GPORT* PO12 .. 132 D3
  NEND PO2 .... 118 C4
  TOTT SO40 .... 50 B5
  TOTT SO40 .... 68 B3
Lyndock Cl *ITCH* SO19 ...... 10 D5
Lyndock Pl *ITCH* SO19 ...... 10 D5
Lyne Pl *HORN* PO8 .... 64 C6
Lynford Av *WINW* SO22 ...... 21 H5
Lynford Wy *WINW* SO22 ...... 21 H5
Lynn Rd *NEND* PO2 .... 118 E2
Lynn Wy *WINC* SO23 .... 22 B1
Lynton Ct *TOTT* SO40 .... 52 D6
Lynton Gdns *FHAM/PORC* PO16 .. 12 E1
Lynton Gv *HSEA* PO3 .... 119 F7
Lynton Rd *HEND* SO30 ...... 58 B5
Lynwood Av *WVILLE* PO7 .... 81 J2
Lynx Cl *ELGH* SO50 .... 45 J1
Lyon St *SHAM* SO14 .... 5 J6
Lysander Wy *WVILLE* PO7 .... 82 B5
Lytham Rd *WEND* SO18 ...... 7 G2
Lytton Rd *FAWY* SO45 ...... 91 J4

M

Mabey Cl *GPORT* PO12 ...... 133 F6
Mablethorpe Rd *CHAM* PO6 .. 100 D5
Macarthur Rd *WEND* SO18 .... 7 C3
Macaulay Av *CHAM* PO6 ..... 99 J5
Macnaghten Rd *WEND* SO18.... 6 B4
Madden Cl *GPORT* PO12 ..... 132 C5
Maddison St *SHAM* SO14 .... 8 F3
Maddoxford Wy *BPWT* SO32.... 58 E3
Madeira Rd *NEND* PO2 ...... 118 D4
Madison Cl
  LSOL/BMARY PO13 .... 116 B7

Mafeking Rd *ENEY* PO4 ...... 19 K7
Magazine La *TOTT* SO40 ...... 70 B2
Magdala Rd *CHAM* PO6 ...... 100 E7
  HISD PO11 .... 137 F5
Magdalene Wy
  FHAM/STUB PO14 .... 95 H5
Magdalen HI *WINC* SO23 ...... 3 G5
Magdalen Rd *NEND* PO2 ...... 118 D4
Magennis Cl
  LSOL/BMARY PO13 .... 132 A1
Magnolia Cl *FAWY* SO45 ...... 90 D3
  FHAM/STUB PO14 .... 12 C7
Magnolia Gv *ELGH* SO50 ...... 46 D1
Magnolia Wy *HORN* PO8 ...... 82 D1
Magpie Dr *TOTT* SO40 .... 52 B5
Magpie Gdns *ITCH* SO19 ...... 11 L2
Magpie La *ELGH* SO50 .... 44 B1
  LSOL/BMARY PO13 .... 131 C1
Magpie Rd *HORN* PO8 .... 65 K7
Magpie Wk *HORN* PO8 .... 81 J1
Maidford Gv *HSEA* PO3 ...... 119 H3
Maidstone Crs *CHAM* PO6 .... 100 D5
Main Dr *FAWY* SO45 .... 127 K2
  WHAM PO17 .... 79 K7
Main Rd *EMRTH* PO10 .... 105 F6
  FAWY SO45 .... 70 B6
  FAWY SO45 .... 109 K1
  WINW SO22 .... 20 D1
  LSOL/BMARY PO13 .... 116 A3
  PSEA PO1 .... 17 K3
  RWIN SO21 .... 32 E7
  TOTT SO40 .... 68 D1
  TOTT SO40 .... 70 A4
Mainsail Dr *FHAM/PORC* PO16 .. 13 J8
Mainstone Rd *RWIN* SO21 .... 34 C4
Mainstream Ct *ELGH* SO50 .... 39 G7
Maisemore Gdns *EMRTH* PO10.. 104 A6
Maitland St *PSEA* PO1 ...... 134 C1
Majestic Rd *ROWN* SO16 .... 41 G7
Malcolm Cl *CHFD* SO53 ..... 38 B1
  HLER SO31 .... 95 C3
Malcolm Rd *CHFD* SO53 ..... 38 B1
Malcroft Ms *TOTT* SO40 ..... 70 B4
Maldon Cl *ELGH* SO50 ...... 39 G7
Maldon Rd *CHAM* PO6 ...... 100 C6
  ITCH SO19 .... 10 D1
Malibres Rd *CHFD* SO53 ..... 38 C2
Malin Cl *FHAM/STUB* PO14 .. 114 C4
  ROWN SO16 .... 41 K7
Malins Rd *NEND* PO2 .... 134 C1
Mallard Cl *BPWT* SO32 ..... 48 B3
  ROMY SO51 .... 52 B5
Mallard Gdns *HEND* SO30 .... 58 B2
  LSOL/BMARY PO13 .... 115 J3
Mallard Rd *ENEY* PO4 ...... 135 K2
  HAV PO9 .... 83 J4
Mallards Rd *HLER* SO31 ..... 73 J6
The Mallards *FHAM/PORC* PO16 .. 13 H1
Mallett Cl *HEND* SO30 ...... 58 C2
Mallory Crs *FHAM/PORC* PO16 .. 13 G2
Mallow Cl *CHAM* PO6 .... 100 E6
  WVILLE PO7 .... 82 A7
Mallow Rd *HEND* SO30 ...... 57 K6
Malmesbury Cl *ELGH* SO50 .. 46 B1
Malmesbury Gdns *WINW* SO22 .. 21 C5
Malmesbury Pl *WSHM* SO15 .. 4 A5
Malmesbury Rd *ROMY* SO51 .. 34 C2
  WSHM SO15 .... 4 A5
Malory Cl *ITCH* SO19 ...... 57 C6
Malta Rd *NEND* PO2 .... 118 D7
Malthouse Cl *ROMY* SO51 .. 34 D2
  RWIN SO21 .... 22 E2
Malthouse Gdns *TOTT* SO40.... 70 A4
Malthouse La
  FHAM/PORC PO16 .... 13 J5
Malthouse Rd *NEND* PO2 .... 118 C7
The Maltings
  FHAM/PORC PO16 .... 98 A4
Malt La *BPWT* SO32 .... 48 D3
Malus Cl *FHAM/STUB* PO14 .. 97 G7
Malvern Av *FHAM/STUB* PO14.. 12 C8
Malvern Cl *BPWT* SO32 ..... 48 E4
Malvern Dr *FAWY* SO45 ..... 90 E3
Malvern Gdns *HEND* SO30 .. 58 C2
Malvern Ms *EMRTH* PO10 .... 104 C5
Malvern Rd *GPORT* PO12 .... 132 C3
  ROWN SO16 .... 54 D2
  SSEA PO5 .... 134 C7
Malwood Av *ROWN* SO16 .... 54 E1
Malwood Cl *HAV* PO9 .... 83 H7
Malwood Gdns *TOTT* SO40.... 52 B4
Malwood Rd *FAWY* SO45 .... 91 G2
Malwood Rd West *FAWY* SO45 .. 91 F2
Manchester Rd *PSEA* PO1 .... 19 H3
Mancroft Av
  FHAM/STUB PO14 .... 114 D6
Mandela Wy *WSHM* SO15 .... 4 C8
Manley Rd *HLER* SO31 ...... 73 J4
Manners La *ENEY* PO4 ...... 19 G5
Manners Rd *ENEY* PO4 ...... 19 H5
Manningford Cl *WINC* SO23 .. 21 K4
Manns Cl *WEND* SO18 .... 57 J2
Mannyngham Wy *ROMY* SO51.... 28 C2
Manor Cl *HLER* SO31 .... 73 J4
  TOTT SO40 .... 52 D6
  WHAM PO17 .... 77 H3
  WINC SO23 .... 3 H3
Manor Crs *CHAM* PO6 .... 101 G7
  HLER SO31 .... 73 J4
Manor Farm Gn *RWIN* SO21 .. 33 J4
Manor Farm Gv *ELGH* SO50 .. 45 H1
Manor Farm Rd *WEND* SO18 .. 56 A3
Manor Gdns *EMRTH* PO10 .... 105 G5
Manor House Av *WSHM* SO15.. 53 K6
Manor Lodge Rd *HAV* PO9 .. 83 J5
Manor Ms *CHAM* PO6 .... 101 H6
Manor Park Av *HSEA* PO3 .... 119 F7
Manor Rd *BPWT* SO32 ...... 47 J4
  ELGH SO50 .... 45 H1
  EMRTH PO10 .... 105 G5
  FAWY SO45 .... 109 K3
  HISD PO11 .... 137 G2
  PSEA PO1 .... 134 D1
  ROWN SO16 .... 42 E2
  RWIN SO21 .... 33 J4
  TOTT SO40 .... 90 B1
Manor Rd North *ITCH* SO19 .. 10 C2
Manor Rd South *ITCH* SO19.... 10 C4

Manor Wy *EMRTH* PO10 ...... 105 G5
  HISD PO11 .... 137 H6
  LSOL/BMARY PO13 .... 131 F2
Mans Br *WEND* SO18 .... 44 C7
Mansbridge Rd *ELGH* SO50 .. 44 A4
  WEND SO18 .... 44 A4
Mansel Cl *ROWN* SO16 ...... 53 H5
Mansell Cl *FAWY* SO45 ..... 91 F6
Mansel Rd East *ROWN* SO16.. 53 H5
Mansel Rd West *ROWN* SO16.. 53 J2
Mansfield La *WHAM* PO17 .... 76 C1
Mansfield Rd
  LSOL/BMARY PO13 .... 115 K3
Mansion Rd *ENEY* PO4 ..... 134 D7
  WSHM SO15 .... 54 D6
Mansvid Av *CHAM* PO6 ..... 101 K7
Mantle Cl *LSOL/BMARY* PO13.. 132 A1
Mantle Sq *NEND* PO2 .... 118 A5
Maple Cl *EMRTH* PO10 ...... 104 C4
  FHAM PO15 .... 96 D5
  LSOL/BMARY PO13 .... 131 C3
  ROMY SO51 .... 35 H4
Maple Dr *WVILLE* PO7 ...... 81 F2
Maple Gdns *TOTT* SO40 ..... 52 B6
Maple Rd *FAWY* SO45 .... 91 J6
  SSEA PO5 .... 134 C6
  WEND SO18 .... 6 D1
Maple Sq *ELGH* SO50 .... 44 B2
Mapleton Rd *HEND* SO30 .... 58 C6
The Maples *CHFD* SO53 ..... 37 K2
Mapletree Av *HORN* PO8 .... 64 D7
Maplewood Cl *TOTT* SO40 .. 52 B6
Maplin Rd *ROWN* SO16 ..... 53 J2
Maralyn Av *WVILLE* PO7 .... 81 K7
Marathon Pl *ELGH* SO50 .... 46 A1
Marchwood By-pass *TOTT* SO40.. 52 C7
Marchwood Rd *HAV* PO9 .... 83 F7
  TOTT SO40 .... 69 H1
  WSHM SO15 .... 54 C6
Marcus Cl *ELGH* SO50 ...... 46 A1
Mardale Rd *ROWN* SO16 .... 53 J4
Mardon Cl *ELGH* SO50 ...... 44 B6
Margam Av *ITCH* SO19 ..... 6 F9
Margaret Cl *WVILLE* PO7 .... 81 J4
Margarita Rd *FHAM* PO15 .. 12 C4
Margate Rd *SSEA* PO5 ...... 18 E6
Margery's Ct *PSEA* PO1 .... 17 M4
Marianne Cl *WSHM* SO15 .... 54 A6
Marie Rd *ITCH* SO19 .... 11 M3
Marigold Cl *FHAM* PO15 .... 12 C4
Marina Cl *EMRTH* PO10 ..... 104 D6
  HSEA PO3 .... 135 G2
Marina Gv *FHAM/PORC* PO16 .. 117 F1
  HSEA PO3 .... 135 G2
Marina Keep *CHAM* PO6 .... 99 K7
Marine Ct *ENEY* PO4 ...... 135 F6
Marine Pde *SHAM* SO14 .... 9 K2
Marine Pde East
  LSOL/BMARY PO13 .... 131 F5
Marine Pde West
  LSOL/BMARY PO13 .... 130 E1
Mariner's Cl *HLER* SO31 .... 93 K2
Mariners Ms *FAWY* SO45 .... 91 H2
Mariners Wk *ENEY* PO4 ..... 135 G3
Mariners Wy *GPORT* PO12 .... 16 C1
  HLER SO31 .... 94 B5
Marine Wk *HISD* PO11 ...... 138 A4
Marion Rd *ENEY* PO4 ...... 134 D6
Maritime Av *TOTT* SO40 .... 70 B2
Maritime Wk *SHAM* SO14 .... 9 J6
Maritime Wy *SHAM* SO14 .... 9 H5
Marjoram Crs *HORN* PO8 .... 82 C2
Marjoram Wy *FHAM* PO15 .. 75 J6
Mark Cl *HSEA* PO3 .... 118 C3
  WSHM SO15 .... 54 B5
Marken Cl *HLER* SO31 ...... 94 C3
Market La *WINC* SO23 ...... 2 E5
Market Pde *HAV* PO9 .... 14 E4
Market Pl *SHAM* SO14 ...... 9 G4
Market St *ELGH* SO50 ...... 44 E2
  WINC SO23 .... 2 E5
Marketway *PSEA* PO1 .... 18 C2
Mark's Rd *FHAM/STUB* PO14 .. 115 F5
Marks Tey Rd
  FHAM/STUB PO14 .... 114 D2
Markway Cl *EMRTH* PO10 .... 104 A5
Marlborough Cl *WVILLE* PO7 .. 101 J1
Marlborough Ct *FAWY* SO45 .. 91 F4
Marlborough Gdns
  HEND SO30 .... 58 B1
Marlborough Gv
  FHAM/PORC PO16 .... 99 F7
Marlborough Pk *HAV* PO9 .. 15 K2
Marlborough Rd *CHFD* SO53 .. 38 B1
  GPORT PO12 .... 132 C2
  WSHM SO15 .... 54 C4
Marlborough Rw *PSEA* PO1 .. 17 M2
Marldell Cl *HAV* PO9 .... 103 H1
Marles Cl *LSOL/BMARY* PO13.. 132 A1
Marlhill Cl *WEND* SO18 ..... 56 C2
Marlin Cl *LSOL/BMARY* PO13 .. 132 A2
Marlow Cl *FHAM* PO15 ..... 97 F2
Marlowe Ct *WVILLE* PO7 .... 81 J4
Marlow Rd *BPWT* SO32 ..... 48 B2
Marlpit La *EMRTH* PO10 ..... 105 K2
Marls Rd *HEND* SO30 ...... 58 C6
Marmion Av *SSEA* PO5 ..... 18 E9
Marmion Rd *SSEA* PO5 ..... 18 D9
Marne Rd *WEND* SO18 ...... 7 H4
Marples Wy *HAV* PO9 ...... 14 B5
Marreis Wd *WVILLE* PO7 .... 101 H2
Marsden Rd *CHAM* PO6 .... 100 A6
Marshall Rd *HISD* PO11 .... 137 K6
Marsh Cl *CHAM* PO6 .... 119 H1
Marshfield Cl *TOTT* SO40 .. 69 J4
Marsh Gdns *HEND* SO30 .... 58 B1
Marshlands Rd *CHAM* PO6 .. 101 J6
Marsh La *FAWY* SO45 ...... 110 E3
  RCCH PO18 .... 123 K3
  SHAM SO14 .... 9 H3
The Marsh *FAWY* SO45 ..... 91 H1
Marshwood Av *WVILLE* PO7.... 82 B6
Marston La *HSEA* PO3 ...... 119 G3
Marston Rd *ITCH* SO19 ..... 57 G7
Martello Ct *GPORT* PO12 .... 132 A5
Martin Av *FHAM/STUB* PO14 .. 114 C5
  WVILLE PO7 .... 81 F1
Martin Cl *BPWT* SO32 ...... 49 J7
  LSOL/BMARY PO13 .... 131 C1
Martin Rd *FHAM/STUB* PO14 .. 114 E5
  HAV PO9 .... 103 H2

  HSEA PO3 .... 119 F7
Martins Flds *RWIN* SO21 .... 25 F7
The Martins *ELGH* SO50 .... 46 C2
Martin St *BPWT* SO32 ...... 48 C4
Martley Gdns *HEND* SO30 .. 58 C2
Marvic Ct *HAV* PO9 .... 83 F7
Marvin Wy *HEND* SO30 ..... 58 C5
  WEND SO18 .... 7 M6
Marybridge Cl *TOTT* SO40 .. 52 D6
Maryfield *SHAM* SO14 ...... 9 J4
Maryland Cl *WEND* SO18 .... 56 C1
Mary Rose Cl *FHAM* PO15 .. 12 C1
The Mary Rose St *PSEA* PO1.. 18 C4
Masefield Av *CHAM* PO6 .... 99 J5
Masefield Cl *ELGH* SO50 .... 38 C7
Masefield Crs *HORN* PO8 .... 82 A2
Masefield Gn *ITCH* SO19 .... 57 G6
Masseys La *BROC* SO42 .... 125 H1
Masten Crs *LSOL/BMARY* PO13 .. 115 K3
Matapan Rd *NEND* PO2 ..... 118 C3
Matheson Rd *ROWN* SO16 .. 42 A5
Matley Gdns *TOTT* SO40 .... 52 A5
Matthews Cl *HAV* PO9 ...... 102 D3
Matthews La *BROC* SO42 .... 125 H2
Maunsell Wy *HEND* SO30 .. 58 B1
Maurepas Wy *WVILLE* PO7 .. 81 J6
Mauretania Rd *ROWN* SO16.. 41 G7
Maurice Rd *ENEY* PO4 ..... 135 H4
Mavis Crs *HAV* PO9 .... 14 E3
Maxstoke Cl *SSEA* PO5 ..... 18 E4
Maxwell Rd *ENEY* PO4 ..... 19 L7
  ITCH SO19 .... 6 C8
Maybray King Wy *WEND* SO18.. 6 F5
Maybush Dr *RCCH* PO18 .... 105 K7
Maybush Rd *ROWN* SO16 .. 53 K2
May Cl *FAWY* SO45 .... 110 A4
May Copse *FAWY* SO45 ..... 110 A4
May Crs *FAWY* SO45 .... 110 A4
Maydman Sq *HSEA* PO3 .... 19 M1
Mayfair Ct *HEND* SO30 ..... 59 F5
Mayfair Gdns *WSHM* SO15 .. 4 E5
Mayfield Av *TOTT* SO40 .... 52 D6
Mayfield Cl *FHAM/STUB* PO14.. 114 E4
Mayfield Rd *GPORT* PO12 .. 16 B7
  NEND PO2 .... 118 D5
  PTSW SO17 .... 55 J1
Mayflower Cl *CHFD* SO53 .. 37 J5
  FHAM/STUB PO14 .... 114 D6
Mayflower Rd *WSHM* SO15 .. 54 D4
Mayflower Rbt *WSHM* SO15 .. 8 E4
The Mayflowers *ROWN* SO16.. 43 H7
Mayhall Rd *HSEA* PO3 ..... 119 F6
Maylands Av *ENEY* PO4 .... 19 M5
Maylands Rd *HAV* PO9 ..... 102 C3
Mayles Cl *WHAM* PO17 ..... 77 H2
Mayles La *WHAM* PO17 ..... 77 H1
Mayles Rd *ENEY* PO4 ...... 118 G3
Maylings Farm Rd
  FHAM/PORC PO16 .... 12 F2
Maynard Cl *LSOL/BMARY* PO13.. 115 K3
Maynard Pl *HORN* PO8 ..... 64 C5
Maynard Rd *TOTT* SO40 .... 52 E5
Mayo Cl *PSEA* PO1 .... 134 C1
Mayridge *FHAM/STUB* PO14 .. 95 H3
May Rd *WSHM* SO15 .... 54 D5
May's La *FHAM/STUB* PO14 .. 114 E3
May Tree Cl *WINW* SO22 .... 25 F4
Maytree Cl *HLER* SO31 ..... 95 F3
Maytree Gdns *HORN* PO8 .. 81 K2
Maytree Rd *CHFD* SO53 .... 31 K7
  FHAM/PORC PO16 .... 13 C6
  HORN PO8 .... 81 K2
Mayvale Cl *TOTT* SO40 ..... 70 A4
Meacher Ct *TOTT* SO40 .... 52 D4
Meadbrook Gdns *CHFD* SO53.. 37 K4
Mead Cl *ROWN* SO16 ...... 35 C3
Mead Crs *WEND* SO18 ..... 56 A1
Meadcroft Cl *HLER* SO31 .... 94 C6
Meadend Cl *HAV* PO9 ...... 103 H1
Meadow Av *HLER* SO31 ..... 95 F2
Meadowbank Rd *FHAM* PO15.. 12 A5
Meadow Cl *BPWT* SO32 .... 49 F7
  HEND SO30 .... 57 H2
  HISD PO11 .... 121 G4
  NBAD SO52 .... 36 B7
  TOTT SO40 .... 52 E7
Meadowcroft Cl *RWIN* SO21.. 33 F6
Meadow Edge *WVILLE* PO7 .. 101 F4
Meadow Gdns *BPWT* SO32 .. 49 F7
Meadowhead Rd *ROWN* SO16 .. 55 C1
Meadowlands *HAV* PO9 .... 15 H5
  HAV PO9 .... 83 K2
Meadow La *HLER* SO31 ..... 93 K4
Meadowmead Av *WSHM* SO15.. 54 B5
Meadow Ri *HORN* PO8 ..... 82 C2
Meadowside Cl *WEND* SO18 .. 44 B7
The Meadows
  FHAM/PORC PO16 .... 13 M1
  LYND SO43 .... 86 D2
Meadow St *SSEA* PO5 ...... 18 B7
Meadowsweet *WVILLE* PO7 .. 82 C4
Meadowsweet Wy *CHAM* PO6 .. 100 C5
  ELGH SO50 .... 46 B5
The Meadow *ROMY* SO51 .. 34 E1
  WVILLE PO7 .... 80 E1
Meadow Wk
  LSOL/BMARY PO13 .... 115 J2
Meadow Wy *FAWY* SO45 .... 110 E4
  WINW SO22 .... 25 F4
Mead Rd *CHFD* SO53 ...... 37 K4
  WINC SO23 .... 25 H4
The Meads *CHFD* SO53 .... 37 H5
  ROMY SO51 .... 34 C3
The Mead *FAWY* SO45 ..... 91 F3
Mead Wy *FHAM/PORC* PO16 .. 13 C2
Meadway *WVILLE* PO7 ...... 82 B4
Mears Rd *ELGH* SO50 ...... 46 C1
Meath Cl *HISD* PO11 ...... 137 K7
Medina Cl *CHFD* SO53 ..... 38 B5
Medina Rd *CHAM* PO6 ..... 100 C6
  WSHM SO15 .... 54 C3
Medlar Cl *HEND* SO30 ..... 58 C6
Medlicott Wy *BPWT* SO32 .. 49 J7
Medstead Rd *HAV* PO9 .... 103 G3
Medwall Gn *ITCH* SO19 .... 57 G7
Medway Dr *CHFD* SO53 .... 37 H2
Medway Rd *NEND* PO2 ..... 118 E2
Megana Wy *ROMY* SO51 .. 29 H4
Megan Rd *HEND* SO30 ..... 57 G2

Meggeson Av *WEND* SO18 .... 56 D1
Melbourne Pl *SSEA* PO5 .... 18 B8
Melbourne Rd *HEND* SO30 .. 58 B5
Melbourne St *SHAM* SO14 .. 9 K1
Melchet Rd *WEND* SO18 .... 7 L1
Melick Cl *TOTT* SO40 ...... 70 A4
Mellor Cl *CHAM* PO6 .... 100 C6
Melrose Cl *ENEY* PO4 ..... 135 G4
Melrose Ct *TOTT* SO40 ..... 52 B4
Melrose Gdns *GPORT* PO12.. 132 C3
Melrose Rd *WSHM* SO15 .... 54 E3
Melville Cl *ROWN* SO16 .... 42 D6
Melville Rd *ENEY* PO4 ..... 135 H4
  GPORT PO12 .... 132 D1
Mendip Gdns *FAWY* SO45 .. 90 E4
Mendip Rd *ROWN* SO16 .... 54 A1
Mendips Rd *FHAM/STUB* PO14.. 12 B8
Mendips Wk *FHAM/STUB* PO14.. 12 B8
Mengham Av *HISD* PO11 .... 137 H6
Mengham La *HISD* PO11 .... 137 H5
Mengham Rd *HISD* PO11 .... 137 H5
Menslands La *WVILLE* PO7 .. 62 A3
Menzies Cl *ROWN* SO16 .... 42 A6
Meon Cl *LSOL/BMARY* PO13 .. 115 J3
  ROMY SO51 .... 35 H3
Meon Crs *CHFD* SO53 ..... 38 A4
Meon Rd *ENEY* PO4 ...... 19 M5
  ROMY SO51 .... 35 H3
Mercer Wy *ROMY* SO51 .... 34 E2
  ROMY SO51 .... 35 F2
Merchants Pl *WINC* SO23 .. 2 F6
Merchistoun Rd *HORN* PO8.. 64 C6
Mercury Cl *ROWN* SO16 .... 42 A7
Mercury Gdns *HLER* SO31 .. 93 K2
Mercury Pl *WVILLE* PO7 .... 101 K4
Merdon Av *CHFD* SO53 .... 38 A2
Merdon Cl *CHFD* SO53 ..... 38 A2
Mere Cft *FHAM* PO15 ...... 95 J3
Meredith Gdns *TOTT* SO40 .. 52 D5
Meredith Rd *NEND* PO2 .... 118 D4
Meredun Cl *RWIN* SO21 .... 31 J2
Merganser Cl *GPORT* PO12 .. 132 E1
Meriden Rd *SSEA* PO5 ..... 18 B5
Merlin Dr *HSEA* PO3 ...... 118 E3
Merlin Cl *BPWT* SO32 ..... 48 C3
Merlin Gdns *FHAM/PORC* PO16.. 98 E5
  HEND SO30 .... 58 A5
Mermaid Rd *FHAM/STUB* PO14.. 115 G2
Mermaid Wy *SHAM* SO14 .. 9 J5
Merrick Wy *CHFD* SO53 .... 37 G2
Merridale Rd *ITCH* SO19 .... 6 D8
Merrieleas Cl *CHFD* SO53 .. 37 K3
Merrieleas Dr *CHFD* SO53 .. 37 K3
Merriemeade Cl *FAWY* SO45.. 91 F5
Merrivale Cl *FAWY* SO45 .... 91 F5
Merrivale Rd *NEND* PO2 .... 118 C4
Merryfield *FHAM/STUB* PO14 .. 95 H2
Merryfield Av *HAV* PO9 .... 102 E1
Merry Gdns *NBAD* SO52 .... 36 B5
Merryoak Gn *ITCH* SO19 .... 6 F9
Merryoak Rd *ITCH* SO19 .... 10 E1
Mersea Gdns *ITCH* SO19 .... 11 G2
Mersham Gdns *WEND* SO18.. 6 F4
Merstone Rd
  LSOL/BMARY PO13 .... 115 K5
Merthyr Av *CHAM* PO6 ..... 101 G5
Merton Av *FHAM/PORC* PO16.. 117 G1
Merton Crs *FHAM/PORC* PO16 .. 117 G1
Merton Rd *PTSW* SO17 .... 55 J2
  SSEA PO5 .... 18 D9
Meryl Rd *ENEY* PO4 ...... 135 H4
Meteor Rd *EMRTH* PO10 .... 122 D4
Methuen Rd *ENEY* PO4 .... 19 L8
Methuen St *SHAM* SO14 .... 5 G5
Metuchen Wy *HEND* SO30 .. 74 B1
Mewsey Ct *HAV* PO9 .... 82 E6
Mews La *WINW* SO22 ...... 2 B5
The Mews *FAWY* SO45 ..... 128 C1
  HAV PO9 .... 103 F2
  ROWN SO16 .... 42 A5
Mey Cl *WVILLE* PO7 .... 82 A6
Meynell Cl *ELGH* SO50 ..... 38 C7
Meyrick Rd *HAV* PO9 ...... 14 B4
  NEND PO2 .... 118 B6
Michael Crook Cl *HAV* PO9 .. 102 D3
Michaels Wy *ELGH* SO50 .... 46 C1
  FAWY SO45 .... 91 G2
Michelmersh Cl *ROWN* SO16.. 41 K6
Michigan Wy *TOTT* SO40 .. 52 A4
Midanbury Crs *WEND* SO18.. 6 E4
Midanbury La *WEND* SO18.... 6 D4
Middlebridge St *ROMY* SO51.. 34 D3
Middlebrook *BPWT* SO32 .. 48 D3
Middle Brook St *WINC* SO23 .. 2 F6
Middlecroft La *GPORT* PO12 .. 132 C2
Middlefield *SELS* PO20 .... 139 K7
Middle Md *FHAM/STUB* PO14.. 96 C5
Middle Park Wy *HAV* PO9 .. 102 E2
Middle Rd *WINW* SO22 .... 2 B3
  HLER SO31 .... 95 G1
  ITCH SO19 .... 11 G4
  NBAD SO52 .... 36 B5
Middlesex Rd *ENEY* PO4 .. 19 M7
Middle St *SHAM* SO14 ..... 5 G5
  SSEA PO5 .... 18 C5
Middleton Cl *FHAM/STUB* PO14.. 12 C9
  WEND SO18 .... 56 D2
Midfield Cl *FHAM/STUB* PO14.. 97 G2
Midlands Est *HEND* SO30 .. 57 F2
Midway *FAWY* SO45 .... 91 G3
Midway Rd *NEND* PO2 ..... 118 D2
Midways *FHAM/STUB* PO14.. 114 D6
Milbeck Cl *HORN* PO8 ..... 82 B2
The Milburns *ROMY* SO51 .. 28 C2
Milbury Crs *WEND* SO18 .... 7 H6
Mildmay St *WINW* SO22 .... 25 G3
Milebush Rd *ENEY* PO4 .... 135 H3
Mile End Rd *PSEA* PO1 ..... 134 B1
Milford Cl *HAV* PO9 .... 102 E3
Milford Gdns *CHFD* SO53 .. 38 A4
Milford Rd *PSEA* PO1 ...... 18 E3
Military Rd *FHAM/PORC* PO16.. 98 A4
  GPORT PO12 .... 132 B4
  GPORT PO12 .... 133 F2
  HSEA PO3 .... 118 C2
  PSEA PO1 .... 18 B1
Milkwood Ct *TOTT* SO40 .. 52 B5
Millais Rd *ITCH* SO19 ..... 10 D3
Milland Rd *WINC* SO23 .... 3 H8

ank St SHAM SO14 ..... 5 L8
ridge Gdns ITCH SO19 ..... 11 J3
rook Cl CHFD SO53 ..... 37 J5
rook Dr HAV PO9 ..... 83 H7
rook Point Rd WSHM SO15.. 54 B6
rook Rd East WSHM SO15 .. 54 D7
rook Rd West WSHM SO15 .. 53 K5
Cl HISD PO11 ..... 121 C5
WN SO16 ..... 41 J6
VILLE PO7 ..... 81 G1
End EMRTH PO10 ..... 104 E6
r Dr FHAM/PORC PO16 ..... 12 F2
ken Cl FAWY SO45 ..... 110 C5
s La WINW SO22 ..... 24 C5
HI HEND SO30 ..... 59 F5
en Cl FAWY SO45 ..... 110 C5
La BPWT SO32 ..... 59 J1
OC SO42 ..... 106 A5
MRTH PO10 ..... 104 E4
AM PO15 ..... 96 B5
ORT PO12 ..... 16 B2
AV PO9 ..... 102 D5
WN SO43 ..... 121 F1
ND SO43 ..... 66 B3
SEA PO1 ..... 134 B1
OMY SO51 ..... 40 D7
HAM PO17 ..... 61 H7
HAM PO17 ..... 100 D2
Pond Rd GPORT PO12 ..... 16 A2
Mill Pond FAWY SO45 ..... 109 J1
n Quay EMRTH PO10 ..... 104 D7
d EMRTH PO10 ..... 104 E2
HAM/PORC PO16 ..... 13 J8
ORT SO40 ..... 132 D2
TT SO40 ..... 53 F5
SHM SO15 ..... 54 B5
VILLE PO7 ..... 81 F1
VILLE PO7 ..... 81 J7
Rythe La HISD PO11 ..... 137 H1
s Rd NEND PO2 ..... 118 C7
stream Ri ROMY SO51 ..... 34 C3
St FHAM/STUB PO14 ..... 96 B6
vina Cl TOTT SO40 ..... 67 J1
Wy TOTT SO40 ..... 52 D7
e Cl FAWY SO45 ..... 90 D4
her Ct WSHM SO15 ..... 54 D4
her Pl WINW SO22 ..... 2 B8
thorpe La WINW SO22 ..... 2 A6
on Gv HLER SO31 ..... 95 C5
on Pde WVILLE PO7 ..... 81 K3
on Park Rd ENEY PO4 ..... 135 G4
on Rd ELGH SO50 ..... 38 E5
NEY PO4 ..... 19 M4
SEA PO3 ..... 19 L1
VILLE PO7 ..... 81 J4
verton Rd WINW SO22 ..... 2 A3
TT SO40 ..... 53 F6
vil Rd LSOL/BMARY PO13 ..... 131 F3
ncingfield La BPWT SO32 ..... 47 J7
nden Wy WINW SO22 ..... 25 F3
nerva Cl WVILLE PO7 ..... 101 K4
ley Ct HAV PO9 ..... 103 J1
nitt Rd GPORT PO12 ..... 17 G5
nstead Cl WINW SO22 ..... 21 G3
nstead Rd ENEY PO4 ..... 135 G5
nster La WINC SO23 ..... 2 E5
ntern Cl ELGH SO50 ..... 39 G5
nters Lepe WVILLE PO7 ..... 101 K3
rror Cl HLER SO31 ..... 94 E5
slingford Rd BPWT SO32 ..... 61 K1
ssenden Acres HEND SO30 ..... 58 B4
sslebrook La NBAD SO52 ..... 36 E6
tchell Rd ROMY SO51 ..... 34 E3
tchells Cl ROMY SO51 ..... 34 E3
tchell Wy ELGH SO50 ..... 44 C4
HAV PO9 ..... 102 C3
tre Copse ELGH SO50 ..... 45 J1
zen Wy LSOL/BMARY PO13 ..... 132 A2
oat Cl FAWY SO45 ..... 109 J4
oat Dr GPORT PO12 ..... 132 A5
oat HI WEND SO18 ..... 56 C1
ole HI WVILLE PO7 ..... 102 A1
olesworth Rd GPORT PO12 .. 16 C6
oneyfield Av HSEA PO3 ..... 119 H5
oneyfield La HSEA PO3 ..... 119 F7
onks Brook Cl ELGH SO50 ..... 44 B2
onk's HI EMRTH PO10 ..... 84 D7
onks Pl TOTT SO40 ..... 52 C6
onks Rd HLER SO31 ..... 72 E7
WINC SO23 ..... 2 E2
onks Wk FAWY SO45 ..... 91 F6
onks Wy ELGH SO50 ..... 44 C2
FHAM/STUB PO14 ..... 114 C7
WEND SO18 ..... 44 B7
onks Wood Cl ELGH SO50 ..... 43 J5
onckton Rd GPORT PO12 ..... 132 B6
onkwood Cl HAV PO9 ..... 102 E1
onmouth Cl CHFD SO53 ..... 37 J4
onmouth Rd NEND PO2 ..... 118 C5
onmouth Sq WINW SO22 ..... 24 E2
onnow Gdns WEND SO18 ..... 56 E3
onroe Cl GPORT PO12 ..... 132 B5
ontague Av ITCH SO19 ..... 73 G2
ontague Rd NEND PO2 ..... 118 D6
onterey Dr HAV PO9 ..... 103 H2
HLER SO31 ..... 95 F4
ontfort Cl ROMY SO51 ..... 35 H3
ontfort Hts ROMY SO51 ..... 35 H3
ontfort Rd ROMY SO51 ..... 35 H4
ontgomerie Rd SSEA PO5 ..... 18 E5
ontgomery Av TOTT SO40 ..... 52 C4
ontgomery Rd HAV PO9 ..... 15 G4

LSOL/BMARY PO13 ..... 115 K3
WEND SO18 ..... 7 G3
Montgomery Wk WVILLE PO7 ..... 101 H1
Montgomery Wy CHFD SO53 ..... 37 J7
Montpelier Cl HLER SO31 ..... 95 H3
Montrose Av FHAM/PORC PO16.. 99 G5
Montrose Cl HEND SO30 ..... 58 D6
Montserrat Rd
 LSOL/BMARY PO13 ..... 131 F2
Monument La RCCH PO18 ..... 85 J6
 WHAM PO17 ..... 98 C2
Moody Rd FHAM/STUB PO14.. 114 C6
Moonhills La BROC SO42 ..... 108 C5
Mooncross Av TOTT SO40 ..... 68 E1
Moore Crs HLER SO31 ..... 72 E7
Moore Gdns GPORT PO12 ..... 132 C4
Moorgreen Rd HAV PO9 ..... 103 H1
 HEND SO30 ..... 57 H3
Moorhill Gdns WEND SO18 ..... 57 H5
Moorhill Rd HEND SO30 ..... 57 G4
The Moorings
 FHAM/PORC PO16 ..... 97 J7
Moorings Wy ENEY PO4 ..... 135 H2
Moorland Cl FAWY SO45 ..... 90 E3
 HLER SO31 ..... 95 F2
Moorland Rd PSEA PO1 ..... 19 H2
Moorlands Crs WEND SO18 ..... 7 H2
Moorlands Rd BPWT SO32 ..... 49 H5
Moor Pk HORN PO8.. ..... 82 C4
Moors Cl RWIN SO21 ..... 39 J1
Moorside Rd WINC SO23 ..... 22 B5
Moortown Av CHAM PO6 ..... 101 H5
Mopley FAWY SO45 ..... 128 C1
Mopley Cl FAWY SO45 ..... 128 C1
Moraunt Cl GPORT PO12 ..... 116 E7
Moraunt Dr FHAM/PORC PO16 .. 116 E1
Moreland Rd GPORT PO12 ..... 16 A4
Morelands Rd WVILLE PO7 ..... 101 K2
Morestead Rd RWIN SO21 ..... 26 D6
 RWIN SO21 ..... 26 D6
Morgan Rd ENEY PO4 ..... 135 H4
 HEND SO30 ..... 58 B7
Morgans Dr FHAM/STUB PO14 .. 114 D2
Morland Rd WSHM SO15 ..... 54 D3
Morley Cl ITCH SO19 ..... 6 E7
Morley Crs HORN PO8.. ..... 82 B2
Morley Dr BPWT SO32 ..... 48 D3
Morley Rd ENEY PO4 ..... 19 M4
Morningside Av
 FHAM/PORC PO16 ..... 99 G5
Mornington Dr WINW SO22 ..... 21 F5
Morpeth Av TOTT SO40 ..... 52 E4
Morris Cl FAWY SO45 ..... 90 E2
 LSOL/BMARY PO13 ..... 115 K3
Morris Rd WSHM SO15 ..... 4 C3
Morshead Crs
 FHAM/PORC PO16 ..... 12 F2
Mortimer Cl HLER SO31 ..... 72 E7
 TOTT SO40 ..... 52 C3
 WINC SO23 ..... 22 A1
Mortimer Rd CHAM PO6 ..... 100 B5
 HEND SO30 ..... 59 F6
 ITCH SO19 ..... 10 C2
Mortimers Dr ELGH SO50 ..... 46 C1
Mortimers La ELGH SO50 ..... 46 C1
Mortimer Wy NBAD SO52 ..... 36 A7
Mortimore Rd GPORT PO12 ..... 132 C2
Mosaic Cl ITCH SO19 ..... 73 J1
Mosdell Rd EMRTH PO10 ..... 105 G4
Moss Dr TOTT SO40 ..... 70 A3
Mossleigh Av ROWN SO16 ..... 42 A6
Moss Rd WINC SO23 ..... 3 H4
Mottisfont Cl WSHM SO15 ..... 54 B6
Mottisfont Rd ELGH SO50 ..... 38 D6
Mound Cl GPORT PO12 ..... 132 D5
Mountain Ash Cl WEND SO18 ..... 7 M5
Mountbatten Av ROMY SO51 ..... 34 E3
Mountbatten Cl
 LSOL/BMARY PO13 ..... 115 K3
Mountbatten Ct WINW SO22 ..... 21 H4
Mountbatten Dr WVILLE PO7 ..... 81 K2
Mountbatten Rd ELGH SO50 ..... 38 D5
 TOTT SO40 ..... 52 A3
Mountbatten Sq ENEY PO4 ..... 135 G6
Mount Cl WINW SO22 ..... 21 H4
Mount Dr CHFD SO53 ..... 38 B6
 FHAM PO15 ..... 96 C6
Mountfield FAWY SO45.. ..... 91 F2
Mount House Cl FAWY SO45 ..... 91 H1
Mount Pleasant WINC SO23 ..... 22 A1
Mount Pleasant Rd
 GPORT PO12 ..... 16 A9
 SHAM SO14 ..... 5 J5
The Mount
 LSOL/BMARY PO13 ..... 116 B6
 ROWN SO16 ..... 43 G7
 ROWN SO16 ..... 54 B3
Mount Vw ELGH SO50.. ..... 38 E6
Mountview Av
 FHAM/PORC PO16 ..... 99 H5
Mountwood Rd EMRTH PO10 ..... 105 G5
Mousehole La FAWY SO45 ..... 91 H3
 WEND SO18 ..... 6 F3
Mousehole Rd CHAM PO6 ..... 99 J5
Mowbray Rd ITCH SO19 ..... 11 K1
Muccleshell Cl HAV PO9 ..... 103 H2
Mulberry Av CHAM PO6 ..... 101 F7
 FHAM/STUB PO14.. ..... 114 D6
Mulberry La GPORT PO12 ..... 16 A6
Mulberry La CHAM PO6 ..... 101 F7
Mulberry Rd TOTT SO40 ..... 70 A4
Mulberry Wk WSHM SO15 ..... 54 D4
Mullen Cl ITCH SO19 ..... 10 C2
Mullin's La FAWY SO45 ..... 91 G4
Mullion Cl CHAM PO6 ..... 100 A7
Mumby Rd GPORT PO12 ..... 16 F4
Mundays Rw HORN PO8.. ..... 64 D3
Munro Crs WSHM SO15 ..... 54 A5
Munster Rd NEND PO2 ..... 118 C5
Murefield Rd PSEA PO1 ..... 18 F3
Muriel Rd WVILLE PO7 ..... 81 K5
Murray Cl HORN PO8.. ..... 64 C5
 ITCH SO19 ..... 57 H6
Murray's La PSEA PO1 ..... 17 K1
Muscliffe Ct HAV PO9 ..... 103 J1
Museum Rd PSEA PO1 ..... 18 A6
Mussett Cl TOTT SO40 ..... 52 D5
Mustang Av FHAM PO15 ..... 75 G6

Myers Cl BPWT SO32 ..... 49 J6
My Lords La HISD PO11 ..... 137 J5
Myrtle Av FHAM/PORC PO16 ..... 99 G7
 TOTT SO40 ..... 99 G7
Myrtle Cl LSOL/BMARY PO13 ..... 115 J4
Myrtle Gv HSEA PO3 ..... 135 G2
Myrtle Rd ROWN SO16 ..... 42 C7
Myvern Cl FAWY SO45 ..... 109 K4

N

Nailsworth Rd CHAM PO6 ..... 100 A5
Naish Ct HAV PO9 ..... 82 D6
Naish Dr GPORT PO12 ..... 116 D6
Napier Crs FHAM PO15 ..... 96 D5
Napier Rd HORN PO8 ..... 64 C5
 ITCH SO19 ..... 57 H7
 SSEA PO5 ..... 18 F9
Narrow La ROMY SO51 ..... 34 D3
Narvik Rd NEND PO2 ..... 118 C3
Nash Cl FAWY SO45 ..... 90 E4
Nashe Cl FHAM PO15 ..... 12 A1
Nashe Wy FHAM PO15 ..... 96 D4
Nash Rd FAWY SO45 ..... 90 E5
Nasmith Cl LSOL/BMARY PO13 .. 132 A4
Navigator's Wy HEND SO30 ..... 58 B4
Navy Rd PSEA PO1 ..... 17 L1
Neath Wy CHFD SO53 ..... 37 H5
Neelands Gv CHAM PO6 ..... 99 H6
Neilson Cl CHFD SO53 ..... 37 K3
Nelson Av FHAM/PORC PO16 ..... 98 E7
 NEND PO2 ..... 118 C5
Nelson Cl FAWY SO45 ..... 109 K4
 ROMY SO51 ..... 34 E2
 ROMY SO51 ..... 35 F2
Nelson Cr FHAM/STUB PO14 ..... 115 G1
Nelson Crs HORN PO8 ..... 64 D5
Nelson La WHAM PO17 ..... 99 F3
Nelson Rd ELGH SO50 ..... 39 G6
 GPORT PO12 ..... 16 B6
 PSEA PO1 ..... 134 C1
 SSEA PO5 ..... 18 D8
 WINC SO23 ..... 3 J6
 WSHM SO15 ..... 54 C6
Nelsons Gdns HEND SO30 ..... 58 B1
Nepean Cl GPORT PO12 ..... 132 E7
Neptune Rd FHAM PO15 ..... 96 C4
 FHAM/STUB PO14.. ..... 115 C2
Neptune Wy SHAM SO14 ..... 9 J5
Nerissa Cl WVILLE PO7 ..... 82 C5
Nerquis Cl HAV PO9 ..... 35 G2
Nesbitt Cl LSOL/BMARY PO13 .. 115 J4
Nessus St NEND PO2 ..... 118 C7
Netherfield Cl HAV PO9 ..... 15 H6
Nether Hill La BPWT SO32 ..... 59 G2
Netherton Rd GPORT PO12 ..... 132 C1
Netley Cl CHFD SO53 ..... 37 J7
Netley Firs Cl ITCH SO19 ..... 73 J1
Netley Hill Est ITCH SO19 ..... 73 J1
Netley Lodge Cl HLER SO31 ..... 93 F1
Netley Rd FHAM/STUB PO14 ..... 95 H5
 SSEA PO5 ..... 134 B6
Netley Ter SSEA PO5 ..... 134 B6
Nettlecombe Av ENEY PO4 ..... 134 D7
Nettlestone HLER SO31 ..... 73 F6
Nettlestone Rd ENEY PO4 ..... 135 F6
Neva Rd WEND SO18.. ..... 6 E2
Neville Av FHAM/PORC PO16 ..... 117 G1
Neville Dr ROMY SO51 ..... 34 E2
Neville Gdns EMRTH PO10 ..... 104 B3
Neville Rd HSEA PO3 ..... 135 F1
Neville Shute Rd SHAM SO14 ..... 119 F4
Newbarn La RCCH PO18 ..... 85 J3
Newbarn Rd NEND PO2 ..... 102 D3
Newbolt Cl HORN PO8 ..... 81 K2
Newbolt Rd CHAM PO6 ..... 99 J5
Newbridge HLER SO31 ..... 73 F7
Newbridge Rd TOTT SO40 ..... 50 C1
New Brighton Rd
 EMRTH PO10 ..... 104 C4
Newbroke Rd
 LSOL/BMARY PO13 ..... 116 B7
Newburgh St WINC SO23 ..... 2 D3
Newbury Cl ELGH SO50 ..... 46 A1
Newbury Pl HLER SO31 ..... 94 E4
Newbury Rd WSHM SO15 ..... 54 D3
New Cliffe Gdns HEND SO30 ..... 58 A7
Newcombe Rd WSHM SO15 ..... 4 D6
Newcomen Rd NEND PO2 ..... 118 B5
Newcome Rd PSEA PO1 ..... 19 H2
New Cut HISD PO11 ..... 121 F4
New Down La WVILLE PO7 ..... 101 F4
Newgate La FHAM/STUB PO14 .. 115 H1
New Inn La BROC SO42 ..... 125 H3
 TOTT SO40 ..... 50 E6
New Inn Rd TOTT SO40 ..... 50 E6
Newland Cl GPORT PO12 ..... 132 D4
Newlands Av WSHM SO15 ..... 54 D5
Newlands Cl FAWY SO45 ..... 110 B7
 NBAD SO52 ..... 37 G3
Newlands Copse FAWY SO45 ..... 110 B7
Newlands La WVILLE PO7 ..... 80 E3
Newlands Rd FAWY SO45 ..... 110 B5
 WVILLE PO7 ..... 101 J1
New La HAV PO9 ..... 15 G3
Newlease Rd WVILLE PO7 ..... 102 A1
Newlyn Wk ROMY SO51 ..... 35 F1
Newlyn Wy CHAM PO6 ..... 99 K7
Newmans HI WHAM PO17 ..... 61 K4
Newman Ct HAV PO9 ..... 82 D7
Newmarket Cl ELGH SO50 ..... 46 C4
Newney Cl NEND PO2 ..... 118 B3
Newnham Ct HAV PO9 ..... 103 J1
Newport Cl CHFD SO53 ..... 37 H6
Newport La ROMY SO51 ..... 29 G3
Newport Rd GPORT PO12 ..... 132 C3
New Rd BPWT SO32 ..... 48 E1
 BPWT SO32 ..... 49 G3
 ELGH SO50 ..... 46 A1
 EMRTH PO10 ..... 104 C3
 EMRTH PO10 ..... 105 H6
 FAWY SO45 ..... 109 J4
 FAWY SO45 ..... 110 B6
 FHAM/PORC PO16 ..... 13 H5
 HLER SO31 ..... 72 E7

HLER SO31 ..... 74 E5
 HLER SO31 ..... 94 E6
 HORN PO8 ..... 63 K6
 NEND PO2 ..... 134 D1
 ROMY SO51 ..... 28 C2
 ROMY SO51 ..... 35 F2
 RWIN SO21 ..... 39 J1
 SHAM SO14 ..... 5 G9
 TOTT SO40 ..... 68 B3
New East Rd NEND PO2 ..... 118 E7
Newton Cl FHAM/STUB PO14 ..... 114 D3
Newton La ROMY SO51 ..... 34 D3
Newton Pl LSOL/BMARY PO13 .. 131 F1
Newton Rd RWIN SO21 ..... 33 K2
 SHAM SO14 ..... 56 B3
Nicholas Crs FHAM PO15 ..... 12 E4
Nicholas Cl FAWY SO45 ..... 128 B1
Nicholl Pl LSOL/BMARY PO13 .. 115 K5
Nichol Rd CHFD SO53 ..... 38 A1
Nicholson Wk ROWN SO16 ..... 41 J5
Nicholson Wy HAV PO9 ..... 14 D1
Nichols Rd SHAM SO14 ..... 5 J8
Nickel Cl WINC SO23 ..... 3 H3
Nickel St SSEA PO5 ..... 18 B7
Nickleby Gdns TOTT SO40 ..... 52 A5
Nickson Cl CHFD SO53 ..... 37 J2
Nightingale Av ELGH SO50 ..... 44 A1
Nightingale Cl WINW SO22 ..... 24 E2
 GPORT PO12 ..... 132 C2
 HAV PO9 ..... 83 H4
 ROMY SO51 ..... 35 G3
Nightingale Crs BPWT SO32 ..... 61 G4
Nightingale Dr TOTT SO40 ..... 52 B4
Nightingale Gv WSHM SO15 ..... 54 D5
Nightingale La RCCH PO18 ..... 105 K3
Nightingale Pk HAV PO9 ..... 15 J5
Nightingale Rd HLER SO31 ..... 73 J5
 SSEA PO5 ..... 18 B9
Nightingale Wk HLER SO31 ..... 93 F2
Nightjar Cl HORN PO8 ..... 64 B6
Nile St EMRTH PO10 ..... 104 C6
Nile St EMRTH PO10 ..... 104 C6
Nimrod Dr LSOL/BMARY PO13.. 132 A2
Nine Elms La WHAM PO17 ..... 98 B2
Ninian Cl ELGH SO50 ..... 46 B2
Ninian Park Rd HSEA PO3 ..... 119 F5
Niton Cl LSOL/BMARY PO13 ..... 115 K5
Noads Cl FAWY SO45 ..... 91 G4
Noads Wy FAWY SO45 ..... 91 F5
Nobbs La PSEA PO1 ..... 17 M6
Nobes Av LSOL/BMARY PO13 ..... 115 K4
Nobes Cl LSOL/BMARY PO13 ..... 116 A5
Noble Rd HEND SO30 ..... 58 C6
Nob's Crook RWIN SO21 ..... 39 K3
Nogarth Cl ROMY SO51 ..... 35 G1
Nomad Cl WEND SO18 ..... 7 J1
The Nook ELGH SO50 ..... 38 E5
 LSOL/BMARY PO13 ..... 116 B6
Norbury Cl CHFD SO53 ..... 37 J3
Norbury Gdns HLER SO31 ..... 93 H4
Norcliffe Rd PTSW SO17 ..... 5 G2
Nordik Gdns HEND SO30 ..... 58 B7
Nore Crs EMRTH PO10 ..... 104 A5
Nore Farm Av EMRTH PO10 ..... 104 A4
Norfolk Rd GPORT PO12 ..... 132 C1
 WSHM SO15 ..... 4 A3
Norfolk St SSEA PO5 ..... 18 C7
Norgett Wy FHAM/PORC PO16.. 116 E1
Norham Av ROWN SO16 ..... 54 D2
Norham Cl ROWN SO16 ..... 54 D2
Norland Rd ENEY PO4 ..... 19 G7
Norlands Dr RWIN SO21 ..... 33 F5
Norley Cl HAV PO9 ..... 103 F1
Norleywood Rd LYMN SO41 ..... 124 C7
Norman Cl FHAM/PORC PO16 ..... 117 G1
Normandy Cl ROWN SO16 ..... 41 J5
Normandy Gdns
 GPORT PO12 ..... 132 C4
Normandy Rd NEND PO2 ..... 118 C3
Normandy Wy TOTT SO40 ..... 70 A2
Norman Gdns HEND SO30 ..... 57 K7
Norman Rd ENEY PO4 ..... 19 G8
 FAWY SO45 ..... 110 C7
 GPORT PO12 ..... 132 D3
 HISD PO11 ..... 137 J6
 WINC SO23 ..... 2 C8
Norman Wy HAV PO9 ..... 102 D4
Norris Cl ROMY SO51 ..... 29 H7
Norris Gdns HAV PO9 ..... 15 H6
Norris HI WEND SO18 ..... 6 D1
Norset Rd FHAM/PORC PO16 ..... 96 D4
Northam Br WSHM SO15 ..... 5 M6
Northam Ms PSEA PO1 ..... 18 E3
Northampton La FAWY SO45 ..... 110 B7
Northam Rd SHAM SO14 ..... 5 K8
Northam St PSEA PO1 ..... 18 F3
Northarbour Rd CHAM PO6 ..... 100 C7
North Av NEND PO2 ..... 118 D2
North Battery Rd NEND PO2 ..... 118 A5
North Bay EMRTH PO10 ..... 122 D4
Northbourne Av FAWY SO45 ..... 91 H5
Northbrook Av WINC SO23 ..... 3 H5
Northbrook Cl PSEA PO1 ..... 134 C1
 WINC SO23 ..... 3 J5
Northbrook Rd SHAM SO14 ..... 5 J5
North Cl GPORT PO12 ..... 132 C4
 HAV PO9 ..... 15 G6
 ROMY SO51 ..... 35 H1
Northcote Av NEND PO2 ..... 118 E1
Northcote Rd ENEY PO4 ..... 19 H8
 PTSW SO17 ..... 55 K2
North Crs HISD PO11 ..... 137 J5
Northcroft Rd GPORT PO12 ..... 132 C2
North Cross St GPORT PO12 ..... 16 F5
Northdene Rd CHFD SO53 ..... 37 K5
North Dr WINW SO22 ..... 20 E2
North East Cl ITCH SO19 ..... 7 K9
North East Rd ITCH SO19 ..... 11 H2
North End Av NEND PO2 ..... 118 C3
North End Cl CHFD SO53 ..... 37 K5
North End Gv NEND PO2 ..... 118 C5
Northern Access Rd
 FAWY SO45 ..... 111 G5
Northern Anchorage ITCH SO19.. 9 M3
Northern Pde NEND PO2 ..... 118 C4

Northern Rd CHAM PO6 ..... 118 E1
Northerwood Av LYND SO43 ..... 86 B1
Northerwood Cl NBAD SO52 ..... 36 A6
Northfield Cl BPWT SO32 ..... 48 B2
 HORN PO8 ..... 64 D2
Northfield Rd WEND SO18 ..... 56 C1
Northfields Farm La
 WHAM PO17 ..... 61 H7
North Front SHAM SO14 ..... 5 H9
North HI CHAM PO6 ..... 100 A4
 FHAM/PORC PO16 ..... 13 J1
North Hill Cl WINW SO22 ..... 21 J5
Northlands Cl TOTT SO40 ..... 52 C4
Northlands Dr WINC SO23 ..... 21 K5
Northlands Gdns WSHM SO15.. 4 B7
North Lands Rd ELGH SO50 ..... 38 D7
 ROMY SO51 ..... 35 H4
 TOTT SO40 ..... 52 C4
 WSHM SO15 ..... 4 D5
North La BROC SO42 ..... 107 K2
North Millers Dl CHFD SO53 ..... 37 H1
Northmore Cl HLER SO31 ..... 95 G1
Northmore Rd HLER SO31 ..... 95 G1
Northney La HISD PO11 ..... 121 K3
Northney Rd HISD PO11 ..... 121 J3
Northolt Gdns ROWN SO16 ..... 42 B7
Northover Rd HSEA PO3 ..... 119 G2
North Rd FAWY SO45 ..... 90 E4
 HORN PO8 ..... 64 D2
 PTSW SO17 ..... 5 M1
 WVILLE PO7 ..... 99 K4
North Rd East WHAM PO17 ..... 79 K7
North Rd West WHAM PO17 ..... 79 J7
North Shore Rd HISD PO11 ..... 136 E3
North St EMRTH PO10 ..... 104 C5
 EMRTH PO10 ..... 104 E2
 HAV PO9 ..... 14 A3
 HAV PO9 ..... 14 F4
 PSEA PO1 ..... 17 M3
 PSEA PO1 ..... 18 E1
North Town RWIN SO21 ..... 33 K2
North Trestle Rd FAWY SO45 ..... 110 E1
Northumberland Rd
 SHAM SO14 ..... 5 K6
 SSEA PO5 ..... 19 G4
North Wallington
 FHAM/PORC PO16 ..... 13 M3
North Walls WINC SO23 ..... 3 G4
Northway FHAM PO15 ..... 95 K3
North Wy HAV PO9 ..... 14 D4
Northways FHAM/STUB PO14.. 114 C5
Northwood Cl ROWN SO16 ..... 43 H5
Northwood La HISD PO11 ..... 121 H6
Northwood Rd NEND PO2 ..... 118 D3
Norton Cl ITCH SO19 ..... 10 C3
 WHAM PO17 ..... 79 J7
 WVILLE PO7 ..... 81 H3
Norton Dr FHAM/PORC PO16 ..... 13 H3
Norton Rd WHAM PO17 ..... 79 J7
Norton Welch Cl NBAD SO52 ..... 36 C6
Norway Rd HSEA PO3 ..... 118 E3
Norwich Cl HLER SO31 ..... 94 D2
Norwich Pl LSOL/BMARY PO13 .. 131 F1
Norwich Rd CHAM PO6 ..... 100 C5
 WEND SO18 ..... 56 C2
Nottingham Pl
 LSOL/BMARY PO13 ..... 131 F1
Novello Gdns WVILLE PO7 ..... 101 K1
Noyce Dr ELGH SO50 ..... 46 C2
Nuns Rd WINC SO23 ..... 2 F1
Nuns Wk WINC SO23 ..... 2 F1
 WINC SO23 ..... 22 A5
Nursery Cl EMRTH PO10 ..... 104 C3
 LSOL/BMARY PO13 ..... 115 J4
Nursery Gdns CHFD SO53 ..... 37 K7
 WINW SO22 ..... 21 G7
 HORN PO8 ..... 64 B7
 ITCH SO19 ..... 7 K6
 ROMY SO51 ..... 35 G3
Nursery Gv HEND SO30 ..... 58 B7
Nursery La FHAM/STUB PO14 ..... 114 D6
Nursery Rd HAV PO9 ..... 102 D4
 WEND SO18 ..... 56 A3
Nursling Crs HAV PO9 ..... 103 H1
Nursling St ROWN SO16 ..... 41 H6
Nutash FHAM PO15 ..... 95 H2
Nutbeem Rd ELGH SO50 ..... 44 D1
Nutbourne Rd CHAM PO6 ..... 101 J7
 HISD PO11 ..... 138 B7
Nutburn Rd NBAD SO52 ..... 36 C5
Nutfield Ct ROWN SO16 ..... 53 K1
Nutfield Pl PSEA PO1 ..... 18 F1
Nutfield Rd ROWN SO16 ..... 41 J5
Nuthatch Cl HAV PO9 ..... 83 J4
Nutley Rd HAV PO9 ..... 102 E1
Nutsey Av TOTT SO40 ..... 52 C2
Nutsey La TOTT SO40 ..... 52 D2
Nutshalling Av ROWN SO16 ..... 41 K6
Nutshalling Cl TOTT SO40 ..... 52 B3
Nutwick Rd HAV PO9 ..... 15 K1
 HAV PO9 ..... 103 J2
Nutwood Wy TOTT SO40 ..... 52 D2
Nyewood Av FHAM/PORC PO16 .. 99 G5
Nyria Wy GPORT PO12 ..... 16 E6

O

Oakapple Gdns CHAM PO6 ..... 101 K6
Oakbank Rd ELGH SO50 ..... 39 F7
 ITCH SO19 ..... 10 A4
Oak Cl FAWY SO45 ..... 91 F5
 HORN PO8 ..... 81 K3
 LYND SO43 ..... 86 C2
 WSHM SO15 ..... 53 H5
Oak Coppice Cl ELGH SO50 ..... 45 K1
Oakcroft La FHAM/STUB PO14 .. 114 D2
Oakdene LSOL/BMARY PO13 ..... 116 A6
 TOTT SO40 ..... 52 A3
Oakdown Rd
 FHAM/STUB PO14.. ..... 114 E4
Oak Dr ELGH SO50 ..... 46 B1
Oakenbrow FAWY SO45 ..... 90 E4
The Oakes FHAM/STUB PO14 ..... 114 C3
Oakfield Ct HAV PO9 ..... 103 J1
Oakfield Rd TOTT SO40 ..... 50 E5
 TOTT SO40 ..... 52 C4
Oakfields ELGH SO50 ..... 38 D7

Oak Green Wy WEND SO18 ..... 7 G2
Oakgrove Rd ELGH SO50 ..... 45 H1
Oakhill HLER SO31 ..... 74 A4
Oakhill Cl CHFD SO53 ..... 38 B5
  HLER SO31 ..... 74 A4
Oakhurst Cl HLER SO31 ..... 73 F7
Oakhurst Dr WVILLE PO7 ..... 82 B5
Oakhurst Gdns PO06 ..... 101 G4
Oakhurst Wy HLER SO31 ..... 73 F7
Oakland Dr TOTT SO40 ..... 70 A4
Oaklands Av TOTT SO40 ..... 52 E5
Oaklands WINW SO22 ..... 24 E3
Oaklands Gdns
  FHAM/STUB PO14 ..... 95 H5
Oaklands Gv HORN PO8 ..... 81 K2
Oaklands HAV PO9 ..... 15 G4
The Oaklands CHFD SO53 ..... 37 K7
Oaklands Wy FAWY SO45 ..... 90 D4
  FHAM/STUB PO14 ..... 95 H5
  ROWN SO16 ..... 43 G2
Oakleigh Crs TOTT SO40 ..... 52 D6
Oakleigh Gdns ROMY SO51 ..... 35 F3
Oakley Cl FAWY SO45 ..... 109 K3
Oakley Rd HAV PO9 ..... 102 E1
  ROWN SO16 ..... 54 A4
Oakmeadow Cl EMRTH PO10 ..... 104 D3
Oakmont Cl WVILLE PO7 ..... 82 A3
Oakmount Av CHFD SO53 ..... 38 A6
  PTSW SO17 ..... 55 H3
  TOTT SO40 ..... 52 E4
Oakmount Rd CHFD SO53 ..... 38 A6
Oak Park Dr HAV PO9 ..... 15 C1
Oakridge Rd WSHM SO15 ..... 53 J4
Oak St BPWT SO32 ..... 48 E3
  FAWY SO45 ..... 91 F5
  FHAM PO15 ..... 12 A4
  HLER SO31 ..... 73 H5
  ITCH SO19 ..... 10 B5
Oaks Coppice HORN PO8 ..... 64 B6
Oakshott Dr HAV PO9 ..... 103 H1
The Oaks HLER SO31 ..... 73 J5
  ITCH SO19 ..... 6 E8
Oak St GPORT PO12 ..... 16 D5
Oakthorn Cl
  LSOL/BMARY PO13 ..... 131 K2
Oak Tree Cl RWIN SO21 ..... 39 J2
Oak Tree Dr EMRTH PO10 ..... 104 D4
Oak Tree Gdns HEND SO30 ..... 58 A6
Oak Tree Rd WEND SO18 ..... 56 A3
Oak Tree Wy ELGH SO50 ..... 38 D5
Oak V HEND SO30 ..... 56 E1
Oakwood Av HAV PO9 ..... 102 C3
  RWIN SO21 ..... 33 F6
Oakwood Cl HLER SO31 ..... 94 C6
  ROMY SO51 ..... 35 H1
  RWIN SO21 ..... 33 F5
Oakwood Ct HEND SO30 ..... 57 H2
Oakwood Dr ROWN SO16 ..... 42 C6
Oakwood Rd CHFD SO53 ..... 38 A2
  HISD PO11 ..... 137 G5
  NEND PO2 ..... 118 E3
Oakwood Wy HLER SO31 ..... 93 K3
Oatfield Gdns TOTT SO40 ..... 52 B6
Oatlands ROMY SO51 ..... 34 E2
Oatlands Cl BPWT SO32 ..... 58 E3
Oatlands Rd BPWT SO32 ..... 58 E3
Obelisk Rd ITCH SO19 ..... 10 B5
Oberon Cl WVILLE PO7 ..... 82 B5
Occupation La
  FHAM/STUB PO14 ..... 95 H5
Ocean Cl FHAM PO15 ..... 12 B3
Ocean Rd FHAM/STUB PO14 ..... 115 G2
  SHAM SO14 ..... 9 H8
Ocean Wy SHAM SO14 ..... 9 J6
Ockendon Cl SSEA PO5 ..... 18 D6
Ocknell Gv FAWY SO45 ..... 90 D3
O'connell Rd ELGH SO50 ..... 44 B1
Octavia Gdns CHFD SO53 ..... 38 C3
Octavia Hl WINW SO22 ..... 25 C2
Octavia Rd WEND SO18 ..... 44 B7
Octavius Ct WVILLE PO7 ..... 82 C4
Odell Cl FHAM/PORC PO16 ..... 12 E1
Odiham Cl ROWN SO16 ..... 42 A7
Oglander Rd WINC SO23 ..... 21 K5
Ogle Rd SHAM SO14 ..... 8 E4
Okement Cl WEND SO18 ..... 56 E2
Olave Cl LSOL/BMARY PO13 ..... 131 F2
Old Agwi Rd FAWY SO45 ..... 111 F2
Oldbarn Cl TOTT SO40 ..... 52 B2
Old Barn Crs WVILLE PO7 ..... 62 B2
Old Bridge House Rd
  HLER SO31 ..... 74 A5
Old Bridge Rd ENEY PO4 ..... 134 D6
Oldbury Ct ROWN SO16 ..... 53 J2
Oldbury Wy FHAM/STUB PO14 ..... 96 D6
Old Canal ENEY PO4 ..... 135 G4
Old Commercial Rd
  PSEA PO1 ..... 134 B1
Old Common HLER SO31 ..... 95 F2
Old Common Gdns HLER SO31 ..... 95 F3
Old Copse Rd HAV PO9 ..... 14 F2
Old Cracknore Cl TOTT SO40 ..... 70 A3
Oldenburg HLER SO31 ..... 75 G5
Old Farm Dr WEND SO18 ..... 56 C2
Old Farm La EMRTH PO10 ..... 104 E3
  FHAM/STUB PO14 ..... 114 D4
Old Farm Wy CHAM PO6 ..... 101 K7
Old Garden Cl
  FHAM/STUB PO14 ..... 95 H4
Old Gdns WINW SO22 ..... 21 J5
Oldgate Gdns NEND PO2 ..... 118 E3
Old Gosport Rd
  FHAM/PORC PO16 ..... 13 K8
Old Hillside Rd WINW SO22 ..... 21 F6
Old Ivy La WEND SO18 ..... 56 C2
Old Kennels Cl WINW SO22 ..... 24 D5
Old Kennels La RWIN SO21 ..... 24 D5
Old Lyndhurst Rd TOTT SO40 ..... 50 C4
Old Magazine Cl TOTT SO40 ..... 70 A3
Old Manor Wy CHAM PO6 ..... 101 G2
Old Mill La HORN PO8 ..... 63 G4
Old Mill Wy ROWN SO16 ..... 54 B3
Old Parsonage Ct RWIN SO21 ..... 33 J4
Old Priory Cl HLER SO31 ..... 93 K4
Old Rectory Cl EMRTH PO10 ..... 104 B3
Old Rectory Gdns WINC SO23 ..... 22 C1
Old Rectory La RWIN SO21 ..... 33 K2
Old Rectory Rd CHAM PO6 ..... 101 K6
Old Redbridge Rd WSHM SO15 ..... 53 H4

Old Reservoir Rd CHAM PO6 ..... 101 J7
Old River WVILLE PO7 ..... 80 E2
Old Rd GPORT PO12 ..... 16 D7
  ROMY SO51 ..... 35 F2
  SHAM SO14 ..... 9 J5
Old Romsey Rd TOTT SO40 ..... 118 E1
Old Romsey Rd TOTT SO40 ..... 50 B4
Old School Cl FAWY SO45 ..... 109 J1
  HLER SO31 ..... 73 G6
Old School Dr HISD PO11 ..... 137 J6
Old School Gdns HEND SO30 ..... 57 H2
Old Shamblehurst La
  HEND SO30 ..... 58 B2
Old Star PSEA PO1 ..... 17 L3
Old Station Ap WINC SO23 ..... 3 H5
Old St FHAM/STUB PO14 ..... 114 C4
Old Timbers HISD PO11 ..... 137 C5
Old Tpk FHAM/PORC PO16 ..... 13 J2
The Old Well Cl ITCH SO19 ..... 11 L4
Old Wymering La CHAM PO6 ..... 100 D6
Oleander Cl HLER SO31 ..... 95 F1
Olinda St PSEA PO1 ..... 19 H2
Olive Crs FHAM/PORC PO16 ..... 117 G1
Olive Rd ROWN SO16 ..... 42 B7
Oliver Rd ENEY PO4 ..... 19 L8
  WEND SO18 ..... 56 A1
Oliver's Battery Crs WINW SO22 ..... 24 E4
Oliver's Battery Gdns
  WINW SO22 ..... 24 E5
Oliver's Battery Rd North
  WINW SO22 ..... 24 E5
Oliver's Battery Rd South
  WINW SO22 ..... 24 E5
Olivers Cl TOTT SO40 ..... 52 A5
Olivia Cl WVILLE PO7 ..... 82 B4
Olympic Wy ELGH SO50 ..... 39 K7
Omdurman Rd PTSW SO17 ..... 55 H2
Omega St SSEA PO5 ..... 18 E4
Onibury Cl WEND SO18 ..... 56 D3
Onibury Rd WEND SO18 ..... 56 D3
Onslow Rd SHAM SO14 ..... 9 H3
  SSEA PO5 ..... 134 C7
Ophir Rd NEND PO2 ..... 118 C5
Oracle Dr WVILLE PO7 ..... 101 K3
Orange Gv
  LSOL/BMARY PO13 ..... 116 A6
Orange Rw EMRTH PO10 ..... 104 C6
Orchard Av ELGH SO50 ..... 45 J2
Orchard Cl FAWY SO45 ..... 110 E4
  GPORT PO12 ..... 116 D6
  HORN PO8 ..... 64 D6
  NBAD SO52 ..... 36 A5
  RWIN SO21 ..... 39 J1
  TOTT SO40 ..... 52 E7
Orchard Ct HEND SO30 ..... 58 D5
Orchard Gv FHAM/PORC PO16 ..... 98 D7
  HORN PO8 ..... 82 A4
Orchard La EMRTH PO10 ..... 104 D6
  ROMY SO51 ..... 34 D3
  SHAM SO14 ..... 9 H3
Orchardlea BPWT SO32 ..... 61 J3
Orchard Pl SHAM SO14 ..... 9 H4
Orchard Rd ELGH SO50 ..... 46 B1
  ENEY PO4 ..... 19 H5
  GPORT PO12 ..... 16 F2
  HAV PO9 ..... 14 F6
  HISD PO11 ..... 137 H6
  HLER SO31 ..... 94 E4
Orchards Wy HEND SO30 ..... 57 G3
  PTSW SO17 ..... 55 H2
The Orchard CHAM PO6 ..... 100 E7
  ROWN SO16 ..... 43 F7
  WVILLE PO7 ..... 80 E1
Orchard Wy FAWY SO45 ..... 91 F4
Ordnance Rd GPORT PO12 ..... 16 E5
  WSHM SO15 ..... 5 G5
Ordnance Rw PSEA PO1 ..... 17 L4
Ordnance Wy TOTT SO40 ..... 70 B2
Oregon Cl ITCH SO19 ..... 11 G1
Oriel Dr FHAM/STUB PO14 ..... 95 H5
Oriel Rd NEND PO2 ..... 118 C5
Orient Dr WINW SO22 ..... 21 H4
Orion Cl FHAM/STUB PO14 ..... 114 E5
  ROWN SO16 ..... 42 A7
Orkney Cl ROWN SO16 ..... 41 K7
Orkney Rd CHAM PO6 ..... 100 C5
Ormesby Dr CHFD SO53 ..... 37 J2
Ormsby Rd SSEA PO5 ..... 18 D8
Orpen Rd ITCH SO19 ..... 11 L3
Orsmond Cl WVILLE PO7 ..... 82 A7
Orwell Cl ROWN SO16 ..... 53 K3
Orwell Crs FHAM/STUB PO14 ..... 95 H4
Osborn Crs LSOL/BMARY PO13 ..... 115 J3
Osborne Cl WVILLE PO7 ..... 82 B6
Osborne Ct CHFD SO53 ..... 38 B5
Osborne Gdns ELGH SO50 ..... 46 C2
Osborne Rd GPORT PO12 ..... 16 E5
  HLER SO31 ..... 94 E6
  LSOL/BMARY PO13 ..... 131 F2
  SSEA PO5 ..... 18 B9
  TOTT SO40 ..... 53 F5
Osborne Rd North PTSW SO17 ..... 5 L3
Osborne Rd South PTSW SO17 ..... 5 L3
Osborne View Rd
  FHAM/STUB PO14 ..... 114 B6
Osborn Rd FHAM/PORC PO16 ..... 13 K5
Osborn Rd South
  FHAM/PORC PO16 ..... 13 J5
Osier Cl NEND PO2 ..... 118 B5
Oslands Dr HLER SO31 ..... 74 C6
Osprey Cl ROWN SO16 ..... 42 C6
  TOTT SO40 ..... 69 K4
Osprey Dr HISD PO11 ..... 137 J5
Osprey Gdns
  LSOL/BMARY PO13 ..... 131 G2
Osprey Quay EMRTH PO10 ..... 104 C4
Osterley Cl HEND SO30 ..... 58 D5
Osterly Rd ITCH SO19 ..... 6 C9
Othello Dr WVILLE PO7 ..... 82 B5
Otterbourne Crs HAV PO9 ..... 102 E1
Otterbourne Hl CHFD SO53 ..... 38 C1
Otterbourne Rd RWIN SO21 ..... 33 F5
Otter Cl ELGH SO50 ..... 45 K1
Ouse Cl CHFD SO53 ..... 37 K1
Outer Cir ROWN SO16 ..... 42 B7
Outlands La HEND SO30 ..... 59 J6
Outram Rd SSEA PO5 ..... 18 F7
Oval Gdns GPORT PO12 ..... 132 C5
Overbrook FAWY SO45 ..... 91 G4
Overbrook Wy NBAD SO52 ..... 35 K5

Overcliff Ri ROWN SO16 ..... 43 F1
Overton Crs HAV PO9 ..... 102 E1
Oviat Cl TOTT SO40 ..... 52 A5
Owen Cl LSOL/BMARY PO13 ..... 131 K1
Owen Rd ELGH SO50 ..... 44 C1
Owen's Rd WINW SO22 ..... 2 C1
Owen St ENEY PO4 ..... 19 M9
Owslebury Gv HAV PO9 ..... 103 G1
Oxburgh Cl ELGH SO50 ..... 38 C5
Oxford Av SHAM SO14 ..... 5 H8
Oxford Cl FHAM/PORC PO16 ..... 12 F3
Oxford Rd GPORT PO12 ..... 132 C3
  SHAM SO14 ..... 5 G4
  SSEA PO5 ..... 18 D9
Oxford St SHAM SO14 ..... 9 H4
Oxlease Cl ROMY SO51 ..... 35 F1
Oxleys Cl FHAM/STUB PO14 ..... 96 C6
Oxted Cl ITCH SO19 ..... 135 G3
Oyster Ms PSEA PO1 ..... 17 L7
Oyster Quay CHAM PO6 ..... 118 A1
Oyster St PSEA PO1 ..... 17 L7
Ozier Rd WEND SO18 ..... 56 D2

P

Pacific Cl SHAM SO14 ..... 9 K6
  SHAM SO14 ..... 9 L6
Packridge La ROMY SO51 ..... 42 A2
Padbury Cl NEND PO2 ..... 118 E3
Paddington Rd NEND PO2 ..... 118 E6
Paddock End WVILLE PO7 ..... 80 E2
The Paddocks FAWY SO45 ..... 110 E4
The Paddock ELGH SO50 ..... 38 E4
  FHAM/STUB PO14 ..... 114 D3
  GPORT PO12 ..... 132 D5
  TOTT SO40 ..... 52 B2
  WINC SO23 ..... 22 B1
Padnell Av HORN PO8 ..... 82 B1
Padnell Rd HORN PO8 ..... 82 C2
Padwell Rd SHAM SO14 ..... 5 G4
Padwick Av CHAM PO6 ..... 101 F6
Paffard Cl LSOL/BMARY PO13 ..... 131 K1
Page Cl FAWY SO45 ..... 110 A5
Pages La BROC SO42 ..... 125 H2
Paget Rd GPORT PO12 ..... 132 D6
Paget St SHAM SO14 ..... 9 K3
Pagham Cl EMRTH PO10 ..... 104 D5
Pagham Gdns HISD PO11 ..... 138 C6
Paignton Av HSEA PO3 ..... 119 F7
Paignton Rd ROWN SO16 ..... 54 A4
Pain's Rd SSEA PO5 ..... 18 E6
Painswick Cl CHAM PO6 ..... 100 B6
  HLER SO31 ..... 74 E7
Palace La BROC SO42 ..... 108 B6
Palk Rd HAV PO9 ..... 14 B4
Pallant Cl FHAM/PORC PO16 ..... 98 A4
The Pallant HAV PO9 ..... 14 F4
Pallet Cl RWIN SO21 ..... 39 J2
Pallot Cl HLER SO31 ..... 73 J5
Palmers Cl ELGH SO50 ..... 46 C1
Palmer's Rd EMRTH PO10 ..... 104 C5
Palmerston Av
  FHAM/PORC PO16 ..... 13 K5
Palmerston Dr
  FHAM/STUB PO14 ..... 97 H7
Palmerston Rd HISD PO11 ..... 137 H4
  SHAM SO14 ..... 5 G9
  SSEA PO5 ..... 134 B6
Palmerston St ROMY SO51 ..... 34 D3
  ROMY SO51 ..... 34 E3
Palm Hall Cl WINC SO23 ..... 3 J5
Palm Rd ROWN SO16 ..... 54 A1
Palmyra Rd GPORT PO12 ..... 132 D5
Pamela Av CHAM PO6 ..... 99 J6
Pangbourne Av CHAM PO6 ..... 101 G7
Pangbourne Cl ITCH SO19 ..... 11 H1
Pannall Rd GPORT PO12 ..... 132 D5
Pan St PSEA PO1 ..... 18 D2
Pansy Rd ROWN SO16 ..... 43 H7
Pantheon Rd CHFD SO53 ..... 38 C3
Panton Cl EMRTH PO10 ..... 104 B3
Panwell Rd WEND SO18 ..... 7 G5
The Parade PSEA PO1 ..... 17 L1
Paradise La BPWT SO32 ..... 49 F5
  EMRTH PO10 ..... 104 E2
  FHAM/PORC PO16 ..... 98 B5
  TOTT SO40 ..... 51 G6
Paradise St PSEA PO1 ..... 18 D3
Parchment St WINC SO23 ..... 2 E4
The Parchment HAV PO9 ..... 14 E5
Pardoe Cl HEND SO30 ..... 58 B7
Parham Dr ELGH SO50 ..... 38 C6
Parham Rd GPORT PO12 ..... 16 D4
Park Av WINC SO23 ..... 2 F3
  WVILLE PO7 ..... 101 H3
Park Cl FAWY SO45 ..... 91 J2
  GPORT PO12 ..... 132 C2
  TOTT SO40 ..... 69 J4
  WINC SO23 ..... 21 K5
Park Crs EMRTH PO10 ..... 104 A5
Parker Cl GPORT PO12 ..... 116 D6
Parker Gdns WVILLE PO7 ..... 101 H4
Park Farm Av FHAM PO15 ..... 96 D2
Park Farm Cl FHAM PO15 ..... 12 A1
Park Farm Rd WVILLE PO7 ..... 101 J2
Park Gln FHAM PO15 ..... 95 H2
Park Gv CHAM PO6 ..... 100 E7
Park Hill Cl FAWY SO45 ..... 109 K4
Park House Farm Wy HAV PO9 ..... 102 C1
Parklands HLER SO31 ..... 95 F2
  WEND SO18 ..... 6 D1
Parklands Av HORN PO8 ..... 64 B7
Parklands Cl CHFD SO53 ..... 37 K3
  GPORT PO12 ..... 16 A2
Park La BPWT SO32 ..... 49 K2
  CHAM PO6 ..... 101 F7
  ELGH SO50 ..... 38 C6
  EMRTH PO10 ..... 104 C2
  FAWY SO45 ..... 109 J3
  FHAM/PORC PO16 ..... 13 G3
  FHAM/STUB PO14 ..... 114 D4
  HAV PO9 ..... 82 D5
  HORN PO8 ..... 82 D5
  HAV PO9 ..... 102 D5
  RWIN SO21 ..... 22 C1
  RWIN SO21 ..... 33 K4
  TOTT SO40 ..... 69 H3

Park Pde HAV PO9 ..... 103 F2
Park Rd BPWT SO32 ..... 48 B3
  CHFD SO53 ..... 37 K2
  EMRTH PO10 ..... 105 G5
  WINW SO22 ..... 21 J5
  GPORT PO12 ..... 16 B9
  HISD PO11 ..... 136 D4
  PSEA PO1 ..... 17 M4
  WSHM SO15 ..... 4 A6
  WSHM SO15 ..... 54 D6
  WVILLE PO7 ..... 62 E7
  WVILLE PO7 ..... 101 H2
Park Rd North HAV PO9 ..... 14 C3
Park Rd South HAV PO9 ..... 14 C3
Parkside HAV PO9 ..... 102 D4
  TOTT SO40 ..... 52 E7
Parkside Av ROWN SO16 ..... 53 J4
Parkside Gdns WINW SO22 ..... 21 F5
Parkstone Av ENEY PO4 ..... 134 D7
Park St GPORT PO12 ..... 16 B4
  ROWN SO16 ..... 54 C4
  SSEA PO5 ..... 18 B6
Park Vw HEND SO30 ..... 58 A5
  HEND SO30 ..... 59 F5
Parkville Rd ROWN SO16 ..... 44 A7
Park Wk SHAM SO14 ..... 5 G9
Parkway FHAM PO15 ..... 75 K6
Park Wy HAV PO9 ..... 14 D4
Parkway Gdns CHFD SO53 ..... 37 K3
The Parkway
  LSOL/BMARY PO13 ..... 115 J5
  ROWN SO16 ..... 43 H6
Parliament Pl WINW SO22 ..... 25 F4
Parnell Rd ELGH SO50 ..... 44 C1
Parr Rd CHAM PO6 ..... 100 C6
Parr Rd North CHAM PO6 ..... 99 K6
Parry Cl CHAM PO6 ..... 99 H6
Parry Rd ITCH SO19 ..... 73 C1
Parsonage La BPWT SO32 ..... 47 C5
Parsonage Rd SHAM SO14 ..... 5 K7
Parsons Cl HSEA PO3 ..... 118 E3
Partridge Cl
  FHAM/PORC PO16 ..... 98 B6
Partridge Down WINW SO22 ..... 24 E5
Partridge Gdns HORN PO8 ..... 81 J1
Partridge Rd FAWY SO45 ..... 91 G5
Partry Cl CHFD SO53 ..... 37 H2
Passage La HLER SO31 ..... 94 A5
Passfield Av ELGH SO50 ..... 44 B1
Passfield Cl ELGH SO50 ..... 44 B1
Passingham Wk HORN PO8 ..... 82 B1
The Pastures
  FHAM/STUB PO14 ..... 95 H2
  WVILLE PO7 ..... 80 D2
Pat Bear Cl WSHM SO15 ..... 53 H4
Patchway Dr FHAM/STUB PO14 ..... 96 D6
Paternoster Rw WINC SO23 ..... 2 F5
Patricia Cl HEND SO30 ..... 57 G2
Patricia Dr HEND SO30 ..... 58 C5
Paulet Cl WEND SO18 ..... 56 D3
Paulet Lacave Av ROWN SO16 ..... 41 J5
Paulet Pl WINW SO22 ..... 2 A9
Pauletts La TOTT SO40 ..... 52 A1
Paulsgrove Rd NEND PO2 ..... 118 C5
Paulson Cl CHFD SO53 ..... 37 K2
Pauncefoot Hl ROMY SO51 ..... 34 B5
Pavilion Cl ELGH SO50 ..... 46 B3
Pavilion Rd HEND SO30 ..... 58 C4
Paxton Cl HEND SO30 ..... 58 C7
Paxton Rd FHAM/STUB PO14 ..... 12 F6
Paynes Hay Rd ROMY SO51 ..... 29 G1
Payne's Rd WSHM SO15 ..... 54 C6
Peach Rd ROWN SO16 ..... 42 B7
Peacock Cl FHAM/PORC PO16 ..... 98 B6
Peacock La PSEA PO1 ..... 17 M7
Peacock Pl WINC SO23 ..... 3 K4
Peak Cl ROWN SO16 ..... 54 A4
Peak Dr FHAM/STUB PO14 ..... 12 F6
Peakfield WVILLE PO7 ..... 80 D1
Peak La FHAM/STUB PO14 ..... 96 F2
The Peak HAV PO9 ..... 83 K3
Pearce Ct GPORT PO12 ..... 16 D4
Peartree Av ITCH SO19 ..... 10 C1
Pear Tree Cl BPWT SO32 ..... 58 E2
Peartree Cl
  FHAM/STUB PO14 ..... 114 E4
  ITCH SO19 ..... 10 B2
Peartree Rd FAWY SO45 ..... 91 F4
  ITCH SO19 ..... 10 B2
Pebble Cl HISD PO11 ..... 137 J6
Pebble Ct TOTT SO40 ..... 70 A3
Pebmarsh Rd CHAM PO6 ..... 100 C6
Pedam Cl ENEY PO4 ..... 19 L8
Pedula Wy ELGH SO50 ..... 39 H5
Peel Cl ROMY SO51 ..... 35 H1
Peel Pl SSEA PO5 ..... 18 C6
Peel Rd GPORT PO12 ..... 16 D4
Peel St SHAM SO14 ..... 5 L8
Peewit Hl HLER SO31 ..... 73 K2
Peewit Hill Cl HLER SO31 ..... 73 K2
Pegasus Cl HLER SO31 ..... 93 J4
  ROWN SO16 ..... 42 A7
Pelham Rd GPORT PO12 ..... 16 A4
  SSEA PO5 ..... 18 D8
Pelham Ter EMRTH PO10 ..... 104 D6
Pelican Cl FHAM/STUB PO14 ..... 115 G2
Pelican Rd FAWY SO45 ..... 91 G5
Pembers Cl ELGH SO50 ..... 46 C1
Pemberton Rd LYND SO43 ..... 86 D1
Pembrey Cl ROWN SO16 ..... 42 A6
Pembroke Cl ELGH SO50 ..... 38 C5
  PSEA PO1 ..... 17 M8
  ROMY SO51 ..... 34 E3
  TOTT SO40 ..... 53 F5
Pembroke Crs
  FHAM/STUB PO14 ..... 114 B5
Pembroke Rd WINW SO22 ..... 21 F2
  ITCH SO19 ..... 11 J1
  PSEA PO1 ..... 17 M7
Pembury Rd
  FHAM/STUB PO14 ..... 114 E3
  HAV PO9 ..... 15 H6
Pemerton Rd WINW SO22 ..... 21 H4
Penarth Av CHAM PO6 ..... 100 C6
Pendennis Rd CHAM PO6 ..... 99 J6
Pendle Cl ROWN SO16 ..... 54 A4
Pendleton Gdns FAWY SO45 ..... 110 B6
Penelope Gdns HLER SO31 ..... 73 J3
Penfolds Paddock
  BPWT SO32 ..... 48 E4

Penhale Gdns
  FHAM/STUB PO14 ..... 95 G5
Penhale Rd PSEA PO1 ..... 19 H5
Penhale Wy TOTT SO40 ..... 52 D7
Peninsula Rd WINW SO22 ..... 2 B6
Penistone Cl ITCH SO19 ..... 11 J7
Penjar Av WVILLE PO7 ..... 101 H2
Penk Rdg CHAM PO6 ..... 102 A5
Pennant Hills HAV PO9 ..... 102 C4
Pennard Wy CHFD SO53 ..... 37 H6
Pennerly Ct HAV PO9 ..... 82 E6
Penner Rd HAV PO9 ..... 14 C8
Pennine Gdns FAWY SO45 ..... 90 E4
Pennine Rd ROWN SO16 ..... 54 A5
Pennine Wy CHFD SO53 ..... 38 A6
  LSOL/BMARY PO13 ..... 131 K4
Pennington Cl ELGH SO50 ..... 39 J2
Pennington Wy FHAM PO15 ..... 12 B1
Penn Wy GPORT PO12 ..... 132 B5
Pennycress HLER SO31 ..... 94 D4
Penny La EMRTH PO10 ..... 104 C4
Penny Pl WVILLE PO7 ..... 101 K3
Penny St PSEA PO1 ..... 17 L8
Penrhyn Cl ELGH SO50 ..... 38 C5
Penrose Cl NEND PO2 ..... 118 C5
Penshurst Wy ELGH SO50 ..... 38 D4
The Pentagon FAWY SO45 ..... 110 B5
Pentere Rd HORN PO8 ..... 64 B6
Pentire Av WSHM SO15 ..... 54 E2
Pentire Wy WSHM SO15 ..... 54 E2
Pentland Cl FAWY SO45 ..... 90 E4
Pentland Ri FHAM/PORC PO16 ..... 99 G5
Penton Ct HAV PO9 ..... 83 J7
Penton Rd RWIN SO21 ..... 33 K2
Pentridge Wy TOTT SO40 ..... 52 C7
Peper Harow HORN PO8 ..... 64 C6
Peppard Cl WEND SO18 ..... 7 H5
Peppercorn Wy HEND SO30 ..... 58 A1
Pepys Av ITCH SO19 ..... 57 G7
Pepys Cl ENEY PO4 ..... 19 J8
  GPORT PO12 ..... 132 C2
Percival Rd NEND PO2 ..... 118 E2
Percy Chandler St PSEA PO1 ..... 18 E2
Percy Cl FAWY SO45 ..... 91 C1
Percy Rd ENEY PO4 ..... 19 C6
  GPORT PO12 ..... 16 C5
  ROWN SO16 ..... 54 B4
Peregrine Cl TOTT SO40 ..... 52 B6
The Peregrines
  FHAM/PORC PO16 ..... 98 C5
Pern Dr WEND SO30 ..... 59 F5
Peronne Cl HSEA PO3 ..... 118 E2
Peronne Rd HSEA PO3 ..... 118 E2
Perran Rd ROWN SO16 ..... 53 J3
Perryvale Rd NBAD SO52 ..... 37 G5
Perrywood Cl FAWY SO45 ..... 109 K4
Perrywood Gdns TOTT SO40 ..... 52 A4
Perseus Pl WVILLE PO7 ..... 102 A3
Pershore Cl HLER SO31 ..... 95 F3
Persian Dr HLER SO31 ..... 75 G5
Perth Rd ENEY PO4 ..... 135 G4
  LSOL/BMARY PO13 ..... 116 A3
Pervin Rd CHAM PO6 ..... 100 E7
Peter Ashley Rd CHAM PO6 ..... 101 J3
Peterborough Rd CHAM PO6 ..... 100 D5
  SHAM SO14 ..... 5 K5
Peters Cl HLER SO31 ..... 94 D3
Peterscroft Av TOTT SO40 ..... 67 K4
Petersfield Rd HAV PO9 ..... 14 F1
  RWIN SO21 ..... 27 K1
  WINC SO23 ..... 3 J6
Petersham Cl WVILLE PO7 ..... 81 J4
Peters Rd HLER SO31 ..... 94 D3
Petrel Wk LSOL/BMARY PO13 ..... 115 J5
Petrie Rd LSOL/BMARY PO13 ..... 131 G2
Pettinger Gdns PTSW SO17 ..... 5 K2
Petty Cl ROMY SO51 ..... 35 F4
Pettycot Crs
  LSOL/BMARY PO13 ..... 115 J4
Petworth Gdns ELGH SO50 ..... 38 D3
  ROWN SO16 ..... 42 D6
Petworth Rd HSEA PO3 ..... 135 G2
Pevensey Cl ROWN SO16 ..... 53 J3
Peverells Rd CHFD SO53 ..... 38 B4
Peverells Wood Av CHFD SO53 ..... 38 B4
Peverells Wood Cl CHFD SO53 ..... 38 B3
Peveril Rd ITCH SO19 ..... 10 C3
Pewsey Pl WSHM SO15 ..... 54 E2
Pheonix Wy
  LSOL/BMARY PO13 ..... 115 K5
Philip Rd WVILLE PO7 ..... 102 A3
Phillimore Rd ROWN SO16 ..... 44 A7
Phillips Cl ROWN SO16 ..... 41 K5
Philpott Dr TOTT SO40 ..... 70 A4
Phoenix Cl HLER SO31 ..... 73 K4
Phoenix Sq NEND PO2 ..... 118 D3
Pickwick Cl TOTT SO40 ..... 52 A5
Pier Head Rd NEND PO2 ..... 118 A1
Pier Rd PSEA PO1 ..... 18 A9
  SSEA PO5 ..... 18 A9
Pier St LSOL/BMARY PO13 ..... 131 F2
Pigeon House La WVILLE PO7 ..... 100 C3
Pikes Hl LYND SO43 ..... 86 B3
Pilands Wood Rd HLER SO31 ..... 73 J5
Pilgrim Pl WEND SO18 ..... 44 B7
Pilgrims Ga WINW SO22 ..... 2 A2
Pilgrims Wy FHAM/STUB PO14 ..... 114 C6
Pilning Cl FHAM/STUB PO14 ..... 96 D6
Pimpernel Cl HLER SO31 ..... 94 D4
Pine Cl FAWY SO45 ..... 91 G4
  WINW SO22 ..... 24 E5
  NBAD SO52 ..... 36 A5
  TOTT SO40 ..... 68 B2
Pine Crs CHFD SO53 ..... 37 K2
Pine Dr WEND SO18 ..... 57 G5
Pine Dr East WEND SO18 ..... 57 H5
Pinefield Rd WEND SO18 ..... 56 C2
Pine Gv HAV PO9 ..... 15 H5
Pinegrove Rd ITCH SO19 ..... 10 F3
Pinehurst Dr HORN PO8 ..... 82 D3
Pinehurst Rd ROWN SO16 ..... 43 G4
Pinelands Rd ROWN SO16 ..... 43 G3
Pine Rd BPWT SO32 ..... 48 E3
  CHFD SO53 ..... 37 K1
  ROWN SO16 ..... 35 H4
The Pines FHAM/PORC PO16 ..... 98 C5
Pine Tree Gdns HORN PO8 ..... 82 B3
Pine Trees FHAM/STUB PO14 ..... 12 B7

Pineview Cl HLER SO31 73 K4
Pine Wk HLER SO31 95 F1
ROWN SO16 43 G4
Pine Wy ROWN SO16 43 G4
Pinewood LSOL/BMARY PO13 116 B6
Pinewood Av HAV PO9 102 C3
Pinewood Cl
FHAM/STUB PO14 114 E3 2
ROMY SO51 35 H1
Pinewood Crs FAWY SO45 91 J4 1
Pinewood Dr FAWY SO45 91 J4
Pinewood Pk ITCH SO19 57 J7
Pinkney La LYND SO43 86 B4
Pink Rd NEND PO2 118 D7 1
Pinks Hl FHAM/PORC PO16 98 A4
Pinsley Dr WHAM PO17 79 K7
Pinto Cl FHAM PO15 75 G6
Pipers Cl TOTT SO40 52 C6
Piping Cl RWIN SO21 39 J2
Piping Rd RWIN SO21 39 J2
Pipit Cl GPORT PO12 132 E1
Pirelli St SHAM SO14 8 E1
WSHM SO15 8 E1
Pirrie Cl WSHM SO15 4 A1
Pitcairn Ms ENEY PO4 135 G6 4
Pitchponds Rd HLER SO31 94 B6
Pitcroft Rd NEND PO2 118 C6
Pitmore Cl ELGH SO50 38 E2
Pitmore Rd ELGH SO50 38 E2
Pitreavie Rd CHAM PO6 119 F1
Pitter Cl WINW SO22 20 E2
Pitt Hill La WVILLE PO7 62 D3
Pitt Rd WSHM SO15 54 D6
Pitymoor La WHAM PO17 100 A2
Place Crs WVILLE PO7 102 A1
Place House Cl FHAM PO15 96 D5
Place La RWIN SO21 33 G1
Plaitford Gv HAV PO9 102 D2
Plantation Dr TOTT SO40 69 K4
The Plantation BPWT SO32 59 K2
Platform Rd SHAM SO14 9 G5
Players Crs TOTT SO40 52 D7
Playfair Rd SSEA PO5 18 E6
Pleasant La EMRTH PO10 123 G6
Pleasant Rd ENEY PO4 135 G4
Plough Wy WINW SO22 25 G4
Plover Cl FHAM/STUB PO14 114 C5
ROWN SO16 42 C6
Plover Reach ENEY PO4 135 G3 1
Plover Rd TOTT SO40 52 B5
Plovers Down WINW SO22 24 E5
Plovers Rd HORN PO8 64 B6
P.l.p.h. Rd FAWY SO45 110 E2
Plumpton Gdns HSEA PO3 119 G4 1
Plumpton Gv WVILLE PO7 82 C4
Plymouth Dr
FHAM/STUB PO14 114 C5
Plymouth St SSEA PO5 18 D5 1
Poets Wy WINW SO22 21 G7
Pointout Cl ROWN SO16 55 F1
Pointout Rd ROWN SO16 55 F1
Polesden Cl CHFD SO53 37 J2 4
Poles La RWIN SO21 31 J3
Pollards Moor Rd TOTT SO40 50 D3
The Polygon WSHM SO15 4 E8
Pond Cl TOTT SO40 70 A3
Pondhead Cl FAWY SO45 109 K4 1
Pond Piece WVILLE PO7 80 E2
Pond Rd HLER SO31 74 E7
Pondside La BPWT SO32 48 D2
Pook La HAV PO9 15 J7
WHAM PO17 97 J2
Pooksgreen TOTT SO40 69 J3
Poole Rd ITCH SO19 10 C2
Popes La TOTT SO40 52 E5
Popham Ct HAV PO9 82 D7
Poplar Dr FHAM/STUB PO14 12 C8
TOTT SO40 69 J4
Poplar Gv HISD PO11 137 H4
Poplar Rd ITCH SO19 6 F7
The Poplars BPWT SO32 60 E1
Poplar Wy HEND SO30 58 C5 2
NBAD SO52 36 A5
Poppy Cl HLER SO31 94 E4
Poppyfields NBAD SO52 37 H4 1
Poppy Rd ROWN SO16 43 K6
Porchester Rd ITCH SO19 10 C4
Porlock Rd ROWN SO16 53 H3
Portal Rd ELGH SO50 39 G7
ITCH SO19 11 J2
LSOL/BMARY PO13 115 K4
TOTT SO40 52 C5
WINC SO23 3 H7
Portchester La WHAM PO17 99 G4
Portchester Ri ELGH SO50 38 D3
Portchester Rd
FHAM/PORC PO16 98 D6
NEND PO2 118 D7
Portelet Pl HEND SO30 58 B7
Porteous Crs CHFD SO53 38 C4
Portersbridge St ROMY SO51 34 D3
Porter's La SHAM SO14 8 F4
Portland Dr GPORT PO12 132 A5
Portland Rd SSEA PO5 18 D9
WVILLE PO7 81 K6
Portland St FHAM/PORC PO16 13 K6
PSEA PO1 18 A3
SHAM SO14 8 F1
Portland Ter SHAM SO14 8 F1
Port La RWIN SO21 31 J2
Portobello Gv
FHAM/PORC PO16 99 G5
Port Royal St SSEA PO5 18 F4 1
Portsdown Av CHAM PO6 101 H6
Portsdown Hill Rd CHAM PO6 100 E5
WHAM PO17 98 D4
Portsdown Rd CHAM PO6 99 H6
Portsmouth Rd CHAM PO6 118 E1
HLER SO31 73 J4
HORN PO8 64 C7
ITCH SO19 10 D4
LSOL/BMARY PO13 131 G4
Portsview Av
FHAM/PORC PO16 99 G6
Portsview Gdns
FHAM/PORC PO16 99 G5
Portswood Av PTSW SO17 5 J2
Portswood Pk PTSW SO17 5 J3
Portswood Rd HAV PO9 82 E7
NEND PO2 118 D2 2
PTSW SO17 5 J3
Portview Rd WEND SO18 56 C2
Port Wy CHAM PO6 99 K6
Portway Cl WEND SO18 7 K4
Posbrooke Rd ENEY PO4 19 M5
Posbrook La
FHAM/STUB PO14 113 K2
Postern Cl FHAM/PORC PO16 99 G6
Post Office Rd WVILLE PO7 101 H1 1
The Potteries
FHAM/PORC PO16 13 K2
Potters Av FHAM/PORC PO16 97 H2
Potters Heron Cl ROMY SO51 31 F6
Potters Heron La ROMY SO51 31 F6
Poulner Cl ITCH SO19 11 G8
Poulner Ct HAV PO9 82 D7
Pound Cl LSOL/BMARY PO13 116 A7
Pound Gate Dr
FHAM/STUB PO14 95 H5
Pound La ROMY SO51 30 C7
TOTT SO40 51 F2
TOTT SO40 68 D2
Pound Lea HISD PO11 137 H3
Pound Rd CHAM PO6 100 A4
HLER SO31 73 J5
SELS PO20 139 J7
Pound St WEND SO18 7 H4
Pound Tree Rd SHAM SO14 9 G1
Powell Crs TOTT SO40 52 E7
Power Rd PSEA PO1 19 H1 3
Powerscourt Rd NEND PO2 118 D7
Poyner Cl FHAM/PORC PO16 13 J3
Poynings Pl PSEA PO1 18 A7 1
Precosa Rd HEND SO30 58 D7
Prelate Wy FHAM/STUB PO14 95 H4
Preshaw Cl ROWN SO16 42 D7
Preston Rd NEND PO2 118 E6
Prestwood Rd HEND SO30 58 B6
Pretoria Rd ENEY PO4 19 K7
HEND SO30 58 A7
Pricketts Hl BPWT SO32 61 G5
Prideaux-Brune Av
LSOL/BMARY PO13 115 K3
Priest Croft Dr FAWY SO45 110 B5
Priestfields FHAM/STUB PO14 95 H4
Priestlands ROMY SO51 34 D2
Priestlands Cl TOTT SO40 51 K6
Priestley Cl TOTT SO40 52 C5 4
Priestwood Cl WEND SO18 57 G5
Primate Rd FHAM/STUB PO14 95 J4
Primrose Cl HEND SO30 58 B7 2
LSOL/BMARY PO13 115 K2
NBAD SO52 37 G6 1
Primrose Rd ROWN SO16 43 H7
Primrose Wy HLER SO31 94 E4
ROMY SO51 35 H1 3
Prince Albert Rd ENEY PO4 19 M8
Prince Alfred St GPORT PO12 16 A7
Prince George's St HAV PO9 14 F4
Prince George St PSEA PO1 17 L3
Prince of Wales Av WSHM SO15 54 B5
Prince of Wales Cl
WVILLE PO7 82 B6 3
Prince of Wales Rd
GPORT PO12 16 D5 3
Prince Rd FHAM/STUB PO14 115 G1
ROWN SO16 41 K4
Princes Cl BPWT SO32 48 C3 3
Princes Ct SHAM SO14 5 L7
Princes Crs LYND SO43 86 D1
Princes Dr WVILLE PO7 82 B4
Princes Pl WINW SO22 2 B9
Princes Rd ROMY SO51 34 D2
WSHM SO15 4 A7
Princess Cl HEND SO30 57 H2
Princess Gdns HORN PO8 64 C5
Princess Rd TOTT SO40 68 A3
Prince's St PSEA PO1 134 C1
SHAM SO14 5 M7
Prinstead Cl WINC SO23 3 G8
Prinsted Crs CHAM PO6 101 J7
Prinsted La EMRTH PO10 105 G7
Priors Barton WINC SO23 2 D9
Priors Cl EMRTH PO10 105 H5
Priorsdean Av HSEA PO3 19 L2
Priorsdean Crs HAV PO9 102 E2
Priors Dean Rd WINW SO22 21 G3
Priors Leaze La RCCH PO18 105 J5
Priors Wy WINW SO22 24 E5
Priory Av PTSW SO17 6 A1
Priory Cl BPWT SO32 48 C3
PTSW SO17 6 A1
Priory Crs ENEY PO4 19 L5
Priory Gdns FHAM/PORC PO16 99 F6
WVILLE PO7 81 K4
Priory Rd ELGH SO50 44 C2
ENEY PO4 19 M9
FHAM PO15 12 A4
HLER SO31 72 E7
PTSW SO17 5 L3
WHAM PO17 79 K7
The Priory BPWT SO32 48 C4
Privett Pl GPORT PO12 132 B3
Privett Rd FHAM PO15 96 D4
GPORT PO12 132 B4
LSOL/BMARY PO13 131 K5
WVILLE PO7 101 J3
Prochurch Rd HORN PO8 82 C1
Proctor Cl ITCH SO19 57 G7
Proctor Dr NBAD SO52 36 A7
Proctor La ENEY PO4 19 J3
The Promenade EMRTH PO10 104 C7
FAWY SO45 91 H1
Prospect La HAV PO9 103 J1
Prospect Pl CHFD SO53 37 K4 1
FAWY SO45 91 H1
Prospect Rd NEND PO2 134 B1
Provene Cl BPWT SO32 49 F7
Provene Gdns BPWT SO32 48 E7
Providence Hl HLER SO31 73 K3
Prunus Cl ROWN SO16 42 D6
Pudbrooke Gdns HEND SO30 58 A4 1
Pudding La WINC SO23 22 A3
Puffin Cl ROWN SO16 42 C6
Puffin Crs FHAM/STUB PO14 114 C4
Puffin Gdns
LSOL/BMARY PO13 115 J4 3
Puffin Wk HORN PO8 81 J1
Pump La HORN PO8 64 B7
LSOL/BMARY PO13 115 K6
Purbeck Dr FHAM/STUB PO14 12 A8
Purbeck St PSEA PO1 18 A4 1
Purbrook Cl ROWN SO16 42 D7 3
Purbrook Gdns WVILLE PO7 101 H1
Purbrook Heath Rd
WVILLE PO7 100 E1
Purbrook Rd PSEA PO1 19 H4
Purbrook Wy HAV PO9 102 E2
WVILLE PO7 102 A2
Purcell Cl WVILLE PO7 101 K1
Purcell Rd ITCH SO19 73 G2
Purkess Cl CHFD SO53 38 A3
Purkiss Cl TOTT SO40 51 F7
Purvis Gdns ITCH SO19 11 L5
Pycroft Cl HISD PO11 121 K4
ITCH SO19 7 G9
Pye St PSEA PO1 18 D1 2
Pyland's La HLER SO31 74 A2
Pyle Cl HORN PO8 82 B1
Pylewell Rd FAWY SO45 91 H2 3
Pyrford Cl GPORT PO12 132 B5
WVILLE PO7 81 J3
Pytchley Cl FHAM/STUB PO14 114 B5

Q

The Quadrangle ELGH SO50 38 D6 2
Quail Wy HORN PO8 64 B6
Quantock Rd ROWN SO16 53 K4
The Quantocks FAWY SO45 90 E4 5
Quarely Rd HAV PO9 82 D7
Quarry Rd WINC SO23 3 H6
Quarterdeck Av NEND PO2 118 A6
Quartremaine Rd HSEA PO3 119 G4
Quay Hvn HLER SO31 74 C5
Quay La GPORT PO12 116 E6
Quayside Rd WEND SO18 6 B5
Quayside Wk TOTT SO40 70 A2
Quay St FHAM/PORC PO16 13 L7
Quebec Gdns HLER SO31 73 J4 4
Queen Anne's Dr HAV PO9 102 D4
Queen Mary Rd
FHAM/PORC PO16 99 G7
Queen Rd FHAM/STUB PO14 115 G1
Queens Cl FAWY SO45 91 H3
LSOL/BMARY PO13 131 F2 3
Queens Crs FHAM/STUB PO14 114 E4
HORN PO8 64 C5
SSEA PO5 18 D8
Queen's Gv SSEA PO5 18 D9
WVILLE PO7 101 J1
Queens Md WINW SO22 25 F2 2
Queen's Pde LYND SO43 86 C1
Queen's Pl SSEA PO5 18 D8 7
Queens Ride NBAD SO52 35 K6
Queen's Rd CHFD SO53 38 A1
FHAM/PORC PO16 13 J6
GPORT PO12 16 C4
HLER SO31 94 B6
LSOL/BMARY PO13 131 G4
NEND PO2 118 D7
PSEA PO1 17 K1
WSHM SO15 54 D2
WVILLE PO7 81 K4
Queen's Ter SHAM SO14 9 H4
Queenstown Rd WSHM SO15 4 A7
Queen St EMRTH PO10 104 D6
PSEA PO1 17 L3
RWIN SO21 33 J4
Queens Vw HLER SO31 72 E7
Queensway HISD PO11 121 H4
Queen's Wy SHAM SO14 9 G4
SSEA PO5 18 D8 3
The Queensway
FHAM/PORC PO16 98 E6
Querida Cl HLER SO31 74 C5 3
Quilter Cl ITCH SO19 73 G1 4
Quinton Cl SSEA PO5 18 E5 6
Quintrell Av FHAM/PORC PO16 98 D6
Quob Farm Cl HEND SO30 57 H1
Quob La HEND SO30 57 H1

R

Racecourse Vw LYND SO43 66 C7 2
Rachel Cl ELGH SO50 46 A1
Racton Av CHAM PO6 101 G7
Racton Rd EMRTH PO10 104 C3
Radcliffe Rd SHAM SO14 5 K7
Radclyffe Rd FHAM/PORC PO16 13 M3
Radleigh Gdns TOTT SO40 52 A4
Radley Cl HEND SO30 58 B3 3
Radnor St SSEA PO5 18 D5
Radstock Rd ITCH SO19 10 C3
Radway Crs WSHM SO15 4 B2
Radway Rd WSHM SO15 4 B2
Raeburn Dr HEND SO30 58 B5
Raglan Cl CHFD SO53 37 G6
Raglan St SSEA PO5 18 E4
Rails La HISD PO11 137 J6
Railway Vw PSEA PO1 18 E3
Railway View Rd PTSW SO17 5 M2
Raley Rd HLER SO31 95 F4
Ramalley La CHFD SO53 37 J3
Rambler Dr LSOL/BMARY PO13 131 K2
Ramblers Wy HORN PO8 82 C4
Rampart Gdns HSEA PO3 118 E2
Rampart Rd WEND SO18 6 A4
Ramsay Pl
LSOL/BMARY PO13 115 K5 6
Ramsdale Av HAV PO9 102 D1
Ramsey Rd HISD PO11 137 H5
Randall Cl TOTT SO40 52 B2
Randall Rd CHFD SO53 32 A7
Randolph Rd NEND PO2 118 D4
Randolph St WSHM SO15 54 D5
Ranelagh Gdns WSHM SO15 4 D5
Ranelagh Rd HAV PO9 14 B4
NEND PO2 118 B6
WINC SO23 2 C8
Ranfurly Gdns FAWY SO45 91 F4
Range Gdns ITCH SO19 11 J4
Range Gn NEND PO2 118 B4
Rannoch Cl FHAM PO15 12 C2
Ransome Cl FHAM/STUB PO14 96 A7
Ranvilles La FHAM/STUB PO14 96 C7
Rapson Cl CHAM PO6 100 B5
Rareridge La BPWT SO32 49 F3
Ratcliffe Rd FAWY SO45 91 G5 4
HEND SO30 58 B5
Ratlake La ROMY SO51 31 G5
Rattigan Gdns HLER SO31 75 H5
Raven Cl LSOL/BMARY PO13 131 K2
Raven Rd SHAM SO14 5 J7
Ravens Cl FHAM/STUB PO14 114 E4
Ravenscroft Cl HLER SO31 73 J4
Ravenscroft Wy BPWT SO32 59 F3
Raven Sq ELGH SO50 44 A1 1
Ravenswood
FHAM/STUB PO14 95 H3 4
Raymond Cl FAWY SO45 110 A4
HEND SO30 57 J1
Raymond Rd CHAM PO6 99 H5
WSHM SO15 4 B4
Rayners Gdns ROWN SO16 44 A7 2
Raynes Rd LSOL/BMARY PO13 131 G4
Reading Room La BPWT SO32 59 J4
The Recess ELGH SO50 38 E5
Record Rd EMRTH PO10 104 B5
Rectory Av CHAM PO6 102 A5
Rectory Cl FHAM/STUB PO14 114 D4
GPORT PO12 132 D6
Rectory Ct HEND SO30 58 E5
Rectory Rd HAV PO9 14 E6
The Redan GPORT PO12 133 F7
Red Barn Av FHAM/PORC PO16 99 F5
Red Barn La FHAM PO15 97 F2
Redbridge Cswy WSHM SO15 53 G4
Redbridge Gv HAV PO9 102 E3
Redbridge Hl ROWN SO16 54 A3
Redbridge La ROWN SO16 53 G2
Redbridge Rd WSHM SO15 53 J4
Redcar Av HSEA PO3 119 F6
Redcote Cl WEND SO18 7 J4
Redcroft La HLER SO31 73 K4
The Redfords TOTT SO40 52 D3
Redhill ROWN SO16 43 F7
Redhill Cl ROWN SO16 43 F7
Red Hill Crs ROWN SO16 43 F7
Redhill Rd HAV PO9 83 J4
Red Hill Wy ROWN SO16 55 F1
Redhouse Park Gdns
LSOL/BMARY PO13 132 B1
Redlands Dr ITCH SO19 6 F6
Redlands Gv ENEY PO4 135 H4
Redlands La EMRTH PO10 104 C2
FHAM/STUB PO14 12 F6
Red Leaves BPWT SO32 61 F2
Red Ldg CHFD SO53 37 J7
Redlynch Cl HAV PO9 103 J2 1
Redmoor Cl ITCH SO19 6 E7
Red Oaks Dr FHAM PO15 95 G1
Redrise Cl FAWY SO45 109 J4
Redshank Rd HORN PO8 64 B5
Redward Rd ROWN SO16 42 A6
Redwing Ct ENEY PO4 135 H3 3
Redwing Gdns TOTT SO40 52 B4 7
Redwood Cl FAWY SO45 90 E3
HEND SO30 57 F2
Redwood Dr FHAM/PORC PO16 98 E6
Redwood Gdns TOTT SO40 52 B5
Redwood Gv HAV PO9 103 H2
Redwood Wy ROWN SO16 43 H5
Reed Dr TOTT SO40 70 A3
Reedmace Cl WVILLE PO7 82 B7 3
Reed's Pl GPORT PO12 16 A2 2
Reeds Rd GPORT PO12 132 E1
Reeves Wy HLER SO31 73 J4 5
Regal Cl CHAM PO6 100 E6
Regency Gdns WVILLE PO7 81 J7 1
Regency Pl FHAM PO15 12 C5
Regent Cl RWIN SO21 33 F5
Regent Pl SSEA PO5 18 B8 2
Regent Rd CHFD SO53 38 A4
Regents Ct HAV PO9 14 E7
Regents Ga HLER SO31 94 D1
Regent's Gv WSHM SO15 54 C4 4
Regent's Park Gdns
WSHM SO15 54 C5 1
Regent's Park Rd WSHM SO15 54 B5
Regent St PSEA PO1 134 B1
SHAM SO14 8 F1
Reginald Rd ENEY PO4 19 M8
Relay Rd WVILLE PO7 81 J5
Reliant Cl CHFD SO53 37 J6 1
Renda Rd FAWY SO45 109 K3
Renny Rd PSEA PO1 19 H4
Renown Cl CHFD SO53 37 J5
Renown Gdns HORN PO8 64 A7
Repton Cl GPORT PO12 132 B4
Reservoir La HEND SO30 57 K6
Rest-a-wyle Av HISD PO11 137 H3
The Retreat ELGH SO50 38 E6
SSEA PO5 18 D8
TOTT SO40 52 E7
Revenge Cl ENEY PO4 135 H2 2
Rewlands Dr WINW SO22 21 F3
Reynolds Dl TOTT SO40 52 C7
Reynolds Rd ELGH SO50 46 C2
WSHM SO15 54 D4
Rhinefield Cl ELGH SO50 45 J1 2
HAV PO9 102 D2 3
Rhyme Hall Ms FAWY SO45 110 E4 3
Ribble Cl CHFD SO53 38 A5
Ribble Ct ROWN SO16 53 K3
Richard Gv GPORT PO12 116 D6
Richards Cl HLER SO31 95 G3
Richlans Rd HEND SO30 58 B6
Richmond Cl CHFD SO53 37 J1
HISD PO11 137 F4
TOTT SO40 52 A3
Richmond Dr HISD PO11 136 E4
Richmond Gdns PTSW SO17 55 J3
Richmond La ROMY SO51 35 F1
Richmond Pk RWIN SO21 33 G5
Richmond Pl PSEA PO1 18 A4
SSEA PO5 18 D9 1
Richmond Ri FHAM/PORC PO16 99 F5
Richmond Rd GPORT PO12 132 D4
LSOL/BMARY PO13 130 E2
SSEA PO5 18 E9 4
WSHM SO15 54 D6
Richmond St SHAM SO14 9 H3
Richville Rd ROWN SO16 54 B4
Ridding Cl WSHM SO15 54 C4
Riders La HAV PO9 103 F2
Ridge La HEND SO30 75 J2
ROMY SO51 40 A2
Ridgemount Av ROWN SO16 43 G6
Ridgeway WINW SO22 25 F3
Ridgeway Cl CHAM PO6 99 J5 1
CHFD SO53 38 B5
The Ridgeway
FHAM/PORC PO16 98 B5
Ridgewood Cl FAWY SO45 90 D3 1
Ridgway HAV PO9 14 A5
The Ridings BPWT SO32 49 F7
ELGH SO50 45 K1
NEND PO2 118 E4
Ridley Cl FAWY SO45 109 K3 3
Rigby Rd PTSW SO17 5 J3
Rimington Rd HORN PO8 82 A2
Ringlet Wy WINC SO23 3 K4
The Ring ROWN SO16 43 F4
Ringwood Dr NBAD SO52 35 K5
Ringwood Rd ENEY PO4 135 G5
TOTT SO40 51 K5
Ripley Gv HSEA PO3 119 F7
Ripon Gdns WVILLE PO7 82 C4
Ripplewood TOTT SO40 70 B4 4
Ripstone Gdns PTSW SO17 55 J1
The Rise WVILLE PO7 101 J4
Ritchie Ct ITCH SO19 11 J1
Riverdale Av WVILLE PO7 82 B6
Riverdene Pl WEND SO18 6 B2
River Gn HLER SO31 93 K4
Riverhead Cl ENEY PO4 135 G3
River La FHAM PO15 76 D7
Rivermead Cl ROMY SO51 34 C3
Riversdale Cl ITCH SO19 10 D9
Riverside ELGH SO50 39 G7
Riverside Av FHAM/PORC PO16 98 A3
Riverside Cl TOTT SO40 51 F6
Riverside Gdns ROMY SO51 34 D4
River's St SSEA PO5 18 E5
River St EMRTH PO10 104 E2
Riverview TOTT SO40 52 E7
River View Rd WEND SO18 56 A2
River Wk WEND SO18 56 B1
River Wy HAV PO9 15 G1
Roads Hl HORN PO8 64 A3
Road Vw NEND PO2 118 B7
Robert Cecil Av WEND SO18 44 B7
Roberts Cl WHAM PO17 77 H1
Roberts Rd FAWY SO45 91 G2
GPORT PO12 132 C2 4
TOTT SO40 52 E7
WSHM SO15 4 B8
Robert Whitworth Dr
ROMY SO51 34 E1
Robina Cl WVILLE PO7 82 B6
Robin Gdns HORN PO8 81 J1
TOTT SO40 52 B4
Robinia Gn ROWN SO16 42 D6
Robins Cl FHAM/STUB PO14 114 D4
Robins Meadow
FHAM/STUB PO14 95 H5
Robinson Rd
FHAM/STUB PO14 114 C6
Robinson Wy HSEA PO3 119 H4
Robin Sq ELGH SO50 43 K2
Rochester Rd ENEY PO4 19 K7
Rochester St SHAM SO14 5 L9
Rochford Rd CHAM PO6 100 C6
Rockall Cl ROWN SO16 41 K6
Rockbourne Cl HAV PO9 102 D2 6
Rockbourne Rd WINW SO22 21 G3
Rockery Cl FAWY SO45 90 D2
Rockingham Wy
FHAM/PORC PO16 98 E6
Rockleigh Dr TOTT SO40 68 C1
Rockleigh Rd ROWN SO16 54 E1
Rockram Cl TOTT SO40 50 E5
Rockram Gdns FAWY SO45 90 D3 2
Rockrose Wy CHAM PO6 99 K4
Rockstone La SHAM SO14 5 H6
Rockstone Pl WSHM SO15 4 F6
Rockville Dr WVILLE PO7 81 K6
Rodney Cl LSOL/BMARY PO13 131 K2
Rodney Rd ENEY PO4 19 K3
Rodney Wy HORN PO8 64 C6
Roebuck Av FHAM PO15 96 E1
Roebuck Cl CHAM PO6 100 E7 3
Roewood Cl FAWY SO45 109 K4 2
Roewood Rd FAWY SO45 109 K4
Rogate Gdns FHAM/PORC PO16 99 F5
Rogers Cl ELGH SO50 39 H6
GPORT PO12 16 A1
Rogers Md HISD PO11 121 G4
Rogers Rd ELGH SO50 39 H6
Roker Wy ELGH SO50 46 A2
Roland Cl HORN PO8 64 C6
Rollestone Rd FAWY SO45 109 J4
Roman Cl CHFD SO53 38 B3
Roman Dr ROWN SO16 43 F4
Roman Gdns FAWY SO45 90 E5 1
Roman Gv FHAM/PORC PO16 117 G1
Roman Landing SELS PO20 139 J6
Roman Rd FAWY SO45 90 D4
FAWY SO45 109 J1
ROWN SO16 43 F2
RWIN SO21 33 K4
Romans' Rd WINC SO23 2 D7
Roman Wy FAWY SO45 90 E5
HAV PO9 102 D4
Romford Rd HLER SO31 94 C6
Romill Cl WEND SO18 56 E1
Romsey Av FHAM/PORC PO16 98 D6
HSEA PO3 135 G2
Romsey Cl ELGH SO50 38 D7
Romsey Rd ELGH SO50 38 D7
WINW SO22 2 A5
HORN PO8 64 D2
LYND SO43 66 C7
ROWN SO16 41 J6
TOTT SO40 50 C4
Romyns Ct FHAM/STUB PO14 12 E6
Rookery Av FHAM PO15 75 H6
HLER SO31 75 G6
The Rookery EMRTH PO10 104 D5
Rookes Cl HORN PO8 64 C6
Rookley HLER SO31 73 F6
Rooksbridge FAWY SO45 90 D3 3
Rooksbury Cft HAV PO9 103 H1 3
Rooks Down Rd WINW SO22 25 G3

Rooksway Gv
  FHAM/PORC PO16 .... 98 B6
Rookwood Cl ELGH SO50 .... 38 E3
Rookwood La SELS SO20 .... 139 K4
Rookwood Rd SELS SO20 .... 139 K4
Rookwood Vw WVILLE PO7 .... 62 E7
Ropley Cl ITCH SO19 .... 11 C9
Ropley Rd HAV PO9 .... 103 J1
Rosebank Cl ROWN SO16 .... 41 K6
Rosebay Cl ELGH SO50 .... 46 B5
Rosebay Ct WVILLE PO7 .... 102 A1
Rosebery Av CHAM PO6 .... 101 F7
Rosebery Crs ELGH SO50 .... 38 E4
Rosebury Av FAWY SO45 .... 91 H5
Rose Cl FAWY SO45 .... 91 H4
  HEND SO30 .... 58 B4
Rosedale Av ROWN SO51 .... 35 F3
Rosedale Cl FHAM/STUB PO14 .... 96 A6
Rose Hl HORN PO8 .... 64 B6
Roselands HEND SO30 .... 57 G4
  HORN PO8 .... 64 B7
Roselands Gdns PTSW SO17 .... 55 H2
Roseleigh Dr TOTT SO40 .... 52 D6
Rosemary Gdns FHAM PO15 .... 75 J5
  HEND SO30 .... 58 B7
Rosemary La PSEA PO1 .... 17 L4
Rosemary Wy HORN PO8 .... 82 C1
Rosemoor Gv CHFD SO53 .... 37 J1
Rosendale Rd CHFD SO53 .... 38 A6
Rose Rd SHAM SO14 .... 5 J3
  TOTT SO40 .... 52 C5
The Rosery GPORT PO12 .... 132 E7
Rosetta Rd ENEY PO4 .... 135 G4
Rosewall Rd ROWN SO16 .... 54 A1
Rosewarne Ct WINC SO23 .... 2 D2
Rosewood LSOL/BMARY PO13 .... 116 B4
Rosewood Gdns TOTT SO40 .... 70 B4
Rosina Cl WVILLE PO7 .... 82 C5
Rosoman Rd ITCH SO19 .... 10 F2
Rossan Av HLER SO31 .... 94 C7
Ross Gdns ROWN SO16 .... 54 B2
Rossington Av WEND SO18 .... 6 F4
Rossington Wy WEND SO18 .... 6 F4
Rosslyn Cl NBAD SO52 .... 36 B6
Ross Wy LSOL/BMARY PO13 .... 131 G5
Rostron Cl WEND SO18 .... 56 D1
Rosyth Rd WEND SO18 .... 6 F4
Rotary Ct HLER SO31 .... 72 E7
Rothbury Cl ITCH SO19 .... 11 H2
  TOTT SO40 .... 52 C3
Rother Cl WEND SO18 .... 56 E3
Rother Dl HITH PO9 .... 73 H2
Rotherwick Cl HAV PO9 .... 103 J1
Rothesay Rd GPORT PO12 .... 132 D1
Rothsbury Dr CHFD SO53 .... 37 J4
Rothschild Cl ITCH SO19 .... 10 C8
Rothville Pl CHFD SO53 .... 31 J7
Rothwell Cl CHAM PO6 .... 99 K5
Roughdown La FAWY SO45 .... 109 K6
Roundcopse FAWY SO45 .... 90 D3
Roundhill Cl WEND SO18 .... 56 D3
Roundhouse Dr TOTT SO40 .... 52 A6
Roundhouse Meadow
  EMRTH PO10 .... 104 D7
Roundhuts Ri WINC SO23 .... 3 K4
Roundway WVILLE PO7 .... 82 A5
Routs Wy ROWN SO16 .... 41 K4
Rowallan Av
  LSOL/BMARY PO13 .... 115 J6
Rowan Av HORN PO8 .... 82 C3
Rowan Cl BPWT SO32 .... 49 J7
  HLER SO31 .... 73 J5
  LSOL/BMARY PO13 .... 131 G3
  ROMY SO51 .... 35 H4
  ROWN SO16 .... 54 A1
  TOTT SO40 .... 52 C6
Rowan Gdns HEND SO30 .... 58 C6
Rowan Rd HAV PO9 .... 103 J5
The Rowans TOTT SO40 .... 70 A4
Rowan Wy FHAM/STUB PO14 .... 96 D6
Rowborough Rd WEND SO18 .... 6 F3
Rowbury Rd HAV PO9 .... 82 E7
Rowe Ashe Wy HLER SO31 .... 94 E3
Rowhill Dr FAWY SO45 .... 90 D3
Rowin Cl HISD PO11 .... 138 C4
Rowland Rd CHAM PO6 .... 99 H5
  FHAM PO15 .... 12 E4
Rowlands Av HAV PO9 .... 81 K4
Rowlands Castle Rd HORN PO8 .... 65 G6
Rowlands Cl CHFD SO53 .... 37 J6
Rowley Cl HEND SO30 .... 58 E4
Rowley Dr HEND SO30 .... 58 E4
Rowlings Rd WINW SO22 .... 21 G4
Rowner Cl LSOL/BMARY PO13 .... 115 K6
Rowner La LSOL/BMARY PO13 .... 115 K7
Rowner Rd LSOL/BMARY PO13 .... 115 J6
Rownhams Cl ROWN SO16 .... 41 K5
Rownhams La NBAD SO52 .... 36 A5
  ROMY SO51 .... 42 A2
  ROWN SO16 .... 42 A4
Rownhams Rd HAV PO9 .... 102 E1
  NBAD SO52 .... 36 B7
  ROWN SO16 .... 54 A2
Rownhams Rd North
  ROWN SO16 .... 42 A6
Rownhams Wy ROWN SO16 .... 41 K5
Rowse Cl ROMY SO51 .... 34 E1
Row Wood La
  LSOL/BMARY PO13 .... 115 J6
Royal Crescent Rd SHAM SO14 .... 9 J4
Royal Gdns HAV PO9 .... 83 H4
Royal Ga ENEY PO4 .... 135 G6
Royal Sovereign Av
  FHAM/STUB PO14 .... 115 G2
Royal Wy WVILLE PO7 .... 82 B6
Royce Cl SELS SO20 .... 139 K7
Royce Wy SELS SO20 .... 139 K7
Roydon Cl WINW SO22 .... 25 G3
Royston Av ELGH SO50 .... 38 D5
Royston Cl PTSW SO17 .... 55 J2
Rozelle Cl WINW SO22 .... 20 D2
Ruby Rd ITCH SO19 .... 7 H7
Rudd La ROMY SO51 .... 28 C1
Rudgwick Cl
  FHAM/PORC PO16 .... 98 E6
Rudmore Sq NEND PO2 .... 118 B7
Ruffield Cl WINW SO22 .... 21 F5
Rufford Cl ELGH SO50 .... 38 D4
Rufus Cl CHFD SO53 .... 38 B7
  ROWN SO16 .... 41 J5

Rufus Gdns TOTT SO40 .... 52 B5
Rugby Rd ENEY PO4 .... 19 H5
Rumbridge Gdns TOTT SO40 .... 53 F5
Rumbridge St TOTT SO40 .... 52 C6
Runnymede FHAM PO15 .... 96 E2
  HEND SO30 .... 57 G3
The Rushes TOTT SO40 .... 70 A3
Rushington Av TOTT SO40 .... 52 B7
Rushington La TOTT SO40 .... 52 D7
Rushmere La WVILLE PO7 .... 62 C5
Ruskin Rd ELGH SO50 .... 38 D5
  ENEY PO4 .... 19 L5
Ruskin Wy HORN PO8 .... 82 A1
Rusland Cl CHFD SO53 .... 37 J3
Russell Cl LSOL/BMARY PO13 .... 131 G2
Russell Pl FHAM/PORC PO16 .... 13 J3
  PTSW SO17 .... 5 J1
Russell Rd HAV PO9 .... 14 F1
  LSOL/BMARY PO13 .... 131 G3
  WINC SO23 .... 21 K5
Russell St GPORT PO12 .... 132 D2
  SHAM SO14 .... 9 H3
Russet Gdns EMRTH PO10 .... 104 E6
Russett Cl BPWT SO32 .... 49 J7
Rustan Cl ELGH SO50 .... 46 C1
  HEND SO30 .... 58 A6
Rutland Gdns HLER SO31 .... 73 K4
Rutland Wy WEND SO18 .... 7 H1
Ruxley Cl FAWY SO45 .... 109 K3
Rydal Cl CHAM PO6 .... 100 A5
Rydal Rd GPORT PO12 .... 116 D7
Ryde Pl LSOL/BMARY PO13 .... 131 H4
Ryde Ter SHAM SO14 .... 9 K3
Rye Cl NBAD SO52 .... 37 G4
Ryecroft FHAM/STUB PO14 .... 95 H4
  HAV PO9 .... 15 K4
Rye Dl TOTT SO40 .... 68 B2
Rye Paddock La FAWY SO45 .... 110 E3
Rylandes Ct ROWN SO16 .... 54 A1

S

Sabre Rd SSEA PO5 .... 122 D4
Sackville St SSEA PO5 .... 18 C6
Saddlers Cl ELGH SO50 .... 38 D4
Sadlers La FAWY SO45 .... 91 H5
Sadlers Wk EMRTH PO10 .... 104 D6
Saffron Wy FHAM PO15 .... 75 J5
Sage Cl WVILLE PO7 .... 82 B7
St Agatha's Rd HLER SO31 .... 93 K2
St Alban's Rd HAV PO9 .... 103 H2
  SHAM SO14 .... 5 J8
St Andrew Cl HORN PO8 .... 64 D2
St Andrews Cl NBAD SO52 .... 35 K5
  ROMY SO51 .... 28 C3
St Andrews Pk ELGH SO50 .... 46 B5
St Andrews Rd SHAM SO14 .... 5 H8
  CHAM PO6 .... 102 A6
  GPORT PO12 .... 16 B6
  HISD PO11 .... 137 J6
  SSEA PO5 .... 18 E7
St Annes Cl WINW SO22 .... 25 F3
St Anne's Gdns ITCH SO19 .... 11 D5
St Anne's Gv FHAM/STUB PO14 .... 97 G7
St Annes La BPWT SO32 .... 60 E5
St Anne's Rd ITCH SO19 .... 10 D6
St Ann's Crs GPORT PO12 .... 132 D2
St Ann's Rd ENEY PO4 .... 19 K8
  HORN PO8 .... 64 D5
St Aubin's Av ITCH SO19 .... 7 H8
St Aubin's Pk HISD PO11 .... 136 E5
St Augustine Gdns PTSW SO17 .... 6 A1
St Augustine Rd ENEY PO4 .... 19 J8
St Austell Cl ITCH SO19 .... 39 H7
St Barbara Wy NEND PO2 .... 118 E3
St Barbe Cl ROMY SO51 .... 35 F4
St Bartholomew's Gdns
  SSEA PO5 .... 18 F7
St Blaize Rd ROMY SO51 .... 35 G2
St Bonnet Dr BPWT SO32 .... 48 D3
St Catherine's Rd ELGH SO50 .... 38 D5
  HISD PO11 .... 136 D5
  WINC SO23 .... 3 H7
St Catherine St SSEA PO5 .... 134 C7
St Catherines Vw HEND SO30 .... 57 K6
St Catherines Wy
  FHAM/PORC PO16 .... 98 B5
St Chad's Av NEND PO2 .... 118 D5
St Christopher Av
  FHAM/PORC PO16 .... 13 K2
St Christophers Cl NBAD SO52 .... 36 A6
St Christopher's Rd HAV PO9 .... 102 D3
St Clares Av HAV PO9 .... 82 E6
St Clements Cl ROMY SO51 .... 34 D2
St Clement St WINC SO23 .... 2 D5
St Colman's Av CHAM PO6 .... 101 F6
St Cross Rd WINC SO23 .... 25 H5
St Cuthberts Cl HLER SO31 .... 95 G2
St Cuthberts La HLER SO31 .... 95 G2
St David's Cl TOTT SO40 .... 52 B3
St Davids Rd HLER SO31 .... 94 E3
  SSEA PO5 .... 18 F6
St Denys' Rd PTSW SO17 .... 5 M1
  PTSW SO17 .... 55 J3
St Edmund Cl FHAM/STUB PO14 .... 95 G5
St Edmund's Rd ROWN SO16 .... 54 C4
St Edward's Rd GPORT PO12 .... 16 B6
  HLER SO31 .... 72 E6
  SSEA PO5 .... 18 C8
St Elizabeth's Av WEND SO18 .... 7 J5
St Evox Cl ROWN SO16 .... 42 A6
St Faith's Cl GPORT PO12 .... 132 D3
St Faith's Rd PSEA PO1 .... 18 D2
  WINC SO23 .... 25 J3
St Francis Av WEND SO18 .... 7 K2
St Francis Cl FAWY SO45 .... 128 B1
St Francis Rd NEND PO2 .... 118 D3
St Francis Pl HAV PO9 .... 103 F3
St Francis Rd FAWY SO45 .... 128 B1
  GPORT PO12 .... 133 F1
St Gabriel's Rd WEND SO18 .... 7 J5
St George Cl HLER SO31 .... 73 J4
St George's Av HAV PO9 .... 15 K4
St Georges Rd HLER SO31 .... 94 E3
  CHAM PO6 .... 100 E6
  ENEY PO4 .... 135 F6
  HISD PO11 .... 136 E5

PSEA PO1 .... 17 L5
St Georges Sq PSEA PO1 .... 17 M4
St Georges St SHAM SO14 .... 9 G2
  WINC SO23 .... 2 E4
St George's Wy PSEA PO1 .... 17 M4
St Giles Cl WINC SO23 .... 3 H6
St Giles Wy HORN PO8 .... 64 D2
St Helena Gdns WEND SO18 .... 56 C1
St Helena Wy
  FHAM/PORC PO16 .... 99 F6
St Helen's Cl ENEY PO4 .... 134 E6
St Helens Rd GPORT PO12 .... 132 B5
  HISD PO11 .... 136 E5
St Hellen's Rd CHAM PO6 .... 101 J6
St Hermans Rd HISD PO11 .... 137 K6
St Hilda Av HORN PO8 .... 64 D2
St Hubert Rd HORN PO8 .... 64 D2
St James' La WINW SO22 .... 2 B1
St James' Rd EMRTH PO10 .... 104 C6
  HEND SO30 .... 57 G2
St James's Cl WSHM SO15 .... 54 D3
St James's Park Rd ROWN SO16 .... 54 D3
St James's Rd SSEA PO5 .... 18 C6
  WSHM SO15 .... 54 D3
St James's St PSEA PO1 .... 18 A3
St James' Ter WINW SO22 .... 2 C5
St James' Vls WINW SO22 .... 2 C6
St James Wy FHAM/PORC PO16 .... 99 G6
St John's Av WVILLE PO7 .... 101 K2
St John's Cl GPORT PO12 .... 16 A3
  HISD PO11 .... 137 F5
  ROWN SO16 .... 41 K4
St Johns Ct TOTT SO40 .... 70 A4
St Johns Dr TOTT SO40 .... 69 K4
St Johns Gdns ROMY SO51 .... 34 E2
St Johns Glebe ROWN SO16 .... 42 A4
St John's Rd CHAM PO6 .... 101 F6
  ELGH SO50 .... 38 E6
  EMRTH PO10 .... 105 F5
  HAV PO9 .... 102 D2
  HEND SO30 .... 73 H1
  HLER SO31 .... 95 G4
  WINC SO23 .... 3 H4
St John's St FAWY SO45 .... 91 H2
St Lawrence Cl ELGH SO50 .... 38 D6
  SHAM SO14 .... 9 G4
St Leonard's Av HISD PO11 .... 137 H5
St Leonards Cl FHAM PO15 .... 95 K3
St Leonard's Rd WINC SO23 .... 3 J7
St Lukes Cl HEND SO30 .... 58 B3
St Luke's Rd GPORT PO12 .... 132 D2
St Margaret's Cl WEND SO18 .... 7 K5
St Margarets La
  FHAM/STUB PO14 .... 95 K5
St Margarets Rd HISD PO11 .... 137 H5
St Mark's Cl GPORT PO12 .... 132 D7
St Mark's Rd GPORT PO12 .... 132 D7
  NEND PO2 .... 118 C6
St Martin's Cl ROWN SO16 .... 53 K1
  WINC SO23 .... 3 H4
St Mary's Av GPORT PO12 .... 132 D6
St Marys Cl WINC SO23 .... 22 B2
St Mary's Pl SHAM SO14 .... 9 H1
St Mary's Rd ELGH SO50 .... 39 G6
  FHAM/STUB PO14 .... 114 D3
  HISD PO11 .... 137 H4
  HLER SO31 .... 73 F7
  PSEA PO1 .... 19 H1
  SHAM SO14 .... 5 H7
St Mary's Ter RWIN SO21 .... 33 K3
St Mary St WINW SO22 .... 25 G3
  SHAM SO14 .... 9 J2
St Matthews Cl SHAM SO14 .... 5 H7
St Matthew's Rd CHAM PO6 .... 100 E6
  WINW SO22 .... 21 G5
St Michaels Cl FAWY SO45 .... 110 B6
St Michaels Ct CHAM PO6 .... 100 A5
St Michael's Gdns WINC SO23 .... 2 B6
St Michael's Gv
  FHAM/STUB PO14 .... 12 F8
St Michaels Rd HLER SO31 .... 94 E4
  HAV PO9 .... 102 D3
  PSEA PO1 .... 18 B5
  TOTT SO40 .... 52 E3
  WINC SO23 .... 2 D7
St Michael's St SHAM SO14 .... 8 F1
St Michaels Wy HORN PO8 .... 64 D2
St Monica Rd ITCH SO19 .... 11 H4
St Nicholas WINC SO23 .... 22 A1
St Nicholas Av
  LSOL/BMARY PO13 .... 131 K1
St Nicholas' Rd HAV PO9 .... 102 D3
St Nicholas St PSEA PO1 .... 17 M7
St Paul's Hl WINW SO22 .... 2 D3
St Paul's Rd HLER SO31 .... 74 D7
  SSEA PO5 .... 18 B5
St Paul's Sq SSEA PO5 .... 18 B6
St Peter's Av HISD PO11 .... 121 K5
St Peter's Gv HISD PO11 .... 18 E7
St Peter's Rd HISD PO11 .... 121 K5
St Peter's Sq EMRTH PO10 .... 104 C6
St Peter's St BPWT SO32 .... 48 D3
St Peter St WINC SO23 .... 2 E4
St Philip's Wy WEND SO18 .... 7 J5
St Piran's Av HSEA PO3 .... 135 F1
St Ronan's Av ENEY PO4 .... 19 H9
St Ronan's Rd ENEY PO4 .... 19 H9
St Sebastian Crs
  FHAM/PORC PO16 .... 13 K1
St Simon Cl HLER SO31 .... 95 G3
St Simon's Rd SSEA PO5 .... 134 C6
St Stephen's Rd WINW SO22 .... 21 G5
  NEND PO2 .... 118 D7
St Swithun Cl BPWT SO32 .... 48 C3
St Swithun's Cl ROMY SO51 .... 35 J1
St Swithun's Rd PSEA PO1 .... 118 E5
St Swithun St WINC SO23 .... 2 D6
St Theresas Cl HAV PO9 .... 102 D3
St Thomas Av HISD PO11 .... 137 H6
St Thomas Cl FHAM/PORC PO16 .... 13 L3
St Thomas's Rd GPORT PO12 .... 116 E7
St Thomas's St PSEA PO1 .... 17 L7
St Tristan Cl HLER SO31 .... 95 G3
St Ursula Gv SSEA PO5 .... 18 E7
St Valerie Rd GPORT PO12 .... 16 B8
St Vigor Wy RWIN SO21 .... 33 J3
St Vincent Crs HORN PO8 .... 64 C6
St Vincent Rd GPORT PO12 .... 16 B1

  SSEA PO5 .... 18 E9
  HSEA PO3 .... 135 H2
Schooner Wy HLER SO31 .... 94 D5
  HSEA PO3 .... 135 H2
The Scimitars
  FHAM/STUB PO14 .... 114 C4
Scivier's La BPWT SO32 .... 47 H1
Scotland Cl ELGH SO50 .... 46 D1
Scotney Ct HAV PO9 .... 83 J7
Scott Cl FHAM/STUB PO14 .... 114 D3
  RWIN SO21 .... 39 K2
Scotter Rd ELGH SO50 .... 39 G7
Scott Rd ELGH SO50 .... 44 C1
  HSEA PO3 .... 118 E2
  ITCH SO19 .... 10 F7
  PSEA PO1 .... 17 K2
Scratchface La HAV PO9 .... 102 C4
  WVILLE PO7 .... 102 A4
Scullards La SHAM SO14 .... 8 E3
Seabird Wy FHAM/PORC PO16 .... 13 K9
Seacombe Rd ROWN SO16 .... 53 J3
Sea Crest Rd
  LSOL/BMARY PO13 .... 131 G3
Seafield Park Rd
  FHAM/STUB PO14 .... 114 C6
Seafield Rd FHAM/PORC PO16 .... 98 E7
  HSEA PO3 .... 119 F6
  ROWN SO16 .... 53 J2
Seafields EMRTH PO10 .... 104 B6
Seaford Cl HLER SO31 .... 73 J4
Sea Front HISD PO11 .... 137 G6
Seagarth La ROWN SO16 .... 54 E1
Seager's Ct PSEA PO1 .... 17 K7
Sea Grove Av HISD PO11 .... 137 H6
Seagrove Rd NEND PO2 .... 118 C6
Seagull Cl ENEY PO4 .... 135 H2
Seagull La EMRTH PO10 .... 104 C5
The Seagulls
  LSOL/BMARY PO13 .... 131 H4
Sea Kings FHAM/STUB PO14 .... 114 C5
Sea La LSOL/BMARY PO13 .... 114 C5
Seamead FHAM/STUB PO14 .... 114 D7
Searles HI RWIN SO21 .... 33 K3
Sea Rd ITCH SO19 .... 10 B2
Seaton Av HSEA PO3 .... 119 F7
Seaton Cl FHAM/STUB PO14 .... 114 D5
  WEND SO18 .... 7 L1
Seaview Av FHAM/PORC PO16 .... 99 F6
Sea View Rd CHAM PO6 .... 101 K6
Seaview Rd HISD PO11 .... 137 K5
Seaward Dr SELS SO20 .... 139 K7
Seaward Rd FAWY SO45 .... 91 J3
  ITCH SO19 .... 10 C1
Seaway Crs ENEY PO4 .... 135 H4
Seaway Gv FHAM/PORC PO16 .... 117 F1
Sebastian Gv WVILLE PO7 .... 82 B5
Second Av CHAM PO6 .... 100 D6
  CHAM PO6 .... 101 K7
  EMRTH PO10 .... 105 G6
  HAV PO9 .... 15 J3
  WSHM SO15 .... 53 J5
Second St FAWY SO45 .... 92 A6
Sedbergh Rd ROWN SO16 .... 53 J3
Sedgefield Cl CHAM PO6 .... 99 J4
  TOTT SO40 .... 52 B4
Sedgeley Gv GPORT PO12 .... 116 D7
Sedgemead HLER SO31 .... 92 E1
Sedgewick Cl
  LSOL/BMARY PO13 .... 115 K7
Sedgewick Rd ELGH SO50 .... 39 G7
  ITCH SO19 .... 7 L9
Sedgley Cl SSEA PO5 .... 18 E6
Segars La RWIN SO21 .... 33 J4
Segensworth Rd FHAM PO15 .... 95 K3
Selangor Av EMRTH PO10 .... 104 A5
Selborne Av HAV PO9 .... 102 E1
  WEND SO18 .... 7 L2
Selborne Gdns GPORT PO12 .... 132 C4
Selborne Pl WINW SO22 .... 25 G3
Selbourne Dr ELGH SO50 .... 38 D6
Selbourne Rd HAV PO9 .... 14 D5
  TOTT SO40 .... 52 C4
Selbourne Ter PSEA PO1 .... 19 H4
Seldon Cl WINW SO22 .... 24 E4
Selhurst Wy ELGH SO50 .... 46 B2
Sellwood Rd HLER SO31 .... 73 F7
Selsdon Av ROMY SO51 .... 35 G2
Selsey Av ENEY PO4 .... 135 F6
  GPORT PO12 .... 116 C7
Selsey Cl HISD PO11 .... 138 C6
  ROWN SO16 .... 53 K2
Selsmore Av HISD PO11 .... 137 K6
Selsmore Rd HISD PO11 .... 137 H5
Selwyn Gdns ELGH SO50 .... 38 C6
Sengana Cl HEND SO30 .... 58 C6
Senlac Rd ROMY SO51 .... 35 G3
Sennen Pl WHAM PO17 .... 99 K7
Sentinel Cl WVILLE PO7 .... 82 C4
Seps 4 Rd FAWY SO45 .... 110 E3
September Cl HEND SO30 .... 57 G3
Serle Cl TOTT SO40 .... 52 A5
Serle Gdns TOTT SO40 .... 52 C6
Sermon Rd WINW SO22 .... 20 E6
Serpentine Rd
  FHAM/PORC PO16 .... 13 J2
  SSEA PO5 .... 18 C9
  WVILLE PO7 .... 101 H3
Setters Cl RWIN SO21 .... 39 J2
Settle Cl ROWN SO16 .... 54 C4
Settlers Cl PSEA PO1 .... 18 E2
Sevenoaks Rd CHAM PO6 .... 100 D6
Severn Cl CHAM PO6 .... 100 A5
Severn Rd FHAM/PORC PO16 .... 98 D6
Severn Rd ROWN SO16 .... 53 K4
Severn Wy HEND SO30 .... 57 G3
Seward Ri ROMY SO51 .... 35 H2
Seymour Cl CHFD SO53 .... 38 B5
  NEND PO2 .... 134 C1
  TOTT SO40 .... 52 B3
Seymour La NBAD SO52 .... 36 A6
Seymour Rd
  LSOL/BMARY PO13 .... 131 G4
  ROWN SO16 .... 54 D1
Shackleton Rd
  LSOL/BMARY PO13 .... 116 A7
Shadwell Rd NEND PO2 .... 118 D5
Shaftesbury Av CHFD SO53 .... 37 K6
  PTSW SO17 .... 55 J2
  WVILLE PO7 .... 101 J2
Shaftesbury Rd GPORT PO12 .... 16 C6
Shaftsbury Rd SSEA PO5 .... 18 C8
Shaggs Meadow LYND SO43 .... 86 C1

Shakespeare Av PTSW SO17	5 J2	The Sidings HLER SO31	93 G1
Shakespeare Dr TOTT SO40	52 C2	Sidlesham Cl HISD PO11	138 C6 ▣
Shakespeare Gdns HORN PO8	81 K2	Sidmouth Av ROWN SO16	119 F7
Shakespeare Rd ELGH SO50	38 C5	Silchester Rd HSEA PO3	135 G1
PSEA PO1	19 H1	Silkin Gdns TOTT SO40	52 C6
Shalbourne Rd GPORT PO12	132 D1	Silksead Av WHAM PO17	83 G7
Shalcombe HLER SO31	73 F6	Silkstead La RWIN SO21	32 C4
Shaldon Cl ROWN SO16	42 C7	Silver Birch Av	
Shaldon Rd HAV PO9	83 J7 ▣	FHAM/STUB SO14	12 C7
Shales Rd WEND SO18	7 J4	Silver Birch Cl ITCH SO19	11 K2
Shamblehurst La HEND SO30	58 B3	Silver Birches HLER SO31	73 J5
Shamblehurst La North		Silverdale Dr WVILLE PO7	81 H3
BPWT SO32	58 C1	Silverdale Rd WSHM SO15	4 D5
Shamblehurst La South		Silver Hl WINC SO23	2 F5
HEND SO30	58 B4	Silverlock Cl NEND PO2	118 C7 ▣
Shamrock Cl GPORT PO12	16 E6	Silversands Gdns HISD PO11	137 J6
Shamrock Rd ITCH SO19	10 D3	Silvers End FAWY SO45	91 H5 ▣
Shamrock Wy FAWY SO45	91 H1	Silver St LYND SO43	86 A1
Shanklin Crs WSHM SO15	54 E3	SSEA PO5	18 B7
Shanklin Rd ENEY PO4	19 H6 ▣	Silvers Wd TOTT SO40	52 B3
WSHM SO15	54 E2	Silverthorne Wy WVILLE PO7	81 J5
Shannon Cl FHAM PO15	12 A3	Silvertrees EMRTH PO10	104 C4
Shannon Rd		Silverwood Cl WINW SO22	25 G3
FHAM/STUB SO14	114 C3 ▣	Silwood Cl WINW SO22	21 G6
FHAM/STUB SO14	115 C2	Simmons Cl HEND SO30	58 B4
Shannon Wy CHFD SO53	37 J4	Simmons Gn HISD PO11	137 K5
Shapton Cl FAWY SO45	109 J3 ▣	Simnel St SHAM SO14	8 F3 ▣
Sharon Rd HEND SO30	57 F2	Simon Wy WEND SO18	57 H5
Sharpness Cl		Simpson Cl FHAM/PORC PO16	99 F5
FHAM/STUB SO14	96 D6 ▣	Simpson Rd NEND PO2	118 B6
Sharps Cl HSEA PO3	119 G4	Sinah La HISD PO11	136 D5
Sharps Rd HAV PO9	103 J1	Sinclair Rd ROWN SO16	42 B6
Shaw Cl TOTT SO40	52 C5 ▣	Singleton Wy TOTT SO40	52 C6
WEND SO18	56 D2	Sir Christopher Cl FAWY SO45	91 J2 ▣
Shawfield Rd HAV PO9	15 H6	Sirdar Rd PTSW SO17	55 K1
Shawford Rd ROWN SO16	43 F7 ▣	Sir Galahad Rd NBAD SO52	37 G4 ▣
TOTT SO40	52 A5 ▣	Sir George's Rd WSHM SO15	4 A7
Shawford Gv HAV PO9	102 D1	Sir Lancelot Cl NBAD SO52	37 G4
Shawford Rd RWIN SO21	33 J3	Siskin Cl BPWT SO32	48 B3
Shearer Rd PSEA PO1	19 H1	ROWN SO16	42 B6
Shears Rd ELGH SO50	39 H7	Siskin Gv WVILLE PO7	82 B7
Shearwater Av		Sissinghurst Cl ITCH SO19	11 H8
FHAM/PORC PO16	98 B6	Sissinghurst Rd	
Shearwater Cl		FHAM/PORC PO16	98 E7 ▣
LSOL/BMARY PO13	115 J5	Six Oaks Rd NBAD SO52	36 B5
Shearwater Dr CHAM PO6	102 A7	Sixpenny Cl FHAM SO31	95 H3
Sheepwash La WVILLE PO7	80 E5	Sixth Av CHAM PO6	100 D6
Sheffield Cl ELGH SO50	39 G5	Sizer Wy FAWY SO45	90 D2
Sheffield Rd PSEA PO1	19 G3	Skew Rd WHAM PO17	99 F4
Sheldrake Gdns ROWN SO16	42 C6	Skipper Wy LSOL/BMARY PO13	131 G3
Shelford Rd ENEY PO4	135 C3	Skipton Rd CHFD SO53	38 A6
Shellcroft HLER SO31	94 C6 ▣	Skylark Mdw FHAM PO15	96 A1
Shelley Av CHAM PO6	99 H5	Skys Wood NBAD SO52	37 G3
Shelley Cl WINW SO22	21 G4	Slades Hl FAWY SO45	110 C5
RWIN SO21	23 K1	Slater Cl TOTT SO40	52 A4
Shelley Gdns HORN PO8	81 K2	Sleepers Delle Gdns WINW SO22	2 A7
Shelley Rd ELGH SO50	44 C2	Sleepers Hl WINW SO22	25 G2
ITCH SO19	57 G6	WINW SO22	25 G2
TOTT SO40	50 E5	Sleepers Hill Gdns WINW SO22	25 G2 ▣
Shenley Cl FHAM PO15	96 D4	Slindon St PSEA PO1	18 D3 ▣
Shepards Cl FHAM/STUB SO14	96 D6	Slingsby Cl PSEA PO1	18 B7 ▣
TOTT SO40	50 E6	Slipper Rd EMRTH PO10	104 E5
Shepherds Hey Rd TOTT SO40	52 A3	Sloane Av FAWY SO45	110 A3 ▣
Shepherds La RWIN SO21	32 C3	Sloane Ct FAWY SO45	110 A3 ▣
Shepherds Purse Cl		Sloane Pk BPWT SO32	60 D1
HLER SO31	94 E4 ▣	Sloe Tree Cl HLER SO31	95 H4 ▣
Shepherds Rd TOTT SO40	50 E6	Smallcutts Av EMRTH PO10	105 C5
WINC SO23	3 K4	Smeeton Rd	
Shepherds Wy ROWN SO16	41 H6	LSOL/BMARY PO13	131 G2
Sheppard Cl HORN PO8	64 B6	Smith Cl FAWY SO45	110 C5
Shepton Br BROC SO42	107 G2	Smithe Cl ELGH SO50	38 D7 ▣
Sherborne Ct ELGH SO50	38 C4	Smith Gv HEND SO30	58 B7
Sherborne Rd PTSW SO17	55 J2	Smith La EMRTH PO10	123 F6
Sherborne Wy HEND SO30	58 B6	Smith's Fld ROMY SO51	35 F1 ▣
Sherfield Av HAV PO9	103 H1	Smiths La BPWT SO32	61 G4
Sheridan Cl WINW SO22	25 F3	Smith St GPORT PO12	132 C6
ITCH SO19	7 M8	The Smithy WVILLE PO7	80 D1
Sheridan Gdns HLER SO31	75 H5	Smythe Rd ITCH SO19	73 G2
TOTT SO40	50 E5	Snakemoor La BPWT SO32	54 D6
Sheringham Rd CHAM PO6	100 C5 ▣	Snapdragon Cl HLER SO31	94 E4 ▣
Sherrington La FAWY SO45	110 E4	Snape Cl LSOL/BMARY PO13	115 K7 ▣
Sherwood Av HEND SO30	74 B1	Snellgrove Cl TOTT SO40	52 B2
Sherwood Cl ROWN SO16	55 F1 ▣	Snellgrove Pl TOTT SO40	52 B2 ▣
Sherwood Gdns HLER SO31	94 D2	Snowberry Crs HAV PO9	103 J3
Sherwood Rd CHFD SO53	38 B1	Snowdon Dr FHAM/STUB PO14	12 C8
GPORT PO12	132 C6	Soake Rd WVILLE PO7	81 G2
Sherwood Wy FAWY SO45	128 B1	Soberton Rd HAV PO9	103 F3
Shetland Cl CHAM PO6	100 C6	Soldridge Cl HAV PO9	83 J7 ▣
TOTT SO40	52 A4	Solent Av ITCH SO19	57 H6
Shetland Ri HLER SO31	75 G7	Solent Cl CHFD SO53	38 B4
Shillinglee WVILLE PO7	101 K3	Solent Dr FAWY SO45	91 G2
Shipbuilding Rd PSEA PO1	133 J1	HISD PO11	137 G6
Shipcote La BPWT SO32	48 D1	HLER SO31	112 C1
Ship Leopard St PSEA PO1	17 L4 ▣	Solent Mdw HLER SO31	93 K5
Shipley Rd RWIN SO21	33 K2	Solent Rd CHAM PO6	101 H6
Shire Cl HLER SO31	75 G6	FAWY SO45	91 F6
HORN PO8	82 C4	FHAM/STUB SO14	114 B4
The Shires HEND SO30	57 K6	HAV PO9	14 C5
Shirley Av ENEY PO4	135 H4	Solent Vw FHAM/PORC PO16	98 E5
WSHM SO15	54 D4	Solent Wy BROC SO42	108 D2
Shirley High St ROWN SO16	54 C3	BROC SO42	126 C1
Shirley Park Rd ROWN SO16	54 C4	FHAM/STUB SO14	114 B6
Shirley Rd SSEA PO5	134 D6	GPORT PO12	16 E9
WSHM SO15	54 D4	GPORT PO12	132 B5
Sholing Ct HAV PO9	82 E4	HAV PO9	14 A7
Sholing Rd ITCH SO19	10 C1	HSEA PO3	135 J2
Shooters Hill Cl ITCH SO19	11 H4	LSOL/BMARY PO13	131 H5
Shoot Hl WHAM PO17	79 G2	PSEA PO1	17 M4 ▣
Shoot La LSOL/BMARY PO13	115 H7	SHAM SO14	9 J6
Shop La HSEA PO3	135 H4	Solomons La BPWT SO32	61 G2
Shore Av HSEA PO3	135 H4	Solona Cl CHFD SO53	38 C3 ▣
Shore Crs BPWT SO32	48 E4 ▣	Somborne Dr HAV PO9	103 G1
Shorefield Rd TOTT SO40	70 A3	Somerford Cl ITCH SO19	7 G8
Shorehaven CHAM PO6	99 J6	Somers Cl WINW SO22	25 G3
Shore La BPWT SO32	48 E4	Somerset Av WEND SO18	7 L5
Shore Rd FAWY SO45	91 J2	Somerset Crs CHFD SO53	37 K7
Shorewell HLER SO31	73 F6 ▣	Somerset Rd PTSW SO17	55 K2
Shorewood Cl HLER SO31	95 F5	SSEA PO5	134 C3
Short Hl WINC SO23	35 H1	Somerset Ter SSEA PO5	54 C6
Short Rd FHAM/STUB SO14	114 B5	Somers Rd North PSEA PO1	18 F4
Short Rw PSEA PO1	17 M2	SSEA PO5	18 E5
Shorts Rd ELGH SO50	46 A1	Somerton Av WEND SO18	7 L4
Shraveshill Cl TOTT SO40	52 B2	Somervell Cl GPORT PO12	16 D1
The Shrubbery GPORT PO12	132 C6	Somervell Dr FHAM/PORC PO16	13 G2
Shrubbs Hill Gdns LYND SO43	86 C2 ▣	Sonnet Wy WVILLE PO7	81 J5
Shrubbs Hill Rd LYND SO43	86 C2	Sopley Cl HAV PO9	83 J7 ▣
Shrubland Cl WEND SO18	7 J2	Sopwith Wy HLER SO31	74 D5
Sibland Cl FHAM/STUB SO14	12 A8	Sorrel Cl ROMY SO51	35 H1
		WVILLE PO7	82 B7

Sorrel Dr FHAM PO15	75 J6	Spenlow Cl NEND PO2	118 C7 ▣
Sorrell Cl HLER SO31	94 E4	Spenser Cl HLER SO31	94 C6 ▣
Southampton Hl		Spicer's Hl TOTT SO40	52 E7
FHAM/STUB SO14	96 A5	Spicer St PSEA PO1	18 D2 ▣
Southampton Rd CHAM PO6	99 J5	Spicewood FHAM PO15	12 C4
ELGH SO50	44 E1	Spindle Cl HAV PO9	15 L1
FAWY SO45	91 H3	Spindle Warren HAV PO9	15 L1
FHAM PO15	95 H1	Spindlewood Cl ROWN SO16	43 H5
FHAM/PORC PO16	13 J4	Spindlewood Wy TOTT SO40	70 A5
FHAM/STUB SO14	95 J4	Spinnaker Cl HISD PO11	137 F4 ▣
LYND SO43	67 F7	LSOL/BMARY PO13	132 A1 ▣
ROMY SO51	35 F4	Spinnaker Dr NEND PO2	118 C3
TOTT SO40	50 E5	Spinnaker Gra HISD PO11	121 K3
Southampton St WSHM SO15	4 F6 ▣	Spinnaker Vw CHAM PO6	102 B5
South Av FAWY SO45	110 B4	Spinney Cl HORN PO8	81 K2
NEND PO2	118 D3	Spinney Gdns FAWY SO45	91 J4
South Bay EMRTH PO10	122 D4	The Spinney ELGH SO50	45 K1
Southbourne Av CHAM PO6	101 G7	FHAM/PORC PO16	98 C5
EMRTH PO10	104 C6	HORN PO8	82 B5
FAWY SO45	109 K3	LSOL/BMARY PO13	116 A6 ▣
Southbrook Rd HAV PO9	14 E7	ROWN SO16	43 G5
ROMY SO51	35 H1	RWIN SO21	33 F2
South Cl GPORT PO12	132 C6	TOTT SO40	52 B3
HAV PO9	14 E8	WVILLE PO7	80 E2
ROMY SO51	35 H1 ▣	Spinney Wk WEND SO18	56 C1
South Ct HSEA PO3	93 H4	Spitfire End WINC SO23	3 L4
Southcroft Rd GPORT PO12	132 C6	Spitfire Loop ELGH SO50	44 C4
South Cross St GPORT PO12	16 F5	Spitfire Wy HLER SO31	93 J4
Southdene Rd CHFD SO53	37 K5	Spithead Av GPORT PO12	133 F7 ▣
Southdown Rd CHAM PO6	101 H6	Spring Cl ELGH SO50	46 B1
HORN PO8	64 D1	ITCH SO19	10 F1
RWIN SO21	33 G3	Spring Crs PTSW SO17	5 J3
South Downs Wy WINC SO23	3 H7	Springcroft	
Southdown Vw WVILLE PO7	81 H3	LSOL/BMARY PO13	115 J2
South Dr WINW SO22	20 D3	Springfield Av FAWY SO45	110 A3
ROMY SO51	28 A6	Springfield Cl HAV PO9	102 C4
South East Crs ITCH SO19	11 G2	Springfield Dr TOTT SO40	52 D6 ▣
South East Rd ITCH SO19	11 G1	Springfield Gv FAWY SO45	110 A3
South End Cl RWIN SO21	31 J3	Springfields Cl RWIN SO21	39 J1
Southern Gdns TOTT SO40	52 D5	Springfield Wy	
Southern La HEND SO30	57 G4	FHAM/STUB SO14	114 D6
WSHM SO15	8 C1	Springford Cl ROWN SO16	42 C7
Southfields Cl BPWT SO32	48 D3	Springford Crs ROWN SO16	54 C1
South Front SHAM SO14	9 H1	Springford Gdns ROWN SO16	42 C7
Southgate St WINC SO23	2 D5	Springford Rd ROWN SO16	54 C1
South La EMRTH PO10	105 H3	Spring Garden La GPORT PO12	16 D4
HORN PO8	65 J1	NBAD SO52	36 A5
South Ldg FHAM PO15	96 C5	PSEA PO1	18 B4 ▣
Southleigh Gv HISD PO11	137 H6	Spring Gdns EMRTH PO10	104 D5
Southleigh Rd EMRTH PO10	104 C6	Spring Gv HLER SO31	75 K4
HAV PO9	15 J5	Springhill Rd CHFD SO53	37 K4
South Millers Dl CHFD SO53	37 J3	Spring Hills ITCH SO19	11 M1
Southmead Rd FHAM PO15	12 B5	Spring La BPWT SO32	49 J6
South Mill Rd WSHM SO15	54 A5	ELGH SO50	39 G7
Southmoor La HAV PO9	14 B8	RWIN SO21	39 J1
South Pde ENEY PO4	134 C7	Springles La FHAM PO15	96 B1
South Pl LSOL/BMARY PO13	131 H4	Spring Pl ROMY SO51	34 D3 ▣
South Rd CHAM PO6	99 K4	Spring Rd FAWY SO45	91 H2
CHAM PO6	101 J7	HLER SO31	74 E7
HISD PO11	137 G5	ITCH SO19	6 F7
HORN PO8	64 D1	The Spring WVILLE PO7	80 E2
PSEA PO1	134 D1	Spring V BPWT SO32	49 H7
PTSW SO17	5 L2	HORN PO8	82 C1
WHAM PO17	79 K7	Springvale Av WINC SO23	22 A1
Southsea Ter SSEA PO5	18 K8	Springvale Rd WINC SO23	22 A1
South Sp CHAM PO6	100 A4	Springwood Av WVILLE PO7	82 B6
South St ELGH SO50	44 D3	Spruce Av WVILLE PO7	82 B6
EMRTH PO10	104 C6	Spruce Cl HLER SO31	94 C6
FAWY SO45	91 H3	Spruce Dr ITCH SO19	57 H7
FHAM/STUB SO14	96 A6	TOTT SO40	52 A2
GPORT PO12	16 E6	Spurlings Rd WHAM PO17	98 A2
HAV PO9	14 F6	Spur Rd CHAM PO6	100 E6
SSEA PO5	18 B7 ▣	WVILLE PO7	81 K6
South Ter PSEA PO1	17 L3 ▣	The Spur GPORT PO12	132 C6
South Trestle Rd FAWY SO45	111 F2	Squires Wk ITCH SO19	10 D8
South Vw WINC SO23	2 B4	Squirrel Cl ELGH SO50	45 J1 ▣
South View Rd WINW SO22	24 E5	Squirrel Dr ITCH SO19	11 G4
Southway FHAM PO15	95 K3	Squirrels Wk FAWY SO45	91 G4
Southways FHAM/STUB SO14	114 D5	Stable Cl FHAM/STUB SO14	95 J4 ▣
Southwick Av		Stacey Ct HAV PO9	82 E6
FHAM/PORC PO16	99 H5	Stafford Rd SSEA PO5	18 E8
Southwick Cl WINW SO22	21 G3 ▣	WSHM SO15	4 A5
Southwick Ct		Staff Rd ROMY SO51	28 A1
FHAM/STUB SO14	115 H1 ▣	Stagbrake Cl FAWY SO45	109 J4 ▣
Southwick Hill Rd CHAM PO6	100 D5	Stag Cl ELGH SO50	45 J1
Southwick Rd CHAM PO6	100 B4	Stagshorn Rd HORN PO8	64 D5 ▣
WHAM PO17	77 K2	Stag Wy FHAM PO15	96 E1
WVILLE PO7	80 D1	Stainer Cl ITCH SO19	73 G2
South Wood Gdns HLER SO31	94 E3	Staith Cl ITCH SO19	7 L8
Southwood Rd HISD PO11	137 K6	Stakes Hill Rd WVILLE PO7	102 A2
NEND PO2	118 D3	Stakes La BPWT SO32	47 K1
Sovereign Crs		Stakes Rd WVILLE PO7	101 J2
FHAM/STUB SO14	95 F5	Stallard Cl EMRTH PO10	104 B5
Sovereign Dr ENEY PO4	135 J3 ▣	Stalybridge Cl HLER SO31	75 F7
HEND SO30	58 C6	Stamford Av HISD PO11	137 F5
Sovereign La WVILLE PO7	101 K3	Stamford St PSEA PO1	18 E2 ▣
Sovereign Wy ELGH SO50	38 C4	Stamford Wy ELGH SO50	46 B2 ▣
Sowden Cl HEND SO30	58 A5	Stamshaw Rd NEND PO2	118 C6
Spalding Rd ITCH SO19	57 G7	Stanbridge La ROMY SO51	28 A6
Spaniard's La ROMY SO51	34 E7	Stanbridge Rd HAV PO9	103 J2
Sparkford Cl WINW SO22	2 B7	Standard Wy FHAM/PORC PO16	13 M1
Sparkford Wy WINW SO22	2 B7	Standen Rd ROWN SO16	41 H6
Spa Rd SHAM SO14	8 F2	Standford St SHAM SO14	9 K2 ▣
Sparrow Cl HORN PO8	82 A1	Stanford Cl CHAM PO6	100 C6
Sparrow Ct		Stanford Ct HAV PO9	103 J1 ▣
LSOL/BMARY PO13	131 G1 ▣	Stanhope Rd PSEA PO1	18 C3
Sparrowgrove RWIN SO21	33 F5	Stanier Wy HEND SO30	58 B2
Sparrow Sq ELGH SO50	44 A1	Stanley Av HSEA PO3	119 G7
Sparsholt Cl HAV PO9	102 D1	Stanley Cl FHAM PO15	12 C5
Sparsholt Rd ITCH SO19	10 E9	GPORT PO12	116 D6
Spartan Cl EMRTH PO10	122 D3	Stanley La PSEA PO1	17 L2
FHAM/STUB SO14	114 D2	Stanley Rd EMRTH PO10	104 D9
Speakers Corner Rbt SHAM SO14	9 G2	FAWY SO45	110 A3
Spear Rd SHAM SO14	5 H3	NEND PO2	118 A6
Specks La ENEY PO4	19 L5	PTSW SO17	5 M1
Speedwell Cl HLER SO31	94 E4 ▣	TOTT SO40	52 C3
Speggs Wk HEND SO30	58 B6	Stanmore La WINW SO22	25 F2
Speltham Hl WVILLE PO7	62 C2	Stannington Crs TOTT SO40	52 E4
Spencer Cl HISD PO11	137 H5 ▣	Stannington Wy TOTT SO40	52 E4
Spencer Dr LSOL/BMARY PO13	131 G5	Stanstead Cl HAV PO9	83 K3
Spencer Gdns HORN PO8	81 K2		
Spencer Rd ELGH SO50	44 B1		
EMRTH PO10	104 B2		
ENEY PO4	134 E6		
ITCH SO19	57 G6		

Stanstead Rd ELGH SO50	38 C6
Stansted Crs HAV PO9	83 J7
Stansted Rd SSEA PO5	18 E6
Stanswood Rd FAWY SO45	128 C4
HAV PO9	82 E7
Stanton Rd WSHM SO15	54 A5
Staple Cl WVILLE PO7	81 J4
Stapleford Cl FHAM SO15	29 G7
Stapleford La BPWT SO32	46 E6
Staple Gdns WINC SO23	2 C4
Staplehurst Cl ITCH SO19	11 J9
Staplers Reach	
LSOL/BMARY PO13	115 J6
Stapleton Rd HSEA PO3	119 F7 ▣
Staplewood La FAWY SO40	69 H4
Stares Cl LSOL/BMARY PO13	131 K1
Starina Gdns WVILLE PO7	82 C5
Starling Sq ELGH SO50	44 A1 ▣
Station Ap PSEA PO1	17 L4
RWIN SO21	23 K1
WHAM PO17	77 H1
Station Hl ELGH SO50	38 C7
HEND SO30	59 H5
HLER SO31	74 A6
RWIN SO21	33 F2
WINC SO23	2 D3 ▣
Station La CHFD SO53	37 K4
Station Rd BPWT SO32	48 B4
CHAM PO6	119 H1
FHAM/PORC PO16	99 G4
GPORT PO12	132 C1
HISD PO11	137 F4
HLER SO31	74 A5
HLER SO31	92 E1
HLER SO31	95 F1
HSEA PO3	119 F7
ITCH SO19	10 F4
ROMY SO51	34 E2
ROWN SO16	41 F6
WHAM PO17	77 H1
WINC SO23	2 C3
WSHM SO15	53 H4
Station Rd North TOTT SO40	53 F5 ▣
Station Rd South TOTT SO40	53 G5 ▣
Station St PSEA PO1	18 C3
Staunton Av HISD PO11	136 E5
Staunton Rd HAV PO9	14 C3
Staunton St PSEA PO1	18 D1
Staunton Wy HAV PO9	14 C2
HAV PO9	102 D6
Stead Cl HISD PO11	137 J5
Steele Cl CHFD SO53	38 A6
Steel St PSEA PO5	18 B7
Steep Cl FHAM/PORC PO16	99 F3 ▣
WEND SO18	7 M3
Steeple Wy FHAM/STUB PO14	95 J3
Steerforth Cl NEND PO2	134 C1
Steinbeck Cl FHAM PO15	75 H5
Stein Rd EMRTH PO10	105 G4
Stenbury Wy HLER SO31	73 F6
Stephen Cl HORN PO8	82 C3
Stephen Rd FHAM PO15	12 C5
Stephenson Cl GPORT PO12	132 D6 ▣
Stephenson Rd TOTT SO40	52 C2
Stephenson Wy HEND SO30	58 A1
Step Ter WINW SO22	2 B4
Steuart Rd WEND SO18	6 A4
Steventon Rd WEND SO18	7 M5
Stewarts Gn WVILLE PO7	62 B1
Stinchar Dr CHFD SO53	37 H5
Stirling Av WVILLE PO7	82 A6
Stirling Cl TOTT SO40	53 F4
Stirling Crs HEND SO30	58 B3
TOTT SO40	53 F4
Stirling St NEND PO2	118 C7
Stockbridge Rd HAV PO9	103 J1 ▣
Stockbridge Rd WINW SO22	2 A1
WINW SO22	21 G6
ROMY SO51	28 B2
Stocker Pl	
LSOL/BMARY PO13	116 A5 ▣
Stockers Av WINW SO22	21 G6
Stockheath La HAV PO9	14 C2
Stockheath Rd HAV PO9	103 G2
Stockheath Wy HAV PO9	103 G5
Stockholm Dr HEND SO30	58 D3 ▣
Stockley Cl FAWY SO45	109 K4 ▣
Stockton Cl HEND SO30	58 C5 ▣
Stoddart Av ITCH SO19	6 E7
Stoke Common Rd ELGH SO50	39 H5
Stoke Gdns GPORT PO12	16 B6
Stoke Park Rd ELGH SO50	39 G6
Stoke Rd GPORT PO12	16 B6
ROWN SO16	54 B3
WINC SO23	21 K4
Stokesay Cl FAWY SO45	91 H6 ▣
Stokes Bay Rd GPORT PO12	132 A6
Stoke Wood Cl ELGH SO50	46 A1 ▣
Stonechat Dr TOTT SO40	52 A4
Stonechat Rd HORN PO8	64 B6
Stone Crop Cl HLER SO31	94 D5
Stoneham Cemetery Rd	
WEND SO18	44 C7
Stoneham Cl ROWN SO16	44 A6 ▣
Stoneham La ELGH SO50	44 A3
ROWN SO16	44 A6
Stoneham Wy ELGH SO50	44 A3
Stonehills FAWY SO45	111 F5
Stone La GPORT PO12	16 B7 ▣
Stoneleigh Cl	
FHAM/PORC PO16	98 E6 ▣
Stoners Cl LSOL/BMARY PO13	115 J4
Stone Sq HAV PO9	103 G2
Stone St SSEA PO5	18 B7
Stoney La WINW SO22	21 G5
Stony La PSEA PO1	17 L2
Stonymoor Cl FAWY SO45	109 K4
Stour Cl WEND SO18	56 D1
Stourvale Gdns CHFD SO53	38 A5
Stowe Cl HEND SO30	58 C3
Stowe Rd ENEY PO4	135 F4
Stradbrook LSOL/BMARY PO13	115 J6
The Straight Mile ROMY SO51	35 K1
Strand SHAM SO14	9 G2
The Strand PSEA PO1	137 K7
Stratfield Dr CHFD SO53	37 J3
Stratford Pl ELGH SO50	38 E6 ▣
Stratford Rd WVILLE PO7	82 B5
Strathmore Rd GPORT PO12	16 D5

Stratton Cl CHAM PO6 ...... 100 B6
Stratton Rd WINC SO23 ...... 3 H6
  WSHM SO15 ...... 54 D3
Strawberry HI HLER SO31 ...... 94 E3
Streamleaze FHAM/STUB PO14 ...... 95 H5
Street End NBAD SO52 ...... 36 C5
Stride Av HSEA PO3 ...... 19 M1
Strides Wy TOTT SO40 ...... 52 A3
Strode Rd NEND PO2 ...... 118 B5
Strongs Cl ROMY SO51 ...... 35 G2
Strouden Ct HAV PO9 ...... 82 E6
Stroud Green La
  FHAM/STUB PO14 ...... 114 E2
Stroudley Av CHAM PO6 ...... 119 H1
Stroudley Wy HEND SO30 ...... 58 C2
Stroudwood Rd HAV PO9 ...... 103 H3
Stuart Cl FHAM/STUB PO14 ...... 114 D5
Stuart Crs WINC SO22 ...... 2 A1
Stubbington Av NEND PO2 ...... 118 D6
Stubbington Gn
  FHAM/STUB PO14 ...... 114 D4
Stubbington La
  FHAM/STUB PO14 ...... 114 D7
Stubbington Wy ELGH SO50 ...... 46 C2
Stubbs Dro HEND SO30 ...... 58 C5
Stubbs Rd ITCH SO19 ...... 11 M6
Studland Rd ROWN SO16 ...... 53 J3
Studland Rd
  LSOL/BMARY PO13 ...... 131 F2
  ROWN SO16 ...... 53 J3
Studley Av FAWY SO45 ...... 109 K4
Sudbury Rd CHAM PO6 ...... 100 C6
Suetts La BPWT SO32 ...... 49 G4
Suffolk Av WSHM SO15 ...... 43 K1
Suffolk Cl CHFD SO53 ...... 43 K1
Suffolk Dr CHFD SO53 ...... 43 K1
  FHAM PO15 ...... 75 G6
  HLER SO31 ...... 75 G6
Suffolk Rd ENEY PO4 ...... 19 M7
Sullivan Cl CHAM PO6 ...... 99 H6
Sullivan Rd ITCH SO19 ...... 73 G2
Sullivan Wy WVILLE PO7 ...... 101 K1
Sultan Rd EMRTH PO10 ...... 104 C5
  NEND PO2 ...... 134 B1
Sumar Cl FHAM/STUB PO14 ...... 114 E2
Summerfield Gdns
  ROWN SO16 ...... 44 A6
Summerfield Rd SELS SO20 ...... 139 K6
Summerfields
  FHAM/STUB PO14 ...... 95 C5
Summerhill Rd HORN PO8 ...... 82 A2
Summerlands Rd ELGH SO50 ...... 46 B1
Summer La BROC SO42 ...... 109 F6
Summerleigh Wk
  FHAM/STUB PO14 ...... 114 E2
Summers St SHAM SO14 ...... 5 K6
Summit Wy WEND SO18 ...... 6 E1
Sunbeam Wy GPORT PO12 ...... 16 B8
Sunbury Ct FHAM PO15 ...... 97 F2
Sundridge Cl CHAM PO6 ...... 100 D6
Sunningdale FAWY SO45 ...... 91 G4
Sunningdale Cl ELGH SO50 ...... 45 J1
  LSOL/BMARY PO13 ...... 115 K6
Sunningdale Rd WEND SO18 ...... 7 K5
Sunningdale Rd
  FHAM/PORC PO16 ...... 99 C7
  HSEA PO3 ...... 19 M1
Sunnydown Rd WINW SO22 ...... 24 D5
Sunnyfield Ri HLER SO31 ...... 73 K4
Sunnyheath HAV PO9 ...... 103 F2
Sunnymead Dr WVILLE PO7 ...... 81 H3
Sunny Wk PSEA PO1 ...... 17 K3
Sunny Wy TOTT SO40 ...... 52 E5
Sunset Av TOTT SO40 ...... 52 D4
Sunset Rd TOTT SO40 ...... 52 D4
Sunshine Av HISD PO11 ...... 137 J6
Sun St PSEA PO1 ...... 17 M4
Sunvale Cl ITCH SO19 ...... 11 J4
Sunwood Rd HAV PO9 ...... 102 E1
Surbiton Rd ELGH SO50 ...... 38 E5
Surrey Cl TOTT SO40 ...... 52 C7
Surrey Rd CHFD SO53 ...... 37 K7
  ITCH SO19 ...... 10 B6
Surrey St PSEA PO1 ...... 18 C3
Sussex Border Pth
  EMRTH PO10 ...... 84 C7
  HAV PO9 ...... 84 A1
Sussex Pl SSEA PO5 ...... 18 C8
Sussex Rd CHFD SO53 ...... 38 A7
  SHAM SO14 ...... 9 C1
  SSEA PO5 ...... 18 C8
Sussex St WINC SO23 ...... 2 C1
Sutherland Cl ROMY SO51 ...... 35 G1
Sutherland Rd ENEY PO4 ...... 19 H7
  ROWN SO16 ...... 42 A6
Sutherlands Ct CHFD SO53 ...... 37 K4
Sutherlands Wy CHFD SO53 ...... 37 J3
Sutton Cl HORN PO8 ...... 81 J2
  HSEA PO3 ...... 119 C3
Sutton Gdns WINC SO23 ...... 2 E4
Sutton Rd HORN PO8 ...... 81 J2
  TOTT SO40 ...... 52 C5
Swale Dr CHFD SO53 ...... 37 H3
Swallow Cl HAV PO9 ...... 15 J1
  TOTT SO40 ...... 52 A6
Swallow Ct
  LSOL/BMARY PO13 ...... 131 C1
Swallow Sq ELGH SO50 ...... 44 A1
Swanage Cl ITCH SO19 ...... 10 C2
Swanage Rd
  LSOL/BMARY PO13 ...... 131 F2
Swan Cl EMRTH PO10 ...... 104 D4
  HLER SO31 ...... 74 C6
Swancote FHAM/PORC PO16 ...... 98 C6
Swan La WINC SO23 ...... 2 D3
Swanley Cl ELGH SO50 ...... 38 D5
Swanmore Av ITCH SO19 ...... 11 K3
Swanmore Rd WINW SO22 ...... 21 C3
Swanmore Rd BPWT SO32 ...... 49 C4
  HAV PO9 ...... 82 E6
Swanton Gdns CHFD SO53 ...... 37 J3
Swanwick La HLER SO31 ...... 74 C5
Swanwick Shore Rd
  HLER SO31 ...... 74 C6
Swarraton Rd HAV PO9 ...... 103 H2
Sway Ct HAV PO9 ...... 103 J1
Swaything Rd HAV PO9 ...... 82 E7
  HEND SO30 ...... 56 E2
Sweetbriar Gdns
  WVILLE PO7 ...... 102 A1

Sweethills Crs HLER SO31 ...... 75 G5
Sweyns Lease BROC SO42 ...... 125 H2
Swift Cl ELGH SO50 ...... 44 A1
  WINW SO22 ...... 25 G3
  HORN PO8 ...... 64 B5
Swift Gdns LSOL/BMARY PO13 ...... 131 G1
Swift Cl ITCH SO19 ...... 10 B7
Swift Hollow ITCH SO19 ...... 10 A7
Swift Rd EMRTH PO10 ...... 122 D4
  ITCH SO19 ...... 10 A7
Swinburn Gdns HORN PO8 ...... 82 A1
Swincombe Ri WEND SO18 ...... 7 K1
Swiss Rd WVILLE PO7 ...... 81 K6
Swivelton La WHAM PO17 ...... 98 D3
Sword Cl GPORT PO12 ...... 132 B6
Sword Sands Rd HSEA PO3 ...... 135 H1
Sycamore Av CHFD SO53 ...... 37 K1
Sycamore Cl
  FHAM/STUB PO14 ...... 95 K5
  HLER SO31 ...... 73 J5
  HORN PO8 ...... 81 K2
  LSOL/BMARY PO13 ...... 116 B6
  NBAD SO52 ...... 36 A5
  ROMY SO51 ...... 35 H4
Sycamore Dr FAWY SO45 ...... 109 J2
  HISD PO11 ...... 137 F4
Sycamore Rd BPWT SO32 ...... 49 F3
  FAWY SO45 ...... 91 G3
  ROWN SO16 ...... 54 B2
Sydenham Ter PSEA PO1 ...... 18 F4
Sydmanton Cl ROMY SO51 ...... 35 F4
Sydmonton Ct HAV PO9 ...... 83 J7
Sydney Av HLER SO31 ...... 93 H3
Sydney Rd ELGH SO50 ...... 39 C6
  GPORT PO12 ...... 16 B5
  WSHM SO15 ...... 54 C3
Sylvan Av ITCH SO19 ...... 7 L7
Sylvan Dr NBAD SO52 ...... 36 A6
Sylvan La HLER SO31 ...... 93 K4
The Sylvans FAWY SO45 ...... 90 E3
Sylvan Vw WVILLE PO7 ...... 82 A7
Sylvia Crs TOTT SO40 ...... 52 D3
Symes Rd ROMY SO51 ...... 35 C3
Symonds Cl CHFD SO53 ...... 38 A6
Symonds St WINC SO23 ...... 2 E6
Sywell Crs HSEA PO3 ...... 119 C3

T

Tadburn Cl CHFD SO53 ...... 38 A5
  ROMY SO51 ...... 35 F3
Tadburn Rd ROMY SO51 ...... 35 F4
Tadfield Rd ROMY SO51 ...... 35 F3
Tagdell La HORN PO8 ...... 64 A4
Tait Pl LSOL/BMARY PO13 ...... 116 A6
Talbot Cl HAV PO9 ...... 102 D3
  ROWN SO16 ...... 43 C7
Talbot Rd ENEY PO4 ...... 19 M5
  FAWY SO45 ...... 90 E5
  HAV PO9 ...... 14 A1
Talland Rd FHAM/STUB PO14 ...... 95 C5
Tamar Cl FHAM/PORC PO16 ...... 98 D5
Tamar Down WVILLE PO7 ...... 82 B6
Tamar Gv FAWY SO45 ...... 91 F5
Tamarisk Cl ENEY PO4 ...... 135 H5
  FHAM/STUB PO14 ...... 114 D6
  WVILLE PO7 ...... 102 B1
Tamarisk Gdns WEND SO18 ...... 6 D3
Tamarisk Rd HEND SO30 ...... 58 A5
Tamella Rd HEND SO30 ...... 58 D6
Tammys Turn
  FHAM/STUB PO14 ...... 96 C6
Tamorisk Dr TOTT SO40 ...... 52 B6
Tamworth Rd HSEA PO3 ...... 19 M1
Tanfield La WHAM PO17 ...... 77 G2
Tanfield Pk WHAM PO17 ...... 77 G2
Tangier La BPWT SO32 ...... 48 A4
Tangier Rd HSEA PO3 ...... 135 F1
Tanglewood
  FHAM/PORC PO16 ...... 13 G1
  TOTT SO40 ...... 70 B4
Tanglewood Cl WVILLE PO7 ...... 101 H2
Tangmere Dr ROWN SO16 ...... 42 A7
Tangyes Cl FHAM/STUB PO14 ...... 114 E4
Tanhouse Cl HEND SO30 ...... 58 B7
Tanhouse La HEND SO30 ...... 58 C7
Tankerton Cl CHAM PO6 ...... 100 D6
Tankerville Rd ITCH SO19 ...... 10 B3
Tanner's Brook Wy WSHM SO15 ...... 54 A6
Tanners La FHAM/STUB PO14 ...... 115 F1
  WVILLE PO7 ...... 82 E7
Tanner's Rdg WVILLE PO7 ...... 101 K3
Tanners Rd NBAD SO52 ...... 36 B6
The Tanners
  FHAM/STUB PO14 ...... 95 H5
Tanner St WINC SO23 ...... 2 F5
Tansy Cl WVILLE PO7 ...... 82 A1
Tansy Meadow NBAD SO52 ...... 37 G6
The Tanyards CHFD SO53 ...... 37 J1
Taplin Dr HEND SO30 ...... 58 B4
Taplings Cl WINW SO22 ...... 21 G4
Taplings Rd WINW SO22 ...... 21 G4
Taranto Rd ROWN SO16 ...... 42 D7
Tarbery Crs HORN PO8 ...... 64 D5
Target Rd NEND PO2 ...... 118 B4
Tarius Cl LSOL/BMARY PO13 ...... 116 A5
Tarleton Rd CHAM PO6 ...... 100 A5
Tarn Ri HORN PO8 ...... 64 D2
Tarrant Gdns HAV PO9 ...... 14 D2
Tasman Cl SHAM SO14 ...... 9 K6
Taswell Rd SSEA PO5 ...... 134 C6
Tatchbury La TOTT SO40 ...... 51 J3
Tate Rd WSHM SO15 ...... 53 H4
Tates Rd FAWY SO45 ...... 91 J3
  FAWY SO45 ...... 91 J4
Tattershall Crs
  FHAM/PORC PO16 ...... 98 E7
Tatwin Cl ITCH SO19 ...... 57 G7
Tatwin Crs ITCH SO19 ...... 57 G7
Taunton Dr WEND SO18 ...... 7 K4
Tavells Cl TOTT SO40 ...... 69 K4
Tavell's La TOTT SO40 ...... 69 K4
Taverners Cl ITCH SO19 ...... 10 C5
Tavistock Cl ROMY SO51 ...... 35 G1
Tavistock Gdns HAV PO9 ...... 15 J3
Tavy Cl CHFD SO53 ...... 37 J4
Taw Dr CHFD SO53 ...... 37 J3

Tawny Owl Cl
  FHAM/STUB PO14 ...... 114 C3
Taylor Cl ITCH SO19 ...... 10 B8
Teachers Wy FAWY SO45 ...... 109 J3
Teal Cl FHAM/PORC PO16 ...... 98 C6
  HISD PO11 ...... 137 J5
  TOTT SO40 ...... 52 B5
Tebourba Dr GPORT PO12 ...... 132 D5
Tebourba Wy WSHM SO15 ...... 54 A5
Tedder Rd LSOL/BMARY PO13 ...... 116 A4
  WEND SO18 ...... 7 C3
Tedder Wy TOTT SO40 ...... 52 C5
Teddington Rd ENEY PO4 ...... 19 M6
Tees Cl CHFD SO53 ...... 37 H3
Teg Down Meads WINW SO22 ...... 20 E6
Teignmouth Rd GPORT PO12 ...... 132 C5
  HSEA PO3 ...... 119 F7
Telegraph Rd HEND SO30 ...... 57 H4
Telephone Rd ENEY PO4 ...... 19 H5
Telford Gdns HEND SO30 ...... 58 C2
Telford Rd NEND PO2 ...... 118 D4
Teme Crs ROWN SO16 ...... 53 K4
Teme Rd ROWN SO16 ...... 53 K4
Tempest Av WVILLE PO7 ...... 82 B5
Templars Mede CHFD SO53 ...... 37 J7
Templars Wy NBAD SO52 ...... 37 G6
Templecombe Rd ELGH SO50 ...... 45 J2
Temple Gdns ITCH SO19 ...... 10 E5
Temple La BPWT SO32 ...... 49 G3
Templemere FHAM/STUB PO14 ...... 96 D7
Temple Rd ITCH SO19 ...... 10 E5
Temple St PSEA PO1 ...... 18 D2
Templeton Cl NEND PO2 ...... 118 D4
Tenby Cl WEND SO18 ...... 7 H3
Tenby Dr CHFD SO53 ...... 37 H6
Tench Wy ROMY SO51 ...... 34 E2
Tennyson Cl BPWT SO32 ...... 49 G3
  FAWY SO45 ...... 109 J2
Tennyson Crs WVILLE PO7 ...... 81 J4
Tennyson Gdns
  FHAM/PORC PO16 ...... 13 C4
Tennyson Rd ELGH SO50 ...... 44 C1
  NEND PO2 ...... 118 E2
  PTSW SO17 ...... 5 K2
  TOTT SO40 ...... 52 C2
Tensing Cl FHAM/PORC PO16 ...... 13 C1
Tenterton Av ITCH SO19 ...... 11 J8
Terminus Ter SHAM SO14 ...... 9 J4
Tern Cl FAWY SO45 ...... 91 J4
Terrier Cl HEND SO30 ...... 58 B1
Terriote Cl CHFD SO53 ...... 37 K3
Testbourne Av TOTT SO40 ...... 52 C5
Testbourne Cl TOTT SO40 ...... 52 C5
Testcombe Rd GPORT PO12 ...... 132 D5
Testlands Av ROWN SO16 ...... 41 J5
Test La ROWN SO16 ...... 53 G3
Test Rd SHAM SO14 ...... 9 J9
Test Wy TOTT SO40 ...... 53 F3
Testwood Av TOTT SO40 ...... 52 D3
Testwood Crs TOTT SO40 ...... 52 C2
Testwood La TOTT SO40 ...... 52 E3
Testwood Pl TOTT SO40 ...... 53 F4
Testwood Rd HAV PO9 ...... 102 E1
  WSHM SO15 ...... 54 C4
Tetney Cl ROWN SO16 ...... 53 K1
Teviot Rd CHFD SO53 ...... 37 H5
Tewkesbury Av FHAM PO15 ...... 96 D3
  GPORT PO12 ...... 132 D1
Tewkesbury Cl CHAM PO6 ...... 100 C6
Texas Dr WINW SO22 ...... 24 E6
Thackeray Rd PTSW SO17 ...... 5 K2
Thames Cl WEND SO18 ...... 56 E2
Thames Dr FHAM PO15 ...... 96 E2
Thamesmead Cl
  FHAM PO15 ...... 132 C1
Theatre Ms SSEA PO5 ...... 18 F9
The Itchen Br SHAM SO14 ...... 9 L4
Theseus Rd LSOL/BMARY PO13 ...... 130 E1
Thetford Gdns CHFD SO53 ...... 37 H3
The Thicket FHAM/PORC PO16 ...... 98 C5
  LSOL/BMARY PO13 ...... 116 B6
  ROMY SO51 ...... 35 H4
  SSEA PO5 ...... 18 E8
  WVILLE PO7 ...... 101 J4
Third Av CHAM PO6 ...... 100 D6
  HAV PO9 ...... 15 H3
  WSHM SO15 ...... 54 A4
Thirlmere ELGH SO50 ...... 44 C1
Thirlmere Cl
  FHAM/STUB PO14 ...... 114 E3
Thirlmere Rd ROWN SO16 ...... 53 K2
Thirlstane Firs CHFD SO53 ...... 37 J6
Thistledown HORN PO8 ...... 64 C7
Thistledowne Gdns
  EMRTH PO10 ...... 104 C6
Thistle Rd HEND SO30 ...... 58 A6
  NBAD SO52 ...... 37 G5
Thomas Cl TOTT SO40 ...... 52 C6
Thomas Lewis Wy PTSW SO17 ...... 55 K2
Thomas Rd NBAD SO52 ...... 36 B6
Thompsons La WVILLE PO7 ...... 62 B7
Thornbrake Rd GPORT PO12 ...... 16 D7
Thornbury Av FAWY SO45 ...... 110 B7
  WSHM SO15 ...... 4 C4
Thornbury Cl
  FHAM/STUB PO14 ...... 96 D6
Thornbury Hts CHFD SO53 ...... 38 C1
Thornbury Wd CHFD SO53 ...... 38 C1
Thorncliffe Cl NEND PO2 ...... 118 E3
Thorn Cl NBAD SO52 ...... 38 D5
Thorncroft Rd PSEA PO1 ...... 19 H4
Thorndike Cl ROWN SO16 ...... 54 B2
Thorness Cl ROWN SO16 ...... 53 H3
Thorney Cl FHAM/STUB PO14 ...... 12 A8
Thorney Old Pk EMRTH PO10 ...... 123 G6
Thorney Rd EMRTH PO10 ...... 122 E2
Thorngate Wy GPORT PO12 ...... 16 F5
Thornham La EMRTH PO10 ...... 122 E1
Thornhill Av ITCH SO19 ...... 57 G1
Thornhill Park Rd WEND SO18 ...... 57 G5
Thornhill Rd FAWY SO45 ...... 110 C5
  ROWN SO16 ...... 42 E7
Thorni Av HEND SO30 ...... 96 D3
Thornleigh Rd ITCH SO19 ...... 10 D5
Thornton Av HLER SO31 ...... 94 B5
Thornton Cl CHAM PO6 ...... 101 C4
Thornton Rd GPORT PO12 ...... 116 E7
Thornycroft Av ITCH SO19 ...... 10 A5
Thorold Rd CHFD SO53 ...... 38 B1

  WEND SO18 ...... 6 C1
Three Acres WVILLE PO7 ...... 81 F2
Three Castles Pth RWIN SO21 ...... 22 B3
Threefield La SHAM SO14 ...... 9 H3
Three Oaks ITCH SO19 ...... 57 H7
Three Tun Cl PSEA PO1 ...... 18 C2
Thresher Cl HORN PO8 ...... 82 D4
Thrush Wk HORN PO8 ...... 81 K1
Thruxton Rd HAV PO9 ...... 102 D1
Thurbern Rd NEND PO2 ...... 118 D5
Thurmell Cl HEND SO30 ...... 74 B1
Thurmond Crs WINW SO22 ...... 25 F2
Thurmond Rd WINW SO22 ...... 25 F2
Thurston Cl CHFD SO53 ...... 38 A3
Thyme Av FHAM PO15 ...... 75 J5
Tichborne Gv HAV PO9 ...... 102 E1
Tichborne Rd ELGH SO50 ...... 44 C3
  WEND SO18 ...... 57 G4
Tichborne Wy
  LSOL/BMARY PO13 ...... 116 A6
Tickleford Dr ITCH SO19 ...... 11 H8
Tickner Cl HEND SO30 ...... 58 C7
Ticonderoga Gdns ITCH SO19 ...... 10 C8
Tides Reach WEND SO18 ...... 6 A3
Tides Wy TOTT SO40 ...... 70 A3
Tideway Gdns ENEY PO4 ...... 135 H4
Tidworth Rd HAV PO9 ...... 103 G2
Tiffield Cl HSEA PO3 ...... 119 H3
Tilbrook Rd WSHM SO15 ...... 54 B4
Tilden Rd RWIN SO21 ...... 33 F4
Tilford Rd HORN PO8 ...... 64 A6
Timberlane WVILLE PO7 ...... 101 J2
Timberly Cl FAWY SO45 ...... 109 K3
The Timbers FHAM PO15 ...... 96 D5
Timor Cl HLER SO31 ...... 75 C5
Timpson Rd PSEA PO1 ...... 18 F1
Timsbury Crs HAV PO9 ...... 14 C1
Timsbury Dr ROWN SO16 ...... 54 A2
Timson Cl TOTT SO40 ...... 52 B6
Tindale Rd ROWN SO16 ...... 53 K2
Tinker Aly ELGH SO50 ...... 44 A1
Tintagel Wy CHAM PO6 ...... 100 A7
Tintern Cl CHAM PO6 ...... 99 J5
Tintern Gv WSHM SO15 ...... 4 C8
Tintern Rd GPORT PO12 ...... 132 C2
Tipner Gn NEND PO2 ...... 118 B5
Tipner La NEND PO2 ...... 118 B4
Tipner Rd NEND PO2 ...... 118 B5
Tiptree Cl ELGH SO50 ...... 38 D5
Tisted Ct HAV PO9 ...... 103 J1
Titchfield Hl FHAM/STUB PO14 ...... 96 B6
Titchfield La FHAM PO15 ...... 76 D5
  WHAM PO17 ...... 76 D4
Titchfield Park Rd FHAM PO15 ...... 95 J3
Titchfield Rd
  FHAM/STUB PO14 ...... 114 D3
The Tithe WVILLE PO7 ...... 80 E2
Tithewood Cl CHFD SO53 ...... 31 J7
Titus Gdns WVILLE PO7 ...... 82 B5
Tivoli Cl CHFD SO53 ...... 38 C3
Toby St PSEA PO1 ...... 18 C2
Tokar St ENEY PO4 ...... 19 M9
Tokio Rd HSEA PO3 ...... 119 F6
Tolefrey Gdns NBAD SO52 ...... 37 G4
Tollbar Wy HEND SO30 ...... 57 K3
Tollgate CHFD SO53 ...... 43 K1
Tollgate Rd HLER SO31 ...... 74 C5
Tonbridge St SSEA PO5 ...... 18 D9
Tonnant Cl
  FHAM/STUB PO14 ...... 114 E6
Toogoods Wy ROWN SO16 ...... 41 J6
Toomer Cl FAWY SO45 ...... 110 C5
Toothill Rd ROMY SO51 ...... 41 H2
Topaz Gv WVILLE PO7 ...... 82 C5
Topiary Gdns HLER SO31 ...... 95 G2
Torch Cl CHFD SO50 ...... 46 A1
Tor Cl FHAM/PORC PO16 ...... 98 B5
Torcross Cl ITCH SO19 ...... 10 C6
Torfrida Ct ENEY PO4 ...... 135 H5
Tormead FAWY SO45 ...... 91 G3
Tornay Gv NBAD SO52 ...... 36 A6
Toronto Pl GPORT PO12 ...... 16 B4
Toronto Rd NEND PO2 ...... 134 D1
Torquay Av GPORT PO12 ...... 116 D7
  WSHM SO15 ...... 54 D4
Torque Cl ITCH SO19 ...... 73 H1
Torre Cl ELGH SO50 ...... 38 D4
Torridge Gdns WEND SO18 ...... 56 E2
Torrington Cl ITCH SO19 ...... 11 H2
Torrington Rd NEND PO2 ...... 118 D5
Tortworth Cl FHAM/STUB PO14 ...... 12 A8
Torwood Gdns ELGH SO50 ...... 45 J1
Tosson Cl ROWN SO16 ...... 53 K2
Totland Cl ROWN SO16 ...... 53 K4
Totland Rd CHAM PO6 ...... 100 D7
  LSOL/BMARY PO13 ...... 115 K5
Totnes Cl ELGH SO50 ...... 38 C5
Tottehale Cl NBAD SO52 ...... 36 A7
Tottenham Rd PSEA PO1 ...... 19 C1
Totton By-pass TOTT SO40 ...... 53 F6
Tournerbury La HISD PO11 ...... 137 H4
Tower Cl GPORT PO12 ...... 132 A5
Tower Gdns HAV PO9 ...... 121 C1
Tower La HLER SO31 ...... 45 F1
Tower Pl HEND SO30 ...... 58 B7
Tower Rd ENEY PO4 ...... 19 K8
  WINC SO23 ...... 2 D3
Tower St EMRTH PO10 ...... 104 D6
  PSEA PO1 ...... 17 K7
  WINC SO23 ...... 2 D4
Town Hall Rd HAV PO9 ...... 7 H2
Townhill Wy WEND SO18 ...... 7 H2
Town Quay SHAM SO14 ...... 8 F5
Towpath Md ENEY PO4 ...... 135 H4
Toynbee Cl ELGH SO50 ...... 38 D7
Toynbee Rd ELGH SO50 ...... 38 D7
Trafalgar Cl CHFD SO53 ...... 37 J5
Trafalgar Dr FHAM/STUB PO14 ...... 97 F2
Trafalgar Pl PSEA PO1 ...... 19 G2
Trafalgar Rd WSHM SO15 ...... 54 D6
Trafalgar Sq GPORT PO12 ...... 16 A3
Trafalgar St WINC SO23 ...... 2 D3
Trafalgar Wy FAWY SO45 ...... 91 J3
Trafford Wy ELGH SO50 ...... 46 A2
Trampers La WHAM PO17 ...... 78 D4
Tranby Rd ENEY PO4 ...... 19 H6
Tranmere Rd ENEY PO4 ...... 135 C5
Treadwheel Rd HORN PO8 ...... 65 H6
Treagore Rd TOTT SO40 ...... 52 B3
Treaman Cl ROWN SO16 ...... 54 A4

Treble Cl WINW SO22 ...... 24 E4
Tredegar Rd ENEY PO4 ...... 19 K7
Treeside Av TOTT SO40 ...... 53 F5
Treeside Rd WSHM SO15 ...... 54 D4
Tree Side Wy WVILLE PO7 ...... 81 K4
Trefoil Cl WVILLE PO7 ...... 82 A6
Tregaron Av CHAM PO6 ...... 101 G7
Treloar Rd HISD PO11 ...... 138 B7
Treloyhan Cl CHFD SO53 ...... 38 A6
Tremona Rd ROWN SO16 ...... 54 C1
Trenley Cl FAWY SO45 ...... 109 K4
Trent Rd WEND SO18 ...... 6 E1
Trentham Rd
  LSOL/BMARY PO13 ...... 131 G2
Tresillian Gdns WEND SO18 ...... 56 E2
Trevis Rd ENEY PO4 ...... 135 H4
Trevone Cl TOTT SO40 ...... 52 D7
Trevor Rd ENEY PO4 ...... 19 H8
Trevose Cl CHFD SO53 ...... 38 A3
  LSOL/BMARY PO13 ...... 115 K6
Trevose Crs CHFD SO53 ...... 38 A5
Trevose Wy FHAM/STUB PO14 ...... 114 D8
Triangle La FHAM/STUB PO14 ...... 113 K3
Tribe Rd GPORT PO12 ...... 132 D3
Trimaran Cl HLER SO31 ...... 94 D5
Trimaran Rd HLER SO31 ...... 94 D5
Trinity Cl GPORT PO12 ...... 16 F6
Trinity Gn CHFD SO53 ...... 17 G6
Trinity Rd SHAM SO14 ...... 5 H8
Trinity St FHAM/PORC PO16 ...... 13 J3
Tristan Cl FAWY SO45 ...... 129 H1
Triumph Cl FHAM PO15 ...... 12 B8
Triumph Rd FHAM/STUB PO14 ...... 115 G2
Trojan Wy WVILLE PO7 ...... 102 A3
Troon Crs CHAM PO6 ...... 101 H5
Trosnant Rd HAV PO9 ...... 14 C2
Trotts La TOTT SO40 ...... 69 H1
Trowbridge Cl ROWN SO16 ...... 41 K5
Truro Ri ELGH SO50 ...... 39 H7
Truro Rd CHAM PO6 ...... 99 J6
Trussell Cl WINW SO22 ...... 21 G4
Trussell Crs WINW SO22 ...... 21 G4
Tudor Av EMRTH PO10 ...... 104 B2
Tudor Cl FHAM/PORC PO16 ...... 98 E5
  HISD PO11 ...... 137 G6
  LSOL/BMARY PO13 ...... 116 A7
  TOTT SO40 ...... 52 B4
Tudor Ct FHAM/STUB PO14 ...... 97 G7
Tudor Crs CHAM PO6 ...... 118 E1
Tudor Gdns HEND SO30 ...... 57 K7
Tudor Wood Cl ROWN SO16 ...... 43 G7
Tuffin Cl ROWN SO16 ...... 41 H6
Tukes Av LSOL/BMARY PO13 ...... 115 J3
Tulip Gdns HAV PO9 ...... 102 D4
  HLER SO31 ...... 94 E3
Tulip Rd ROWN SO16 ...... 43 K7
Tumulus Cl ITCH SO19 ...... 73 J1
Tunstall Rd CHAM PO6 ...... 100 C5
  ITCH SO19 ...... 73 H1
Tunworth Ct HAV PO9 ...... 103 J1
Tuppenny La EMRTH PO10 ...... 105 F6
Turner Av LSOL/BMARY PO13 ...... 116 B6
Turnpike Down WINC SO23 ...... 3 K4
Turnpike Wy HEND SO30 ...... 57 K6
Turnstone Gdns ROWN SO16 ...... 42 C6
Turtle Cl FHAM/STUB PO14 ...... 114 C3
Tuscan Wk CHFD SO53 ...... 38 B4
Tuscany Wy WVILLE PO7 ...... 82 C5
The Tussocks TOTT SO40 ...... 70 A3
Tutland Rd NBAD SO52 ...... 36 A6
Tutor Cl HLER SO31 ...... 93 J3
Tweed Cl CHFD SO53 ...... 37 H5
Twiggs End Cl HLER SO31 ...... 94 E2
Twiggs La TOTT SO40 ...... 69 J7
Twiggs Lane End TOTT SO40 ...... 89 H1
Twyford Av NEND PO2 ...... 118 C6
  WSHM SO15 ...... 54 D3
Twyford Rd ELGH SO50 ...... 38 E4
Twynhams Hl BPWT SO32 ...... 61 H4
The Tyleshades ROMY SO51 ...... 35 F4
Tyne Cl CHFD SO53 ...... 37 H5
Tynedale Cl GPORT PO12 ...... 116 C7
Tyne Wy HEND SO30 ...... 57 K3
Tyrell Rd CHFD SO53 ...... 37 K3
Tyseley Rd SSEA PO5 ...... 18 D5
Tytherley Rd WEND SO18 ...... 7 L3

U

Ullswater Av WEND SO18 ...... 56 E3
Ullswater Rd ROWN SO16 ...... 53 K3
Underdown Av WVILLE PO7 ...... 101 J4
Underwood Cl ROWN SO16 ...... 43 F7
Underwood Rd ELGH SO50 ...... 39 G6
  ROWN SO16 ...... 43 F7
Unicorn Rd LSOL/BMARY PO13 ...... 130 E1
  PSEA PO1 ...... 18 C2
Union Pl PSEA PO1 ...... 18 E2
Union Rd HAV PO9 ...... 14 D4
  SHAM SO14 ...... 5 L8
Union St FHAM/PORC PO16 ...... 13 M6
  PSEA PO1 ...... 17 M3
  WINC SO23 ...... 3 G4
University Crs PTSW SO17 ...... 55 J1
University Pkwy ROWN SO16 ...... 42 D2
University Rd PTSW SO17 ...... 55 H1
Unwin Cl ITCH SO19 ...... 10 A8
Uphill Rd WINW SO22 ...... 20 E2
Uplands Crs FHAM/PORC PO16 ...... 13 J3
Uplands Rd CHAM PO6 ...... 101 H5
  WINW SO22 ...... 21 H4
  HAV PO9 ...... 83 K3
  WVILLE PO7 ...... 62 A6
Uplands Wy PTSW SO17 ...... 55 H2
Upper Arundel St PSEA PO1 ...... 18 D2
Upper Banister St WSHM SO15 ...... 4 F6
Upper Bere Wd WVILLE PO7 ...... 82 A7
Upper Brook Dr HLER SO31 ...... 94 D4
Upper Brownhill Rd
  ROWN SO16 ...... 54 A1
Upper Bugle St SHAM SO14 ...... 8 F3
Upper Church Rd BPWT SO32 ...... 61 F5
Upper Cornaway La
  FHAM/PORC PO16 ...... 98 E6
Upper Crabbick La WVILLE PO7 ...... 62 B7
Upper Crescent Rd NBAD SO52 ...... 36 A6
Upper Deacon Rd ITCH SO19 ...... 7 K7
Upper High St WINW SO22 ...... 2 C3

Upper House Ct WHAM PO17 ...... 77 H2
Upper Market St ELGH SO50 ...... 38 E7
Upper Mead Cl ELGH SO50 ...... 46 C1 4
Upper Moors Rd ELGH SO50 ...... 39 J1
RWIN SO21 ...... 39 J2
Upper Mullin's La FAWY SO45 ...... 91 F3
Upper New Rd HEND SO30 ...... 57 G3
Upper Northam Cl HEND SO30 ...... 57 K6
Upper Northam Dr HEND SO30 .. 57 H6
Upper Northam Rd HEND SO30 .. 57 K5
Upper Old St
FHAM/STUB PO14 ...... 114 C3
Upper Piece WVILLE PO7 ...... 81 F2
Upper St Helens Rd HEND SO30 .. 74 A1
Upper Shaftesbury Av
PTSW SO17 ...... 55 J2
Upper Shirley Av WSHM SO15 ...... 54 D3
Upper Spinney HLER SO31 ...... 94 B6
Upper Toothill Rd ROWN SO16 ...... 41 K2
Upper Weston La ITCH SO19 ...... 11 H6
Upper Whf FHAM/PORC PO16 ...... 13 L7
Upton Cl HAV PO9 ...... 82 E6
Upton Crs ROWN SO16 ...... 41 H4
Upton Grey Cl WINW SO22 ...... 21 G4
Upton La ROWN SO16 ...... 41 G6

V

Vadne Gdns GPORT PO12 ...... 16 A1 1
Vale Dr WEND SO18 ...... 6 F1
Vale Gv GPORT PO12 ...... 132 D1
Valentine Av ITCH SO19 ...... 11 M4
Valentine Cl FHAM PO15 ...... 96 D3
Valentine Ct WVILLE PO7 ...... 82 B5 5
Valerian Cl ELGH SO50 ...... 46 B5 5
Valerian Rd HEND SO30 ...... 58 B6
Vale Rd WINC SO23 ...... 3 J7
The Vale FAWY SO45 ...... 91 G3
HLER SO31 ...... 95 G4
HORN PO8 ...... 64 D3
SSEA PO5 ...... 134 B6 7
Valetta Pk EMRTH PO10 ...... 104 B6
Valetta Rd EMRTH PO10 ...... 123 G6
Valiant Gdns NEND PO2 ...... 118 C3
Valiant Rd EMRTH PO10 ...... 123 G6
Valley Cl FAWY SO45 ...... 110 C6 1
RWIN SO21 ...... 39 J2
WVILLE PO7 ...... 101 H3
Valleydene FAWY SO45 ...... 91 G4
Valley Hl WINW SO22 ...... 21 F2
Valley Park Dr HORN PO8 ...... 64 E1
Valley Ri HLER SO31 ...... 94 D2
Valley Rd CHFD SO53 ...... 37 K3
WINW SO22 ...... 20 E2
TOTT SO40 ...... 52 E7
The Valley WINW SO22 ...... 25 G2
Valsheba Dr FHAM/STUB PO14 .. 114 C6
Vanburgh Wy CHFD SO53 ...... 37 J1 7
Vanguard Hl WINW SO22 ...... 21 F1
Vanguard Rd WEND SO18 ...... 7 H3
Vanstone Rd
LSOL/BMARY PO13 ...... 116 A7
Vardy Cl ITCH SO19 ...... 73 G2 4
Varna Rd WSHM SO15 ...... 54 D7
Varos Cl GPORT PO12 ...... 132 D2
Varsity Rd EMRTH PO10 ...... 123 G6
Vaudrey Cl WSHM SO15 ...... 54 D3 3
Vaughan Cl ITCH SO19 ...... 57 H7
Vaughan Rd FAWY SO45 ...... 90 D2 4
Veal's La TOTT SO40 ...... 70 C6
Vear's La RWIN SO21 ...... 39 K2
Vectis Rd GPORT PO12 ...... 132 B5
Vectis Wy CHAM PO6 ...... 100 E7
Velder Av ENEY PO4 ...... 19 M4
Vellan Ct ROWN SO16 ...... 53 H3
Velmore Rd CHFD SO53 ...... 37 J6
Velsheda Ct FAWY SO45 ...... 91 H1
Venerable Rd
FHAM/STUB PO14 ...... 115 H2
Vengeance Rd
LSOL/BMARY PO13 ...... 131 F1
Venice Cl WVILLE PO7 ...... 82 B5
Ventnor Rd ENEY PO4 ...... 19 H6 2
LSOL/BMARY PO13 ...... 115 J4
Ventnor Wy FHAM/PORC PO16 ...... 98 B5
Venture Rd ROWN SO16 ...... 42 E2
Verbena Crs HORN PO8 ...... 82 C1
Verbena Wy HEND SO30 ...... 58 C6 8
Verdon Av HLER SO31 ...... 93 H3
Verger Cl FHAM/STUB PO14 ...... 95 H3 5
Vermont Cl ROWN SO16 ...... 43 G7
Vernham Rd WINW SO22 ...... 21 G5
Vernon Av ENEY PO4 ...... 19 L4
Vernon Cl GPORT PO12 ...... 132 D3
Vernon Hl BPWT SO32 ...... 48 D1
Vernon Rd GPORT PO12 ...... 132 D3
HSEA PO3 ...... 119 F5
Verona Rd CHFD SO53 ...... 38 B3
Verulam Rd SHAM SO14 ...... 5 J4
Verwood Rd HAV PO9 ...... 83 J7 12
Veryan FHAM PO15 ...... 12 C6
Vespasian Rd WEND SO18 ...... 6 A4
Vespasian Wy CHFD SO53 ...... 38 B4
Vesta Wy CHFD SO53 ...... 38 B3
Vian Cl LSOL/BMARY PO13 ...... 115 K3
Vian Rd WVILLE PO7 ...... 81 J7
Vicarage Dr HEND SO30 ...... 58 A7
Vicarage La BPWT SO32 ...... 49 K5
BPWT SO32 ...... 59 H4
FHAM/STUB PO14 ...... 114 D4
TOTT SO40 ...... 50 E3
WVILLE PO7 ...... 62 C1
Vicarage Rd TOTT SO40 ...... 70 A4
Viceroy Rd ITCH SO19 ...... 11 H4
Victena Rd ELGH SO50 ...... 46 B1
Victoria Av HISD PO11 ...... 137 G5
WVILLE PO7 ...... 101 G3
Victoria Cl HLER SO31 ...... 95 F5
Victoria Gld HLER SO31 ...... 93 F1
Victoria Gv SSEA PO5 ...... 18 F8
Victoria Pl GPORT PO12 ...... 16 B6 3
Victoria Rd BPWT SO32 ...... 48 C3
ELGH SO50 ...... 38 E5
EMRTH PO10 ...... 104 B5
HISD PO11 ...... 121 G5
HLER SO31 ...... 72 D7
ITCH SO19 ...... 10 A5
PSEA PO1 ...... 17 L1
WINC SO23 ...... 2 D2
WVILLE PO7 ...... 81 K6 1
Victoria Rd North SSEA PO5 ...... 18 F6
Victoria Sq LSOL/BMARY PO13 .. 131 F2
Victoria St GPORT PO12 ...... 16 C4
PSEA PO1 ...... 134 B1
SHAM SO14 ...... 5 L9
Victor Rd EMRTH PO10 ...... 123 G6
HSEA PO3 ...... 134 E1 1
Victor St WSHM SO15 ...... 54 D4 2
Victory Av HORN PO8 ...... 64 B6
Victory Cl CHFD SO53 ...... 37 J5
Victory Crs WSHM SO15 ...... 54 C6 1
Victory Gn NEND PO2 ...... 118 B5 2
Victory Rd FHAM/STUB PO14 ...... 114 E5
PSEA PO1 ...... 17 L4 6
WSHM SO15 ...... 54 C6
Victory Sq WSHM SO15 ...... 54 C6 2
Viking Cl FAWY SO45 ...... 110 C7
FHAM/STUB PO14 ...... 114 C4
ROWN SO16 ...... 41 K6
The Vikings ROMY SO51 ...... 35 G3 5
Viking Wy HORN PO8 ...... 64 D1
Villa Gdns WVILLE PO7 ...... 81 K5
Village Cl FHAM/STUB PO14 ...... 114 D5
Village Rd GPORT PO12 ...... 132 C6
Ville De Paris Rd
FHAM/STUB PO14 ...... 115 H2
Villiers Rd FAWY SO45 ...... 91 G6
SSEA PO5 ...... 134 C7 7
WSHM SO15 ...... 54 D5
Vincent Av ROWN SO16 ...... 54 D2
Vincent Gv FHAM/PORC PO16 ...... 99 F7
Vincent Rd WSHM SO15 ...... 54 D4
Vincent's Gv WSHM SO15 ...... 54 D4 3
Vincent St WSHM SO15 ...... 54 C4
Vincent's Wk SHAM SO14 ...... 9 G2
Vine Bank WEND SO18 ...... 7 K2
Vine Cl HLER SO31 ...... 94 C3
Vine Coppice WVILLE PO7 ...... 101 K2
Vine Rd ROWN SO16 ...... 54 B1
Vinery Gdns ROWN SO16 ...... 54 C2
Vinery Rd ROWN SO16 ...... 54 D2 1
Vineside LSOL/BMARY PO13 ...... 116 B6
Vineyard Cl ITCH SO19 ...... 10 B3
The Vineyards NBAD SO52 ...... 36 B6
Viney Av ROMY SO51 ...... 35 G2
Violet Av FHAM/STUB PO14 ...... 114 C5
Violet Cl NBAD SO52 ...... 37 H4
Violet Rd ROWN SO16 ...... 43 H7
Virginia Park Rd GPORT PO12 ...... 132 C2
Vita Rd NEND PO2 ...... 118 D4
Vivash Rd PSEA PO1 ...... 19 G4 5
Vixen Cl FHAM/STUB PO14 ...... 114 C5
Vokes Cl ITCH SO19 ...... 7 J9
Vulcan Cl WSHM SO15 ...... 54 A6
Vulcan Rd EMRTH PO10 ...... 123 G6
WSHM SO15 ...... 54 A6
Vyse La SHAM SO14 ...... 8 F4 2

W

Wade Court Rd HAV PO9 ...... 15 G6
Wade La HAV PO9 ...... 15 G8
Wadham Rd NEND PO2 ...... 118 C5
Wadhurst Gdns ITCH SO19 ...... 11 H9
Wadhurst Rd HEND SO30 ...... 58 B6
The Wad SELS PO20 ...... 139 J7
Wagtail Rd HORN PO8 ...... 64 B6
Wagtail Wy FHAM/PORC PO16 ...... 98 C6
Wainscott Rd ENEY PO4 ...... 19 L9
Wainwright Cl CHAM PO6 ...... 119 H1
Wait End Rd WVILLE PO7 ...... 81 K7
Wakefield Av FHAM/PORC PO16 .. 12 F1
Wakefield Ct WEND SO18 ...... 7 G1
Wakefield Rd WEND SO18 ...... 7 G1
Wakefords Wy HAV PO9 ...... 83 J7
Walberton Av CHAM PO6 ...... 101 F6
Waldegrave Cl ITCH SO19 ...... 10 A8
Walden Gdns HORN PO8 ...... 64 C5
Walden Rd NEND PO2 ...... 118 B5
Waldon Gdns WEND SO18 ...... 56 E2 5
Wales St WINC SO23 ...... 3 G4
Walford Rd CHAM PO6 ...... 100 B6
Walker Pl LSOL/BMARY PO13 .. 116 A6 4
Walker Rd NEND PO2 ...... 118 B5
Walkers Cl ELGH SO50 ...... 46 C1 5
Walkers La North FAWY SO45 ...... 110 C6
Walker's La South FAWY SO45 .. 128 C1
Wallace La BROC SO42 ...... 125 H2
Wallace Rd ITCH SO19 ...... 10 E8
NEND PO2 ...... 118 E7
Wallington Ct
FHAM/STUB PO14 ...... 115 G1 1
Wallington Dr CHFD SO53 ...... 37 H2
Wallington Hl
FHAM/PORC PO16 ...... 13 L4
Wallington Rd NEND PO2 ...... 118 E6
Wallington Shore Rd
FHAM/PORC PO16 ...... 13 M4
Wallington Wy
FHAM/PORC PO16 ...... 13 L4
Wallisdean Av
FHAM/STUB PO14 ...... 12 E8
HSEA PO3 ...... 135 G1
Wallis Gdns WVILLE PO7 ...... 81 K4
Wallis Rd WVILLE PO7 ...... 81 K4
Walmer Cl ELGH SO50 ...... 38 D3
Walmer Rd PSEA PO1 ...... 19 H4
Walnut Av WEND SO18 ...... 44 B6
Walnut Cl CHFD SO53 ...... 31 K7
ROWN SO16 ...... 54 A3
Walnut Dr FHAM/STUB PO14 ...... 114 C5
Walnut Gv WINW SO22 ...... 21 G6
ROWN SO16 ...... 54 A4
Walnut Tree Cl HISD PO11 ...... 137 G5 1
Walnut Tree Dr EMRTH PO10 ...... 105 H3
Walnwright Gdns HEND SO30 ...... 58 B1
Walpole La HLER SO31 ...... 74 D6
Walpole Rd WINW SO22 ...... 25 F3
GPORT PO12 ...... 16 D5
Walsall Rd HSEA PO3 ...... 19 M1
Walsingham Cl CHAM PO6 ...... 100 C5 3
Walsingham Gdns WEND SO18 .... 56 B1
Waltham Cl FHAM/PORC PO16 ...... 99 F4
Waltham Crs ROWN SO16 ...... 42 C7
Waltham St SSEA PO5 ...... 18 B5 5
Walton Cl GPORT PO12 ...... 132 D4
WVILLE PO7 ...... 101 K1
Walton Ct FHAM PO15 ...... 96 E2
Walton Pl WINW SO22 ...... 25 G3
Walton Rd CHAM PO6 ...... 119 H1
GPORT PO12 ...... 132 D4
ITCH SO19 ...... 73 G1 5
Waltons Av FAWY SO45 ...... 110 A3
Wandesford Pl GPORT PO12 ...... 116 D6
Wangfield La BPWT SO32 ...... 59 H3
Wansbeck Cl CHFD SO53 ...... 37 J5 2
Warbler Cl HORN PO8 ...... 64 B5
ROWN SO16 ...... 42 C5
Warblington Av HAV PO9 ...... 15 K5
Warblington Cl CHFD SO53 ...... 37 J7 3
Warblington Rd EMRTH PO10 ...... 104 B7
Warblington St PSEA PO1 ...... 17 M6
Warbrook Ct HAV PO9 ...... 103 J1 18
Warburton Cl ITCH SO19 ...... 73 H1 1
Warburton Rd ITCH SO19 ...... 57 G7
Ward Crs EMRTH PO10 ...... 104 D3
Warden Cl HEND SO30 ...... 57 G3 6
Wardens Cl HISD PO11 ...... 137 G3
Wardle Rd ELGH SO50 ...... 39 G3
Ward Rd ENEY PO4 ...... 19 L9
Wardroom Rd NEND PO2 ...... 118 A6
Warfield Av WVILLE PO7 ...... 81 K6
Warfield Crs WVILLE PO7 ...... 81 K6
Warlock Cl ITCH SO19 ...... 73 G2 5
Warnford Cl GPORT PO12 ...... 132 C4 6
Warnford Crs HAV PO9 ...... 102 E1
Warren Av CHFD SO53 ...... 38 B5
ENEY PO4 ...... 19 M4
HSEA PO3 ...... 119 F3
ROWN SO16 ...... 54 C3
Warren Cl CHFD SO53 ...... 38 B5
HISD PO11 ...... 136 D4
ROWN SO16 ...... 54 B2
Warren Crs ROWN SO16 ...... 54 B2
Warren Pl TOTT SO40 ...... 52 B2
Warren Rd WINC SO23 ...... 3 K3
The Warren FAWY SO45 ...... 109 J2
Warrior Cl CHFD SO53 ...... 37 J6
Warrys Cl FAWY SO45 ...... 91 H6
Warsash Cl HAV PO9 ...... 83 F7 6
Warsash Gv
LSOL/BMARY PO13 ...... 115 K5 7
Warsash Rd FHAM/STUB PO14 ...... 95 K5
HLER SO31 ...... 94 C5
Warspite Cl NEND PO2 ...... 118 C3
Warton Cl BROC SO42 ...... 125 H2
Warwick Cl CHFD SO53 ...... 37 H6 4
LSOL/BMARY PO13 ...... 131 H4
Warwick Crs SSEA PO5 ...... 18 D6
Warwick Rd TOTT SO40 ...... 52 E4 1
WSHM SO15 ...... 54 E2
Wasdale Cl HORN PO8 ...... 64 D2
Washbrook Rd CHAM PO6 ...... 100 C6
Washington Rd EMRTH PO10 ...... 104 C5
NEND PO2 ...... 118 C7
Waterbeech Dr HEND SO30 ...... 58 B4 6
Waterberry Dr WVILLE PO7 ...... 81 H4
Waterhouse La WSHM SO15 ...... 54 C6 3
Waterhouse Wy WSHM SO15 ...... 54 C5
Water La FAWY SO45 ...... 91 F4
TOTT SO40 ...... 52 C4
WINC SO23 ...... 3 G4
Waterlock Gdns ENEY PO4 ...... 135 J4
Waterloo Cl HORN PO8 ...... 81 J2
Waterloo Rd GPORT PO12 ...... 133 F7
HAV PO9 ...... 14 F3
WSHM SO15 ...... 54 D6
Waterloo St SSEA PO5 ...... 18 D5
Waterloo Ter WSHM SO15 ...... 4 F7
Watermans La FAWY SO45 ...... 91 F5
Watermead Rd CHAM PO6 ...... 101 K7 1
Water's Edge HEND SO30 ...... 58 A6
Waters Edge Gdns
EMRTH PO10 ...... 104 C6
Watersedge Rd CHAM PO6 ...... 99 K6 2
Waterside FAWY SO45 ...... 91 G1
Waterside Gdns
FHAM/PORC PO16 ...... 98 A5 1
Waterside La
FHAM/PORC PO16 ...... 117 H1
Waterside Rd ROMY SO51 ...... 35 F1 4
Watersmeet
FHAM/PORC PO16 ...... 115 J1
The Waters WHAM PO17 ...... 97 F1
Waterworks Rd CHAM PO6 ...... 101 J6
RWIN SO21 ...... 33 F5
Watkin Rd HEND SO30 ...... 58 D2 1
Watley Cl ROWN SO16 ...... 41 J6
Watley La RWIN SO21 ...... 20 A3
Watson Wk TOTT SO40 ...... 52 B5 3
Watton Rd FAWY SO45 ...... 109 K4
Watts Cl ROWN SO16 ...... 53 K2
Watts Rd HEND SO30 ...... 58 B5
PSEA PO1 ...... 134 C1
Wavell Rd LSOL/BMARY PO13 ...... 116 A4
WEND SO18 ...... 7 G4
Wavell Wy WINW SO22 ...... 25 F3
Waveney Cl
LSOL/BMARY PO13 ...... 131 G2 9
Waveney Gn ROWN SO16 ...... 53 K3
Waverley Av HLER SO31 ...... 73 F7
Waverley Cl ROMY SO51 ...... 35 G1 6
Waverley Ct HLER SO31 ...... 93 F1 2
Waverley Gv ENEY PO4 ...... 134 D6 2
Waverley Rd CHAM PO6 ...... 101 H6
ENEY PO4 ...... 134 D6
SSEA PO5 ...... 19 G9
WSHM SO15 ...... 4 A6
Wayfarer Cl ENEY PO4 ...... 135 H3 4
HLER SO31 ...... 94 E5
Wayfarers LSOL/BMARY PO13 ...... 132 A1
Wayfarer's Wk HAV PO9 ...... 102 D4
WVILLE PO7 ...... 80 E5
Waylands Pl HEND SO30 ...... 73 K1
Waynflete Cl BPWT SO32 ...... 48 D3
Waynflete Pl WINW SO22 ...... 25 G2 2
Wayside HLER SO31 ...... 74 C5
Wayte St CHAM PO6 ...... 100 E7
Weald Cl HLER SO31 ...... 95 F2
Weardale Rd CHFD SO53 ...... 38 A6
Weavers Gn HAV PO9 ...... 15 L1
Weavers Pl CHFD SO53 ...... 37 J2
Weavills Rd ELGH SO50 ...... 45 K1
Webb Cl HISD PO11 ...... 137 H6
Webb La HISD PO11 ...... 137 H6
Webb Rd FHAM/PORC PO16 ...... 117 G1
Webburn Gdns WEND SO18 ...... 56 D1 3
Webster Rd WINW SO22 ...... 20 E6
Wedgewood Cl FAWY SO45 ...... 109 K3
FHAM/STUB PO14 ...... 114 D5 1
Wedgewood Wy WVILLE PO7 ...... 81 K3
Wedmore Cl WINW SO22 ...... 24 D5
Weeke Manor Cl WINW SO22 ...... 21 G5
Weevil La GPORT PO12 ...... 16 E2
Welbeck Av PTSW SO17 ...... 55 J2
Welch Rd ENEY PO4 ...... 134 D6
GPORT PO12 ...... 132 D1
Welch Wy ROWN SO16 ...... 41 K6
Welchwood Cl HORN PO8 ...... 64 A6
Welland Gdns WEND SO18 ...... 56 E2
Welland Gn ROWN SO16 ...... 53 K4
Wellands Rd LYND SO43 ...... 86 C1 3
Wellbrooke Gdns CHFD SO53 ...... 37 J3
Well Copse Cl HORN PO8 ...... 64 D3
Wellers Cl TOTT SO40 ...... 52 A5
Wellesley Cl WVILLE PO7 ...... 81 K6
Welles Rd CHFD SO53 ...... 38 A4
Well House La WINW SO22 ...... 21 H2
Wellington Av WEND SO18 ...... 7 K4
Wellington Cl FAWY SO45 ...... 90 E5
HORN PO8 ...... 64 E6
Wellington Gv
FHAM/PORC PO16 ...... 99 F7
Wellington Pk HEND SO30 ...... 57 K3
Wellington Rd WEND SO18 ...... 56 A2
Wellington St SSEA PO5 ...... 18 C5
Wellington Wy WVILLE PO7 ...... 81 K6 2
Well La BPWT SO32 ...... 49 J4
HLER SO31 ...... 93 K4
Well Meadow HAV PO9 ...... 83 F7
Wellowbrook Cl CHFD SO53 ...... 37 H4 2
Wellow Cl HAV PO9 ...... 14 B1
WEND SO18 ...... 7 L5
Wellow Gdns FHAM/STUB PO14 .. 95 H4
Wellsfield SELS PO20 ...... 139 K7
Wellsmoor FHAM/STUB PO14 ...... 95 H3
Wells Pl ELGH SO50 ...... 44 E1
Wellswood Gdns HAV PO9 ...... 83 K2
Wellsworth La HAV PO9 ...... 83 K2
Wembley Gv CHAM PO6 ...... 119 F1 1
Wendover Rd HAV PO9 ...... 14 C3
Wensley Gdns EMRTH PO10 ...... 104 C3
Wentworth Dr HORN PO8 ...... 64 C5
Wentworth Gdns
FAWY SO45 ...... 110 A5 1
ITCH SO19 ...... 11 J8
Wentworth Gra WINW SO22 ...... 2 B7
Wentworth Gv FAWY SO45 ...... 110 A4
Wesermarsch Rd HORN PO8 ...... 82 B1
Wesley Cl ITCH SO19 ...... 73 G1
Wesley Gv HSEA PO3 ...... 118 E4
Wessex Cl FAWY SO45 ...... 110 C6
Wessex Dr WINW SO22 ...... 21 H5
Wessex Gdns
FHAM/PORC PO16 ...... 98 E7
ROMY SO51 ...... 35 G3
Wessex La WEND SO18 ...... 44 A7
Wessex Rd HORN PO8 ...... 64 D1
Wessex Wy RWIN SO21 ...... 39 K2
West Bargate SHAM SO14 ...... 8 F2 1
West Battery Rd NEND PO2 ...... 118 A6
Westborn Rd FHAM/PORC PO16 .. 13 K5
Westbourne Av EMRTH PO10 ...... 104 D4
FAWY SO45 ...... 109 K3
Westbourne Cl EMRTH PO10 .. 104 D4 1
Westbourne Crs PTSW SO17 ...... 55 G3
Westbourne Rd EMRTH PO10 ...... 104 D3
NEND PO2 ...... 118 E7
Westbroke Gdns ROMY SO51 ...... 34 E1 3
Westbrook Cl HLER SO31 ...... 95 F1
Westbrooke Cl HORN PO8 ...... 64 B6
Westbrook Gv WVILLE PO7 ...... 101 J1
Westbrook Rd
FHAM/PORC PO16 ...... 117 G1
Westbrook Wy WEND SO18 ...... 44 B7 3
Westbury Cl CHAM PO6 ...... 100 A5 6
Westbury Ct HEND SO30 ...... 58 B7
Westbury Rd WSHM SO15 ...... 54 A5
Westcliff Cl LSOL/BMARY PO13 .. 131 F1
West Common FAWY SO45 ...... 128 A1
Westcot Rd FAWY SO45 ...... 109 J4 3
Westcroft Rd GPORT PO12 ...... 132 C3
West Downs Cl
FHAM/PORC PO16 ...... 97 H2
West Dr ELGH SO50 ...... 39 G6
West End Cl WINW SO22 ...... 2 B4
West End Rd HEND SO30 ...... 57 G3
HEND SO30 ...... 73 J1
Westend Rd WEND SO18 ...... 7 G5
West End Rd WEND SO18 ...... 7 H3
West End Ter WINW SO22 ...... 2 B4
Westerham Cl CHAM PO6 ...... 100 D6
Westering ROMY SO51 ...... 35 H1 7
ROMY SO51 ...... 35 H2 2
Westerley Cl HLER SO31 ...... 94 D5 3
Western Av EMRTH PO10 ...... 104 A6
Western District Cut
WSHM SO15 ...... 4 A5
Western Esp SHAM SO14 ...... 4 D9
Western Pde EMRTH PO10 ...... 104 B7
SSEA PO5 ...... 18 B8
Western Rd CHAM PO6 ...... 100 C7
CHFD SO53 ...... 38 B1
FHAM/PORC PO16 ...... 13 J6
WINW SO22 ...... 2 B3
HAV PO9 ...... 14 C3
HEND SO30 ...... 57 G3
Western Wy FHAM/PORC PO16 .. 13 H5
GPORT PO12 ...... 132 B5
Westfield Av FHAM/STUB PO14 .. 12 F8
HISD PO11 ...... 137 F5
Westfield Cl ELGH SO50 ...... 46 B4
HLER SO31 ...... 93 H4
Westfield Common
HLER SO31 ...... 93 G4 1
Westfield Crs CHFD SO53 ...... 37 K7
Westfield Rd CHFD SO53 ...... 37 K7
ENEY PO4 ...... 19 L7
WINW SO22 ...... 20 E2
GPORT PO12 ...... 132 C3
TOTT SO40 ...... 52 E4
WSHM SO15 ...... 54 B5
Westgate FHAM/STUB PO14 ...... 114 D6
Westgate St SHAM SO14 ...... 8 F4
West Haye Rd HISD PO11 ...... 138 A7
West Hill Dr FAWY SO45 ...... 91 G1
WINW SO22 ...... 2 A4
West Hill Pk WINW SO22 ...... 21 G7
West Hoe La BPWT SO32 ...... 49 G3
West Horton La ELGH SO50 ...... 45 J2
Westland Dr WVILLE PO7 ...... 101 K2
Westland Gdns GPORT PO12 ...... 132 D5
Westlands Gv
FHAM/PORC PO16 ...... 99 F7
West La HISD PO11 ...... 137 F3
NBAD SO52 ...... 35 K5
Westley Cl WINW SO22 ...... 21 G6
Westley Gv FHAM/STUB PO14 ...... 12 E7
Westman Rd WINW SO22 ...... 21 G5
West Marlands Rd SHAM SO14 ...... 4 F9
Westmead Cl HISD PO11 ...... 136 E5
Westminster Gdns
FHAM/STUB PO14 ...... 95 H3 6
Westminster Ga WINW SO22 ...... 24 E3
Westmorland Wy CHFD SO53 ...... 38 B5
Weston Av ENEY PO4 ...... 135 G4
Weston Cl ITCH SO19 ...... 10 E8
Weston Crs WEND SO18 ...... 7 L4
Weston Grove Rd ITCH SO19 ...... 10 A6
Weston La ITCH SO19 ...... 10 C9
ROWN SO16 ...... 41 F7
Weston Pde ITCH SO19 ...... 10 D9
Weston Rd ELGH SO50 ...... 38 D7
Westover Rd HSEA PO3 ...... 119 G7
ROWN SO16 ...... 53 G4
West Park Rd WSHM SO15 ...... 4 E9
West Quay Rd WSHM SO15 ...... 8 E3
Westridge Rd PTSW SO17 ...... 5 K2
West Rd EMRTH PO10 ...... 104 B6
FAWY SO45 ...... 90 E5
FAWY SO45 ...... 92 A5
HEND SO30 ...... 57 J6
ITCH SO19 ...... 10 C5
SHAM SO14 ...... 9 G5
WHAM PO17 ...... 79 K7
Westrow Gdns WSHM SO15 ...... 4 D4
Westrow Rd WSHM SO15 ...... 4 D4
West St EMRTH PO10 ...... 104 C6
FAWY SO45 ...... 91 G1
FHAM/PORC PO16 ...... 13 H6
FHAM/STUB PO14 ...... 96 A6
HAV PO9 ...... 14 B4
PSEA PO1 ...... 17 K7
SHAM SO14 ...... 8 F3
WHAM PO17 ...... 79 H7
WVILLE PO7 ...... 62 B3
Westview Rd WINW SO22 ...... 20 D5
Westward Rd HEND SO30 ...... 58 B4
Westway FHAM PO15 ...... 95 K3
Westway Cl ROWN SO16 ...... 41 J5
Westways CHAM PO6 ...... 102 A6
FHAM/STUB PO14 ...... 114 E5
Westways Cl ROWN SO16 ...... 41 J6 1
Westwood Cl EMRTH PO10 ...... 104 D3
Westwood Gdns CHFD SO53 ...... 38 B2
Westwood Rd HLER SO31 ...... 72 E6
LYND SO43 ...... 66 C7
NEND PO2 ...... 118 D3
PTSW SO17 ...... 5 G2
Wetherby Gdns TOTT SO40 ...... 52 B4
Weyhill Cl FHAM/PORC PO16 ...... 99 F5
HAV PO9 ...... 102 E1 5
Weymouth Av GPORT PO12 ...... 116 C7
Whaddon Cha
FHAM/STUB PO14 ...... 114 C5
Whaddon Ct HAV PO9 ...... 82 D7
Whale Island Wy NEND PO2 ...... 118 B6
Whalesmead Cl ELGH SO50 ...... 45 J2
Whalesmead Rd ELGH SO50 ...... 45 J2
Whaley Rd NEND PO2 ...... 118 A6
Wharf Hl WINC SO23 ...... 3 G7
Wharf Rd ITCH SO19 ...... 10 A4
NEND PO2 ...... 118 B7
Wharncliffe Rd ITCH SO19 ...... 10 A3
Whartons La TOTT SO40 ...... 68 B1
Wheat Cl NBAD SO52 ...... 37 G4
Wheatcroft Dr WEND SO18 ...... 56 E3 5
WEND SO18 ...... 7 K1 2
Wheatcroft Rd
LSOL/BMARY PO13 ...... 131 G2
Wheatland Cl WINW SO22 ...... 25 G3
Wheatlands FHAM/STUB PO14 ...... 95 H2
Wheatlands Av HISD PO11 ...... 138 B7
Wheatlands Crs HISD PO11 ...... 138 B7 1
Wheatsheaf Ct HEND SO30 ...... 58 A6 5
Wheatsheaf Dr HORN PO8 ...... 81 J2
Wheatstone Rd ENEY PO4 ...... 19 H8
Wheeler Cl GPORT PO12 ...... 16 A1
Wheelers Wk FAWY SO45 ...... 110 B7
Whernside Cl ROWN SO16 ...... 54 A4 3
Wherwell Ct HAV PO9 ...... 103 J1 19
Whichers Cl HAV PO9 ...... 83 J5
Whichers Gate Rd HAV PO9 ...... 83 J5
Whimbrel Cl ENEY PO4 ...... 135 H3
Whinchat Cl FHAM PO15 ...... 96 D2
ROWN SO16 ...... 42 C5
Whinfield Rd FAWY SO45 ...... 91 F5
Whippingham Cl CHAM PO6 ...... 100 C6
Whistler Cl ITCH SO19 ...... 11 L4
Whistler Rd ITCH SO19 ...... 11 L4
Whitcombe Cl TOTT SO40 ...... 52 D5 2
Whitcombe Gdns HSEA PO3 ...... 19 K2
Whitebeam Cl
FHAM/STUB PO14 ...... 12 C7
HORN PO8 ...... 64 D7 1
RWIN SO21 ...... 39 K2
Whitebeam Rd HEND SO30 ...... 58 C6
Whitebeam Wy NBAD SO52 ...... 36 B5
Whitechimney Rw
EMRTH PO10 ...... 104 E3
Whitecliffe Av HSEA PO3 ...... 135 F1
White Cloud Pk ENEY PO4 ...... 19 K8
Whitecross Gdns NEND PO2 ...... 118 E4
Whitedell La WHAM PO17 ...... 98 A2
White Dirt La HORN PO8 ...... 64 C2
Whitefield Rd FAWY SO45 ...... 109 K4
White Gates BPWT SO32 ...... 47 G6
White Hart La
FHAM/PORC PO16 ...... 98 E7
TOTT SO40 ...... 50 C4
White Hart Rd ELGH SO50 ...... 46 B2
GPORT PO12 ...... 16 B6 4
PSEA PO1 ...... 17 L7
Whitehaven FHAM/PORC PO16 .. 98 E7
HORN PO8 ...... 64 E6
White Heather Ct FAWY SO45 ...... 91 H1

Whitehill CI *WEND* SO18 .... 7 L4 🔟
White Horse La *WVILLE* PO7 ...... 63 F6
White House Gdns *WSHM* SO15 .. 54 B6
White La *RWIN* SO21 .... 15 C5
White Ladies CI *HAV* PO9 .... 33 K1
Whitelaw Rd *WSHM* SO15 .... 54 C5
Whiteley La *FHAM* PO15............. 75 J4
  FHAM PO15............................... 96 A2
  HLER SO31 .... 75 H4
Whiteley Wy *FHAM* PO15 .... 75 J7
Whitenap CI *ROMY* SO51 .... 35 G4
Whitenap La *ROMY* SO51 .... 35 H4
White Rd *ELGH* SO50.................. 39 C6
Whiteshute La *WINC* SO23.......... 25 H4
Whites La *FAWY* SO45 .... 110 E4 🔟
White's Rd *ITCH* SO19................ 7 H7
Whitestone CI *ROWN* SO16 ...... 54 A4 🔟
Whitethorn Rd *HISD* PO11 ...... 137 H5 🔟
Whitewater Ri *FAWY* SO45 .... 91 G4
Whithedwood Av *WSHM* SO15..... 4 A2
Withers La *BROC* SO42............... 125 H2
Whitley CI *EMRTH* PO10............. 104 E1
Whitley Rd *HORN* PO8................ 64 A6
Whitsbury Rd *HAV* PO9 .... 103 H1
Whitstable Rd *CHAM* PO6 .... 100 D6
Whittington CI *FAWY* SO45 .... 91 G4
Whittington Ct *EMRTH* PO10 ...... 104 C6
Whittle Av *FHAM* PO15............... 95 H1
Whitwell *HLER* SO31 .... 73 F6 🔟
Whitwell Rd *ENEY* PO4............... 134 D7
Whitworth CI *GPORT* PO12 .... 132 D4
Whitworth Crs *WEND* SO18.......... 6 B3
Whitworth Rd *GPORT* PO12 .... 132 D3
  NEND PO2 .... 118 E2
  WEND SO18 .... 6 B3
Whyte CI *FAWY* SO45 .... 109 J4
Whyteways *ELGH* SO50 .... 38 C6
The Wicket *FAWY* SO45.............. 91 G4
Wickham Rd *FHAM/PORC* PO16 ... 13 J1
  WHAM PO17 .... 97 J2
Wickham St *PSEA* PO1 .... 17 L3
Wicklow Dr *CHFD* SO53 .... 37 H5
Wickor CI *EMRTH* PO10 .... 104 D4
Wickor Wy *EMRTH* PO10 .... 104 C3
Wicor Mill La
  FHAM/PORC PO16 .... 116 E1
Wicor Pth *FHAM/PORC* PO16 ...... 117 H1
Widecombe Dr *FAWY* SO45 .... 91 F2
Wide La *ELGH* SO50.................... 44 C4
  WEND SO18 .... 44 B6
Widgeon CI *GPORT* PO12 .... 132 B1
  ROWN SO16 .... 42 C5
Widley Ct *FHAM/STUB* PO14 ...... 115 C1
Widley Court Dr *CHAM* PO6 .... 101 F7
Widley Gdns *WVILLE* PO7 .... 101 J3
Widley Rd *CHAM* PO6 .... 101 F6
  NEND PO2 .... 118 B5
Widley Wk *CHAM* PO6 .... 100 E4
Wield CI *HAV* PO9...................... 102 D2
Wigan Crs *HAV* PO9 .... 102 C4
Wilberforce CI *WINW* SO22 ...... 25 F2 🔟
Wilberforce Rd *GPORT* PO12 ... 133 F7 🔟
  SSEA PO5 .... 18 C7 🔟
Wild Arum Wy *NBAD* SO52.......... 37 G5
Wildburn CI *TOTT* SO40............. 52 B2
Wild Cherry Wy *NBAD* SO52 ...... 37 H4 🔟
Wilde CI *TOTT* SO40 .... 52 C5 🔟
Wildern CI *HLER* SO31 .... 94 E3 🔟
Wilderness Hts *WEND* SO18......... 7 M1
Wildern La *HEND* SO30 .... 58 A4
Wild Ridings *FHAM/STUB* PO14... 96 C6
Wild Rose Crs *HLER* SO31.......... 94 D4
Wilks CI *ROWN* SO16 .... 41 H6
Willersley CI *CHAM* PO6 .... 100 B5
William CI *FHAM/STUB* PO14 ...... 114 E6
William Macleod Wy
  ROWN SO16 .... 54 B4
William Price Gdns
  FHAM/PORC PO16 .... 13 J3
  LSOL/BMARY PO13 .... 132 A1
Williams CI *FAWY* SO45.............. 110 A4
Williams Rd *HSEA* PO3 .... 119 G4
William St *SHAM* SO14 .... 5 M8
Willis Av *NBAD* SO52 .... 36 C6
Willis Rd *GPORT* PO12 .... 16 D5
  PSEA PO1 .... 18 C3
  ROWN SO16 .... 44 A6
Willis Waye *WINC* SO23.............. 22 B2
Willow CI *HAV* PO9..................... 15 C5
  HEND SO30 .... 57 H2 🔟
  HEND SO30 .... 58 C6
Willow Ct *ROWN* SO16 .... 54 B1 🔟
Willowdene CI *HAV* PO9 .... 102 C2

Willow Dr *TOTT* SO40 .... 70 A5
Willow Gdns *EMRTH* PO10 .... 104 E2 🔟
  NBAD SO52 .... 36 A5
Willow Gn *RWIN* SO21 .... 39 K2
Willow Gv *ELGH* SO50 .... 46 C1
Willow Herb CI *HLER* SO31 .... 94 D4
Willow PI *GPORT* PO12 .... 16 B3
Willow Rd *BPWT* SO32 .... 49 F4
The Willows *WVILLE* PO7 .... 80 D1
Willow Tree Av *HORN* PO8.......... 82 C3
Willow Tree Gdns
  FHAM/STUB PO14........................ 12 C7
Willow Tree Wk *ITCH* SO19 .... 11 K3
Willow Wood Rd *HISD* PO11 .... 137 H5 🔟
Wills Wy *ROMY* SO51................. 35 F4
Wilmer Rd *ELGH* SO50................ 44 D1
Wilmington CI *WEND* SO18.......... 56 C1
Wilmot CI *ELGH* SO50................. 39 H5
Wilmott CI *GPORT* PO12 .... 132 C3
Wilmott La *GPORT* PO12 .... 132 C3
Wilson Gv *SSEA* PO5 .... 18 F7
Wilson Rd *NEND* PO2.................. 118 B5
Wilson St *SHAM* SO14 .... 5 L8
Wilton Av *WSHM* SO15 .... 4 D6
Wilton Crs *WSHM* SO15 .... 54 E3
Wilton Dr *HORN* PO8................... 64 B7
Wilton Gdns *WSHM* SO15 .... 54 E3
Wilton PI *SSEA* PO5 .... 18 D9
Wilton Rd *WSHM* SO15 .... 54 E3
Wilton Ter *SSEA* PO5 .... 18 E9 🔟
Wiltshire Rd *CHFD* SO53 .... 38 A7
Wiltshire St *SSEA* PO5 .... 18 B5
Wilverley Av *HAV* PO9 .... 103 H2
Wilverley PI *FAWY* SO45 .... 110 B6
Wimbledon Park Rd
  SSEA PO5 .... 134 C6 🔟
Wimborne Rd *ENEY* PO4............. 19 L6
Wimpole St *PSEA* PO1 .... 18 F2
Wimpson Gdns *ROWN* SO16 .... 54 A3
Wimpson La *ROWN* SO16 .... 53 K4
Wincanton Wy *WVILLE* PO7 .... 82 C4
Winchcombe Rd *CHAM* PO6 ...... 100 A5
Winchester By-pass *WINC* SO23... 22 C1
Winchester HI *ROMY* SO51 .... 35 G2
Winchester Rd *BPWT* SO32 .... 58 D1
  BPWT SO32 .... 61 F4
  CHFD SO53............................... 38 A4
  NEND PO2 .... 118 D7
  ROMY SO51 .... 35 F3
  ROMY SO51 .... 35 J1 🔟
  ROWN SO16 .... 54 B3
  RWIN SO21................................ 33 G2
  WHAM PO17 .... 61 G7
Winchester St *HEND* SO30 .... 59 F4
  WSHM SO15............................... 4 F7
Winchester Wy *TOTT* SO40 ..... 52 B5 🔟
Winchfield CI *WVILLE* PO7 .... 11 G9
Winchfield Crs *HAV* PO9.............. 102 D2
Windbury Rd *ROWN* SO16 .... 53 K2
Windermere Av
  FHAM/STUB PO14........................ 114 E3
  ROWN SO16 .... 53 J2
Windermere Gdns *TOTT* SO40..... 52 D4
Windermere Rd *NEND* PO2 .... 118 E4
  WEND SO18 .... 56 E3
Windfield Dr *ROMY* SO51 .... 35 G2 🔟
Windmill Copse *FAWY* SO45 ..... 91 G5 🔟
Windmill Fld *WVILLE* PO7 .... 81 F1
Windmill Gv *FHAM/PORC* PO16... 116 F1
Windmill La *HLER* SO31 .... 73 K3
Windover CI *ITCH* SO19............... 7 M6
Windrush Gdns *WVILLE* PO7 .... 81 J6
Windrush Rd *ROWN* SO16 .... 53 K3
Windrush Wy *FAWY* SO45 .... 91 H3
Windsor Ct *ELGH* SO50 .... 39 G6 🔟
Windsor Ga *ELGH* SO50.............. 38 D4
Windsor Rd *CHAM* PO6................ 100 E7
  FHAM/PORC PO16 .... 99 G7
  GPORT PO12 .... 132 D4
  WVILLE PO7 .... 81 J3
Winfield Wy *EMRTH* PO10 .... 104 C2 🔟
Winfrith Wy *ROWN* SO16 .... 41 J6
Wingate Dr *ITCH* SO19 .... 7 J9
Wingate Rd *TOTT* SO40.............. 52 C4
Wingfield St *PSEA* PO1 .... 134 C1
Wingrove Rd *TOTT* SO40 .... 68 B2 🔟
Winifred Rd *WVILLE* PO7 .... 81 K5
Winkfield Rw *HORN* PO8.............. 64 C7
Winkle St *SHAM* SO14 .... 8 F5
Winkton CI *HAV* PO9 .... 14 B1
Winnall CI *WINC* SO23 .... 3 K2
Winnall Manor Rd *WINC* SO23 ..... 3 K4
Winnall Valley Rd *WINC* SO23 ..... 3 J3
Winnards Pk *HLER* SO31 .... 94 C3

Winnham Dr *FHAM/PORC* PO16 ... 98 D6
Winnington *FHAM* PO15 .... 96 E2
Winn Rd *PTSW* SO17 .... 5 G2
Winscombe Av *HORN* PO8........... 82 B3
Winsford Av *ELGH* SO50 .... 45 K2
Winsford CI *ELGH* SO50 .... 45 K2 🔟
Winsford Gdns *ELGH* SO50 ...... 45 K2 🔟
Winslade Rd *WINW* SO22 .... 21 F3
  HAV PO9 .... 102 E1 🔟
Winsor CI *HISD* PO11.................. 138 A1
Winsor La *TOTT* SO40................. 51 G4
Winsor Rd *TOTT* SO40 .... 50 E5
  TOTT SO40 .... 53 F6
Winstanley Rd *NEND* PO2 .... 118 B6
  ROWN SO16 .... 41 H6
Winston Churchill Av *SSEA* PO5... 18 D5
Winston CI *ELGH* SO50 .... 38 D6
  HISD PO11 .... 137 F5
  ROWN SO16 .... 54 A2
Winstone Crs *NBAD* SO52........... 36 B7
Winterbourne Rd *CHAM* PO6 ...... 99 J5 🔟
  ROMY SO51 .... 35 H1 🔟
Winterhill Rd *CHAM* PO6 .... 100 C6
Winter Rd *ENEY* PO4.................. 19 L8
Winters CI *FAWY* SO45 .... 110 A4
Winters HI *BPWT* SO32 .... 47 K3
Winterslow Dr *HAV* PO9 .... 83 F7 🔟
Winters Rd *BPWT* SO32 .... 61 H4
Winton Rd *NEND* PO2.................. 118 E5
Winton St *SHAM* SO14 .... 5 H9 🔟
Wisborough Rd *SSEA* PO5 .... 18 F9
Wish PI *SSEA* PO5 .... 19 G9
Wisteria Gdns *HAV* PO9 .... 103 J2
Witchampton CI *HAV* PO9 .... 103 H1 🔟
Witham CI *CHFD* SO53 .... 37 H4
Witherbed La *FHAM* PO15 .... 95 J2
Withies Rd *LSOL/BMARY* PO13 .. 116 A7
Withy CI *ROMY* SO51 .... 34 E2 🔟
Wittering Rd *HISD* PO11.............. 138 C6
  ROWN SO16 .... 42 A6
Witt Rd *ELGH* SO50 .... 46 B1
Witts HI *WEND* SO18 .... 6 F1
Winton CI *WINW* SO22 .... 21 J5
Woburn CI *ELGH* SO50 .... 38 D4
Woburn Rd *ROWN* SO16 .... 42 C6
Wode CI *HORN* PO8.................... 64 D1
Wodehouse Rd *ITCH* SO19 .... 10 D2
Wolfe CI *WINW* SO22 .... 25 F3
Wolseley Rd *WSHM* SO15 .... 54 D5
Wolverley Ct *ROWN* SO16 .... 54 E1 🔟
Wolverton Rd *HAV* PO9 .... 103 F1
  SHAM SO14 .... 5 K8 🔟
Wolverton Wy *SHAM* SO14 .... 5 J8
Wolvesey PI *CHFD* SO53 .... 37 H6 🔟
Wonston Ct *HAV* PO9 .... 83 J7 🔟
Wonston Rd *ROWN* SO16 .... 42 C7
Wood Barn Rd *FHAM* PO15 .... 12 A5
Woodberry La *EMRTH* PO10 ...... 84 C6
  HAV PO9 .... 84 A4
Woodbourne CI *FHAM* PO15 .... 12 A6
Woodbury Av *HAV* PO9 .... 14 E7
Woodbury Gv *HORN* PO8............ 64 A7
Wood CI *ITCH* SO19 .... 11 M3
Woodcot Crs *HAV* PO9................ 83 H7
Woodcote La
  FHAM/STUB PO14........................ 115 H5
Woodcote Rd *PTSW* SO17 .... 55 K1 🔟
Woodcroft La *HORN* PO8............. 63 K7
Wood End Wy *NBAD* SO52 .... 37 H3
Wooden House La *LYMN* SO41 ... 124 A6
Woodfield Av *CHAM* PO6 .... 101 K5
Woodfield Dr *WINW* SO22 .... 24 E2
Woodfield Park Rd
  EMRTH PO10 .... 104 E5
Woodgason La *HISD* PO11 .... 121 K6
Wood Glade *TOTT* SO40 .... 70 A4
Woodgreen Av *HAV* PO9 .... 14 B2
Woodgreen Rd *WINW* SO22........ 21 G3
Woodhall Wy *FHAM* PO15 .... 12 D1
Woodhouse La *HAV* PO9 .... 83 K1
  HEND SO30 .... 58 D4
  HORN PO8 .... 65 H6
Woodhouse Rd *HORN* PO8.......... 65 G5
Woodington CI *HAV* PO9 .... 83 H7 🔟
Woodland CI *WEND* SO18............ 57 G5
Woodland Dro *RWIN* SO21.......... 33 K6
Woodland Ms *HEND* SO30 .... 57 G3
Woodlands *FHAM/PORC* PO16 .... 98 A4
Woodlands CI *CHFD* SO53 .... 32 A7
  FAWY SO45 .... 91 F5
  HLER SO31 .... 74 E7
  LSOL/BMARY PO13 .... 131 K4
Woodlands Ct *FAWY* SO45 ...... 91 F5 🔟

Woodlands Dr *HLER* SO31 .... 73 G7
Woodlands Dro *TOTT* SO40 .... 67 J2
Woodlands Gv *WVILLE* PO7 .... 101 J1
Woodlands La *HISD* PO11 .... 137 F3
  RCCH PO18 .... 85 H3
Woodlands Rd *TOTT* SO40 .... 67 H1
The Woodlands *WINC* SO23........ 22 B1
Woodlands St *PSEA* PO1 .... 19 J6
Woodlands Wy *HAV* PO9 .... 103 G2 🔟
  HLER SO31 .... 73 J5
  NBAD SO52 .... 35 K6
  WSHM SO15............................... 4 E2
Woodland Vw *HLER* SO31 .... 73 J5
  HORN PO8 .... 64 A6
Wood La *WHAM* PO17 .... 79 K6
Woodlea CI *WINW* SO22 .... 21 H5
Woodlea Gdns *HEND* SO30 .... 57 H3
Woodlea Wy *ROMY* SO51 .... 31 G7
Woodleigh CI *HAV* PO9 .... 103 K3
Woodley CI *ROMY* SO51 .... 29 H7
Woodley La *ROMY* SO51............. 35 F1
Woodley Rd *GPORT* PO12 .... 16 C6 🔟
  ITCH SO19 .... 11 H5
Woodley Wy *ROMY* SO51 .... 29 H7 🔟
Wood Ldg *TOTT* SO40 .... 52 A3
Woodman CI *RWIN* SO21............. 20 A5
Woodmancote La
  EMRTH PO10 .... 105 H2
Woodmancote Rd *ENEY* PO4 ...... 19 M6
Woodman La *RWIN* SO21 .... 20 B4
Woodman Rd *WEND* SO18 .... 56 A1
Woodmoor CI *TOTT* SO40 .... 70 B4 🔟
Woodpath *SSEA* PO5 .... 18 D8
Woodpecker CI *HAV* PO9 .... 15 A4
Woodpecker Copse *HLER* SO31 .. 95 C3
Woodpecker Dr *WINW* SO22 ...... 21 F5
  TOTT SO40 .... 69 K4
Wood Rd *TOTT* SO40 .... 68 A3
Woodrow *WVILLE* PO7 .... 80 D1
Woodrush Crs *HLER* SO31 .... 94 D4
Woodsedge *WVILLE* PO7............. 82 B7
Woodside *LSOL/BMARY* PO13 .... 115 J2
  ROWN SO16 .... 43 F1
Woodside Av *ELGH* SO50 .... 38 B7
Woodside CI *TOTT* SO40 .... 69 K4
Woodside Crs *ROWN* SO16 ...... 42 E1 🔟
Woodside Gdns *TOTT* SO40 .... 68 B3
Woodside Rd *ELGH* SO50 .... 38 B6
  NBAD SO52 .... 36 A6 🔟
  PTSW SO17 .... 5 K3
Woodstock Av *HORN* PO8........... 64 B7
Woodstock CI *FHAM* PO15 .... 12 C5
  HEND SO30 .... 58 C7 🔟
Woodstock Dr *PTSW* SO17 ...... 55 H3 🔟
Woodstock Rd *GPORT* PO12 ...... 16 C6
  HAV PO9 .... 102 D4
Woodthorpe Gdns *HLER* SO31 .... 74 E7
Woodvale *FHAM* PO15 .... 12 A4
Woodview CI *ROWN* SO16 .... 43 H5
Woodville Dr *PSEA* PO1 .... 18 A7
Woodville Rd *FAWY* SO45 .... 110 E4
  HAV PO9 .... 102 C4
Woodward CI *GPORT* PO12 .... 132 C4
Woofferton Rd *CHAM* PO6 .... 99 K5
Woolford CI *WINW* SO22 .... 25 F2
Woolmer Ct *HAV* PO9 .... 103 J1 🔟
Woolmer St *EMRTH* PO10 .... 104 B2
Woolner Av *CHAM* PO6................ 101 F6
Woolston Rd *HAV* PO9 .... 82 D7
  HLER SO31 .... 11 K9
Woolwich CI *HLER* SO31 .... 73 J3
Wootton Av *LSOL/BMARY* PO13 .. 131 H4
Wootton *HLER* SO31 .... 73 F6 🔟
Wootton St *CHAM* PO6 .... 100 E7
Worcester PI *ITCH* SO19 .... 11 J6
Wordsworth Av *CHAM* PO6 .... 99 H5
Wordsworth CI *BPWT* SO32 .... 49 F3
  WSHM SO15............................... 21 G7 🔟
Wordsworth PI *HLER* SO31 .... 75 C4
Wordsworth Rd *ROWN* SO16 ...... 54 D3
Workman's La *HLER* SO31 .... 112 D2
Workshop Rd *WVILLE* PO7 .... 99 K4
Worldham Rd *HAV* PO9 .... 83 J7
Worsley Rd *SSEA* PO5 .... 18 D8 🔟
Worsley St *ENEY* PO4 .... 135 F6 🔟
Worthing Av *GPORT* PO12 .... 116 C7
Worthing Rd *SSEA* PO5 .... 134 C6
Worthy Ct *HAV* PO9 .... 103 J1 🔟
Worthy La *WINC* SO23 .... 2 D1
Worthy Rd *WINC* SO23................ 21 K5
Wraysbury Park Dr
  EMRTH PO10 .... 104 C3

Wren CI *WINW* SO22 .... 25 G3
Wren Rd *ELGH* SO50................... 44 B2
Wren Wy *FHAM/PORC* PO16 ..... 98 C6 🔟
Wrexham Gv *HORN* PO8.............. 64 C2 🔟
Wright's HI *ITCH* SO19................ 11 G5
Wryneck CI *ROWN* SO16............. 42 C5
Wyborn CI *HISD* PO11 .... 137 H6
Wych La *LSOL/BMARY* PO13 ...... 115 J2
Wychwood Dr *FAWY* SO45 .... 128 B3
Wychwood Gv *CHFD* SO53.......... 38 B2
Wycote Rd *LSOL/BMARY* PO13 .. 115 J3
Wyeford CI *HAV* PO9 .... 83 J7 🔟
Wykeham CI *ROWN* SO16 .... 43 F7 🔟
Wykeham Fld *WHAM* PO17 .... 77 H2
Wykeham PI *WINW* SO22 .... 25 G3
Wykeham Rd *HLER* SO31 .... 72 E7
  NEND PO2 .... 118 D6
Wyllie Rd *NEND* PO2 .... 118 D3
Wylye CI *WEND* SO18 .... 56 E1
Wymering La *CHAM* PO6 .... 100 D6
Wymering Manor CI
  CHAM PO6 .... 100 D6 🔟
Wymering Rd *NEND* PO2 .... 118 D7
Wyndcliffe Rd *ENEY* PO4 .... 19 H8
Wyndham CI *HORN* PO8.............. 82 C1
Wyndham Ms *PSEA* PO1 .... 17 M7 🔟
Wyndham PI *WSHM* SO15 .... 4 D8
Wynter Rd *WEND* SO18 .... 7 J3
Wynton Wy *FHAM* PO15.............. 96 D3
Wynyards Gap *NBAD* SO52......... 36 A6
Wyre CI *CHFD* SO53.................... 37 J4
Wyvern CI *CHFD* SO53................ 38 A4

Y

Yaldhurst Ct *HAV* PO9 .... 83 J7 🔟
Yapton St *PSEA* PO1 .... 18 C3
Yarborough Rd *SSEA* PO5 .... 18 C8
Yardlea CI *HAV* PO9 .... 83 J4
Yardley CI *HSEA* PO3.................. 119 H3
Yardley Rd *HEND* SO30............... 58 A7
Yarmouth Gdns *WSHM* SO15....... 54 C3
Yarrow Wy *HLER* SO31 .... 94 D4
Yateley CI *HAV* PO9 .... 102 D1
Yaverland *HLER* SO31 .... 73 F7
Yelverton Av *FAWY* SO45 .... 91 H5
Yeo Ct *ENEY* PO4 .... 135 H5
Yeomans Wy *TOTT* SO40............ 52 E4
Yeovil Cha *WEND* SO18 .... 7 K3
Yew Rd *WEND* SO18 .... 7 H3
Yewside *LSOL/BMARY* PO13 .... 116 B6 🔟
The Yews *HORN* PO8................... 64 E5
Yewtree CI *FAWY* SO45............... 91 H6
Yew Tree Dr *FHAM* PO15 .... 75 H5
  HLER SO31 .... 75 G6
Yew Tree Gdns *WVILLE* PO7....... 80 D1
Yewtree La *ROWN* SO16 .... 53 H1
Yew Tree Rd *HISD* PO11............. 121 H7
Yoells Crs *HORN* PO8................. 64 A6
Yoells La *HORN* PO8................... 64 A6
Yokesford HI *ROMY* SO51 .... 28 D4
Yonge CI *ELGH* SO50 .... 38 E7
York Buildings *SHAM* SO14 .... 9 G2 🔟
York CI *ELGH* SO50..................... 46 C4
  NBAD SO52 .... 37 G6
  SHAM SO14 .... 5 M7
  TOTT SO40 .... 53 F4
York Crs *LSOL/BMARY* PO13 ...... 131 H4
York Dro *WEND* SO18 .... 7 J5
Yorke St *SSEA* PO5 .... 18 B6
Yorke Wy *HLER* SO31 .... 93 H3
York Gdns *FHAM/PORC* PO16 ..... 117 G1
York PI *PSEA* PO1 .... 18 A2
York Rd *ELGH* SO50.................... 44 D2
  WSHM SO15............................... 54 D5
Yves Ms *SSEA* PO5 .... 18 E9 🔟

Z

Zetland Rd *CHAM* PO6 .... 101 J7
  GPORT PO12 .... 16 A4
Zeus La *WVILLE* PO7................... 102 A3

Index - featured places

Abbey Chiropractic Clinic
  ROMY SO51 .... 34 D3
Abbey Mead Surgery
  ROMY SO51 .... 34 C3
Abbotswood Junior School
  TOTT SO40 .... 52 C5
Abraham Gallery
  SSEA PO5 .... 18 D8
Acorn Business Centre
  CHAM PO6 .... 100 D6
Admiral Lord Nelson School
  HSEA PO3 .... 119 G6
Albany Business Centre
  WHAM PO17 .... 77 J6
Alderman Quilley
  Secondary School
  ELGH SO50 .... 44 C2
Aldermoor Health Centre
  ROWN SO16 .... 42 D7
Allington Manor
  Business Centre
  ELGH SO50 .... 45 H4
All Saints Community
  Primary School
  WINC SO23 .... 3 H7
Alma Road Surgery
  PTSW SO17 .... 5 G2
Alma Road Surgery
  ROMY SO51 .... 34 E3

The Alpha Business Park
  SHAM SO14 .... 5 L5
Alverstoke C of E
  Junior School
  GPORT PO12 .... 132 D5
Alverstoke County
  Infant School
  GPORT PO12 .... 132 D6
A M F Bowling
  ITCH SO19 .... 7 G5
A M F Bowling
  PSEA PO1 .... 18 D3
Ampfield Primary School
  ROMY SO51 .... 30 D5
Anchor Business Centre
  CHFD SO53............................... 37 J4
Andover Road Retail Park
  WINW SO22 .... 2 C2
Anne Dale County
  Junior & Infant School
  FHAM/STUB PO14........................ 114 D5
Apple Industrial Estate
  FHAM PO15 .... 95 H1
Applemore College
  FAWY SO45 .... 90 D4
Applemore Recreation
  Centre
  FAWY SO45 .... 90 D3
The Art Gallery
  EMRTH PO10 .... 104 E2

Art Space School
  PSEA PO1 .... 134 B1
Arundel Court Junior &
  Infant School
  PSEA PO1 .... 18 E2
Ashurst Hospital
  TOTT SO40 .... 68 A4
Associated Football Club
  TOTT SO40 .... 53 F4
Atherley House Surgery
  WSHM SO15............................... 4 B6
The Atherley School
  ROWN SO16 .... 41 G5
Avington Park
  RWIN SO21................................ 23 K2
Baddesley Park
  Industrial Estate
  NBAD SO52 .... 36 C6
Badger Farm Surgery
  WINW SO22 .... 25 F4
Banister School
  WSHM SO15............................... 4 E5
Bargate Museum
  SHAM SO14 .... 9 G2
Bargate Shopping Centre
  SHAM SO14 .... 9 G2
Barncroft Infant School
  HAV PO9 .... 102 E2
Barncroft Junior School
  HAV PO9 .... 102 D2

Barratt Industrial Park
  FHAM PO15 .... 95 H1
Bartley C of E Middle School
  TOTT SO40 .... 50 E5
Barton Peveril College
  ELGH SO50 .... 44 C2
Bassett Green Junior School
  ROWN SO16 .... 43 J7
Baycroft School
  FHAM/STUB PO14........................ 114 E5
Bay House School
  GPORT PO12 .... 132 B6
BBC South TV & Radio Solent
  WSHM SO15............................... 4 E8
Beaulieu CP School
  BROC SO42............................... 108 A6
Bedenham County
  Junior & Infant School
  LSOL/BMARY PO13 .... 116 A4
Beechwood Middle School
  WEND SO18 .... 6 C1
Belbins Business Park
  ROMY SO51 .... 29 F6
Belgrave Industrial Estate
  PTSW SO17 .... 55 K2
Bellemoor Secondary School
  ROWN SO16 .... 54 C4
Berrywood Primary School
  HEND SO30 .... 58 D4

Bevois Town Primary School
  SHAM SO14 .... 5 H4
Bidbury Junior & Infant School
  HAV PO9 .... 14 A2
Bishops Waltham
  County Infant School
  BPWT SO32 .... 48 E3
Bitterne C of E First School
  ITCH SO19 .... 6 F6
Bitterne C of E Infant School
  ITCH SO19 .... 6 F6
Bitterne Health Centre
  WEND SO18 .... 7 H5
Bitterne Leisure Centre
  ITCH SO19 .... 7 G5
Bitterne Manor Primary School
  ITCH SO19 .... 6 B4
Bitterne Middle School
  ITCH SO19 .... 6 F6
Bitterne Park Clinic
  WEND SO18 .... 6 C2
Bitterne Park Junior &
  Infant School
  WEND SO18 .... 56 A2
Bitterne Park
  Secondary School
  WEND SO18 .... 56 B2
Bitterne Park Surgery
  WEND SO18 .... 6 C2

Blackbrook Business Park
FHAM PO15 .... 12 C5
Blackfield Health Centre
FAWY SO45 .... 110 A5
Blackfield Junior &
Infant School
FAWY SO45 .... 110 B6
The Boatyard
Industrial Estate
FHAM/PORC PO16 .... 13 H8
Bosmere Junior School
HAV PO9 .... 14 E5
Botley Junior & Infant School
HEND SO30 .... 59 F5
Botley Park Hotel &
Country Club
BPWT SO32 .... 58 E2
Boundary Oak School
WHAM PO17 .... 97 J1
The Bourne
Community College
EMRTH PO10 .... 105 F5
Boyatt Shopping Centre
ELGH SO50 .... 38 D5
Boyatt Wood Surgery
ELGH SO50 .... 38 C5
Braishfield CP School
ROMY SO51 .... 29 J3
Brickfield Trading Estate
CHFD SO53 .... 37 J5
Bridge Gallery
WSHM SO15 .... 4 F6
Bridgemary Community
School
LSOL/BMARY PO13 .... 115 K5
The Bridge Shopping Centre
PSEA PO1 .... 18 F3
Broadlands House
ROMY SO51 .... 34 D5
Brockhurst County
Infant School
GPORT PO12 .... 132 C1
Brockhurst County
Junior School
GPORT PO12 .... 132 D2
Brockhurst Medical Centre
GPORT PO12 .... 132 C1
Brompton Gallery
SHAM SO14 .... 5 H9
Brookes Hill Industrial Estate
TOTT SO40 .... 40 A7
Brookfield Secondary School
HLER SO31 .... 94 D2
Brookwood Industrial Estate
ELGH SO50 .... 38 C7
The Brownhill Surgery
CHFD SO53 .... 38 A3
Brune Park Community School
LSOL/BMARY PO13 .... 116 B7
Buckland Medical Centre
NEND PO2 .... 118 C7
Burgess Road Surgery
ROWN SO16 .... 43 K7
Burrfields Retail Park
HSEA PO3 .... 119 G6
Burridge Social & Sports Club
HLER SO31 .... 75 G3
Bursledon C of E
Junior & Infant School
HLER SO31 .... 73 K5
Bursledon Windmill Museum
HLER SO31 .... 73 K3
Business Centre
SHAM SO14 .... 9 J5
Byngs Business Park
WVILLE PO7 .... 81 G3
By Pass Football Club
ROMY SO51 .... 34 E4
Cadnam Surgery
TOTT SO40 .... 50 D5
Calmore County
Junior & Infant School
TOTT SO40 .... 52 B2
Calmore Industrial Estate
TOTT SO40 .... 52 D2
Calmore Sports Club
TOTT SO40 .... 51 K2
Calshot Castle
FAWY SO45 .... 112 A6
Cameleon Theatre
WSHM SO15 .... 4 A6
Campbell Surgery
SSEA PO5 .... 18 F7
Cams Hill School
FHAM/PORC PO16 .... 98 B6
Cantell Secondary School
ROWN SO16 .... 43 H7
The Canute Surgery
ITCH SO19 .... 10 C4
Castle County Primary School
FHAM/PORC PO16 .... 99 G7
Catherine Corbett Clinic
HAV PO9 .... 14 F3
Catherington C of E
Controlled Infant School
HORN PO8 .... 64 C3
The Cedar School
ROWN SO16 .... 41 K7
Central Trading Estate
SHAM SO14 .... 9 L1
Centurion Industrial Park
SHAM SO14 .... 5 L5
Chamberlayne Park School
ITCH SO19 .... 11 G8
Chandlers Ford Infant School
CHFD SO53 .... 38 A3
Chesil Theatre
WINC SO23 .... 3 G6
Chevron Business Park
FAWY SO45 .... 109 J1
Christchurch Medical Centre
HAV PO9 .... 103 K3
Churchill Yard
Industrial Estate
WVILLE PO7 .... 81 K4
City Business Centre
WINC SO23 .... 2 E2

City Grove Trading Estate
ELGH SO50 .... 38 B6
City Industrial Park
WSHM SO15 .... 8 C2
City Museum
PSEA PO1 .... 18 A7
City Museum & Art Gallery
PSEA PO1 .... 18 A7
City Offices
WINC SO23 .... 2 F5
The City of Portsmouth
Boys School
NEND PO2 .... 118 D3
The City of Portsmouth
Girls School
PSEA PO1 .... 19 G1
City of Portsmouth
Sports Club
NEND PO2 .... 118 C4
Civic Centre
SHAM SO14 .... 4 F9
Civic Centre
TOTT SO40 .... 53 F4
Civil Service Sports Ground
HSEA PO3 .... 119 F4
Clayfields Sports Centre
FAWY SO45 .... 90 E2
Cliffdale Primary School
NEND PO2 .... 118 E5
Cluster Industrial Estate
HSEA PO3 .... 19 L3
The Coast Clinic
FAWY SO45 .... 110 E4
Colden Common
Primary School
RWIN SO21 .... 39 J1
College Art School
WINC SO23 .... 2 D8
College Park Infant School
NEND PO2 .... 118 E5
Collingwood Business Park
FHAM/STUB PO14 .... 115 J1
Commercial Business Centre
CHFD SO53 .... 37 K4
Compton All Saints C of E
Primary School
RWIN SO21 .... 33 G1
Continental Ferry Port
NEND PO2 .... 118 B7
Copnor Infant School
HSEA PO3 .... 119 F6
Copnor Junior School
NEND PO2 .... 118 E6
Copythorne First School
TOTT SO40 .... 50 E2
Corpus Christi RC
Primary School
NEND PO2 .... 118 C6
Cosham Health Centre
CHAM PO6 .... 100 E7
Cottage Grove
Primary School
SSEA PO5 .... 18 D7
County and Magistrates
Court
PSEA PO1 .... 18 C5
Court Lane Junior &
Infant School
CHAM PO6 .... 101 F7
Cowplain School
HORN PO8 .... 81 K3
Craneswater Junior School
ENEY PO4 .... 19 H9
Crescent Primary School
ELGH SO50 .... 38 D7
The Crestwood
Community School
ELGH SO50 .... 38 C5
Crofton School
FHAM/STUB PO14 .... 115 F5
The Crookhorn
Community School
WVILLE PO7 .... 102 A2
Cumberland Business Centre
SSEA PO5 .... 18 F4
Cumberland Infant School
ENEY PO4 .... 19 L8
Cupernham County
Junior & Infants School
ROMY SO51 .... 35 G1
Curdridge Primary School
BPWT SO32 .... 59 J3
D Day Museum
SSEA PO5 .... 134 B7
Deacon Trading Estate
ELGH SO50 .... 45 F1
Deanery Campus
SHAM SO14 .... 9 J3
Dean Farm Estate
WHAM PO17 .... 97 H1
Delta Business Park
FHAM/PORC PO16 .... 97 J7
Denmead Health Centre
WVILLE PO7 .... 62 D7
Denmead Infant School
WVILLE PO7 .... 81 F1
Denmead Junior School
WVILLE PO7 .... 80 E1
Derby Road Surgery
NEND PO2 .... 118 C6
Devonshire Infant School
ENEY PO4 .... 19 H6
Devonshire Practice
ENEY PO4 .... 135 G5
Discover Bible School
WSHM SO15 .... 54 D6
Dockyard Apprentice
Exhibition
PSEA PO1 .... 17 K3
Dorset Healthcare NHS Trust
WEND SO18 .... 7 L4
Dorset Medical Centre
SHAM SO14 .... 5 G9
Dr Munroe & Partners
TOTT SO40 .... 52 E4
Durley Primary School
BPWT SO32 .... 47 F5

Eastern Industrial Centre
CHAM PO6 .... 119 H1
Eastleigh Borough Council
ELGH SO50 .... 38 C7
Eastleigh College of Further
Education
ELGH SO50 .... 44 D1
Eastleigh Football Club
ELGH SO50 .... 44 B4
Eastleigh Health Centre
ELGH SO50 .... 38 D7
Eastleigh Museum
ELGH SO50 .... 44 D1
Eastleigh Rugby Club
ELGH SO50 .... 39 F7
Eastney Health Centre
ENEY PO4 .... 19 M8
Eastney Swimming Baths
ENEY PO4 .... 135 H6
Easton Lane Business Park
WINC SO23 .... 3 J3
East Shore School
HSEA PO3 .... 135 G2
East Street Shopping Centre
SHAM SO14 .... 9 H2
Eling County Infant School
TOTT SO40 .... 53 F6
Elmhurst Business Park
GPORT PO12 .... 16 B5
Elson County Infant School
GPORT PO12 .... 116 D7
Elson County Junior School
GPORT PO12 .... 116 D7
Emsworth Museum
EMRTH PO10 .... 104 C5
Emsworth Primary School
EMRTH PO10 .... 104 B5
Emsworth Surgery
EMRTH PO10 .... 104 C5
English Gallery
HAV PO9 .... 83 K3
Enterprise Industrial Estate
HORN PO8 .... 64 D4
Fairfield Infant School
HAV PO9 .... 15 G4
Fairisle Junior &
Infant School
ROWN SO16 .... 41 K7
Fairlands Montessori
School
BPWT SO32 .... 61 F5
Fair Oak Junior &
Infant School
ELGH SO50 .... 46 C2
Fairway Business Centre
HSEA PO3 .... 119 H4
Fareham Borough Council
FHAM PO15 .... 95 J1
Fareham Borough Council
FHAM/PORC PO16 .... 13 K5
Fareham Borough Council
FHAM/PORC PO16 .... 98 D7
Fareham College
FHAM/STUB PO14 .... 12 D6
The Fareham Gallery
FHAM/PORC PO16 .... 13 J6
Fareham Leisure Centre
FHAM/PORC PO16 .... 13 H4
Fareham Megabowl
FHAM/STUB PO14 .... 115 J2
Fareham Park C of E
Controlled Junior School
FHAM PO15 .... 96 D3
Fareham Park Infant School
FHAM PO15 .... 96 D3
Fawley Business Centre
FAWY SO45 .... 110 D4
Fawley County First School
FAWY SO45 .... 110 D4
Fenwick Hospital
LYND SO43 .... 66 B7
Fernhurst Junior School
ENEY PO4 .... 19 J4
Flanders Industrial Park
HEND SO30 .... 58 A4
Fleming Park Leisure Centre
ELGH SO50 .... 38 B7
Flying Bull Junior &
Infant School
NEND PO2 .... 118 C7
Forest Edge School
TOTT SO40 .... 52 D5
Forest End Surgery
WVILLE PO7 .... 81 J6
Forest Gate Surgery
TOTT SO40 .... 52 B5
Forestside Medical Practice
FAWY SO45 .... 91 F6
Fort Brockhurst
LSOL/BMARY PO13 .... 116 C6
Fort Cumberland
ENEY PO4 .... 135 K5
Forton Road Surgery
GPORT PO12 .... 16 A2
Fort Wallington
Industrial Estate
FHAM/PORC PO16 .... 98 A4
Foundry Lane
Middle & Primary School
WSHM SO15 .... 54 C4
Foxhills County First School
TOTT SO40 .... 68 C1
Freeground Junior &
Infant School
HEND SO30 .... 58 C6
Freemantle Business Centre
WSHM SO15 .... 54 D7
Friarsgate Medical Centre
WINC SO23 .... 2 F5
Frobisher Industrial Centre
ROMY SO51 .... 34 C1
Front Lawn GM Junior School
HAV PO9 .... 83 G7
Front Lawn Infant School
HAV PO9 .... 103 G1
Fryern Junior &
Infant School
CHFD SO53 .... 38 B4

The Fryern Surgery
CHFD SO53 .... 38 B3
The Futcher School
CHAM PO6 .... 101 H6
The Gallery
SSEA PO5 .... 18 D9
Gasholders
SHAM SO14 .... 5 K9
Gatcombe Park Infant School
NEND PO2 .... 118 E3
George & Dragon Surgery
EMRTH PO10 .... 104 E3
George Street School
Branch Clinic
PSEA PO1 .... 134 E1
Glenfield Infant School
WEND SO18 .... 6 F4
Glenhurst School
HAV PO9 .... 15 G4
Glenwood School
EMRTH PO10 .... 104 B5
Goldfield Gallery
PSEA PO1 .... 17 M7
Goldsmith Infant School
ENEY PO4 .... 19 H7
Gomer County Junior &
Infant School
GPORT PO12 .... 132 B5
Goodway Sea School
GPORT PO12 .... 116 D7
Goodwyn Gallery
PSEA PO1 .... 19 G3
Gosport Health Centre
GPORT PO12 .... 132 D4
Gosport Ice Rink
LSOL/BMARY PO13 .... 116 B6
Gosport Museum
GPORT PO12 .... 16 F5
Gosport War Memorial
Hospital
GPORT PO12 .... 132 D4
Grange County Junior &
Infant School
LSOL/BMARY PO13 .... 131 K1
Grange Farm Business Park
BPWT SO32 .... 60 D4
Gravaton Business Centre
BPWT SO32 .... 48 C3
Greatbridge Business Park
ROMY SO51 .... 34 C1
Greenacres School
WINW SO22 .... 21 H5
The Gregg School
WEND SO18 .... 56 D1
Greggs School
PTSW SO17 .... 5 G1
Grey Welles Surgery
HAV PO9 .... 103 G2
Group Surgery
ROWN SO16 .... 44 A7
Grove Medical Practice
WSHM SO15 .... 54 D5
Gudge Heath Surgery
FHAM PO15 .... 12 B2
Gurdwara Sikh Temple
SHAM SO14 .... 5 H6
Hall of Aviation
SHAM SO14 .... 9 K4
Halterworth CP School
ROMY SO51 .... 35 H3
Hamble County
Primary School
HLER SO31 .... 93 H2
Hamble County
Secondary School
HLER SO31 .... 93 H1
Hambledon Infant School
WVILLE PO7 .... 62 C1
Hammond County
Junior & Infant School
FHAM/STUB PO14 .... 114 D5
Hammond Industrial Estate
FHAM/STUB PO14 .... 114 E6
Hampshire County Council
ELGH SO50 .... 38 B7
Hampshire County Council
ELGH SO50 .... 38 E7
Hampshire County Council
FHAM/PORC PO16 .... 13 K5
Hampshire County Council
GPORT PO12 .... 16 C6
Hampshire County Council
HAV PO9 .... 15 G5
Hampshire County Council
TOTT SO40 .... 68 E1
Hampshire County Council
WINC SO23 .... 2 C4
Hampshire
County Cricket Club
WSHM SO15 .... 4 E3
Hamwic College
SHAM SO14 .... 9 H2
Hanway Group Practice
NEND PO2 .... 118 D6
Hanway Surgery
PSEA PO1 .... 134 C1
Hardley School
FAWY SO45 .... 109 K2
Harefield Clinic
WEND SO18 .... 7 H5
Harefield Junior &
Infant School
WEND SO18 .... 7 K3
Harestock Infant School
WINW SO22 .... 21 G4
Harrison County
Primary School
FHAM/PORC PO16 .... 13 K4
Hart Plain Infant School
HORN PO8 .... 81 K3
Hart Plain Junior School
WVILLE PO7 .... 81 K3
Haselworth County
Primary School
GPORT PO12 .... 16 B7
Havant Business Centre
HAV PO9 .... 14 A6

Havant College
HAV PO9 .... 14 D1
Havant Leisure Centre
HAV PO9 .... 14 E2
Havant Museum
HAV PO9 .... 14 F5
Havant Retail Park
HAV PO9 .... 102 C5
Havant Rugby Football Club
HAV PO9 .... 14 A2
Havant Sports Club
HAV PO9 .... 14 E3
Havant Town Football Club
HAV PO9 .... 103 H1
Havant War
Memorial Hospital
HAV PO9 .... 14 D3
Hayling Billy Business Centre
HISD PO11 .... 136 E4
Hayling Island Health Centre
HISD PO11 .... 137 H5
Hayward Business Centre
HAV PO9 .... 103 J3
Hazel Wood 1st School
TOTT SO40 .... 52 B5
Heathfield Infant &
Middle School
ITCH SO19 .... 11 M4
Heathfield School
FHAM/STUB PO14 .... 96 D6
Hedge End Business Centre
HEND SO30 .... 58 A4
Hedge End Retail Park
HEND SO30 .... 57 K5
Hedge End Town Council
HEND SO30 .... 58 A6
Henry Beaufort School
WINW SO22 .... 21 H4
Henry Cort
Community School
FHAM PO15 .... 96 C3
The Heritage Centre &
Museum
TOTT SO40 .... 53 G6
Highbury College
CHAM PO6 .... 119 F2
Highbury College
PSEA PO1 .... 18 D3
Highbury College of
Technology
PSEA PO1 .... 18 B1
Highbury Primary School
CHAM PO6 .... 119 F1
Highcroft Industrial Estate
HORN PO8 .... 64 D4
Highfield C of E (a)
Primary School
PTSW SO17 .... 55 H2
Highgrove Industrial Park
HSEA PO3 .... 119 G4
Highlands Medical Centre
FHAM PO15 .... 12 A2
Highlands Medical Centre
FHAM PO15 .... 96 D3
Hightown Primary School
ITCH SO19 .... 73 H1
Hill Lane Surgery
WSHM SO15 .... 4 C5
Hill Park Clinic
FHAM PO15 .... 12 D1
Hillside Industrial Estate
HORN PO8 .... 64 D4
Hiltingbury County
Junior & Infant School
CHFD SO53 .... 37 K1
Hindu Temple
SHAM SO14 .... 5 K7
Hiscock Gallery
SSEA PO5 .... 18 D9
Holbrook County
Junior & Infant School
LSOL/BMARY PO13 .... 115 K4
Holbrook Recreation Centre
LSOL/BMARY PO13 .... 116 B6
Holbury County JMI School
FAWY SO45 .... 109 K4
Hollybrook First School
ROWN SO16 .... 54 E1
Hollybrook Middle School
ROWN SO16 .... 54 E1
Holy Family RC
Primary School
ROWN SO16 .... 53 H2
Homewood Chiropractic
Health Centre
FHAM/PORC PO16 .... 13 K4
Hook with Warsash
Primary School
HLER SO31 .... 94 C6
Horndean C of E Junior School
HORN PO8 .... 64 D5
Horndean Community School
HORN PO8 .... 64 C5
Horndean Football Club
HORN PO8 .... 64 C5
Horndean Health Centre
HORN PO8 .... 64 E5
Horndean Infant School
HORN PO8 .... 64 D5
Housndown School
TOTT SO40 .... 68 E1
Hovercraft Terminal
SSEA PO5 .... 133 K6
Hulbert Junior School
WVILLE PO7 .... 82 A7
Hythe CP School
FAWY SO45 .... 91 H2
Hythe Medical Centre
FAWY SO45 .... 91 G4
Isambard Brunel
Junior School
NEND PO2 .... 118 D7
Isle of Wight
Car Ferry Terminal
PSEA PO1 .... 17 L6
Itchen College
ITCH SO19 .... 7 H8

J M L Trading Estate
WSHM SO15 .... 4 C9
Jubilee Business Centre
WVILLE PO7 .... 81 K5
Jubilee Surgery
FHAM/STUB PO14 .... 96 A6
Just Ahead Business School
PSEA PO1 .... 18 D1
Kanes Hill Primary School
ITCH SO19 .... 57 H6
Keble Memorial
Primary School
RWIN SO21 .... 31 J3
King Alfred's College
WINW SO22 .... 21 G7
King Alfreds College of
Higher Education
WINW SO22 .... 2 A6
King Edward VI School
WSHM SO15 .... 4 C7
King Richard School
CHAM PO6 .... 99 J2
Kings Copse Primary School
HEND SO30 .... 58 D7
Kingsland Market
SHAM SO14 .... 9 H1
The Kings Primary School
HEND SO30 .... 57 G1
Kings School
ELGH SO50 .... 46 A2
Kings School
WINW SO22 .... 24 E2
Kings Theatre
SSEA PO5 .... 18 F8
Kingsworthy Primary School
WINC SO23 .... 22 B1
Kin Hon Clinic
SSEA PO5 .... 18 B5
Knightwood Primary School
NBAD SO52 .... 37 G3
Lacey Lodge School
HSEA PO3 .... 135 G2
Langdown County
Infants School
FAWY SO45 .... 91 J4
Langdown County
Junior School
FAWY SO45 .... 91 J3
Langstone Junior School
HSEA PO3 .... 135 F1
Lankhills School
WINC SO23 .... 2 D1
Lee on Solent Health Centre
LSOL/BMARY PO13 .... 131 F2
Lee-on-the-solent
Infant School
LSOL/BMARY PO13 .... 131 G3
Lee-on-the-solent
Junior School
LSOL/BMARY PO13 .... 131 G3
Leesland C of E
Infant School
GPORT PO12 .... 16 A5
Leesland C of E
Junior School
GPORT PO12 .... 16 A5
Leigh House Hospital
CHFD SO53 .... 37 J2
Lido Sports Club
WINC SO23 .... 2 E2
Liner Industrial Estate
WSHM SO15 .... 54 D6
Locksheath County
Infants & Primary School
HLER SO31 .... 95 F5
Locks Road Surgery
HLER SO31 .... 95 F4
Lockswood Surgery
HLER SO31 .... 95 F3
Longbridge Industrial Park
SHAM SO14 .... 9 K4
Longdown Estates
TOTT SO40 .... 68 D5
Lordshill Health Centre
ROWN SO16 .... 42 A7
LSU College of
Higher Education
WSHM SO15 .... 4 F5
Lucia Foster Welch College
SHAM SO14 .... 9 J4
Ludlow Infant School
ITCH SO19 .... 10 C3
Ludlow Middle School
ITCH SO19 .... 10 D2
Lulworth Business Centre
TOTT SO40 .... 52 D2
Lydlynch County First School
TOTT SO40 .... 52 D5
Lyndhurst Infant School
LYND SO43 .... 86 C1
Lyndhurst Junior School
NEND PO2 .... 118 E6
Lyndhurst Surgery
LYND SO43 .... 86 C1
Malvern Business Centre
ROWN SO16 .... 54 E2
Manor Infant School
FAWY SO45 .... 109 K2
Manor Infant School
PSEA PO1 .... 134 D1
Mansbridge Primary School
WEND SO18 .... 44 B7
Mansel Infant &
Junior Schools
ROWN SO16 .... 53 J2
Marchwood C of E
Infant School
TOTT SO40 .... 69 K5
Marchwood Junior School
TOTT SO40 .... 70 A4
Marchwood Priory Hospital
TOTT SO40 .... 70 B6
Maritime Museum
BROC SO42 .... 126 E4
Marlands Shopping Centre
SHAM SO14 .... 8 F1

Marycourt Co-educational
School
GPORT PO12 .... 132 D7
Mary Rose Exhibition
PSEA PO1 .... 17 K3
Mary Rose Ship Hall
PSEA PO1 .... 17 K2
Mason Manor Primary School
ROWN SO16 .... 54 A4
Mayflower Theatre
WSHM SO15 .... 4 D8
Mayville High School
SSEA PO5 .... 134 D6
Meadowlands Infant School
HORN PO8 .... 63 K7
Meadowlands Junior School
HORN PO8 .... 63 K7
Medina Primary School
CHAM PO6 .... 100 D7
Mengham Infant School
HISD PO11 .... 137 H4
Mengham Junior School
HISD PO11 .... 137 H4
Meoncross School
FHAM/STUB PO14 .... 114 E3
Meon Infant School
ENEY PO4 .... 135 G4
Meon Junior School
ENEY PO4 .... 135 G3
Meon Valley Golf &
Country Club
BPWT SO32 .... 60 E4
Meon Valley Police Station
BPWT SO32 .... 48 E3
Merdon Junior School
CHFD SO53 .... 38 A3
Meredith Infant School
NEND PO2 .... 118 D7
Meridian TV Studios
SHAM SO14 .... 5 L6
Middle Park Medical Centre
HAV PO9 .... 102 D2
Millbrook Clinic
ROWN SO16 .... 53 K4
Millbrook Community School
ROWN SO16 .... 53 K1
Millbrook Secondary School
ROWN SO16 .... 53 K1
Millbrook Trading Estate
WSHM SO15 .... 53 K5
Millers Dale Surgery
CHFD SO53 .... 37 J2
Millhouse Business Centre
ITCH SO19 .... 10 A1
Milton Park Infant School
ENEY PO4 .... 135 G4
Milton Park Junior School
ENEY PO4 .... 135 G4
Monks Brook Industrial Park
CHFD SO53 .... 37 J5
Moorgreen Hospital
HEND SO30 .... 57 J2
Moorings Way Infant School
ENEY PO4 .... 135 H2
Moorlands Infant School
WEND SO18 .... 7 J1
Morelands Primary School
WVILLE PO7 .... 101 K4
Mountbatten
Business Centre
WSHM SO15 .... 4 B8
Mountbatten
Secondary School
ROMY SO51 .... 35 H4
The Mount Hospital
ELGH SO50 .... 39 G5
Mount Pleasant
Industrial Estate
SHAM SO14 .... 5 K5
Mount Pleasant
Junior School
SHAM SO14 .... 5 J5
National Motor Museum
BROC SO42 .... 108 A5
National Museum of Artillery
WHAM PO17 .... 98 E3
Natural Sciences Museum
ENEY PO4 .... 134 E7
Nelson Industrial Park
HEND SO30 .... 58 A3
Nethercliffe School
WINW SO22 .... 2 B2
Netley Abbey Infant School
HLER SO31 .... 72 E6
Netley Court School
HLER SO31 .... 92 E1
Netley Marsh C of E
Controlled Infant School
TOTT SO40 .... 51 K5
Neville Lovett
Community School
FHAM/STUB PO14 .... 12 E8
Newbridge Junior School
NEND PO2 .... 134 E1
New Forest Golf Club
LYND SO43 .... 66 E7
New Forest Museum &
Visitors Centre
LYND SO43 .... 86 D1
Newlands Infant &
Middle School
ROWN SO16 .... 53 K3
New Theatre Royal
PSEA PO1 .... 18 B4
The Newton Health Clinic
SHAM SO14 .... 5 H6
Nightingale County
Junior & Infant School
ELGH SO50 .... 44 A2
Nightingale Surgery
ROMY SO51 .... 35 F2
Northam Business Centre
SHAM SO14 .... 5 L6
Northam Primary School
SHAM SO14 .... 5 L8
North Baddesley
County Infants School
NBAD SO52 .... 36 C6

North Baddesley
Junior School
NBAD SO52 .... 36 C6
Northbrook Industrial
Estate
ROWN SO16 .... 54 D2
Northern County
Junior & Infant School
FHAM/PORC PO16 .... 99 F5
Northern Parade Clinic
NEND PO2 .... 118 D3
Northern Parade
Infant School
NEND PO2 .... 118 D4
Northern Parade
Junior School
NEND PO2 .... 118 D4
Northview Gallery
HLER SO31 .... 74 B5
Norwood CP School
ELGH SO50 .... 38 D7
Nuffield Theatre
PTSW SO17 .... 55 H1
Nursling C of E
Primary School
ROWN SO16 .... 41 J6
Nursling Industrial Estate
ROWN SO16 .... 41 J6
Nursling Industrial Estate
ROWN SO16 .... 53 G1
Oakfield Primary School
TOTT SO32 .... 52 D4
Oaklands Community School
ROWN SO16 .... 42 A6
Oaklands RC School
WVILLE PO7 .... 102 A1
Oak Lodge School
FAWY SO45 .... 90 D3
Oakwood First School
ROWN SO16 .... 42 C6
Oakwood Junior School
ROWN SO16 .... 42 C6
Oatlands House Health Clinic
ROWN SO16 .... 54 D2
Oceanographic Centre
SHAM SO14 .... 9 K6
Odeon Cinema
NEND PO2 .... 118 C6
Odeon Cinema
WSHM SO15 .... 8 D2
Oil Refinery
FAWY SO45 .... 110 C3
O Jays Industrial Park
HSEA PO3 .... 119 F5
Old Anchor Inn Surgery
ELGH SO50 .... 39 F7
Oldfield Gallery
SSEA PO5 .... 18 D7
The Old Fire Station Surgery
ITCH SO19 .... 10 D5
Olivers Battery
Primary School
WINW SO22 .... 25 F5
On Line Gallery
WSHM SO15 .... 4 F7
Orchard County
Infant & Junior School
FAWY SO45 .... 91 F4
Orchard Lea Junior &
Infant Schools
FHAM PO15 .... 97 F2
Orion Business Centre
WEND SO18 .... 44 B6
The Osborn Clinic
FHAM/PORC PO16 .... 13 L5
Osborne Practice Surgery
SSEA PO5 .... 18 C9
Otterbourne Primary School
RWIN SO21 .... 32 E7
Padnell Infant School
HORN PO8 .... 82 B3
Padnell Junior School
HORN PO8 .... 82 C2
Palace House
BROC SO42 .... 107 K6
Palmerston Business Park
FHAM/STUB PO14 .... 97 H7
Park Community School
HAV PO9 .... 102 D1
Park Gate Business Centre
HLER SO31 .... 75 G7
Park Gate Junior School
HLER SO31 .... 95 G1
Park House Primary School
HAV PO9 .... 102 D1
Parklands Business Park
WVILLE PO7 .... 80 E2
Park Lane Medical Centre
HAV PO9 .... 102 E3
The Pascoe Practice
PSEA PO1 .... 18 A6
Paulsgrove Industrial Centre
CHAM PO6 .... 100 A6
Paulsgrove Primary School
CHAM PO6 .... 100 A6
Peacock Trading Estate
ELGH SO50 .... 38 B6
Peacock Trading Estate
ELGH SO50 .... 38 C5
Peel Common County
Junior & Infant School
LSOL/BMARY PO13 .... 115 H5
Pegham Industrial Park
FHAM PO15 .... 76 C7
Penhale Infant School
PSEA PO1 .... 19 H3
Peter Dyer Gallery
SSEA PO5 .... 18 D9
Peter Dyer Gallery
SSEA PO5 .... 134 B6
Peter Symonds College
WINW SO22 .... 2 C1
Phoenix Industrial Park
ELGH SO50 .... 45 F1
Pilgrims School
WINC SO23 .... 2 F6
Pipers Wood Industrial Park
WVILLE PO7 .... 81 H5

Pitmore School
CHFD SO53 .... 38 C2
Plaza Theatre
ROMY SO51 .... 34 E3
Police Station & Courts
SHAM SO14 .... 4 F8
The Polygon School
WSHM SO15 .... 4 D7
Portchester Castle
FHAM/PORC PO16 .... 117 H2
Portchester
Community School
FHAM/PORC PO16 .... 99 F7
Portchester Health Centre
FHAM/PORC PO16 .... 99 F6
Portsdown Group Practice
WVILLE PO7 .... 101 K3
Portsmouth City Council
CHAM PO6 .... 100 A5
Portsmouth City Council
CHAM PO6 .... 100 D7
Portsmouth City Council
CHAM PO6 .... 100 E6
Portsmouth City Council
HAV PO9 .... 103 G2
Portsmouth City Council
PSEA PO1 .... 17 M7
Portsmouth City Council
PSEA PO1 .... 19 C1
Portsmouth City Council
PSEA PO1 .... 134 D1
Portsmouth City Council
SSEA PO5 .... 18 C8
Portsmouth City Council
SSEA PO5 .... 18 D4
Portsmouth City Council
SSEA PO5 .... 18 E7
Portsmouth County Court
PSEA PO1 .... 18 C4
Portsmouth Crown Court
PSEA PO1 .... 18 C5
Portsmouth Grammar School
PSEA PO1 .... 18 A6
Portsmouth High School
SSEA PO5 .... 18 B8
Portsmouth Natural
Health Centre
SSEA PO5 .... 18 B6
Portsmouth Rugby
Football Club
HSEA PO3 .... 119 F3
Portsmouth Sixth
Form College
HSEA PO3 .... 135 H1
Portswood Primary School
PTSW SO17 .... 55 K2
The Practice
Doctors Surgery
FHAM/PORC PO16 .... 13 H5
Premier Business Park
FHAM/STUB PO14 .... 12 C7
Princes Mead School
RWIN SO21 .... 22 D1
Princess Anne Hospital
ROWN SO16 .... 54 C1
Priory School
SSEA PO5 .... 19 G5
Purbrook Cricket Club
WVILLE PO7 .... 101 G2
Purbrook Junior &
Infant School
WVILLE PO7 .... 101 J1
Purbrook Park School
WVILLE PO7 .... 101 J3
Queen Alexandra Hospital
CHAM PO6 .... 100 D5
Queens Enclosure
Primary School
WVILLE PO7 .... 82 B4
Queens Road Surgery
NEND PO2 .... 118 D7
Rachel Madocks School
HORN PO8 .... 81 J1
Ranvilles Junior &
Infant School
FHAM/STUB PO14 .... 96 D6
Red Barn County
Primary School
FHAM/PORC PO16 .... 98 E6
Redbridge Community School
ROWN SO16 .... 53 J4
Redbridge Primary School
ROWN SO16 .... 53 J4
Red Funnel Ferry Terminal
SHAM SO14 .... 8 F5
Red Gallery
SSEA PO5 .... 18 E9
Redlands County
Primary School
FHAM/PORC PO16 .... 13 H9
Red Lodge School
ROWN SO16 .... 43 F7
Redwood Park School
CHAM PO6 .... 119 G1
Regents Park Girls School
ROWN SO16 .... 54 B4
Regents Park Surgery
WSHM SO15 .... 54 C4
Regional Film Theatre
SHAM SO14 .... 9 J6
Rex Industrial Estate
CHFD SO53 .... 37 K5
Richard Martin Gallery &
Bookshop
GPORT PO12 .... 16 D6
Riders Junior & Infant School
HAV PO9 .... 102 E1
Ridgemede Junior School
BPWT SO32 .... 48 E3
Ridgeway House
Special School
ITCH SO19 .... 6 E8
River Park Leisure Centre
WINC SO23 .... 2 F2
Riverside School
WVILLE PO7 .... 102 A3

Romsey Abbey C of E
Primary School
ROMY SO51 .... 34 C3
Romsey County Junior School
ROMY SO51 .... 35 F2
Romsey Cricket Club
ROMY SO51 .... 34 E4
Romsey Hospital
ROMY SO51 .... 35 F3
Romsey Industrial Estate
ROMY SO51 .... 34 D1
Romsey Infant School
ROMY SO51 .... 34 E3
Romsey Rugby Football Club
ROMY SO51 .... 34 E4
The Romsey School
ROMY SO51 .... 34 D2
Romsey Sports Centre
ROMY SO51 .... 34 E4
Rookesbury Park School
WHAM PO17 .... 78 A1
Rowmans House
Industrial Estate
ROWN SO16 .... 41 K5
Rowner County Infant School
LSOL/BMARY PO13 .... 116 A6
Rowner County Junior School
LSOL/BMARY PO13 .... 116 A6
Rowner Health Centre
LSOL/BMARY PO13 .... 115 K7
Rowner Swimming Centre
LSOL/BMARY PO13 .... 131 K5
Royal Hampshire
County Hospital
WINW SO22 .... 2 B5
Royal Hampshire
County Hospital
WINW SO22 .... 25 E4
Royal Hampshire
Regiment Museum
WINC SO23 .... 2 D5
Royal Hospital Haslar
GPORT PO12 .... 16 F9
Royal Hospital Haslar
GPORT PO12 .... 133 H1
Royal Marines Museum
ENEY PO4 .... 135 G6
Royal Naval Museum
PSEA PO1 .... 17 J3
Royal Navy Submarine
Museum Offices
GPORT PO12 .... 17 G8
Royal South Hants Hospital
SHAM SO14 .... 5 H6
Royal Winchester Golf Club
WINW SO22 .... 24 E1
Rushington Business Park
TOTT SO40 .... 52 D7
Russell Hicks & Temple
ROMY SO51 .... 34 E3
St Albans C of E
Primary School
HAV PO9 .... 103 H3
St Andrews Surgery
ELGH SO50 .... 44 D1
St Annes School
LSOL/BMARY PO13 .... 131 F1
St Anthonys RC
Primary School
FHAM/STUB PO14 .... 95 H2
St Bedes C of E
Primary School
WINC SO23 .... 2 E5
St Catherines Road
Junior School
ELGH SO50 .... 38 D7
St Christophers Hospital
FHAM/PORC PO16 .... 13 L2
St Christophers School
WEND SO18 .... 6 D3
St Denys Primary School
PTSW SO17 .... 5 M1
St Edmunds Catholic School
PSEA PO1 .... 18 E3
St Faiths Primary School
WINC SO23 .... 25 J3
St Francis Primary School
NBAD SO52 .... 37 G5
St Francis School
FHAM/STUB PO14 .... 96 D5
St Georges Beneficial C of E
Primary School
PSEA PO1 .... 17 M4
St Georges Business Centre
PSEA PO1 .... 17 M4
St Georges Catholic
Boys School
ELGH SO50 .... 43 K5
St Georges Industrial Estate
ENEY PO4 .... 19 L4
St Georges University
School of Medicine
WINC SO23 .... 2 E4
St James C of E
Primary School
EMRTH PO10 .... 104 B4
St James Hospital
ENEY PO4 .... 135 G3
St James Primary School
HEND SO30 .... 57 J2
St Johns Cathedral
Primary School
PSEA PO1 .... 18 F3
St Johns C of E
Infant School
HLER SO31 .... 95 H4
St Johns C of E
Primary School
GPORT PO12 .... 132 E1
St Johns C of E
Primary School
HAV PO9 .... 83 J5
St Johns College
SSEA PO5 .... 18 E8
St Johns RC Cathedral
PSEA PO1 .... 18 B2
St John the Baptist School
BPWT SO32 .... 61 G2

St Judes Catholic
Primary School
FHAM/STUB PO14...................... 12 C6
St Judes C of E
Primary School
PSEA PO1.............................. 18 A7
St Lukes C of E School
SSEA PO5.............................. 18 D4
St Lukes Surgery
HEND SO30............................ 58 A3
St Marks C of E Junior School
WSHM SO15............................ 4 A5
St Marys C of E Primary School
SHAM SO14............................ 5 J9
St Marys C of E Primary School
SHAM SO14............................ 5 K9
St Marys College
WEND SO18............................ 6 D3
St Marys Hospital
HSEA PO3............................. 19 M2
St Marys RC Primary School
GPORT PO12.......................... 132 D3
St Marys Surgery
SHAM SO14............................ 9 J1
St Monica Infant School
ITCH SO19........................... 11 H4
St Monica Middle School
ITCH SO19........................... 11 G3
St Patricks RC Primary School
ITCH SO19........................... 10 C4
St Pauls Hospital
WINW SO22............................ 2 C3
St Pauls RC Primary School
CHAM PO6........................... 100 A6
St Peters School
WINW SO22........................... 24 E3
St Swithuns RC
Primary School
SSEA PO5........................... 134 C6
St Swithuns School
RWIN SO21............................ 3 M4
St Swithun Wells RC
Primary School
CHFD SO53........................... 38 A5
St Thomas Mores RC
Primary School
HAV PO9............................. 14 A1
St Vincent College
GPORT PO12.......................... 16 B3
Salterns School
TOTT SO40........................... 53 F4
Sarisbury Green C of E
Primary School
HLER SO31........................... 94 D1
Sarisbury Infant School
HLER SO31........................... 94 D2
Sarum Road Hospital
WINW SO22........................... 25 F1
Saxon Shore Infant School
CHAM PO6........................... 99 H6
Scantabout Primary School
CHFD SO53........................... 38 C3
School
SHAM SO14............................ 8 F4
Shakespeare Business Centre
ELGH SO50........................... 38 E6
Shakespeare County
Infant School
ELGH SO50........................... 38 D6
Shamblehurst CP School
HEND SO30........................... 58 B4
Sharps Copse Junior &
Infant School
HAV PO9............................ 103 J1
Shawcross Industrial Park
HSEA PO3........................... 119 F2
Shepherds Down School
RWIN SO21........................... 33 F3
Sherborne House School
CHFD SO53........................... 38 A2
Shirley Business Park
WSHM SO15............................ 4 A6
Shirley Business Park
WSHM SO15........................... 54 D5
Shirley First & Middle School
WSHM SO15........................... 54 D3
The Shirley Health Centre
WSHM SO15........................... 54 D5
Shirley Swimming Pool
WSHM SO15........................... 54 D5
Shirley Warren Primary School
ROWN SO16........................... 54 B2
Sholing First School
ITCH SO19............................ 7 G9
Sholing Girls School
ITCH SO19........................... 10 F1
Sholing Infants School
ITCH SO19............................ 7 G9
Sholing Middle School
ITCH SO19............................ 7 G9
Sidings Industrial Estate
HLER SO31........................... 93 G1
Sikh Temple
SSEA PO5............................ 18 E6
Simcoe Clinic
WSHM SO15............................ 4 D5
Sinclair First & Junior School
ROWN SO16........................... 42 B6
Siskin County Junior &
Infant School
LSOL/BMARY PO13.................. 132 A2
Solent Business Centre
WSHM SO15........................... 54 C6
Solent Industrial Centre
WSHM SO15........................... 54 D5
Solent Industrial Estate
HEND SO30........................... 58 A3
Solent Infant School
CHAM PO6.......................... 101 J6
Solent Junior School
CHAM PO6.......................... 101 J6
Solent Peoples Theatre
ITCH SO19........................... 11 L4
Somers Park Primary School
SSEA PO5............................ 18 E4
Somers Town Health Centre
SSEA PO5............................ 18 E5

Southampton Airport
Parkway Station
ELGH SO50........................... 44 C5
Southampton Central Mosque
SHAM SO14............................ 5 K6
Southampton City College
SHAM SO14............................ 9 J2
Southampton City Council
PTSW SO17........................... 55 K2
Southampton City Council
ROWN SO16........................... 42 E6
Southampton City Council
ROWN SO16........................... 53 H2
Southampton City Council
ROWN SO16........................... 54 C3
Southampton City Council
SHAM SO14............................ 5 J9
Southampton City Council
SHAM SO14............................ 8 F3
Southampton City Council
SHAM SO14............................ 8 F4
Southampton City Council
SHAM SO14............................ 9 K1
Southampton City Council
WEND SO18............................ 7 L4
Southampton City Council
WSHM SO15............................ 4 C9
Southampton City Council
WSHM SO15............................ 4 F7
Southampton Football Club
WSHM SO15............................ 4 D6
Southampton General Hospital
ROWN SO16........................... 54 C1
Southampton Institute & Millais
Gallery
WSHM SO15............................ 5 C8
Southampton Magistrates Court
WSHM SO15............................ 4 F6
Southampton & New Forest
Magistrates Courts
WSHM SO15............................ 4 D8
Southampton Sports Centre
ROWN SO16........................... 42 E7
Southampton Sports Club
ROWN SO16........................... 53 H2
Southampton Technical College
SHAM SO14............................ 9 M3
Southampton University
ROWN SO16........................... 42 D2
Southbourne County
Junior & Infant School
EMRTH PO10......................... 105 H6
Southbourne Surgery
EMRTH PO10......................... 105 H6
Southdown School
RWIN SO21........................... 33 F3
The South Downs College
WVILLE PO7......................... 102 B3
South Hants Country Club
WHAM PO17........................... 78 D4
South Parade Pier
SSEA PO5.......................... 134 D7
Southsea Castle Museum
SSEA PO5.......................... 134 A5
Southsea Infant School
SSEA PO5............................ 19 G9
South West Health Authority
HEND SO30........................... 74 A1
Southwick Park Naval
Recreation Centre
WHAM PO17........................... 99 K1
Sparsholt Primary School
RWIN SO21........................... 20 A4
Spitfire Court Surgery
SHAM SO14............................ 9 M4
Springfield School
CHAM PO6.......................... 101 H7
Springhill RC Primary School
WSHM SO15............................ 4 D0
Stakes Hill Infant School
WVILLE PO7"......................... 82 A7
Stakes Lodge Surgery
WVILLE PO7.......................... 82 B7
Stamshaw Infant School
NEND PO2.......................... 118 C5
Stamshaw Junior School
NEND PO2.......................... 118 B4
Stamshaw & Tipner
Leisure Centre
NEND PO2.......................... 118 B5
Stanbridge Earls School
ROMY SO51........................... 28 A6
Stanmore Primary School
WINW SO22........................... 25 H3
Stanton Industrial Estate
WSHM SO15........................... 54 B5
Station Theatre
HISD PO11......................... 136 E4
Staunton Park
Community School
HAV PO9............................ 83 J6
Stoke Gallery
GPORT PO12.......................... 16 B7
Stoke Park County
Junior School
ELGH SO50........................... 39 H7
Stoke Park Infant School
ELGH SO50........................... 45 H1
Stokewood Surgery
ELGH SO50........................... 45 K1
Stroud School
ROMY SO51........................... 35 K2
Sunnyside Doctors Surgery
PSEA PO1............................ 19 G3
Sun Valley Business Park
WINC SO23............................ 3 K2
Super Bowl
WSHM SO15........................... 54 A5
Superstore
SHAM SO14............................ 4 E9
Superstore
SHAM SO14............................ 8 E1
Surrey House First School
ITCH SO19........................... 11 M3
Surrey House Health Centre
ITCH SO19........................... 11 M3
Swanmore Business Park
BPWT SO32........................... 49 G6

Swanmore C of E School
BPWT SO32........................... 49 J5
Swanmore County Secondary School
BPWT SO32........................... 49 H6
Swanwick Business Park
HLER SO31........................... 74 C6
Swaythling Clinic
PTSW SO17........................... 55 K1
Swaythling Primary School
PTSW SO17........................... 55 J1
The Synagogue
SHAM SO14............................ 5 G5
Talisman Business Centre
HLER SO31........................... 75 G7
Tankerville School
ELGH SO50........................... 38 E7
Tanners Brook Infant School
WSHM SO15........................... 54 A5
Tanners Brook Junior School
ROWN SO16........................... 54 A5
Tatchbury Manor House
TOTT SO40........................... 51 J3
Tatchbury Mount Hospital
TOTT SO40........................... 51 K2
Terminus Industrial Estate
PSEA PO1............................ 18 E4
Test Vale Surgery
TOTT SO40........................... 52 E4
Test Valley Business Centre
TOTT SO40........................... 53 G2
Testwood School
TOTT SO40........................... 52 E3
Thornden School
CHFD SO53........................... 38 C2
Thorney County
Primary School
EMRTH PO10......................... 122 D4
Thornhill Clinic
ITCH SO19........................... 57 G7
Thornhill First School
ITCH SO19............................ 7 M7
Thornhill Junior School
ITCH SO19............................ 7 L8
Thornhill Park Surgery
ITCH SO19........................... 57 G6
Titchfield County
Primary School
FHAM/STUB PO14..................... 96 A5
Totton College
TOTT SO40........................... 52 C4
Totton College
TOTT SO40........................... 52 D7
Totton Recreation Centre
TOTT SO40........................... 52 C4
Tower Industrial Estate
ELGH SO50........................... 45 F1
Town Hall
GPORT PO12.......................... 16 E5
Townhill Infant School
WEND SO18........................... 56 D2
Townhill Middle School
WEND SO18........................... 56 D2
Townhill Park Health Clinic
WEND SO18........................... 56 D2
Townhill Surgery
WEND SO18........................... 56 E1
The Toynbee School
CHFD SO53........................... 38 A5
Treadgold Museum
PSEA PO1............................ 17 M3
Trinity Business Centre
TOTT SO40........................... 52 D2
Trinity Industrial Estate
WSHM SO15........................... 54 A5
Trojans Sports Club
ELGH SO50........................... 43 K4
Tudor House Museum
SHAM SO14............................ 8 F3
Turnpike Business Park
FHAM/PORC PO16..................... 13 K3
Twyford C of E Primary School
RWIN SO21........................... 33 J3
Twyford School
RWIN SO21........................... 33 K3
Twyford Surgery
RWIN SO21........................... 39 J1
United Services Cricket Ground
PSEA PO1............................ 17 M5
United Services Rugby Club
PSEA PO1............................ 18 A4
University of Portsmouth
ENEY PO4............................ 19 J9
University of Portsmouth
ENEY PO4.......................... 135 G4
University of Portsmouth
HISD PO11......................... 136 A4
University of Portsmouth
PSEA PO1............................ 17 M3
University of Portsmouth
PSEA PO1............................ 17 M6
University of Portsmouth
PSEA PO1............................ 18 A4
University of Portsmouth
PSEA PO1............................ 18 A5
University of Portsmouth
PSEA PO1............................ 18 C2
University of Portsmouth
PSEA PO1............................ 18 F4
University of Portsmouth
SSEA PO5............................ 18 B8
University of Portsmouth
SSEA PO5............................ 18 C5
University of Portsmouth
SSEA PO5............................ 18 D6
University of Southampton
PTSW SO17........................... 55 J1
University of Southampton
ROWN SO16........................... 55 G1
University of Southampton
WSHM SO15............................ 4 F5
University Practice
SSEA PO5............................ 18 B6
Uplands County
Primary School
FHAM/PORC PO16..................... 13 G2
Venture Industrial Park
LSOL/BMARY PO13................... 116 A4

Vermont School
ROWN SO16........................... 43 F7
Victoria Cottage Hospital
EMRTH PO10......................... 104 C4
Victoria Park
Swimming Centre
PSEA PO1............................ 18 B3
Victor Street Surgery
WSHM SO15........................... 54 C3
Victory Business Centre
PSEA PO1............................ 19 G4
Victory Retail Park
PSEA PO1.......................... 134 B1
Victory Trading Estate
HSEA PO3.......................... 119 G5
The Vine School
BPWT SO32........................... 59 J4
Virgin Cinemas
SHAM SO14............................ 9 J5
Wallisdean County
Infant School
FHAM/STUB PO14..................... 12 D7
Wallisdean County
Junior School
FHAM/STUB PO14..................... 12 E7
Waltham Business Park
BPWT SO32........................... 49 H7
Warblington School
HAV PO9............................ 15 J4
Warren Avenue
Industrial Estate
ENEY PO4.......................... 135 G3
Warren Park Primary School
HAV PO9............................ 82 E6
Warrior Business Centre
CHAM PO6.......................... 101 K7
Waterfront Garden Surgery
FAWY SO45........................... 91 H1
Waterloo Industrial Estate
HEND SO30........................... 58 A3
The Waterloo School
WVILLE PO7.......................... 81 K6
Waterlooville Football Club
WVILLE PO7.......................... 81 K5
Waterlooville Health Centre
WVILLE PO7.......................... 81 J3
The Waterside Health Centre
FAWY SO45........................... 91 H4
Waterside School
NEND PO2.......................... 118 A4
Weeke CP School
WINW SO22........................... 21 G5
Wellington Sports Club
ELGH SO50........................... 44 A4
Wessex Nuffield Hospital
CHFD SO53........................... 38 C1
Wessex Nuffield Hospital
ELGH SO50........................... 38 E7
Wessex Regional
Health Authority
HEND SO30........................... 58 A3
Wessex Superbowl
CHAM PO6.......................... 102 B5
Westbourne County
Primary School
EMRTH PO10......................... 104 E2
Westbourne Surgery
EMRTH PO10......................... 104 E3
West End Surgery
HEND SO30........................... 57 H2
Western Community Hospital
ROWN SO16........................... 54 B3
Western Primary School
WINW SO22........................... 21 G7
Westfield Junior School
CHAM PO6........................... 99 H6
The Westgate School
WINW SO22............................ 2 A2
The Westgate School
WINW SO22........................... 21 G6
West Hill Park School
FHAM/STUB PO14..................... 95 K6
Westlands Medical Centre
FHAM/PORC PO16..................... 99 F7
Weston Park Boys School
ITCH SO19........................... 11 L7
Weston Park First School
ITCH SO19........................... 11 H6
Weston Park Junior School
ITCH SO19........................... 11 G7
Weston Shore First School
ITCH SO19........................... 72 C5
Westover Primary School
HSEA PO3.......................... 119 G7
West Quay Retail Park
WSHM SO15............................ 8 D1
West Quay Shopping Centre
SHAM SO14............................ 8 E1
West Wittering
Parochial School
SELS PO20......................... 139 J7
Westwood Business Park
TOTT SO40........................... 52 E2
Whiteley County
Primary School
FHAM PO15........................... 75 H6
The Whiteley Surgery
HLER SO31........................... 75 G5
Wickham C of E
Controlled Primary School
WHAM PO17........................... 61 G7
Wickham Park Golf Club
WHAM PO17........................... 77 F1
Wickham Riding School
WHAM PO17........................... 78 B3
Wickham Surgery
WHAM PO17........................... 77 H1
Wicor County Primary School
FHAM/PORC PO16..................... 98 D6
Wildern Clinic
HEND SO30........................... 58 B5
The Wildern School
HEND SO30........................... 58 B5
Wildground County
Infant School
FAWY SO45........................... 91 G5

Wildground County
Junior School
FAWY SO45........................... 91 G5
Willments Industrial Estate
ITCH SO19............................ 6 B8
Wimbledon Park
Sports Centre
SSEA PO5.......................... 134 C6
Wimborne Junior &
Infant School
ENEY PO4............................ 19 L6
Winchester Agricultural
Museum
WINC SO23............................ 2 E2
Winchester City Museum
WINC SO23............................ 2 E5
Winchester College
WINC SO23............................ 2 E7
The Winchester Gallery
ROWN SO16........................... 55 F1
Winchester Lawn
Tennis Club
WINW SO22........................... 21 G5
Winchester Rugby
Football Club
WINC SO23............................ 3 G1
Winchester School of Art
WINC SO23............................ 3 G3
Winnall CP School
WINC SO23............................ 3 J4
Winnall Farm Industrial Estate
WINC SO23............................ 3 H3
Wolvesey Palace
WINC SO23............................ 2 F6
Woodhill Preparatory School
CHFD SO53........................... 38 A1
Woodhills School
HEND SO30........................... 58 E5
Woodlands Community School
WEND SO18........................... 57 G4
Wool House Maritime Museum
SHAM SO14............................ 8 F4
Woolston First School
ITCH SO19........................... 10 C5
Wooiston School
ITCH SO19........................... 10 D4
Wordsworth Infant School
WSHM SO15........................... 54 D3
Wykeham House School
FHAM/PORC PO16..................... 13 M5
Wykeham Industrial Estate
WINC SO23............................ 3 J1
Wynford Farm Industrial Estate
ROMY SO51........................... 28 E5
The Wyvern Community
Secondary School
ELGH SO50........................... 46 B2
Yeoman Industrial Park
TOTT SO40........................... 53 G2